THE TIMES

MINI

ATLAS

OF THE WORLD

TIMES BOOKS
LONDON

Published by Times Books
An imprint of HarperCollins Publishers
Westerhill Road
Bishopbriggs
Glasgow G64 2QT
www.harpercollins.co.uk

First published 1991
Published as The Times Atlas
of the World Mini Edition 1994
Second Edition 1999
Third Edition 2006
Fourth Edition 2009
Fifth Edition 2012

Sixth Edition 2015
Reprinted with changes 2016

A catalogue record for this book is available from the British Library

ISBN 978-0-00-810497-9

10 9 8 7 6 5 4 3 2
Printed in Hong Kong

All mapping in this atlas is generated from Collins Bartholomew™ digital databases.
Collins Bartholomew™, the UK's leading independent geographical information supplier,
can provide a digital, custom, and premium mapping service to a variety of markets.
For further information:
Tel: +44 (0) 208 307 4515
e-mail: collinsbartholomew@harpercollins.co.uk
or visit our website at: www.collinsbartholomew.com

If you would like to comment on any aspect of this atlas,
please contact us at the above address or online.
www.timesatlas.com
email: timesatlases@harpercollins.co.uk
 facebook.com/thetimesatlas
 @TimesAtlas

Pages	Title	Scale

GEOGRAPHICAL INFORMATION

6–19	**COUNTRIES of the WORLD**	
20–21	**OCEANIA** Physical Features	
22–23	**ASIA** Physical Features	
24–25	**EUROPE** Physical Features	
26–27	**AFRICA** Physical Features	
28–29	**NORTH AMERICA** Physical Features	
30–31	**SOUTH AMERICA** Physical Features	
32–33	**OCEANS and POLES** Physical Features	
34–35	**CLIMATE**	
36–37	**LAND COVER**	
38–39	**POPULATION**	
40–41	**URBANIZATION**	
42–43	**SYMBOLS and ABBREVIATIONS**	

WORLD

44–45	**WORLD** Physical Features	1:170 000 000
46–47	**WORLD** Countries	1:170 000 000

OCEANIA 1:70 000 000

50–51	**AUSTRALIA**	1:25 000 000
52–53	**AUSTRALIA** Southeast	1:10 000 000
54	**NEW ZEALAND**	1:10 000 000

ANTARCTICA 1:60 000 000

55		

ASIA 1:70 000 000

58–59	**SOUTHEAST ASIA**	1:30 000 000
60–61	**MALAYSIA and INDONESIA** West	1:15 000 000
62–63	**CONTINENTAL SOUTHEAST ASIA**	1:15 000 000
64	**PHILIPPINES**	1:15 000 000

CONTENTS

Pages	Title	Scale
65	**NORTH KOREA and SOUTH KOREA**	1:9 000 000
66–67	**JAPAN**	1:10 000 000
68–69	**CHINA and MONGOLIA**	1:30 000 000
70–71	**CHINA** Central	1:15 000 000
72–73	**SOUTH ASIA**	1:20 000 000
74–75	**PAKISTAN, INDIA and BANGLADESH**	1:15 000 000
76–77	**CENTRAL ASIA**	1:20 000 000
78–79	**ARABIAN PENINSULA**	1:15 000 000
80–81	**EAST MEDITERRANEAN**	1:15 000 000
82–83	**RUSSIA**	1:42 000 000
84–85	EUROPE	1:40 000 000
86–87	**EUROPEAN RUSSIA**	1:20 000 000
88–89	**NORTHEAST EUROPE**	1:8 000 000
90–91	**UKRAINE and MOLDOVA**	1:8 000 000
92–93	**SCANDINAVIA and ICELAND**	1:10 000 000
94–95	**BRITISH ISLES**	1:8 000 000
96	**SCOTLAND**	1:4 000 000
97	**IRELAND**	1:4 000 000
98–99	**ENGLAND and WALES**	1:4 000 000
100–101	**NORTHWEST EUROPE**	1:4 000 000
102–103	**CENTRAL EUROPE**	1:8 000 000
104–105	**FRANCE and SWITZERLAND**	1:8 000 000
106–107	**SPAIN and PORTUGAL**	1:8 000 000
108–109	**ITALY and THE BALKANS**	1:8 000 000
110–111	**GREECE, ROMANIA and BULGARIA**	1:8 000 000
112–113	AFRICA	1:60 000 000
114–115	**NORTHWEST AFRICA**	1:26 000 000

CONTENTS

Pages	Title	Scale
116–117	**NORTHEAST AFRICA**	1:26 000 000
118–119	**CENTRAL AFRICA**	1:20 000 000
120–121	**SOUTHERN AFRICA**	1:20 000 000
122–123	**SOUTH AFRICA**	1:10 000 000
124–125	NORTH AMERICA	1:70 000 000
126–127	**CANADA**	1:30 000 000
128–129	**CANADA** West	1:15 000 000
130–131	**CANADA** East	1:15 000 000
132–133	**UNITED STATES OF AMERICA**	1:25 000 000
134–135	**USA** West	1:11 000 000
136–137	**USA** North Central	1:11 000 000
138–139	**USA** South Central	1:11 000 000
140–141	**USA** Northeast	1:11 000 000
142–143	**USA** Southeast	1:11 000 000
144–145	**MEXICO**	1:15 000 000
146–147	**CARIBBEAN**	1:20 000 000
148–149	SOUTH AMERICA	1:70 000 000
150–151	**SOUTH AMERICA** North	1:25 000 000
152–153	**SOUTH AMERICA** South	1:25 000 000
154–155	**BRAZIL** Southeast	1:10 000 000
	OCEANS	
156–157	**PACIFIC OCEAN**	1:120 000 000
158	**ATLANTIC OCEAN**	1:120 000 000
159	**INDIAN OCEAN**	1:120 000 000
160	**ARCTIC OCEAN**	1:60 000 000
161–256	INDEX	

COUNTRIES OF THE WORLD

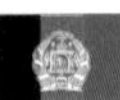

AFGHANISTAN
Islamic Republic of Afghanistan
Capital Kābul

Area sq km	652 225	**Currency**	Afghani
Area sq miles	251 825	**Languages**	Dari, Pashto
Population	30 552 000		(Pashtu), Uzbek,
			Turkmen

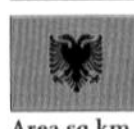

ALBANIA
Republic of Albania
Capital Tirana (Tiranë)

Area sq km	28 748	**Currency**	Lek
Area sq miles	11 100	**Languages**	Albanian, Greek
Population	3 173 000		

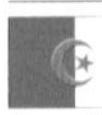

ALGERIA
People's Democratic Republic of Algeria
Capital Algiers (Alger)

Area sq km	2 381 741	**Currency**	Algerian dinar
Area sq miles	919 595	**Languages**	Arabic, French,
Population	39 208 000		Berber

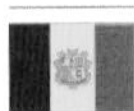

ANDORRA
Principality of Andorra
Capital Andorra la Vella

Area sq km	465	**Currency**	Euro
Area sq miles	180	**Languages**	Catalan, Spanish,
Population	79 000		French

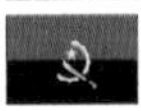

ANGOLA
Republic of Angola
Capital Luanda

Area sq km	1 246 700	**Currency**	Kwanza
Area sq miles	481 354	**Languages**	Portuguese,
Population	21 472 000		Bantu, other local
			lang.

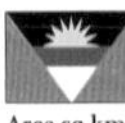

ANTIGUA AND BARBUDA
Capital St John's

Area sq km	442	**Currency**	East Caribbean
Area sq miles	171		dollar
Population	90 000	**Languages**	English, creole

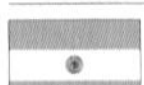

ARGENTINA
Argentine Republic
Capital Buenos Aires

Area sq km	2 766 889	**Currency**	Argentinian peso
Area sq miles	1 068 302	**Languages**	Spanish, Italian,
Population	41 446 000		Amerindian lang.

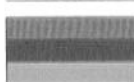

ARMENIA
Republic of Armenia
Capital Yerevan (Erevan)

Area sq km	29 800	**Currency**	Dram
Area sq miles	11 506	**Languages**	Armenian,
Population	2 977 000		Kurdish

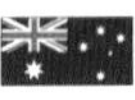

AUSTRALIA
Commonwealth of Australia
Capital Canberra

Area sq km	7 692 024	**Currency**	Australian dollar
Area sq miles	2 969 907	**Languages**	English, Italian,
Population	23 343 000		Greek

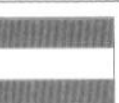

AUSTRIA
Republic of Austria
Capital Vienna (Wien)

Area sq km	83 855	**Currency**	Euro
Area sq miles	32 377	**Languages**	German,
Population	8 495 000		Croatian, Turkish

AZERBAIJAN
Republic of Azerbaijan
Capital Baku (Bakı)

Area sq km	86 600	**Currency**	Azerbaijani manat
Area sq miles	33 436	**Languages**	Azeri, Armenian,
Population	9 413 000		Russian, Lezgian

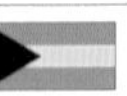

THE BAHAMAS
Commonwealth of The Bahamas
Capital Nassau

Area sq km	13 939	**Currency**	Bahamian dollar
Area sq miles	5 382	**Languages**	English, creole
Population	377 000		

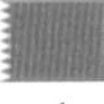

BAHRAIN
Kingdom of Bahrain
Capital Manama (Al Manāmah)

Area sq km	691	**Currency**	Bahraini dinar
Area sq miles	267	**Languages**	Arabic, English
Population	1 332 000		

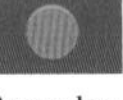

BANGLADESH
People's Republic of Bangladesh
Capital Dhaka (Dacca)

Area sq km	143 998	**Currency**	Taka
Area sq miles	55 598	**Languages**	Bengali, English
Population	156 595 000		

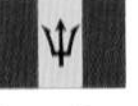

BARBADOS
Capital Bridgetown

Area sq km	430	**Currency**	Barbadian dollar
Area sq miles	166	**Languages**	English, creole
Population	285 000		

BELARUS
Republic of Belarus
Capital Minsk

Area sq km	207 600	Currency	Belarusian rouble
Area sq miles	80 155	Languages	Belarusian,
Population	9 357 000		Russian

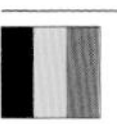

BELGIUM
Kingdom of Belgium
Capital Brussels (Brussel/Bruxelles)

Area sq km	30 520	Currency	Euro
Area sq miles	11 784	Languages	Dutch (Flemish),
Population	11 104 000		French (Walloon),
			German

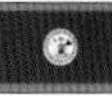

BELIZE
Capital Belmopan

Area sq km	22 965	Currency	Belize dollar
Area sq miles	8 867	Languages	English, Spanish,
Population	332 000		Mayan, creole

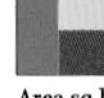

BENIN
Republic of Benin
Capital Porto-Novo

Area sq km	112 620	Currency	CFA franc*
Area sq miles	43 483	Languages	French, Fon,
Population	10 323 000		Yoruba, Adja,
			other local lang.

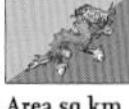

BHUTAN
Kingdom of Bhutan
Capital Thimphu

Area sq km	46 620	Currency	Ngultrum,
Area sq miles	18 000		Indian rupee
Population	754 000	Languages	Dzongkha,
			Nepali, Assamese

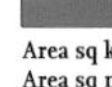

BOLIVIA
Plurinational State of Bolivia
Capital La Paz/Sucre

Area sq km	1 098 581	Currency	Boliviano
Area sq miles	424 164	Languages	Spanish, Quechua,
Population	10 671 000		Aymara

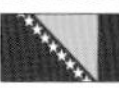

BOSNIA AND HERZEGOVINA
Capital Sarajevo

Area sq km	51 130	Currency	Convertible mark
Area sq miles	19 741	Languages	Bosnian, Serbian,
Population	3 829 000		Croatian

BOTSWANA
Republic of Botswana
Capital Gaborone

Area sq km	581 370	Currency	Pula
Area sq miles	224 468	Languages	English, Setswana,
Population	2 021 000		Shona, other local
			lang.

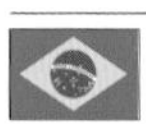

BRAZIL
Federative Republic of Brazil
Capital Brasília

Area sq km	8 514 879	Currency	Real
Area sq miles	3 287 613	Languages	Portuguese
Population	200 362 000		

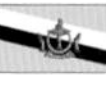

BRUNEI
Brunei Darussalam
Capital Bandar Seri Begawan

Area sq km	5 765	Currency	Bruneian dollar
Area sq miles	2 226	Languages	Malay, English,
Population	418 000		Chinese

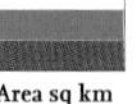

BULGARIA
Republic of Bulgaria
Capital Sofia

Area sq km	110 994	Currency	Lev
Area sq miles	42 855	Languages	Bulgarian,
Population	7 223 000		Turkish, Romany,
			Macedonian

BURKINA FASO
Capital Ouagadougou

Area sq km	274 200	Currency	CFA franc*
Area sq miles	105 869	Languages	French, Moore
Population	16 935 000		(Mossi), Fulani,
			other local lang.

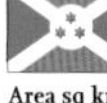

BURUNDI
Republic of Burundi
Capital Bujumbura

Area sq km	27 835	Currency	Burundian franc
Area sq miles	10 747	Languages	Kirundi (Hutu,
Population	10 163 000		Tutsi), French

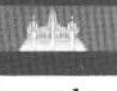

CAMBODIA
Kingdom of Cambodia
Capital Phnom Penh

Area sq km	181 035	Currency	Riel
Area sq miles	69 884	Languages	Khmer,
Population	15 135 000		Vietnamese

* CFA Communauté Financière Africaine

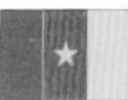

CAMEROON
Republic of Cameroon
Capital Yaoundé

Area sq km	475 442	**Currency**	CFA franc*
Area sq miles	183 569	**Languages**	French, English,
Population	22 254 000		Fang, Bamileke,
			other local lang.

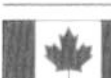

CANADA
Capital Ottawa

Area sq km	9 984 670	**Currency**	Canadian dollar
Area sq miles	3 855 103	**Languages**	English, French,
Population	35 182 000		other local lang.

CAPE VERDE (CABO VERDE)
Republic of Cabo Verde
Capital Praia

Area sq km	4 033	**Currency**	Cape Verdean
Area sq miles	1 557		escudo
Population	499 000	**Languages**	Portuguese, creole

CENTRAL AFRICAN REPUBLIC
Capital Bangui

Area sq km	622 436	**Currency**	CFA franc*
Area sq miles	240 324	**Languages**	French, Sango,
Population	4 616 000		Banda, Baya,
			other local lang.

CHAD
Republic of Chad
Capital Ndjamena

Area sq km	1 284 000	**Currency**	CFA franc*
Area sq miles	495 755	**Languages**	Arabic, French,
Population	12 825 000		Sara, other local
			lang.

CHILE
Republic of Chile
Capital Santiago

Area sq km	756 945	**Currency**	Chilean peso
Area sq miles	292 258	**Languages**	Spanish,
Population	17 620 000		Amerindian lang.

CHINA
People's Republic of China
Capital Beijing (Peking)

Area sq km	9 606 802	**Currency**	Yuan, HK dollar,
Area sq miles	3 709 186		Macao pataca
Population	1 369 993 000	**Languages**	Mandarin
			(Putonghua), Wu,
			Cantonese, Hsiang,
			regional lang.

COLOMBIA
Republic of Colombia
Capital Bogotá

Area sq km	1 141 748	**Currency**	Colombian peso
Area sq miles	440 831	**Languages**	Spanish,
Population	48 321 000		Amerindian lang.

COMOROS
Union of the Comoros
Capital Moroni

Area sq km	1 862	**Currency**	Comorian franc
Area sq miles	719	**Languages**	Shikomor
Population	735 000		(Comorian),
			French, Arabic

CONGO
Republic of the Congo
Capital Brazzaville

Area sq km	342 000	**Currency**	CFA franc*
Area sq miles	132 047	**Languages**	French, Kongo,
Population	4 448 000		Monokutuba,
			other local lang.

CONGO, DEMOCRATIC REPUBLIC OF THE
Capital Kinshasa

Area sq km	2 345 410	**Currency**	Congolese franc
Area sq miles	905 568	**Languages**	French, Lingala,
Population	67 514 000		Swahili, Kongo,
			other local lang.

COSTA RICA
Republic of Costa Rica
Capital San José

Area sq km	51 100	**Currency**	Costa Rican colón
Area sq miles	19 730	**Languages**	Spanish
Population	4 872 000		

CÔTE D'IVOIRE (IVORY COAST)
Republic of Côte d'Ivoire
Capital Yamoussoukro

Area sq km	322 463	**Currency**	CFA franc*
Area sq miles	124 504	**Languages**	French, creole,
Population	20 316 000		Akan, other local
			lang.

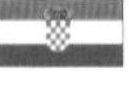

CROATIA
Republic of Croatia
Capital Zagreb

Area sq km	56 538	**Currency**	Kuna
Area sq miles	21 829	**Languages**	Croatian, Serbian
Population	4 290 000		

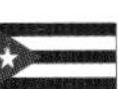

CUBA
Republic of Cuba
Capital Havana (La Habana)

Area sq km	110 860	**Currency**	Cuban peso
Area sq miles	42 803	**Languages**	Spanish
Population	11 266 000		

CYPRUS
Republic of Cyprus
Capital Nicosia (Lefkosia)

Area sq km	9 251	**Currency**	Euro
Area sq miles	3 572	**Languages**	Greek, Turkish,
Population	1 141 000		English

CZECH REPUBLIC
Capital Prague (Praha)

Area sq km	78 864	**Currency**	Czech koruna
Area sq miles	30 450	**Languages**	Czech, Moravian,
Population	10 702 000		Slovakian

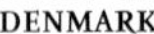

DENMARK
Kingdom of Denmark
Capital Copenhagen (København)

Area sq km	43 075	**Currency**	Danish krone
Area sq miles	16 631	**Languages**	Danish
Population	5 619 000		

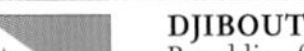

DJIBOUTI
Republic of Djibouti
Capital Djibouti

Area sq km	23 200	**Currency**	Djiboutian franc
Area sq miles	8 958	**Languages**	Somali, Afar,
Population	873 000		French, Arabic

DOMINICA
Commonwealth of Dominica
Capital Roseau

Area sq km	750	**Currency**	East Caribbean
Area sq miles	290		dollar
Population	72 000	**Languages**	English, creole

DOMINICAN REPUBLIC
Capital Santo Domingo

Area sq km	48 442	**Currency**	Dominican peso
Area sq miles	18 704	**Languages**	Spanish, creole
Population	10 404 000		

EAST TIMOR (TIMOR-LESTE)
Democratic Republic of Timor-Leste
Capital Dili

Area sq km	14 874	**Currency**	US dollar
Area sq miles	5 743	**Languages**	Portuguese, Tetun,
Population	1 133 000		English

ECUADOR
Republic of Ecuador
Capital Quito

Area sq km	272 045	**Currency**	US dollar
Area sq miles	105 037	**Languages**	Spanish, Quechua,
Population	15 738 000		Amerindian lang.

EGYPT
Arab Republic of Egypt
Capital Cairo (Al Qāhirah)

Area sq km	1 000 250	**Currency**	Egyptian pound
Area sq miles	386 199	**Languages**	Arabic
Population	82 056 000		

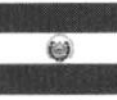

EL SALVADOR
Republic of El Salvador
Capital San Salvador

Area sq km	21 041	**Currency**	US dollar
Area sq miles	8 124	**Languages**	Spanish
Population	6 340 000		

EQUATORIAL GUINEA
Republic of Equatorial Guinea
Capital Malabo

Area sq km	28 051	**Currency**	CFA franc*
Area sq miles	10 831	**Languages**	Spanish, French,
Population	757 000		Fang

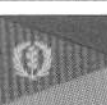

ERITREA
State of Eritrea
Capital Asmara

Area sq km	117 400	**Currency**	Nakfa
Area sq miles	45 328	**Languages**	Tigrinya, Tigre
Population	6 333 000		

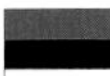

ESTONIA
Republic of Estonia
Capital Tallinn

Area sq km	45 200	**Currency**	Euro
Area sq miles	17 452	**Languages**	Estonian, Russian
Population	1 287 000		

ETHIOPIA
Federal Democratic Republic of Ethiopia
Capital Addis Ababa (Ādīs Ābeba)

Area sq km	1 133 880	**Currency**	Birr
Area sq miles	437 794	**Languages**	Oromo, Amharic,
Population	94 101 000		Tigrinya, other
			local lang.

FIJI
Republic of Fiji
Capital Suva

Area sq km	18 330	**Currency**	Fijian dollar
Area sq miles	7 077	**Languages**	English, Fijian,
Population	881 000		Hindi

FINLAND
Republic of Finland
Capital Helsinki (Helsingfors)

Area sq km	338 145	**Currency**	Euro
Area sq miles	130 559	**Languages**	Finnish, Swedish,
Population	5 426 000		Sami

FRANCE
French Republic
Capital Paris

Area sq km	543 965	**Currency**	Euro
Area sq miles	210 026	**Languages**	French, German
Population	64 291 000		dialects, Italian,
			Arabic, Breton

GABON
Gabonese Republic
Capital Libreville

Area sq km	267 667	**Currency**	CFA franc*
Area sq miles	103 347	**Languages**	French, Fang,
Population	1 672 000		other local lang.

THE GAMBIA
Republic of The Gambia
Capital Banjul

Area sq km	11 295	**Currency**	Dalasi
Area sq miles	4 361	**Languages**	English, Malinke,
Population	1 849 000		Fulani, Wolof

Gaza
Disputed territory
Capital Gaza

Area sq km	363	**Currency**	Israeli shekel
Area sq miles	140	**Languages**	Arabic
Population	1 701 437		

GEORGIA
Capital Tbilisi

Area sq km	69 700	**Currency**	Lari
Area sq miles	26 911	**Languages**	Georgian, Russian,
Population	4 341 000		Armenian, Azeri,
			Ossetian, Abkhaz

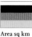
GERMANY
Federal Republic of Germany
Capital Berlin

Area sq km	357 022	**Currency**	Euro
Area sq miles	137 849	**Languages**	German, Turkish
Population	82 727 000		

GHANA
Republic of Ghana
Capital Accra

Area sq km	238 537	**Currency**	Cedi
Area sq miles	92 100	**Languages**	English, Hausa,
Population	25 905 000		Akan, other local
			lang.

GREECE
Hellenic Republic
Capital Athens (Athina)

Area sq km	131 957	**Currency**	Euro
Area sq miles	50 949	**Languages**	Greek
Population	11 128 000		

GRENADA
Capital St George's

Area sq km	378	**Currency**	East Caribbean
Area sq miles	146		dollar
Population	106 000	**Languages**	English, creole

GUATEMALA
Republic of Guatemala
Capital Guatemala City

Area sq km	108 890	**Currency**	Quetzal
Area sq miles	42 043	**Languages**	Spanish,
Population	15 468 000		Mayan lang.

GUINEA
Republic of Guinea
Capital Conakry

Area sq km	245 857	**Currency**	Guinean franc
Area sq miles	94 926	**Languages**	French, Fulani,
Population	11 745 000		Malinke, other
			local lang.

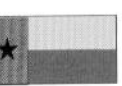

GUINEA-BISSAU
Republic of Guinea-Bissau
Capital Bissau

Area sq km	36 125	**Currency**	CFA franc*
Area sq miles	13 948	**Languages**	Portuguese,
Population	1 704 000		crioulo, other
			local lang.

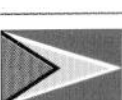

GUYANA
Co-operative Republic of Guyana
Capital Georgetown

Area sq km	214 969	**Currency**	Guyana dollar
Area sq miles	83 000	**Languages**	English, creole,
Population	800 000		Amerindian lang.

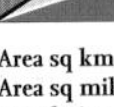

HAITI
Republic of Haiti
Capital Port-au-Prince

Area sq km	27 750	**Currency**	Gourde
Area sq miles	10 714	**Languages**	French, creole
Population	10 317 000		

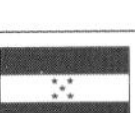

HONDURAS
Republic of Honduras
Capital Tegucigalpa

Area sq km	112 088	**Currency**	Lempira
Area sq miles	43 277	**Languages**	Spanish,
Population	8 098 000		Amerindian lang.

HUNGARY
Capital Budapest

Area sq km	93 030	**Currency**	Forint
Area sq miles	35 919	**Languages**	Hungarian
Population	9 955 000		

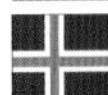

ICELAND
Republic of Iceland
Capital Reykjavík

Area sq km	102 820	**Currency**	Icelandic króna
Area sq miles	39 699	**Languages**	Icelandic
Population	330 000		

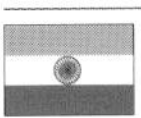

INDIA
Republic of India
Capital New Delhi

Area sq km	3 166 620	**Currency**	Indian rupee
Area sq miles	1 222 632	**Languages**	Hindi, English,
Population	1 252 140 000		many regional
			lang.

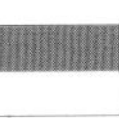

INDONESIA
Republic of Indonesia
Capital Jakarta

Area sq km	1 919 445	**Currency**	Rupiah
Area sq miles	741 102	**Languages**	Indonesian,
Population	249 866 000		other local
			lang.

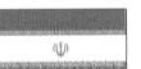

IRAN
Islamic Republic of Iran
Capital Tehrān

Area sq km	1 648 000	**Currency**	Iranian rial
Area sq miles	636 296	**Languages**	Farsi, Azeri,
Population	77 447 000		Kurdish,
			regional lang.

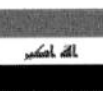

IRAQ
Republic of Iraq
Capital Baghdād

Area sq km	438 317	**Currency**	Iraqi dinar
Area sq miles	169 235	**Languages**	Arabic, Kurdish,
Population	33 765 000		Turkmen

IRELAND
Capital Dublin (Baile Átha Cliath)

Area sq km	70 282	**Currency**	Euro
Area sq miles	27 136	**Languages**	English, Irish
Population	4 627 000		

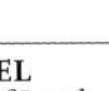

ISRAEL
State of Israel
Capital Jerusalem* (Yerushalayim) (El Quds)

Area sq km	22 072	**Currency**	Shekel
Area sq miles	8 522	**Languages**	Hebrew, Arabic
Population	7 733 000		

* De facto capital. Disputed.

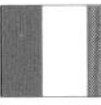

ITALY
Italian Republic
Capital Rome (Roma)

Area sq km	301 245	**Currency**	Euro
Area sq miles	116 311	**Languages**	Italian
Population	60 990 000		

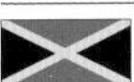

JAMAICA
Capital Kingston

Area sq km	10 991	**Currency**	Jamaican dollar
Area sq miles	4 244	**Languages**	English, creole
Population	2 784 000		

JAPAN
Capital Tōkyō

Area sq km	377 727	Currency	Yen
Area sq miles	145 841	Languages	Japanese
Population	127 144 000		

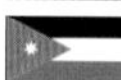

JORDAN
Hashemite Kingdom of Jordan
Capital 'Ammān

Area sq km	89 206	Currency	Jordanian dinar
Area sq miles	34 443	Languages	Arabic
Population	7 274 000		

KAZAKHSTAN
Republic of Kazakhstan
Capital Astana (Akmola)

Area sq km	2 717 300	Currency	Tenge
Area sq miles	1 049 155	Languages	Kazakh, Russian,
Population	16 441 000		Ukrainian, German,
			Uzbek, Tatar

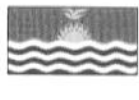

KENYA
Republic of Kenya
Capital Nairobi

Area sq km	582 646	Currency	Kenyan shilling
Area sq miles	224 961	Languages	Swahili, English,
Population	44 354 000		other local lang.

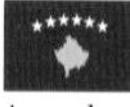

KIRIBATI
Republic of Kiribati
Capital Bairiki

Area sq km	717	Currency	Australian dollar
Area sq miles	277	Languages	Gilbertese,
Population	102 000		English

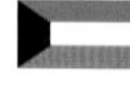

KOSOVO
Republic of Kosovo
Capital Prishtinë (Priština)

Area sq km	10 908	Currency	Euro
Area sq miles	4 212	Languages	Albanian, Serbian
Population	1 815 606		

KUWAIT
State of Kuwait
Capital Kuwait (Al Kuwayt)

Area sq km	17 818	Currency	Kuwaiti dinar
Area sq miles	6 880	Languages	Arabic
Population	3 369 000		

KYRGYZSTAN
Kyrgyz Republic
Capital Bishkek (Frunze)

Area sq km	198 500	Currency	Kyrgyz som
Area sq miles	76 641	Languages	Kyrgyz, Russian,
Population	5 548 000		Uzbek

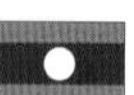

LAOS
Lao People's Democratic Republic
Capital Vientiane (Viangchan)

Area sq km	236 800	Currency	Kip
Area sq miles	91 429	Languages	Lao, other local
Population	6 770 000		lang.

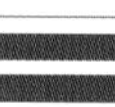

LATVIA
Republic of Latvia
Capital Rīga

Area sq km	64 589	Currency	Euro
Area sq miles	24 938	Languages	Latvian, Russian
Population	2 050 000		

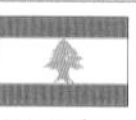

LEBANON
Lebanese Republic
Capital Beirut (Beyrouth)

Area sq km	10 452	Currency	Lebanese pound
Area sq miles	4 036	Languages	Arabic, Armenian,
Population	4 822 000		French

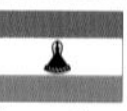

LESOTHO
Kingdom of Lesotho
Capital Maseru

Area sq km	30 355	Currency	Loti,
Area sq miles	11 720		S. African rand
Population	2 074 000	Languages	Sesotho, English,
			Zulu

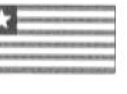

LIBERIA
Republic of Liberia
Capital Monrovia

Area sq km	111 369	Currency	Liberian dollar
Area sq miles	43 000	Languages	English, creole,
Population	4 294 000		other local lang.

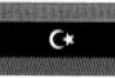

LIBYA
State of Libya
Capital Tripoli (Ṭarābulus)

Area sq km	1 759 540	Currency	Libyan dinar
Area sq miles	679 362	Languages	Arabic, Berber
Population	6 202 000		

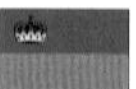

LIECHTENSTEIN
Principality of Liechtenstein
Capital Vaduz

Area sq km	160	Currency	Swiss franc
Area sq miles	62	Languages	German
Population	37 000		

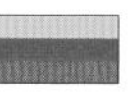

LITHUANIA
Republic of Lithuania
Capital Vilnius

Area sq km	65 200	**Currency**	Euro
Area sq miles	25 174	**Languages**	Lithuanian,
Population	3 017 000		Russian, Polish

LUXEMBOURG
Grand Duchy of Luxembourg
Capital Luxembourg

Area sq km	2 586	**Currency**	Euro
Area sq miles	998	**Languages**	Letzeburgish,
Population	530 000		German, French

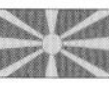

MACEDONIA (F.Y.R.O.M.)
Republic of Macedonia
Capital Skopje

Area sq km	25 713	**Currency**	Macedonian denar
Area sq miles	9 928	**Languages**	Macedonian,
Population	2 107 000		Albanian, Turkish

MADAGASCAR
Republic of Madagascar
Capital Antananarivo

Area sq km	587 041	**Currency**	Ariary
Area sq miles	226 658	**Languages**	Malagasy, French
Population	22 925 000		

MALAWI
Republic of Malawi
Capital Lilongwe

Area sq km	118 484	**Currency**	Malawian kwacha
Area sq miles	45 747	**Languages**	Chichewa,
Population	16 363 000		English, other
			local lang.

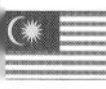

MALAYSIA
Capital Kuala Lumpur/Putrajaya

Area sq km	332 965	**Currency**	Ringgit
Area sq miles	128 559	**Languages**	Malay, English,
Population	29 717 000		Chinese, Tamil,
			other local lang.

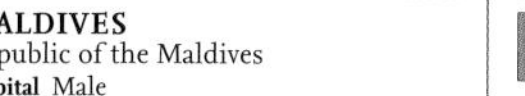

MALDIVES
Republic of the Maldives
Capital Male

Area sq km	298	**Currency**	Rufiyaa
Area sq miles	115	**Languages**	Divehi
Population	345 000		(Maldivian)

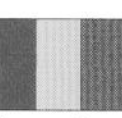

MALI
Republic of Mali
Capital Bamako

Area sq km	1 240 140	**Currency**	CFA franc*
Area sq miles	478 821	**Languages**	French, Bambara,
Population	15 302 000		other local lang.

MALTA
Republic of Malta
Capital Valletta

Area sq km	316	**Currency**	Euro
Area sq miles	122	**Languages**	Maltese, English
Population	429 000		

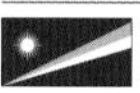

MARSHALL ISLANDS
Republic of the Marshall Islands
Capital Delap-Uliga-Djarrit

Area sq km	181	**Currency**	US dollar
Area sq miles	70	**Languages**	English,
Population	53 000		Marshallese

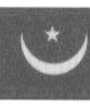

MAURITANIA
Islamic Republic of Mauritania
Capital Nouakchott

Area sq km	1 030 700	**Currency**	Ouguiya
Area sq miles	397 955	**Languages**	Arabic, French,
Population	3 890 000		other local lang.

MAURITIUS
Republic of Mauritius
Capital Port Louis

Area sq km	2 040	**Currency**	Mauritius rupee
Area sq miles	788	**Languages**	English, creole,
Population	1 244 000		Hindi, Bhojpuri,
			French

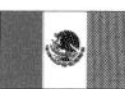

MEXICO
United Mexican States
Capital Mexico City

Area sq km	1 972 545	**Currency**	Mexican peso
Area sq miles	761 604	**Languages**	Spanish,
Population	122 332 000		Amerindian lang.

MICRONESIA, FEDERATED STATES OF
Capital Palikir

Area sq km	701	**Currency**	US dollar
Area sq miles	271	**Languages**	English, Chuukese,
Population	104 000		Pohnpeian, other
			local lang.

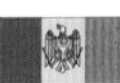

MOLDOVA
Republic of Moldova
Capital Chişinău (Kishinev)

Area sq km	33 700	**Currency**	Moldovan leu
Area sq miles	13 012	**Languages**	Romanian,
Population	3 487 000		Ukrainian,
			Gagauz, Russian

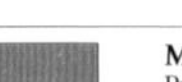

MONACO
Principality of Monaco
Capital Monaco-Ville

Area sq km	2	**Currency**	Euro
Area sq miles	1	**Languages**	French,
Population	38 000		Monégasque,
			Italian

MONGOLIA
Capital Ulan Bator (Ulaanbaatar)

Area sq km	1 565 000	**Currency**	Tugrik (tögrög)
Area sq miles	604 250	**Languages**	Khalka
Population	2 839 000		(Mongolian),
			Kazakh, other
			local lang.

MONTENEGRO
Republic of Montenegro
Capital Podgorica

Area sq km	13 812	**Currency**	Euro
Area sq miles	5 333	**Languages**	Serbian
Population	621 000		(Montenegrin),
			Albanian

MOROCCO
Kingdom of Morocco
Capital Rabat

Area sq km	446 550	**Currency**	Moroccan dirham
Area sq miles	172 414	**Languages**	Arabic, Berber,
Population	33 008 000		French

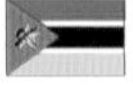

MOZAMBIQUE
Republic of Mozambique
Capital Maputo

Area sq km	799 380	**Currency**	Metical
Area sq miles	308 642	**Languages**	Portuguese,
Population	25 834 000		Makua, Tsonga,
			other local lang.

MYANMAR (Burma)
Republic of the Union of Myanmar
Capital Nay Pyi Taw

Area sq km	676 577	**Currency**	Kyat
Area sq miles	261 228	**Languages**	Burmese, Shan,
Population	53 259 000		Karen, other
			local lang.

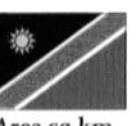

NAMIBIA
Republic of Namibia
Capital Windhoek

Area sq km	824 292	**Currency**	Namibian dollar
Area sq miles	318 261	**Languages**	English, Afrikaan
Population	2 303 000		German, Ovambo
			other local lang.

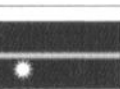

NAURU
Republic of Nauru
Capital Yaren (de facto)

Area sq km	21	**Currency**	Australian dollar
Area sq miles	8	**Languages**	Nauruan, English
Population	10 000		

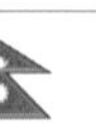

NEPAL
Federal Democratic Republic of Nepal
Capital Kathmandu

Area sq km	147 181	**Currency**	Nepalese rupee
Area sq miles	56 827	**Languages**	Nepali, Maithili,
Population	27 797 000		Bhojpuri, English
			other local lang.

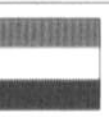

NETHERLANDS
Kingdom of the Netherlands
Capital Amsterdam/The Hague ('s-Gravenhag

Area sq km	41 526	**Currency**	Euro
Area sq miles	16 033	**Languages**	Dutch, Frisian
Population	16 759 000		

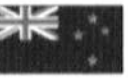

NEW ZEALAND
Capital Wellington

Area sq km	270 534	**Currency**	New Zealand
Area sq miles	104 454		dollar
Population	4 506 000	**Languages**	English, Maori

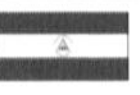

NICARAGUA
Republic of Nicaragua
Capital Managua

Area sq km	130 000	**Currency**	Córdoba
Area sq miles	50 193	**Languages**	Spanish,
Population	6 080 000		Amerindian lang.

NIGER
Republic of Niger
Capital Niamey

Area sq km	1 267 000	**Currency**	CFA franc★
Area sq miles	489 191	**Languages**	French, Hausa,
Population	17 831 000		Fulani, other loca
			lang.

NIGERIA
Federal Republic of Nigeria
Capital Abuja

Area sq km	923 768	**Currency**	Naira
Area sq miles	356 669	**Languages**	English, Hausa, Yoruba, Ibo, Fulani, other local lang.
Population	173 615 000		

NORTH KOREA
Democratic People's Republic of Korea
Capital P'yŏngyang

Area sq km	120 538	**Currency**	North Korean won
Area sq miles	46 540	**Languages**	Korean
Population	24 895 000		

NORWAY
Kingdom of Norway
Capital Oslo

Area sq km	323 878	**Currency**	Norwegian krone
Area sq miles	125 050	**Languages**	Norwegian, Sami
Population	5 043 000		

OMAN
Sultanate of Oman
Capital Muscat (Masqat)

Area sq km	309 500	**Currency**	Omani rial
Area sq miles	119 499	**Languages**	Arabic, Baluchi, Indian lang.
Population	3 632 000		

PAKISTAN
Islamic Republic of Pakistan
Capital Islamabad

Area sq km	881 888	**Currency**	Pakistani rupee
Area sq miles	340 497	**Languages**	Urdu, Punjabi, Sindhi, Pashto (Pashtu), English, Balochi
Population	182 143 000		

PALAU
Republic of Palau
Capital Melekeok (Ngerulmud)

Area sq km	497	**Currency**	US dollar
Area sq miles	192	**Languages**	Palauan, English
Population	21 000		

PANAMA
Republic of Panama
Capital Panama City

Area sq km	77 082	**Currency**	Balboa
Area sq miles	29 762	**Languages**	Spanish, English, Amerindian lang.
Population	3 864 000		

PAPUA NEW GUINEA
Independent State of Papua New Guinea
Capital Port Moresby

Area sq km	462 840	**Currency**	Kina
Area sq miles	178 704	**Languages**	English, Tok Pisin (creole), other local lang.
Population	7 321 000		

PARAGUAY
Republic of Paraguay
Capital Asunción

Area sq km	406 752	**Currency**	Guaraní
Area sq miles	157 048	**Languages**	Spanish, Guaraní
Population	6 802 000		

PERU
Republic of Peru
Capital Lima

Area sq km	1 285 216	**Currency**	Nuevo sol
Area sq miles	496 225	**Languages**	Spanish, Quechua, Aymara
Population	30 376 000		

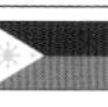

PHILIPPINES
Republic of the Philippines
Capital Manila

Area sq km	300 000	**Currency**	Philippine peso
Area sq miles	115 831	**Languages**	English, Filipino, Tagalog, Cebuano, other local lang.
Population	98 394 000		

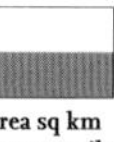

POLAND
Republic of Poland
Capital Warsaw (Warszawa)

Area sq km	312 683	**Currency**	Złoty
Area sq miles	120 728	**Languages**	Polish, German
Population	38 217 0000		

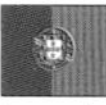

PORTUGAL
Portuguese Republic
Capital Lisbon (Lisboa)

Area sq km	88 940	**Currency**	Euro
Area sq miles	34 340	**Languages**	Portuguese
Population	10 608 000		

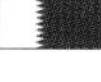

QATAR
State of Qatar
Capital Doha (Ad Dawḥah)

Area sq km	11 437	**Currency**	Qatari riyal
Area sq miles	4 416	**Languages**	Arabic
Population	2 169 000		

COUNTRIES OF THE WORLD

ROMANIA
Capital Bucharest (Bucureşti)

Area sq km	237 500	**Currency**	Romanian leu
Area sq miles	91 699	**Languages**	Romanian,
Population	21 699 000		Hungarian

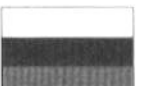

RUSSIA
Capital Moscow (Moskva)

Area sq km	17 075 400	**Currency**	Russian rouble
Area sq miles	6 592 849	**Languages**	Russian, Tatar,
Population	142 834 000		Ukrainian, other
			local lang.

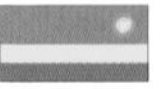

RWANDA
Republic of Rwanda
Capital Kigali

Area sq km	26 338	**Currency**	Rwandan franc
Area sq miles	10 169	**Languages**	Kinyarwanda,
Population	11 777 000		French, English

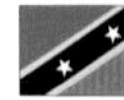

ST KITTS AND NEVIS
Federation of St Kitts and Nevis
Capital Basseterre

Area sq km	261	**Currency**	East Caribbean
Area sq miles	101		dollar
Population	54 000	**Languages**	English, creole

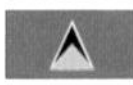

ST LUCIA
Capital Castries

Area sq km	616	**Currency**	East Caribbean
Area sq miles	238		dollar
Population	182 000	**Languages**	English, creole

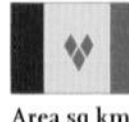

ST VINCENT AND THE GRENADINES
Capital Kingstown

Area sq km	389	**Currency**	East Caribbean
Area sq miles	150		dollar
Population	109 000	**Languages**	English, creole

SAMOA
Independent State of Samoa
Capital Apia

Area sq km	2 831	**Currency**	Tala
Area sq miles	1 093	**Languages**	Samoan, English
Population	190 000		

SAN MARINO
Republic of San Marino
Capital San Marino

Area sq km	61	**Currency**	Euro
Area sq miles	24	**Languages**	Italian
Population	31 000		

SÃO TOMÉ AND PRÍNCIPE
Democratic Rep. of São Tomé and Prínci
Capital São Tomé

Area sq km	964	**Currency**	Dobra
Area sq miles	372	**Languages**	Portuguese, creo
Population	193 000		

SAUDI ARABIA
Kingdom of Saudi Arabia
Capital Riyadh (Ar Riyāḍ)

Area sq km	2 200 000	**Currency**	Saudi Arabian
Area sq miles	849 425		riyal
Population	28 829 000	**Languages**	Arabic

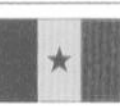

SENEGAL
Republic of Senegal
Capital Dakar

Area sq km	196 720	**Currency**	CFA franc*
Area sq miles	75 954	**Languages**	French, Wolof,
Population	14 133 000		Fulani, other loc
			lang.

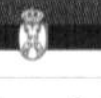

SERBIA
Republic of Serbia
Capital Belgrade (Beograd)

Area sq km	77 453	**Currency**	Serbian dinar,
Area sq miles	29 904	**Languages**	Serbian,
Population	7 181 505		Hungarian

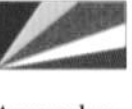

SEYCHELLES
Republic of Seychelles
Capital Victoria

Area sq km	455	**Currency**	Seychelles rupee
Area sq miles	176	**Languages**	English, French,
Population	93 000		creole

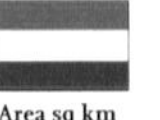

SIERRA LEONE
Republic of Sierra Leone
Capital Freetown

Area sq km	71 740	**Currency**	Leone
Area sq miles	27 699	**Languages**	English, creole,
Population	6 092 000		Mende, Temne,
			other local lang.

SINGAPORE
Republic of Singapore
Capital Singapore

Area sq km	639	**Currency**	Singapore dolla
Area sq miles	247	**Languages**	Chinese, English
Population	5 412 000		Malay, Tamil

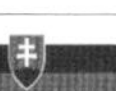

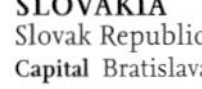

SLOVAKIA
Slovak Republic
Capital Bratislava

Area sq km	49 035	**Currency**	Euro
Area sq miles	18 933	**Languages**	Slovak,
Population	5 450 000		Hungarian, Czech

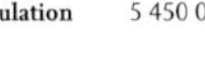

SLOVENIA
Republic of Slovenia
Capital Ljubljana

Area sq km	20 251	**Currency**	Euro
Area sq miles	7 819	**Languages**	Slovene, Croatian,
Population	2 072 000		Serbian

SOLOMON ISLANDS
Capital Honiara

Area sq km	28 370	**Currency**	Solomon Islands
Area sq miles	10 954		dollar
Population	561 000	**Languages**	English, creole,
			other local lang.

SOMALIA
Federal Republic of Somalia
Capital Mogadishu (Muqdisho)

Area sq km	637 657	**Currency**	Somali shilling
Area sq miles	246 201	**Languages**	Somali, Arabic
Population	10 496 000		

SOUTH AFRICA
Capital Pretoria (Tshwane)/
Cape Town/Bloemfontein

Area sq km	1 219 090	**Currency**	Rand
Area sq miles	470 693	**Languages**	Afrikaans,
Population	52 776 000		English, nine
			official local lang.

SOUTH KOREA
Republic of Korea
Capital Seoul (Sŏul)

Area sq km	99 274	**Currency**	South Korean
Area sq miles	38 330		won
Population	49 263 000	**Languages**	Korean

SOUTH SUDAN
Republic of South Sudan
Capital Juba

Area sq km	644 329	**Currency**	South Sudan
Area sq miles	248 775		pound
Population	11 296 000	**Languages**	English, Arabic,
			Dinka, Nuer, other
			local lang.

SPAIN
Kingdom of Spain
Capital Madrid

Area sq km	504 782	**Currency**	Euro
Area sq miles	194 897	**Languages**	Spanish (Castilian),
Population	46 927 000		Catalan, Galician,
			Basque

SRI LANKA
Democratic Socialist Republic of Sri Lanka
Capital Sri Jayewardenepura Kotte

Area sq km	65 610	**Currency**	Sri Lankan rupee
Area sq miles	25 332	**Languages**	Sinhalese,
Population	21 273 000		Tamil, English

SUDAN
Republic of the Sudan
Capital Khartoum

Area sq km	1 861 484	**Currency**	Sudanese pound
Area sq miles	718 725		(Sudani)
Population	37 964 000	**Languages**	Arabic, English,
			Nubian, Beja, Fur,
			other local lang.

SURINAME
Republic of Suriname
Capital Paramaribo

Area sq km	163 820	**Currency**	Surinamese guilder
Area sq miles	63 251	**Languages**	Dutch,
Population	539 000		Surinamese,
			English, Hindi

SWAZILAND
Kingdom of Swaziland
Capital Mbabane

Area sq km	17 364	**Currency**	Lilangeni ,
Area sq miles	6 704		South African
Population	1 250 000		rand
		Languages	Swazi, English

SWEDEN
Kingdom of Sweden
Capital Stockholm

Area sq km	449 964	**Currency**	Swedish krona
Area sq miles	173 732	**Languages**	Swedish, Sami
Population	9 571 000		

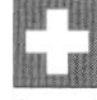

SWITZERLAND
Swiss Confederation
Capital Bern (Berne)

Area sq km	41 293	**Currency**	Swiss franc
Area sq miles	15 943	**Languages**	German, French,
Population	8 078 000		Italian, Romansch

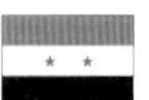

SYRIA
Syrian Arab Republic
Capital Damascus (Dimashq)

Area sq km	184 026	**Currency**	Syrian pound
Area sq miles	71 052	**Languages**	Arabic, Kurdish,
Population	21 898 000		Armenian

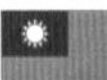

TAIWAN
Republic of China
Capital Taibei

Area sq km	36 179	**Currency**	New Taiwan dollar
Area sq miles	13 969	**Languages**	Mandarin
Population	23 344 000		(Putonghua), Min,
			Hakka, other local
			lang.

The People's Republic of China claims Taiwan as its 23rd province.

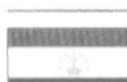

TAJIKISTAN
Republic of Tajikistan
Capital Dushanbe

Area sq km	143 100	**Currency**	Somoni
Area sq miles	55 251	**Languages**	Tajik, Uzbek,
Population	8 208 000		Russian

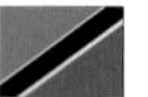

TANZANIA
United Republic of Tanzania
Capital Dodoma

Area sq km	945 087	**Currency**	Tanzanian shilling
Area sq miles	364 900	**Languages**	Swahili, English,
Population	49 253 000		Nyamwezi, other
			local lang.

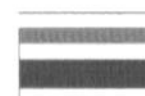

THAILAND
Kingdom of Thailand
Capital Bangkok (Krung Thep)

Area sq km	513 115	**Currency**	Baht
Area sq miles	198 115	**Languages**	Thai, Lao,
Population	67 011 000		Chinese, Malay,
			Mon-Khmer lang.

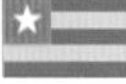

TOGO
Togolese Republic
Capital Lomé

Area sq km	56 785	**Currency**	CFA franc*
Area sq miles	21 925	**Languages**	French, Ewe,
Population	6 817 000		Kabre, other local
			lang.

TONGA
Kingdom of Tonga
Capital Nuku'alofa

Area sq km	748	**Currency**	Pa'anga
Area sq miles	289	**Languages**	Tongan, English
Population	105 000		

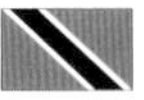

TRINIDAD AND TOBAGO
Republic of Trinidad and Tobago
Capital Port of Spain

Area sq km	5 130	**Currency**	Trinidad and
Area sq miles	1 981		Tobago dollar
Population	1 341 000	**Languages**	English, creole,
			Hindi

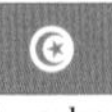

TUNISIA
Republic of Tunisia
Capital Tunis

Area sq km	164 150	**Currency**	Tunisian dinar
Area sq miles	63 379	**Languages**	Arabic, French
Population	10 997 000		

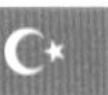

TURKEY
Republic of Turkey
Capital Ankara

Area sq km	779 452	**Currency**	Lira
Area sq miles	300 948	**Languages**	Turkish, Kurdish
Population	74 933 000		

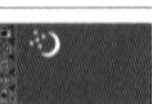

TURKMENISTAN
Capital Aşgabat (Ashkhabad)

Area sq km	488 100	**Currency**	Turkmen manat
Area sq miles	188 456	**Languages**	Turkmen, Uzbek,
Population	5 240 000		Russian

TUVALU
Capital Vaiaku

Area sq km	25	**Currency**	Australian dollar
Area sq miles	10	**Languages**	Tuvaluan, English
Population	10 000		

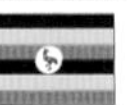

UGANDA
Republic of Uganda
Capital Kampala

Area sq km	241 038	**Currency**	Ugandan shilling
Area sq miles	93 065	**Languages**	English, Swahili,
Population	37 579 000		Luganda, other
			local lang.

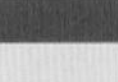

UKRAINE
Capital Kiev (Kyiv)

Area sq km	603 700	**Currency**	Hryvnia
Area sq miles	233 090	**Languages**	Ukrainian,
Population	45 239 000		Russian

UNITED ARAB EMIRATES
Federation of Emirates
Capital Abu Dhabi (Abū Ẓaby)

Area sq km	77 700	**Currency** UAE dirham
Area sq miles	30 000	**Languages** Arabic, English
Population	9 346 000	

UNITED KINGDOM
United Kingdom of Great Britain and
Northern Ireland
Capital London

Area sq km	243 609	**Currency** Pound sterling
Area sq miles	94 058	**Languages** English, Welsh,
Population	63 136 000	Gaelic

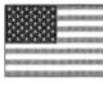

UNITED STATES OF AMERICA
Capital Washington D.C.

Area sq km	9 826 635	**Currency** US dollar
Area sq miles	3 794 085	**Languages** English, Spanish
Population	320 051 000	

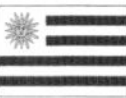

URUGUAY
Oriental Republic of Uruguay
Capital Montevideo

Area sq km	176 215	**Currency** Uruguayan peso
Area sq miles	68 037	**Languages** Spanish
Population	3 407 000	

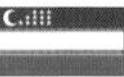

UZBEKISTAN
Republic of Uzbekistan
Capital Tashkent

Area sq km	447 400	**Currency** Uzbek som
Area sq miles	172 742	**Languages** Uzbek, Russian,
Population	28 934 000	Tajik, Kazakh

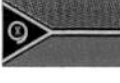

VANUATU
Republic of Vanuatu
Capital Port Vila

Area sq km	12 190	**Currency** Vatu
Area sq miles	4 707	**Languages** English,
Population	253 000	Bislama (creole),
		French

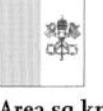

VATICAN CITY
Vatican City State or Holy See
Capital Vatican City

Area sq km	0.5	**Currency** Euro
Area sq miles	0.2	**Languages** Italian
Population	800	

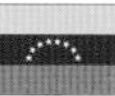

VENEZUELA
Bolivarian Republic of Venezuela
Capital Caracas

Area sq km	912 050	**Currency** Bolívar
Area sq miles	352 144	**Languages** Spanish,
Population	30 405 000	Amerindian lang.

VIETNAM
Socialist Republic of Vietnam
Capital Ha Nôi (Hanoi)

Area sq km	329 565	**Currency** Dong
Area sq miles	127 246	**Languages** Vietnamese, Thai,
Population	91 680 000	Khmer, Chinese,
		other local lang.

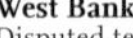

West Bank
Disputed territory

Area sq km	5 860	**Currency** Jordanian dinar,
Area sq miles	2 263	Israeli shekel
Population	2 719 112	**Languages** Arabic, Hebrew

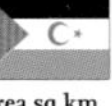

Western Sahara
Disputed territory (Morocco)
Capital Laâyoune

Area sq km	266 000	**Currency** Moroccan dirham
Area sq miles	102 703	**Languages** Arabic
Population	567 000	

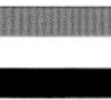

YEMEN
Republic of Yemen
Capital Şan'a'

Area sq km	527 968	**Currency** Yemeni riyal
Area sq miles	203 850	**Languages** Arabic
Population	24 407 000	

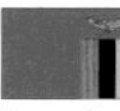

ZAMBIA
Republic of Zambia
Capital Lusaka

Area sq km	752 614	**Currency** Zambian kwacha
Area sq miles	290 586	**Languages** English, Bemba,
Population	14 539 000	Nyanja, Tonga,
		other local lang.

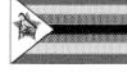

ZIMBABWE
Republic of Zimbabwe
Capital Harare

Area sq km	390 759	**Currency** US dollar and
Area sq miles	150 873	other currencies
Population	14 150 000	**Languages** 16 local languages
		including English,
		Shona, Ndebele

Total Land Area 8 844 516 sq km / 3 414 868 sq miles
(includes New Guinea and Pacific Island nations)

HIGHEST MOUNTAIN
Puncak Jaya
4 884 m / 16 023 feet

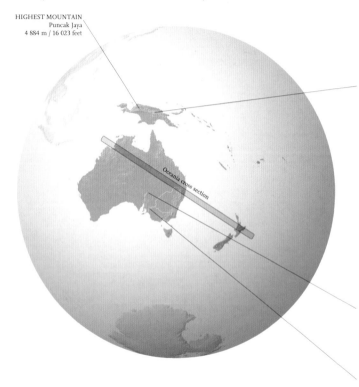

Oceania cross section

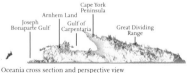

Joseph
Bonaparte Gulf

Arnhem Land

Gulf of
Carpentaria

Cape York
Peninsula

Great Dividing
Range

Oceania cross section and perspective view

Cook Strait

North Island

North Cape

Tasman Sea

HIGHEST MOUNTAINS	metres	feet	Map page
Puncak Jaya, Indonesia	4 884	16 023	59 D3
Puncak Trikora, Indonesia	4 730	15 518	59 D3
Puncak Mandala, Indonesia	4 700	15 420	59 D3
Puncak Yamin, Indonesia	4 595	15 075	—
Mt Wilhelm, Papua New Guinea	4 509	14 793	59 D3
Mt Kubor, Papua New Guinea	4 359	14 301	—

LARGEST ISLAND
New Guinea
808 510 sq km /
312 166 sq miles

LARGEST ISLANDS	sq km	sq miles	Map page
New Guinea	808 510	312 166	59 D3
South Island (Te Waipounamu)	151 215	58 384	54 B2
North Island (Te Ika-a-Māui)	115 777	44 701	54 B1
Tasmania	67 800	26 178	51 D4

LONGEST RIVERS	km	miles	Map page
Murray-Darling	3 672	2 282	52 B2
Darling	2 844	1 767	52 B2
Murray	2 375	1 476	52 B3
Murrumbidgee	1 485	923	52 B2
Lachlan	1 339	832	53 C2
Cooper Creek	1 113	692	52 B1

LARGEST LAKES	sq km	sq miles	Map page
Kati Thanda-Lake Eyre	0–8 900	0–3 436	52 A1
Lake Torrens	0–5 780	0–2 232	52 A1

LARGEST LAKE AND LOWEST POINT
Kati Thanda-Lake Eyre
0-8 900 sq km / 0-3 436 sq miles
16 m / 52 feet below sea level

LONGEST RIVER AND
LARGEST DRAINAGE BASIN
Murray-Darling
3 672 km / 2 282 miles
1 058 000 sq km / 409 000 sq miles

Total Land Area 45 036 492 sq km / 17 388 590 sq miles

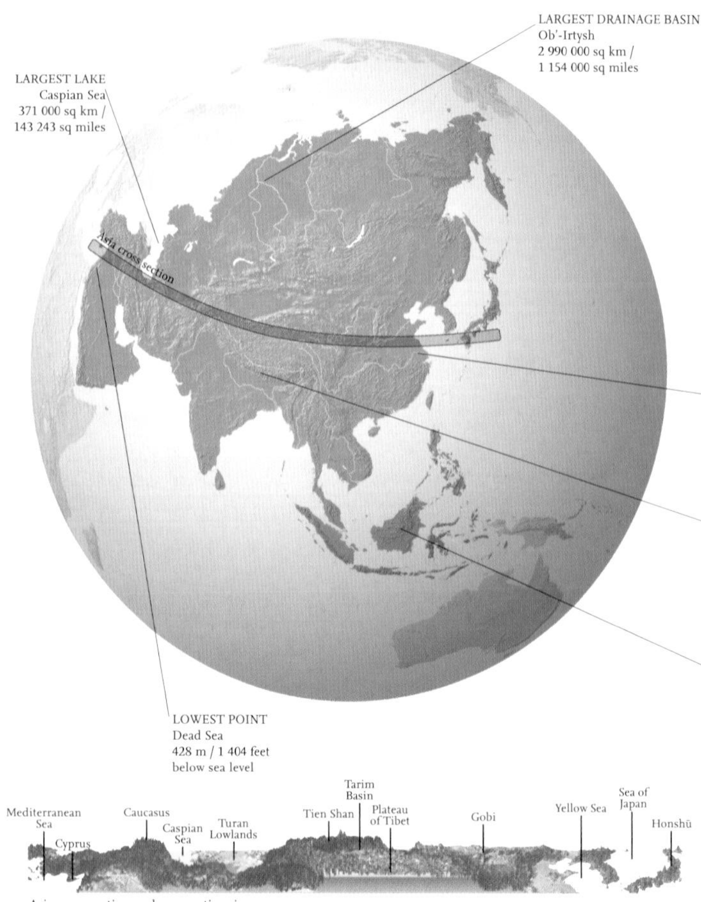

LARGEST DRAINAGE BASIN
Ob'-Irtysh
2 990 000 sq km /
1 154 000 sq miles

LARGEST LAKE
Caspian Sea
371 000 sq km /
143 243 sq miles

Asia cross section

LOWEST POINT
Dead Sea
428 m / 1 404 feet
below sea level

Mediterranean
Sea
Cyprus
Caucasus
Caspian
Sea
Turan
Lowlands
Tien Shan
Tarim
Basin
Plateau
of Tibet
Gobi
Yellow Sea
Sea of
Japan
Honshū

Asia cross section and perspective view

HIGHEST MOUNTAINS	metres	feet	Map page
Mt Everest (Sagarmatha/ Qomolangma Feng), China/Nepal	8 848	29 028	75 C2
K2 (Qogir Feng), China/Pakistan	8 611	28 251	74 B1
Kangchenjunga, India/Nepal	8 586	28 169	75 C2
Lhotse, China/Nepal	8 516	27 939	—
Makalu, China/Nepal	8 463	27 765	—
Cho Oyu, China/Nepal	8 201	26 906	—

LARGEST ISLANDS	sq km	sq miles	Map page
Borneo	745 561	287 861	61 C1
Sumatra (Sumatera)	473 606	182 859	60 A1
Honshū	227 414	87 805	67 B3
Celebes (Sulawesi)	189 216	73 056	58 C3
Java (Jawa)	132 188	51 038	61 B2
Luzon	104 690	40 421	64 B1

LONGEST RIVER
Yangtze (Chang Jiang)
6 380 km /
3 965 miles

LONGEST RIVERS	km	miles	Map page
Yangtze (Chang Jiang)	6 380	3 965	70 C2
Ob'-Irtysh	5 568	3 460	86 F2
Yenisey-Angara-Selenga	5 550	3 449	83 H3
Yellow (Huang He)	5 464	3 395	70 B2
Irtysh	4 440	2 759	86 F2
Mekong	4 425	2 750	63 B2

HIGHEST MOUNTAIN
Mt Everest
8 848 m / 29 028 feet

LARGEST LAKES	sq km	sq miles	Map page
Caspian Sea	371 000	143 243	81 C1
Lake Baikal (Ozero Baykal)	30 500	11 776	69 D1
Lake Balkhash (Ozero Balkash)	17 400	6 718	77 D2
Aral Sea (Aral'skoye More)	17 158	6 625	76 B2
Ysyk-Köl	6 200	2 394	77 D2

LARGEST ISLAND
Borneo
745 561 sq km /
287 861 sq miles

Total Land Area 9 908 599 sq km / 3 825 710 sq miles

LARGEST ISLAND
Great Britain
218 476 sq km /
84 354 sq miles

Europe cross section

HIGHEST MOUNTAIN
El'brus
5 642 m / 18 510 feet

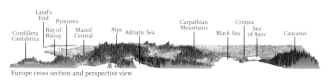

Cordillera
Cantabrica · Land's End · Bay of Biscay · Pyrenees · Massif Central · Alps · Adriatic Sea · Carpathian Mountains · Black Sea · Crimea · Sea of Azov · Caucasus

Europe cross section and perspective view

HIGHEST MOUNTAINS	metres	feet	Map pages
El'brus, Russian Federation	5 642	18 510	87 D4
Gora Dykh-Tau, Russian Federation	5 204	17 073	—
Shkhara, Georgia/Russian Federation	5 201	17 063	—
Kazbek, Georgia/Russian Federation	5 047	16 558	76 A2
Mont Blanc, France/Italy	4 810	15 781	105 D2
Dufourspitze, Italy/Switzerland	4 634	15 203	—

LARGEST ISLANDS	sq km	sq miles	Map pages
Great Britain	218 476	84 354	95 C3
Iceland	102 820	39 699	92 A3
Ireland	83 045	32 064	97 C2
Ostrov Severnyy (part of Novaya Zemlya)	47 079	18 177	86 E1
Spitsbergen	37 814	14 600	82 C1

LONGEST RIVER AND
LARGEST DRAINAGE BASIN
Volga
3 688 km / 2 292 miles
1 380 000 sq km / 533 000 sq miles

LONGEST RIVERS	km	miles	Map pages
Volga	3 688	2 292	89 F2
Danube	2 850	1 771	110 A1
Dnieper	2 285	1 420	91 C2
Kama	2 028	1 260	86 E3
Don	1 931	1 200	89 E3
Pechora	1 802	1 120	86 E2

LARGEST LAKE AND LOWEST POINT
Caspian Sea
371 000 sq km / 143 243 sq miles
28m / 92 feet below sea level

LARGEST LAKES	sq km	sq miles	Map pages
Caspian Sea	371 000	143 243	81 C1
Lake Ladoga (Ladozhskoye Ozero)	18 390	7 100	86 C2
Lake Onega (Onezhskoye Ozero)	9 600	3 707	86 C2
Vänern	5 585	2 156	93 F4
Rybinskoye Vodokhranilishche	5 180	2 000	89 E2

Total Land Area 30 343 578 sq km / 11 715 655 sq miles

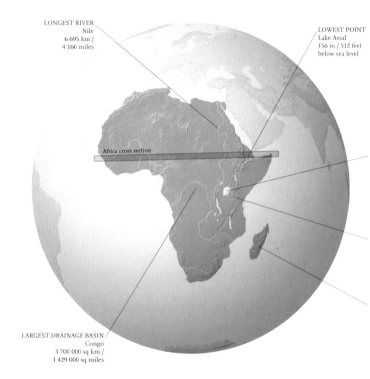

LONGEST RIVER
Nile
6 695 km /
4 160 miles

LOWEST POINT
Lake Assal
156 m / 512 feet
below sea level

Africa cross section

LARGEST DRAINAGE BASIN
Congo
3 700 000 sq km /
1 429 000 sq miles

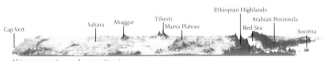

Cap Vert · Sahara · Ahaggar · Tibesti · Marra Plateau · Ethiopian Highlands · Red Sea · Arabian Peninsula · Socotra

Africa cross section and perspective view

HIGHEST MOUNTAINS	metres	feet	Map page
Kilimanjaro, Tanzania	5 892	19 330	119 D3
Mt Kenya (Kirinyaga), Kenya	5 199	17 057	119 D3
Margherita Peak, Democratic Republic of the Congo/Uganda	5 110	16 765	119 C2
Meru, Tanzania	4 565	14 977	119 D3
Ras Dejen, Ethiopia	4 533	14 872	117 B3
Mt Karisimbi, Rwanda	4 510	14 796	—

LARGEST ISLANDS	sq km	sq miles	Map page
Madagascar	587 040	226 656	121 D3

LONGEST RIVERS	km	miles	Map page
Nile	6 695	4 160	116 B1
Congo	4 667	2 900	118 B3
Niger	4 184	2 600	115 C4
Zambezi	2 736	1 700	120 C2
Wabē Shebelē Wenz	2 490	1 547	117 C4
Ubangi	2 250	1 398	118 B3

LARGEST LAKES	sq km	sq miles	Map page
Lake Victoria	68 870	26 591	52 B2
Lake Tanganyika	32 600	12 587	119 C3
Lake Nyasa (Lake Malawi)	29 500	11 390	121 C1
Lake Volta	8 482	3 275	114 C4
Lake Turkana	6 500	2 510	119 D2
Lake Albert	5 600	2 162	119 D2

LARGEST LAKE
Lake Victoria
68 870 sq km /
26 591 sq miles

HIGHEST MOUNTAIN
Kilimanjaro
5 892 m / 19 330 feet

LARGEST ISLAND
Madagascar
587 040 sq km /
226 656 sq miles

Total Land Area 24 680 331 sq km / 9 529 076 sq miles
(including Hawaiian Islands)

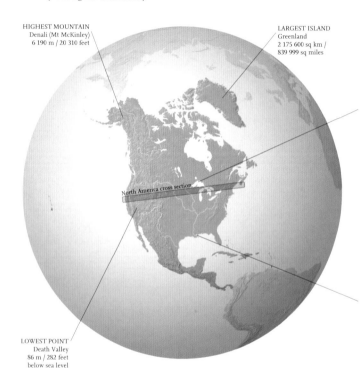

HIGHEST MOUNTAIN
Denali (Mt McKinley)
6 190 m / 20 310 feet

LARGEST ISLAND
Greenland
2 175 600 sq km /
839 999 sq miles

North America cross section

LOWEST POINT
Death Valley
86 m / 282 feet
below sea level

Coast Ranges | Rocky Mountains | Great Plains | Lake Michigan | Lake Huron | Lake Erie | Chesapeake Bay | Appalachian Mountains | Long Island | Cape Cod | Nova Scotia

North America cross section and perspective view

HIGHEST MOUNTAINS	metres	feet	Map page
Denali, USA	6 190	20 310	124 F2
Mt Logan, Canada	5 959	19 550	126 B2
Pico de Orizaba, Mexico	5 610	18 405	145 C3
Mt St Elias, USA	5 489	18 008	126 B2
Volcán Popocatépetl, Mexico	5 452	17 887	145 C3
Mt Foraker, USA	5 303	17 398	—

LARGEST LAKE
Lake Superior
82 100 sq km /
31 699 sq miles

LARGEST ISLANDS	sq km	sq miles	Map page
Greenland	2 175 600	839 999	127 I2
Baffin Island	507 451	195 927	127 G2
Victoria Island	217 291	83 896	126 D2
Ellesmere Island	196 236	75 767	127 F1
Cuba	110 860	42 803	146 B2
Newfoundland	108 860	42 031	131 E2
Hispaniola	76 192	29 418	147 C2

LONGEST RIVERS	km	miles	Map page
Mississippi-Missouri	5 969	3 709	133 D3
Mackenzie-Peace-Finlay	4 241	2 635	126 C2
Missouri	4 086	2 539	137 E3
Mississippi	3 765	2 340	142 C3
Yukon	3 185	1 979	126 A2
St Lawrence	3 058	1 900	131 D2

LONGEST RIVER AND
LARGEST DRAINAGE BASIN
Mississippi-Missouri
5 969 km / 3 709 miles
3 250 000 sq km / 1 255 000
sq miles

LARGEST LAKES	sq km	sq miles	Map page
Lake Superior	82 100	31 699	140 B1
Lake Huron	59 600	23 012	140 C2
Lake Michigan	57 800	22 317	140 B2
Great Bear Lake	31 328	12 096	126 C2
Great Slave Lake	28 568	11 030	128 C1
Lake Erie	25 700	9 923	140 C2
Lake Winnipeg	24 387	9 416	129 E2
Lake Ontario	18 960	7 320	141 D2

Total Land Area 17 815 420 sq km / 6 878 534 sq miles

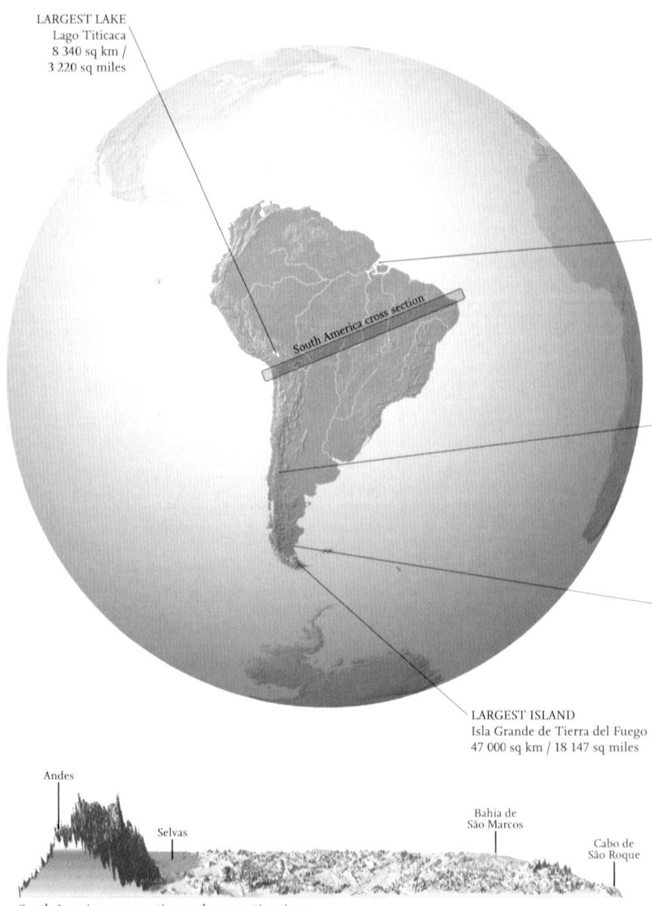

LARGEST LAKE
Lago Titicaca
8 340 sq km /
3 220 sq miles

South America cross section

LARGEST ISLAND
Isla Grande de Tierra del Fuego
47 000 sq km / 18 147 sq miles

Andes

Selvas

Bahia de
São Marcos

Cabo de
São Roque

South America cross section and perspective view

HIGHEST MOUNTAINS	metres	feet	Map page
Cerro Aconcagua, Argentina	6 959	22 831	153 B4
Nevado Ojos del Salado, Argentina/Chile	6 908	22 664	152 B3
Cerro Bonete, Argentina	6 872	22 546	—
Cerro Pissis, Argentina	6 858	22 500	—
Cerro Tupungato, Argentina/Chile	6 800	22 309	—
Cerro Mercedario, Argentina	6 770	22 211	—

LARGEST ISLANDS	sq km	sq miles	Map page
Isla Grande de Tierra del Fuego	47 000	18 147	153 B6
Isla de Chiloé	8 394	3 241	153 A5
East Falkland	6 760	2 610	153 C6
West Falkland	5 413	2 090	153 B6

LONGEST RIVER AND
LARGEST DRAINAGE BASIN
Amazon
8 516 km / 4 049 miles
7 050 000 sq km / 2 722 000 sq miles

LONGEST RIVERS	km	miles	Map page
Amazon (Amazonas)	6 516	4 049	150 C1
Río de la Plata-Paraná	4 500	2 796	153 C4
Purus	3 218	2 000	150 B2
Madeira	3 200	1 988	150 C2
São Francisco	2 900	1 802	151 E3
Tocantins	2 750	1 709	151 D2

HIGHEST MOUNTAIN
Cerro Aconcagua
6 959 m / 22 831 feet

LARGEST LAKES	sq km	sq miles	Map page
Lake Titicaca	8 340	3 220	152 B2

LOWEST POINT
Laguna del Carbón
105 m / 344 feet below sea level

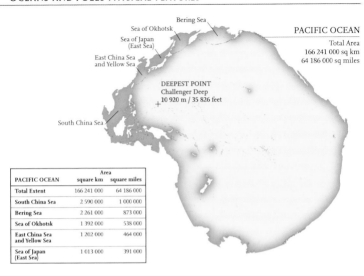

PACIFIC OCEAN

Total Area
166 241 000 sq km
64 186 000 sq miles

Bering Sea

Sea of Okhotsk

Sea of Japan
(East Sea)

East China Sea
and Yellow Sea

DEEPEST POINT
Challenger Deep
10 920 m / 35 826 feet

South China Sea

PACIFIC OCEAN	Area square km	square miles
Total Extent	166 241 000	64 186 000
South China Sea	2 590 000	1 000 000
Bering Sea	2 261 000	873 000
Sea of Okhotsk	1 392 000	538 000
East China Sea and Yellow Sea	1 202 000	464 000
Sea of Japan (East Sea)	1 013 000	391 000

ANTARCTICA

Total Land Area 12 093 000 sq km /
4 669 107 sq miles (excluding ice shelves)

HIGHEST MOUNTAIN
Mount Vinson
4 897 m / 16 066 feet

HIGHEST MOUNTAINS	Height metres	feet
Mount Vinson	4 897	16 066
Mt Tyree	4 852	15 918
Mt Kirkpatrick	4 528	14 855
Mt Markham	4 351	14 275
Mt Sidley	4 285	14 058
Mt Minto	4 165	13 665

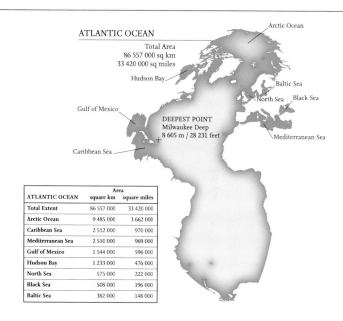

ATLANTIC OCEAN

Total Area
86 557 000 sq km
33 420 000 sq miles

Arctic Ocean

Hudson Bay

Baltic Sea

North Sea   Black Sea

Gulf of Mexico

DEEPEST POINT
Milwaukee Deep
8 605 m / 28 231 feet

Mediterranean Sea

Caribbean Sea

ATLANTIC OCEAN	Area	
	square km	square miles
Total Extent	86 557 000	33 420 000
Arctic Ocean	9 485 000	3 662 000
Caribbean Sea	2 512 000	970 000
Mediterranean Sea	2 510 000	969 000
Gulf of Mexico	1 544 000	596 000
Hudson Bay	1 233 000	476 000
North Sea	575 000	222 000
Black Sea	508 000	196 000
Baltic Sea	382 000	148 000

The Gulf

Red Sea

Bay of Bengal

DEEPEST POINT
Java Trench
7 125 m / 23 376 feet

INDIAN OCEAN	Area	
	square km	square miles
Total Extent	73 427 000	28 350 000
Bay of Bengal	2 172 000	839 000
Red Sea	453 000	175 000
The Gulf	238 000	92 000

INDIAN OCEAN

Total Area
73 427 000 sq km
28 350 000 sq miles

MAJOR CLIMATIC REGIONS AND SUB-TYPES
Köppen classification system
Winkel Tripel Projection
scale 1:200 000 000

• Weather
  extreme location

WORLD WEATHER EXTREMES

	Location
Highest shade temperature	56.7°C / 134°F Furnace Creek, Death Valley, California, USA (10 July 1913)
Hottest place – Annual mean	34.4°C / 93.9°F Dalol, Ethiopia
Driest place – Annual mean	0.1 mm / 0.004 inches Atacama Desert, Chile
Most sunshine – Annual mean	90% Yuma, Arizona, USA (over 4 000 hours)
Least sunshine	Nil for 182 days each year, South Pole
Lowest screen temperature	-89.2°C / -128.6°F Vostok Station, Antarctica (21 July 1983)
Coldest place – Annual mean	-56.6°C / -69.9°F Plateau Station, Antarctica
Wettest place – Annual mean	11 873 mm / 467.4 inches Meghalaya, India
Highest surface wind speed	
- High altitude	372 km per hour/231 miles per hour Mount Washington, New Hampshire, USA, (12 April 1934)
- Low altitude	408 km per hour/254 miles per hour Barrow Island, Australia (10 April 1996)
- Tornado	512 km per hour / 318 miles per hour in a tornado, Oklahoma City, Oklahoma, USA (3 May 1999)
Greatest snowfall	31 102 mm / 1 224.5 inches Mount Rainier, Washington, USA (19 February 1971 – 18 February 1972)

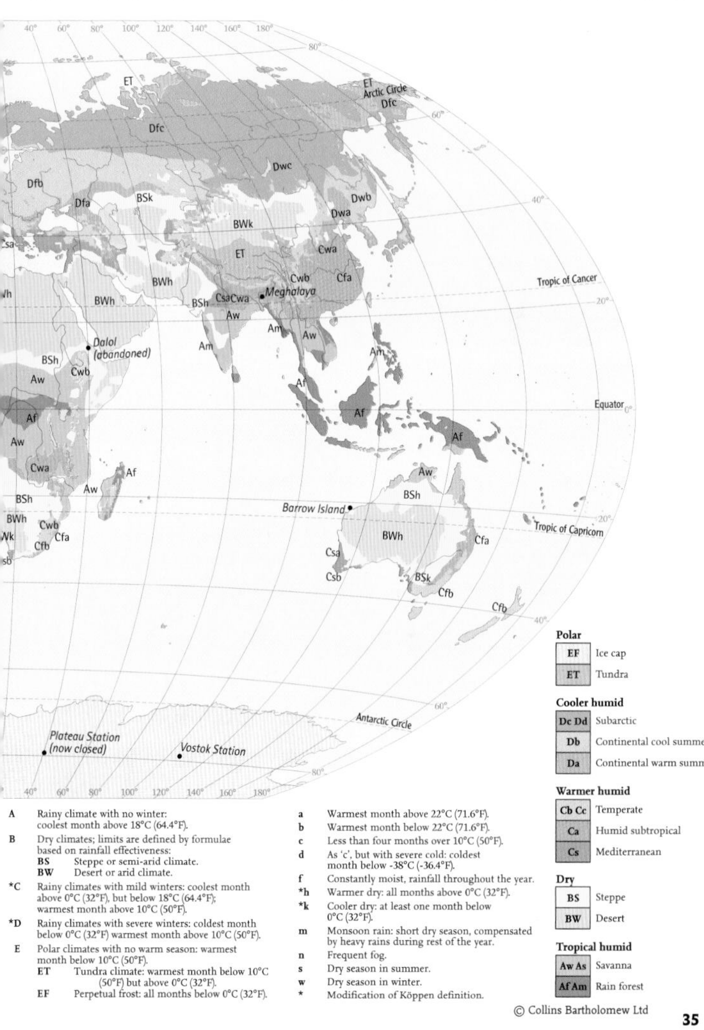

A Rainy climate with no winter: coolest month above 18°C (64.4°F).

B Dry climates; limits are defined by formulae based on rainfall effectiveness:
   BS Steppe or semi-arid climate.
   BW Desert or arid climate.

*C Rainy climates with mild winters: coolest month above 0°C (32°F), but below 18°C (64.4°F); warmest month above 10°C (50°F).

*D Rainy climates with severe winters: coldest month below 0°C (32°F) warmest month above 10°C (50°F).

E Polar climates with no warm season: warmest month below 10°C (50°F).
   ET Tundra climate: warmest month below 10°C (50°F) but above 0°C (32°F).
   EF Perpetual frost: all months below 0°C (32°F).

a Warmest month above 22°C (71.6°F).
b Warmest month below 22°C (71.6°F).
c Less than four months over 10°C (50°F).
d As 'c', but with severe cold: coldest month below -38°C (-36.4°F).
f Constantly moist, rainfall throughout the year.
*h Warmer dry: all months above 0°C (32°F).
*k Cooler dry: at least one month below 0°C (32°F).
m Monsoon rain: short dry season, compensated by heavy rains during rest of the year.
n Frequent fog.
s Dry season in summer.
w Dry season in winter.
* Modification of Köppen definition.

Polar

EF	Ice cap
ET	Tundra

Cooler humid

Dc Dd	Subarctic
Db	Continental cool summer
Da	Continental warm summer

Warmer humid

Cb Cc	Temperate
Ca	Humid subtropical
Cs	Mediterranean

Dry

BS	Steppe
BW	Desert

Tropical humid

Aw As	Savanna
Af Am	Rain forest

© Collins Bartholomew Ltd

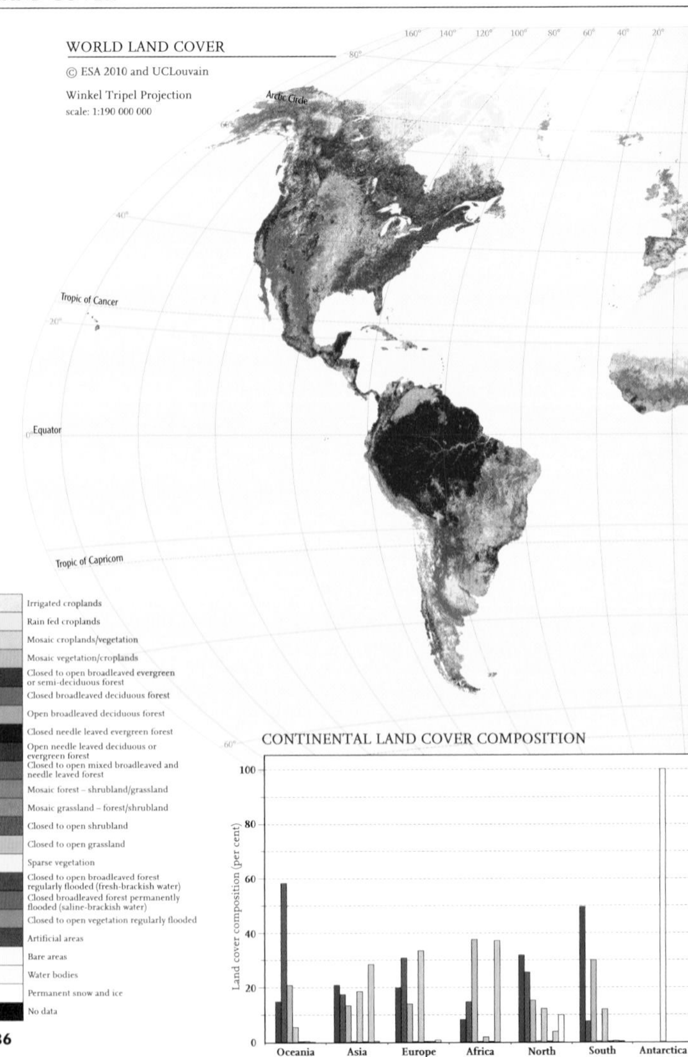

WORLD LAND COVER

© ESA 2010 and UCLouvain

Winkel Tripel Projection
scale: 1:190 000 000

Irrigated croplands
Rain fed croplands
Mosaic croplands/vegetation
Mosaic vegetation/croplands
Closed to open broadleaved evergreen or semi-deciduous forest
Closed broadleaved deciduous forest
Open broadleaved deciduous forest
Closed needle leaved evergreen forest
Open needle leaved deciduous or evergreen forest
Closed to open mixed broadleaved and needle leaved forest
Mosaic forest – shrubland/grassland
Mosaic grassland – forest/shrubland
Closed to open shrubland
Closed to open grassland
Sparse vegetation
Closed to open broadleaved forest regularly flooded (fresh-brackish water)
Closed broadleaved forest permanently flooded (saline-brackish water)
Closed to open vegetation regularly flooded
Artificial areas
Bare areas
Water bodies
Permanent snow and ice
No data

CONTINENTAL LAND COVER COMPOSITION

36

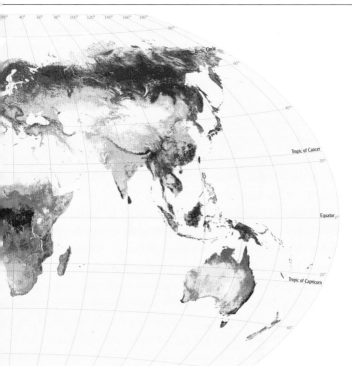

LAND COVER GRAPHS - CLASSIFICATION

Class description	Map classes
Forest/Woodland	Evergreen needleleaf forest
	Evergreen broadleaf forest
	Deciduous needleleaf forest
	Deciduous broadleaf forest
	Mixed forest
Shrubland	Closed shrublands
	Open shrublands
Grass/Savanna	Woody savannas
	Savannas
	Grasslands
Wetland	Permanent wetlands
Crops/Mosaic	Croplands
	Cropland/Natural vegetation mosaic
Urban	Urban and built-up
Snow/Ice	Snow and Ice
Barren	Barren or sparsely vegetated

GLOBAL LAND COVER COMPOSITION

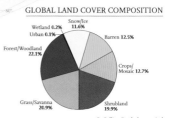

Wetland **0.2%**
Urban **0.1%**
Snow/Ice **11.6%**
Barren **12.5%**
Forest/Woodland **22.1%**
Crops/Mosaic **12.7%**
Shrubland **19.9%**
Grass/Savanna **20.9%**

WORLD POPULATION DISTRIBUTION

Population Density
Winkel Tripel Projection
scale 1:190 000 000

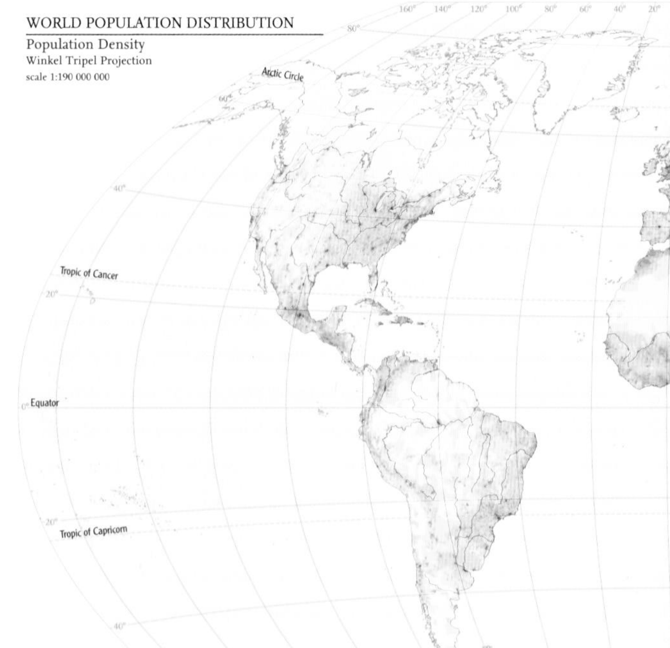

KEY POPULATION STATISTICS FOR MAJOR REGIONS

	Population 2013 (millions)	Growth (per cent)	Infant mortality rate	Total fertility rate	Life expectancy (years)
World	7 162	1.1	37	2.5	70
More developed regions[1]	1 253	0.3	6	1.7	78
Less developed regions[2]	5 909	1.3	40	2.6	67
Africa	1 111	2.5	64	4.7	58
Asia	4 299	1.0	31	2.2	71
Europe[3]	742	0.1	6	1.6	76
Latin America and the Caribbean[4]	617	1.1	18	2.2	75
North America	355	0.9	6	1.9	79
Oceania	38	1.4	20	2.4	78

1. Europe, North America, Australia, New Zealand and Japan.

2. Africa, Asia (excluding Japan), Latin America and the Caribbean, and Oceania (excluding Australia and New Zealand).

3. Includes Russia.

4. South America, Central America (including Mexico) and all Caribbean Islands.

Except for population (2013) the data are annual averages projected for the period 2010–2015.

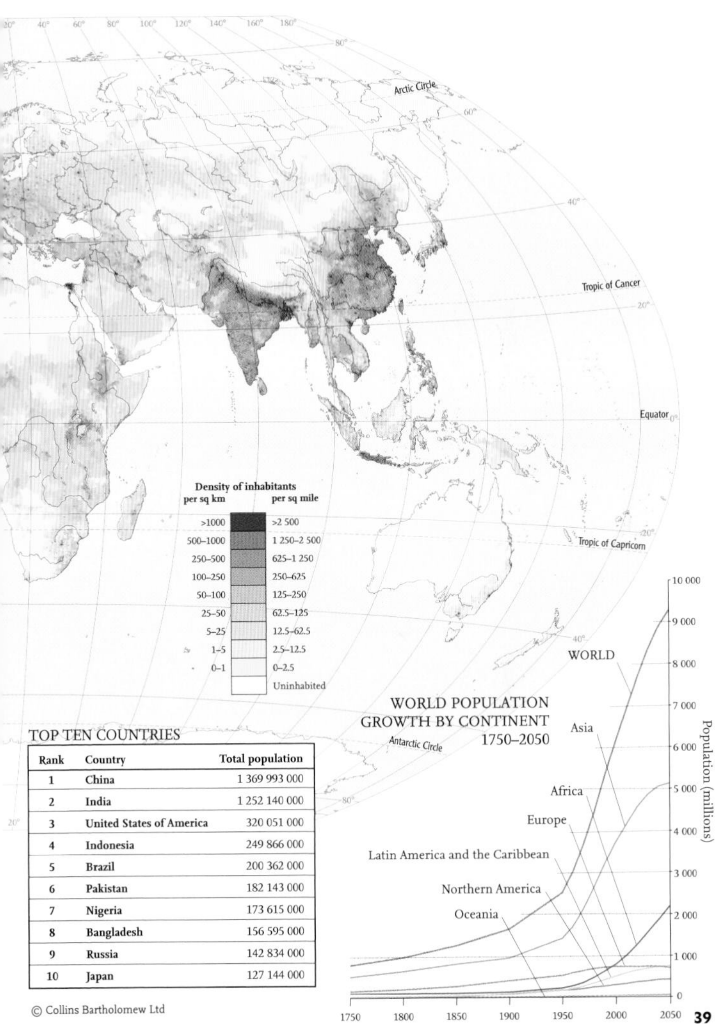

Density of inhabitants

per sq km	per sq mile
>1000	>2 500
500–1000	1 250–2 500
250–500	625–1 250
100–250	250–625
50–100	125–250
25–50	62.5–125
5–25	12.5–62.5
1–5	2.5–12.5
0–1	0–2.5
	Uninhabited

WORLD POPULATION GROWTH BY CONTINENT 1750–2050

WORLD
Asia
Africa
Europe
Latin America and the Caribbean
Northern America
Oceania

TOP TEN COUNTRIES

Rank	Country	Total population
1	China	1 369 993 000
2	India	1 252 140 000
3	United States of America	320 051 000
4	Indonesia	249 866 000
5	Brazil	200 362 000
6	Pakistan	182 143 000
7	Nigeria	173 615 000
8	Bangladesh	156 595 000
9	Russia	142 834 000
10	Japan	127 144 000

© Collins Bartholomew Ltd

THE WORLD'S MAJOR CITIES

Urban agglomerations with over
1 million inhabitants.
Winkel Tripel Projection
scale 1:190 000 000

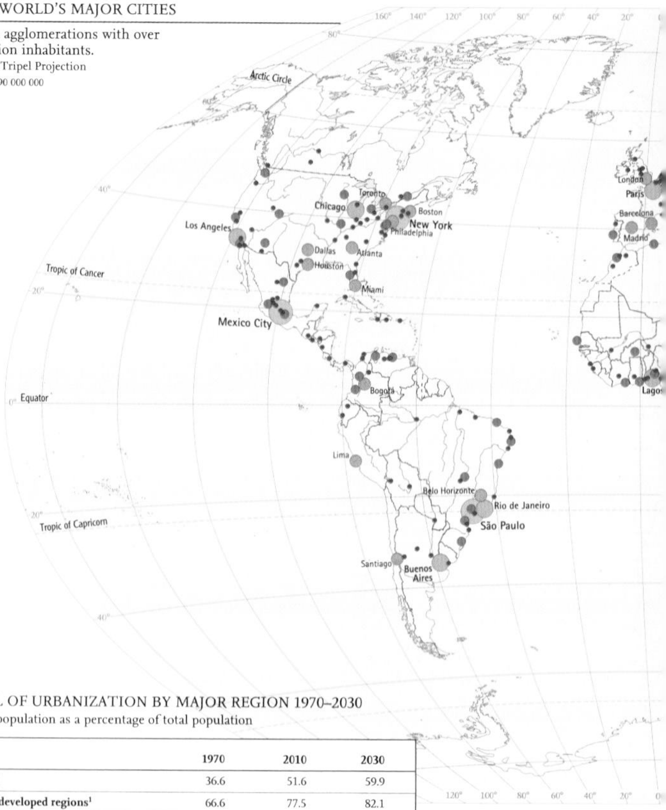

LEVEL OF URBANIZATION BY MAJOR REGION 1970–2030

Urban population as a percentage of total population

	1970	2010	2030
World	36.6	51.6	59.9
More developed regions[1]	66.6	77.5	82.1
Less developed regions[2]	25.3	46.0	55.8
Africa	23.5	39.2	47.7
Asia	23.7	44.4	55.5
Europe[3]	62.8	72.7	77.4
Latin America and the Caribbean[4]	57.1	78.8	83.4
Northern America	73.8	82.0	85.8
Oceania	71.2	70.7	71.4

1. Europe, North America, Australia,
New Zealand and Japan.

2. Africa, Asia (excluding Japan), Latin
America and the Caribbean, and
Oceania (excluding Australia and
New Zealand).

3. Includes Russia.

4. South America, Central America
(including Mexico) and all Caribbean
Islands.

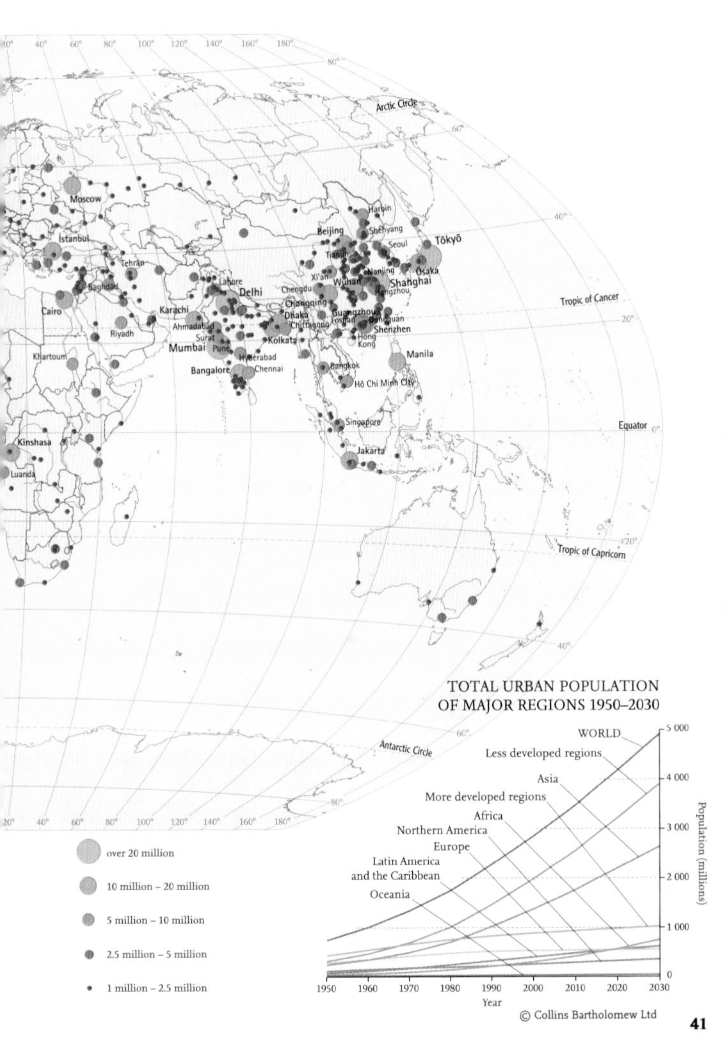

TOTAL URBAN POPULATION
OF MAJOR REGIONS 1950–2030

over 20 million

10 million – 20 million

5 million – 10 million

2.5 million – 5 million

1 million – 2.5 million

© Collins Bartholomew Ltd

SYMBOLS

Map symbols used on the map pages are explained here. The depiction of relief follows the tradition of layer-colouring, with colours depicting altitude bands. Ocean pages have a different contour interval. Settlements are classified in terms of both population and administrative significance. The abbreviations listed are those used in place names on the map pages and within the index.

LAND AND WATER FEATURES

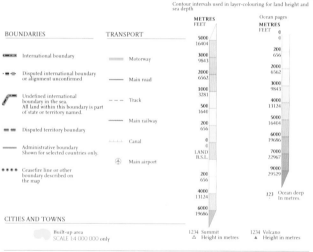

Lake	River
Impermanent lake	Impermanent river
Salt lake or lagoon	Ice cap / Glacier
Impermanent salt lake	123 Pass height in metres
Dry salt lake or salt pan	∴ Site of special interest
	Wall

BOUNDARIES

▭▬▭	International boundary
▪▬◆	Disputed international boundary or alignment unconfirmed
	Undefined international boundary in the sea. All land within this boundary is part of state or territory named.
▬▬	Disputed territory boundary
	Administrative boundary Shown for selected countries only.
✶✶✶✶	Ceasefire line or other boundary described on the map

TRANSPORT

Motorway	
Main road	
Track	
Main railway	
Canal	
✈ Main airport	

RELIEF

Contour intervals used in layer-colouring for land height and sea depth

METRES FEET		Ocean pages METRES FEET
5000 16404		0 0
3000 9843		200 656
2000 6562		2000 6562
1000 3281		3000 9843
500 1640		4000 13124
200 656		5000 16404
0 0		6000 19686
LAND B.S.L.		7000 22967
200 656		9000 29529
4000 13124		123 Ocean deep In metres.
6000 19686		

1234 Summit △ Height in metres

1234 Volcano ▲ Height in metres

CITIES AND TOWNS

Built-up area
SCALE 1:4 000 000 only

Population	National Capital	Administrative Capital Shown for selected countries only	Other City or Town
over 10 million	**BEIJING** ■	**São Paulo** ◉	**New York** ◉
5 to 10 million	**MADRID** ▣	**Toronto** ◉	**Philadelphia** ◉
1 to 5 million	**KUWAIT** ▢	**Sydney** ○	**Seattle** ○
500 000 to 1 million	**BANGUI** ▢	**Winnipeg** ○	**Warangal** ○
100 000 to 500 000	WELLINGTON ▢	Edinburgh ○	Apucarana ○
50 000 to 100 000	PORT OF SPAIN ▢	Bismarck ○	Invercargill ○
under 50 000	MALABO ▫	Charlottetown ○	Ceres ○

STYLES OF LETTERING

Cities and towns are explained separately

		Physical features	
Country	**FRANCE**	Island	*Gran Canaria*
Overseas Territory/Dependency	**Guadeloupe**	Lake	*Lake Erie*
Disputed Territory	WESTERN SAHARA	Mountain	*Mt Blanc*
Administrative name Shown for selected countries only.	**SCOTLAND**	River	*Thames*
Area name	PATAGONIA	Region	*LAPPLAND*

CONTINENTAL MAPS

BOUNDARIES

------- International boundary

- - - - - - Disputed international boundary

•••••••• Ceasefire line

CITIES AND TOWNS

National capital	Other city or town
Kuwait □	Seattle ○

ABBREVIATIONS

Arch.	Archipelago		
B.	Bay		
	Bahía, Baía	Portuguese	bay
	Bahía	Spanish	bay
	Baie	French	bay
C.	Cape		
	Cabo	Portuguese, Spanish	cape, headland
	Cap	French	cape, headland
Co	Cerro	Spanish	hill, peak, summit
E.	East, Eastern		
Est.	Estrecho	Spanish	strait
Gt	Great		
I.	Island, Isle		
	Ilha	Portuguese	island
	Islas	Spanish	island
Is	Islands, Isles		
	Islas	Spanish	islands
Khr.	Khrebet	Russian	mountain range
L.	Lake		
	Loch	(Scotland)	lake
	Lough	(Ireland)	lake
	Lac	French	lake
	Lago	Portuguese, Spanish	lake
M.	Mys	Russian	cape, point
Mt	Mount		
	Mont	French	hill, mountain
Mt.	Mountain		

Mts	Mountains		
	Monts	French	hills, mountains
N.	North, Northern		
O.	Ostrov	Russian	island
Pt	Point		
Pta	Punta	Italian, Spanish	cape, point
R.	River		
	Rio	Portuguese	river
	Río	Spanish	river
	Rivière	French	river
Ra.	Range		
S.	South, Southern		
	Salar, Salina, Salinas	Spanish	saltpan, saltpans
Sa	Serra	Portuguese	mountain range
	Sierra	Spanish	mountain range
Sd	Sound		
S.E.	Southeast, Southeastern		
St	Saint		
	Sankt	German	
	Sint	Dutch	saint
Sta	Santa	Italian, Portuguese, Spanish	saint
Ste	Sainte	French	saint
Str.	Strait		
W.	West, Western		
	Wadi, Wādī	Arabic	watercourse

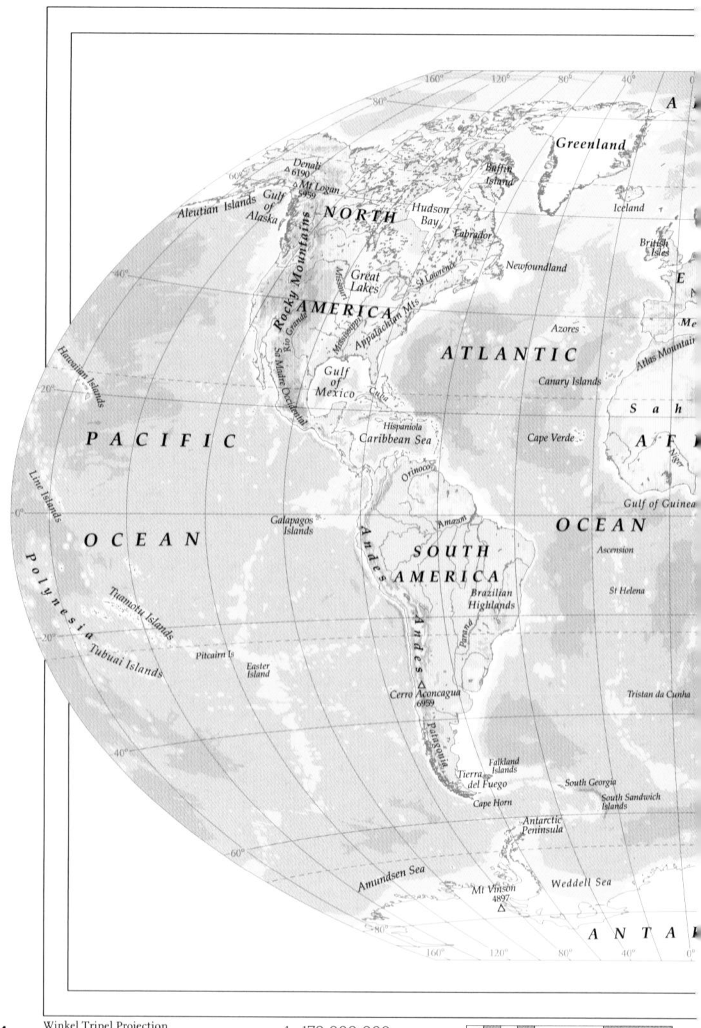

Greenland

Iceland

Denali 6190
Mt Logan 5959
Aleutian Islands
Gulf of Alaska
NORTH
Hudson Bay
Baffin Island
Labrador
British Isles

Rocky Mountains
Great Lakes
St Lawrence
Newfoundland

AMERICA
Rio Grande
Mississippi
Appalachian Mts
Azores
ATLANTIC

Hawaiian Islands
Sierra Madre Occidental
Gulf of Mexico
Cuba
Canary Islands
Atlas Mountains

Hispaniola
Caribbean Sea
Cape Verde
S a h

A F

PACIFIC
Gulf of Guinea

Line Islands

OCEAN
Galapagos Islands
Orinoco
OCEAN
Ascension

P o l y n e s i a
Amazon
SOUTH
AMERICA
Brazilian Highlands
St Helena

Tuamotu Islands
Andes

Pitcairn I.
Easter Island
Parana
Tristan da Cunha
Tubuai Islands

Cerro Aconcagua 6959
Andes

Patagonia

Falkland Islands
South Georgia
Tierra del Fuego
Cape Horn
South Sandwich Islands

Antarctic Peninsula

Amundsen Sea
Mt Vinson 4897
Weddell Sea

A N T A

Winkel Tripel Projection

1 : 170 000 000

MILES 0   1000   2000   3000

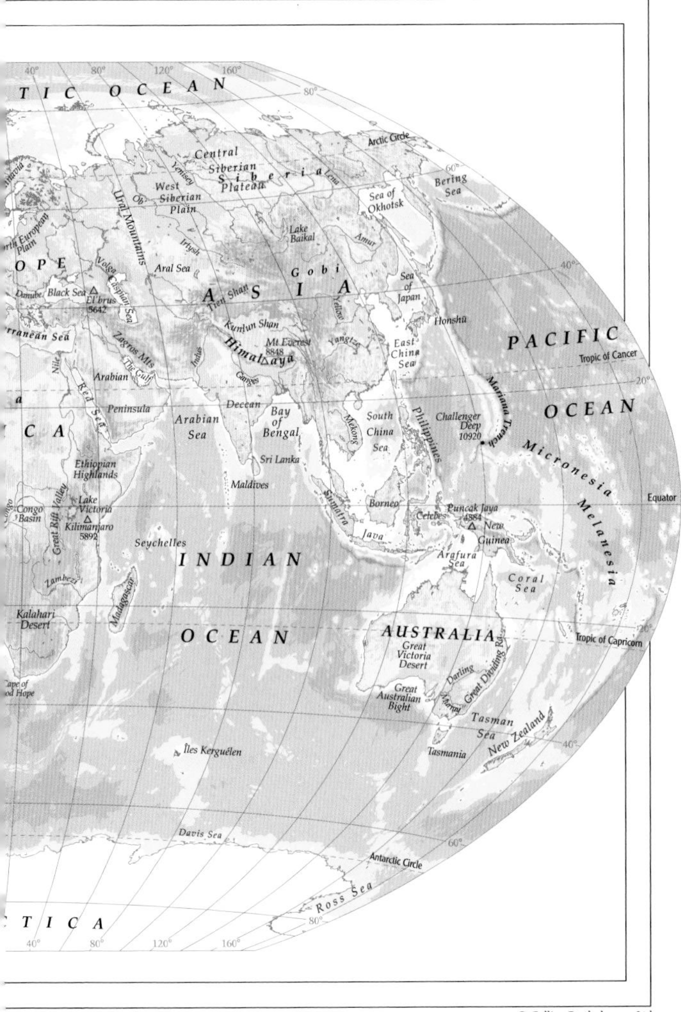

TIC OCEAN

ATLANTIC OCEAN

Arctic Circle

Central
Siberian
Plateau

West
Siberian
Plain

Ural Mountains

Ob

Yenisey

S i b e r i a

Bering
Sea

Sea of
Okhotsk

OPE

North European
Plain

Danube

Black Sea

Volga

El'brus
5642

Caspian Sea

Aral Sea

Lake
Baikal

Amur

Irtysh

Gobi

Tien Shan

A   S   I   A

Sea
of
Japan

Honshū

Kunlun Shan

Mt Everest
8848

Himalaya

Yangtze

East
China
Sea

PACIFIC

Tropic of Cancer

Zagros Mts

Indus

Ganges

Mekong

South
China
Sea

Philippines

Mariana Trench

Challenger
Deep
10920

OCEAN

Micronesia

Melanesia

Equator

terranean Sea

Nile

Red Sea

The Gulf

Arabian
Peninsula

Arabian
Sea

Deccan

Bay
of
Bengal

Sri Lanka

Maldives

CA

AFRICA

Ethiopian
Highlands

Congo
Basin

Great Rift Valley

Lake
Victoria

Kilimanjaro
5892

Seychelles

Zambezi

Sumatra

Borneo

Celebes

Java

Puncak Jaya
4884

New
Guinea

Arafura
Sea

Coral
Sea

INDIAN

Kalahari
Desert

Cape of
Good Hope

Madagascar

OCEAN

AUSTRALIA

Great
Victoria
Desert

Great
Australian
Bight

Darling

Murray

Great Dividing Range

Tropic of Capricorn

Tasman
Sea

New Zealand

Iles Kerguélen

Tasmania

Davis Sea

Antarctic Circle

TICA

ANTARCTICA

Ross Sea

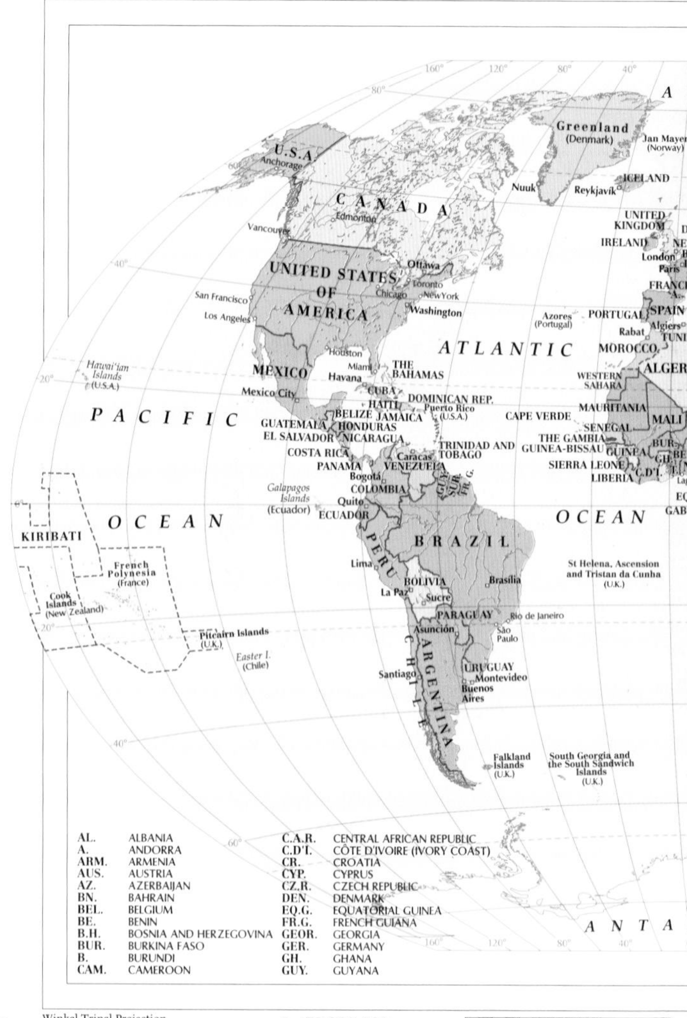

AL.	ALBANIA	C.A.R.	CENTRAL AFRICAN REPUBLIC
A.	ANDORRA	C.D'I.	CÔTE D'IVOIRE (IVORY COAST)
ARM.	ARMENIA	CR.	CROATIA
AUS.	AUSTRIA	CYP.	CYPRUS
AZ.	AZERBAIJAN	CZ.R.	CZECH REPUBLIC
BN.	BAHRAIN	DEN.	DENMARK
BEL.	BELGIUM	EQ.G.	EQUATORIAL GUINEA
BE.	BENIN	FR.G.	FRENCH GUIANA
B.H.	BOSNIA AND HERZEGOVINA	GEOR.	GEORGIA
BUR.	BURKINA FASO	GER.	GERMANY
B.	BURUNDI	GH.	GHANA
CAM.	CAMEROON	GUY.	GUYANA

Winkel Tripel Projection

1 : 170 000 000   MILES 0   1000   2000   3000

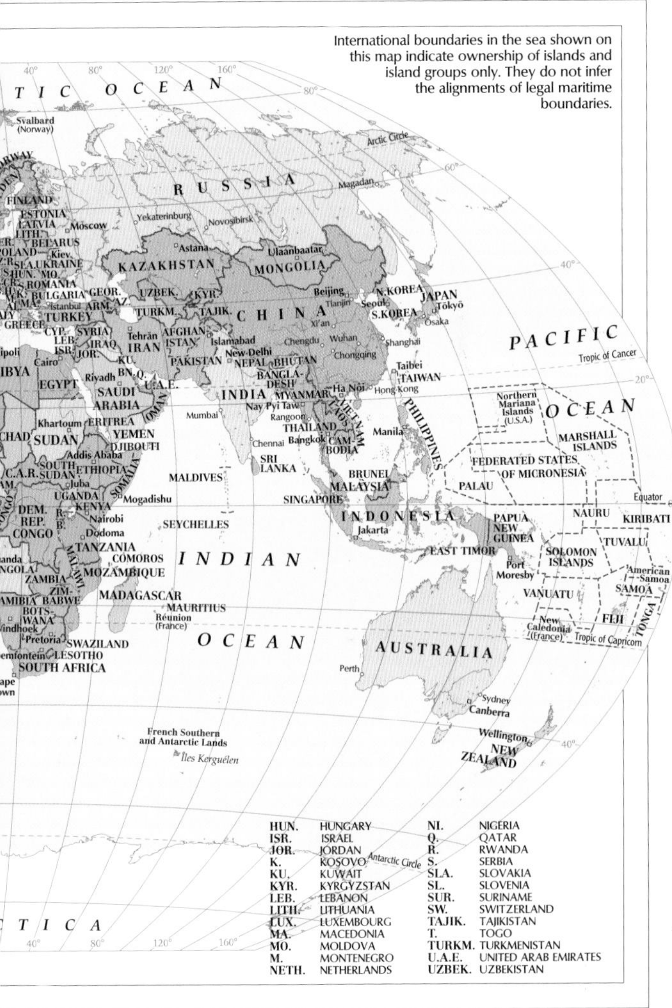

International boundaries in the sea shown on this map indicate ownership of islands and island groups only. They do not infer the alignments of legal maritime boundaries.

HUN.	HUNGARY	NI.	NIGERIA
ISR.	ISRAEL	Q.	QATAR
JOR.	JORDAN	R.	RWANDA
K.	KOSOVO	S.	SERBIA
KU.	KUWAIT	SLA.	SLOVAKIA
KYR.	KYRGYZSTAN	SL.	SLOVENIA
LEB.	LEBANON	SUR.	SURINAME
LITH.	LITHUANIA	SW.	SWITZERLAND
LUX.	LUXEMBOURG	TAJIK.	TAJIKISTAN
MA.	MACEDONIA	T.	TOGO
MO.	MOLDOVA	TURKM.	TURKMENISTAN
M.	MONTENEGRO	U.A.E.	UNITED ARAB EMIRATES
NETH.	NETHERLANDS	UZBEK.	UZBEKISTAN

0   1000   2000   3000   4000   5000 KILOMETRES

© Collins Bartholomew Ltd

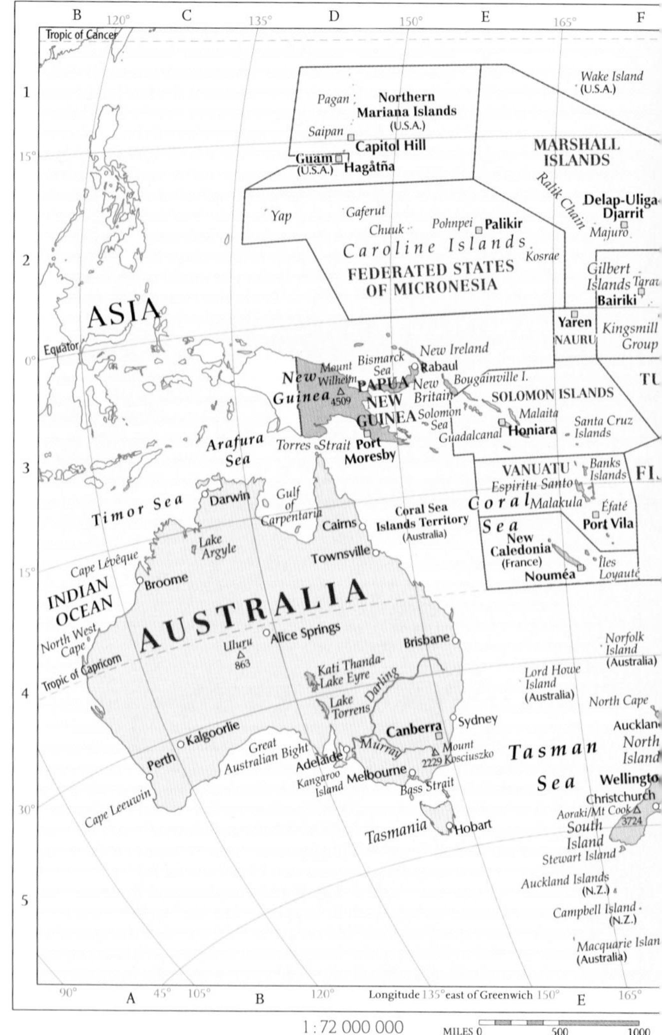

B 120° C 135° D 150° E 165° F

Tropic of Cancer

1

Pagan **Northern**
Mariana Islands
(U.S.A.)

Saipan

□ **Capitol Hill**

Guam □ **Hagåtña**
(U.S.A.)

Wake Island
(U.S.A.)

**MARSHALL
ISLANDS**

Ralik Chain

15°

Yap *Gaferut*

Chuuk *Pohnpei* □ **Palikir**

Kosrae

**Delap-Uliga-
Djarrit**
□
Majuro

2

C a r o l i n e   I s l a n d s

**FEDERATED STATES
OF MICRONESIA**

Gilbert *Tarawa*
Islands □
Bairiki

Equator

ASIA

New Bismarck *New Ireland*
Guinea Sea

Mount □ **Rabaul**
Wilhelm *New*
4509 *Britain* *Bougainville I.*

**PAPUA
NEW
GUINEA**

Solomon
Sea

Yaren □
NAURU

Kingsmill
Group

TU

0°

SOLOMON ISLANDS

Malaita

Honiara □ *Guadalcanal*

Santa Cruz
Islands

3

Arafura
Sea

Port
Torres Strait **Moresby**

VANUATU *Banks*
Espiritu Santo *Islands*

FI.

Efaté
Malakula □ **Port Vila**

Timor Sea Darwin □ *Gulf*
of
Carpentaria

Cairns □

**Coral Sea
Islands Territory**
(Australia)

C o r a l
S e a

**New
Caledonia**
(France) *Îles*
Nouméa □ *Loyauté*

15°

**INDIAN
OCEAN**

Cape Lévêque ○
Broome ○

North West
Cape

Lake ○
Argyle

Townsville □

Norfolk
Island
(Australia)

Tropic of Capricorn

Uluru Alice Springs □
△
863

AUSTRALIA

Kati Thanda-
Lake Eyre △

Brisbane □

Lord Howe
Island
(Australia)

North Cape

Tas man *Auckland*
North
Sea *Island*

4

Perth ○ Kalgoorlie ○

Great
Australian Bight

Lake
Torrens △

Adelaide □

Kangaroo
Island

Darling
Murray □ **Canberra** Sydney □

Melbourne □ △ Mount
2229 Kosciuszko

Bass Strait

Wellingto
Christchurch ○
Aoraki/Mt Cook △
South 3724
Island
Stewart Island

30°

Cape Leeuwin ○

Tasmania

Hobart □

Auckland Islands
(N.Z.)

Campbell Island
(N.Z.)

5

Macquarie Islan
(Australia)

90° A 45° 105° B 120° Longitude 135°east of Greenwich 150° E 165°

48

1 : 72 000 000

MILES 0 ___ 500 ___ 1000

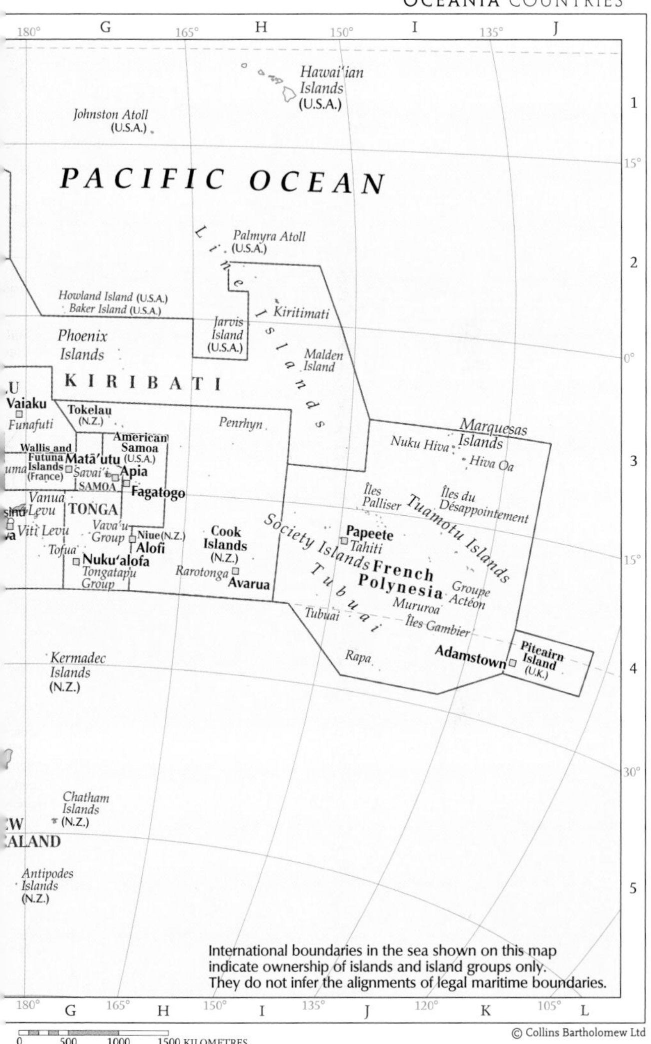

180°   G   165°   H   150°   I   135°   J

Hawai'ian Islands (U.S.A.)

1

Johnston Atoll (U.S.A.)

15°

PACIFIC OCEAN

L
i
n
e

Palmyra Atoll (U.S.A.)

2

Howland Island (U.S.A.)
Baker Island (U.S.A.)

I
s
l
a
n
d
s

Kiritimati

Phoenix Islands

Jarvis Island (U.S.A.)

Malden Island

0°

...U

Vaiaku

Funafuti

K I R I B A T I

Tokelau (N.Z.)

Penrhyn

Marquesas Islands

Nuku Hiva

Hiva Oa

3

Wallis and Futuna Islands (France)

uma

Savai'i

SAMOA

American Samoa (U.S.A.)

Matā'utu

Apia

Fagatogo

Îles Palliser

Îles du Désappointement

Tuamotu Islands

Vanua

Viti Levu

va

Levu

TONGA

Vava'u Group

Tofua'

Niue (N.Z.)

Alofi

Cook Islands (N.Z.)

Society Islands

Papeete

Tahiti

French

15°

Nuku'alofa

Tongatapu Group

Rarotonga

Avarua

Polynesia

Groupe Actéon

Tubuai

Mururoa

Îles Gambier

Kermadec Islands (N.Z.)

Tubuai

Rapa

Adamstown

Pitcairn Island (U.K.)

4

Chatham Islands (N.Z.)

30°

W
...ALAND

Antipodes Islands (N.Z.)

5

International boundaries in the sea shown on this map indicate ownership of islands and island groups only. They do not infer the alignments of legal maritime boundaries.

180°   G   165°   H   150°   I   135°   J   120°   K   105°   L

0   500   1000   1500 KILOMETRES

© Collins Bartholomew Ltd

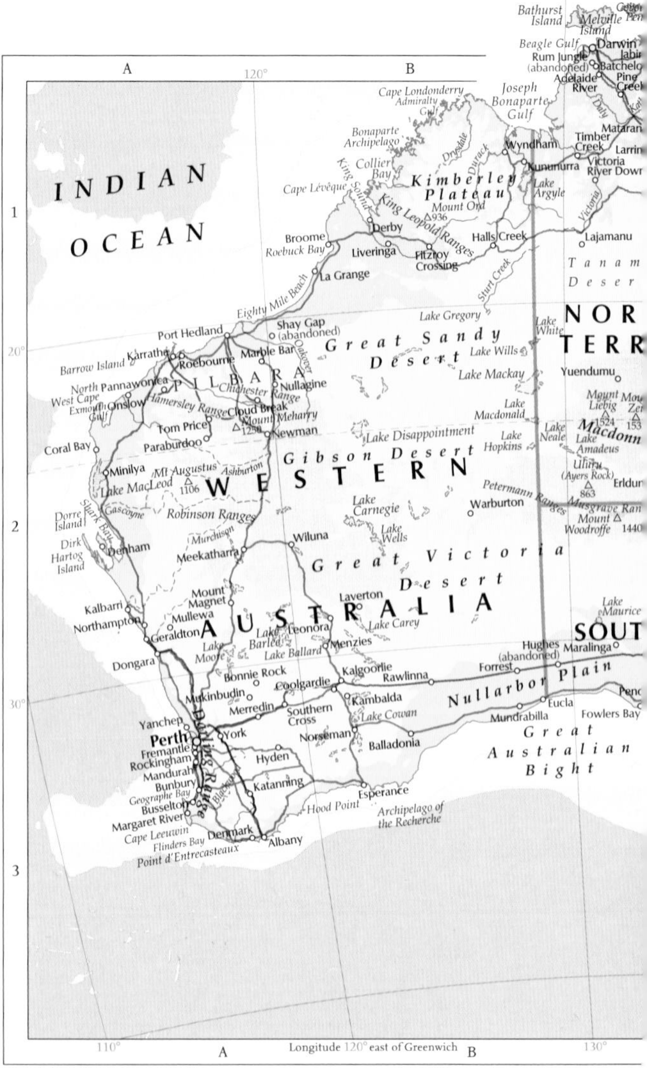
A
B
120°
1
2
3
INDIAN OCEAN
Bathurst Island
Melville Island
Beagle Gulf
Darwin
Rum Jungle (abandoned)
Batchelor
Adelaide River
Pine Creek
Joseph Bonaparte Gulf
Cape Londonderry
Admiralty Gulf
Bonaparte Archipelago
Collier Bay
King Sound
Cape Lévêque
Drysdale
Durack
Kimberley Plateau
Wyndham
Kununurra
Timber Creek
Victoria River Downs
Lake Argyle
Victoria
King Leopold Ranges
Mount Ord
936
Derby
Broome
Roebuck Bay
Liveringa
Fitzroy Crossing
Halls Creek
Lajamanu
Tanami Desert
La Grange
Eighty Mile Beach
Sturt Creek
Lake Gregory
Lake White
NORTHERN TERRITORY
Port Hedland
Shay Gap (abandoned)
Great Sandy Desert
Lake Wills
Lake Mackay
Yuendumu
20°
Barrow Island
Karratha
Roebourne
Marble Bar
Oakover
Nullagine
PILBARA
Chichester Range
North West Cape
Pannawonica
Exmouth Gulf
Onslow
Hamersley Range
Cloud Break
Mount Meharry
1250
Tom Price
Newman
Paraburdoo
Lake Macdonald
Mount Liebig
1524
Lake Neale
Lake Amadeus
Lake Disappointment
Lake Hopkins
Gibson Desert
Coral Bay
Minilya
Mt Augustus
1106
Ashburton
WESTERN
Lake MacLeod
Uluru (Ayers Rock)
863
Petermann Ranges
Musgrave Ranges
Mount Woodroffe
1440
Warburton
Lake Carnegie
Lake Wells
Dorre Island
Shark Bay
Gascoyne
Robinson Ranges
Dirk Hartog Island
Denham
Murchison
Meekatharra
Wiluna
Great Victoria Desert
Mount Magnet
Laverton
Kalbarri
Northampton
Mullewa
Geraldton
AUSTRALIA
Lake Barlee
Leonora
Lake Carey
Lake Maurice
Lake Moore
Lake Ballard
Menzies
Dongara
Bonnie Rock
Kalgoorlie
Rawlinna
Forrest
Hughes (abandoned)
Maralinga
SOUTH
Nullarbor Plain
Mukinbudin
Coolgardie
Kambalda
Merredin
Southern Cross
Lake Cowan
Eucla
Mundrabilla
Fowlers Bay
30°
Yanchep
Perth
Darling Range
York
Norseman
Balladonia
Fremantle
Rockingham
Hyden
Mandurah
Bunbury
Geographe Bay
Katanning
Blackwood
Esperance
Busselton
Margaret River
Hood Point
Archipelago of the Recherche
Cape Leeuwin
Flinders Bay
Denmark
Albany
Point d'Entrecasteaux
Great Australian Bight
110°
Longitude 120° east of Greenwich
130°

Lambert Azimuthal Equal Area Projection

1 : 25 000 000

MILES 0 250 500

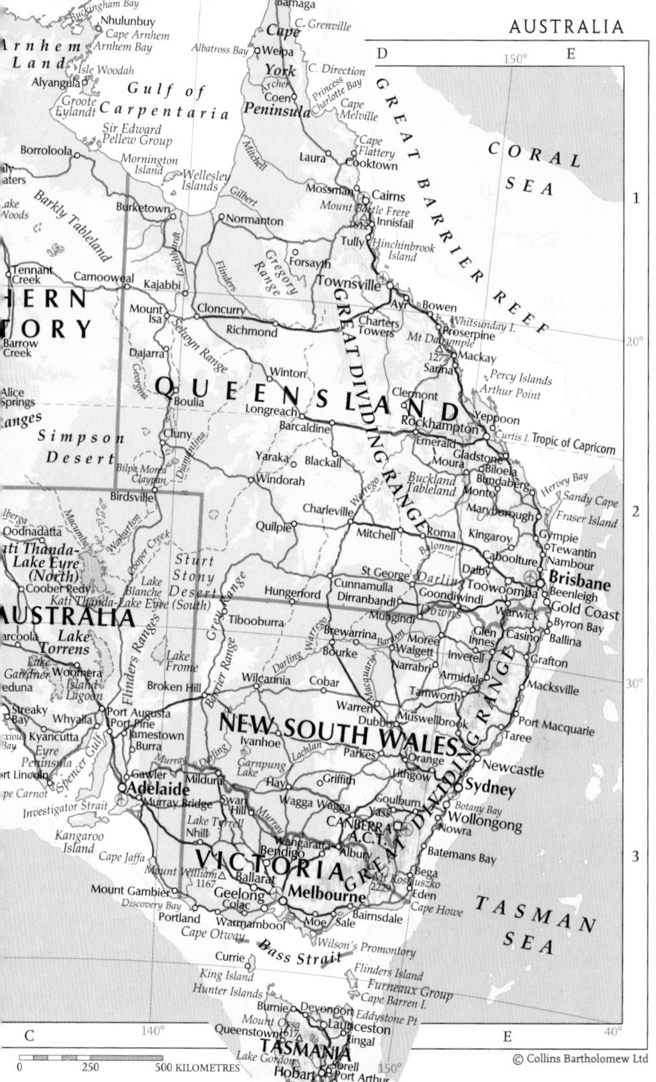

Wessel Is. Cape Wessel
Buckingham Bay
Nhulunbuy
Arnhem Arnhem Bay
Land Cape Arnhem
Alyangula Isle Woodah
Groote
Eylandt

Cape York
Bamaga
C. Grenville
Cape
Albatross Bay Weipa
York C. Direction
Ychel
Princess Charlotte Bay
Peninsula Cape
Melville

AUSTRALIA

CORAL
SEA

Borroloola
aly
aters
Lake
Noods

Gulf of
Carpentaria
Sir Edward
Pellew Group
Mornington
Island
Wellesley
Islands

Cape
Flattery
Cooktown

Mossman
Cairns
Mount Bartle Frere
Innisfail

GREAT BARRIER REEF

Tennant
Creek
Camooweal

Barkly Tableland
Burketown

Normanton
Forsayth
Tully Hinchinbrook
Island

HERN
TORY
Barrow
Creek

Mount
Isa
Cloncurry
Richmond
Dajarra

Kajabbi

Gregory Range
Flinders

Townsville
Ayr Bowen
Charters
Towers
Mt Dalrymple
1273

Whitsunday I.
Proserpine
Mackay

GREAT DIVIDING RANGE

Alice
Springs
anges

Boulia
Winton

Longreach
Barcaldine

Clermont
Rockhampton
Emerald
Moura
Monto

Percy Islands
Arthur Point

Curtis I. Tropic of Capricorn
Gladstone
Biloela

Simpson
Desert

Cluny
Bilpa Morea
Claypan

Yaraka Blackall
Windorah

Buckland
Tableland

Maryborough
Harvey Bay
Sandy Cape
Fraser Island

Birdsville

Charleville
Quilpie

Mitchell
Roma
Miles

Kingaroy
Gympie
Tewantin
Nambour
Caboolture

QUEENSLAND

Oodnadatta
ati Thanda-
Lake Eyre
(North)
Coober Pedy

Sturt
Stony
Desert
Lake
Blanche

Cooper Creek

Kati Thanda-Lake Eyre (South)

Hungerford

St George
Cunnamulla
Dirranbandi

Goondiwindi
Mungindi

Dalby
Toowoomba
Warwick

Brisbane
Beenleigh
Gold Coast
Byron Bay
Casino Ballina

AUSTRALIA
arcoola
Lake
Gairdner
eduna

Lake
Torrens
Woomera
Island

Lake
Frome

Tibooburra

Brewarrina
Bourke

Moree
Walgett
Narrabri

Glen
Innes
Inverell
Grafton

Macksville

Streaky
Bay
Whyalla
xious
Bay
Port Augusta
Port Pirie

Broken Hill

Wilcannia

Cobar

Warren
Dubbo

Tamworth
Armidale

Port Macquarie
Taree

Kyancutta
Eyre
Peninsula
rt Lincoln
pe Jervis

Jamestown
Burra

Billiker Range

Cobar

Muswellbrook

Newcastle

NEW SOUTH WALES

Ivanhoe
Garnpung
Lake
Hay

Parkes
Orange
Lithgow

Sydney
Wollongong

Gawler
Adelaide
Mildura
Murray Bridge
Swan
Hill

Wagga Wagga
Yass
Goulburn

Botany Bay
Kowra

Investigator Strait
Kangaroo
Island
Cape Jaffa

Lake Tyrrell
Nhill

Bendigo
Ballarat

Hopetoun
Horsham

CANBERRA
A.C.T.
Albury

Batemans Bay

Mount William △
1167

VICTORIA
Melbourne
Geelong

Bega
Eden
Cape Howe

TASMAN
SEA

Mount Gambier
Discovery Bay
Portland
Cape Otway
Warrnambool
Colac

Moe
Sale
Bairnsdale

Wilson's Promontory

Currie
King Island
Hunter Islands

Burnie Devonport
Queenstown
Mount Ossa
1617

Flinders Island
Furneaux Group
Cape Barren I.

Launceston
Fingal

Bass Strait

TASMANIA
Lake Gordon
Eddystone Pt

Hobart Port Arthur

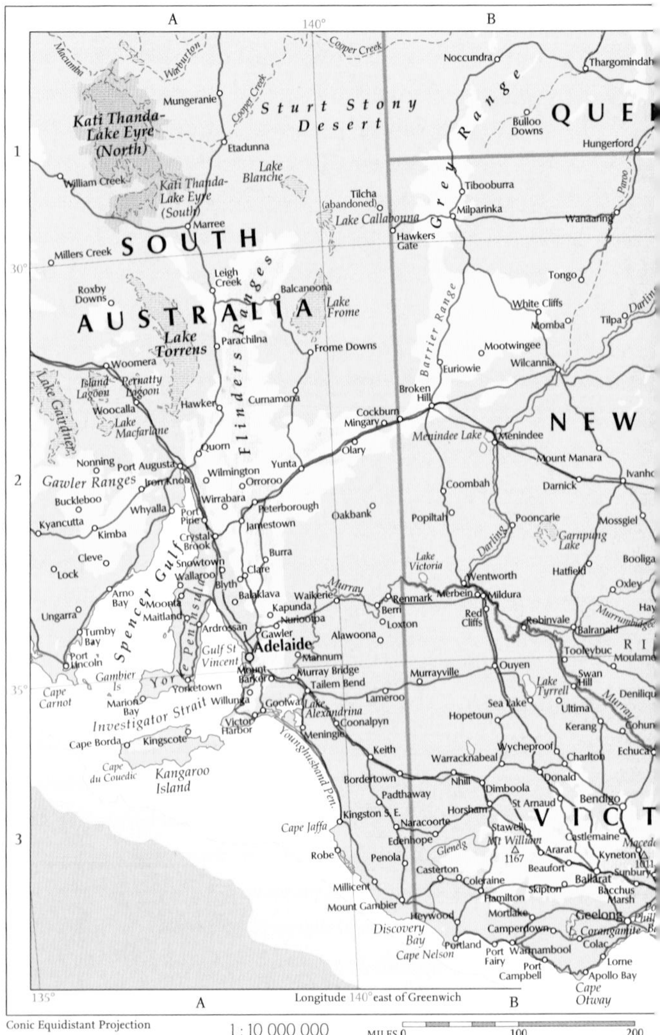

Mooraberie
Haddon
Cooper Creek
Noccundra
Thargomindah

Mungeranie
Sturt Stony Desert
Bulloo Downs
Hungerford

QUE

Kati Thanda-
Lake Eyre
(North)
Etadunna
Lake Blanche
Tilcha (abandoned)
Lake Callabonna
Tibooburra
Milparinka
Wanaaring

William Creek
Kati Thanda-
Lake Eyre
(South)
Marree
Hawkers Gate
Tongo

Millers Creek
SOUTH
Leigh Creek
Balcanoona
White Cliffs
Momba
Tilpa

Roxby Downs
AUSTRALIA
Lake Frome
Grey Range

Lake Torrens
Parachilna
Frome Downs
Euriowie
Wilcannia

Woomera
Island Lagoon
Pernatty Lagoon
Hawker
Curnamona
Cockburn
Mingary
Broken Hill
NEW

Woocalla
Lake Macfarlane
Quorn
Olary
Menindee Lake
Menindee
Mount Manara
Ivanho

Nonning
Gawler Ranges
Port Augusta
Iron Knob
Wilmington
Yunta
Coombah
Darnick

Buckleboo
Whyalla
Port Pirie
Wirrabara
Peterborough
Oakbank
Popiltah
Pooncarie
Garnpung Lake
Mossgiel

Kyancutta
Kimba
Crystal Brook
Jamestown
Booliga

Cleve
Snowtown
Burra
Lake Victoria
Wentworth
Hatfield
Oxley

Lock
Arno Bay
Moonta
Wallaroo
Blyth
Clare
Murray
Waikerie
Renmark
Merbein
Mildura
Balranald
Hay

Ungarra
Tumby Bay
Maitland
Babakala
Kapunda
Berri
Loxton
Red Cliffs
Robinvale
Tooleybuc
Moulame

Port Lincoln
Ardrossan
Gawler
Alawoona
RI

Spencer Gulf
Yorketown
Adelaide
Mannum
Ouyen
Swan Hill
Deniliqu

Cape Carnot
Gambier Is
Marion Bay
Mount Barker
Murray Bridge
Tailem Bend
Lake Tyrrell
Ultima
Cohuna

Investigator Strait
Willunga
Victor Harbor
Meningie
Lake Alexandrina
Coonalpyn
Murrayville
Hopetoun
Sea Lake
Kerang
Echuca

Cape Borda
Kingscote
Goolwa
Keith
Warracknabeal
Wycheproof
Charlton
VICT

Cape du Couedic
Kangaroo Island
Cape Jaffa
Bordertown
Padthaway
Dimboola
Nhill
Horsham
Donald
St Arnaud
Bendigo

Kingston S.E.
Naracoorte
Stawell
Mt William 1167
Ararat
Castlemaine
Macede

Robe
Edenhope
Penola
Casterton
Beaufort
Skipton
Ballarat
Kyneton
Bacchus Marsh

Millicent
Glenelg
Coleraine
Hamilton
Mortlake
Geelong
Coranganite
Be

Mount Gambier
Heywood
Camperdown
Colac

Discovery Bay
Cape Nelson
Portland
Port Fairy
Warrnambool
Port Campbell
Apollo Bay
Lome
Cape Otway

1

30°

2

35°

3

135°

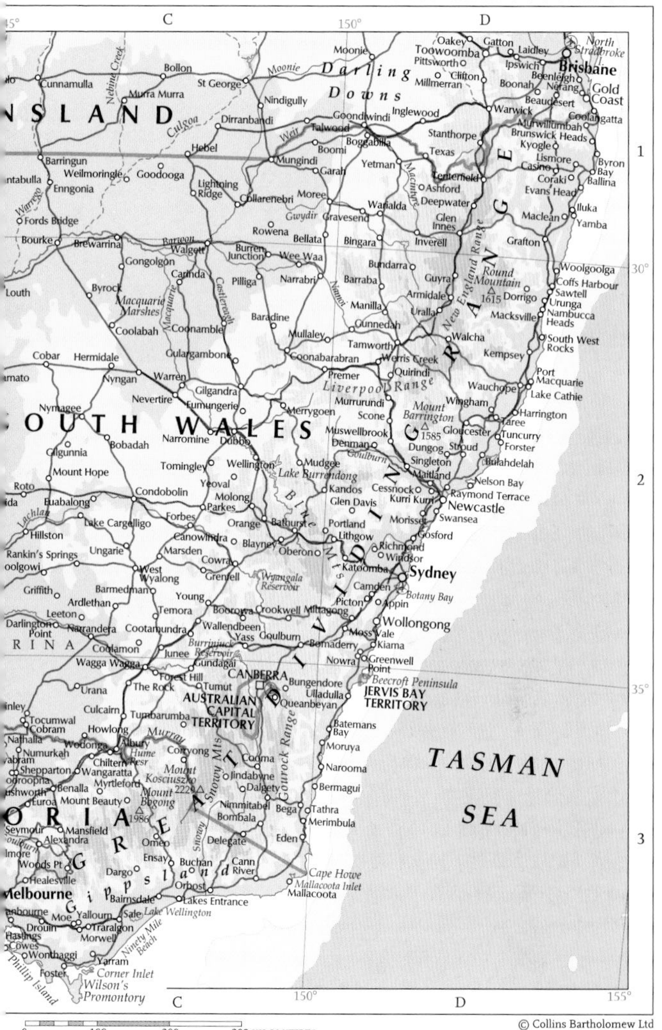

Cunnamulla
Bollon
St George
Moonie
Oakey
Toowoomba
Gatton
Laidley
North Stradbroke
Pittsworth
Clifton
Millmerran
Ipswich
Boonah
Brisbane
Gold Coast
Nobby
Murra Murra
Nindigully
Inglewood
Stanthorpe
Warwick
Beaudesert
Brunswick Heads
Byron Bay
Dirranbandi
Wyaralong
Talwood
Boggabilla
Texas
Tenterfield
Kyogle
Casino
Ballina
Barringun
Weilmoringle
Goodooga
Hebel
Mungindi
Boomi
Yetman
Ashford
Deepwater
Evans Head
ntabulla
Enngonia
Lightning Ridge
Collarenebri
Moree
Warialda
Glen Innes
Maclean
Yamba
Fords Bridge
Rowena
Bellata
Bingara
Inverell
Grafton
Bourke
Brewarrina
Walgett
Burren Junction
Wee Waa
Bundarra
Guyra
Round Mountain
Woolgoolga
Coffs Harbour
Louth
Gongolgon
Carinda
Pilliga
Narrabri
Barraba
1615
Dorrigo
Sawtell
Urunga
Byrock
Macquarie Marshes
Baradine
Manilla
Armidale
Macksville
Nambucca Heads
Cobar
Hermidale
Coolabah
Coonamble
Mullaley
Uralla
South West Rocks
arnato
Nyngan
Gulargambone
Coonabarabran
Quirindi
Walcha
Kempsey
Port Macquarie
Nymagee
Warren
Gilgandra
Tamworth
Werris Creek
Wauchope
Lake Cathie
Nevertire
Dubbo
Premer
Murrurundi
Wingham
Harrington
Bobadah
Narromine
Mendooran
Merrygoen
Scone
Mount Barrington
Gloucester
Taree
Tuncurry
Gilgunnia
Mount Hope
Condobolin
Yeoval
Wellington
Mudgee
Denman
Muswellbrook
Dungog
Stroud
Bulahdelah
Forster
Roto
Euabalong
Lake Cargelligo
Forbes
Parkes
Molong
Lake Burrendong
Kandos
Glen Davis
Singleton
Kurri Kurri
Cessnock
Raymond Terrace
Maitland
Nelson Bay
Newcastle
Hillston
Ungarie
Marsden
Orange
Bathurst
Portland
Lithgow
Morisset
Swansea
Rankin's Springs
oolgowi
West Wyalong
Cowra
Blayney
Oberon
Richmond
Windsor
Gosford
Griffith
Ardlethan
Temora
Grenfell
Young
Boorowa
Crookwell
Katoomba
Sydney
Leeton
Barmedman
Wyangala Reservoir
Camden
Botany Bay
Darlington Point
Narrandera
Cootamundra
Junee
Murrumburrah
Yass
Goulburn
Picton
Appin
Wollongong
RINA
Coolamon
Wagga Wagga
Gundagai
Bungendore
Mittagong
Bowral
Kiama
Urana
The Rock
Tumut
CANBERRA
Nowra
Greenwell Point
inley
Culcairn
Tumbarumba
Batemans Bay
Tocumwal
Cobram
Howlong
AUSTRALIAN CAPITAL TERRITORY
Bungendore
Queanbeyan
Ulladulla
JERVIS BAY TERRITORY
Nathalia
Numurkah
Wodonga
Albury
Corryong
Cooma
Moruya
abram
Shepparton
Wangaratta
Chiltern
Mount Kosciuszko
Jindabyne
Narooma
ogrooyba
Benalla
Myrtleford
Dalgety
Bermagui
Euroa
Mount Beauty
Mount Bogong
Nimmitabel
Bega
Tathra
ORIA
Seymour
Mansfield
Omeo
Bombala
Merimbula
Alexandra
Delegate
Imore
Woods Pt
Dargo
Ensay
Buchan
Cann River
Cape Howe
Healesville
Bairnsdale
Orbost
Mallacoota Inlet
Mallacoota
elbourne
Moe
Yallourn
Sale
Lake Wellington
Lakes Entrance
Melbourne
Drouin
Traralgon
Morwell
Hastings
owes
Wonthaggi
Foster
Yarram
Corner Inlet
Wilson's Promontory

QUEENSLAND

NEW SOUTH WALES

Darling Downs

Great Dividing Range

New England Range

Liverpool Range

TASMAN SEA

0   100   200   300 KILOMETRES

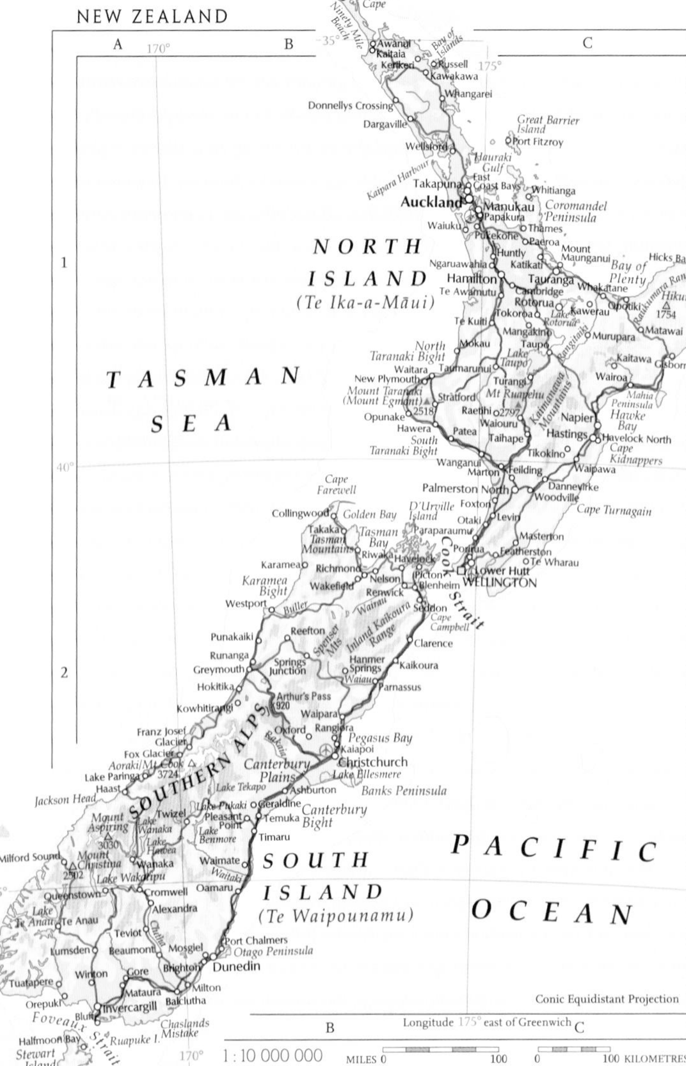

NEW ZEALAND

Te Paki
North Cape
North Cape
Awanui
Kaitaia
Kerikeri
Bay of
Islands
Russell
Kawakawa
Kawakawa
Whangarei

A   170°   B   175°   C

-35°

Donnellys Crossing
Dargaville
Wellsford
Port Fitzroy
Great Barrier
Island

Kaipara Harbour
Takapuna
East Bays
Whitianga
Hauraki
Gulf
Coromandel
Peninsula

Auckland
Manukau
Papakura
Waiuku
Pukekohe
Paeroa
Thames
Mount
Maunganui
Hicks Bay

N O R T H
I S L A N D
(Te Ika-a-Māui)

Ngaruawahia
Huntly
Hamilton
Te Awamutu
Cambridge
Katikati
Tauranga
Whakatane
Ōpōtiki
Bay of
Plenty
Kaitaia
Matawai
Te Kuiti
Tokoroa
Lake
Rotoiti
Rotorua
Murupara
Hikurangi
1754

T A S M A N
Mokau
Lake
Taupo
Taupo
Kawerau
Gisborne

S E A
North
Taranaki
Bight
Waitara
New Plymouth
Taumarunui
Turangi
Mt Ruapehu
2797
Mahia
Peninsula
Wairoa
Kaitaia

Mount Taranaki
(Mount Egmont)
2518
Stratford
Raetihi
Waiouru
Napier
Hastings
Havelock North
Cape
Kidnappers
Hawke
Bay

40°
Opunake
Hawera
Patea
Taihape
Tikokino
Waipawa

South
Taranaki
Bight
Wanganui
Marton
Feilding
Dannevirke
Woodville
Waipawa
Cape Turnagain

Cape
Farewell
Collingwood
Golden Bay
Palmerston North
Foxton
Otaki
Levin
D'Urville
Island
Paraparaumu

Takaka
Tasman
Mountains
Tasman
Bay
Riwaka
Havelock
Nelson
Picton
Porirua
WELLINGTON
Lower Hutt
Masterton
Te Wharau

Karamea
Richmond
Wakefield
Blenheim
Renwick
Cook
Strait

Karamea
Bight
Westport
Buller
Inland Kaikoura
Range
St Arnaud
Cape
Campbell

Punakaiki
Reefton
Springs
Junction
Hanmer
Springs
Clarence

Runanga
Greymouth
Hokitika
Arthur's Pass
920
Waiau
Kaikoura
Parnassus

Kowhitirangi
Waipara
Pegasus Bay
SOUTHERN ALPS
Oxford
Rangiora
Kaiapoi
Christchurch

Franz Josef
Glacier
Fox Glacier
Aoraki/Mt Cook
3724
Canterbury
Plains
Lake Ellesmere
Banks Peninsula

Jackson Head
Lake Pukaki
Geraldine
Ashburton

Mount
Aspiring
3030
Lake
Hawea
Twizel
Pleasant
Point
Temuka
Lake
Tekapo
Canterbury
Bight

Milford Sound
Mount
Christina
2502
Lake
Wanaka
Wanaka
Lake
Benmore
Timaru

Lake
Te Anau
Queenstown
Cromwell
Waimate
Oamaru
Waitaki

45°
Lumsden
Te Anau
Teviot
Alexandra
S O U T H
I S L A N D
(Te Waipounamu)

P A C I F I C

O C E A N

Tuatapere
Winton
Gore
Beaumont
Mosgiel
Port Chalmers
Brighton
Dunedin
Otago Peninsula

Orepuki
Mataura
Milton
Balclutha

Halfmoon Bay
Bluff
Invercargill
Ruapuke I.
Chaslands
Mistake

Stewart
Island
Foveaux
Strait

170°

1 : 10 000 000

Conic Equidistant Projection

B   Longitude 175° east of Greenwich   C

MILES 0   100   0   100 KILOMETRES

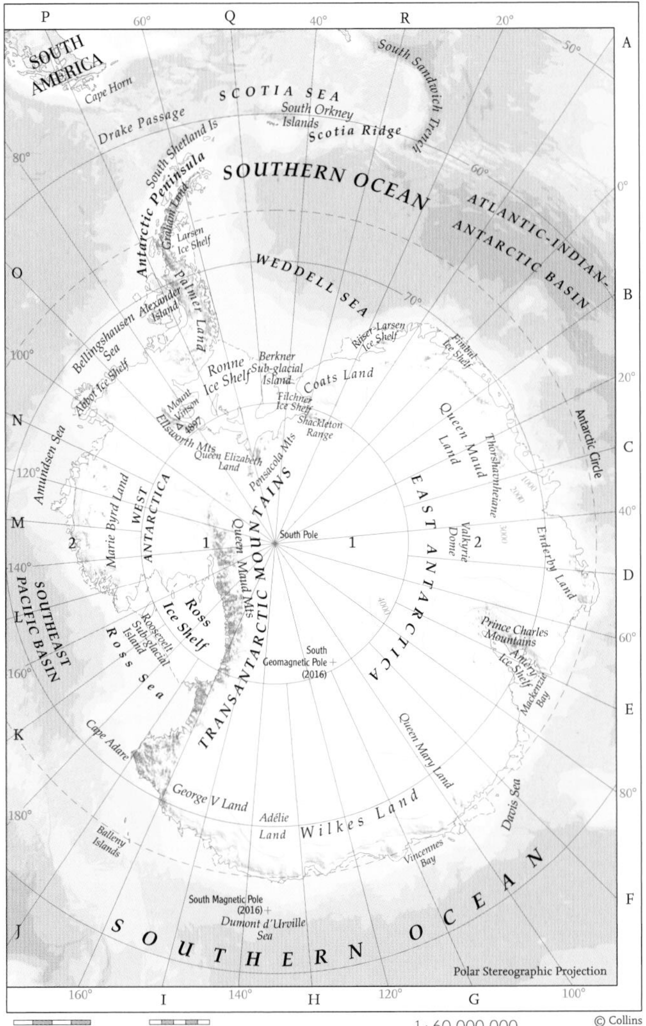

1 : 60 000 000

© Collins
Bartholomew Ltd

Polar Stereographic Projection

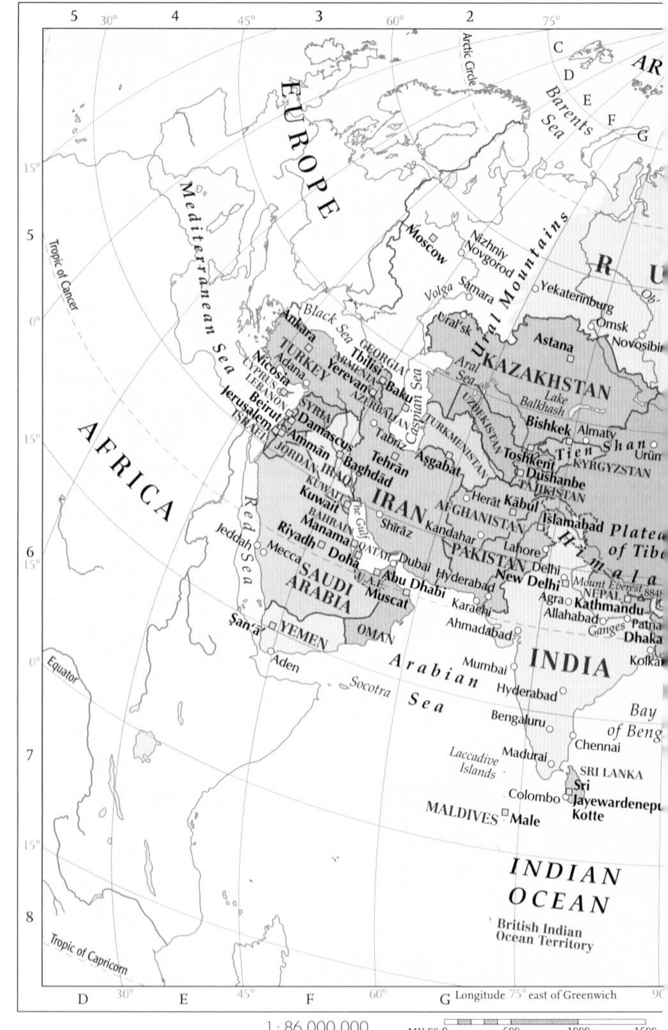

5 30° 4 45° 3 60° 2 75°

Arctic Circle

C
D
E
F
G

EUROPE

AR

Barents
Sea

R U

Mediterranean Sea

Moscow

Nžhniy
Novgorod

Volga Samara

Ural Mountains

Yekaterinburg

Ob'

Omsk

Novosibir

Ural'sk

15°

5

0°

Tropic of Cancer

AFRICA

Ankara
Black Sea
NICOSIA
CYPRUS
LEBANON
Beirut
ISRAEL
Jerusalem
Amman
JORDAN

TURKEY
GEORGIA
Tbilisi
ARMENIA
Yerevan
AZERBAIJAN
Baku
Adana
Syria
Damascus
IRAQ
Baghdad

Aral
Sea

Lake
Balkhash

KAZAKHSTAN

Astana

Bishkek Almaty

Caspian Sea

UZBEKISTAN
Toshkent
TURKMENISTAN

T i e n   S h a n
Ürün
KYRGYZSTAN

Dushanbe
TAJIKISTAN

15°

Kuwait
KUWAIT
BAHRAIN
Manama
Riyadh
QATAR
Doha

Tabriz
Tehran
Asgabat

Herät Käbul

IRAN

AFGHANISTAN

Islamabad

Shiräz
Kandahar
Dubai
Abu Dhabi
U.A.E.
Muscat

Lahore

Delhi

New Delhi

H i m a l a

Plate
of Tibe

6
15°

Jeddah
Mecca

SAUDI
ARABIA

Hyderabad

PAKISTAN

NEPAL
Kathmandu

Mount Everest 884

0°

Equator

San'a

YEMEN

OMAN

Aden

Red Sea

Karachi

Ahmadabad

Agra
Allahabad
Ganges
Patna

Dhaka

Kolkta

Arabian
Sea

Socotra

Mumbai

INDIA

Hyderabad

Bay
of Beng

Bengaluru

Chennai

7

Laccadive
Islands

Madurai

MALDIVES Male

Colombo

SRI LANKA
Sri
Jayewardenepu
Kotte

15°

INDIAN
OCEAN

8

Tropic of Capricorn

British Indian
Ocean Territory

D 30° E 45° F 60° G Longitude 75° east of Greenwich 90

1 : 86 000 000   MILES 0   500   1000   1500

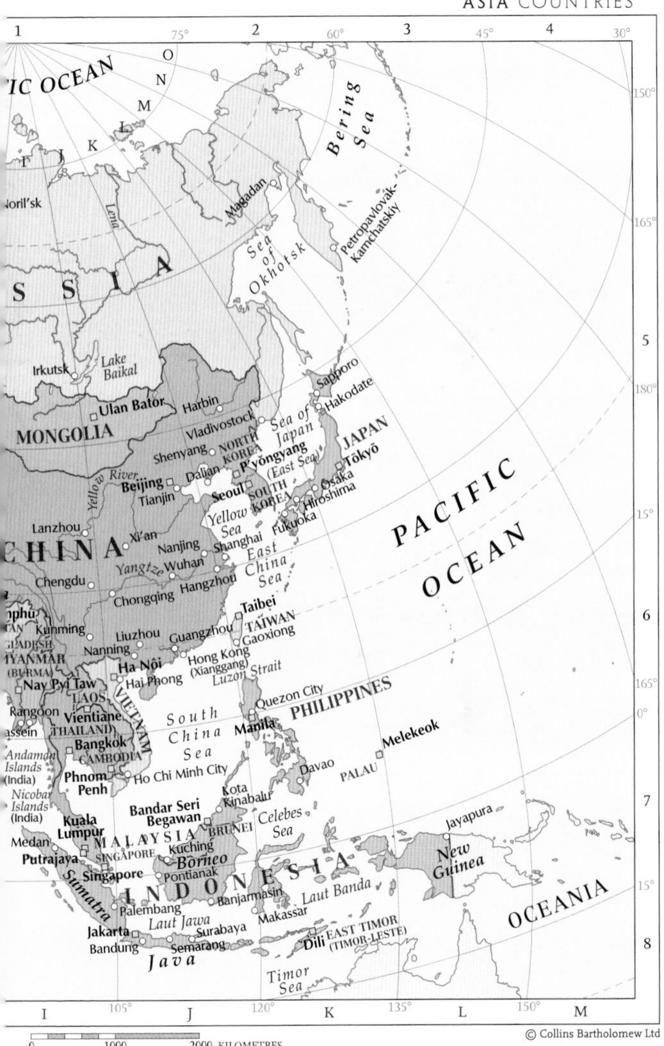

IC OCEAN

Bering Sea

Noril'sk

Lena

Magadan

Petropavlovsk-Kamchatskiy

Sea of Okhotsk

R U S S I A

Irkutsk
Lake Baikal

Sapporo

MONGOLIA

Ulan Bator
Harbin

Hakodate

Vladivostock

Shenyang NORTH KOREA Sea of Japan
(East Sea)

JAPAN

Beijing
Dalian P'yŏngyang
Tōkyō

Yellow River

Tianjin
Seoul SOUTH KOREA
Ōsaka

Lanzhou
Xi'an
Yellow Sea
Shanghai Hiroshima Fukuoka

C H I N A

Nanjing
Yangtze Wuhan
East China Sea

Chengdu

Chongqing Hangzhou

PACIFIC

OCEAN

phu
Kunming
Liuzhou Guangzhou
Taibei

TAN
DADISH
(BURMA)
MYANMAR

Nanning
Hong Kong (Xianggang)
Gaoxiong

TAIWAN

Nay Pyi Taw
Ha Nôi
Hai Phong
Luzon Strait

LAOS

Rangoon
Vientiane

Quezon City

PHILIPPINES

assein
THAILAND
South China Sea
Manila

VIETNAM

Andaman Islands (India)

Bangkok
CAMBODIA
Davao
Melekeok

Nicobar Islands (India)

Phnom Penh
Ho Chi Minh City

PALAU

Kota Kinabalu

Bandar Seri Begawan

Celebes Sea

Jayapura

Medan
Kuala Lumpur
MALAYSIA
BRUNEI

Putrajaya
SINGAPORE
Kuching
Borneo

New Guinea

Singapore
Pontianak

I N D O N E S I A

Sumatra

Banjarmasin
Laut Banda

Palembang
Makassar

OCEANIA

Jakarta
Laut Jawa
Surabaya

Bandung
Semarang
Dili EAST TIMOR
(TIMOR-LESTE)

Java

Timor Sea

0   1000   2000 KILOMETRES

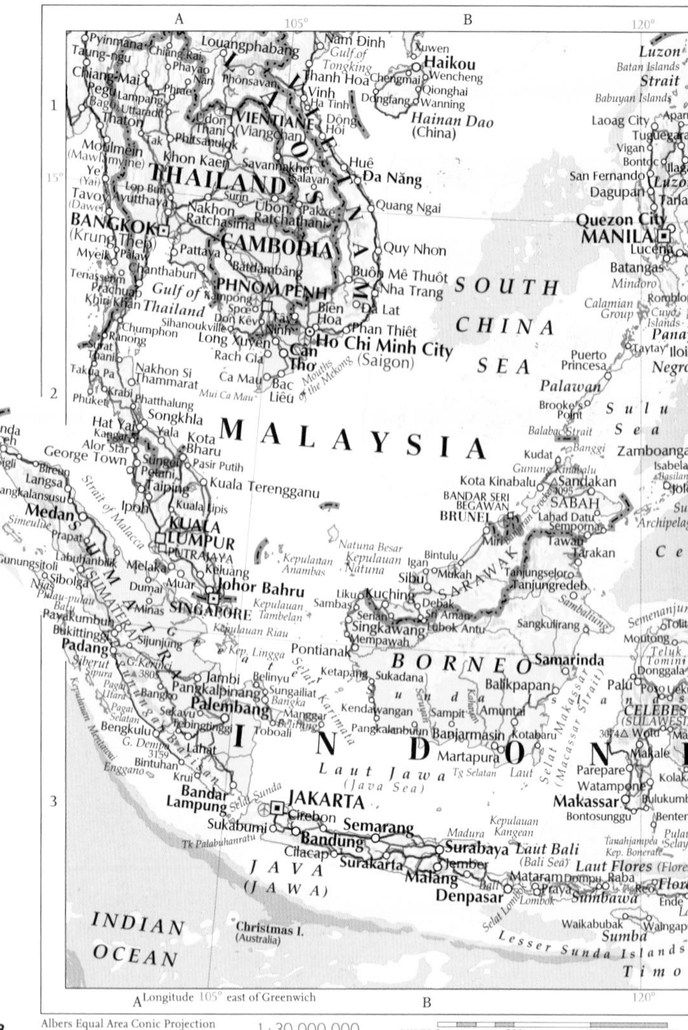

A   105°   B   120°

Pyinmana
Taung-ngu
Chiang-Mai
Pegu   Lampang
Phrae
Bago   Uttaradit
Louangphabang   Nam Đinh
Gulf of
Tongking
Thanh Hoa   Chengmai
Phav   Nan   Phônsavan
Vinh
Ha Tinh
Luzon
Batan Islands
Strait
Babuyan Islands

Chiang-Mai
Phôngsali
VIENTIANE
(Viangchan)
Đông
Hội
Haikou
Wencheng
Qionghai
Wanning

Laoag
Tuguegarao
Aparri

Mohnyin
(Mawlamyine)
Ye
(Yai)
Tavoy
(Dawei)
Khon Kaen
Savannakhet
Phitsanulok
Udon
Thani
Malayan
Lop Buri
Huê
Quang Ngai
Đa Nẵng
Hainan Dao
(China)

Vigan
Bontoc
San Fernando
Dagupan
Ilagan
Luzon
Tarlac

THAILAND
Ayutthaya
Nakhon
Ratchasima
Ubon
Ratchathani
Pakse

BANGKOK
(Krung Thep)
Pattaya
CAMBODIA
PHNOM PENH
Quy Nhon
SOUTH
Quezon City
MANILA
Lucena
Batangas

Myeik
Tenasserim
Prachuap
Khiri Khan
Chanthaburi
Gulf of
Thailand
Battambang
Kampong
Speu
Don Kev
Buôn Mê Thuôt
Nha Trang
Đa Lat
CHINA
Mindoro
Calamian
Group
Romblon
Cuyo
Islands

Chumphon
Ranong
Sihanoukville
Bien
Hoa
Phan Thiết
SEA
Panay

Takua Pa
Surat
Thani
Nakhon Si
Thammarat
Long Xuyên
Rach Gia
Can
Tho
Ho Chi Minh City
(Saigon)
Palawan
Puerto
Princesa
Cuytay
Iloilo
Negro

Phuket
Krabi
Phatthalung
Ca Mau
Mui Ca Mau
Bac
Liêu
Mouths
of the Mekong
Brooke's
Point
Sulu
Sea

Hat Yai
Songkhla
Banda
Aceh
Sigli
Bireun
Langsa
Pangkalansusu
MALAYSIA
Kota
Bharu
Pasir Putih
Balabac
Strait
Banggi
Kudat
Gunung Kinabalu
Kota Kinabalu
Sandakan
SABAH
Labad Datu
Tawau
Zamboanga
Isabela
Basilan
Jolo
Sul
Archipelag
Ce

George Town
Alor
Star
Yala
Kangar
Taiping
Kuala Lipis
Kuala Terengganu
BANDAR SERI
BEGAWAN
BRUNEI
SARAWAK
Tarakan

Medan
Prapat
Pematangsiantar
Ipoh
Kuantan
Natuna Besar
Kepulauan
Natuna
Igan
Bintulu
Mukah
Tanjungselor
Tanjungredeb

Gunungsitoli
Sibolga
Labuhanbilik
KUALA
LUMPUR
PUTRAJAYA
Melaka
Dumai
Muar
Johor Bahru
Kepulauan
Anambas
Sibu
Kuching
Debak
Tanjungpura
Celebes

Simeulue
Pulau-pulau
Batu
Padang
Bukittinggi
Pekanbaru
Minas
SINGAPORE
Sijunjung
Kepulauan
Riau
Kepulauan
Lingga
Pontianak
Singkawang
Sambas
Semitau
Tebok Antu
Sangkuliang
Semenanjung
Tolitoli
Moutong
Teluk
Tomini
Donggala

G. Kerinci
▲ 380
Sungaipinang
Belinyu
Pangkalpinang
Bangka
Ketapang
Likusdana
Sukadana
Pangkalanbuun
u   n   d   a
Balikpapan
Samarinda
Palu
Poso
CELEBES
(SULAWESI)
Mamuju

Siberut
Krui
Lahat
Jambi
Sungailiat
Manggar
Kendawangan
Sampit
Amuntai
Kotabaru
Martapura
Parepare
Watampone

INDONI

Pagai
Selatan
Bengkulu
G. Dempo
▲
Palembang
Toboali
BORNEO
Banjarmasin
Pangkalanbuun
Laut
Tg Selatan
Selat Makassar
Makassar

Bintuhan
Enggano
Krui
Bandar
Lampung
Sukabumi
JAKARTA
Cirebon
Bandung
Semarang
Laut Jawa
(Java Sea)
Pulau
Selayar

Christmas I.
(Australia)
Selat Sunda
Cilacap
Surakarta
Surabaya
Malang
JAVA
(JAWA)
Denpasar
Jember
Mataram
Bali
Madura
Kepulauan
Kangean
Laut Bali
(Bali Sea)
Praya
Lombok
Sumbawa
Raba
Laut Flores
Ende
Flore

INDIAN
OCEAN
Waikabubak
Sumba
Selat Lombok
Lesser   Sunda   Islands
Timo

A   Longitude 105° east of Greenwich   B   120°

Albers Equal Area Conic Projection   1 : 30 000 000   MILES 0   200   400   600

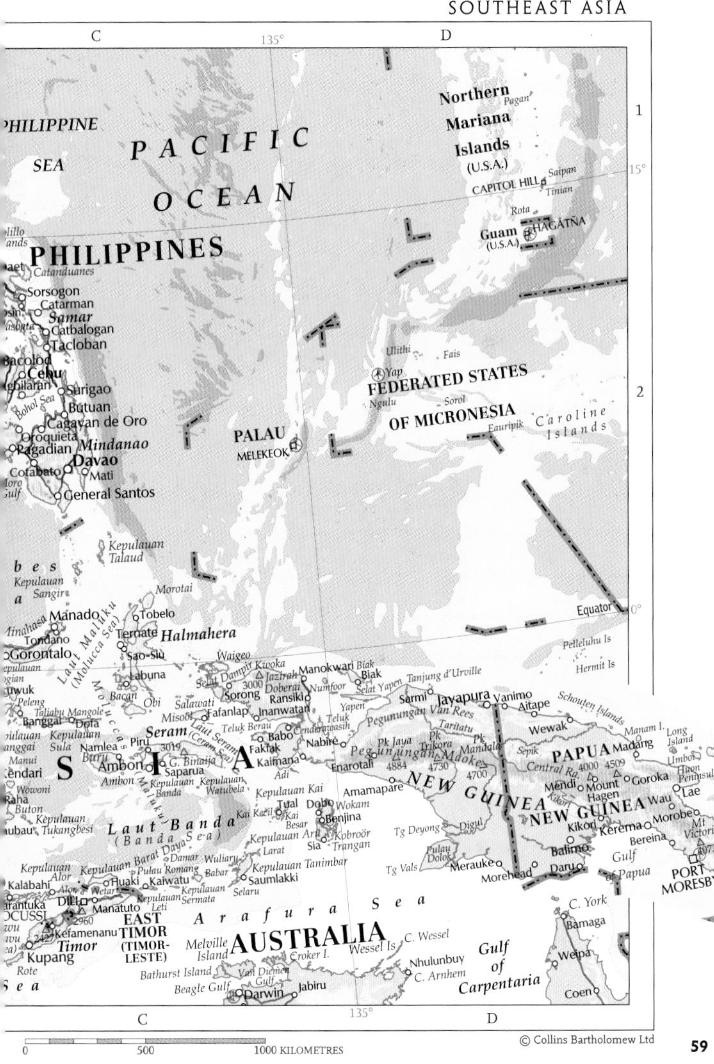
PACIFIC OCEAN
PHILIPPINE SEA
PHILIPPINES
Northern Mariana Islands (U.S.A.)
Pagan
Saipan
CAPITOL HILL
Tinian
Rota
Guam (U.S.A.)
HAGÅTÑA
Catanduanes
Sorsogon
Catarman
Samar
Catbalogan
Tacloban
Cebu
Surigao
Bohol Sea
Butuan
Cagayan de Oro
Oroquieta
Pagadian
Mindanao
Davao
Cotabato
Mati
General Santos
Ulithi
Fais
Yap
FEDERATED STATES OF MICRONESIA
Ngulu
Sorol
Eauripik
Caroline Islands
PALAU
MELEKEOK
Kepulauan Talaud
Kepulauan Sangir
Morotai
Manado
Tobelo
Tondano
Gorontalo
Ternate
Halmahera
Sao-Siu
Laut Maluku (Molucca Sea)
Equator
Pelleluhu Is
Hermit Is
Waigeo
Selat Dampir
Kwoka
Jazirah Doberai
Manokwari
Biak
Numfoor
Labuna
Sorong
Ransiki
Selat Yapen
Tanjung d'Urville
Sarmi
Jayapura
Vanimo
Aitape
Schouten Islands
Bacan
Obi
Salawati
Misool
Fafanlap
Inanwatan
Yapen
Pegunungan Van Rees
Taritatu
Wewak
Manam I.
Long Island
Peleng
Taliabu
Mangole
Banggai
Dofa
Kepulauan Sula
Seram
Laut Seram (Ceram Sea)
Teluk Berau
Babo
Teluk Cenderawasih
Nabire
Pk Jaya
Pk Trikora
Pk Mandala
Sepik
PAPUA
Madang
Umboi
Huon Peninsula
Namlea
Piru
3019
Fakfak
Pegunungan Maoke
4884
4730
Central Ra.
4000
4509
Buru
Ambon
G. Binaija
Saparua
Kaimana
Enarotali
4700
Mendi
Mount Hagen
Goroka
Lae
Kendari
Ambon
Kepulauan Banda
Kepulauan Watubela
Adi
NEW GUINEA
Amamapare
Kepulauan Kai
Kikori
Wowoni
Raha
Buton
Kepulauan Tukangbesi
Laut Banda (Banda Sea)
Kai Kecil
Tual
Kai Besar
Dobo
Wokam
Benjina
PAPUA NEW GUINEA
Wau
Morobe
Kikori
Kerema
Mt Victoria
Bereina
4073
Kepulauan Aru
Kobroör
Trangan
Sia
Larat
Tg Deyong
Digul
Pulau Dolok
Balimo
Gulf of Papua
Kepulauan Barat Daya
Damar
Wuliaru
Pulau Romang
Babar
Kepulauan Tanimbar
Saumlakki
Tg Vals
Merauke
Morehead
Daru
PORT MORESBY
Kalabahi
Alor
Huaki
Kaiwatu
Wetar
Kepulauan Leti
Kepulauan Sermata
Selaru
DILI
Manatuto
2960
EAST TIMOR (TIMOR-LESTE)
Arafura Sea
C. York
Bamaga
Kefamenanu
2427
Timor
Kupang
Rote
AUSTRALIA
Melville Island
Wessel Is
C. Wessel
Croker I.
Weipa
Nhulunbuy
Gulf of Carpentaria
Bathurst Island
Van Diemen Gulf
C. Arnhem
Beagle Gulf
Darwin
Jabiru
Coen
135°
15°
0°
C
D
1
2
0
500
1000 KILOMETRES

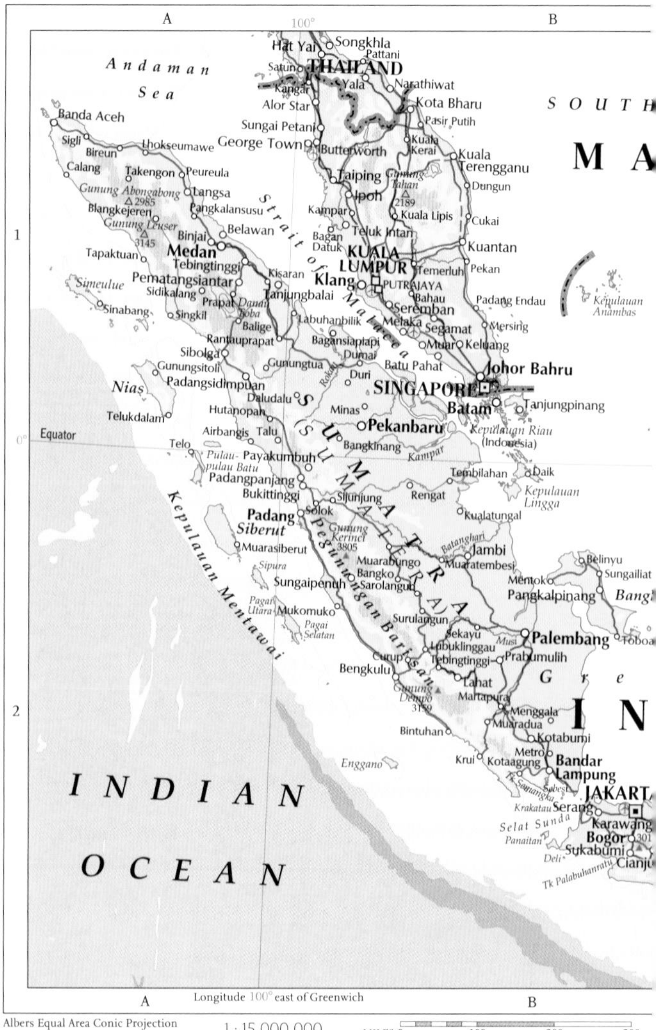

Andaman Sea

S O U T H

M A

Banda Aceh
Sigli
Bireun
Calang
Lhokseumawe
Takengon
Peureula
Gunung Abongabong
△2985
Langsa
Blangkejeren
Pangkalansusu
Gunung Leuser
Belawan
3145
Binjai
Tapaktuan
Medan
Tebingtinggi
Kisaran
Simeulue
Pematangsiantar
Sidikalang
Prapat
Tanjungbalai
Sinabang
Singkil
Baline
Labuhanbilik
Nias
Rantauprapat
Gunungtua
Bagansiapiapi
Gunungsitoli
Dumai
Sibolga
Duri
Padangsidimpuan
Daludalu
Telukdalam
Hutanopan
Minas
Airbangis
Talu
Pulau-pulau Batu
Payakumbuh
Bangkinang
Telo
Padangpanjang
Bukittinggi
Sijunjung
Rengat
Padang
Solok
Siberut
Gunung Kerinci
3805
Sipura
Muarasiberut
Muarabungo
Bangko
Sungaipenuh
Pagai Utara
Sarolangun
Sekayu
Mukomuko
Surulangun
Pagai Selatan
Lubuklinggau
Curup
Tebingtinggi
Prabumulih
Bengkulu
Gunung Dempo
3159
Lahat
Martapura
Menggala
Bintuhan
Muaradua
Krui
Kotaagung
Metro
Enggano
Bandar Lampung
Serang
Krakatau
301
Karawang
Bogor
Sukabumi
Panaitan
Cianju
Deli
Tk Palabuhanratu

Songkhla
Pattani
Hat Yai
Satun
THAILAND
Narathiwat
Kangar
Yala
Alor Star
Kota Bharu
Sungai Petani
Pasir Putih
George Town
Butterworth
Kuala Kerai
Kuala Terengganu
Taiping
Gunung Tahan
2189
Ipoh
Dungun
Kampar
Kuala Lipis
Teluk Intan
Cukai
Bagan Datuk
KUALA LUMPUR
Kuantan
Klang
PUTRAJAYA
Temerluh
Pekan
Seremban
Bahau
Padang Endau
Melaka
Segamat
Muar
Mersing
Batu Pahat
Keluang
SINGAPORE
Johor Bahru
Batam
Tanjungpinang
Pekanbaru
Kepulauan Riau (Indonesia)
Kampar
Tembilahan
Daik
Kepulauan Lingga
Kualatungal
Batanghari
Jambi
Muaratembesi
Belinyu
Sungailiat
Mentok
Pangkalpinang
Bang
Musi
Palembang
Tobo
G r e
I N

Kepulauan Anambas

Strait of Malacca
Danau Toba

Equator   0°

I N D I A N

O C E A N

Selat Sunda

JAKART

Kotaburni

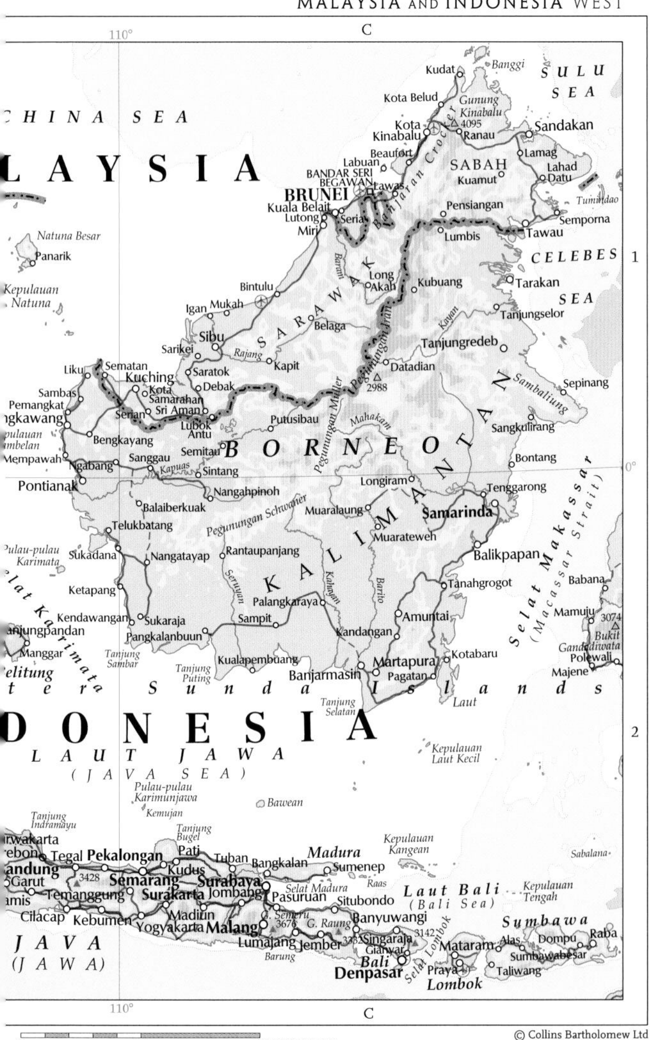

110°

C

CHINA SEA

LAYSIA

SULU SEA

Kudat ○ ·Banggi

Kota Belud ○

Kota ○ Gunung
Kinabalu Kinabalu
△4095
○Ranau ○Sandakan

Beaufort ○

·Labuan ○Lamag ○Lahad
Datu

BANDAR SERI ○Kawas SABAH
BEGAWAN
BRUNEI ○Pensiangan Tumindao

Kuala Belait
Lutong○ ○Seria ○Lumbis ○Tawau
Miri *CELEBES*

○Kubuang ○Tarakan 1

Bintulu Long
○Pakah ○Tanjungselor SEA

Igan○Mukah Belaga ○Tanjungredeb

○Sarikei Kapit ○Datadian ○Sepinang

Sibu
Saratok ○ 2988
Liku ○Sematan ○Debak
Kuching ○Kota ○Putusibau ○Sangkulirang
Sambas○ Samarahan
Pemangkat○ Sri Aman ○Bontang
○Serian Lubok
ngkawang○ Antu
ulauan Bengkayang ○Semitau ○Sintang *BORNEO* ○Sangkularang
mbelan ○Sanggau
Mempawah○ ○Longiram ○Tenggarong 0°

Pontianak ○Nangahpinoh ○Muaralaung **Samarinda**

○Balaiberkuak ○Muarateweh

Telukbatang *KALIMANTAN* ○Balikpapan

Pulau-pulau ○Nangatayap ○Rantaupanjang ○Tanahgrogot ○Babala
Karimata
○Ketapang Mamuju
Palangkaraya ○ 3074
anjungpandan ○Sukaraja ○Amuntai ·Bukit
○Kendawangan ○Sampit Gandadiwata
Pangkalanbuun ○Kotabaru Polewali·
Manggar Kualapembuang ○ ○Martapura Majene·
Tanjung ○Banjarmasin ○Pagatan
Selatan *Tanjung* ○
elitung *Puting* Sunda Islands
tera *Laut*
Tanjung
Selatan
2

DONESIA

LAUT JAWA
(JAVA SEA)

Kepulauan
Laut Kecil

Pulau-pulau
Karimunjawa ○Bawean *Sabalana*

Kemujan

Tanjung
Indramayu *Tanjung*
awakarta *Bugel* *Kepulauan*
rebon ○Pati ○Tuban *Kangean* *Kepulauan*
andung○ Tegal ○Pekalongan ○ *Madura* *Tengah*
Garut 3428 ○Kudus Bangkalan ○Sumenep
amis○ Temanggung **Semarang** *Selat Madura* ○Raas *Laut Bali*
Cilacap○ ○Madiun **Surakarta** **Surabaya** ○Situbondo *(Bali Sea)*
○Kebumen **Yogyakarta** ○Jombang ○Pasuruan ○Banyuwangi *Sumbawa*
G.Raung△
JAVA △3676 ○Lumajang ○Jember △3332 ○Singaraja △3142 ·Raba
(JAWA) **Malang** ·Dompu
Barung *Bali* Gilimanuk ○ ○Mataram
Denpasar ○Sumbawabesar
○Praya ○Taliwang
Lombok

110°

C

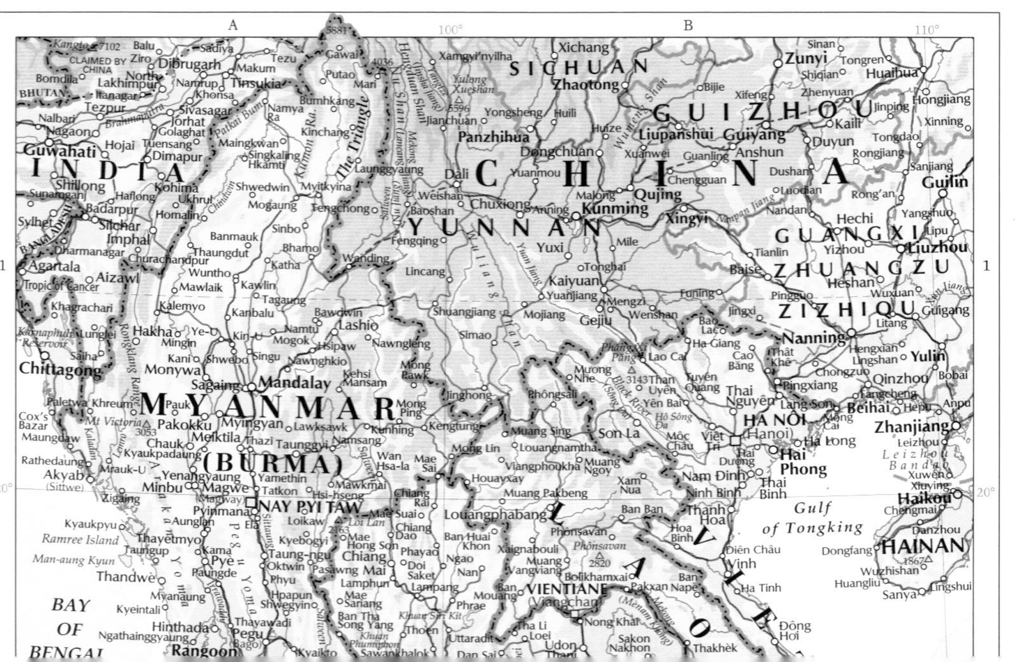

Albers Equal Area Conic Projection

1 : 15 000 000   MILES 0   100   200   300

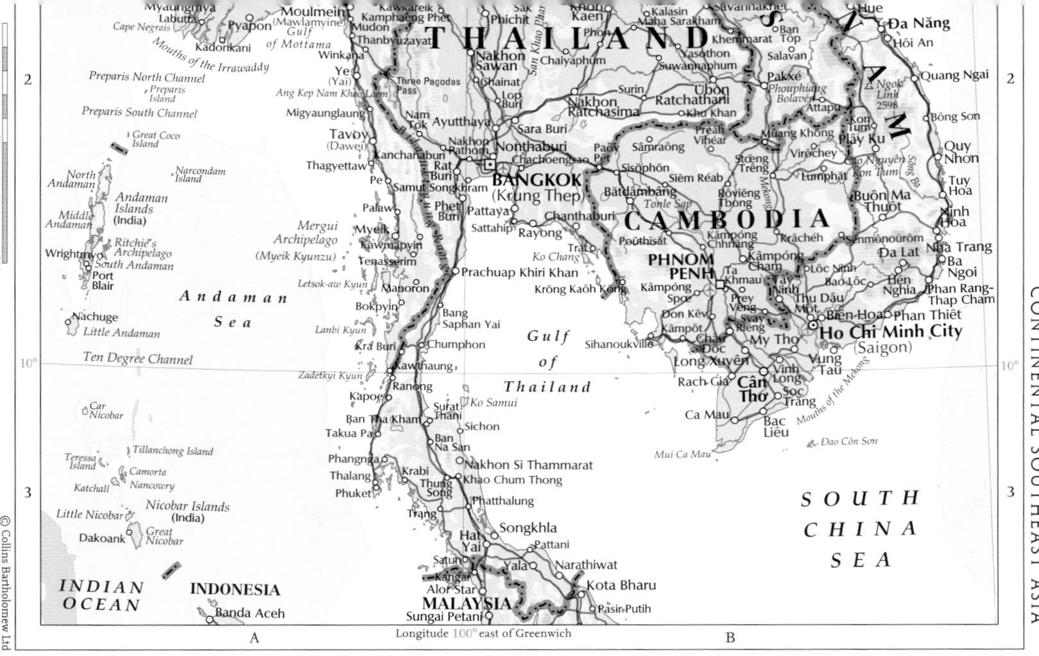

Longitude 100° east of Greenwich

© Collins Bartholomew Ltd

0   250   500 KILOMETRES

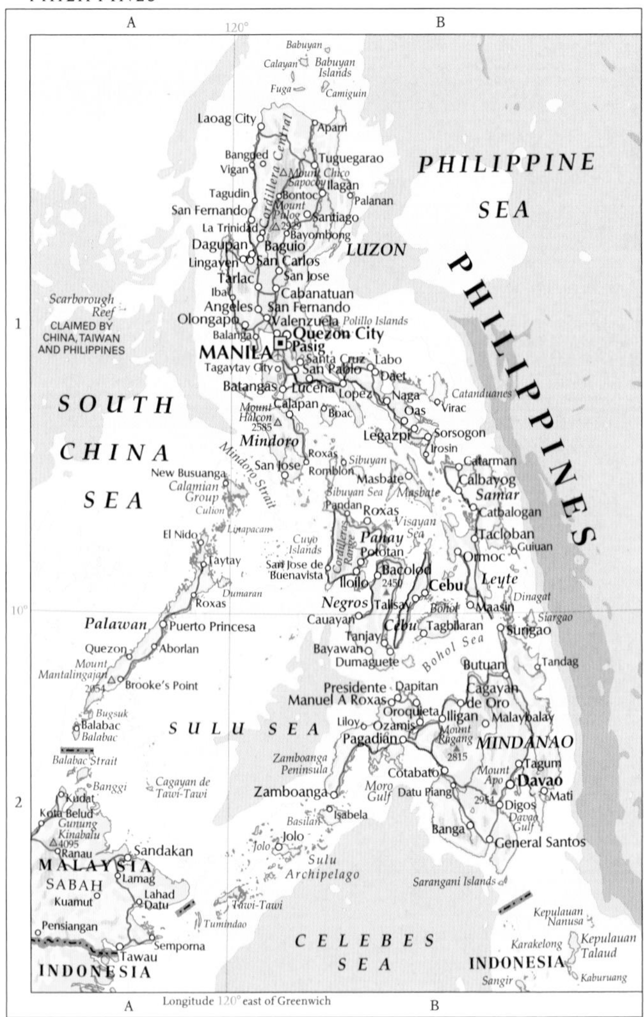

A   120°   B

Babuyan
Calayan   *Babuyan*
  Islands
Fuga   *Camiguin*

Laoag City
Bangged   Pamplona
Vigan   Tuguegarao
Tagudin   *Mount Chico* Ilagan
San Fernando   Bontoc *Sapocoil*
La Trinidad   *Mount Nov* Santiago
Dagupan   Baguio   Bayombong
Lingayen   San Carlos
Tarlac   San Jose   **LUZON**
Iba   Cabanatuan
Angeles   San Fernando
Olongapo   Valenzuela   Polillo Islands
Balanga   **Quezon City**
MANILA   Pasig
Tagaytay City   Santa Cruz   Labo
Batangas   Lucena   Naga
  Lopez   Oas
Calapan   Boac   Legazpi
Mount
Halcon   Irosin
2585   Sorsogon
Mindoro   San Jose   Romblon   Calamian
  Roxas   *Sibuyan*
New Busuanga   Masbate   Calbayog
Calamian   Pandan   *Masbate*   **Samar**
Group   Roxas   *Sibuyan Sea*   Catbalogan
Culion   *Visayan*   Tacloban
El Nido   *Linapacan*   **Panay**   Ormoc   Guiuan
  Cuyo   Pototan
Taytay   *Islands*   **Bacolod**   **Leyte**
San Jose de   Iloilo   *2450*   **Cebu**
Buenavista   **Negros**   Talisay   Maasin
Roxas   *Dumaran*   *Bohol*   *Dinagat*
  Cauayan   **Cebu**   Tagbilaran   *Siargao*
Palawan   Puerto Princesa   Tanjay   Surigao
Quezon   Bayawan   Dumaguete   *Bohol Sea*   Tandag
Mount   Aborlan   Butuan
Mantalingajan   Brooke's Point   Presidente   Dapitan   Cagayan
2085   Manuel A Roxas   de Oro
Bugsuk   Oroquieta   Iligan   Malaybalay
Balabac   Liloy   Ozamis   *Mount*
Balabac   **SULU SEA**   Pagadian   *Ragang*
Balabac Strait   *2815*   **MINDANAO**
  Banggi   *Zamboanga*   Cotabato   Tagum
Kudat   *Cagayan de*   *Peninsula*   *Mount*   **Davao**
Gunung   *Tawi-Tawi*   Zamboanga   Datu Piang   *Apo*   Digos
Kinabalu   Isabela   *Moro*   *2954*   *Davao*
4095   *Gulf*   Banga   *Gulf*   Mati
Ranau   *Basilan*   General Santos
Sandakan   Jolo   *Jolo*
MALAYSIA   Lamag   *Sulu*
SABAH   Lahad   *Archipelago*   Sarangani Islands
Kuamut   Datu
  Kepulauan
Pensiangan   *Tawi-Tawi*   *Nanusa*
  Tumindao   **CELEBES**   *Karakelong*   *Kepulauan*
Semporna   **SEA**   *Talaud*
Tawau   *Sangir*   *Kaburuang*
INDONESIA   **INDONESIA**

**PHILIPPINE
SEA**

PHILIPPINES

Catanduanes
Virac

SOUTH

CHINA

SEA

Scarborough
Reef
CLAIMED BY
CHINA, TAIWAN
AND PHILIPPINES

Mindoro Strait

1

10°

2

Longitude 120° east of Greenwich

A   B

Albers Equal Area Conic
Projection   1 : 15 000 000   MILES 0   100   0   250 KILOMETRES

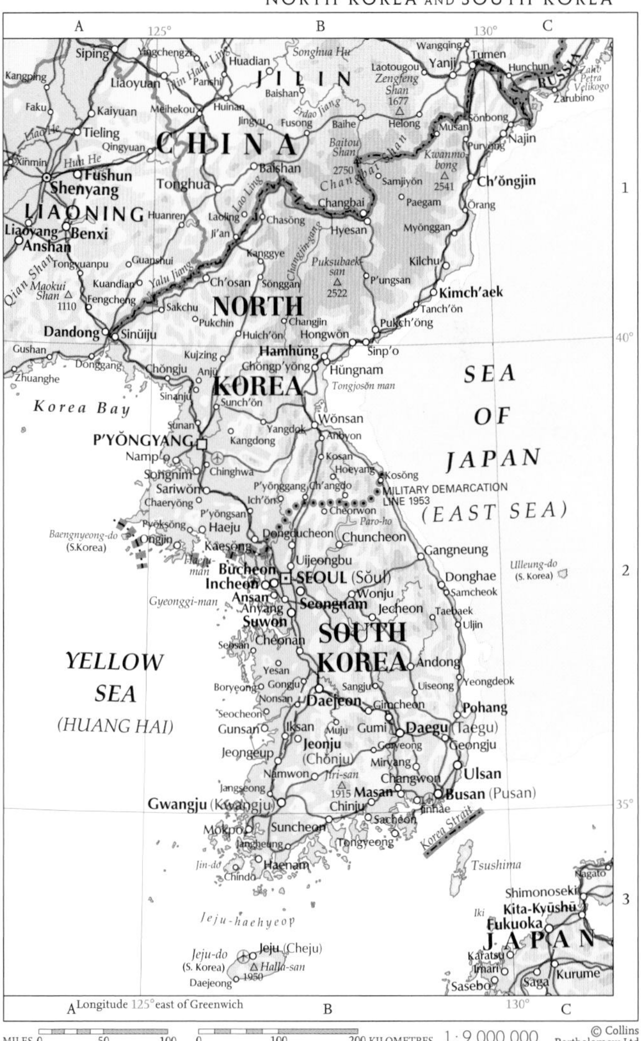
CHINA
NORTH KOREA
SOUTH KOREA
JAPAN
RUSSIA
JILIN
LIAONING
SEA OF JAPAN (EAST SEA)
YELLOW SEA (HUANG HAI)
Korea Bay
Korea Strait
Jeju-haehyeop
Gyeonggi-man
Tongjosŏn man
MILITARY DEMARCATION LINE 1953
P'YŎNGYANG
SEOUL (Sŏul)
Shenyang
Fushun
Benxi
Anshan
Liaoyang
Dandong
Sinŭiju
Hamhŭng
Hŭngnam
Ch'ŏngjin
Kimch'aek
Wŏnsan
Kaesŏng
Incheon
Bucheon
Suwon
Seongnam
Daejeon
Daegu (Taegu)
Ulsan
Busan (Pusan)
Gwangju (Kwangju)
Jeonju (Chŏnju)
Pohang
Masan
Changwon
Jeju (Cheju)
Jeju-do (S. Korea)
Halla-san 1950
Ulleung-do (S. Korea)
Baengnyeong-do (S.Korea)
Tsushima
Fukuoka
Kita-Kyūshū
Shimonoseki
Kurume
Saga
Sasebo
Paektu-san (Baitou Shan) 2750
Puksubaek-san 2522
Kwanmo-bong 2541
Changbai Shan
Yalu Jiang
Longitude 125° east of Greenwich
125°
130°
35°
40°
A
B
C
1
2
3
MILES 0 50 100
0 100 200 KILOMETRES
1 : 9 000 000
© Collins Bartholomew Ltd

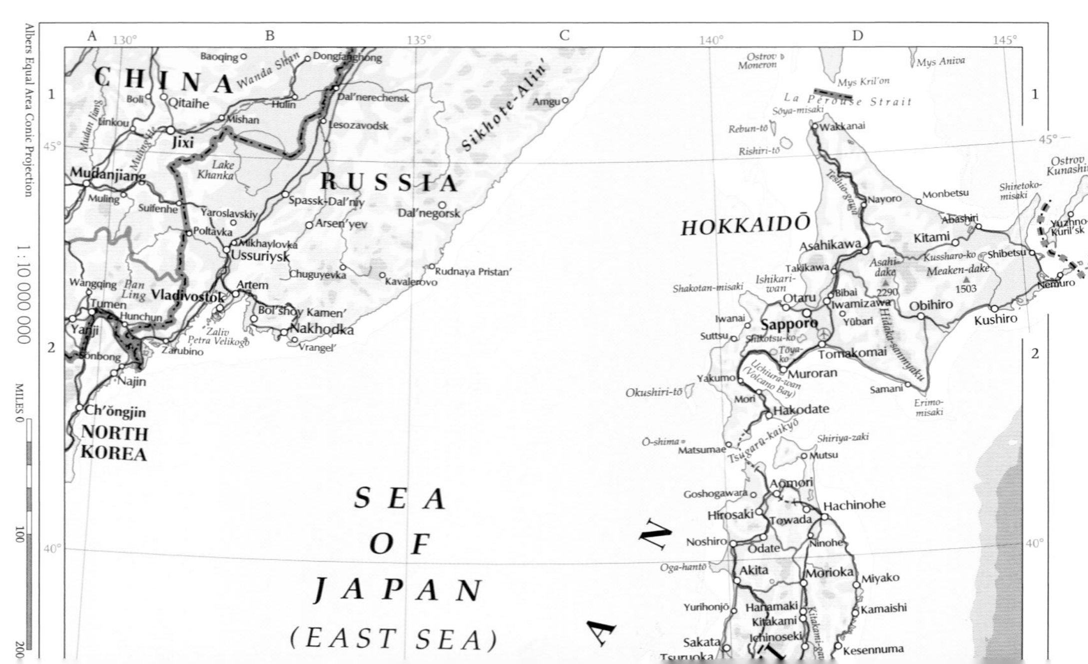

Albers Equal Area Conic Projection

1 : 10 000 000

MILES 0   100   200

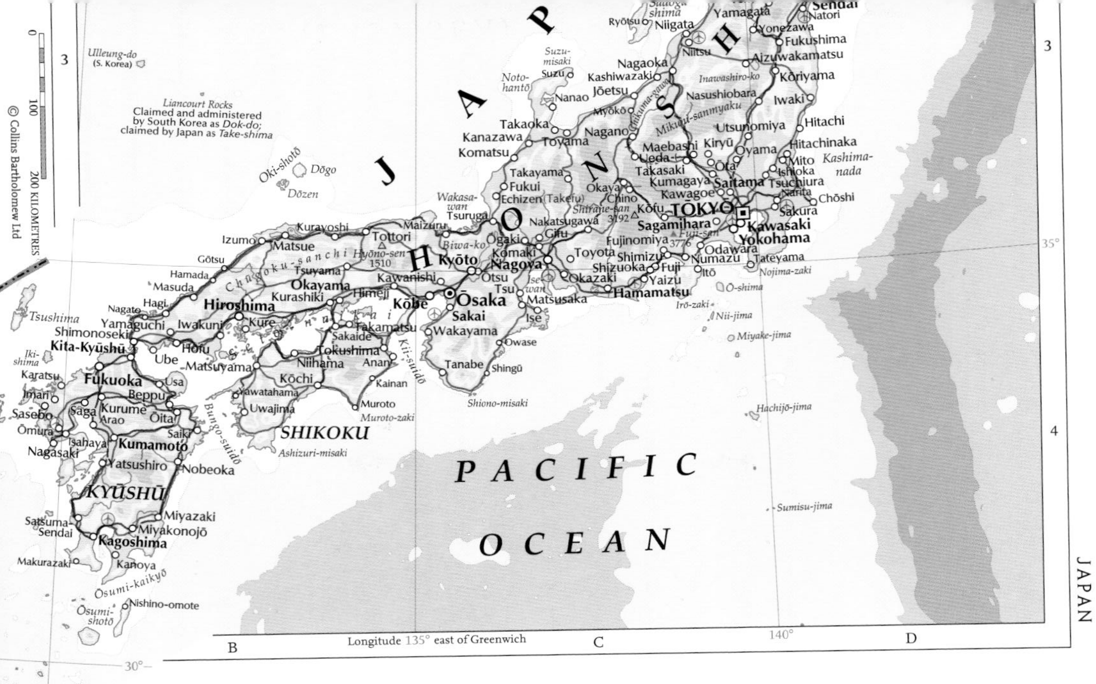

PACIFIC

OCEAN

Longitude 135° east of Greenwich

Liancourt Rocks
Claimed and administered
by South Korea as Dokdo;
claimed by Japan as Take-shima

Ullung-do (S. Korea)

0   100   200 KILOMETRES

© Collins Bartholomew Ltd

69

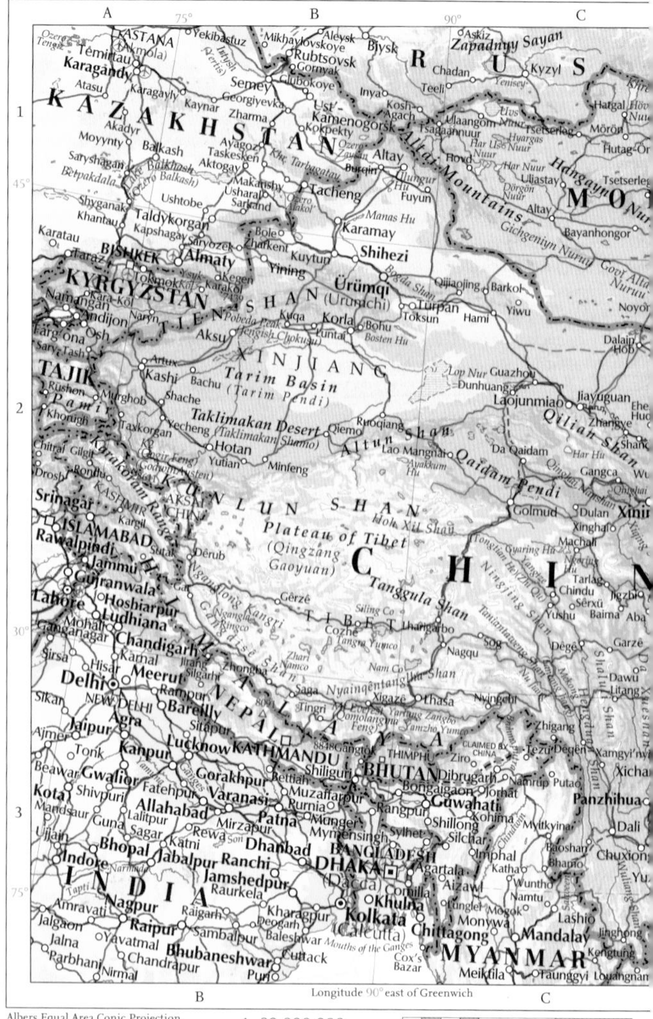

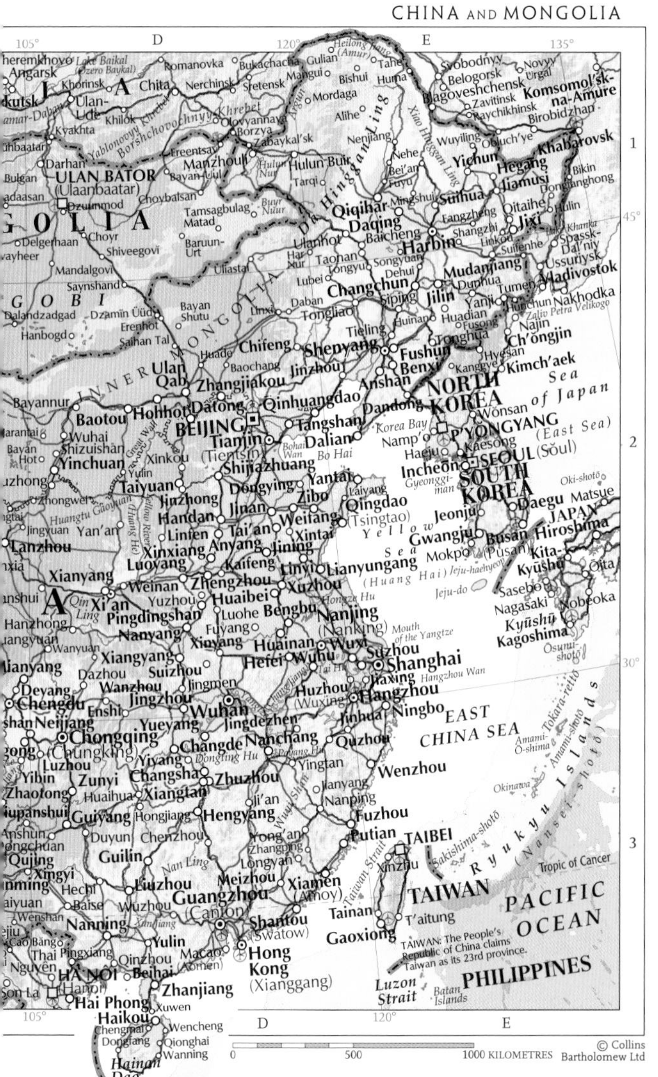

105°   D   120°   E   135°

Sheremkhovo
Angarsk
Khorinsk
Ulan-Ude
Khilok
Kyakhta

Romanovka   Bukachacha   Gulian
Nerchinsk   Sretensk   Mangui   Bishui   Huma   Tahe
Chita   Oloyyannaya   Mordaga
Borzya   Zabaykal'sk

Lake Baikal
(Ozero Baykal)

Svobodnyy   Novyy
Belogorsk   Urgal
Blagoveshchensk   Zavitinsk   Birobidzhan
Raychikhinsk   Obluch'ye   Khabarovsk

Komsomol'sk-
na-Amure

1

ULAN BATOR
(Ulaanbaatar)
Dzuunmod

Manzhouli   Hailar   Nur   Tarqi   Nehe
Choybalsan   Tamsagbulag   Ullanhot   Taonan   Dehui
Matad   Baruun-Urt   Uliastai   Lubei   Songyuan

Yichun   Hegang   Jiamusi   Bikin
Suihua   Qitaihe   Dongning   Kang
Tangzheng   Shangzhi   Jixi
Harbin   Mudanjiang   Ussuriysk

Vladivostok

45°

GOBI

Saynshand
Mandalgovi
Dzamin Üüd
Saihan Tal

Changchun   Jilin
Siping   Huadian
Tongliao   Tieling   Fusong
Chifeng   Shenyang   Gongzhuling   Ch'ongjin

Kimch'aek

2

Baotou   Hohhot   Datong   Zhangjiakou   Qinhuangdao
BEIJING   Tangshan
Tianjin   Dandong
(Tientsin)   Bo Hai
Shijiazhuang   Yantai

Korea Bay   Namp'o
Haeju   PYONGYANG

Wonsan   Sea of Japan
(East Sea)

Incheon   SEOUL
Gyeonggi-man   (Sŏul)   Oki-shotō

SOUTH
KOREA

Daegu   Matsue
Hiroshima

JAPAN

Yinchuan   Taiyuan   Jinzhong   Zibo   Qingdao
Linfen   Jinan   Weifang   (Tsingtao)
Handan   Tai'an   Xintai   Yellow
Xinxiang   Anyang   Sea
Luoyang   Kaifeng   Linyi   Lianyungang   (Huang Hai)

Jeonju
Gwangju   Busan
Mokpo   (Pusan)   Kyūshū
Jeju-haehyeop   Ōita

Lanzhou   Xianyang   Weinan   Zhengzhou   Huaibei   Xuzhou
Xi'an   Yuzhou   Luohe   Bengbu   Hongze Hu
Pingdingshan   Fuyang   Huainan
Nanyang   Xinyang   Hefei   Wuhu   Suzhou   Shanghai
Xiangyang   Suizhou   Jingmen   Jiaxing   Hangzhou Wan
Deyang   Wanzhou   Jingzhou   Huzhou   Hangzhou
Chengdu   Enshi   (Wuxing)   Ningbo

Jeju-do   Sasebo
Kita-
Nagasaki   Kyūshū
Kagoshima   Ōsumi-shotō

Mouth of the Yangtze

EAST
CHINA SEA

30°

Chongqing
(Chungking)   Yueyang   Nanchang
Changde   Dongting Hu   Jingdezhen
Yiyang   Zhuzhou   Ji'an   Yingtan   Wenzhou

Zunyi   Changsha
Zhaotong   Huaihua   Xiangtan
Tupanshui   Guiyang   Hongjiang   Hengyang

Xinyang   Nanping
Yanpingzhang   Fuzhou

Okinawa   Ryukyu Islands (Nansei-shotō)

Anshun   Duyun   Chenzhou
Qujing   Xingyi   Guilin   Nan Ling   Longyan
Hechi   Baise   Wuzhou   Meizhou   Xiamen
aiyuan   Wenshan   Nanning   Xunjiang   Guangzhou   Zhangzhou
Thai   Pingxiang   Qinzhou   (Canton)   Shantou
Nguyen   Yulin   Macao   (Amoy)   (Swatow)
HÀ NỘI   Beihai   (Aomen)   Hong   Tainan
Son La   (Hanoi)   Zhanjiang   Kong   Gaoxiong
Hai Phong   Xuwen   (Xianggang)

Putian   TAIBEI
Xinzhu

TAIWAN   T'aitung

3

Tropic of Cancer

PACIFIC
OCEAN

Haikou
Chengmai   Wenchang
Dongjiao   Qionghai
Hainan   Qionghai   Wanning
Dao

Luzon   Batan
Strait   Islands

PHILIPPINES

TAIWAN: The People's
Republic of China claims
Taiwan as its 23rd province.

105°   D   120°   E

0   500   1000 KILOMETRES

© Collins
Bartholomew Ltd   69

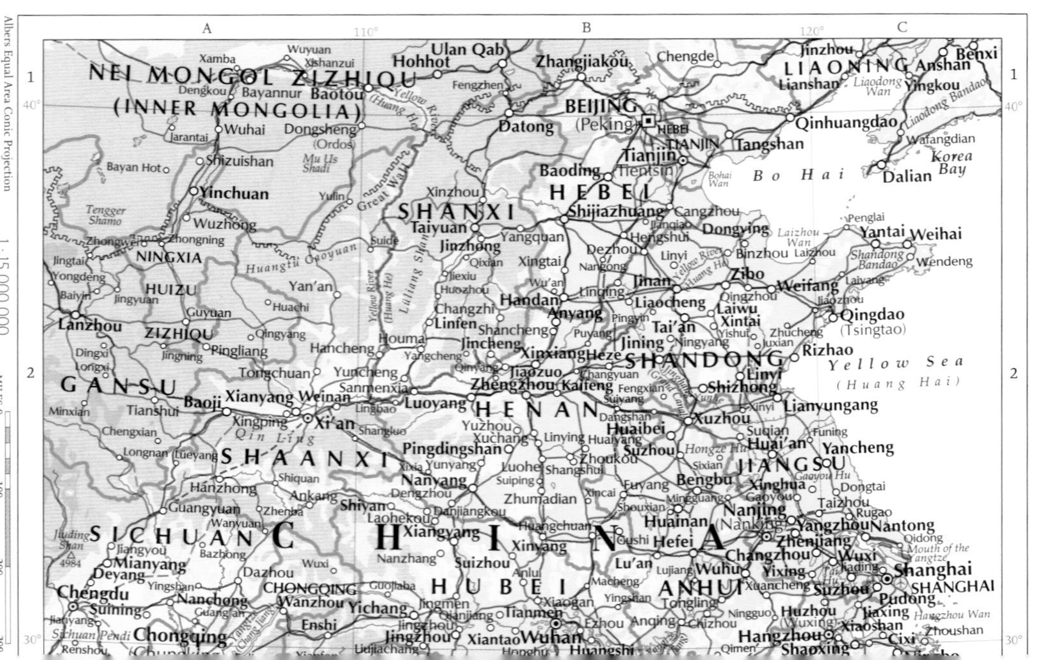

Albers Equal Area Conic Projection   1 : 15 000 000   MILES 0   100   200   300

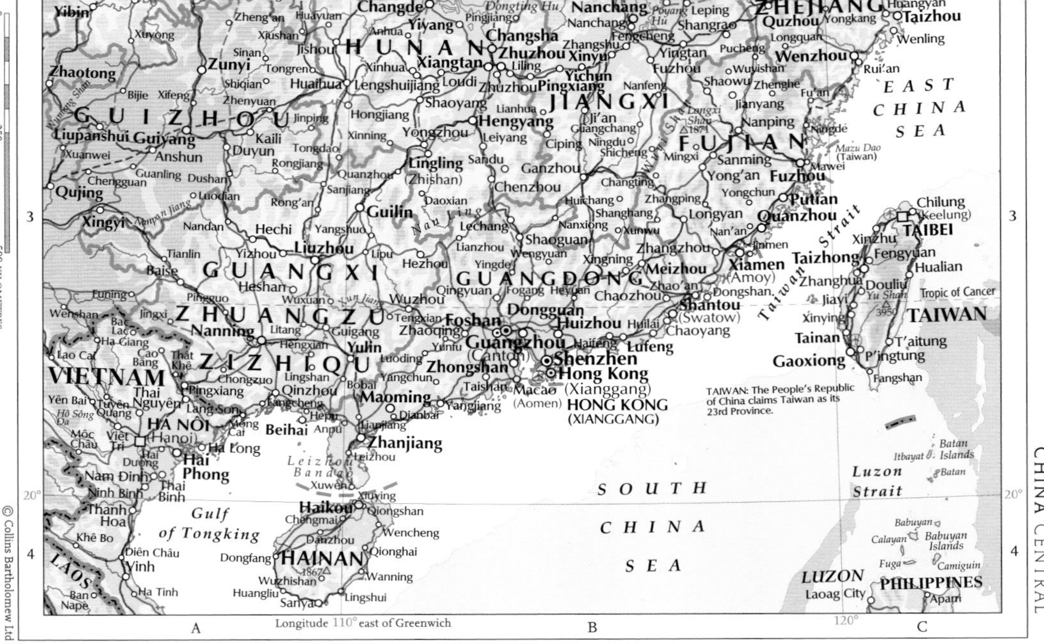
EAST CHINA SEA
SOUTH CHINA SEA
Taiwan Strait
Luzon Strait
Gulf of Tongking
ZHEJIANG
FUJIAN
JIANGXI
HUNAN
GUIZHOU
GUANGDONG
GUANGXI ZHUANGZU ZIZHIQU
HAINAN
TAIWAN
VIETNAM
LAOS
PHILIPPINES
LUZON
TAIBEI
HONG KONG (XIANGGANG)
Hong Kong (Xianggang)
Macao (Aomen)
Guangzhou (Canton)
Shenzhen
Dongguan
Foshan
Zhongshan
Shantou (Swatow)
Xiamen (Amoy)
Fuzhou
Quanzhou
Putian
Wenzhou
Taizhou
Nanchang
Changsha
Zhuzhou
Xiangtan
Hengyang
Changde
Guilin
Liuzhou
Nanning
Guiyang
Zunyi
Zhanjiang
Haikou
Sanya
Beihai
HÀ NỘI (Hanoi)
Hai Phong
Gaoxiong
Tainan
Taizhong
Hualian
Tropic of Cancer
TAIWAN: The People's Republic of China claims Taiwan as its 23rd Province.
Longitude 110° east of Greenwich
0
250
500 KILOMETRES

© Collins Bartholomew Ltd

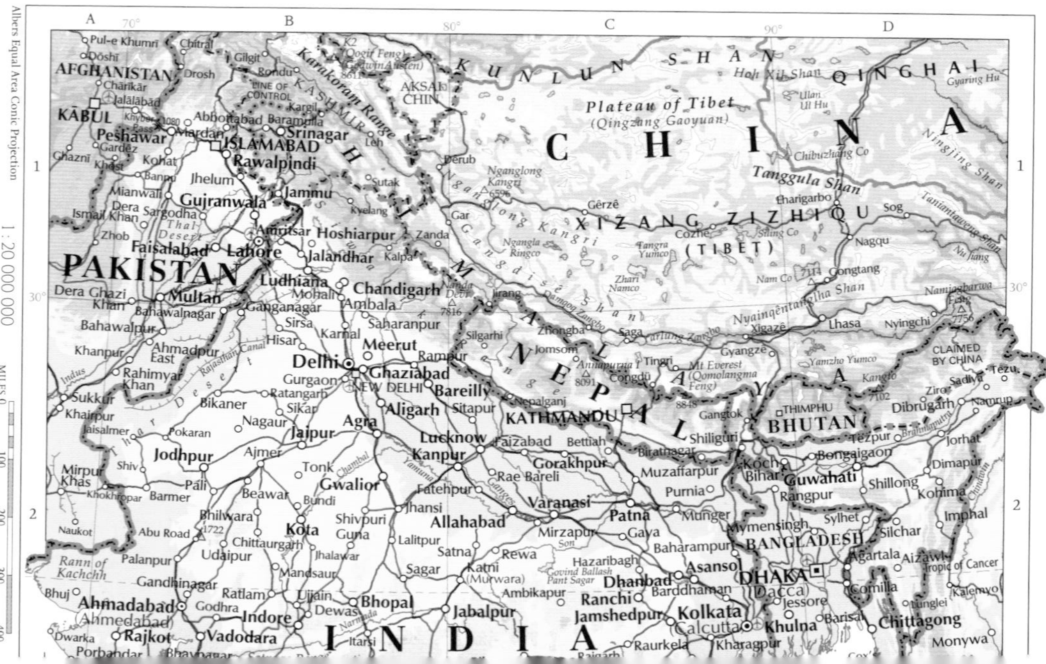

Albers Equal Area Conic Projection

1 : 20 000 000

MILES 0   100   200   300   400

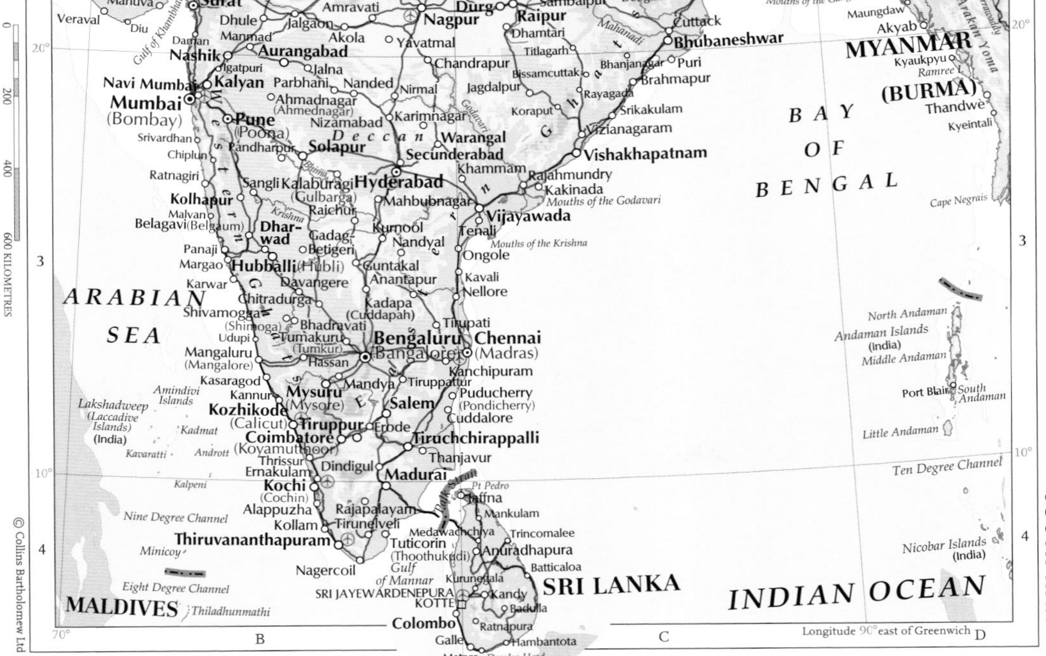

MYANMAR
(BURMA)

Arakan Yoma

Irrawaddy

Maungdaw
Akyab
Kyaukpyu
Ramree
Thandwe
Kyeintali

Cape Negrais

Mouths of the Ganga

B A Y

O F

B E N G A L

North Andaman
Andaman Islands
(India)
Middle Andaman

Port Blair South
Andaman
Little Andaman

Ten Degree Channel

Nicobar Islands
(India)

INDIAN OCEAN

Cuttack
Bhubaneshwar
Puri
Brahmapur

Sambalpur
Raipur
Durg
Nagpur
Amravati
Akola
Yavatmal
Jalna
Aurangabad
Ahmadnagar
(Ahmednagar)
Nanded
Parbhani
Nashik
Kalyan
Navi Mumbai
Mumbai
(Bombay)
Pune
(Poona)
Solapur
Kolhapur
Sangli
Kalaburagi
Gulbarga
Hyderabad
Secunderabad
Warangal
Karimnagar
Nizamabad
Nirmal

Chandrapur
Jagdalpur
Koraput
Vijayanagaram
Vishakhapatnam
Rajahmundry
Kakinada
Eluru
Vijayawada

Mouths of the Godavari
Mouths of the Krishna

Guntur
Ongole
Kavali
Nellore

Mahbubnagar
Kurnool
Anantapur
Nandyal
Kadapa
(Cuddapah)
Tirupati
Chennai
(Madras)
Kanchipuram
Tiruppur
Puducherry
(Pondicherry)
Cuddalore

Bengaluru
(Bangalore)
Mysuru
(Mysore)
Mandya
Salem
Erode
Tiruchchirappalli
Thanjavur
Madurai
Dindigul
Rajapalayam
Karur
Tuticorin
(Thoothukudi)
Tirunelveli
Nagercoil

Jaffna
Trincomalee
Batticaloa
Kandy
SRI JAYEWARDENEPURA KOTTE
Colombo
SRI LANKA
Galle
Hambantota
Matara
Dondra Head

Gulf of Mannar

Pt Pedro

MALDIVES

Lakshadweep
(Laccadive
Islands)
(India)

Minicoy

Eight Degree Channel
Nine Degree Channel

A R A B I A N
S E A

Veraval
Diu
Daman
Surat
Navsari
Dhule
Jalgaon

Gulf of Khambhat

Mangaluru
(Mangalore)
Kasaragod
Kannur
Kozhikode
Calicut
(Kozhikode)
Thrissur
Ernakulam
Kochi
(Cochin)
Alappuzha
Kollam
Thiruvananthapuram

Hubballi
Dharwad
Belagavi
(Belgaum)
Panaji
Margao
Karwar
Ratnagiri

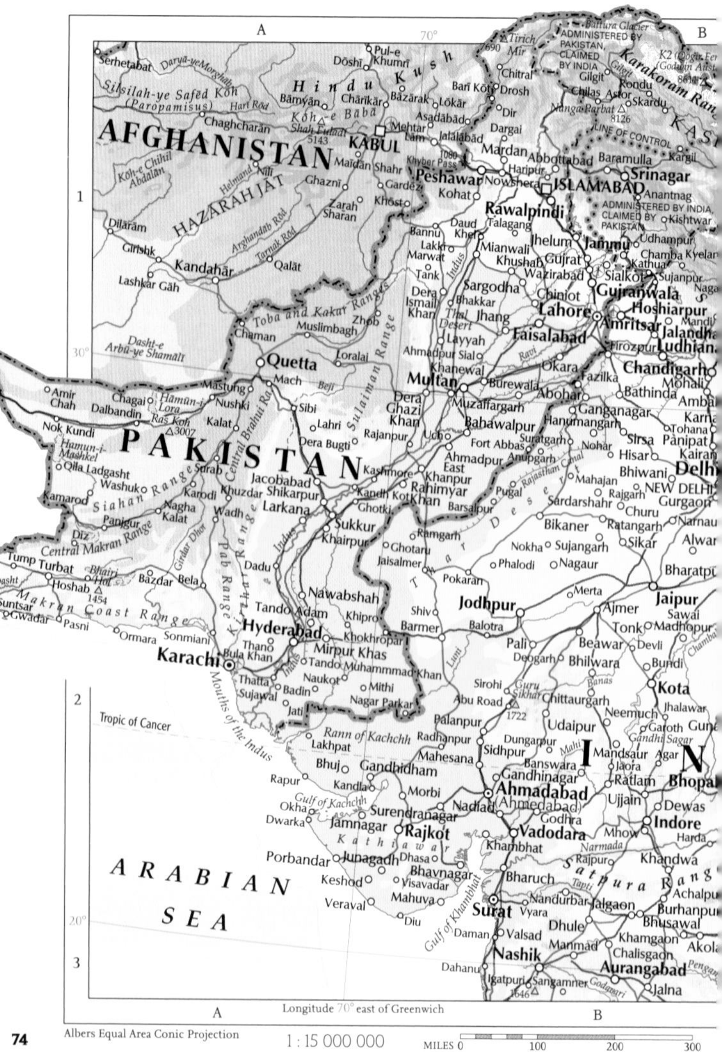

Tirich Glacier
ADMINISTERED BY
PAKISTAN,
CLAIMED
BY INDIA
Serhetabat   Tirich
        Darya-ye Morghāb   Mir   K2 (Qogir Feng)
                                          Pul-e   8611
Silsilah-ye Safed Koh   Dōshī Khumrī Bārī Kol Chitral Drosh Chilas Askore Gilgit 8126 Karakoram Ran. KAS
(Paropamisus)   Hari Rud   Bāmyān Bāzārak   Nangaparbat Skardu
Chaghcharan   Koh-i   Shāh Foladī Chārīkār Lōkar Dir Dargai   LINE OF CONTROL
                  Bābā   5143   Asadābād Mardan Abbottābād Baramulla Kargil
AFGHANISTAN   KĀBUL Jalālābād   Peshāwar   Haripur   Srinagar
                  Maidān Shahr Gardēz Khost   Nowshera Kohat ISLĀMĀBĀD Anantnag ADMINISTERED BY INDIA,
        Ghaznī   Rawalpindi Kishtwar CLAIMED BY
Dīlārām   HAZĀRAJĀT Zarah Sharan Bannu Daud Khel Talagang Jhelum Jammu Udhampur Chamba Kyelang
                      Argbandāb Rud   Lakki Talagang Mianwali Gujrat Sialkot Sujanpur
Girishk Lashkar Gāh Nīlī Helmand Road Tarnak Rud Marwat Sargodha Wazīrābād Gujrānwala Hoshiarpur
        Kandahār Qalāt   Dera Thal Jhang Chiniot Lahore Amritsar Jalandhar Ludhiana
        Toba and Kakar Ranges   Ismail Desert Faisalabad Firozpur Chandigarh
        Chaman Zhob   Khan   Leyyah   Abohar Mohali Amb.
Amīr Chagai Hills Nushki Toralai Suleiman Range Ahmadpur Sial Khanewal Multan Bathinda Karn.
Chah Nok Kundi Dalbandin Ras Koh Mastung Mach Beji Dera Burewala Ganganagar Sirsa Panipat
  Qila Ladgasht Washuk 3002 Quetta Sibi Lahri Ghazi Khan Muzaffargarh Hanumangarh Hisar Kaith.
Kamaror Hamun-i- Kalat Central Brahui Range Dera Bugti Babarwala Suratgarh Nohar Bhiwani NEW DELHI
        Mashkel Surab Khuzdar Rajanpur Fort Abbas Mahajan Rajgarh Gurgaon Narnaul
Dīz Siahan Range Nagha Wadh Jacobābād Kashmore Ahmadpur East Anupgarh Pugal Sardarshahr Churu Ratangarh Sikar Alwar
Tump Turbat Central Makran Range Kalat Khairpur Khanpur Rahimyar Barsalpur Bikaner Nokha Sujangarh Nagaur Bharatp.
        Bāzdār Bela   Larkana Ghotki Thar Desert Merta Jaipur
Dasht Hoshab 1454 Gidar Dhor Dadu Sukkur Khmgarh Phalodi Ajmer Sawai Madhopur
Suntsar Makran Coast Range Panjgur Ghotarru Jodhpur Beawar Devli Bundi
Gwadar Pasni Ormara Sonmiani Nawābshāh Shiv Jaisalmer Pokaran Pali Bhilwara Kota Jhalawar
        Tando Adam Khipro Barmer Balotra Sirohi Chittaurgarh
        Hyderābād Mirpur Khas Abu Road Neemuch Mandsaur Agar I N
Karāchi Thano Tando Muhamm'ad Khan Nagar Parkar Radhanpur 1722 Dungarpur Banswara Jaora Ratlam Bhopa.
        Bula Khan Naukot Badin Palanpur Sidhpur Udaipur Dewas
        Thatta Sujāwal Jati Rann of Kachchh Mahesana Gandhinagar Ujjain Indore
        Tropic of Cancer   Lakhpat Bhuj Gandhidhām Godhra Mhow Harda
                          Rapur Kandla Morbi Nadiād Ahmadābād Dahod Narmada Khandwa Khanwa
                Okha Dwarka Jāmnagar Surendranagar Vadodara Ratlam Bhusawal
ARABIAN Gulf of Kachchh Kathiawar Rajkot Dhasa Khambhat Bharuch Rajpur Satpura Range Akal.
        Porbandar Junagadh Bhavnagar Nandurbar Jalgaon Achalpur
SEA Keshod Visavadar Mahuva Diu Gulf of Khambhat Surat Dhule Chaligaon Akola
        Veraval Daman Valsad Mandad Khamgaon Pengan.
                          Dahanu Nandurbar Jalna
20°   Igatpuri Sangamner Godavari
                          1646 Nashik Aurangabad

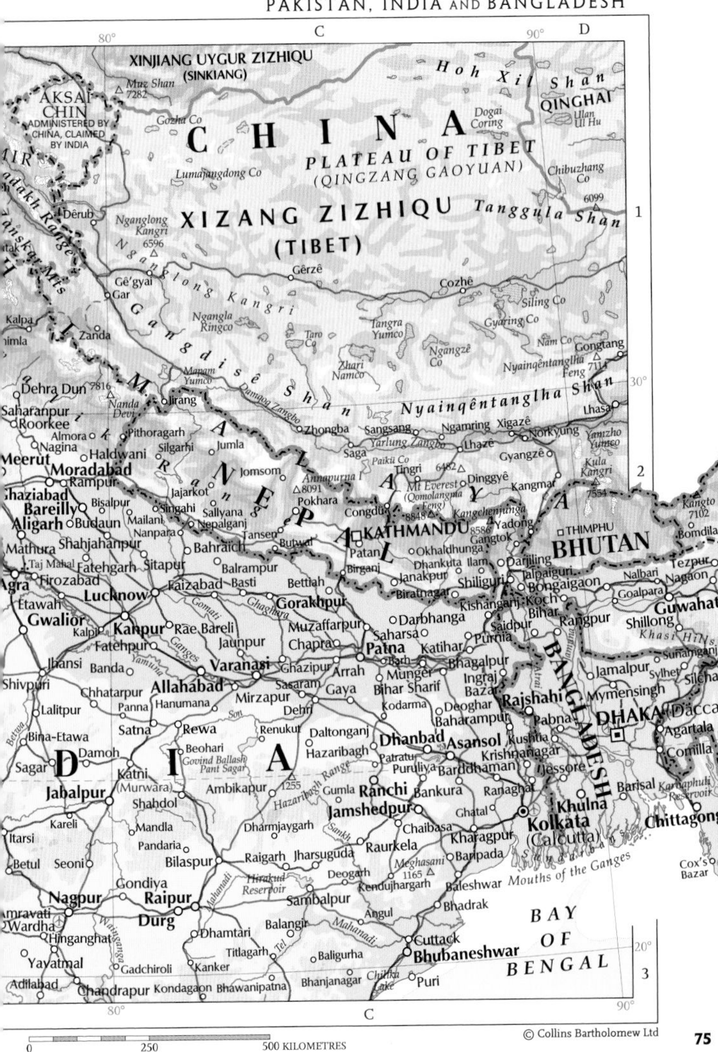

△ Muz Shan
7282

XINJIANG UYGUR ZIZHIQU (SINKIANG)

Hoh Xil Shan

QINGHAI

AKSAI CHIN
ADMINISTERED BY CHINA, CLAIMED BY INDIA

Gozha Co

Dogai
Coring

Ulan
Ul Hu

C H I N A

PLATEAU OF TIBET
(QINGZANG GAOYUAN)

Lumajangdong Co

Chibuzhang Co

6099
△

Ngangiong
Kangri
6596
△

XIZANG ZIZHIQU
(TIBET)

Tanggula Shan

Dêrub

Gê'gyai

Gar

Gêrzê

Cozhê

Siling Co

Gongtang
Feng 7114
△

1

Kalpa

Zanda

Ngangla
Ringco

Tangra
Yumco

Gyaring Co

Nam Co

Nyainqêntanglha
Feng 7111
△

Dampa Zangbo

Zhari
Namco

Ngangzê
Co

Lhasa
Yamzho
Yumco

30°

Dehra Dun 7816
△

Nanda
Devi

Oilkang

Zhongba

Sangsang

Nyainqêntanglha Shan

Saharanpur
Roorkee

Almora

Pithoragarh

Silgarhi

Jumla

Ngamring

Xigazê

Norkyung

Nagina
Haldwani

Jajarkot

Jomsom

Saga

Yarlung Zangbo
Lhazê

Gyangzê

Lhaze

Gyangzê

Kulu
Kangri
7554
△

2

Meerut
Moradabad

Bisalpur

Sallyana

Annapurna I
8091
△

Congdün

Mt Everest
(Qomolangma
Feng)
8848
△

Dinggyê

Kangmar

Kangto
7102
△

Rampur

Bareilly

Budaun

Singahi

Mailani

Pokhara

Kangchenjunga 8586 △

Yadong

THIMPHU

Bomdila

Aligarh

Shahjahanpur

Nanpara

Tansen

Butwal

KATHMANDU

Gangtok

Darjiling

Jalpaiguri

BHUTAN

Nalbari

Tezpur

Mathura

Fatehgarh

Sitapur

Bahraich

Patan

Birganj

Dhankuta

Ilam

Shiliguri

Bongaigaon

Goalpara

Nagaon

Taj Mahal
Firozabad

Balrampur

Bettiah

Janakpur

Biratnagar

Bihar

Rangpur

Shillong

Guwahati

Agra

Lucknow

Faizabad

Basti

Gorakhpur

Kishanganj

Purnia

Khasi Hills

Jamalpur

Etawah
Gwalior

Kalpi

Rae Bareli

Jaunpur

Muzaffarpur

Darbhanga

Saidpur

Sylhet

Silchar

Kanpur

Gomati

Chhapra

Patna

Katihar

BANGLADESH

Mymensingh

Fatehpur

Ghaghara

Ganges

Munger

Bhagalpur

Ingraj
Bazar

Rajshahi

Shivpuri

Banda

Ghazipur

Arrah

Bihar Sharif

Deoghar

Pabna

DHAKA (Dacca)

Agartala

Jhansi
Lalitpur

Chhatarpur

Panna

Allahabad

Mirzapur

Yamuna

Sasaram

Gaya

Kodarma

Dhanbad

Asansol

Kushtia

Krishnanagar

Baharampur

Comilla

Bina-Etawa

Sagar

Damoh

Hanumana

Rewa

Renukut

Daltonganj

Hazaribagh

Patratu

Puruliya

Barddhaman

Jessore

Khulna

Barisal

Chittagong

I N D I A

Katni
(Murwara)

Satna

Ambikapur

1255
△

Gumla

Ranchi

Bankura

Raniganj

Karnaphuli

Jabalpur

Shahdol

Govind Ballash
Pant Sagar

Hazaribagh Range

Ranchi

Jamshedpur

Chaibasa

Kharagpur

Baleshwar

Cox's
Bazar

Kareli

Mandla

Dharmjaygarh

Raigarh

Jharsuguda

Raurkela

Baripada

Itarsi

Seoni

Bilaspur

Hirakud
Reservoir

Deogarh

Kendujhargarh

Bhadrak

Mouths of the Ganges

Betul

Pandaria

1165
△

Baleshwar

Nagpur

Gondiya

Raipur

Sambalpur

Angul

Cuttack

Kolkata
(Calcutta)

BAY

Amravati
Wardha

Durg

Dhamtari

Balangir

Mahanadi

Bhubaneshwar

20°

OF

Hinganghat

Yavatmal

Gadchiroli

Kondagaon

Titlagarh

Baligurha

Bhanjanagar

Chilka
Lake

Puri

BENGAL

3

Adilabad

Chandrapur

Bhawanipatna

80°

C

90°

© Collins Bartholomew Ltd

0   250   500 KILOMETRES

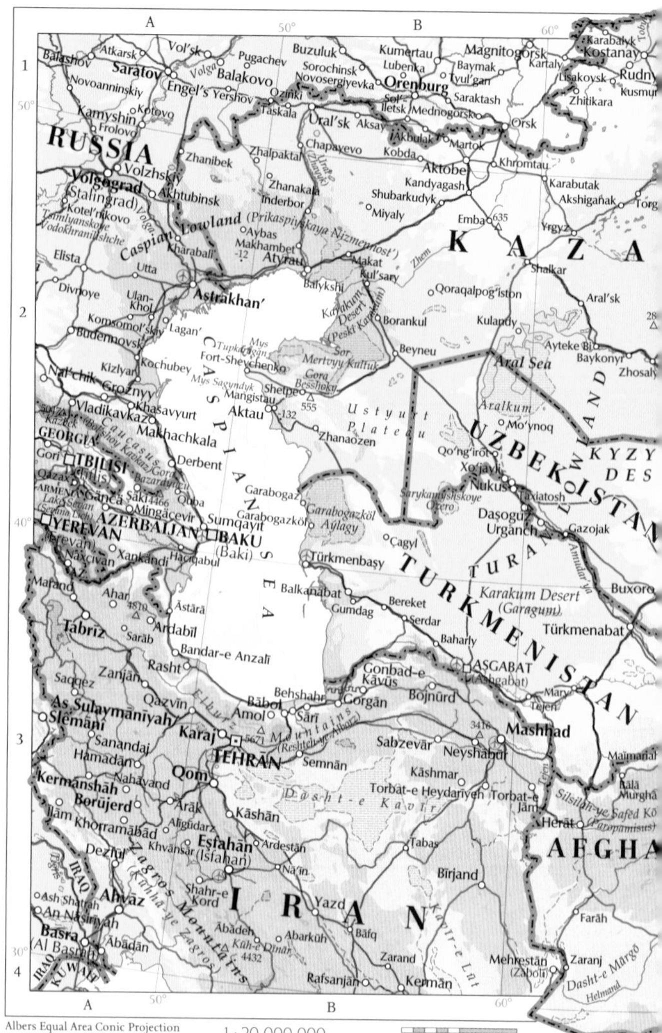

Albers Equal Area Conic Projection   1 : 20 000 000   MILES 0   100   200

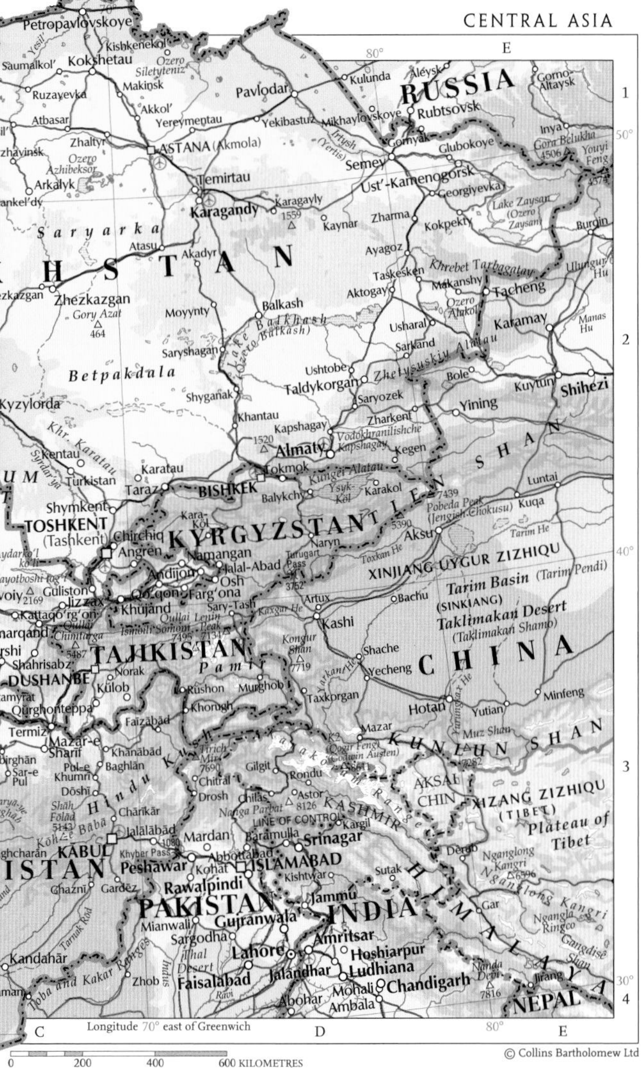

Petropavlovskoye
Yesil'
Saumalkol' Kishkenekol'
Kokshetau
Makinsk
Ruzayevka 'Akkol'
Atbasar Yereymentau Pavlodar
Zhaltyr (Akmola)
Erzhayinsk Ozero Zhibek
Azhibekşor
Arkalyk
nankel'dy ASTANA
Temirtau
Karagandy

RUSSIA
80° E
Kulunda Aleysk
Mikhaylovskoye Rubtsovsk
Semey Glubokoye
Ust'-Kamenogorsk
Georgiyevka
Zharma Kokpekty Lake Zaysan
Kaynar (Ozero Zaysan)
Ayagoz
Taskesken
Aktogay
Makanshy Tacheng
Ozero Karamay

Gora Belukha
Inya 4506
Gora
Gorno-
Altaysk
Youyi
Feng

Saryarka
ezkazgan Zhezkazgan
Gora Aazt
464
Moyynty
Balkash
Balkash
(Ozero Balkash)
Betpakdala
Saryshagan
Ushtobe
Shyganak

RHRebet Tarbagatay
Usharal
Sarkand
Zharkent

TIEN
Yining
Kuytun

SHAN
Shihezi

Kyzylorda
Kentau
Turkistan Karatau
Shymkent
TOSHKENT
(Tashkent)
Chirchiq Angren
Guliston Namangan
Kattaqo'rg'on
Khujand Jalal-Abad
Jizzax
narqand Andijon Osh
rshi
Shahrisabz Norak
DUSHANBE
Kulob

BISHKEK
Balykchy
Kara-
Kol
Toqmok
Almaty
Kegen
Kapshagay
Saryozek
Zhetigen
Karakol
Ysyk-
Köl
Köl Kungei Alatau
KYRGYZSTAN
Tarugart
Pass
Sary-Tash
TAJIKISTAN
Pamir
Murghob

XINJIANG UYGUR ZIZHIQU
(SINKIANG)
Aksu
Taklimakan Desert
(Taklimakan Shamo)
Kuqa
Tarim He
Luntai
Pobeda Peak
(Jengish Chokusu)
Bachu
Kashi
Tarim Basin (Tarim Pendi)
Yecheng
Shache
CHINA

KAZAKHSTAN

Longitude 70° east of Greenwich D 80° E

© Collins Bartholomew Ltd

0 200 400 600 KILOMETRES

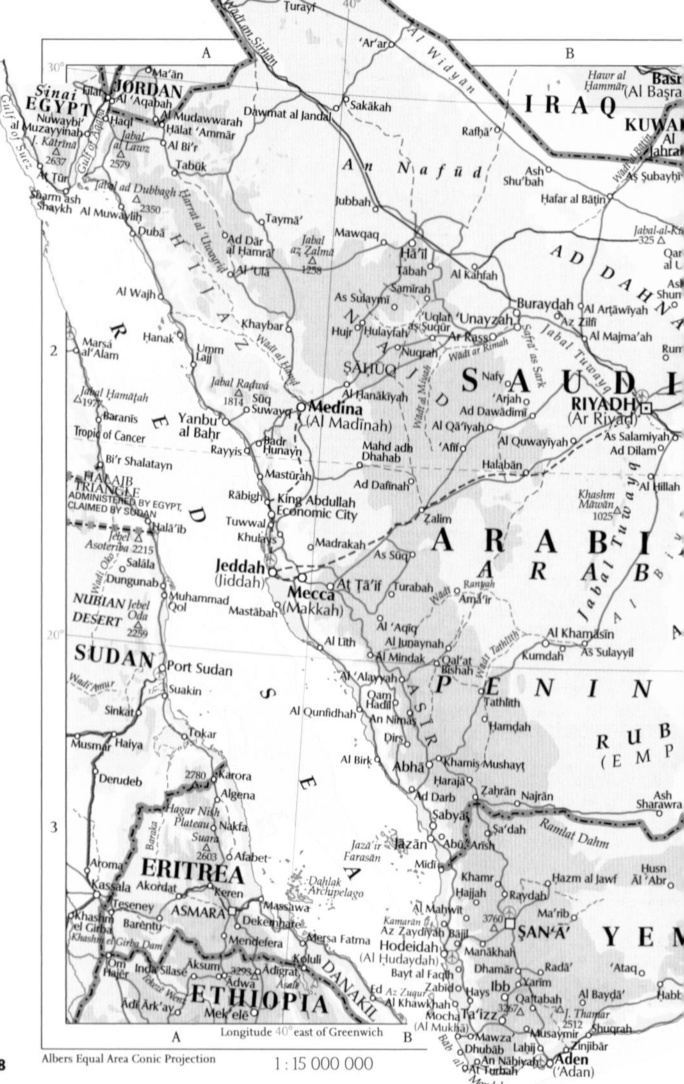

Ṭurayf 40°
'Ar'ar Al Widyān
30° A JORDAN B
Ma'ān Ḥawr al IRAQ Baṣr
Sinai EGYPT Ēlat 'Aqaba Ḥammār Al Baṣra
Nuwaybi' Al Mudawwara Ṣakākah
Muzayyinah Ḥaql Dawmat al Jandal KUWA
Kātrīna Jabal al Lawz Ḥālat 'Ammār Rafḥā' Aṣ Zahrā
2637 2579 Al Bi'r Ash As Ṣubayḥī
Tabūk Shu'bah Ḥafar al Bāṭin Jabal-al-U
Jabal ad Dubbagh Jubbah 325
Al Tūr 2350 An Nafūd AD DAHNA Qar
Sharm ash Al Muwayliḥ Taymā' Mawqaq
Shaykh Ḥarrat al 'Uwayriḍ Jabal Ḥā'il As Shun
Ad Dār az Zalma Tābah Al Kahfah Buraydah Al Arṭāwīyah Rum
Dubā Al Ḥamrā' 1258 Samirah 'Uqlat 'Unayzah Az Zilfī
REED As Sulaymī As Ṣuqūr Ar Rass Al Majma'ah
Al Wajh Khaybar Hujr Ḥulayfah Nugrah Wādī ar Rimah Salma as Sark
Ḥanak Umm Nafy Jabal Ţuwayq
Laji Wādī ar Rimah 'Arjah Ad Dawādimi As Salamīyah
Marsā al 'Alam Jabal Raḍwa Suwayr Al Hanākīyah Ad Dilam
Jabal Ḥamāṭah 1814 Sūq Medina SAUDI RIYADH As Salamīyah
1977 Baranis (Al Madīnah) Al Qā'īyah (Ar Riyāḍ) Ad Dilam
Tropic of Cancer Yanbu' Badr Al Quwayyīyah Al Hillah
Bi'r Shalatayn al Baḥr Ḥunayn Mahd adh 'Affīf Khashm Mawin
Rayyis Dhahab Ḥalabān 1025
HALAIB TRIANGLE Masṭūrah Ad Dafinah Zālim ARABI
ADMINISTERED BY EGYPT, Rābigh King Abdullah
CLAIMED BY SUDAN Economic City Madrakah As Sūq
Jebel Ḥalā'ib Tuwwal Khulays Turabah Wādī Ranyah
Asoteriba 2215 Jeddah Aṭ Ṭā'if Amā'ir Jabal Ţuwayq Biy
Ole (Jiddah) Bişah
NUBIAN Jebel Mecca Al 'Aqiq ASIR PENIN
DESERT Oda Mastābah (Makkah) Al Mindak Al Khamasin (EMP
Dungunab 2259 Al Līth Al Junaynah Qal'at Bishah Kumdah As Sulayyil
Muhammad Al 'Alayrah Qarn Ḥadid Tathlīth RUB
Qol Al Birk An Nimāṣ (E M P
SUDAN Al Qunfidhah Dirs Ḥamdah
20° Port Sudan Abha Khamis Mushayṭ
Suakin Harajah Zahrān Najrān Ramlat Dahm
Sinkat Ad Darb Ṣabyā Ṣa'dah Ash
Musmar Haiya Khamr Sharawra
Derudeb 2780 Algena Jazā'ir Abū 'Arīsh Midi Hazm Al Jawf Husn
Karora Farasān Al 'Abr
Hagar Nish 2603 Raydah YEM
3 Plateau Suara Dahlak 3760 Ma'rib
Atoma Nafka Archipelago Al Maḥwīt
Kassala Akordat Keren Massawa Al Mahwit Ḥajjah ŞAN'Ā'
ERITREA Az Zaydīyah Bajil Manākhah 'Ataq
Khashm Barentu Dekemhare Mersa Fatma Hodeidah Dhamār
el Girba Teseney ASMARA (Al Ḥudaydah) Ibb Yarim Al Bayḍā'
Khashm el Girba Dam Koluli DANAKIL Bayt al Faqīh Qa'ṭabah J. Thamar Habl
'Om Mendefera Ḥays Ta'izz 2512 Shuqrah
Hajer Inda Silase Adigrat Asale Zabīd Al Khawkhah Mocha Laḥij Zinjibār
Adwa Ed Zuqur (Al Makhā') An Nabīyah Aden
Adi Ark'ay ETHIOPIA Mek'ele Mawza Ḍhubab Turbah ('Adan)
A Longitude 40° east of Greenwich B Musaymīr

78 Albers Equal Area Conic Projection 1 : 15 000 000

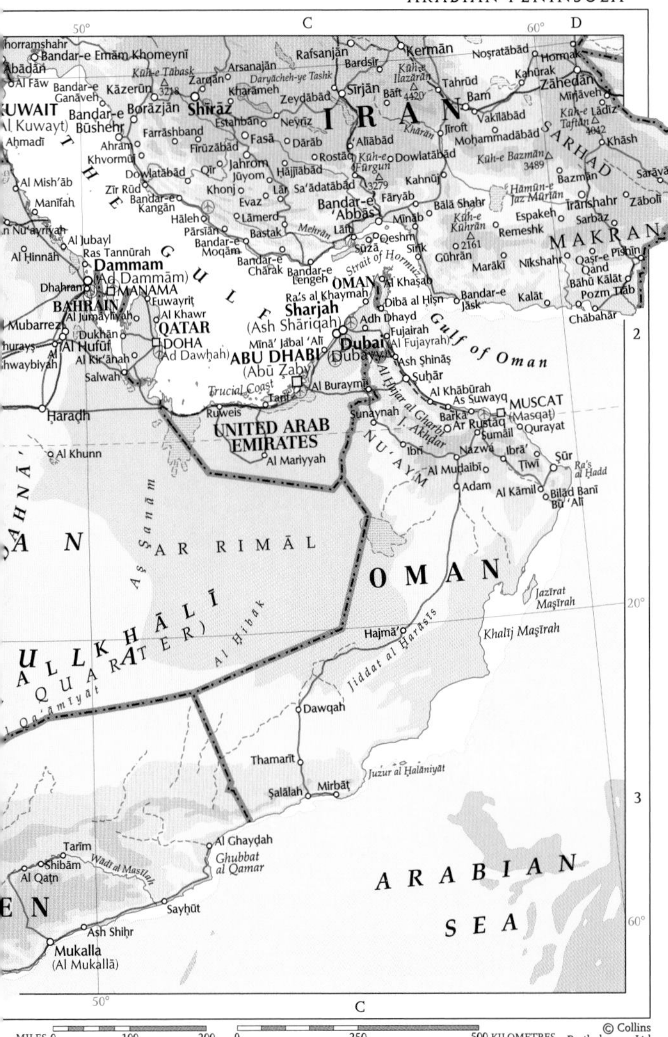

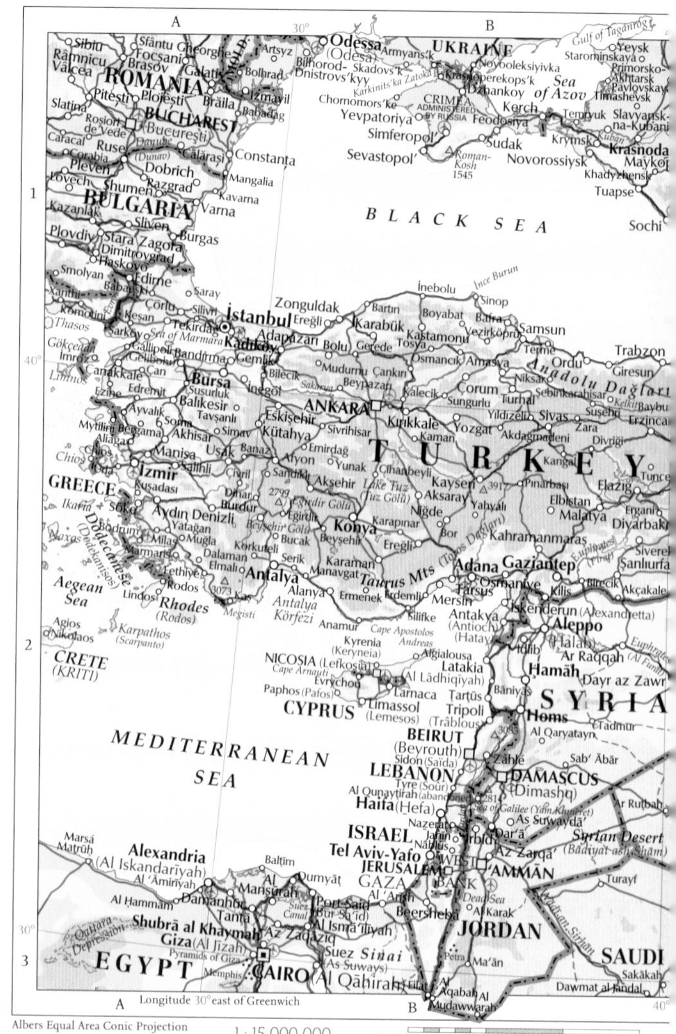

Albers Equal Area Conic Projection

1 : 15 000 000

MILES 0   100   200   300

C   50'   D

al'sk   Proletarskoye
Vodokhranilishche   Elista   Utta   Borankul   Karakum Desert   Beyneu

horetsk   Ipatovo   Divnoye   Astrakhan'
mavir   Stavropol'   Ulan-Khol   Komsomol'skiy   Mys
Vozryshennost'   Budennovsk   Tupkaragan   Fort-Shevchenko   Gora
Stavropol'skaya   Beshtau   555   Ustyurt
abinsk   Nevinnomyssk   Georgiyevsk   Kizlyar   Shetpe   555   Plateau
bay   Cherkessk   Pyatigorsk   Prokhladnyy   Aktau   332   Mangistau
Kislovodsk   Nal'chik   Grozny   Khasavyurt   Zhanaozen

RUSSIA

KAZAKHSTAN

Sokhumi   Nal'chik   Grozny   Khasavyurt   Makhachkala
aga   Vladikavkaz   Izberbash   Kazakhskiy Zaliv
T'q'varcheli   CAUCASUS   Buynaksk   Derbent
ugdidi   Samt'redia   Derbent
Poti   GEORGIA   Kutaisi   Gora
'umi   TBILISI   Bazardüzü   Qoba   Garabogaz   Garabogazköl
(Tiflis)   4466   Sumqayit   Z   Garabogaz   Aylagy
af   Artvin   Ardahan   Gori   Şäki   Göyçay Samax   Abşeron   Garabogazköl
ze   Yusufeli   Mingäçevir   Yarimadası
Gyumri   Kars   ARMENIA   Ganca   BAKU   Türkmenbaşy   Janña
navir   Sarıkamış   AZERBAIJAN   (Baki)   Hazar   Balkanabat
Horasan   Doğubeyazıt   Hacıqabul   Qumdag
zurum   Ağrı   YEREVAN   Aĝdam   Salyan
göl   Matazgirt   Patnos   Erevan   Xankändi   Länkäran
Muş   Ahlat   AZER.   Sisian   Astara   Gonbad-e Kāvūs   Gorgan
ilvanTatvan Lake Van   Van   Naxçıvan   Maku   Khvoy   Marand
Slirt (Van Gölü)   Salmas   Ahar   4810   Bandar-e Anzalī
atman   Başkale   Tabriz   Sarāb   Ārdabīl   Tähijān   Rasht   Nowshahr   Bābol   Behshahr
Şemdinli   Lake Urmia   Miāneh   Qazvīn   Amol   Sārī   Shāhrūd
Mardin   Hakkâri   (Daryācheh-ye   Mīāndoāb   Zanjān   Rasht   Elburz Mountains   (Reshteh-ye)   Dāmghān
Qāmishlī   Zākhū   Orūmīyeh)   Maḩābād   Qazvīn   5671   Semnān
Hasakah   Zaxo   Oshnavīyeh   Saqqez   Bijar   Karaj   TEHRAN
Tall Afar   Mosul   Arbil/Hewlêr   Sanandaj   Hamadān   Qom   Dasht-e
'Anah   As Sulaymānīyah/Slêmanî   Kirkūk   Halabjah/Helebce   Ravānsar   Malāyer   Kāshān   Kavīr   Jandaq
Ash   Tikrit   Dast-e   Kermānshāh   Nahāvand   IRAN
Bayjī   Sharqat   Kifri   Shīrīn   Kerend-e   Borūjerd   Golpāyegān   Ardestān
Al Hadīthah   Sāmarrā'   Ghar   Eslāmābād-e   Nahāvand   Arāk   Āʾīn
uhayrat al Tharthar   Ar Ramādī   Ba'qūbah   Gharb   Khorramābād   Alīgūdarz   Dārān   Eşfahān   Nāʾīn
Haur al Habbaniyah   BAGHDAD   Īlām   Dezfūl   Najafābād   (Isfahan)
Buhayrat ar Razāzah   Hillah   Al Kūt   Shūshtar   Shahr-e Kord   Yazd
IRAQ   Karbalā'   Al Hayy   Masjed   Shahrezā   Ābādeh   Abarkūh
An Najaf   Ad Dīwānīyah   Soleymān   Kūh-e Dīnār
As Samāwah   Ash Shaṭrah   Ahvāz   Rāmhormoz   4432   Arsanājān
Haur al   An Nāṣirīyah   Shuyūkh   Kūh-e Tabask
RABIA   Ḩammār   Sūq ash   Khorramshahr   Bandar-e Emām Khomeynī   Zargān   Daryācheh-ye   Shiraz
Ar'ar   Basra   Ābādān   Bandar-e Kāzerūn   kharamah   Tashk
(Al Baṣrah)   Al Fāw   Ganāveh
KUWAIT   Bandar-e

1

40'

C   A   S   P   I   A   N   S   E   A

T   U   R   K   M   E   N   I   S   T   A   N

2

3

30'

50'

C   D

0   250   500 KILOMETRES
© Collins Bartholomew Ltd

81

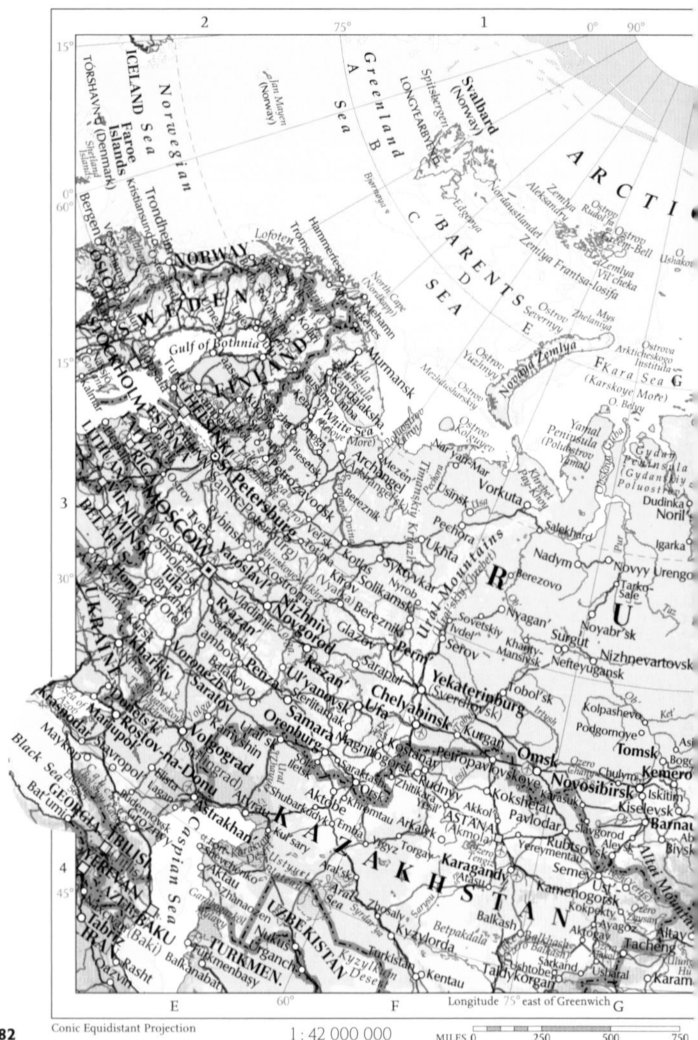

Conic Equidistant Projection

1 : 42 000 000

MILES 0   250   500   750

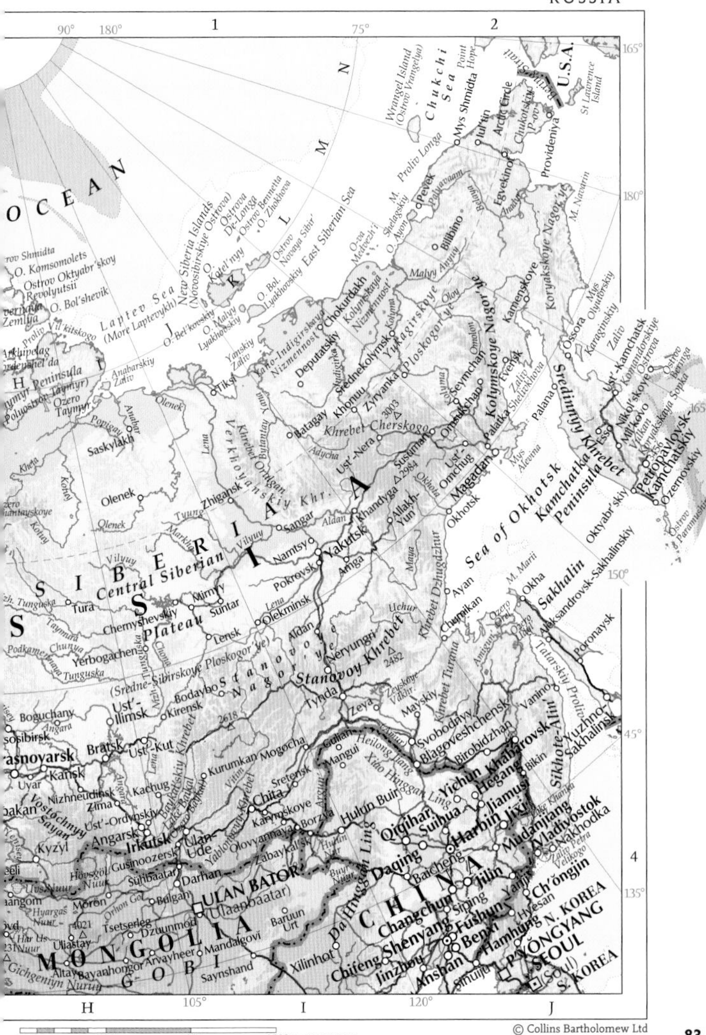

© Collins Bartholomew Ltd

0   500   1000   1500 KILOMETRES

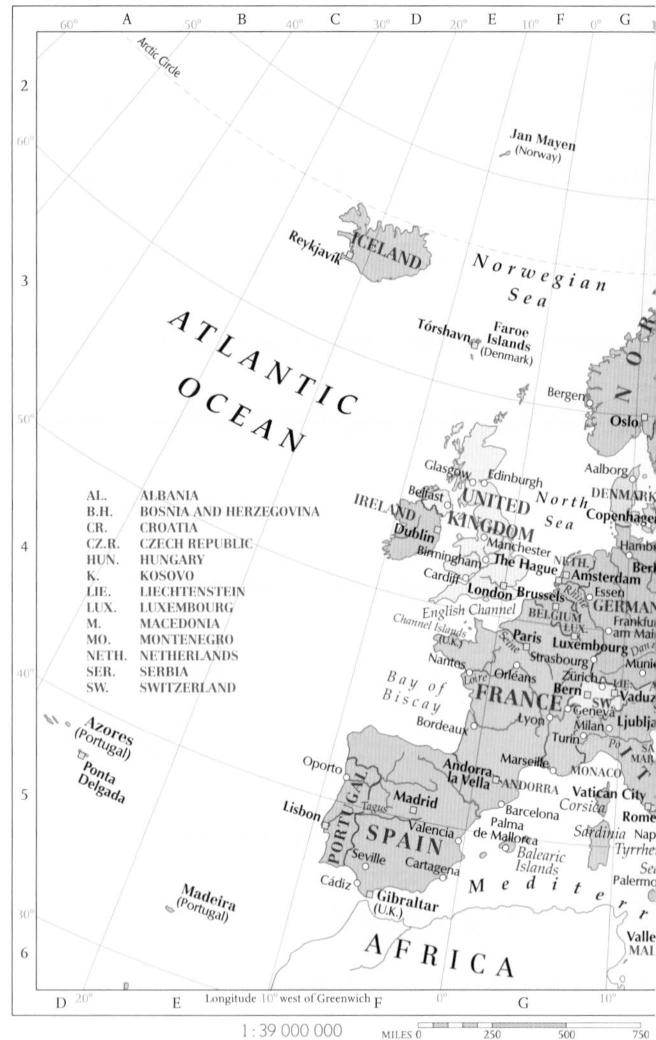

A   B   C   D   E   F   G

60°   50°   40°   30°   20°   10°   0°

Arctic Circle

2

60°

Jan Mayen
(Norway)

ICELAND
Reykjavík

3

Norwegian
Sea

Tórshavn   Faroe
Islands
(Denmark)

A T L A N T I C

O C E A N

50°

Bergen

N O R

Oslo

Glasgow   Edinburgh   North   Aalborg

Belfast   UNITED   Sea   DENMARK
IRELAND   KINGDOM   Copenhagen

4   Dublin   Manchester   Hamb
Birmingham   The Hague   NETH.
Cardiff   London Brussels   Amsterdam   Ber
English Channel   BELGIUM   Essen   GERMAN
Channel Islands   LUX.   Frankfu
(U.K.)   Paris   Luxembourg   am Mai
Nantes   Strasbourg   Dan   Muni
Orleans   Zürich   Bern   LIE.   Vaduz
SW.   Geneva   Vaduz

AL.	ALBANIA
B.H.	BOSNIA AND HERZEGOVINA
CR.	CROATIA
CZ.R.	CZECH REPUBLIC
HUN.	HUNGARY
K.	KOSOVO
LIE.	LIECHTENSTEIN
LUX.	LUXEMBOURG
M.	MACEDONIA
MO.	MONTENEGRO
NETH.	NETHERLANDS
SER.	SERBIA
SW.	SWITZERLAND

40°

Bay of
Biscay

FRANCE   Milan   Ljublja
Lyon   Turin   Po   SA
MAR.

Bordeaux   Marseille   Vatican City

Azores
(Portugal)

Ponta
Delgada

Oporto

Andorra
la Vella   ANDORRA   Corsica   Rome

5   Madrid   Barcelona   Vatican City
Lisbon   Valencia   Palma   Sardinia   Nap
Tagus   SPAIN   de Mallorca   Tyrrhe
Seville   Cartagena   Balearic   Se
Islands   M e d i t e   Palermo

Cádiz   Gibraltar
(U.K.)   r

Madeira
(Portugal)   Valle
MAI

30°

6   A F R I C A

D   20°   E   Longitude 10° west of Greenwich   F   0°   G   10°

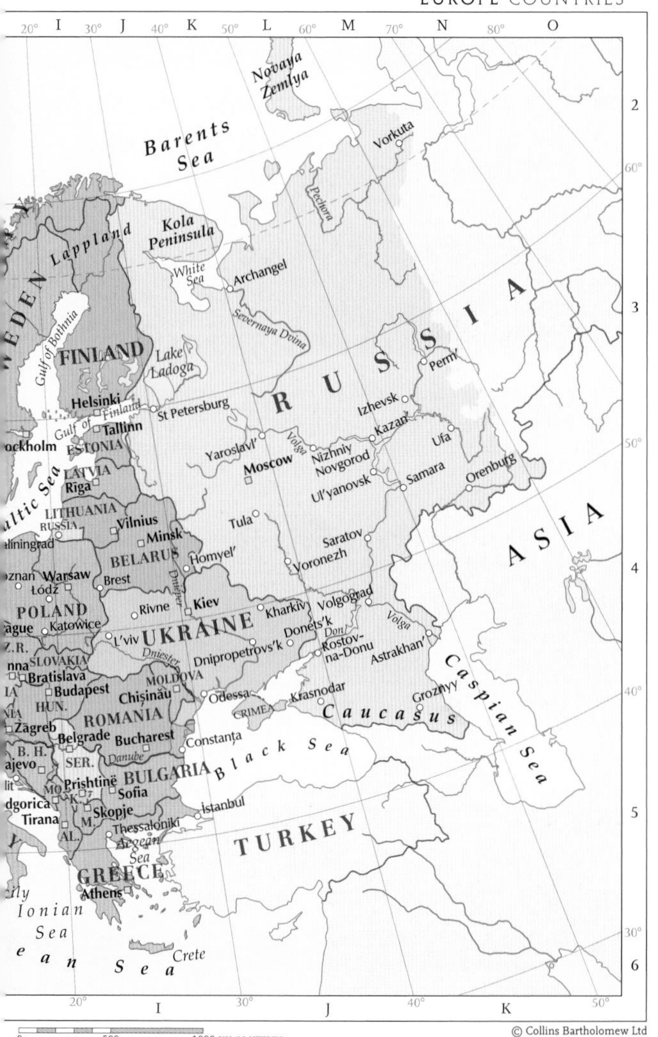
Novaya Zemlya
Barents Sea
Vorkuta
Pechora
Kola Peninsula
Lappland
White Sea
Archangel
Severnaya Dvina
FINLAND
Gulf of Bothnia
Lake Ladoga
Helsinki
Gulf of Finland
Tallinn
ESTONIA
St Petersburg
R U S S I A
Perm'
Izhevsk
Kazan'
Ufa
Yaroslavl'
Volga
Nizhniy Novgorod
Moscow
Ul'yanovsk
Samara
Orenburg
LATVIA
Rīga
LITHUANIA
RUSSIA
Vilnius
Minsk
BELARUS
Tula
Saratov
Homyel'
Voronezh
ASIA
Warsaw
Łódź
Brest
Dnieper
POLAND
Katowice
Rivne
Kiev
Kharkiv
Volgograd
UKRAINE
L'viv
Dnipropetrovs'k
Donets'k
Don
Rostov-na-Donu
Astrakhan'
SLOVAKIA
Bratislava
Dniester
MOLDOVA
Budapest
Chişinău
Odessa
Krasnodar
Groznyy
HUN.
ROMANIA
CRIMEA
Caucasus
Caspian Sea
Zagreb
Belgrade
Bucharest
Constanța
Black Sea
Danube
SER.
BULGARIA
Prishtinë
Sofia
Skopje
İstanbul
Tirana
Thessaloniki
Aegean Sea
TURKEY
GREECE
Athens
Ionian Sea
Crete
Sea
0 500 1000 KILOMETRES

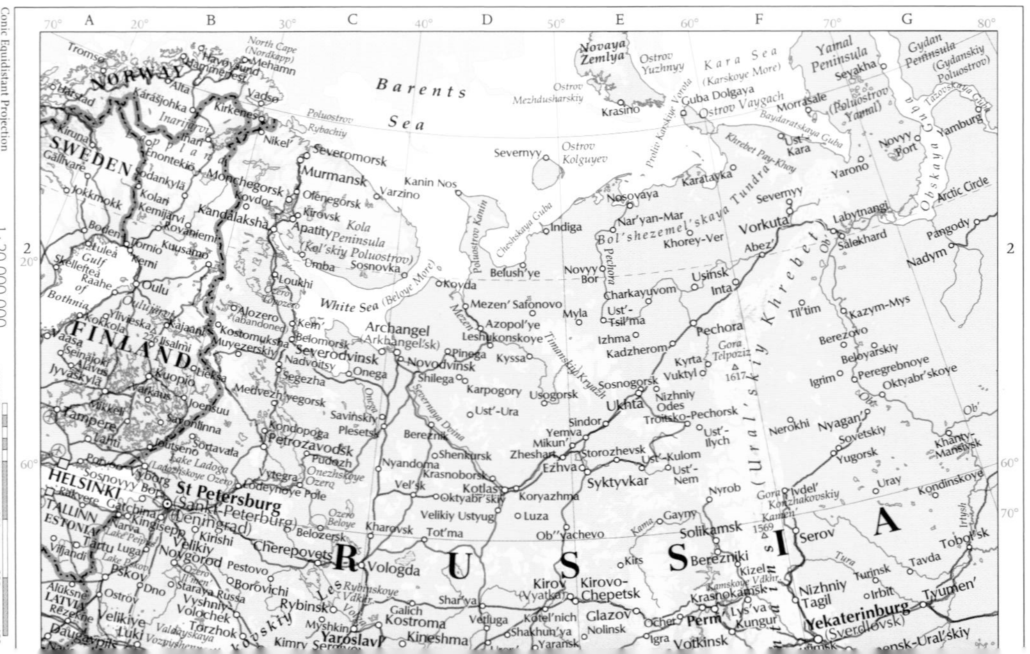

NORWAY

SWEDEN

FINLAND

ESTONIA

LATVIA

Barents Sea

White Sea

Kara Sea (Karskoye More)

Novaya Zemlya

Yamal Peninsula

Kola Peninsula

Gulf of Bothnia

St Petersburg

HELSINKI

TALLINN

RUSSIA

Murmansk

Arkhangel'sk

Vorkuta

Yekaterinburg

Tyumen'

Tobol'sk

Serov

Nizhniy Tagil'

Perm'

Syktyvkar

Vologda

Yaroslavl'

Kostroma

Arctic Circle

Conic Equidistant Projection

1 : 20 000 000

MILES 0   100   200   300   400

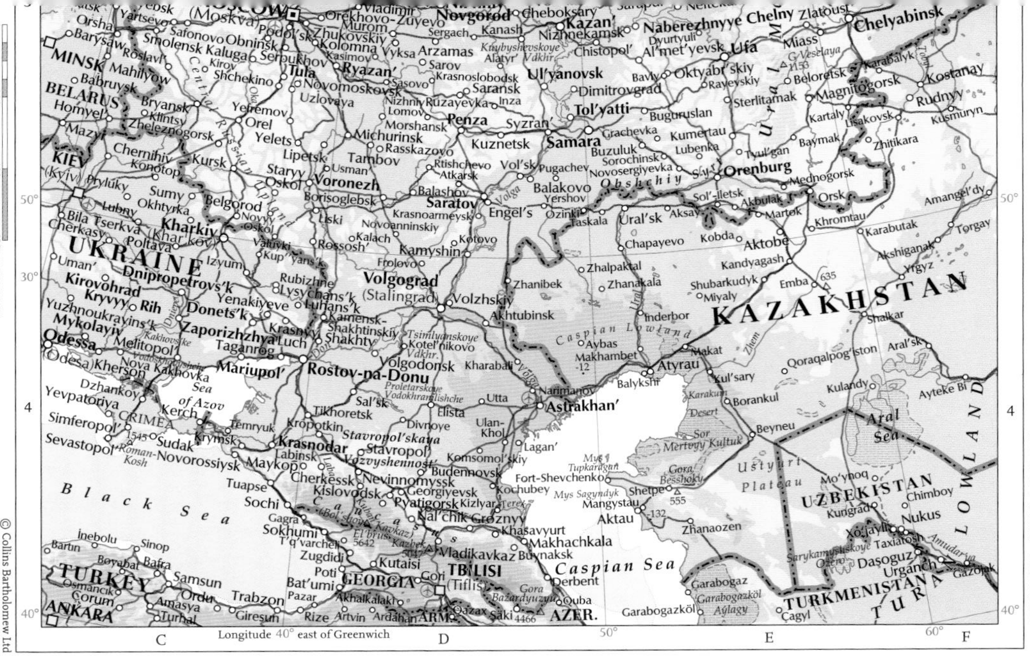

© Collins Bartholomew Ltd

0   200   400   600 KILOMETRES

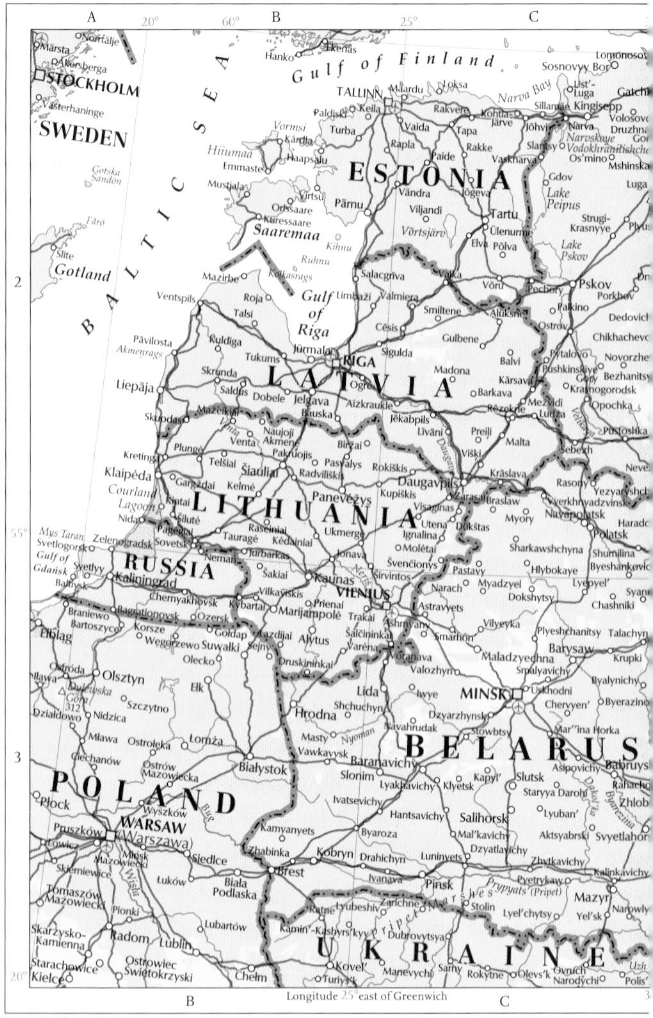

Conic Equidistant Projection   1 : 8 000 000   MILES 0   50   100   150

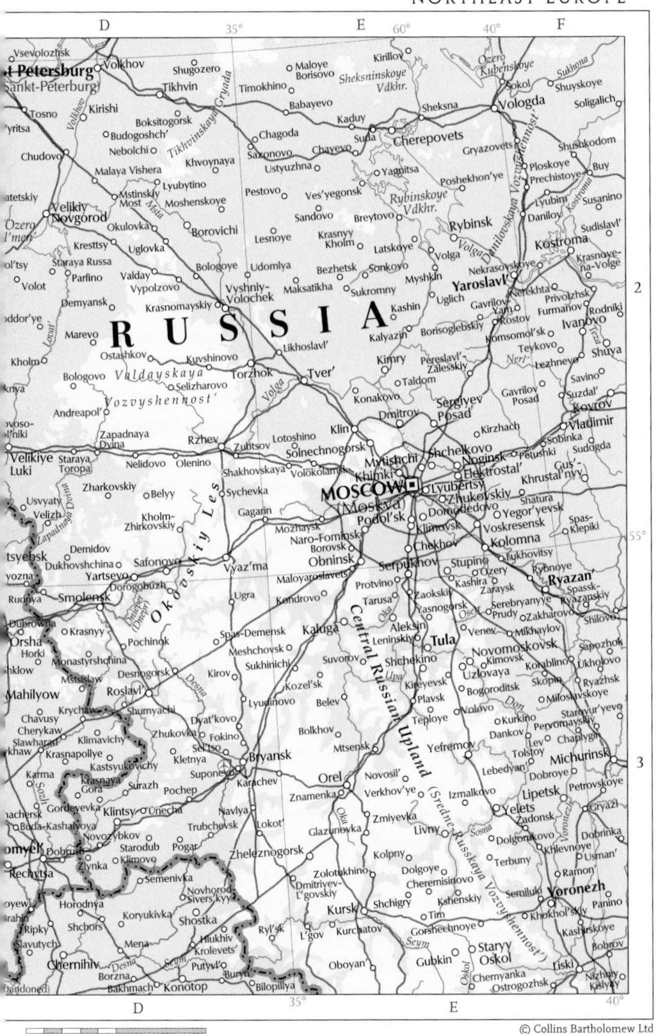

D   35°   E   60°   40°   F

Vsevolozhsk
t Petersburg   Volkhov   Shugozero   Maloye   Kirillov   Ozero
Sankt-Peterburg   Tikhvin   Timokhino   Borisovo   Kubenskoye
°Tosno   Kirishi   Babayevo   Sheksna   Sokol   Shuyskoye   Soligalich
yritsa   Chudovo   Boksitogorsk   Chagoda   Chayevo   Cherepovets   Gryazovets   Shushkodom
         Budogoshch'   Ustyuzhna   Gryazovets   Ploskoye   Buy
Neboliki   Malaya Vishera   Khvoynaya   Yagnitsa   Poshekhon'ye   Prechistoye   Lyubim   Danilov   Susanino
atetskiy   Lyubytino   Moshenskoye   Pestovo   Ves'yegonsk   Rybinskoye   Sudislavl'
Velikiy   Mstinskiy   Borovichi   Sandovo   Breytovo   Vdkhr.   Nekrasovskoye   Kostroma
Novgorod   Most   Okulovka   Lesnoye   Krasnyy   Latskoye   Rybinsk   Krasnoye-
'l'men   Krestsy   Uglovka   Bologoye   Udomlya   Kholm   Sonkovo   Myshkin   Yaroslavl'   na-Volge   2
'ty   Staraya Russa   Valday   Vyshniy-   Maksatikha   Sukromny   Gavrilov   Furmanov   Rodniki
Volot   Parfino   Vypolzovo   Volochek   Bezhetsk   Kashin   Kalyazin   Komsomol'sk   Ivanovo   Shuya
Demyansk   Krasnomayskiy   Likhoslavl'   Kimry   Pereslavl'   Teykovo   Savino
Marevo   Ostashkov   Kuvshinovo   Torzhok   Konakovo   Taldom   Zalesskiy   Gavrilov   Suzdal'   Kovrov
Kholm   Bologovo   Selizharovo   Tver'   Dmitrov   Sergiyev   Posad   Vladimir
kriya   Andreapol'   Rzhev   Lotoshino   Klin   Mytishchi   Shchelkovo   Kirzhach   Feushki   Sudogda
osa-   Zapadnaya   Zubtsov   Solnechnogorsk   Khimki   Noginsk   Elektrostal'   Gus'-
Velikiye   Dvina   Nelidovo   Olenino   Shakhovskaya   Volokolamsk   MOSCOW   Lyubertsy   Zhukovskiy   Khrustal'nyy   55°
Luki   Staraya   Zharkovskiy   Belyy   Sychevka   (Moskva)   Voskresensk   Yegor'yevsk   Spas-
Usvyaty   Toropa'   Kholm-   Gagarin   Naro-Fominsk   Podol'sk   Klimovsk   Kolomna   Klepiki
Velizh   Demidov   Zhirkovskiy   Mozhaysk   Borovsk   Chekhov   Stupino   Lukhovitsy
tsyebsk   Dukhovshchina   Safonovo   Vyaz'ma   Maloyaroslavets   Obninsk   Serpukhov   Kashira   Zaraysk   Ryazan'
yozna   Yartsevo   Dorogobuzh   Ugra   Kondrovo   Protvino   Tarusa   Zaoksk   Serebryanyye   Ozakharovo   Shilovo
Rudnya   Smolensk   Spas-Demensk   Meshchovsk   Kaluga   Aleksin   Yasnogorsk   Venev   Prudy
Orsha   Krasnyy   Pochinok   Sukhinichi   Suvorov   Leninskiy   Tula   Novomoskovsk   Skopin   Ukholovo
Horki   Monastyrshchina   Kozel'sk   Shchekino   Uzlovaya   Kimovsk   Kosimovskoye
khlov   Mstsislaw   Roslavl'   Kirov   Lyudinovo   Belev   Yasnogorsk   Plavsk   Yepifan'   Kurkino   Dankov   Staroyur'yevo   Michurinsk
Mahilyow   Desnogorsk   Dyat'kovo   Bolkhov   Teploye   Kireyevsk   Novosil'   Lebedyan'   Dobroye   Petrovskoye
huy   Krychaw   Shumyachi   Zhukovka   Seltso   Mtsensk   Yefremov   Tolstoy   Lipetsk
Chavusy   Klimavichy   Bryansk   Orel   Dankov   Zadonsk   Gryazi
Cherykaw   Krasnapolye   Kastsyukovichy   Karachev   Novosil'   Verkhov'ye   Izmalkovo   Yelets   Dobrinka
khaw   Krasnaya   Surazh   Pochep   Navlya   Znamenka   Zmiyevka   Livny   Dolgorukovo   Dobrinka   Ramon'
Karma   Gordeyevka   Klintsy   Unecha   Trubchevsk   Lokot'   Glazunovka   Kolpny   Dolgoye   Terbuny   Semiluki   Voronezh
achersk   Novozybkov   Starodub   Pogar   Zheleznogorsk   Zolotukhino   Dmitriyev-   Cheremisinovo   Khokhol'skiy   Panino
omyel'   Dobrush   Zlynka   Semenovka   Novhorod-   Dmitriyev-   l'govskiy   Shchigry   Tim   Gubkin   Starry   Liski
Rechytsa   Zynka   Sivers'kyy   Shostka   Kursk   Kurchatov   Oboyan'   Semiluki   Oskol   Ostrogozhsk   Nizhniy
Ripky   Horodnya   Koryukivka   Ryl'sk   L'gov   Sudzha   Seym   Okol   Chernyanka   Robrov
Slavutych   Shchors   Mena   Hlukhiv   Krolevets'   Putyvl'   40°
honded)   Chernihiv   Borzna   Bakhmach   Konotop   Bilopillya   3

D   35°   E   40°

0   100   200 KILOMETRES   © Collins Bartholomew Ltd   89

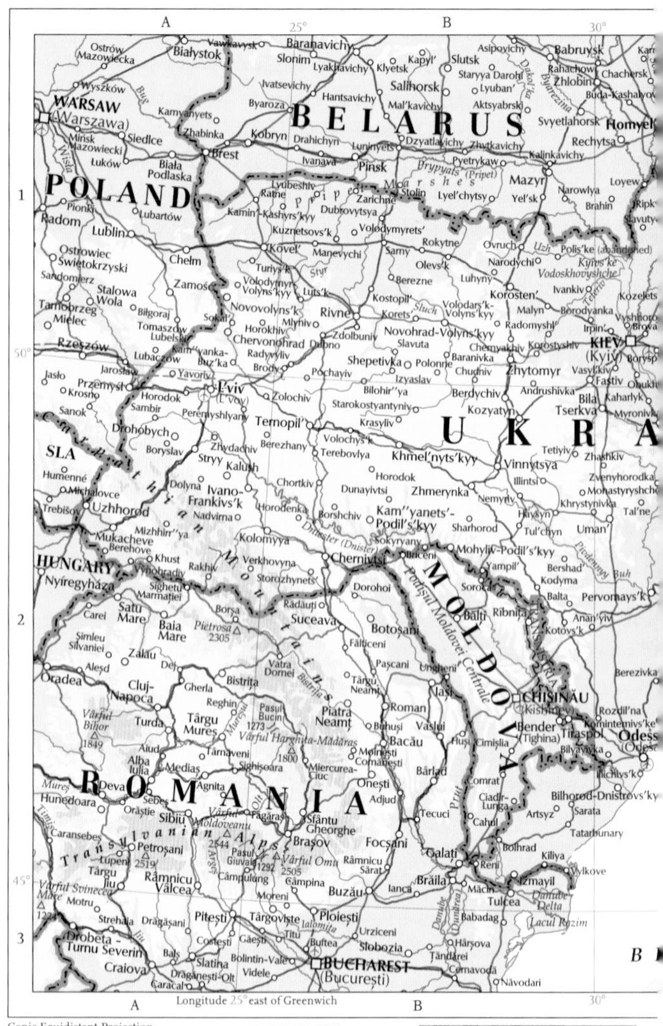

Conic Equidistant Projection

Longitude 25° east of Greenwich

1 : 8 000 000

MILES 0   50   100   150

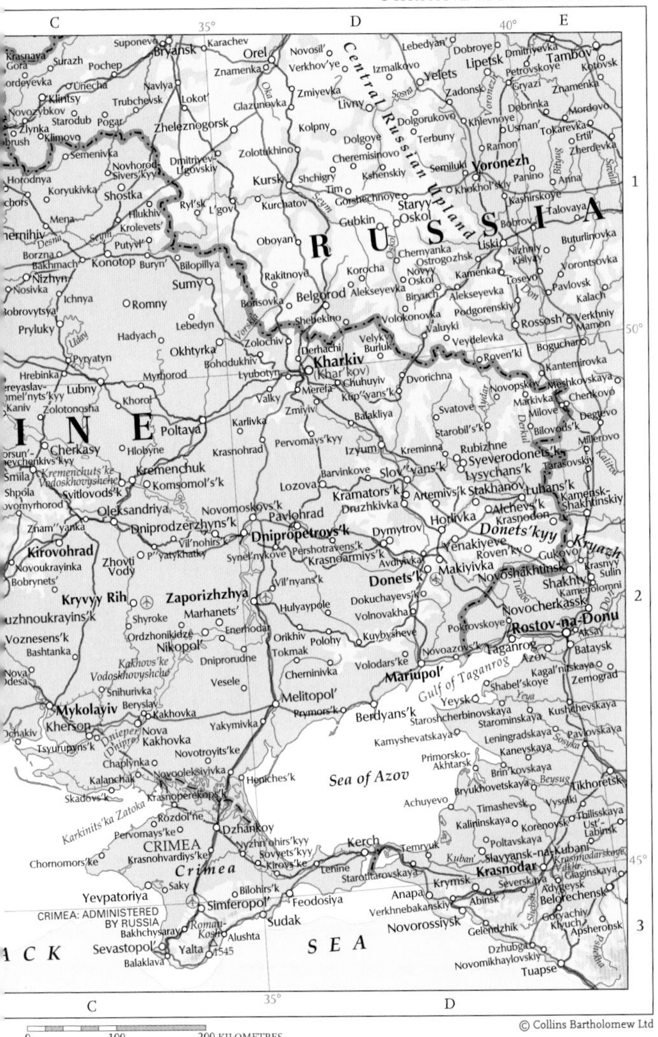
C
D
E
35°
40°
50°
45°
1
2
3
RUSSIA
UKRAINE
Central Russian Upland
Donets'kyy Kryazh
Sea of Azov
Gulf of Taganrog
Karkinits'ka Zatoka
BLACK SEA
CRIMEA
Crimea
CRIMEA: ADMINISTERED BY RUSSIA
Bryansk
Orel
Kursk
Belgorod
Kharkiv
(Khar'kov)
Voronezh
Lipetsk
Tambov
Yelets
Staryy Oskol
Sumy
Poltava
Cherkasy
Kremenchuk
Kirovohrad
Dnipropetrovs'k
Dniprodzerzhyns'k
Zaporizhzhya
Kryvyy Rih
Donets'k
Luhans'k
Mariupol'
Melitopol'
Berdyans'k
Mykolayiv
Kherson
Nova Kakhovka
Nikopol'
Rostov-na-Donu
Taganrog
Novocherkassk
Shakhty
Krasnodar
Novorossiysk
Anapa
Tuapse
Tikhoretsk
Yeysk
Kerch
Dzhankoy
Simferopol'
Sevastopol'
Yalta
Yevpatoriya
Feodosiya
Sudak
Alushta
Konotop
Shostka
Chernihiv
Nizhyn
Pryluky
Romny
Okhtyrka
Lubny
Myrhorod
Izyum
Slov"yans'k
Kramators'k
Horlivka
Makiyivka
Alchevs'k
Syeverodonets'k
Lysychans'k
Stakhanov
Pavlohrad
Lozova
Novomoskovs'k
Oleksandriya
Svitlovods'k
Smila
Voznesens'k
Kakhovs'ke Vodoskhovyshche
Kremenchuts'ke Vodoskhovyshche
Rossosh'
Millerovo
Kamensk-Shakhtinskiy
Azov
Bataysk
Belorechensk
Slavyansk-na-Kubani
Dnieper (Dnipro)
Don
Seym
Desna
Oskol
Vorskla
Sosna
Voronezh
Bitiug
Kuban'
1545

0 100 200 KILOMETRES

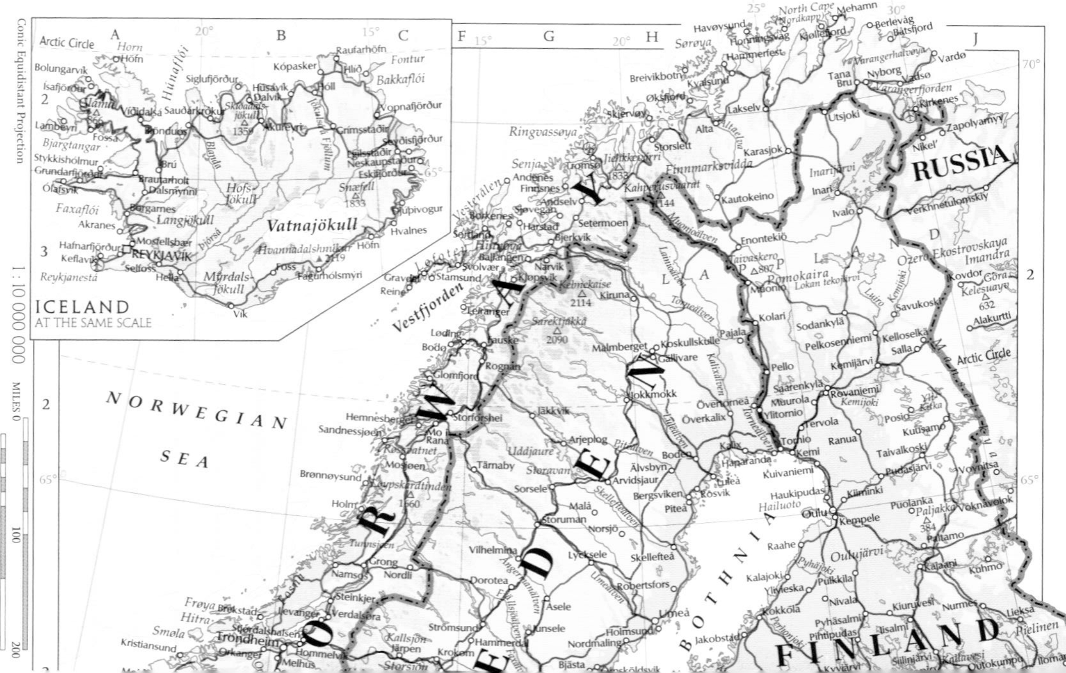

Conic Equidistant Projection

1 : 10 000 000   MILES 0   100   200

KILOMETRES 0   100   200   300

ICELAND
AT THE SAME SCALE

RUSSIA

FINLAND

NORWEGIAN SEA

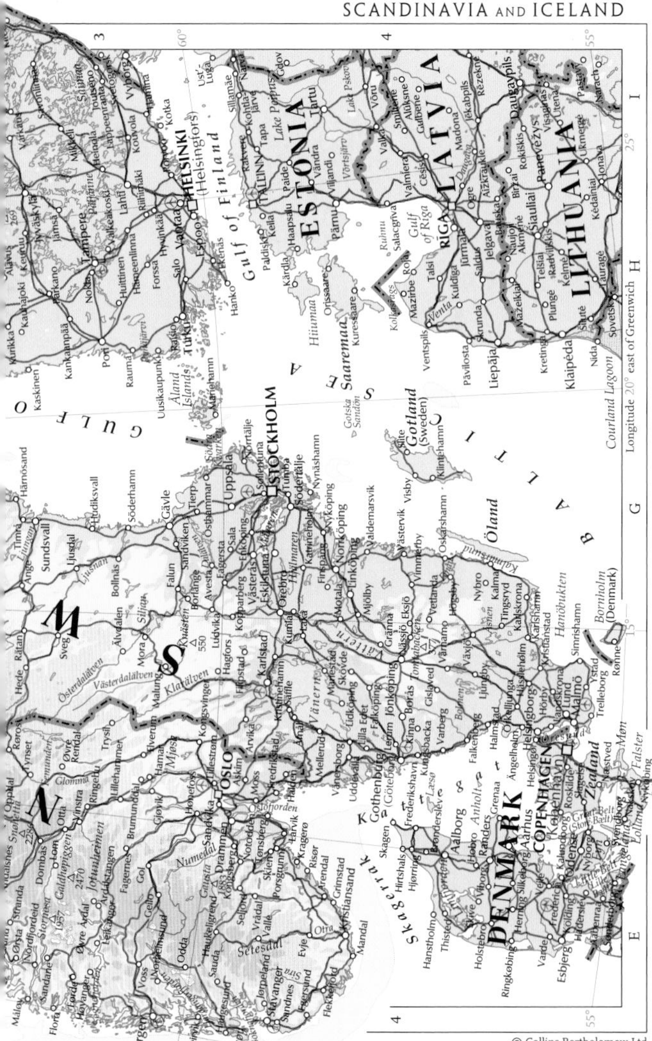

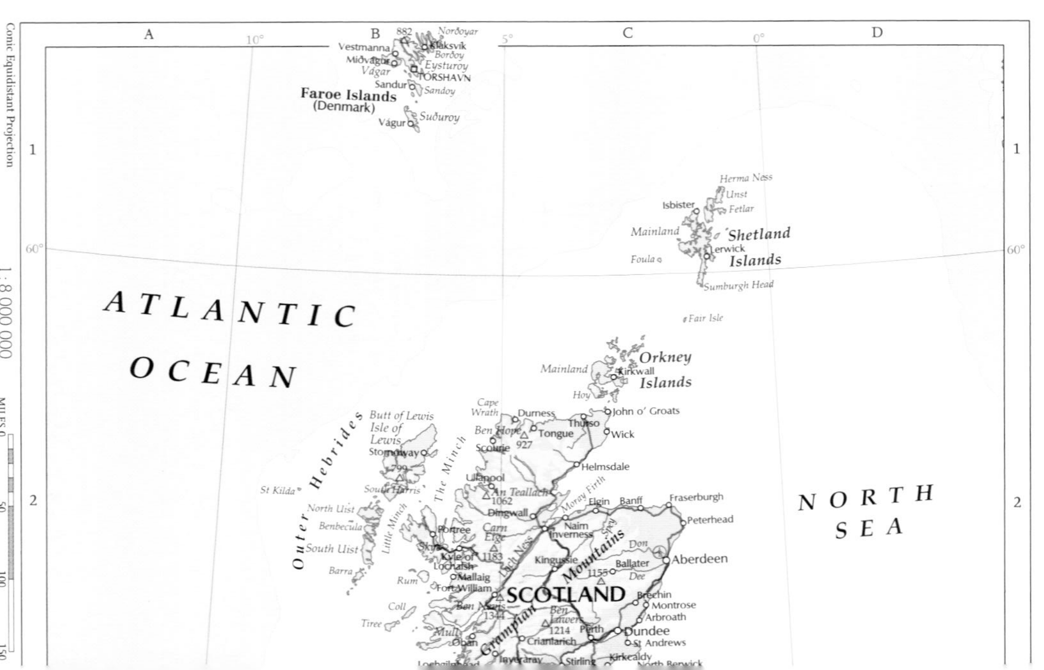

ATLANTIC OCEAN

NORTH SEA

Faroe Islands (Denmark)

Vestmanna · Norðoyar
882 · Bordoy
Miðvágur · Klaksvík · Eysturoy
Vágar · STREYMOY · TÓRSHAVN
Sandur · Sandoy
Vágur · Suðuroy

Shetland Islands
Hermaness
Unst
Fetlar
Isbister · Yell
Mainland · Lerwick
Foula · Sumburgh Head
Fair Isle

Orkney Islands
Kirkwall
Mainland · St John o' Groats
Hoy · Wick

Cape Wrath · Durness
Scourie · 927 · Tongue · Thurso · Helmsdale
Ullapool · Ben More · Lairg
Cairngorm · Inverness
Dingwall · Nairn · Elgin · Banff · Fraserburgh
The Minch · Gairloch · Beauly · Spey · Peterhead

Butt of Lewis
Isle of Lewis
Stornoway
Little Minch
North Uist
Benbecula
South Uist
Barra · St Kilda

Outer Hebrides

Dee · Aberdeen
Ballater · Montrose
Kingussie · Arbroath
1214 · St Andrews
Dundee
Perth
Stirling
Dumbarton

SCOTLAND
Grampian

The Minch
Skye · Portree · Mallaig
Rum · Fort William · Ben Nevis 1344
Coll · Mull · Oban
Tiree

94   Conic Equidistant Projection   1 : 8 000 000   MILES 0   50   100   150

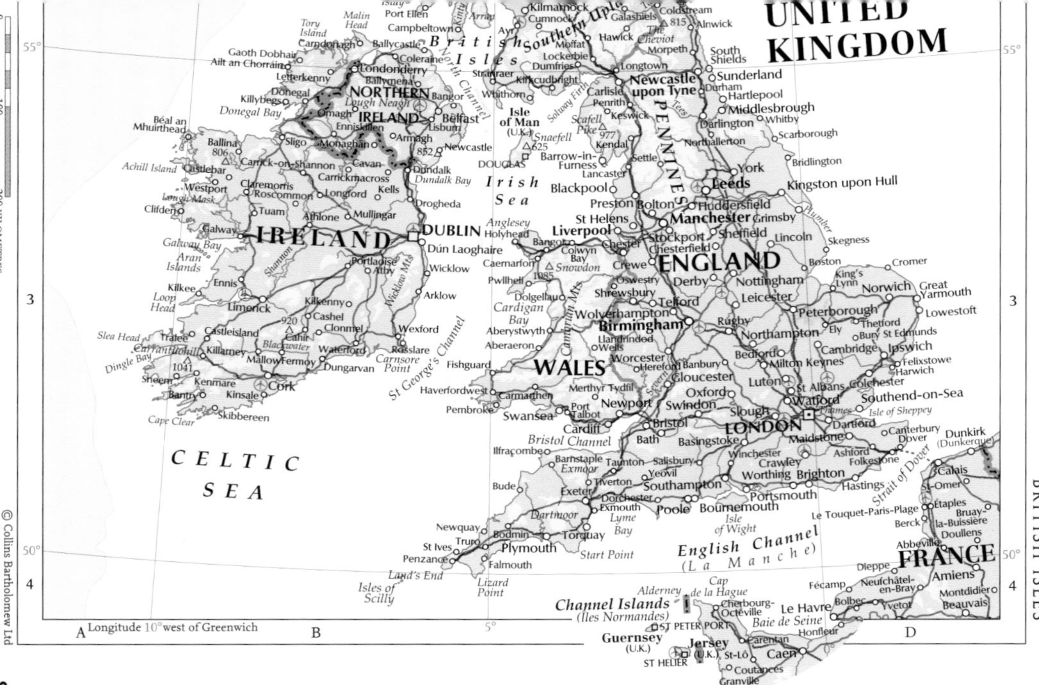

UNITED KINGDOM

Shetland Islands

FRANCE

PENNINE

ENGLAND

WALES

NORTHERN IRELAND

IRELAND

English Channel (La Manche)

Irish Sea

North Channel

Bristol Channel

St George's Channel

Cardigan Bay

CELTIC SEA

Channel Islands (Îles Normandes)

GUERNSEY (U.K.)

ST HELIER • JERSEY (U.K.)

British Isles

© Collins Bartholomew Ltd

0   100   200 KILOMETRES

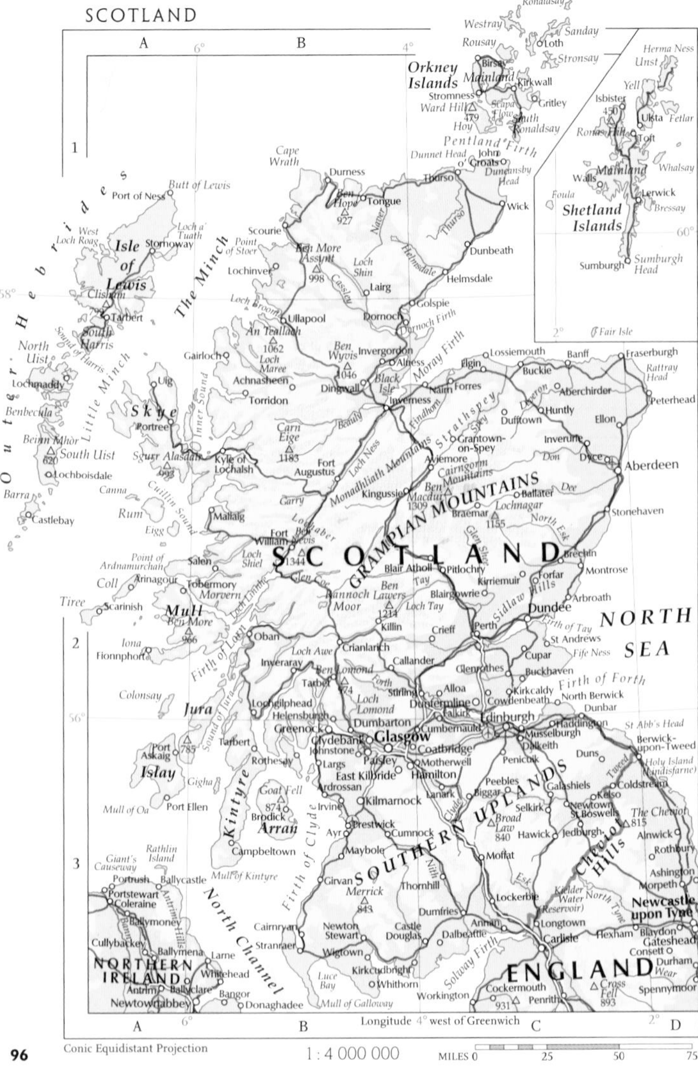

A B

North Ronaldsay
Westray
Rousay Sanday
Loth Stronsay
Orkney Birsay Mainland
Islands Kirkwall
Stromness Grimsby
Ward Hill Gritley
179 Hoy South
Ronaldsay
Cape Pentland Firth
Wrath Dunnet Head John
Durness o'Groats Dunncansby
Head
Kyle Hope Tongue
More Thurso Wick
Scourie 927 Naver
Assynt
Point of Loch Helmsdale Dunbeath
Stoer More Shin
Assynt Laing Helmsdale
998 Canisp
Lochinver Ullapool Golspie
Dornoch Firth
An Teallach Lossiemouth Banff
Gairloch 1062 Invergordon Moray Firth Buckie Fraserburgh
Loch Black Elgin Rattray
Maree Dingwall Isle Nairn Forres Head
Torridon Beauly Peterhead
Carn Ben Inverness Strathspey Dufftown Huntly
Eige Wyvis Nethy Aberchirder
1046 Bridge Ellon
Fort Grantown-on-Spey Inverurie
Kyle of Augustus Aviemore Dyce Aberdeen
Lochalsh Cairngorm Don
Monadhliath Mountains Mountains
Carrn Ben Stonehaven
Mallaig Eige Macdui
1183 1309 Ballater Dee
Lochnagar
Fort Glen Braemar 1155 Brechin
William Spean Blair Atholl North Esk
SCOTLAND Kirriemuir
Ben Montrose
Glen Nevis Pitlochry Forfar
1344 Kinloch Sidlaw
Ben Rannoch Blairgowrie Arbroath
Tobermory Lawers Moor Dundee
Morvern 1214 Loch Tay
Salen Killin Perth Firth of Tay
Oban Loch Tay St Andrews
Loch Awe Crianlarich Crieff Fife Ness
Inveraray Callander Cupar
Loch Lomond Glenrothes Buckhaven
Colonsay Tarbet 974 Stirling Kirkcaldy North Berwick
Loch Alloa Cowdenbeath Dunbar
Helensburgh Lomond Dunfermline
Greenock Dumbarton Edinburgh
Clydebank Glasgow Musselburgh
Paisley Coatbridge Dalkeith
East Kilbride Motherwell Penicuik
Hamilton Duns Berwick-
Rothesay upon-Tweed
Ardrossan Peebles Galashiels
Goat Fell Biggar Selkirk Coldstream
874 Kilmarnock Broad St Boswells
Arran Irvine Law Hawick Jedburgh
Prestwick 840
Ayr Moffat Rothbury
Cumnock Lockerbie
Maybole SOUTHERN UPLANDS Ashington
Girvan Thornhill Morpeth
Merrick Dumfries Annan Newcastle
843 upon Tyne
Newton Castle Carlisle Gateshead
Stewart Douglas Dalbeattie Consett
Wigtown Solway Firth Cross
Kirkcudbright Cockermouth Penrith Fell
Whithorn Workington 893 Spennymoor
Mull of Galloway

Conic Equidistant Projection 1 : 4 000 000 MILES 0 25 50 75

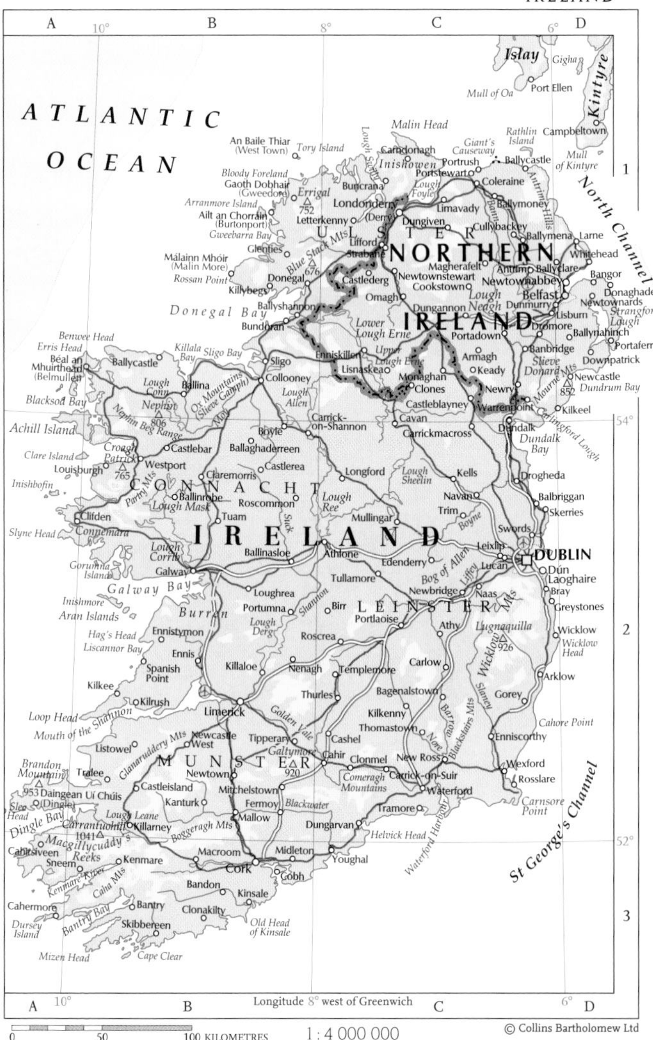
ATLANTIC OCEAN
NORTHERN IRELAND
IRELAND
ULSTER
CONNACHT
LEINSTER
MUNSTER
North Channel
St George's Channel
Islay
Gigha
Kintyre
Port Ellen
Mull of Oa
Campbeltown
Rathlin Island
Mull of Kintyre
Malin Head
Giant's Causeway
Ballycastle
Tory Island
An Baile Thiar (West Town)
Bloody Foreland
Gaoth Dobhair (Gweedore)
Errigal 752
Arranmore Island
Ailt an Chorráin (Burtonport)
Gweebarra Bay
Glenties
Málainn Mhóir (Malin More)
Rossan Point
Killybegs
Donegal
Blue Stack Mts 676
Letterkenny
Buncrana
Carndonagh
Inishowen
Lough Swilly
Lough Foyle
Londonderry (Derry)
Portrush
Portstewart
Coleraine
Limavady
Dungiven
Ballymoney
Cullybackey
Ballymena
Larne
Whitehead
Antrim Hills
Bann
Lifford
Strabane
Castlederg
Newtownstewart
Cookstown
Magherafelt
Antrim
Ballyclare
Newtownabbey
Bangor
Belfast
Donaghadee
Newtownards
Dunmurry
Lisburn
Strangford Lough
Omagh
Lough Neagh
Dungannon
Ballyshannon
Bundoran
Donegal Bay
Lower Lough Erne
Upper Lough Erne
Portadown
Dromore
Ballynahinch
Portaferry
Banbridge
Downpatrick
Armagh
Keady
Slieve Donard
Mourne Mts
Newcastle
852
Dundrum Bay
Enniskillen
Lisnaskea
Monaghan
Clones
Newry
Castleblayney
Warrenpoint
Kilkeel
Carlingford Lough
Benwee Head
Erris Head
Béal an Mhuirthead (Belmullet)
Ballycastle
Killala Bay
Sligo Bay
Sligo
Collooney
Lough Conn
Ballina
Ox Mountains (Slieve Gamph)
Nephin 806
Nephin Beg Range
Blacksod Bay
Achill Island
Lough Allen
Carrick-on-Shannon
Cavan
Carrickmacross
Dundalk
Dundalk Bay
Boyle
Ballaghaderreen
Castlebar
Croagh Patrick 765
Clare Island
Westport
Louisburgh
Castlerea
Claremorris
Longford
Lough Sheelin
Kells
Drogheda
Inishbofin
Partry Mts
Ballinrobe
Lough Mask
Roscommon
Lough Ree
Navan
Balbriggan
Trim
Skerries
Clifden
Tuam
Suck
Mullingar
Boyne
Swords
Slyne Head
Connemara
Moy
Ballinasloe
Athlone
Leixlip
Lucan
DUBLIN
Dún Laoghaire
Edenderry
Lough Corrib
Gorumna Island
Galway
Galway Bay
Tullamore
Bog of Allen
Liffey
Newbridge
Naas
Bray
Greystones
Loughrea
Inishmore
Aran Islands
Burren
Portumna
Shannon
Birr
Portlaoise
Lough Derg
Athy
Lugnaquilla 926
Wicklow Mts
Wicklow
Wicklow Head
Hag's Head
Liscannor Bay
Ennistymon
Roscrea
Ennis
Spanish Point
Killaloe
Nenagh
Templemore
Carlow
Arklow
Kilkee
Kilrush
Thurles
Bagenalstown
Barrow
Slaney
Gorey
Blackstairs Mts
Loop Head
Mouth of the Shannon
Limerick
Golden Vale
Kilkenny
Thomastown
Nore
Cahore Point
Listowel
Glanaruddery Mts
Newcastle West
Tipperary
Cashel
Enniscorthy
Galtymore 920
Cahir
Clonmel
New Ross
Wexford
Brandon Mountain
953
Tralee
Newtown
Carrick-on-Suir
Rosslare
Castleisland
Comeragh Mountains
Mitchelstown
Waterford
Daingean Uí Chúis (Dingle)
Kanturk
Fermoy
Blackwater
Carnsore Point
Slea Head
Dingle Bay
Lough Leane
Tramore
Waterford Harbour
Carrantuohill 1041
Killarney
Mallow
Boggeragh Mts
Dungarvan
Helvick Head
Macgillycuddy's Reeks
Cahirsiveen
Sneem
Macroom
Midleton
Youghal
Kenmare
Kenmare River
Cork
Cobh
Caha Mts
Bandon
Kinsale
Cahermore
Bantry
Bantry Bay
Clonakilty
Dursey Island
Skibbereen
Old Head of Kinsale
Mizen Head
Cape Clear
A
B
C
D
1
2
3
10°
8°
6°
54°
52°
Longitude 8° west of Greenwich
0
50
100 KILOMETRES
1 : 4 000 000

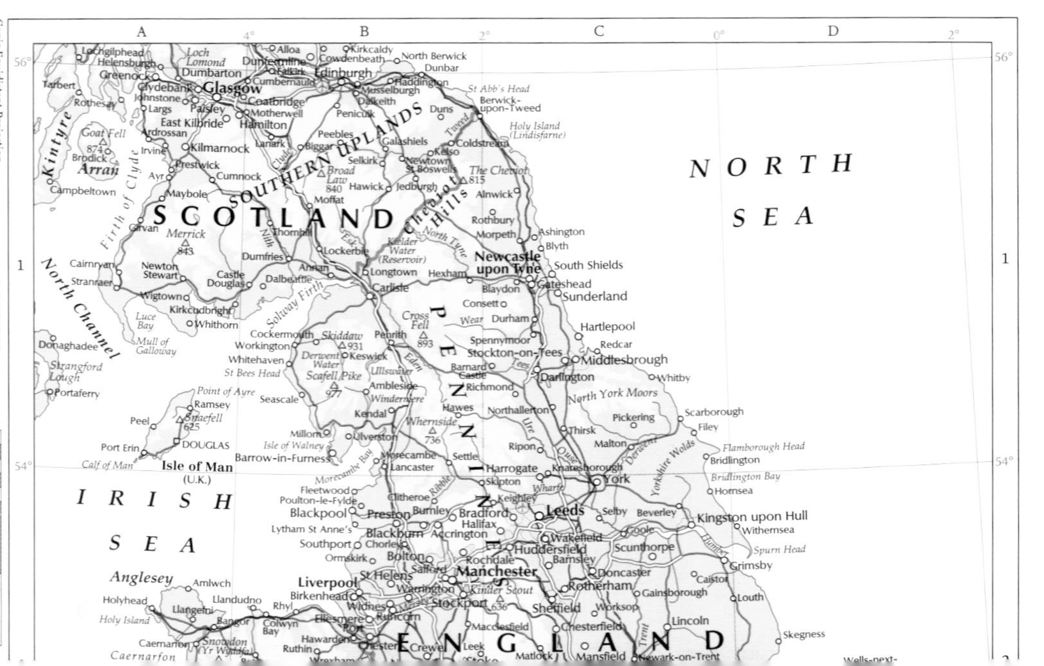

Conic Equidistant Projection

1 : 4 000 000

MILES 0   25   50   75

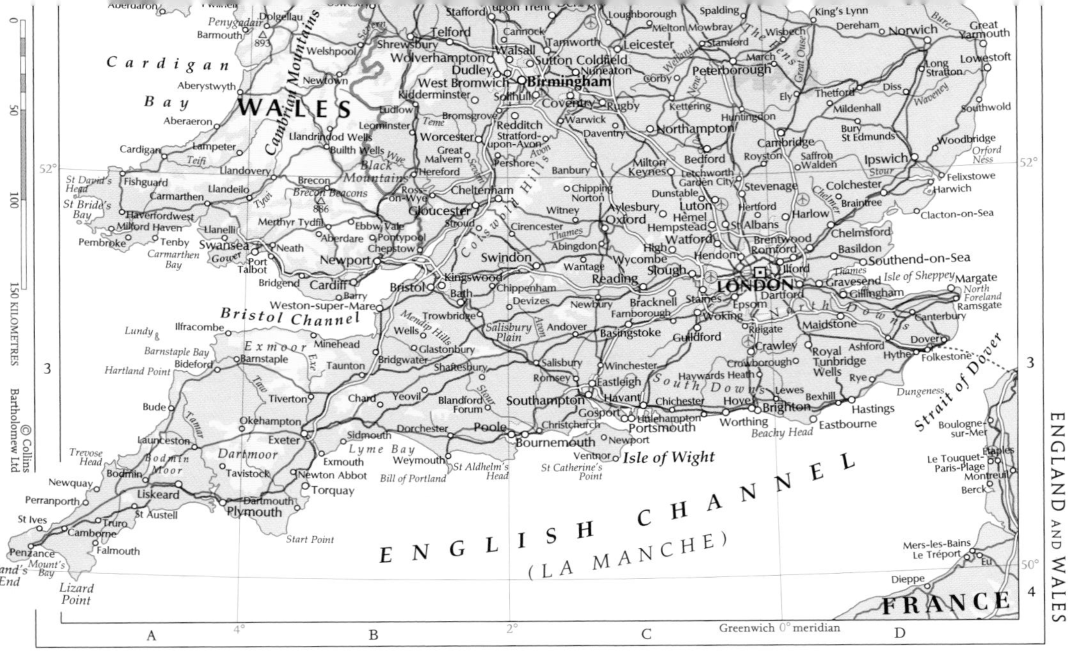
ENGLISH CHANNEL
(LA MANCHE)
FRANCE
WALES
Cardigan Bay
Bristol Channel
Strait of Dover
Isle of Wight
LONDON
Birmingham
Norwich
Great Yarmouth
Lowestoft
Southwold
Woodbridge
Orford Ness
Felixstowe
Harwich
Clacton-on-Sea
Ipswich
Colchester
Braintree
Chelmsford
Southend-on-Sea
Margate
Ramsgate
North Foreland
Canterbury
Dover
Folkestone
Hythe
Dungeness
Hastings
Eastbourne
Beachy Head
Brighton
Worthing
Portsmouth
Southampton
Bournemouth
Poole
Weymouth
Exeter
Plymouth
Torquay
Penzance
Land's End
Lizard Point
Falmouth
Truro
Bristol
Cardiff
Newport
Swansea
Gloucester
Cheltenham
Oxford
Reading
Cambridge
Peterborough
Leicester
Northampton
Coventry
Wolverhampton
Cambrian Mountains
Black Mountains
Brecon Beacons
Cotswold Hills
Mendip Hills
Salisbury Plain
Exmoor
Dartmoor
Bodmin Moor
North Downs
South Downs
The Fens
Greenwich 0° meridian
Boulogne-sur-Mer
Le Touquet-Paris-Plage
Montreuil
Berck
Mers-les-Bains
Le Tréport
Eu
Dieppe
52°
50°
2°
4°
3
4
A
B
C
D
0
50
100
150 KILOMETRES
© Collins Bartholomew Ltd

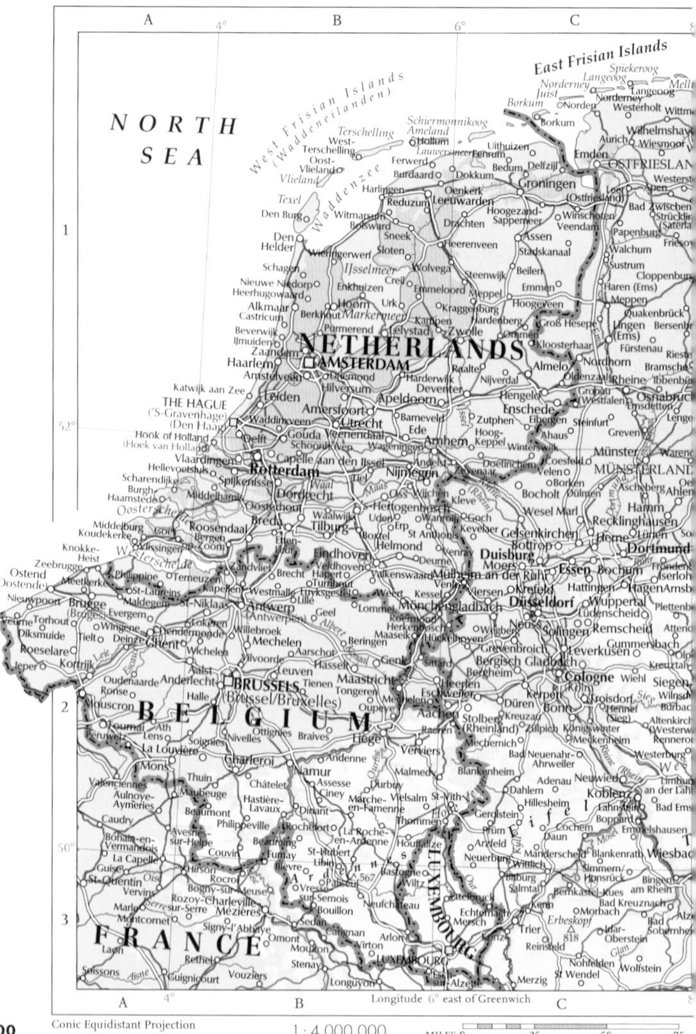

1 : 4 000 000

MILES 0   25   50   75

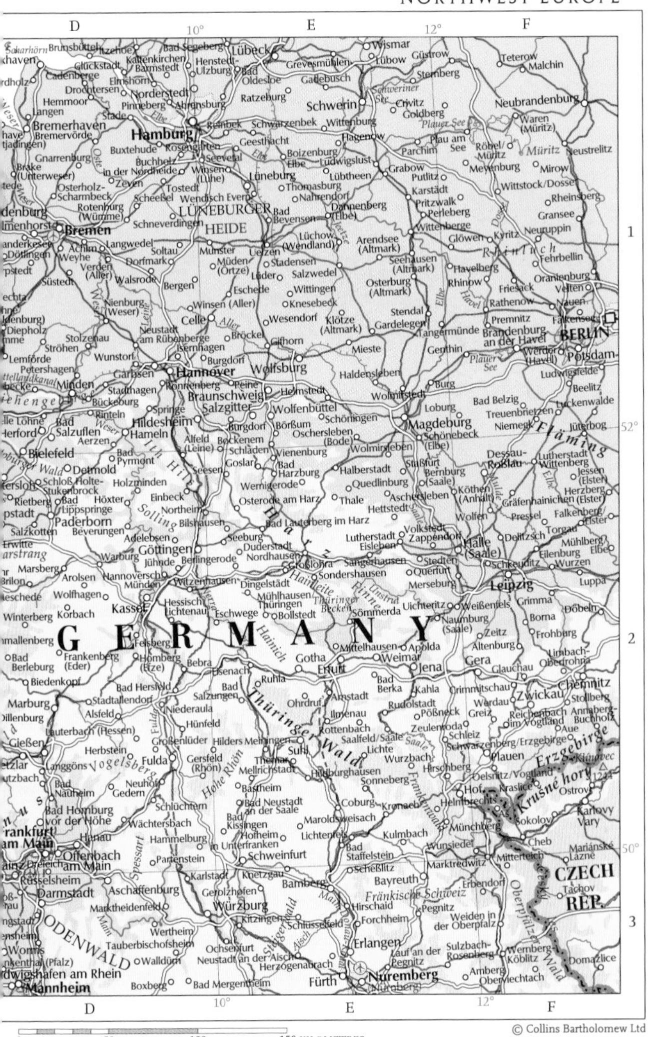

© Collins Bartholomew Ltd

0   50   100   150 KILOMETRES

12°
F
2
3
52°
GERMANY
CZECH REP.
Hamburg
Bremen
Bremerhaven
Lübeck
Wismar
Schwerin
Neubrandenburg
Lüneburg
LÜNEBURGER HEIDE
Celle
Hannover
Wolfsburg
Braunschweig
Salzgitter
Hildesheim
Hameln
Bielefeld
Detmold
Paderborn
Göttingen
Kassel
Magdeburg
Dessau-Roßlau
Halle (Saale)
Leipzig
Berlin
Potsdam
Brandenburg an der Havel
Erfurt
Weimar
Jena
Gera
Zwickau
Chemnitz
Plauen
Hof
Bayreuth
Bamberg
Würzburg
Schweinfurt
Erlangen
Fürth
Nuremberg
Frankfurt am Main
Offenbach am Main
Darmstadt
Mannheim
Marburg
Gießen
Fulda
Harz
Thüringer Wald
Erzgebirge
Krušné hory
Fläming
ODENWALD
Vogelsberg
Fränkische Schweiz
Karlovy Vary
Mariánské Lázně
Domažlice

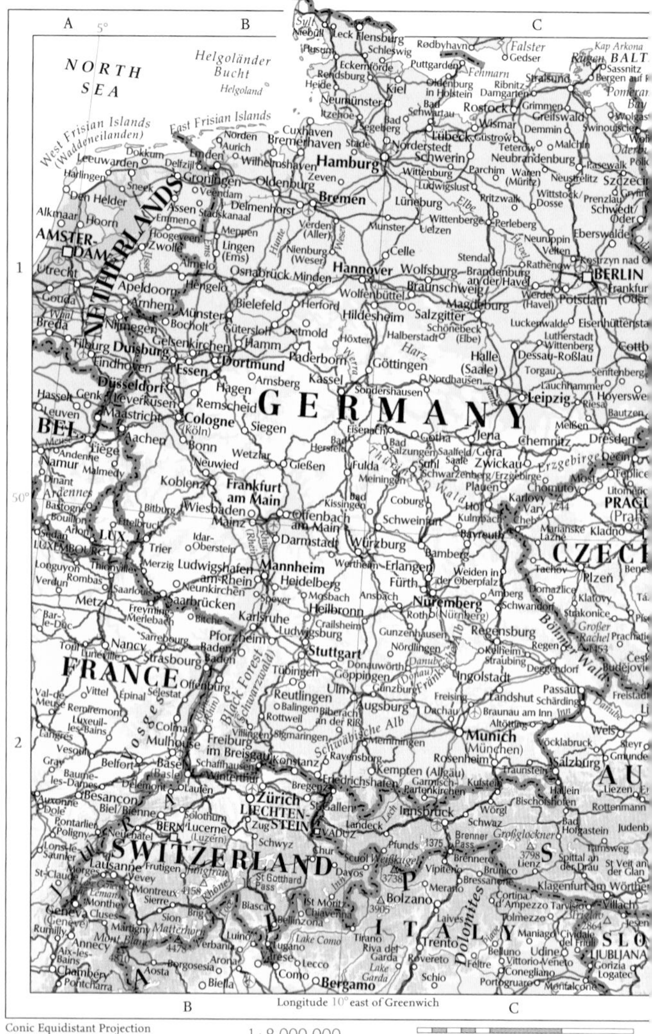

Grid references

Top: A 5° B C

Major labels and features

NORTH SEA

Helgoländer Bucht
Helgoland

West Frisian Islands (Waddeneilanden)
East Frisian Islands

NETHERLANDS
AMSTER-DAM
Utrecht
Leeuwarden
Den Helder
Alkmaar
Hoorn
Groningen
Assen
Zwolle
Apeldoorn
Arnhem
Nijmegen
Eindhoven
Tilburg
Breda
's-Hertogenbosch

BELGIUM (BEL.)
Leuven
Namur
Dinant
Andenne
Malmedy

GERMANY
Hamburg
Bremen
Bremerhaven
Cuxhaven
Wilhelmshaven
Oldenburg
Emden
Norden
Kiel
Neumünster
Lübeck
Rostock
Schwerin
Lüneburg
Hannover
Braunschweig
Wolfsburg
Magdeburg
Münster
Osnabrück
Minden
Bielefeld
Herford
Detmold
Paderborn
Dortmund
Essen
Duisburg
Düsseldorf
Cologne (Köln)
Aachen
Bonn
Koblenz
Wiesbaden
Mainz
Frankfurt am Main
Offenbach am Main
Darmstadt
Mannheim
Heidelberg
Ludwigshafen am Rhein
Saarbrücken
Kaiserslautern
Karlsruhe
Pforzheim
Stuttgart
Heilbronn
Würzburg
Nuremberg (Nürnberg)
Fürth
Erlangen
Bamberg
Bayreuth
Regensburg
Ingolstadt
Augsburg
Ulm
Munich (München)
Kassel
Göttingen
Halle (Saale)
Leipzig
Dresden
Chemnitz
Erfurt
Jena
Gera
Zwickau
Plauen
Hof
Potsdam
BERLIN
Frankfurt (Oder)
Dessau-Roßlau
Eberswalde
Brandenburg an der Havel
Cottbus

POLAND
Szczecin
Pomeranian Bay

CZECH (CZECH REPUBLIC)
PRAGUE (Praha)
Plzeň
Karlovy Vary

FRANCE
Metz
Nancy
Strasbourg
Mulhouse
Belfort
Besançon
Colmar
Épinal
Verdun

LUXEMBOURG (LUX.)
Trier

SWITZERLAND
BERN
Zürich
Basel
Lucerne (Luzern)
Lausanne
Geneva (Genève)
Lugano

LIECHTENSTEIN
VADUZ

AUSTRIA (AU...)
Innsbruck
Salzburg
Klagenfurt am Wörther

ITALY
Bolzano
Trento
Bergamo
Como
Udine

SLOVENIA (SLO...)
LJUBLJANA

Black Forest (Schwarzwald)
Swabian Alb (Schwäbische Alb)
Lake Constance (Bodensee)
Matterhorn
Lake Como (Lago di Como)
Lake Garda (Lago di Garda)
Danube (Donau)

Longitude 10° east of Greenwich

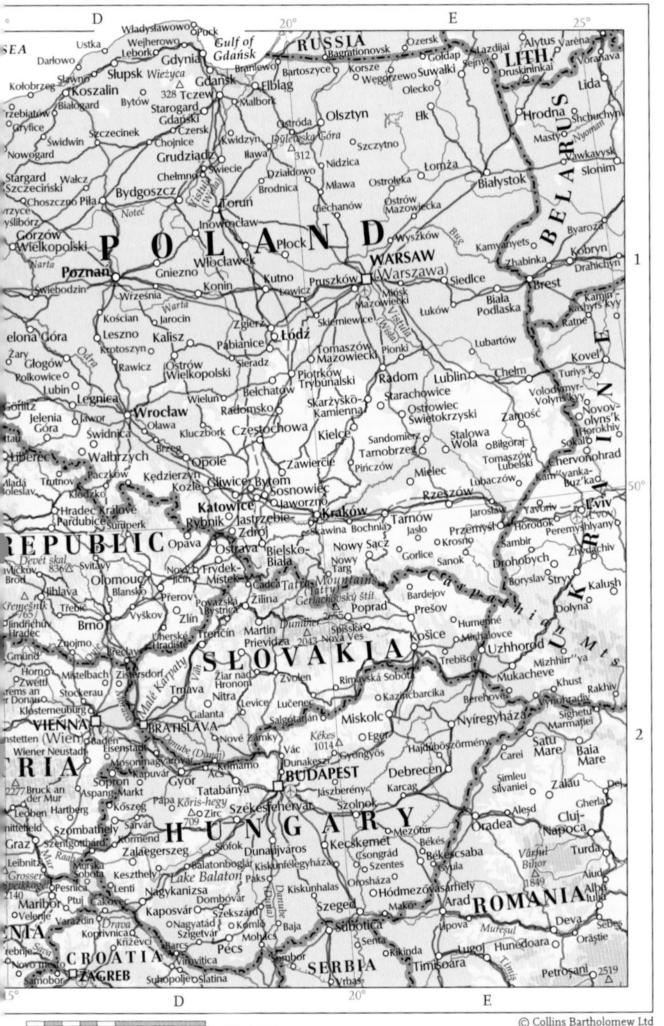
POLAND
SLOVAKIA
HUNGARY
ROMANIA
CROATIA
SERBIA
RUSSIA
LITH.
BELARUS
UKRAINE
REPUBLIC
TRIA
WARSAW
(Warszawa)
BUDAPEST
VIENNA
(Wien)
BRATISLAVA
ZAGREB
Gulf of
Gdańsk
Gdańsk
Gdynia
Elbląg
Olsztyn
Białystok
Bydgoszcz
Toruń
Poznań
Łódź
Wrocław
Katowice
Kraków
Lublin
Radom
Kielce
Częstochowa
Rzeszów
Przemyśl
Opole
Gliwice
Bytom
Sosnowiec
Tarnów
Nowy Sącz
Ostrava
Olomouc
Brno
Žilina
Poprad
Košice
Prešov
Uzhhorod
L'viv
(L'vov)
Brest
Hrodna
Miskolc
Debrecen
Nyíregyháza
Szeged
Pécs
Győr
Székesfehérvár
Kecskemét
Oradea
Cluj-
Napoca
Arad
Timișoara
Subotica
Graz
Maribor
Carpathian Mts
Tatra Mountains
Lake Balaton
Vistula
(Wisła)
Danube
(Duna)
Odra
Warta
Bug
1
2
D
E
20°
25°
50°
0
100
200 KILOMETRES

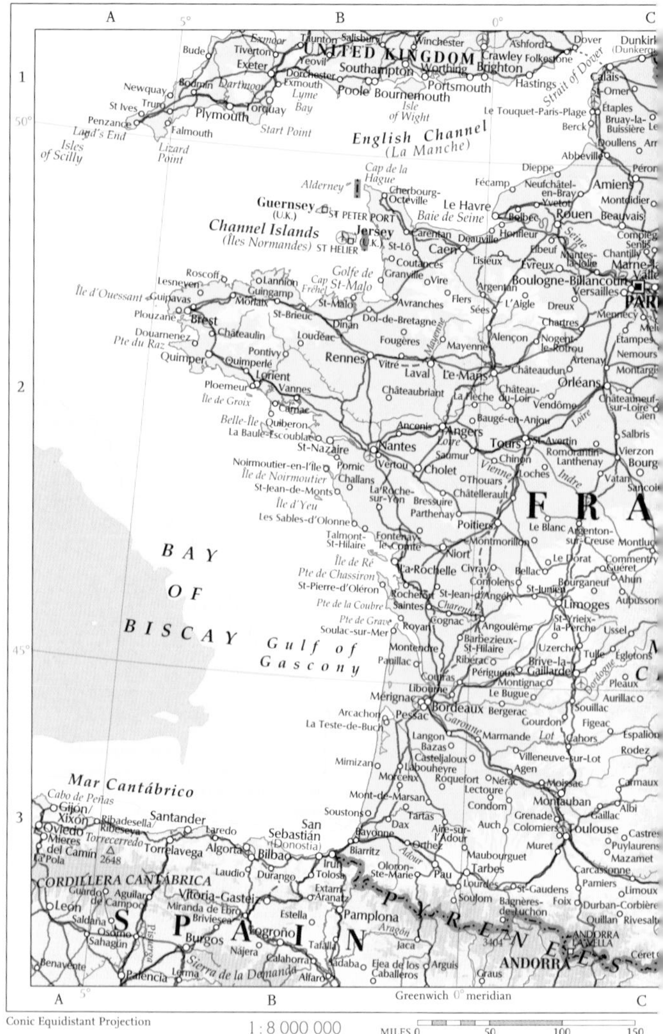

A

1

Trevose Head
Bude
Newquay
St Ives
Penzance
Land's End
Isles
of Scilly

Tiverton
Dartmouth
Truro
Falmouth
Lizard
Point

Bodmin
Plymouth

Start Point

Taunton
Exeter
Dorchester
Torquay
Lyme
Bay

B

Salisbury
Yeovil
Poole

UNITED KINGDOM
Southampton
Bournemouth
Isle
of Wight

Winchester
Portsmouth
Worthing

Crawley
Brighton

Ashford
Folkestone

Dover
Dunkir
(Dunkerque)

Hastings
Calais
Étaples
Berck

Le Touquet-Paris-Plage
Bruay-la-
Buissière

Roullens

Abbeville

Péro

Amiens
Montdidier
Beauvais

Chantilly
Creil
Senlis

Versailles
PARIS

C

English Channel
(La Manche)

Dieppe
Neufchâtel-
en-Bray
Yvetot

Cap de la
Hague

Alderney

Cherbourg-
Octeville

Le Havre
Baie de Seine
Carentan

Honfleur
Deauville

Fécamp

Rouen

Guernsey
(U.K.)
ST PETER PORT

Channel Islands
(Îles Normandes)
ST HELIER
Jersey
(U.K.)

St-Lô
Coutances
Granville

Caen
Lisieux
Évreux

Elbeuf

L'Aigle
Dreux

Mantes

Roscoff
Île d'Ouessant
Plouzané
Brest
Douarnenez
Pte du Raz

Lesneven
Guipavas

Lannion
Guingamp

Cap
Fréhel

Morlaix
St-Brieuc

Châteaulin
Quimper

Pontivy
Quimperlé

Loudéac

Dol-de-Bretagne
Dinan
Fougères

Avranches
Vire
Flers

Mayenne

Sées
Alençon

Chartres

Nogent-
le-Rotrou

Étampes

Nemours
Montargis

2

Ploemeur
Lorient
Vannes

Île de Groix

Belle-Île
Quiberon
Carnac

La Baule-Escoublac
St-Nazaire

Rennes
Vitré
Laval

Château-
Gontier

Châteaubriant
Ancenis

Nantes
Vertou

Le Mans

La Flèche
Baugé-en-Anjou

Angers
Saumur

Vendôme

Orléans
Châteauneuf-
sur-Loire
Gien

Salbris
Vierzon
Romorantin-
Lanthenay
Bourg

FRA

Tours
Loches

Chinon

Avon
Sancoi

Noirmoutier-en-l'Île
Île de Noirmoutier
St-Jean-de-Monts
Île d'Yeu

Pornic
Challans
La Roche-
sur-Yon

Cholet

Bressuire
Thouars

Châtellerault

Parthenay

Poitiers

Le Blanc

Argenton-
sur-Creuse

Montluc
St-Amand-
Montro

Commentry
Guéret
Ahun

A

BAY
OF
BISCAY

Les Sables-d'Olonne

Île de Ré

La Rochelle

Île d'Oléron

Talmont-
St-Hilaire

Fontenay-
le-Comte

Niort

Surgères
Rochefort

St-Pierre-d'Oléron

Civray

Bellac

Le Dorat

St-Junien

Limoges

St-Yrieix-
la-Perche

Ussel

Aubusson

Confolens

Pte de Chassiron

Gulf of
Gascony

Pte de la Coubre
Royan
Soulac-sur-Mer
Pte de Grave
Pauillac

Saintes
Cognac

Angoulême

Barbezieux-
St-Hilaire

Uzerche

Montendre
Riberac

Montignac

Mérignac
Pessac
La Teste-de-Buch

Arcachon

Libourne
Coutras

Bordeaux
Bergerac

Le Bugue
Périgueux

Brive-la-
Gaillarde

Tulle

Égletons

Aurillac

M
A
C

3

Mar Cantábrico
Cabo de Peñas

Gijón
Xixón
Oviedo
Mieres
del Camin

Ribadesella

Ribeseya
Torrecerredo
del Prida
2648

Santander
Laredo
Torrelavega

Mimizan

Langon
Bazas

Mont-de-Marsan

Roquefort
Nérac

Marmande
Villeneuve-sur-Lot

Agen
Lectoure
Condom

Lot

Gourdon

Cahors

Souillac
Figeac

Rodez

Espalion

Gaillac

Castres
Puylaurens
Mazamet

Caylus
Montauban

Grenade
Colomiers

Toulouse

Muret

Carmaux

CORDILLERA CANTÁBRICA

Guardo
Osorno
Aguilar de
Campoo
Saldaña

León
Sahagún
Benavente

Santoña
Castro Urdiales
Bilbao

Laudio

Durango
Éibar

Vitoria-Gasteiz

Miranda de Ebro
Briviesca

San
Sebastián
(Donostia)

Bayonne
Biarritz

Irún

Estella
Pamplona

Zarautz
Oloron-
Ste-Marie

Dax
St-Sever

Tartas
Aire-sur-
l'Adour

Orthez
Pau

Maubourguet
Tarbes

Lourdes
Bagnères-
de-Luchon

St-Gaudens
Foix

Pamiers

Mirepoix

Limoux

Durban-Corbières

Quillan
Rivesalte

Céret

ANDORRA
LA VELLA
ANDORRA

PYRENEES

Logroño
Nájera
Calahorra
Tafalla

Briones
Aranda
de Duero
Burgos

SPAIN
Palencia

Sierra de la Demanda

Haro
Ólvega
Soria

Ejea de los
Caballeros

Sádaba

Jaca

Aragón

Graus

Arriés

A   B   Greenwich 0° meridian   C

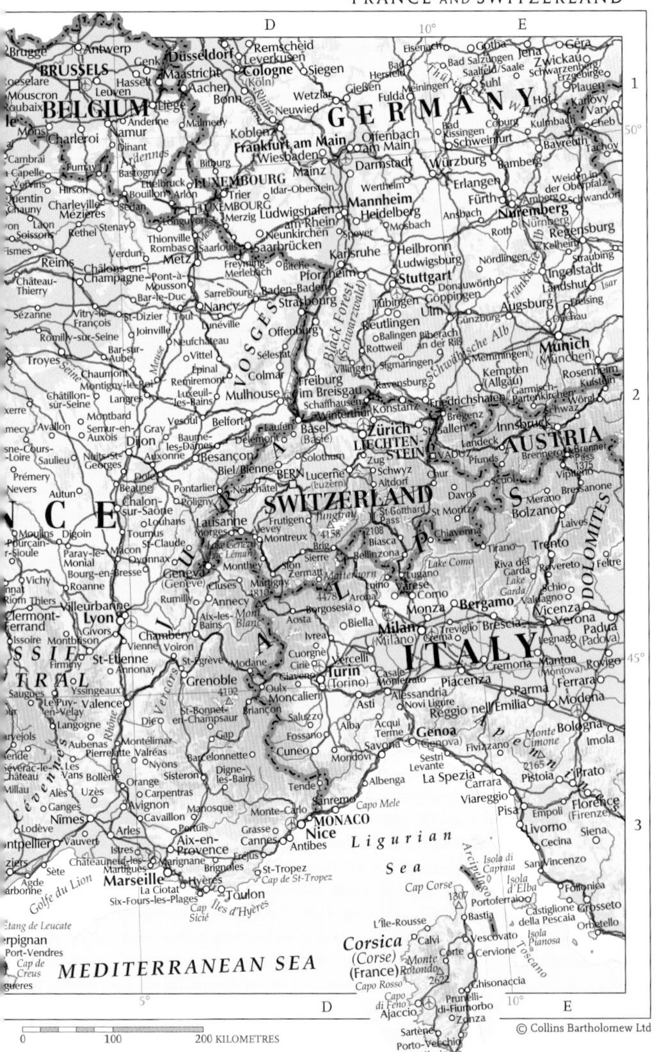

MEDITERRANEAN SEA

© Collins Bartholomew Ltd

0   100   200 KILOMETRES

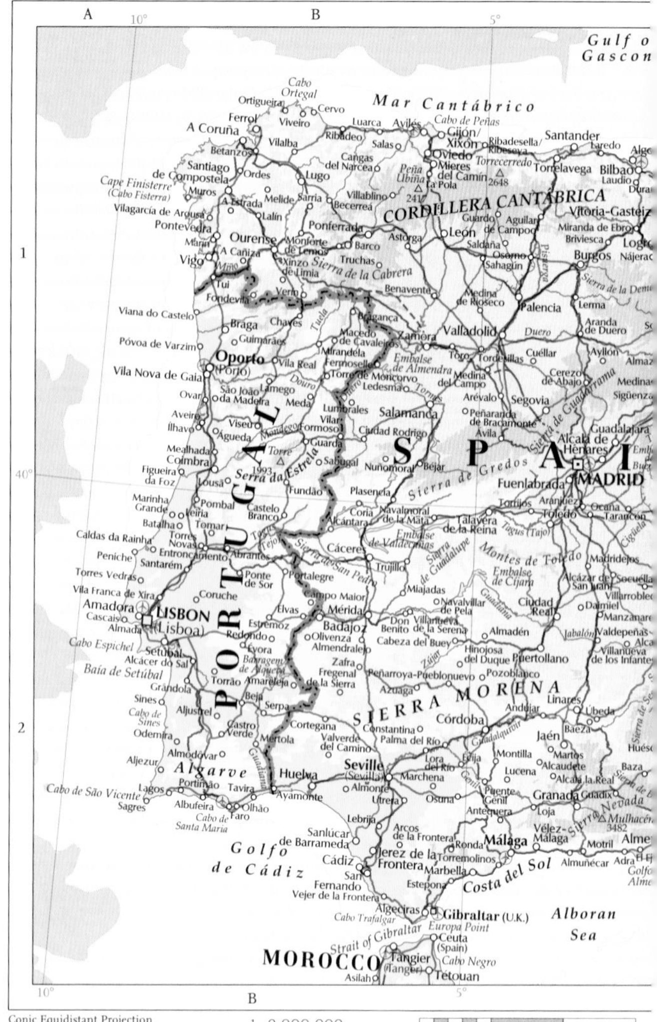

Conic Equidistant Projection   1 : 8 000 000   MILES 0   50   100   150

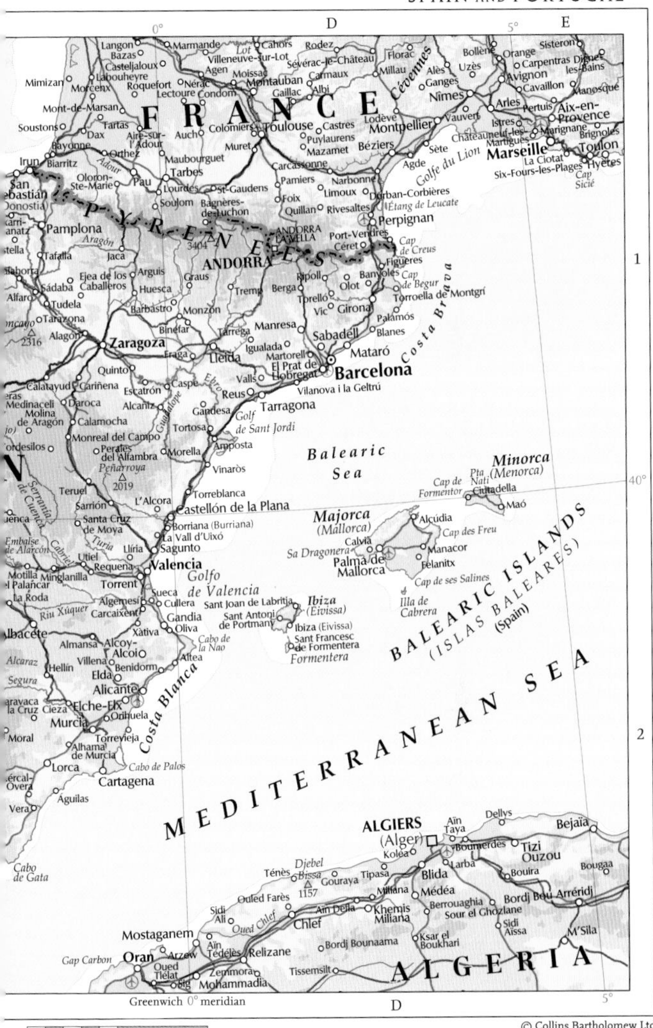

Greenwich 0° meridian

0   100   200 KILOMETRES

© Collins Bartholomew Ltd

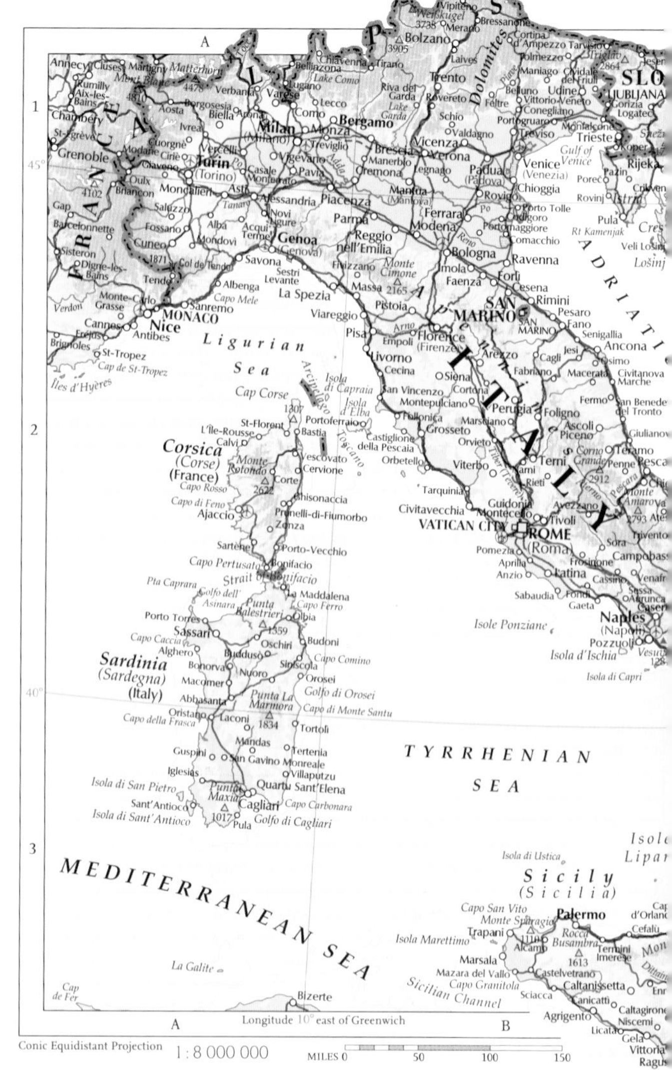

Conic Equidistant Projection   1 : 8 000 000   MILES 0   50   100   150

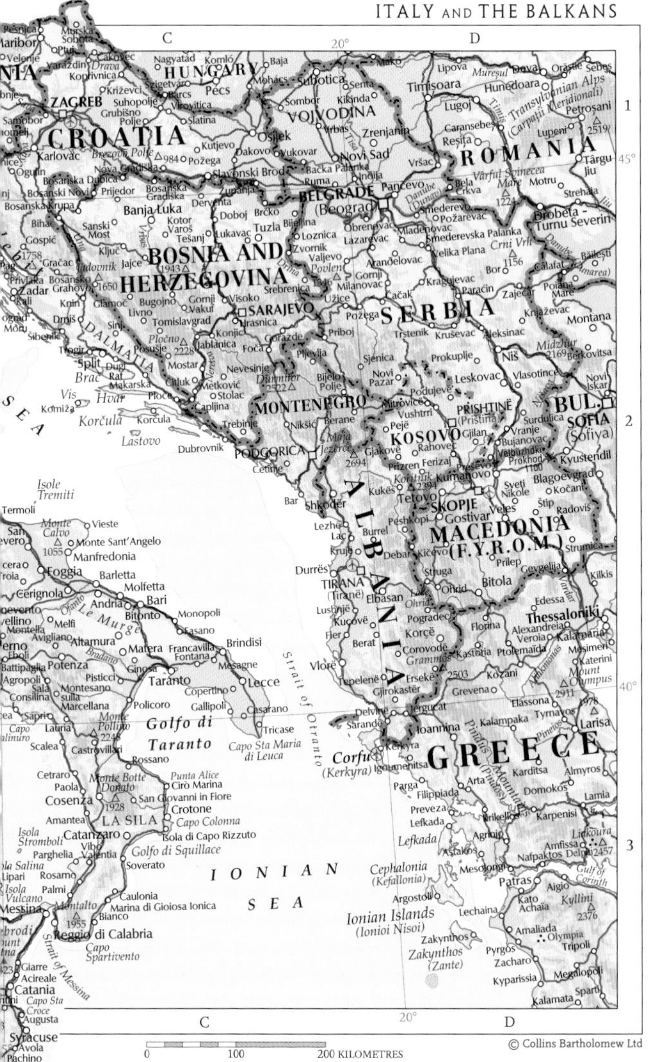
C
D
20°
1
2
3
45°
40°
HUNGARY
CROATIA
ZAGREB
BOSNIA AND HERZEGOVINA
SARAJEVO
VOJVODINA
ROMANIA
SERBIA
BELGRADE
(Beograd)
MONTENEGRO
PODGORICA
KOSOVO
PRISHTINË
(Priština)
ALBANIA
TIRANA
(Tiranë)
MACEDONIA
(F.Y.R.O.M.)
SKOPJE
BUL.
SOFIA
(Sofiya)
GREECE
DALMATIA
Transylvanian Alps
(Carpații Meridionali)
Danube
(Dunav)
Drava
Tisa
Drina
Neretva
Morava
Vardar
Pindus Mountains
(Pindos)
Mount Olympus
2911
Golfo di Taranto
IONIAN
SEA
Strait of Otranto
Strait of Messina
Golfo di Squillace
Gulf of Corinth
Capo Sta Maria di Leuca
Capo Colonna
Punta Alice
Capo Spartivento
LA SILA
Le Murge
Isole Tremiti
Monte Calvo
Monte Pollino
2248
Monte Botte Donato
1928
Lastovo
Korčula
Hvar
Vis
Brač
Corfu
(Kerkyra)
Lefkada
Cephalonia
(Kefallonia)
Ionian Islands
(Ionioi Nisoi)
Zakynthos
(Zante)
Varaždin
Koprivnica
Karlovac
Osijek
Vukovar
Slavonski Brod
Banja Luka
Tuzla
Zenica
Mostar
Split
Šibenik
Zadar
Dubrovnik
Subotica
Novi Sad
Zrenjanin
Pančevo
Niš
Kragujevac
Čačak
Užice
Novi Pazar
Leskovac
Timișoara
Lugoj
Reșița
Hunedoara
Petroșani
Drobeta-Turnu Severin
Montana
Kyustendil
Blagoevgrad
Shkodër
Durrës
Elbasan
Vlorë
Fier
Korçë
Gjirokastër
Sarandë
Tetovo
Kumanovo
Veles
Bitola
Ohrid
Struga
Prilep
Thessaloniki
Kozani
Larisa
Ioannina
Arta
Patras
Tripoli
Kalamata
Foggia
Bari
Barletta
Brindisi
Lecce
Taranto
Matera
Potenza
Crotone
Catanzaro
Cosenza
Reggio di Calabria
Messina
Catania
Syracuse
Termoli
Manfredonia
Vieste

0 100 200 KILOMETRES

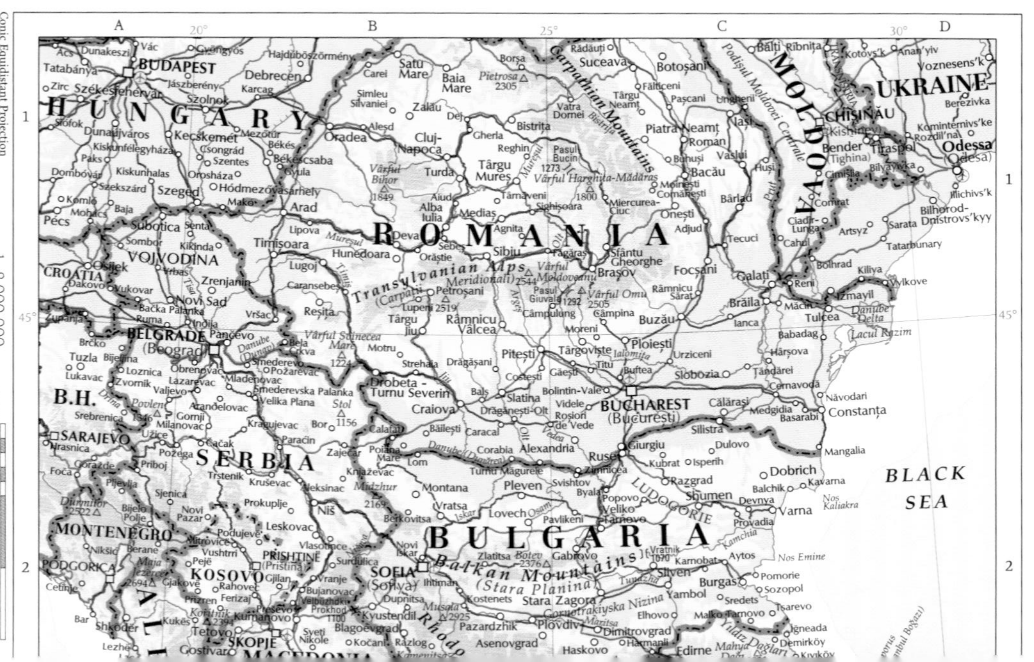

Conic Equidistant Projection

1 : 8 000 000

MILES 0   50   100   150

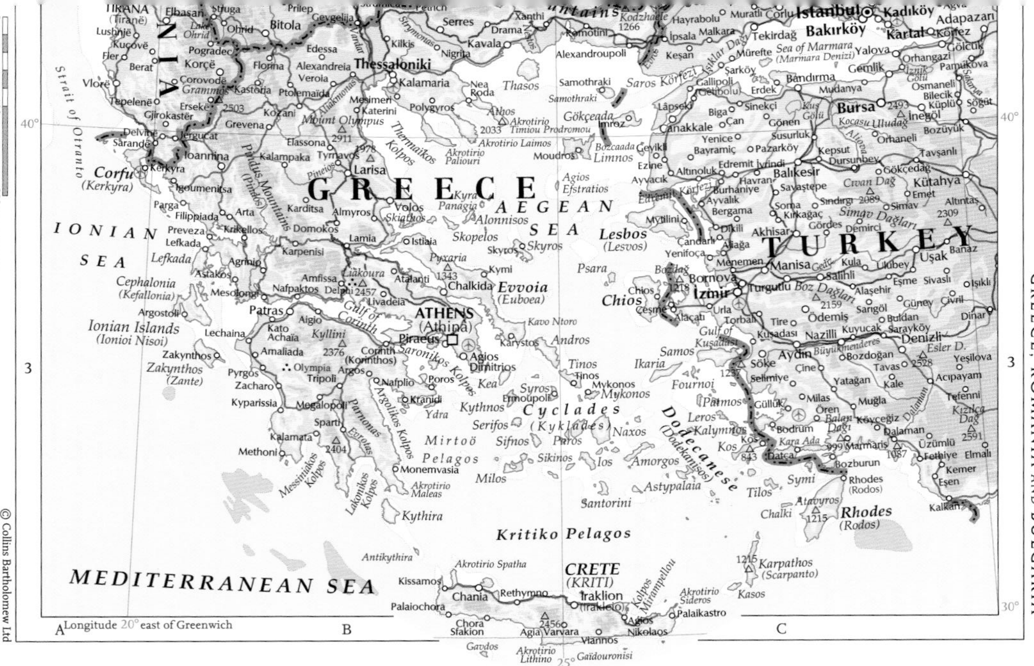

GREECE, ROMANIA and BULGARIA

MEDITERRANEAN SEA

IONIAN SEA

AEGEAN SEA

GREECE

TURKEY

Istanbul

Bursa

İzmir

ATHENS

Rhodes
(Ródos)

CRETE
(KRITI)

Cyclades
(Kykládes)

Dodecanese
(Dodekánisa)

Kritiko Pelagos

Ionian Islands
(Ionioi Nisoi)

Pindus Mountains
(Pindos)

Corfu
(Kerkyra)

Lesbos
(Lésvos)

Chios

Samos

Naxos

Santorini

Strait of Otranto

A Longitude 20° east of Greenwich

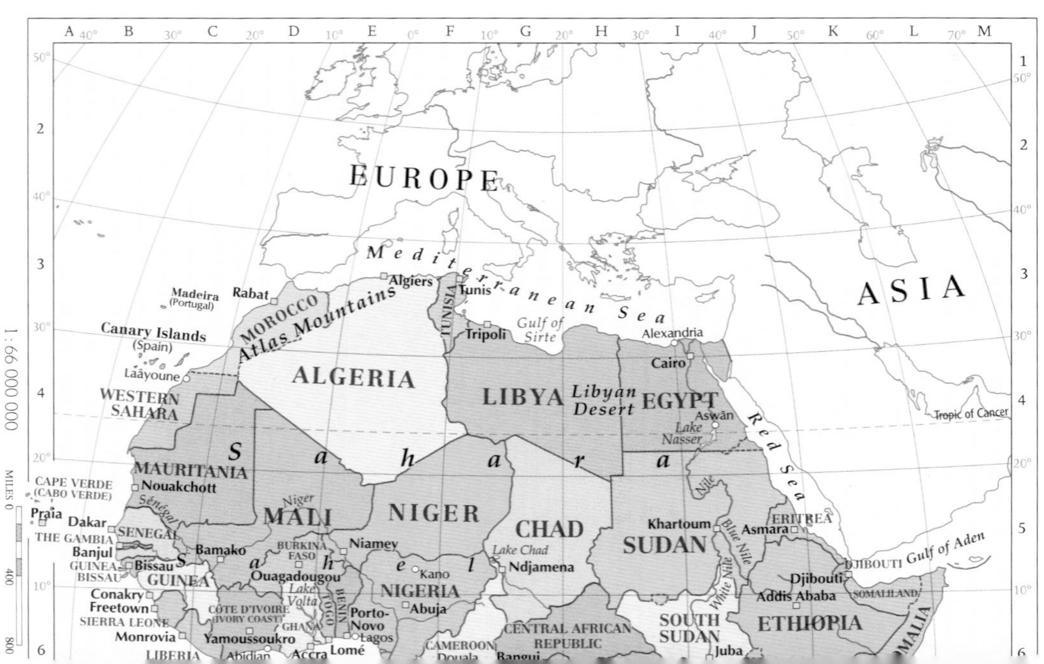

EUROPE
ASIA
Mediterranean Sea
Gulf of Sirte
Red Sea
Gulf of Aden
Tropic of Cancer
Sahara
Atlas Mountains
Libyan Desert
Madeira (Portugal)
Rabat
MOROCCO
Algiers
Tunis
TUNISIA
Tripoli
Alexandria
Cairo
Canary Islands (Spain)
Laâyoune
ALGERIA
LIBYA
EGYPT
Aswân
Lake Nasser
WESTERN SAHARA
MAURITANIA
Nouakchott
CAPE VERDE (CABO VERDE)
Praia
Dakar
Sénégal
SENEGAL
THE GAMBIA
Banjul
GUINEA-BISSAU
Bissau
GUINEA
Bamako
Niger
MALI
NIGER
Niamey
BURKINA FASO
Ouagadougou
Kano
Lake Chad
Ndjamena
CHAD
Nile
Khartoum
Blue Nile
White Nile
SUDAN
Asmara
ERITREA
DJIBOUTI
Djibouti
Addis Ababa
SOMALILAND
ETHIOPIA
Conakry
Freetown
SIERRA LEONE
Monrovia
LIBERIA
CÔTE D'IVOIRE (IVORY COAST)
Yamoussoukro
Abidjan
Lake Volta
GHANA
Accra
TOGO
Lomé
BENIN
Porto-Novo
Lagos
NIGERIA
Abuja
CAMEROON
Douala
CENTRAL AFRICAN REPUBLIC
Bangui
SOUTH SUDAN
Juba
1 : 66 000 000
MILES 0 400 800

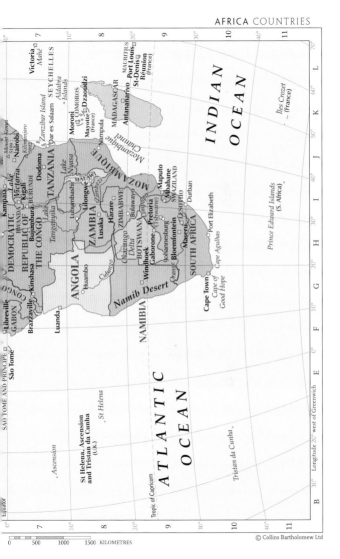

Victoria
Mahé
SEYCHELLES
Aldabra
Islands

MAURITIUS
Port Louis
Réunion
(France)

Mount Kenya
5199
Nairobi
Kilimanjaro
5895

Kampala
Lake
Victoria
Kigali
RWANDA
BURUNDI
Bujumbura

DEMOCRATIC
REPUBLIC OF
THE CONGO
Kinshasa

Brazzaville
CONGO

Libreville
GABON

SÃO TOMÉ AND PRÍNCIPE
São Tomé

Lubumbashi

Luanda

Huambo

ANGOLA

Cabinda

Lake
Nyasa

Dodoma
TANZANIA

Zanzibar Island
Dar es Salaam

Lake
Tanganyika

Lilongwe
MALAWI
Lake
Kariba

ZAMBIA
Lusaka

Harare
ZIMBABWE
Bulawayo

Okavango
Delta

BOTSWANA
Gaborone

Windhoek

NAMIBIA

Namib Desert

Moroni
COMOROS
Dzaoudzi
Mayotte
(France)

MOZAMBIQUE

Nampula

Antananarivo

MADAGASCAR

Mozambique Channel

Maputo

Mbabane
SWAZILAND

Pretoria
(Tshwane)
Johannesburg

Bloemfontein
Maseru
LESOTHO

SOUTH AFRICA

Durban

Port Elizabeth

Cape Town
Cape of
Good Hope

Cape Agulhas

Orange

Limpopo

INDIAN

OCEAN

Îles Crozet
(France)

Prince Edward Islands
(S. Africa)

L

K

J

I

H

G

F

E

ATLANTIC

OCEAN

St Helena

Ascension

St Helena, Ascension
and Tristan da Cunha
(U.K.)

Tristan da Cunha

Tropic of Capricorn

Equator

Longitude 20° west of Greenwich

B

7

8

9

10

11

© Collins Bartholomew Ltd

0   500   1000   1500 KILOMETRES

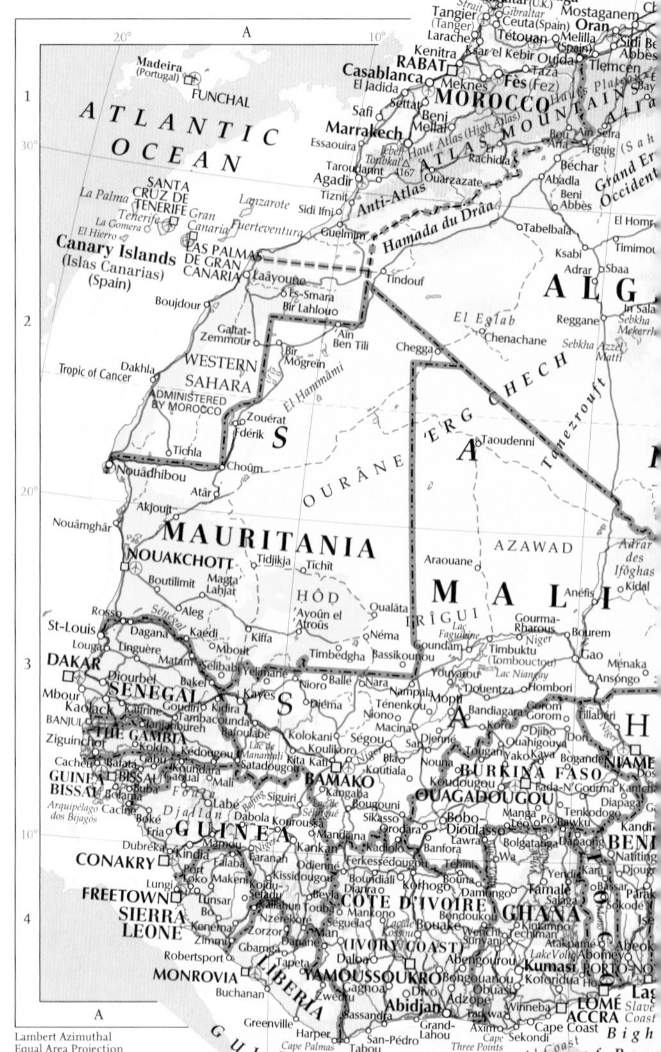
ATLANTIC OCEAN
MOROCCO
WESTERN SAHARA
ADMINISTERED BY MOROCCO
MAURITANIA
MALI
SENEGAL
THE GAMBIA
GUINEA-BISSAU
GUINEA
SIERRA LEONE
LIBERIA
CÔTE D'IVOIRE
(IVORY COAST)
BURKINA FASO
GHANA
GULF OF GUINEA
Canary Islands
(Islas Canarias)
(Spain)
Madeira
(Portugal)
RABAT
DAKAR
NOUAKCHOTT
BAMAKO
CONAKRY
FREETOWN
MONROVIA
YAMOUSSOUKRO
OUAGADOUGOU
ACCRA
LOMÉ
Tropic of Cancer
Lambert Azimuthal
Equal Area Projection

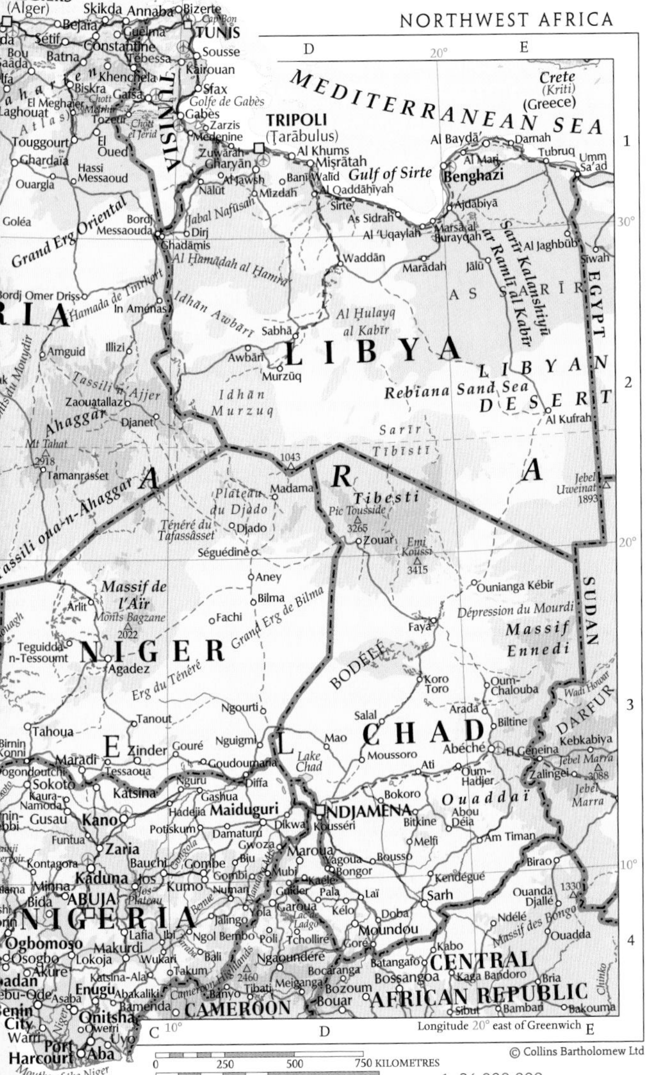

ALGIERS
(Alger)
Skikda Annaba Bizerte
Bejaïa
Sétif
da
Bou
Batna Constantine Tébessa
TUNIS
Sousse
Ifa
Khenchela Gafsa
Biskra
Kairouan
Sfax
El Meghaïer
Tozeur
Golfe de Gabès
Gabès
aghout
Atlas
Touggourt
El
Oued
Médenine
Zarzis

MEDITERRANEAN SEA

Crete
(Kriti)
(Greece)

TRIPOLI
(Ṭarābulus)
Ghardaïa
Hassi
Messaoud
Ouargla
Goléa
Grand Erg Oriental
Bordj
Messaouda
Ghadāmis
Dirj
Nālūt

Al Khums Miṣrātah
Zuwārah Al Khums
Al Mawshī
Gharyān
Banī Walīd
Mizdah
Sirte
Al Qaddāḥiyah
As Sidrah
Gulf of Sirte
Al ʿUqaylah
Waddān
Marādah
Jālū

Al Bayḍāʾ Darnah
Al Marj Tubruq
Benghazi
Ajdābiyā
Marsá al
Burayqah
Sarīr Kalanshiyū
ar Ramlī al Kabīr
Al Jaghbūb

EGYPT

Bordj Omer Driss
Hamada de Tinrhert
In Amenas
Amguid
Illizi
Tassili n'Ajjer
Zaouatallaz
Djanet
Mt Tahat
2918
Tamanrasset
Idhan Awbārī
Awbārī
Sabhā
Murzūq
Idhan
Murzuq

Al Ḥamādah al Ḥamrāʾ
Jabal Nafūsah

AS

RĪR

LIBYA

Rebiana Sand Sea

LIBYAN
DESERT

Al Hulayq
al Kabīr

Sarīr Tībistī

1043
Madama
Tibesti
Pic Toussidé
3265
Emi
Koussi
3415
Zouar

Jebel
Uweinat
1893

Plateau
du Djado
Ténéré du
Tafassâsset
Séguédine
Djado
Aney
Bilma
Fachi
Grand Erg de Bilma

Al Kufrah

Ounianga Kébir

Dépression du Mourdi
Massif
Ennedi

SUDAN

Arlit
Massif de
l'Aïr
Monts Bagzane
2022
Teguiddа
n-Tessoum
Agadez
Erg du Ténéré

Faya
Koro
Toro
Oum-
Chalouba
Arada
Wadi Hawar
Biltine
DARFUR
Kebkabiya

NIGER

Tahoua
Tanout
Ngourti
Salal

BODÉLÉ

Mao
CHAD
Abéché
Zinder
Goudoumaria
Nguigmi
Lake
Chad
Moussoro
Ati
Oum-
Hadjer
El Geneina
Jebel Marra
3088
Zalingei
Jebel
Marra

Birni
Konni
Maradi
Goure
Tessaoua
Diffa
Bokoro
Abou
Déia
Am Timan

Sokoto
Katsina
Gashua
Nguru
Hadejia Maiduguri
Damaturu
Dikwa Kousséri
Bitkine
Melfi

Kano
Potiskum
Bauchi
Gombe
Biu
Gwoza
Bongor
Mubi
Kendégué

Zaria

Guider
Pala
Laï
Birao

ABUJA
NIGERIA
Jos
Kumo
Numan
Garoua
Kélo
Doba
Sarh
Ouanda
Djallé
1330

Minna
Bida
Kontagora
Kaduna
Lafia
Makurdi
Wukari
Ngaoundéré
Moundou
Ndélé
Ouadda

Ogbomoso
Oshogbo
Akure
Lokoja
Bali
Poli
Tignère
Bocaranga
Bozoum
Kabo
Bossangoa
Kaga Bandoro
Bria
Bamouka

Enugu
Onitsha
Owerri
Benue
Cameroun
2460
Banyo
Meiganga
CENTRAL
AFRICAN REPUBLIC
Sibut

Benin
City
Warri
Port
Harcourt
Aba
Mouths of the Niger
CAMEROON
Bouar
Baoro
Ouadda

Longitude 20° east of Greenwich

© Collins Bartholomew Ltd

115

0   250   500   750 KILOMETRES
0   250   500 MILES
1 : 26 000 000

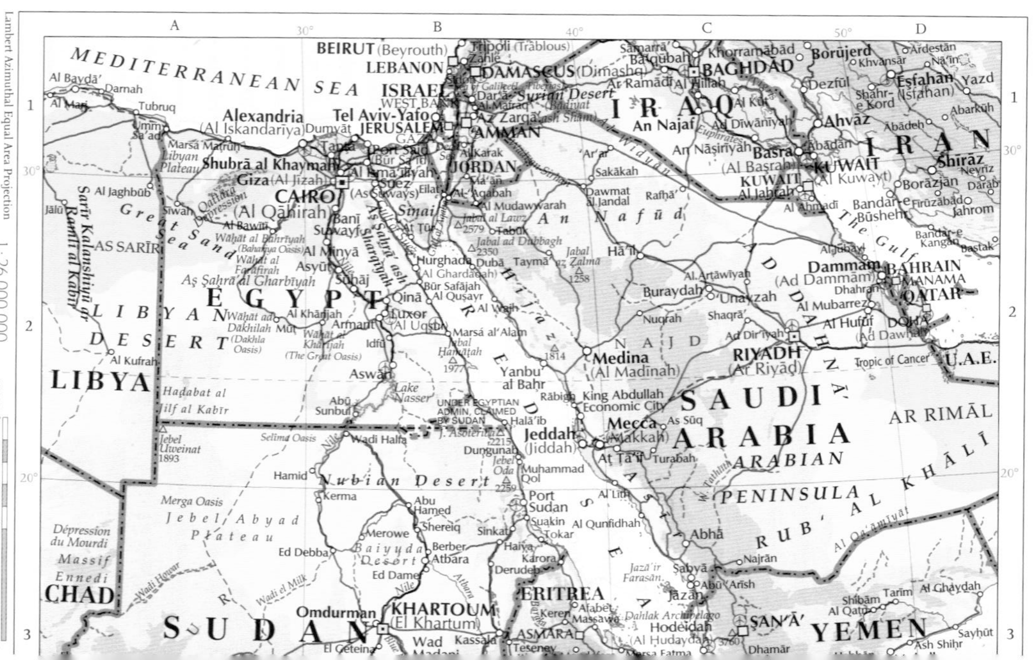

Lambert Azimuthal Equal Area Projection   1 : 26 000 000   MILES 0   250   500

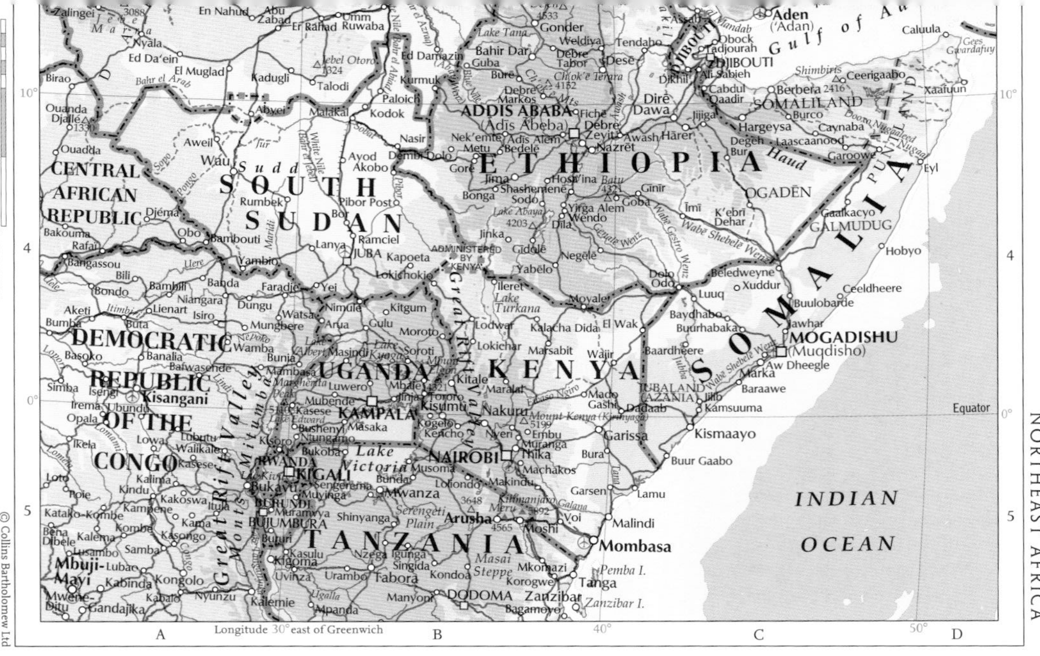

10°
0°
4
5

Equator

D

Caluula
Gandumy
Raas Xaafuun
Qardho
Ceerigaabo Xaafuun
Ceelaayo
Hobyo
Burco
Garoowe Eyl
Beledweyne
Xuddur
Buuhoodle
Beletweyne
Buulobarde
Ceeldheere

INDIAN
OCEAN

C

MOGADISHU
(Muqdisho)
Aw Dheegle
Baraawe
Jamaame
Kismaayo
Buur Gaabo
Lamu
Malindi
Pemba I.

Mombasa
Tanga
Zanzibar
Zanzibar I.

B

INDIAN OCEAN

40°

KENYA
NAIROBI
Great Rift Valley

TANZANIA
DODOMA

Longitude 30° east of Greenwich

A

ETHIOPIA
ADDIS ABABA

SOUTH
SUDAN

UGANDA
KAMPALA
Lake Victoria

DEMOCRATIC
REPUBLIC
OF THE
CONGO

CENTRAL
AFRICAN
REPUBLIC

Great Rift Valley
Mitumba Mons

10°

0°

5

© Collins Bartholomew Ltd

117

0   250   500   750 KILOMETRES

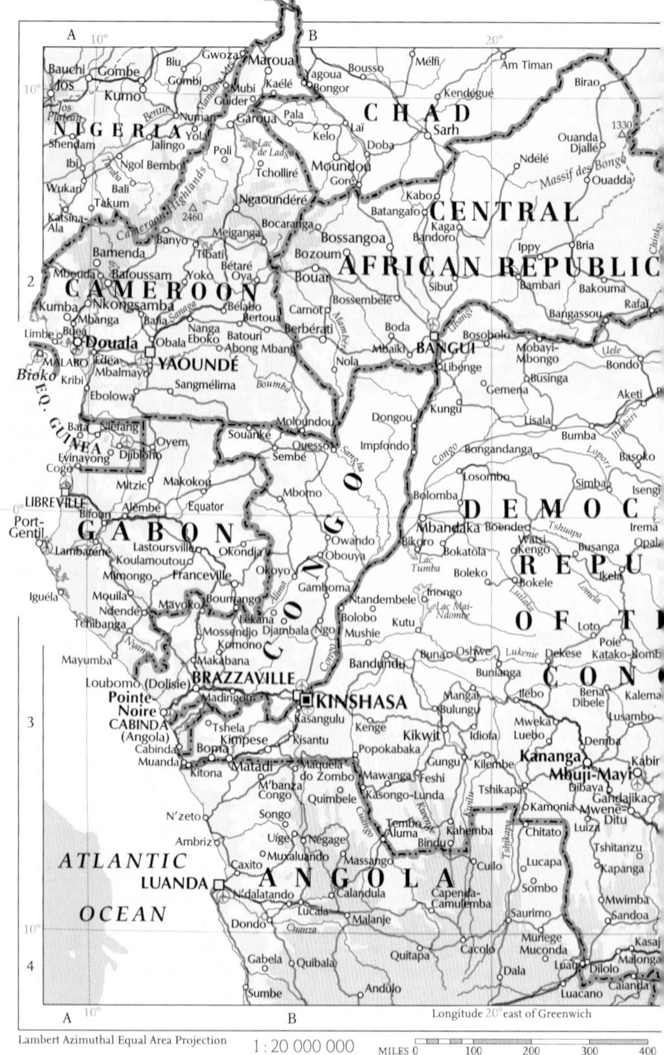

A | 10° | B | 20°

Gwoza oMaroua Bousso oMélfi Am Timan
Biu Gombi oYagoua Bongor Kendégué Birao
Bauchi Gombe Mubi Kaélé 1330
Jos Kumo Guider Garoua Pala Lai Doba Sarh Ouanda Djallé Massif des Bongo
NIGERIA Numan Kelo Moundou Gore Kabo Ouadda
Shendam Jalingo Yola Tchollíré Batangafo Kaga Ippy Bria Chinko
Ibi Ngol Bembo Poli Ngaoundéré Bozoum Bandoro Bambari Bakouma
Wukari Takum 2460 Meiganga Bocaranga Bossangoa CENTRAL Bangassou Rafaï
Katsina- Bali Banyo Tibati Bétaré AFRICAN REPUBLIC Ouesso
Ala Bamenda Oya Bouar Sibut Bangui
Mbouda Banyo Belabo Bossembélé Boda Bimbo Mobayi Bosobolo Aketi
CAMEROON Bafoussam Bertoua Carnot Berbérati Mbaïki BANGUI Mbongo Bondo Businga
Kumba Nkongsamba Nanga Eboko Batouri Nola Dongou Kungu Gemena Lisala Bumba Basoko
Mbanga Bana Ebolo Abong Mbang Moloundou Ouesso Impfondo Bongandanga Simba
Limbe Buéa Douala Obala Sangmélima Souanké Sembé Losombo DEMOC
MALABO Mbalmayo YAOUNDÉ Ebolowa Makokou Mbomo Mbandaka Boende Watsi Busanga Isengi Irema
Bioko Kribi Nsibang Oyem Djibloho Mitzic Equator Owando Ikoro Bokatola Boleko Bokele Ikela Lukenie REPU
EQ. GUINEA Bata Evinayong Cogo Bifoun Alembé Makoko Okondja Obouya Tumba Bolomba Lac Mango Inongo OF TI
LIBREVILLE Port- Lambaréné Koulamoutou Franceville Boumango Ntandembele Mushie Kutu Loto Katako-Kombi CON
Gentil GABON Mouila Mayoko Lekana Djambala Ngo Bunduki Oshwe Dekese Kalema
Iguéla Ndendé Mossendjo Komono Makabana Bandundu Bena Dibele Lusambo
Mayumba Tchibanga Loubomo (Dolisie) Madingou BRAZZAVILLE KINSHASA Manga Ilebo Lodja Kabir
Pointe- Noire Tshela Kimpese Kenge Kikwit Idiofa Luebo Kanga Mbuji-Mayi Kabir
CABINDA (Angola) Cabinda Boma Matadi Popokabaka Gungu Kilembe Kananga Tshibaya Gandajika
Muanda Kitona M'banza Congo Manguela do Zombo Kasongo-Lunda Tshikapa Kamonia Mwene-Ditu
N'zeto Songo Uige Negage Feshi Temba Aluma Bindu Kahemba Chitato Luiza Tshitanzu
Ambriz Muxaluando Massango Cullo Lucapa Kapanga
ATLANTIC Caxito Calandula Capenda- Sombo Mwimba
OCEAN LUANDA N'dalatando ANGOLA Camulemba Saurimo Muriege Sandoa
Dondo Lucala Malanje Cacolo Muconda Kasaji
Gabela Quibala Quitapa Dala Luau Dilolo Calanda
Sumbe Andulo Longa

Longitude 20° east of Greenwich

A | 10° | B

118 Lambert Azimuthal Equal Area Projection 1 : 20 000 000 MILES 0   100   200   300   400

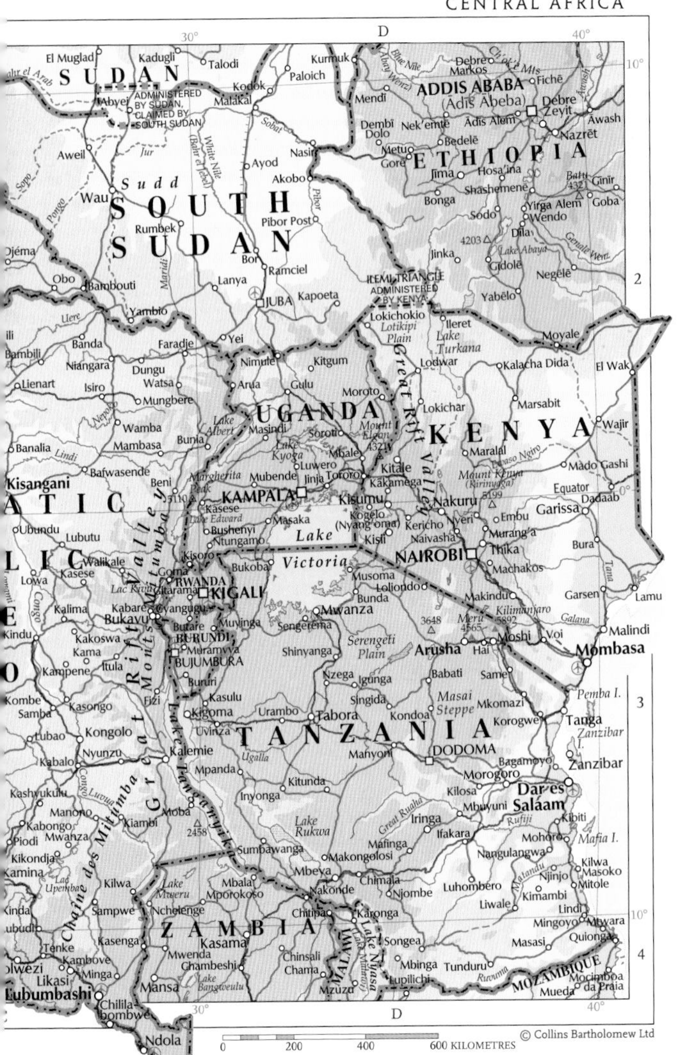

El Muglad Kadugli Talodi Kurmuk Blue Nile Debre Mt 10°
Abyei Kodok Paloich Mendi Markos Fiche
SUDAN Malakal ADDIS ABABA Debre
ADMINISTERED (Adis Abeba) Zeyit Awash
Aweil BY SUDAN, Nek'emte Adis Alem
CLAIMED BY Nasir Dembi Bedele Nazrēt
Sopo SOUTH SUDAN Dolo Metu
Wau White Nile (Bahr al Jabal) Gore Jima Hosa'ina Balti Ginir
Djema Sudd Ayod Bonga Shashemene Goba
SOUTH Akobo Sodo Irga Alem Wendo
Rumbek SUDAN Pibor Post Jinka Dila Lake Abaya Beru
Obo Bambouti Bor Pibor 4203 Gidole Negēle
Banda Lanya Ramciel Yabelo 2
Niangara Faradje JUBA Kapoeta ILEMI TRIANGLE
ili Yambio Yei ADMINISTERED
Bambili BY KENYA Moyale
Lienart Dungu Nimule Kitgum Lokichokio Ileret Kalacha Dida El Wak
Isiro Watsa Arua Lotikipi Lake
Wamba Mungbere UGANDA Gulu Moroto Plain Turkana Lodwar
Banalia Mambasa Masindi Soroti Lokichar Marsabit
Bafwasende Beni Bunia Lake Mount Elgon Kitale Wajir
Kisangani Margherita Albert Lira 4321 Kakamega Marsabit
Lubutu KAMPALA Luwero Mubende Jinja Tororo Kisumu Mount Kenya (Kirinyaga) Mado Gashi
Walikale Lake Kasese Masaka Nakuru 5199 Embu Garissa
Kasese Edward Bushenyi Kisii Kogelo Kericho Nyeri Dadaab
Kalima Butembo Ntungamo (Nyang'oma) Naivasha Murang'a
Kindu Lac Kivu Bukoba Lake NAIROBI Thika Bura
Kakoswa Bukavu Kabare RWANDA Victoria Musoma Machakos Lamu
Kama Uvira KIGALI Mwanza Loliondo Makindu Garsen
Kampene Itula Gitarama Muyinga Bunda Kilimanjaro Galana Malindi
Kombe Kasongo BURUNDI Butare Sengerema Serengeti 5892 Voi
Samba Fizi BUJUMBURA Shinyanga Plain Arusha Moshi Mombasa
tubao Kongolo Bururi Nzega 3648 Hai
Kabalo Nyunzu Kigoma Kasulu Igunga Singida Masai Same Pemba I. 3
Kashwuku Kalemie Uvinza Urambo Tabora Steppe Mkomazi Korogwe Tanga
Manono Moba Mpanda Kondoa DODOMA Bagamoyo Zanzibar
Kabongo Ugalla Kitunda Manyoni Kilosa Morogoro Dar es Salaam
Piodi Mwanza Inyonga Great Ruaha Mbwuyni Kibiti
Kikondja Lake TANZANIA Iringa Mohoro Mafia I.
Kamina 2458 Sumbawanga Rukwa Makongolosi Mafinga Ifakara Nangulangwa
Luena Mbala Mbeya Chimala Njombe Luhombero Kilwa Masoko
ubudi Lake Mporokoso Nakonde Liwale Njinjo Mitole
Tenke Mweru Nchelenge Karonga Kimambi Lindi
olwezi Kambove Sampwe ZAMBIA Chitipa Masasi Mingoyo Mtwara 10°
Likasi Minga Kasenga Mwenda Kasama Songea Quionga
Lubumbashi Mansa Lake Chinsali Mbinga Tunduru MOZAMBIQUE
Chilila Bangweulu Chambeshi Chama Lupilichi Mocimboa
bombwe Mzuzu Rovuma Mueda da Praia
Ndola MALAWI

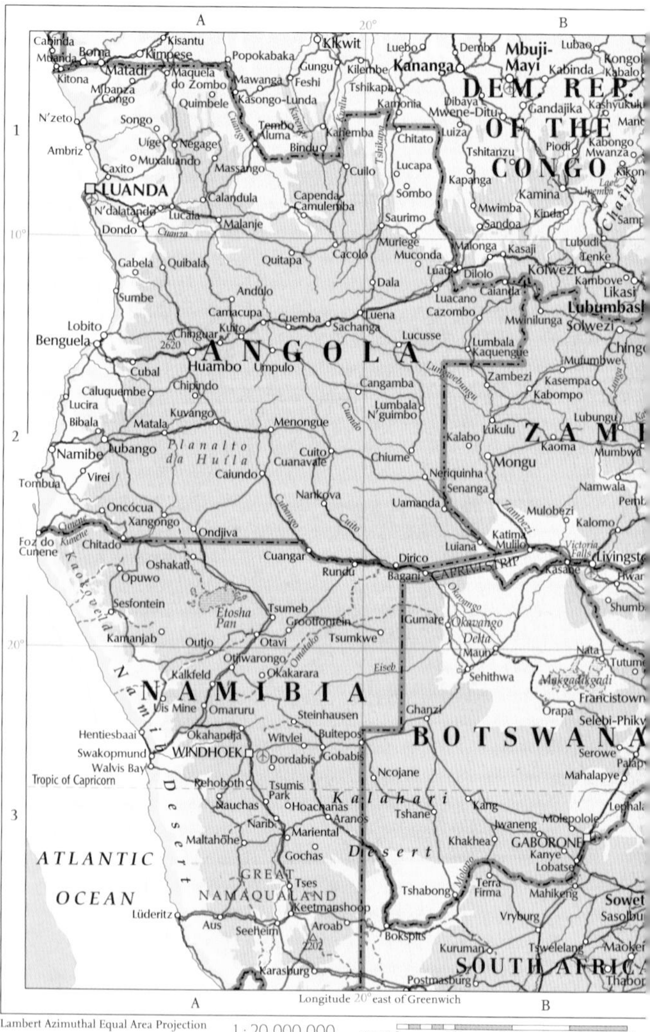

Lambert Azimuthal Equal Area Projection   1 : 20 000 000   MILES 0   100   200   300   400

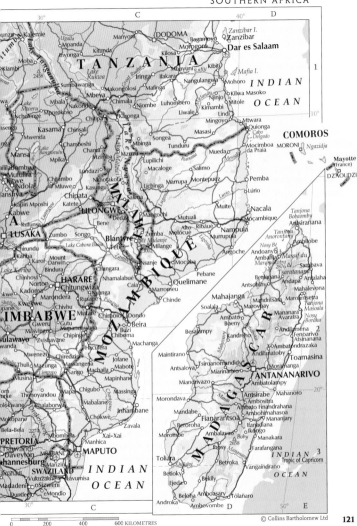

SOUTHERN AFRICA

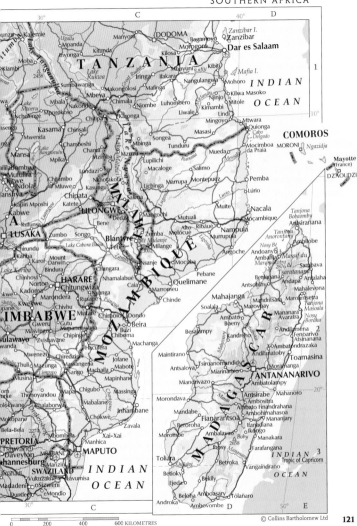

© Collins Bartholomew Ltd

0   200   400   600 KILOMETRES

121

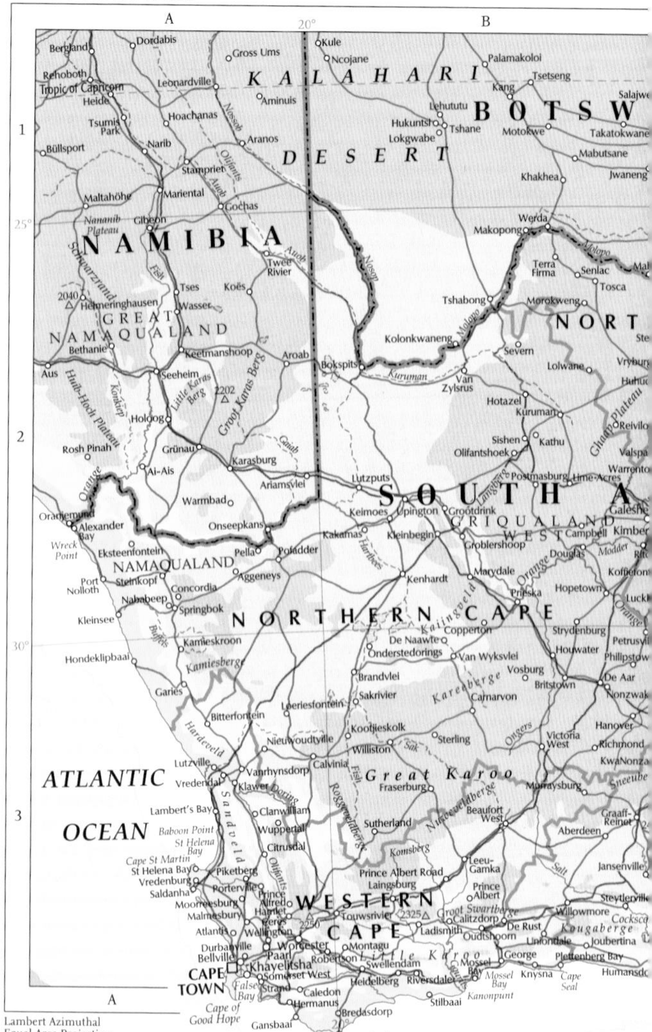
A
20°
B
1
2
3
25°
30°
KALAHARI
DESERT
BOTSW
NAMIBIA
GREAT
NAMAQUALAND
NAMAQUALAND
SOUTH A
NORT
NORTHERN CAPE
GRIQUALAND WEST
WESTERN CAPE
ATLANTIC
OCEAN
Great Karoo
Little Karoo
Dordabis
Bergland
Rehoboth
Tropic of Capricorn
Heide
Tsumis Park
Büllsport
Maltahöhe
Nananib Plateau
Gibeon
Mariental
Stampriet
Narib
Hoachanas
Leonardville
Gross Ums
Aminuis
Aranos
Gochas
Kule
Ncojane
Palamakoloi
Tsetseng
Kang
Salajwe
Lehututu
Hukuntsi
Tshane
Lokgwabe
Motokwe
Takatokwane
Mabutsane
Jwaneng
Khakhea
Werda
Makopong
Molopo
Terra Firma
Senlac
Tosca
Tshabong
Morokweng
Kolonkwaneng
Severn
Lolwane
Vryburg
Van Zylsrus
Kuruman
Hotazel
Kathu
Sishen
Olifantshoek
Reivilo
Ghaap Plateau
Valspan
Warrenton
Postmasburg
Lime Acres
Langberg
Nossob
Olifants
Auob
Fish
Twee Rivier
Tses
Koës
Wasser
Helmeringhausen
2040
Schwarzrand
Bethanie
Aus
Keetmanshoop
Aroab
Bokspits
Seeheim
Little Karas Berg
Groot Karas Berg
2202
Huib-Hoch Plateau
Konkiep
Holoog
Grünau
Gaiab
Karasburg
Rosh Pinah
Ai-Ais
Orange
Ariamsvlei
Lutzputs
Warmbad
Oranjemund
Alexander Bay
Onseepkans
Keimoes
Upington
Grootdrink
Kakamas
Kleinbegin
Campbell
Kimberley
Wreck Point
Eksteenfontein
Pella
Pofadder
Groblershoop
Douglas
Modder
Hartbees
Port Nolloth
Steinkopf
Aggeneys
Concordia
Kenhardt
Marydale
Koffiefontein
Prieska
Hopetown
Nababeep
Springbok
Kleinsee
Buffels
Kaiingveld
Copperton
Strydenburg
De Naawte
Onderstedorings
Van Wyksvlei
Houwater
Petrusville
Philipstown
Kamieskroon
Hondeklipbaai
Kamiesberge
Vosburg
Britstown
De Aar
Brandvlei
Kareeberge
Carnarvon
Garies
Sakrivier
Loeriesfontein
Bitterfontein
Hardeveld
Kootjieskolk
Sterling
Ongers
Victoria West
Hanover
Richmond
Nieuwoudtville
Williston
Sak
KwaNonzame
Lutzville
Vredendal
Vanrhynsdorp
Calvinia
Klawer
Doring
Roggeveldberge
Fraserburg
Murraysburg
Sneeuberge
Lambert's Bay
Sandveld
Clanwilliam
Wuppertal
Nuweveldberge
Beaufort West
Graaff-Reinet
Sutherland
Aberdeen
Baboon Point
St Helena Bay
Citrusdal
Komsberg
Cape St Martin
St Helena Bay
Vredenburg
Saldanha
Piketberg
Leeu-Gamka
Jansenville
Prince Albert Road
Laingsburg
Prince Albert
Salt
Porterville
Moorreesburg
Prince Alfred Hamlet
Malmesbury
Ceres
2250
Touwsrivier
2325
Groot Swartberge
Calitzdorp
Steytlerville
Willowmore
De Rust
Cockscomb
Atlantis
Wellington
Ladismith
Oudtshoorn
Uniondale
Kougaberge
Joubertina
Durbanville
Worcester
Montagu
Bellville
Paarl
Khayelitsha
Robertson
Swellendam
George
Plettenberg Bay
Mossel Bay
CAPE TOWN
Somerset West
Heidelberg
Riversdale
Mossel Bay
Knysna
Cape Seal
Humansdorp
False Bay
Strand
Caledon
Stilbaai
Kanonpunt
Hermanus
Cape of Good Hope
Gansbaai
Bredasdorp
Struis Bay
Cape Agulhas

Lambert Azimuthal
Equal Area Projection

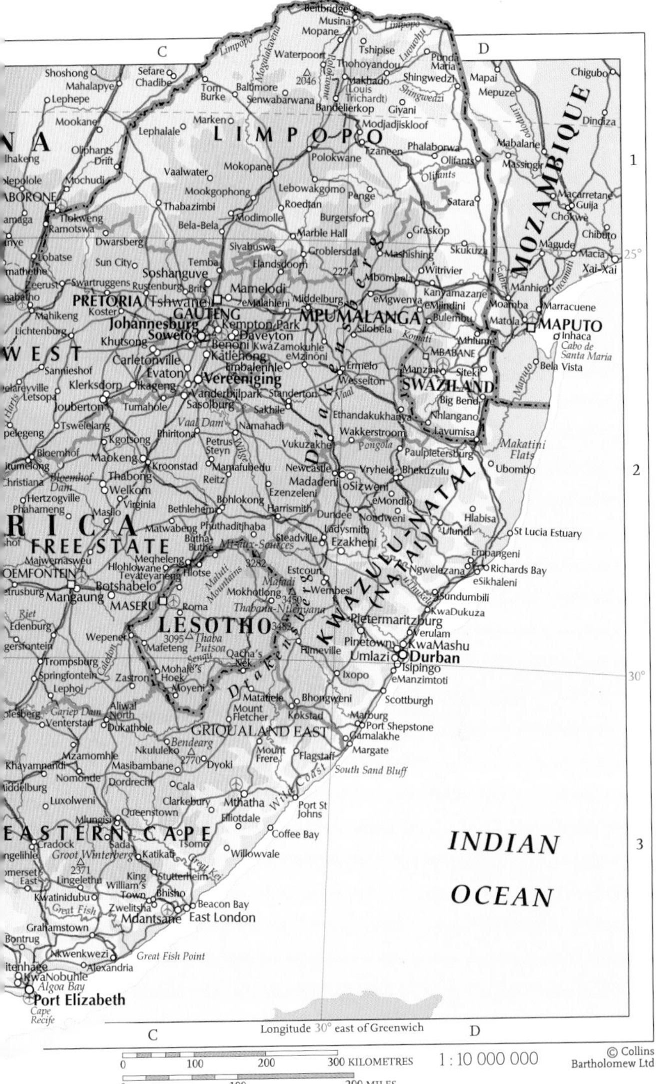

Longitude 30° east of Greenwich

1 : 10 000 000

© Collins
Bartholomew Ltd

0   100   200   300 KILOMETRES
0   100   200 MILES

MOZAMBIQUE

LIMPO-PO

Beitbridge
Musina
Mopane
Tshipise
Tshohoyandou
Pondi
Mapai
Chigubo
Chibuto
Dindiza

Waterpoort
Makhado
Shingwedzi
Mepuze
Swangedzi

Shoshong
Sefare
Chadibe
Baltimore
Tom
Burke
Senwabarwana
Bandelierkop
Giyani
Massingir
Macarretane

Mookane
Lephalale
Vaalwater
Mokopane
Polokwane
Tzaneen
Phalaborwa
Olifants
Mabalane
Guija
Chokwe
Macia
Xai-Xai

Mochudi
Drift
Mookgophong
Lebowakgomo
Roedtan
Pange
Satara
Skukuza
Magude
Manhiça

GAUTENG
MPUMALANGA

PRETORIA
Tshwane
Mamelodi
Middelburg
eMgwenya
Manzini
Moamba
Marracuene

Johannesburg
Soweto
Kempton Park
Daveyton
Benoni
KwaZamokuhle
eMzinoni
Siteki
MAPUTO
Inhaca

SWAZILAND

Evaton
Vereeniging
Vanderbijlpark
Sasolburg
Standerton
Ermelo
Wesselton
MBABANE
Big Bend
Bela Vista

FREE STATE
KWAZULU-NATAL

LESOTHO
MASERU

EASTERN CAPE

INDIAN

OCEAN

Port Elizabeth
East London
Durban

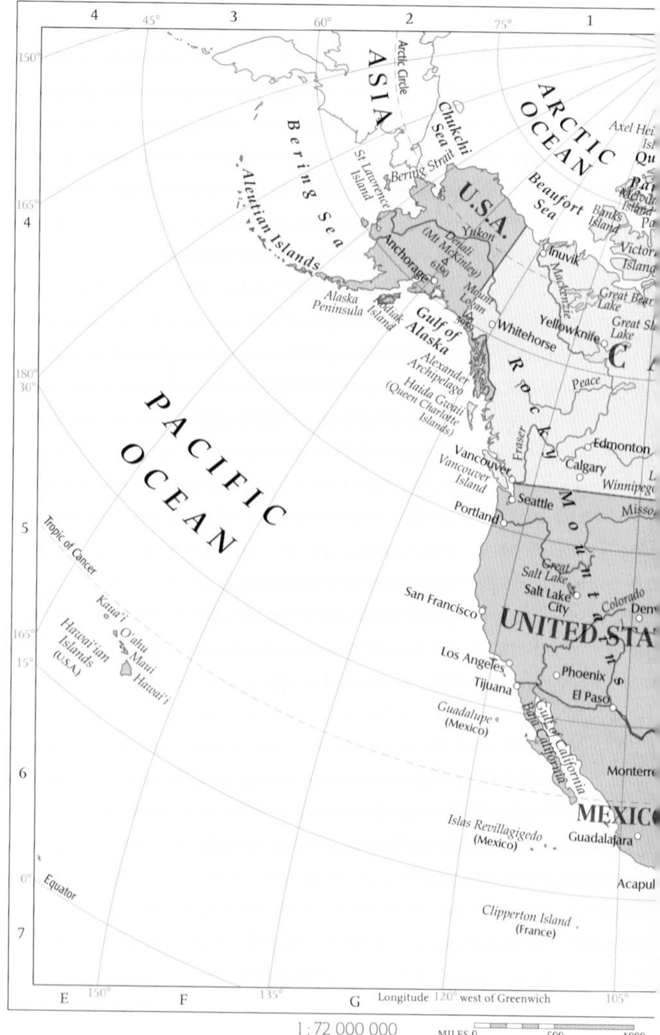

ASIA
Arctic Circle
Chukchi Sea
ARCTIC OCEAN
Bering Sea
Aleutian Islands
St Lawrence Island
Bering Strait
U.S.A.
Beaufort Sea
Banks Island
Yukon
Denali (Mt McKinley) 6190
Anchorage
Inuvik
Mackenzie
Alaska Peninsula
Kodiak Island
Mount Logan 5959
Gulf of Alaska
Whitehorse
Yellowknife
Great Bear Lake
Great Slave Lake
Alexander Archipelago
Haida Gwaii (Queen Charlotte Islands)
Peace
PACIFIC OCEAN
Rocky Mountains
Fraser
Edmonton
Calgary
Vancouver
Vancouver Island
Seattle
Portland
Tropic of Cancer
Great Salt Lake
Salt Lake City
San Francisco
Colorado
UNITED STA
Kaua'i
O'ahu
Maui
Hawai'i
Hawai'ian Islands (U.S.A.)
Los Angeles
Tijuana
Phoenix
El Paso
Guadalupe (Mexico)
Gulf of California
Baja California
MEXIC
Islas Revillagigedo (Mexico)
Guadalajara
Equator
Acapul
Clipperton Island (France)
Longitude 120° west of Greenwich
1 : 72 000 000
MILES 0 500 1000

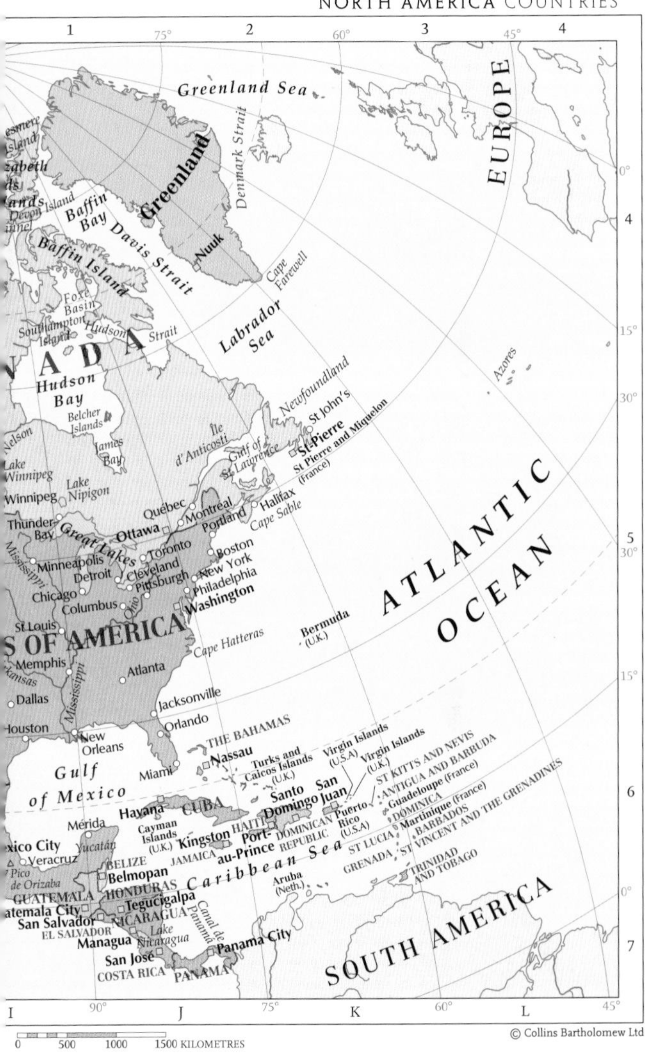

Greenland Sea

Denmark Strait

EUROPE

Ellesmere Island

Elizabeth Islands

Devon Island

Baffin Bay

Greenland

Baffin Island

Nuuk

Davis Strait

Baffin Bay

Foxe Basin

Southampton Island

Hudson Strait

Cape Farewell

Labrador Sea

CANADA

Hudson Bay

Belcher Islands

James Bay

Newfoundland

Nelson

Lake Winnipeg

Lake Nipigon

Ile d'Anticosti

Gulf of St Lawrence

St John's

St-Pierre

St Pierre and Miquelon (France)

Thunder Bay

Great Lakes

Québec

Montreal

Ottawa

Toronto

Portland

Halifax

Cape Sable

Minneapolis

Detroit

Cleveland

Boston

Chicago

Pittsburgh

New York

Columbus

Philadelphia

Washington

St Louis

Ohio

ATLANTIC

OCEAN

Memphis

Kansas

Mississippi

Dallas

Atlanta

UNITED STATES OF AMERICA

Cape Hatteras

Bermuda (U.K.)

Houston

Jacksonville

New Orleans

Orlando

Gulf of Mexico

Miami

THE BAHAMAS

Nassau

Turks and Caicos Islands (U.K.)

Virgin Islands (U.S.A.)

Virgin Islands (U.K.)

ST KITTS AND NEVIS

ANTIGUA AND BARBUDA

Guadeloupe (France)

Merida

Havana

CUBA

Cayman Islands (U.K.)

Santo Domingo

San Juan

Puerto Rico (U.S.A.)

DOMINICA

Martinique (France)

xico City

Yucatán

JAMAICA

Kingston

HAITI

DOMINICAN REPUBLIC

Port-au-Prince

ST LUCIA

BARBADOS

Veracruz

Pico de Orizaba

BELIZE

Belmopan

HONDURAS

Caribbean Sea

Aruba (Neth.)

GRENADA

ST VINCENT AND THE GRENADINES

TRINIDAD AND TOBAGO

GUATEMALA

Guatemala City

Tegucigalpa

San Salvador

EL SALVADOR

NICARAGUA

Managua

Lake Nicaragua

San José

COSTA RICA

PANAMA

Golfo de Panamá

Panama City

SOUTH AMERICA

© Collins Bartholomew Ltd

0   500   1000   1500 KILOMETRES

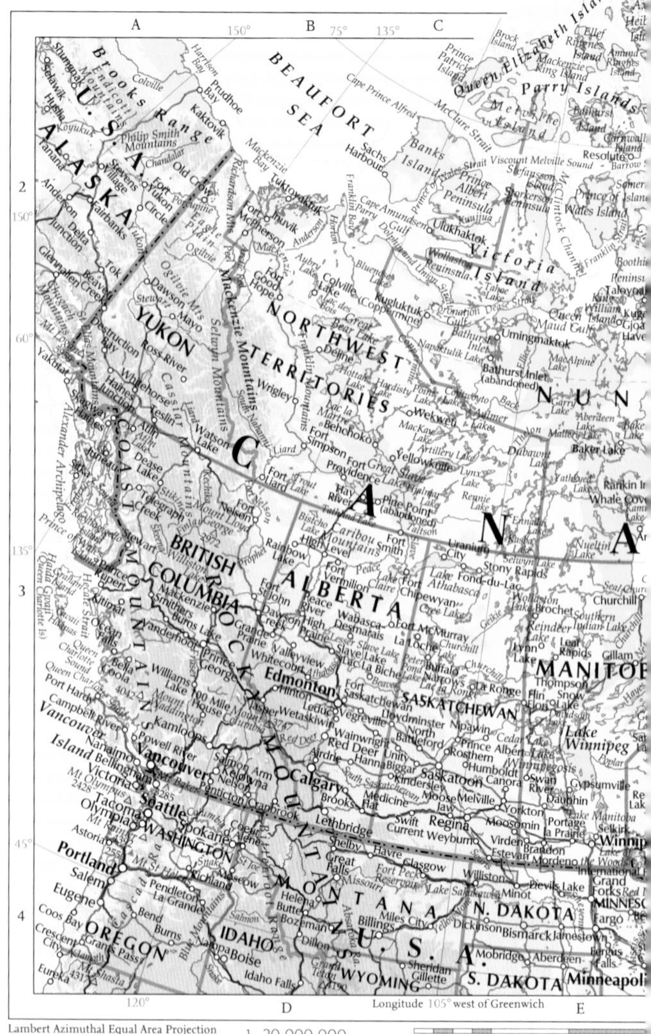

Lambert Azimuthal Equal Area Projection   1 : 30 000 000   MILES 0   200   400   60

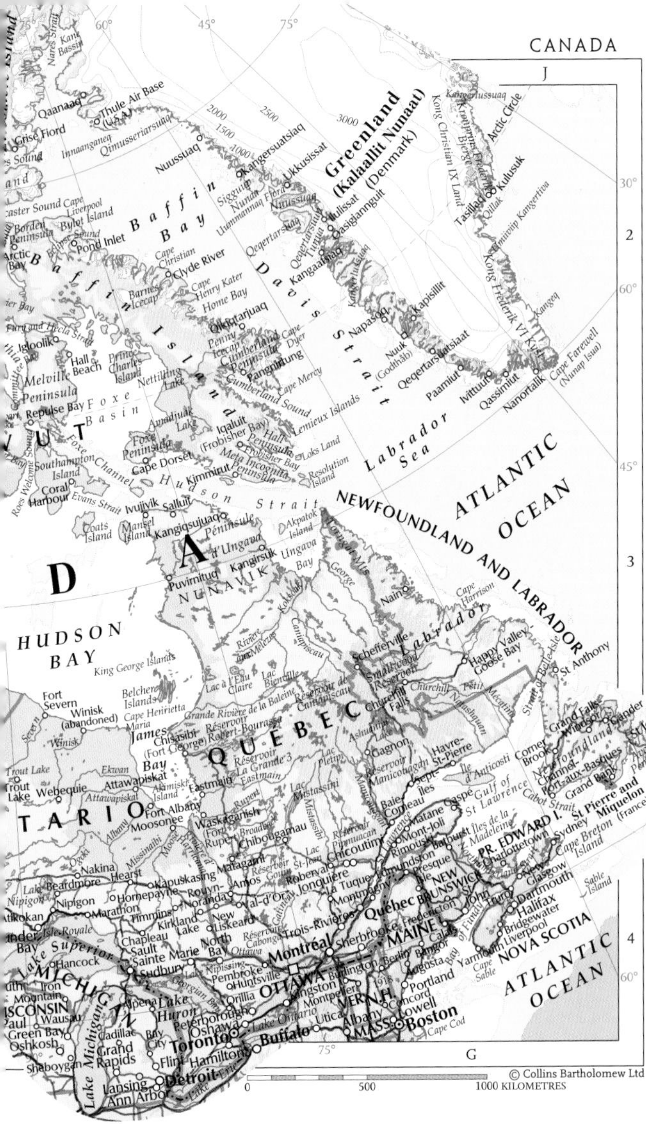
J
G
2
3
4
30°
45°
60°
75°
Greenland
(Kalaallit Nunaat)
(Denmark)
Baffin Bay
Baffin Island
Davis Strait
Labrador Sea
ATLANTIC OCEAN
NEWFOUNDLAND AND LABRADOR
HUDSON BAY
James Bay
QUEBEC
NUNAVIK
Hudson Strait
Foxe Basin
Foxe Channel
Ungava Bay
Gulf of St Lawrence
NEW BRUNSWICK
NOVA SCOTIA
PR. EDWARD I.
St Pierre and Miquelon (France)
MAINE
VER.
N.H.
MASS.
MICHIGAN
Lake Superior
Lake Huron
Lake Michigan
Lake Ontario
Qaanaaq
Thule Air Base (USA)
Grise Fiord
Nuussuaq
Kangersuatsiaq
Ukkusissat
Ilulissat
Qasigiannguit
Qeqertarsuaq
Kangaatsiaq
Kangerlussuaq
Arctic Circle
Kulusuk
Tasiilaq
Kong Christian IX Land
Kong Frederik VI Kyst
Napasoq
Kapisillit
Nuuk (Godthåb)
Qeqertarsuatsiaat
Paamiut
Ivittuut
Qassimiut
Nanortalik
Cape Farewell (Nunap Isua)
Pond Inlet
Bylot Island
Clyde River
Cape Christian
Home Bay
Qikiqtarjuaq
Cumberland Peninsula
Cape Dyer
Pangnirtung
Cumberland Sound
Cape Mercy
Lemieux Islands
Iqaluit (Frobisher Bay)
Hall Peninsula
Frobisher Bay
Loks Land
Meta Incognita Peninsula
Resolution Island
Kimmirut
Cape Dorset
Foxe Peninsula
Nettilling Lake
Amadjuak Lake
Igloolik
Hall Beach
Prince Charles Island
Melville Peninsula
Repulse Bay
Southampton Island
Coral Harbour
Evans Strait
Coats Island
Mansel Island
Ivujivik
Salluit
Kangiqsujuaq
Péninsule d'Ungava
Akpatok Island
Kangirsuk
Puvirnituq
Nain
Cape Harrison
Labrador
Schefferville
Smallwood Reservoir
Churchill Falls
Happy Valley-Goose Bay
St Anthony
Strait of Belle Isle
Grand Falls-Windsor
Gander
St John's
Avalon Peninsula
Cape Race
Corner Brook
Channel-Port-aux-Basques
Grand Bank
Cabot Strait
Newfoundland
Île d'Anticosti
Havre-St-Pierre
Sept-Îles
Gagnon
Réservoir Manicouagan
Baie-Comeau
Gaspé
Matane
Mont-Joli
Rimouski
Îles de la Madeleine
Charlottetown
Sydney
Cape Breton Island
Sable Island
New Glasgow
Dartmouth
Halifax
Truro
Bridgewater
Liverpool
Yarmouth
Cape Sable
Bay of Fundy
Saint John
Fredericton
Edmundston
Presque Isle
Bathurst
Calais
Bangor
Augusta
Portland
Concord
Lowell
Boston
Cape Cod
Berlin
Burlington
Montpelier
Albany
Utica
Buffalo
Québec
Trois-Rivières
Sherbrooke
Montréal
OTTAWA
Kingston
Pembroke
Huntsville
Orillia
Peterborough
Oshawa
Toronto
Hamilton
Detroit
Lansing
Ann Arbor
Flint
Bay City
Grand Rapids
Cadillac
Alpena
Sudbury
North Bay
Sault Sainte Marie
Chapleau
Timmins
Kirkland Lake
New Liskeard
Rouyn-Noranda
Val-d'Or
Amos
La Tuque
Jonquière
Chicoutimi
Roberval
Lac St-Jean
Chibougamau
Matagami
Lac Mistassini
Waskaganish (Fort Rupert)
Eastmain
Réservoir La Grande 3
Réservoir Robert-Bourassa
Chisasibi (Fort George)
Grande Rivière de la Baleine
Lac à l'Eau Claire
Lac Bienville
Réservoir de Caniapiscau
Kuujjuaq
King George Islands
Belcher Islands
Cape Henrietta Maria
Fort Severn
Winisk (abandoned)
Trout Lake
Webequie
Attawapiskat
Akimiski Island
Fort Albany
Moosonee
Kapuskasing
Hearst
Hornepayne
Nakina
Lake Nipigon
Nipigon
Marathon
Thunder Bay
Isle Royale
Hancock
Iron Mountain
WISCONSIN
Wausau
Green Bay
Oshkosh
Sheboygan
Atikokan
Beardmore
ONTARIO
0
500
1000 KILOMETRES

© Collins Bartholomew Ltd

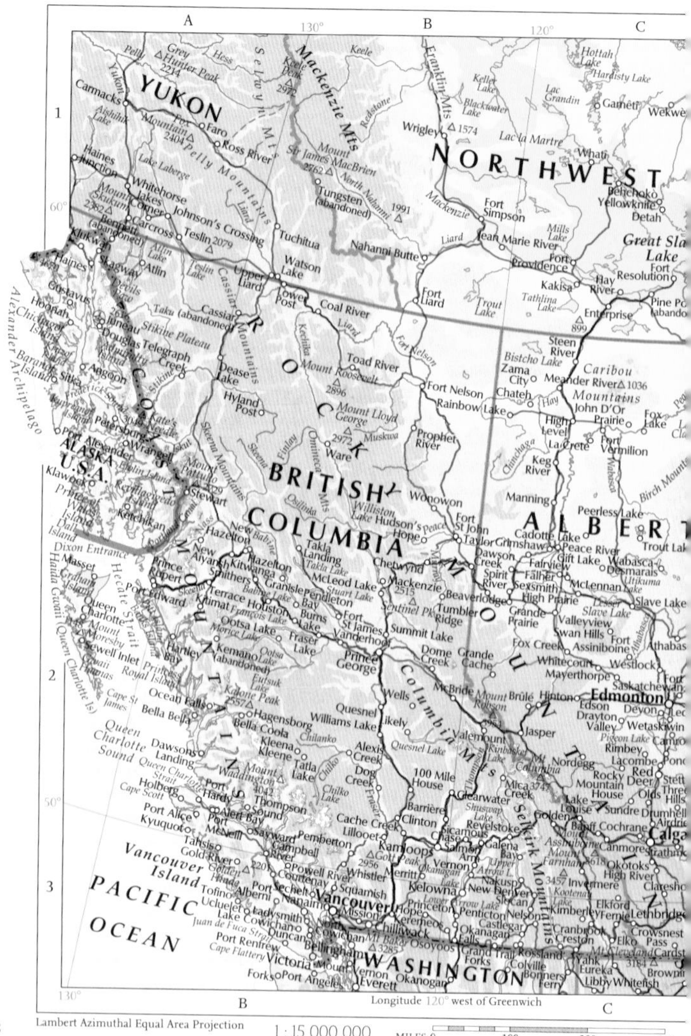

Lambert Azimuthal Equal Area Projection   1 : 15 000 000   MILES 0   100   200   300

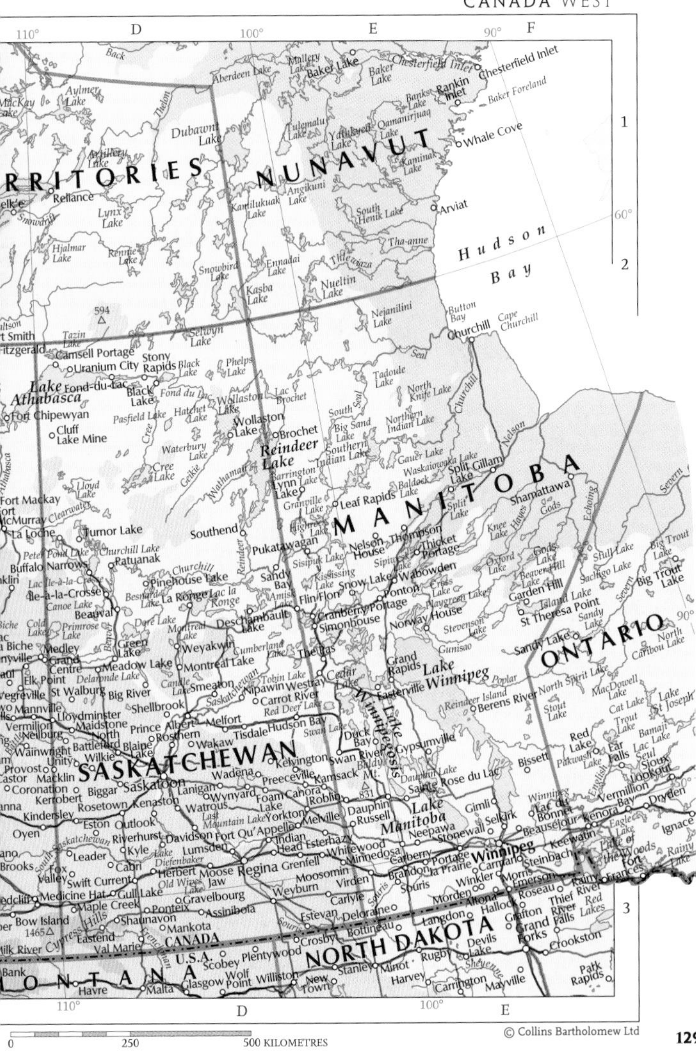

TERRITORIES

NUNAVUT

Back

Aberdeen Lake

Mackay Lake
Aylmer Lake

Artillery Lake

Reliance

Lynx Lake

Hjalmar Lake

Kasba Lake

Dubawnt Lake

Mallery

Baker Lake

Chesterfield Inlet

Chesterfield Inlet

Banks Lake

Rankin Inlet

Baker Foreland

Whale Cove

Arviat

Angikuni Lake

Kaminak Lake

South Henik Lake

Tulemalu Lake

Yathkyed Lake

Qamanirjuaq Lake

Tha-anne

Hudson Bay

60°

Snowbird Lake

Ennadai Lake

Nueltin Lake

Nejanilini Lake

Button Bay

Cape Churchill

594

Selwyn Lake

Kasba Lake

Churchill

Seal

Camsell Portage

Uranium City

Fond-du-Lac

Stony Rapids

Black Lake

Phelps Lake

Tadoule Lake

North Knife Lake

Lake Athabasca

Fort Chipewyan

Fitzgerald

Cluff Lake Mine

Pasfield Lake

Fond du Lac

Black Lake

Hatchet Lake

Wollaston Lake

Lac Brochet

Big Sand Lake

Northern Indian Lake

Split Lake

Gillam

Reindeer Lake

Brochet

Waterbury Lake

Cree Lake

Southern Indian Lake

Nelson

Shamattawa

Lloyd Lake

Waskaiowaka Lake

Gauer Lake

Baldock Lake

Fort McMurray

La Loche

Turnor Lake

Southend

Pukatawagan

MANITOBA

Leaf Rapids

Granville Lake

Lynn Lake

Barrington Lake

Stull Lake

Big Trout Lake

ONTARIO

Buffalo Narrows

Patuanak

Churchill

Sisipuk Lake

Nelson House

Thompson

Wabowden

Knee Lake

Oxford Lake

Gods Lake

Island Lake

Gods

Echoing

Sachigo Lake

Ile-à-la-Crosse

Canoe Lake

Pinehouse Lake

La Ronge

Lac la Ronge

Sandy Bay

Kississing Lake

Snow Lake

Flin Flon

Ponton

Setting Lake

Cross Lake

Garden Hill

St Theresa Point

Sandy Lake

Cold Lake

Primrose Lake

Beauval

Dore Lake

Deschambault Lake

Cranberry Portage

Simonhouse

Norway House

Nayaweun Lake

Stevenson

North Caribou Lake

Lac la Biche

Bonnyville

Weyakwin

Meadow Lake

Montreal Lake

Cumberland Lake

The Pas

Gunisao

Sandy Lake

Elk Point

St Walburg

Delaronde Lake

Big River

Smeaton

Tobin Lake

Nipawin

Carrot River

Cedar Lake

Grand Rapids

Lake Winnipeg

Poplar

Reindeer Island

Berens River

Red Lake

Cat Lake

Lac Seul

Ear Falls

Vermilion

Mannville

Vegreville

Vermilion

Shellbrook

Prince Albert

Melfort

Tisdale

Hudson Bay

Swan River

Duck Bay

Gypsumville

Berens River

Stout Lake

Pikwitonei Lake

Red Lake

Trout Lake

Barriere

Dryden

Ignace

Lloydminster

Maidstone

North Battleford

Rosthern

Wakaw

Kelvington

Preeceville

Swan Lake

Dauphin

Ste Rose du Lac

Bissett

Winnipeg

Lac Seul

Keewatin

Kenora

Wainwright

Unity

Wilkie

Biggar

Saskatoon

Watrous

Wadena

Kamsack Mt.

Roblin

Dauphin Lake

Gimli

Stonewall

Beausejour

Keewatin

SASKATCHEWAN

Lanigan

Wynyard

Yorkton

Melville

Neepawa

Selkirk

Sioux Lookout

Macklin

Kerrobert

Rosetown

Kenaston

Last Mountain Lake

Esterhazy

Manitoba

Russell

Portage la Prairie

Steinbach

Vermilion

Coronation

Kindersley

Biggar

Outlook

Davidson

Lumsden

Indian Head

Whitewood

Brandon

Winkler

Morris

Sprague

Lake of the Woods

Oyen

Saskatchewan

Riverhurst

Kyle

Regina

Grenfell

Moosomin

Virden

Souris

Morden

Emerson

Roseau

Warroad

Rainy Lake

Brooks

Swift Current

Herbert

Moose Jaw

Old Wives Lake

Weyburn

Carlyle

Deloraine

Boissevain

Pilot Mound

Altona

Halkett

Grand Forks

Crookston

Park Rapids

Medicine Hat

Maple Creek

Gull Lake

Cabri

Gravelbourg

Assiniboia

Estevan

Carnduff

CANADA

U.S.A.

Bottineau

Rolla

Devils Lake

Thief River Falls

Red Lake Falls

Cypress Hills

Val Marie

Mankota

Scobey

Plentywood

NORTH DAKOTA

Stanley

Minot

Rugby

Shryenne

Carrington

Mayville

Bow Island

1465∆

Shaunavon

Milk River

Havre

Malta

Glasgow

Wolf Point

Williston

New Town

Harvey

MONTANA

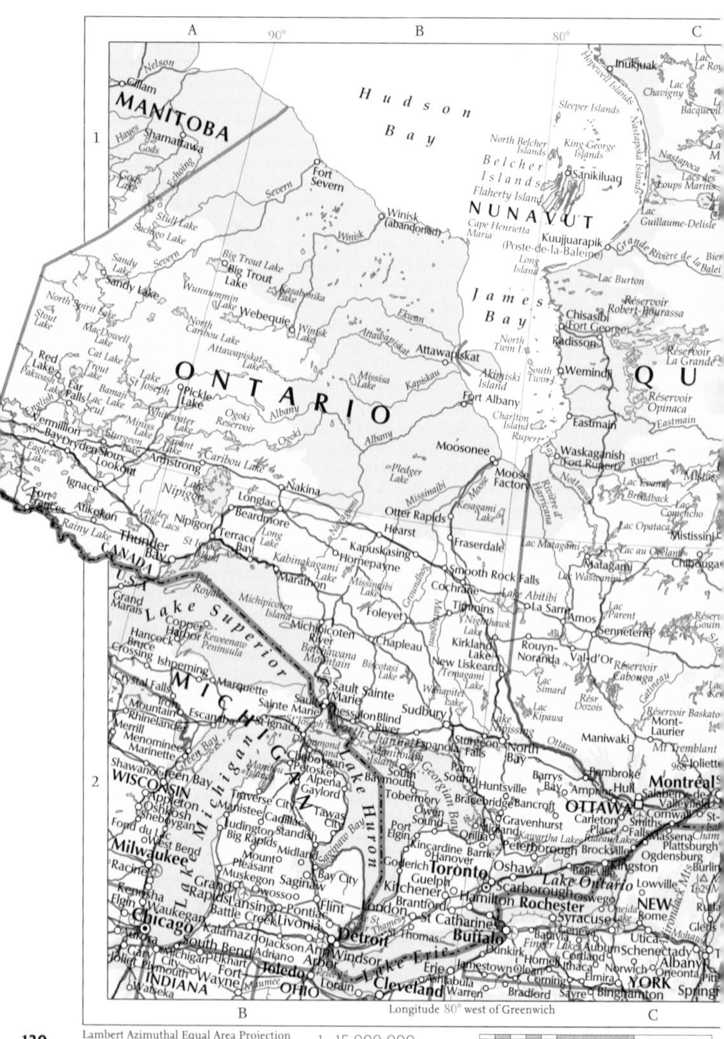

Lambert Azimuthal Equal Area Projection   1 : 15 000 000   MILES 0   100   200   300

Longitude 80° west of Greenwich

70° D 60° E

1

2

ATLANTIC OCEAN

NEWFOUNDLAND AND LABRADOR

Labrador

Hebron
Cod Island
Kangiqsualujjuaq
Tasiujaq
Kuujjuaq (Fort Chimo)
Nain
Voisey's Bay
Natuashish
Davis Inlet (abandoned)
Hopedale
Makkovik
Cape Harrison
Groswater Bay
Sandwich Bay
Rigolet
Cartwright
Caniapiscau
Schefferville
Menihek
Esker
Smallwood Reservoir
Churchill Falls
Lake Melville
North West River
Happy Valley-Goose Bay
Mealy Mountains
Port Hope Simpson
Labrador City
Fermont
Gagnon
Réservoir Manicouagan
Red Bay
Belle Isle
Cook's Harbour
Blanc-Sablon
St Anthony
Grey Islands
Roddickton
St-Augustin
Port aux Choix
Horse Islands
La Tabatière
Harrington Harbour
Notre Dame Bay
Fogo Island
Twillingate
Long Range Mts
White Bay
Mingan
Havre-St-Pierre
Natashquan
Sept-Îles
Port-Menier
Île d'Anticosti
Springdale
Grand Falls-Windsor
Gander
Bonavista Bay
Bonavista
Deer Lake
Corner Brook
Newfoundland
Stephenville
Gambo
Clarenville
Trinity Bay
Pouch Cove
Carbonear
St John's
Avalon Peninsula
Terrenceville
Placentia
Burin
Trepassey
Cape Race
Channel-Port-aux-Basques
Burgeo
Harbour Breton
Grand Bank
St Pierre and Miquelon (France)
ST-PIERRE
Gulf of St Lawrence (Golfe du St-Laurent)
Cabot Strait
Îles de la Madeleine
Havre-Aubert
Gaspé
Mt Jacques-Cartier 1268
Pén. de Gaspésie
Grande-Rivière
Baie-Comeau
Hauterive
Ste-Anne-des-Monts
Matane
Betsiamites
Forestville
Mont-Joli
Rimouski
Causapscal
Dalhousie
Chaleur Bay
Caraquet
Campbellton
Bathurst
St Quentin
Chicoutimi
Jonquière
Alma
Dolbeau-Mistassini
St-Siméon
Rivière-du-Loup
Edmundston
Van Buren
Grand Falls
Miramichi
Tignish
PRINCE EDWARD ISLAND
Chéticamp
Cape Breton Island
Summerside
Souris
Sydney Mines
Glace Bay
Sydney
Bras d'Or Lake
Inverness
Charlottetown
Port Hawkesbury
NEW BRUNSWICK
Bouctouche
Caribou
Presque Isle
Woodstock
Minto
Moncton
Riverview
Springhill
Amherst
New Glasgow
Antigonish
Fredericton
Sussex
Truro
Sherbrooke
Saint John
Wolfville
NOVA SCOTIA
Dartmouth
Halifax
Bridgewater
Digby
Bay of Fundy
Liverpool
Yarmouth
Shelburne
Cape Sable
Sable Island
MAINE
Mt Katahdin 1606
Millinocket
Lincoln
Dover-Foxcroft
Bangor
Calais
Machias
Bucksport
Ellsworth
Bar Harbor
Belfast
Waterville
Augusta
Lewiston
Brunswick
Portland
Biddeford
Sanford
Portsmouth
Manchester
Nashua
Lowell
Boston
Quincy
Massachusetts Bay
Cape Cod
Worcester
N.H.
Conway
Laconia
Mont Notre-Dame
St Lawrence

70° D 60° E

0 250 500 KILOMETRES

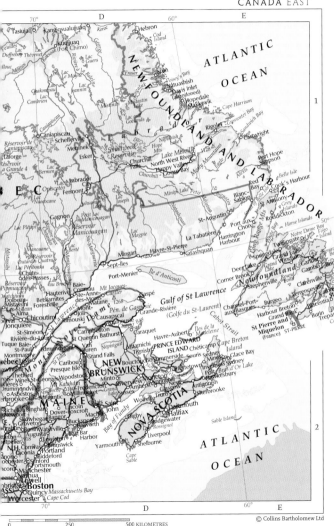

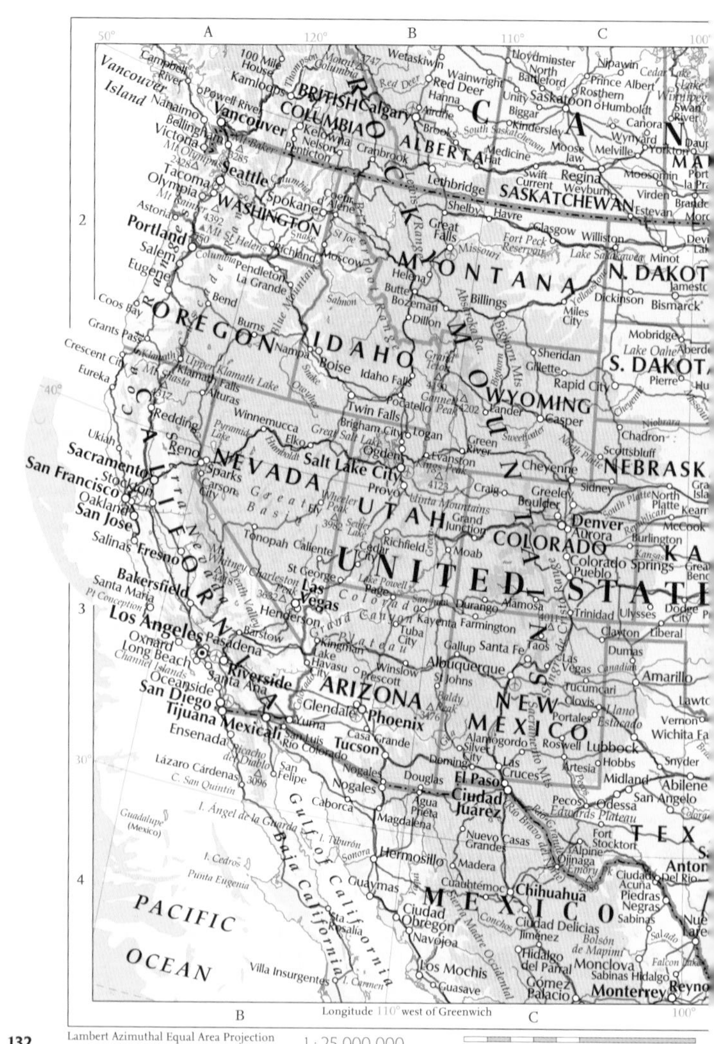

Lambert Azimuthal Equal Area Projection   1 : 25 000 000   MILES 0   250   500

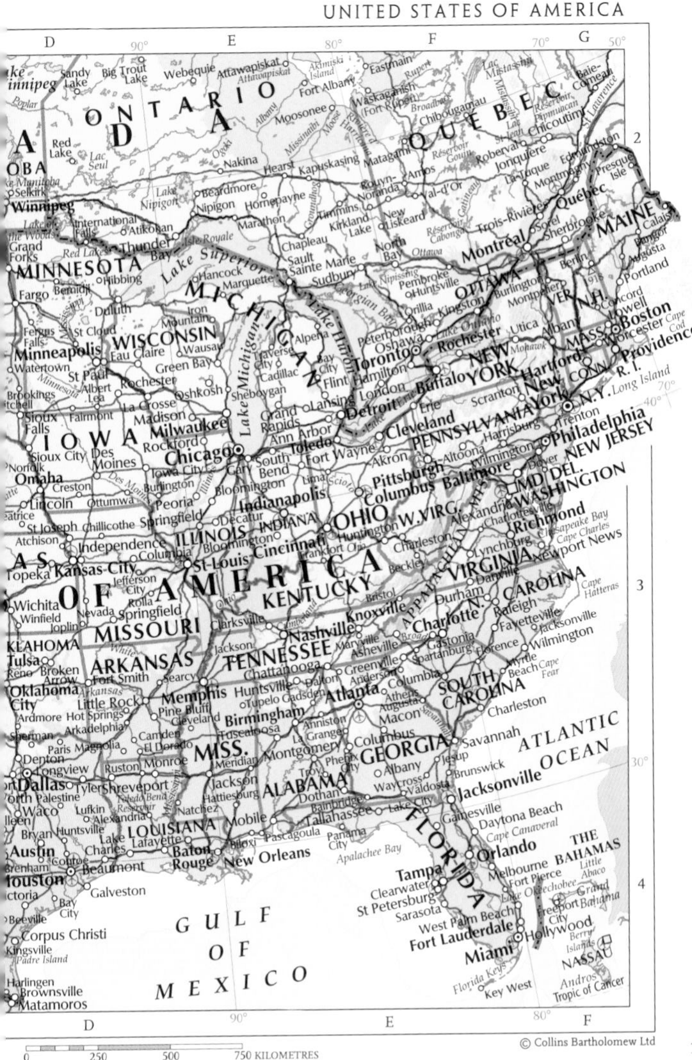

ke
innipeg   Sandy   Big Trout
        Lake   Lake   Webequie   Attawapiskat   Eastmain   Rupert
                                                                Calaba
as   ONTARIO   Fort Albany   Kapuskasing   QUEBEC   Pennimaq
OBA   Red
Lake   Lac   Nakina   Moosonee   Matagami   Chicoutimi   Baie-
        Seul   Roberval   Jonquiere   Comeau
Winnipeg   Atikokan   Beardmore   Kapuskasing   Rouyn-   Val-d'Or   Quebec   Portland
        Lake   Nipigon   Hornepayne   Noranda   New   Sherbrooke   MAINE
the Woods   Thunder   Marathon   Chapleau   Liskeard   Montreal
Grand
Forks   International   Atikokan   Timmins   Sudbury   North Bay   Ottawa   N.H.   Concord
MINNESOTA   Lake Superior   Sault   Sturgeon Bay   Pembroke   Kingston   Burlington   Boston
Fargo   Bemidji   Hibbing   Ironwood   Sainte Marie   Orillia   VER   Cape
Duluth   Marquette   Sudbury   Peterborough   Rochester   Utica   MASS.   Cod
        MICHIGAN   Alpena   Orillia   Toronto   N.Y.   Providence
Minneapolis   Eau Claire   WISCONSIN   Cadillac   Hamilton   Buffalo   Hartford   CONN.   R.I.
Watertown   St Cloud   Wausau   Cheboygan   London   Erie   Scranton   NEW YORK   N.Y.   Long Island
Brookings   Green Bay   Grand   Flint   Detroit   Cleveland   PENNSYLVANIA   Philadelphia
Sioux   Rochester   Oshkosh   Rapids   Lansing   Toledo   Akron   Harrisburg   Wilmington   NEW JERSEY
Falls   IOWA   Milwaukee   Ann Arbor   Fort Wayne   Pittsburgh   Baltimore   DEL.
Sioux City   Des   Rockford   South   Columbus   MD.   WASHINGTON
Omaha   Moines   Iowa City   Chicago   Bend   INDIANA   OHIO   W.VIRG.   Richmond
        Creston   Peoria   Indianapolis   Huntington   Charleston   VIRGINIA   Newport News
S   St Joseph   Chillicothe   Springfield   Cincinnati   Lynchburg   Cape Charles
Topeka   Kansas City   St Louis   Frankfort   Durham   Cape
Atchison   OF   AMERICA   KENTUCKY   Bristol   Raleigh   Hatteras
AS   Jefferson   ILLINOIS   Knoxville   Charlotte   CAROLINA
Wichita   Rolla   Clarksville   Nashville   Greenville   Fayetteville
Winfield   Joplin   MISSOURI   Jackson   Chattanooga   Spartanburg   Wilmington
KLAHOMA   Fort Smith   Searcy   TENNESSEE   Gadsden   SOUTH   Myrtle Beach
Tulsa   Broken   Memphis   Huntsville   Atlanta   Columbia   CAROLINA   Cape Fear
        Arrow   ARKANSAS   Little Rock   Tupelo   Gastonia
Oklahoma   Pine Bluff   Birmingham   Macon   Charleston
City   Hot Springs   Cleveland   GEORGIA   Savannah
Ardmore   Camden   Tuscaloosa   Montgomery   ATLANTIC
Sherman   Magnolia   El Dorado   MISS.   Columbus   Albany
Paris   Monroe   Meridian   Troy   Brunswick   OCEAN
Dallas   Ruston   Jackson   ALABAMA   Dothan   Waycross   Jacksonville
        Shreveport   Hattiesburg   Tallahassee   Valdosta   Gainesville
Waco   Lufkin   Mobile   Pascagoula   Panama   FLORIDA   Daytona Beach
leen   LOUISIANA   City   Apalachee Bay   Cape Canaveral
Austin   Lake   Lafayette   Melbourne   THE
Beaumont   Charles   Baton   New Orleans   Orlando   Fort Pierce   BAHAMAS   Little
ouston   Rouge   Abaco
        Galveston   Clearwater   Tampa   West Palm Beach   Freeport   Grand
Corpus Christi   St Petersburg   Bahama
        Sarasota   Fort Lauderdale   Hollywood   Berry
Kingsville   Miami   Islands
Harlingen   GULF   Key West   Andros   NASSAU
Brownsville   OF   Florida Keys   Tropic of Cancer
Matamoros   MEXICO

0   250   500   750 KILOMETRES

133

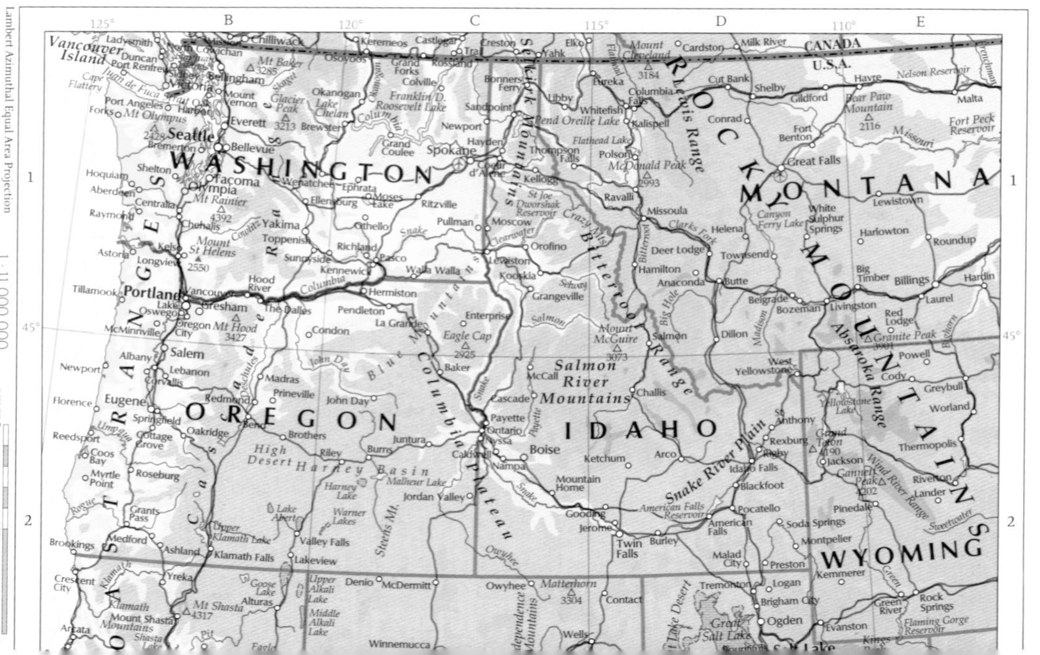

Lambert Azimuthal Equal Area Projection

1 : 11 000 000

MILES 0   100   200

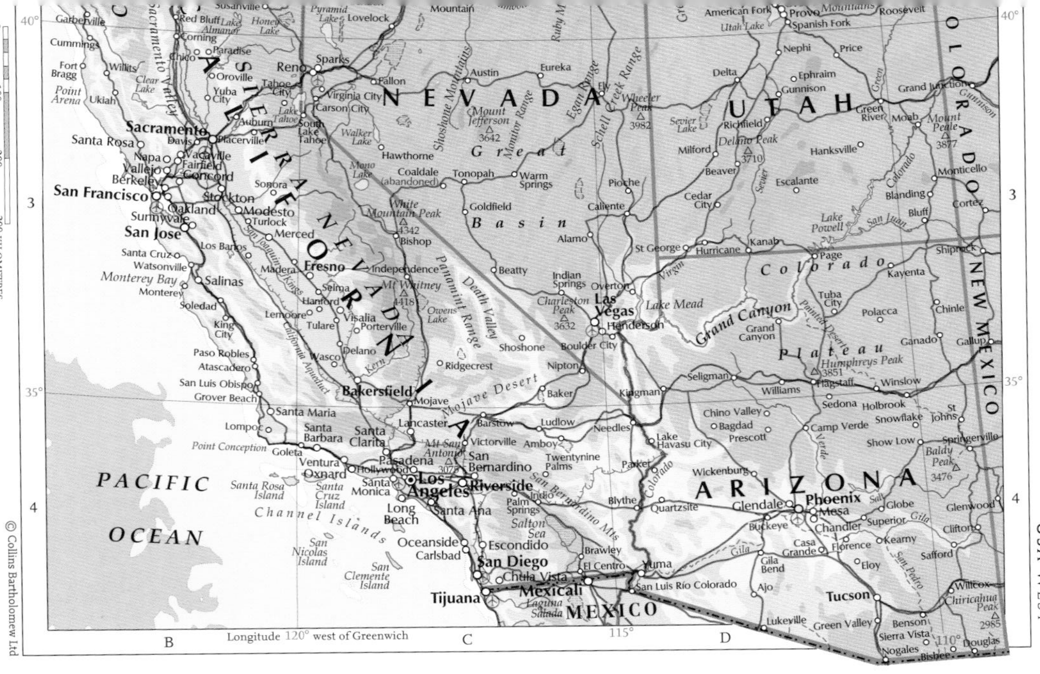

© Collins Bartholomew Ltd

0   100   200   300 KILOMETRES

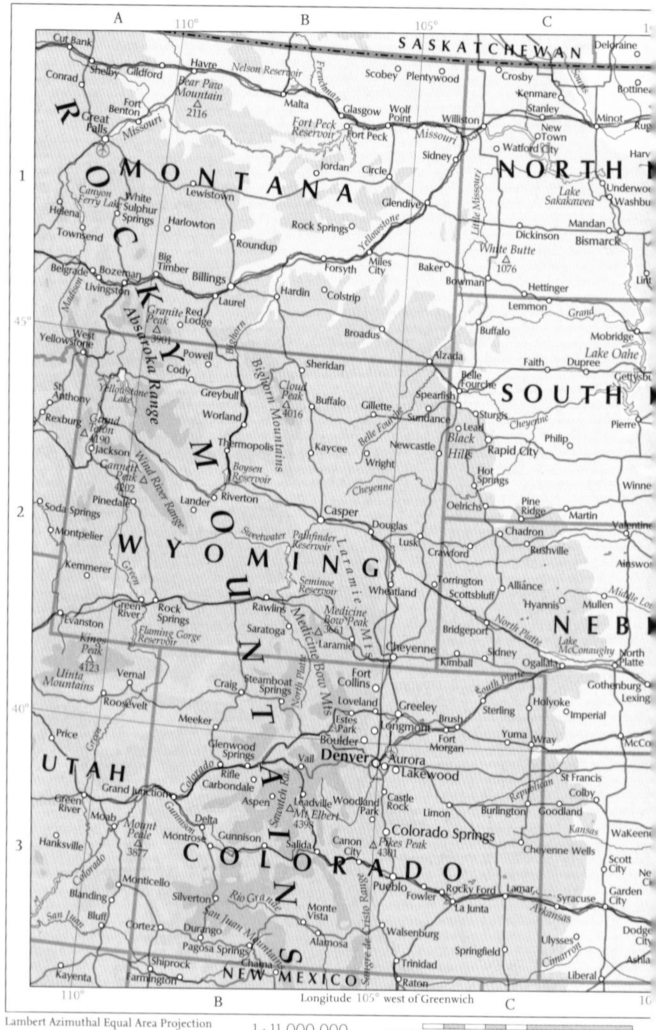

Lambert Azimuthal Equal Area Projection

1 : 11 000 000

MILES 0   100   200

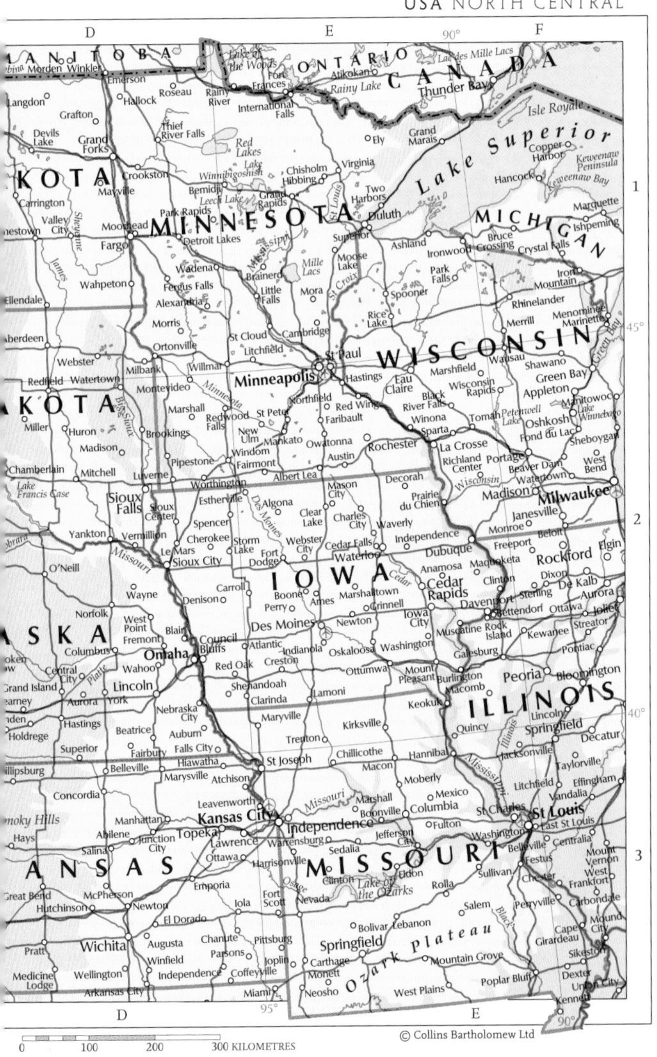
D
E
F
90°
MANITOBA
Morden
Winkler
Emerson
Lake of the Woods
ONTARIO
Fort Frances
Atikokan
Rainy Lake
Lac des Mille Lacs
CANADA
Thunder Bay
Isle Royale
Langdon
Roseau
Hallock
Rainy River
International Falls
Grafton
Devils Lake
Grand Forks
Thief River Falls
Red Lakes
Lake Winnibigoshish
Ely
Grand Marais
Lake Superior
Copper Harbor
Keweenaw Peninsula
Keweenaw Bay
Hancock
KOTA
Crookston
Mayville
Chisholm
Hibbing
Virginia
Bemidji
Leech Lake
Grand Rapids
Two Harbors
Carrington
Park Rapids
MINNESOTA
St Louis
Duluth
MICHIGAN
Marquette
Ishpeming
Valley City
Sheyenne
Jamestown
Moorhead
Fargo
Detroit Lakes
Mississippi
Superior
Ashland
Ironwood
Bruce Crossing
Crystal Falls
James
Wadena
Brainerd
Mille Lacs
Moose Lake
Park Falls
Iron Mountain
Wahpeton
Fergus Falls
Little Falls
Mora
St Croix
Spooner
Rhinelander
Ellendale
Alexandria
Rice Lake
Merrill
Menominee
Marinette
Green Bay
45°
Morris
Cambridge
Aberdeen
St Cloud
Ortonville
Litchfield
WISCONSIN
Wausau
Shawano
St Paul
Webster
Milbank
Willmar
Marshfield
Green Bay
Redfield
Watertown
Minneapolis
Hastings
Eau Claire
Wisconsin Rapids
Appleton
Montevideo
Minnesota
Manitowoc
AKOTA
Northfield
Black River Falls
Big Sioux
Marshall
Red Wing
Winona
Tomah
Petenwell Lake
Oshkosh
Lake Winnebago
Miller
Redwood Falls
St Peter
Faribault
Sparta
Fond du Lac
Huron
Brookings
New Ulm
Mankato
Owatonna
Rochester
La Crosse
Sheboygan
Madison
Windom
Austin
Richland Center
Portage
West Bend
Pipestone
Fairmont
Beaver Dam
Chamberlain
Mitchell
Luverne
Albert Lea
Decorah
Wisconsin
Watertown
Lake Francis Case
Worthington
Mason City
Prairie du Chien
Madison
Milwaukee
Sioux Falls
Estherville
Algona
Sioux Center
Des Moines
Clear Lake
Charles City
Janesville
2
Spencer
Waverly
Monroe
Beloit
Yankton
Vermillion
Cherokee
Storm Lake
Webster City
Cedar Falls
Independence
Freeport
Elgin
Le Mars
Fort Dodge
Waterloo
Dubuque
Rockford
Missouri
Sioux City
Maquoketa
O'Neill
IOWA
Anamosa
Dixon
Cedar
Cedar Rapids
Clinton
De Kalb
Carroll
Wayne
Denison
Boone
Marshalltown
Sterling
Aurora
Ames
Perry
Grinnell
Davenport
Bettendorf
Ottawa
Joliet
Norfolk
West Point
Iowa City
Blair
Des Moines
Newton
Muscatine
Rock Island
Kewanee
Streator
Fremont
Council Bluffs
NEBRASKA
Columbus
Omaha
Atlantic
Indianola
Oskaloosa
Washington
Galesburg
Pontiac
Wahoo
Red Oak
Creston
Central City
Platte
Ottumwa
Mount Pleasant
Burlington
Peoria
Bloomington
Grand Island
Lincoln
Shenandoah
Aurora
York
Clarinda
Lamoni
Macomb
ILLINOIS
Kearney
Nebraska City
Keokuk
Hastings
Maryville
Kirksville
Illinois
Lincoln
Springfield
40°
Beatrice
Auburn
Quincy
Decatur
Holdrege
Superior
Fairbury
Falls City
Trenton
Chillicothe
Hannibal
Jacksonville
Hiawatha
St Joseph
Macon
Taylorville
Phillipsburg
Belleville
Marysville
Atchison
Moberly
Mississippi
Litchfield
Effingham
Concordia
Leavenworth
Missouri
Marshall
Mexico
Vandalia
Smoky Hills
Manhattan
Kansas City
Boonville
Columbia
St Charles
St Louis
Independence
Fulton
East St Louis
Hays
Abilene
Junction City
Topeka
Lawrence
Warrensburg
Jefferson City
Washington
Centralia
Salina
Sedalia
Belleville
Mount Vernon
KANSAS
Ottawa
Harrisonville
MISSOURI
Festus
Sullivan
3
Clinton
Lake of the Ozarks
Eldon
Osage
Chester
West Frankfort
Great Bend
McPherson
Emporia
Fort Scott
Rolla
Hutchinson
Newton
Iola
Nevada
Salem
Perryville
Carbondale
El Dorado
Black
Bolivar
Lebanon
Mound City
Augusta
Chanute
Pittsburg
Springfield
Ozark Plateau
Cape Girardeau
Pratt
Wichita
Parsons
Joplin
Carthage
Mountain Grove
Sikeston
Winfield
Monett
Medicine Lodge
Wellington
Independence
Coffeyville
Poplar Bluff
Dexter
Arkansas City
Miami
Neosho
West Plains
Union City
Kennett
95°
D
E
90°
0
100
200
300 KILOMETRES

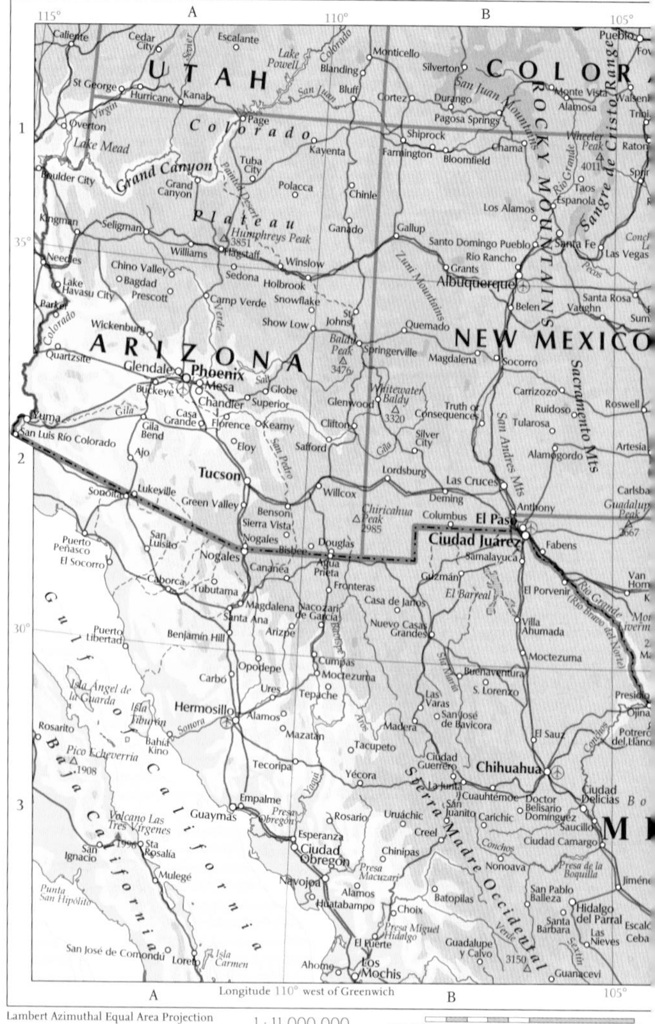

Lambert Azimuthal Equal Area Projection   1 : 11 000 000   MILES 0   100   200

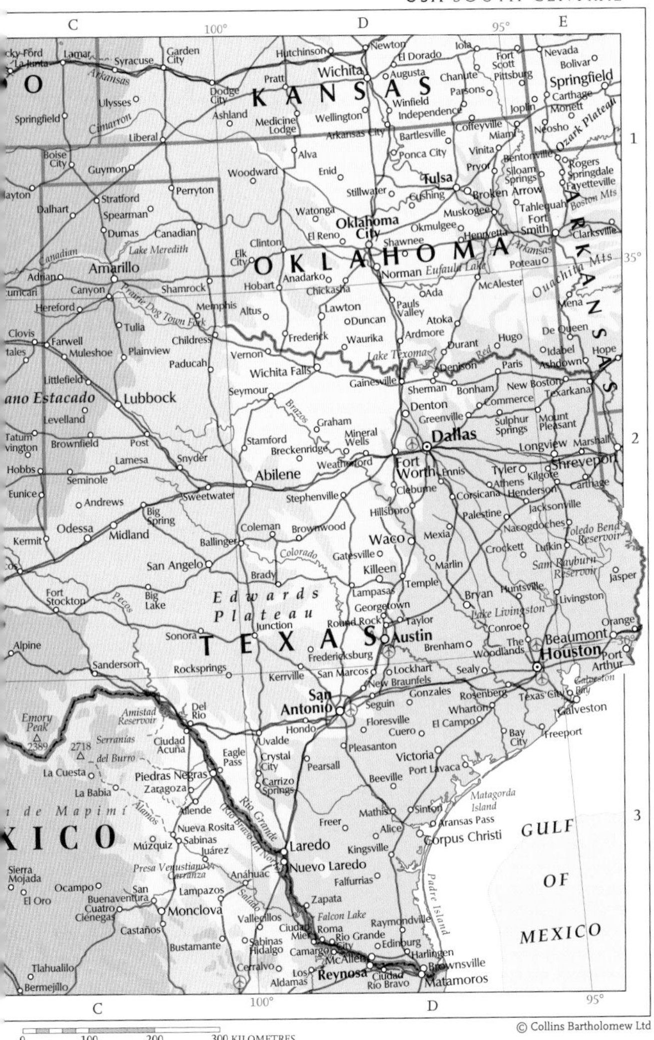

© Collins Bartholomew Ltd

KANSAS
OKLAHOMA
TEXAS
ARKANSAS
MEXICO
GULF OF MEXICO
Wichita
Tulsa
Oklahoma City
Amarillo
Lubbock
Dallas
Fort Worth
Abilene
Waco
Austin
San Antonio
Houston
Beaumont
Laredo
Nuevo Laredo
Corpus Christi
Brownsville
Matamoros
Reynosa
McAllen
Monclova
Shreveport
Springfield
Edwards Plateau
Llano Estacado
Rio Grande
Ozark Plateau
Ouachita Mts
Lake Texoma
Padre Island
0 100 200 300 KILOMETRES

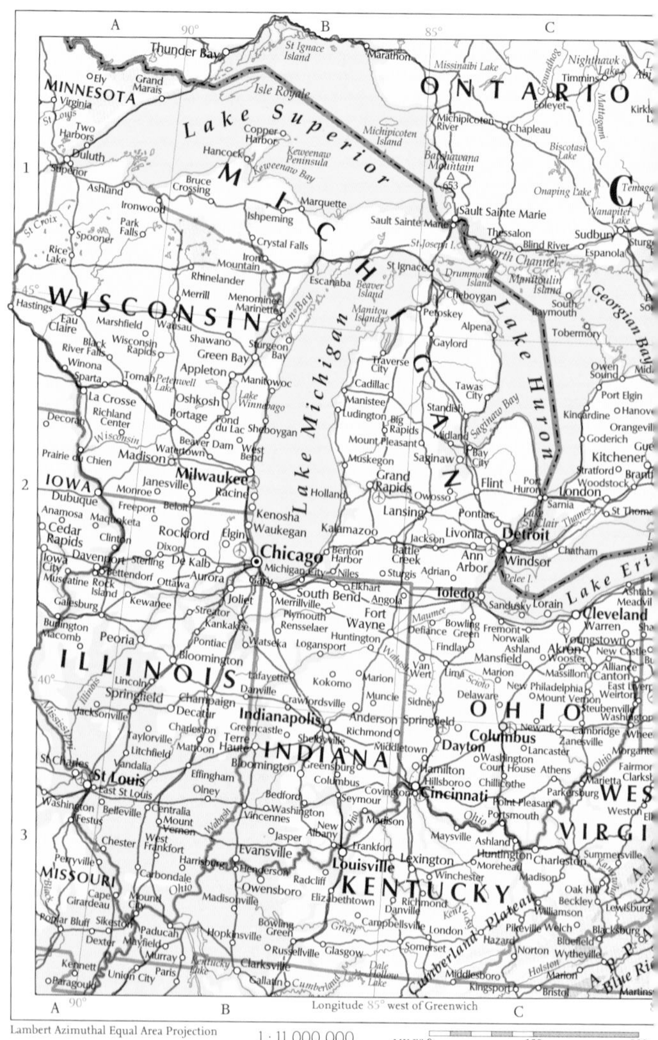

MINNESOTA
Thunder Bay
St Ignace Island
Marathon
Missinaibi Lake
Nighthawk Lake
Timmins
Ely
Grand Marais
Isle Royale
ONTARIO
Foleyet
Kirkl
Virginia
Two Harbors
Lake Superior
Michipicoten River
Chapleau
Biscotasi Lake
Duluth
Superior
Copper Harbor
Keweenaw Bay
Keweenaw Peninsula
Michipicoten Island
Onaping Lake
Wanapitei Lake
Ashland
Ironwood
Hancock
MICHIGAN
Batchawana Mountain
Sudbury
Espanola
Park Falls
Bruce Crossing
Marquette
Ishpeming
Sault Sainte Marie
Sault Sainte Marie
Thessalon
Blind River
Sturg
Rice Lake
Spooner
Crystal Falls
Iron Mountain
St Joseph I
North Channel
Drummond Island
Manitoulin Island
Georgian Bay
Hastings
Eau Claire
WISCONSIN
Rhinelander
Merrill
Menominee
Marinette
Escanaba
Beaver Island
St Ignace
Cheboygan
South Baymouth
Tobermory
Owen Sound
Black River Falls
Marshfield
Wausau
Shawano
Green Bay
Sturgeon Bay
Green Bay
Manitou Islands
Petoskey
Alpena
Port Elgin
Kincardine
Hanove
Winona
Sparta
Appleton
Gaylord
Orangeville
La Crosse
Oshkosh
Lake Winnebago
Manitowoc
Cadillac
Traverse City
Tawas City
Goderich
Stratford
Kitchener
Brant
Decorah
Richland Center
Portage
Fond du Lac
Sheboygan
Manistee
Big Rapids
Midland
Saginaw Bay
Woodstock
London
St Thom
Prairie du Chien
Beaver Dam
West Bend
Ludington
Mount Pleasant
Saginaw
Bay City
IOWA
Madison
Watertown
Milwaukee
Muskegon
Grand Rapids
Flint
Port Huron
Sarnia
Dubuque
Janesville
Monroe
Beloit
Racine
Holland
Lansing
Owosso
Pontiac
Detroit
Clair
St Clair
London
St Thom
Anamosa
Maquoketa
Freeport
Rockford
Elgin
Kenosha
Waukegan
Kalamazoo
Jackson
Livonia
Windsor
Chatham
Cedar Rapids
Clinton
Dixon
De Kalb
Chicago
Benton Harbor
Battle Creek
Ann Arbor
Adrian
Lake Erie
Iowa City
Davenport
Sterling
Aurora
Michigan City
Niles
Sturgis
Toledo
Sandusky
Lorain
Cleveland
Muscatine
Rock Island
Ottawa
Joliet
South Bend
Elkhart
Bowling Green
Fremont
Norwalk
Akron
Youngstown
New Castle
Galesburg
Kewanee
Streator
Kankakee
Merrillville
Plymouth
Fort Wayne
Defiance
Findlay
Ashland
Mansfield
Wooster
Massillon
Canton
Alliance
East Liver
Weirton
Burlington
Macomb
Peoria
Pontiac
Catska
Rensselaer
Huntington
Logansport
Van Wert
Lima
Marion
Delaware
New Philadelphia
Mount Vernon
Washington
Wheel
ILLINOIS
Bloomington
Lincoln
Danville
Lafayette
Kokomo
Marion
Muncie
Sidney
Springfield
Newark
Columbus
Cambridge
Zanesville
Morgan
Springfield
Decatur
Champaign
Crawfordsville
Anderson
Springfield
OHIO
Lancaster
Jacksonville
Charleston
Taylorville
Terre Haute
Greencastle
Indianapolis
Shelbyville
Richmond
Middletown
Dayton
Hamilton
Washington Court House
Athens
Marietta
Clarks
Fairmon
St Charles
St Louis
Litchfield
Mattoon
INDIANA
Bloomington
Greensburg
Columbus
Hillsboro
Chillicothe
Cincinnati
Portsmouth
Mount Pleasant
Parkersburg
WES
East St Louis
Vandalia
Effingham
Olney
Bedford
Washington
Seymour
Covington
Maysville
Ashland
Huntington
Charleston
VIRGI
Washington
Belleville
Centralia
Mount Vernon
Vincennes
Jasper
New Albany
Frankfort
Morehead
Madison
Oak Hill
Summersville
Lewisburg
Weston
Prestou
Chester
West Frankfort
Harrisburg
Shawneetown
Evansville
Louisville
Lexington
London
Beckley
MISSOURI
Perryville
Carbondale
Olton
Madisonville
Owensboro
Radcliff
Elizabethtown
KENTUCKY
Campbellsville
Danville
Somerset
Williamson
Welch
Blacksburg
Princet
Bluefiel
Cape Girardeau
Mount
Paducah
Hopkinsville
Bowling Green
Russellville
Glasgow
Cumberland Plateau
Hazard
Norton
Wytheville
Marion
Poplar Bluff
Sikeston
Mayfield
Dexter
Murray
Clarksville
Dale Hollow Lake
Middlesboro
Kingsport
Bristol
Abe Rive
Kennett
Piragould
Union City
Paris
Gallatin
Cumberland

A 90°
B
Longitude 85° west of Greenwich
C

Lambert Azimuthal Equal Area Projection
1 : 11 000 000
MILES 0
100
200

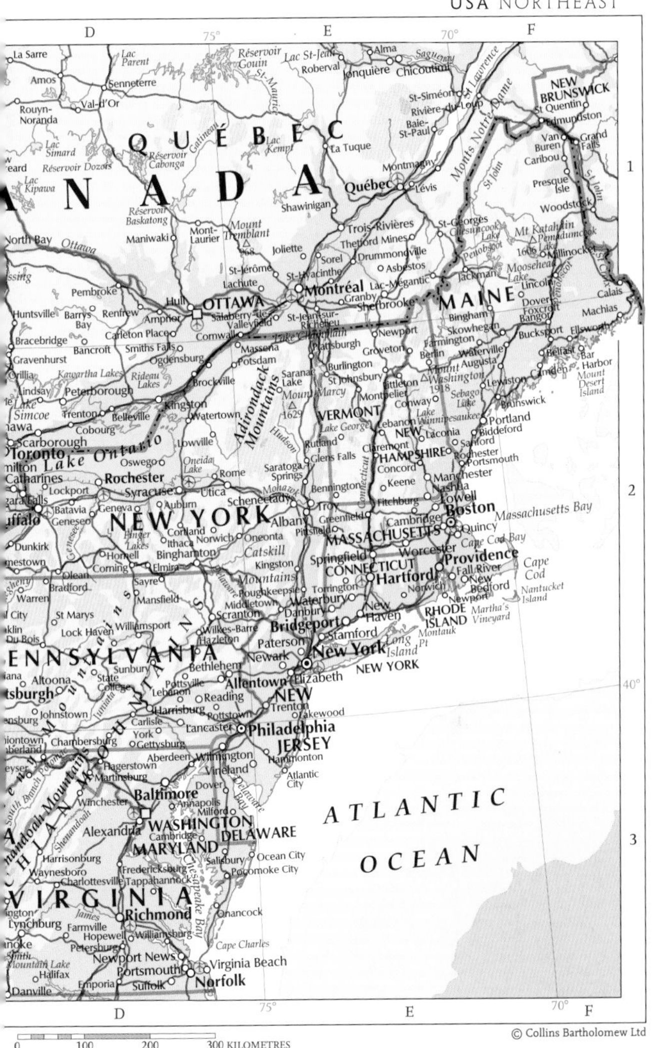
QUÉBEC
CANADA
NEW BRUNSWICK
MAINE
VERMONT
NEW HAMPSHIRE
MASSACHUSETTS
CONNECTICUT
RHODE ISLAND
NEW YORK
PENNSYLVANIA
NEW JERSEY
DELAWARE
MARYLAND
VIRGINIA
WASHINGTON
OTTAWA
Montréal
Québec
Boston
New York
Philadelphia
Baltimore
Providence
Hartford
Richmond
Norfolk
Rochester
Toronto
Lake Ontario
Adirondack Mountains
Catskill Mountains
Massachusetts Bay
Cape Cod
ATLANTIC OCEAN
300 KILOMETRES

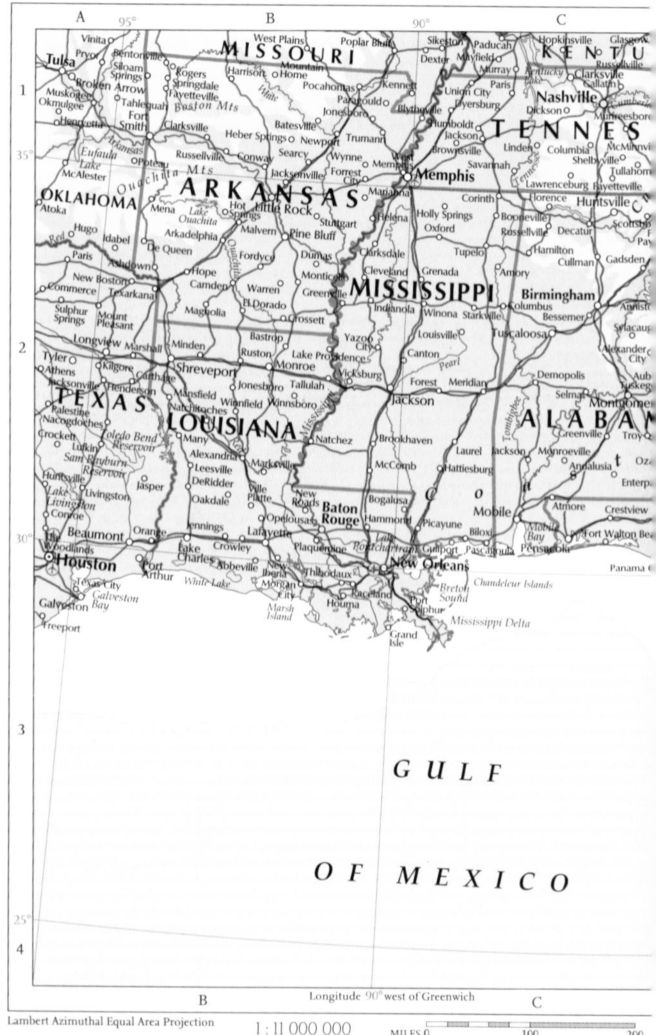

Lambert Azimuthal Equal Area Projection   1 : 11 000 000   MILES 0   100   200

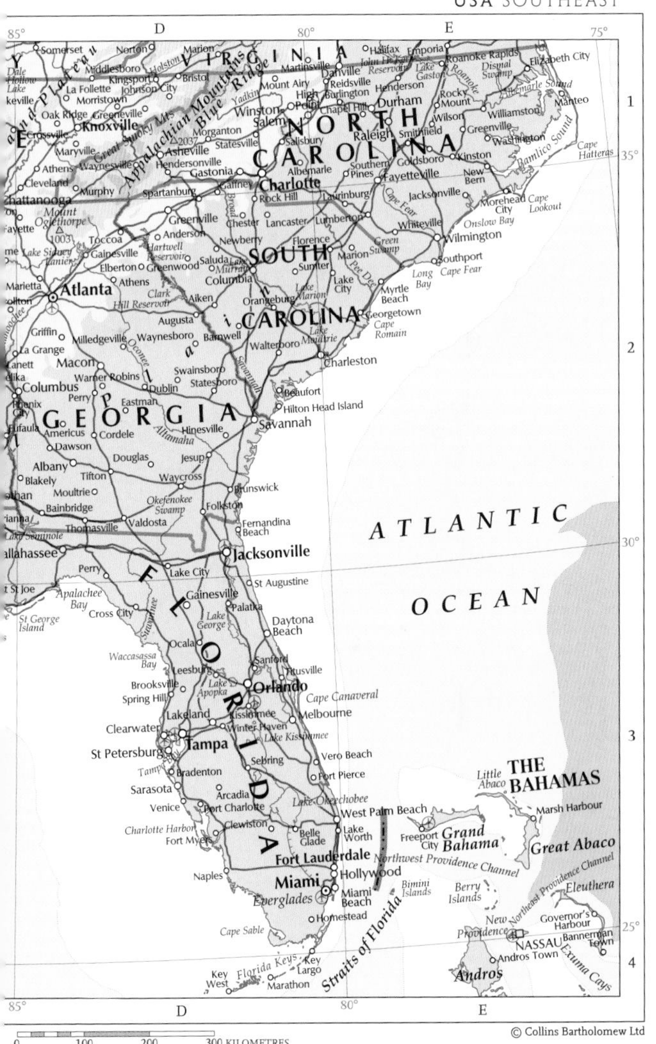

0 100 200 300 KILOMETRES

© Collins Bartholomew Ltd

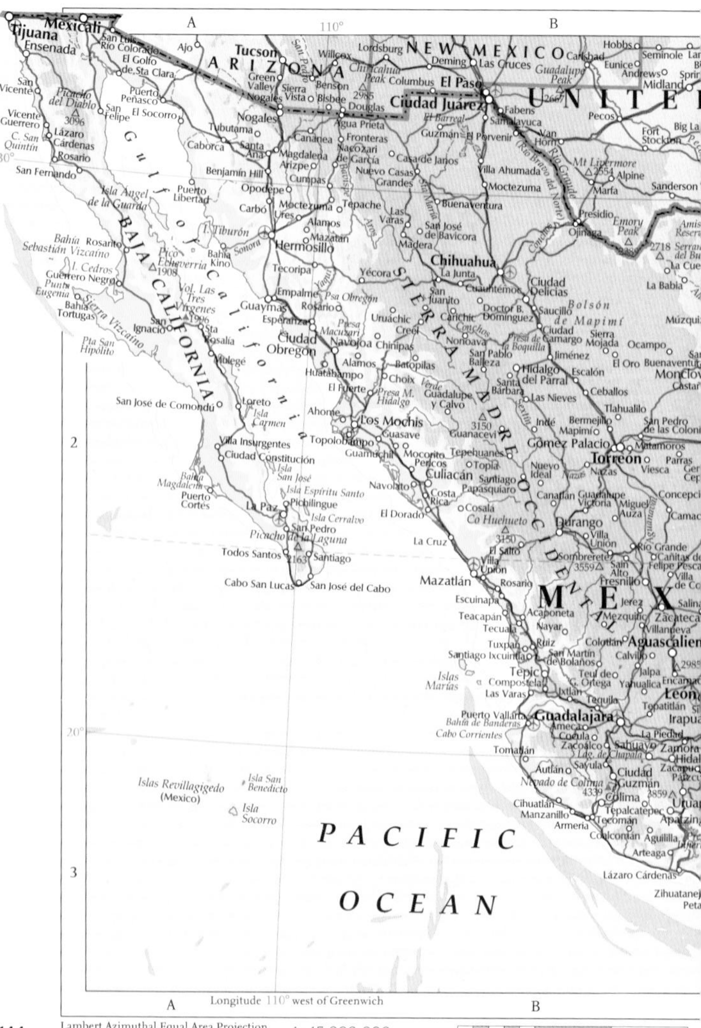

A B

110°

Mexicali Tijuana
Ensenada

San Luis
Río Colorado
El Golfo
de Sta. Clara

NEW MEXICO

ARIZONA

Tucson

Lordsburg
Deming Las Cruces
Peak Columbus El Paso

Carlsbad

Hobbs

Seminole
Eunice Andrews
Sprin

San
Vicente
Guerrero
C. San
Quintín

Ajo

Willcox
Green Sierra Benson
Valley Vista
Nogales
Douglas
Bisbee

Ciudad Juárez

Fabens

UNITE
Pecos

Midland

Big La

San Felipe
Pinacho
del Diablo
3096

San
Felipe
San
Pedro
Puerto
Peñasco
El Socorro

Nogales
Cananea
Fronteras
Naco
de García
Agua Prieta

Guzmán

El Porvenir
Samalayuca

Van
Horn

Fort
Stockton

Rosario
San Fernando

Tubutama
Caborca
Magdalena
Arizpe
Casas Janos
Villa Ahumada

Moctezuma

Presidio

Marfa

Alpine

Sanderson

30°

Benjamín Hill
Opodepe
Cumpas
Nuevo Casas
Grandes

Buenaventura

Emory
Peak

Ojinaga

Amis
Reserv

2718 Serran
del Bu
Que C

La Babia

Isla Ángel
de la Guarda

Carbó
Tres

Moctezuma
Tepache

Chihuahua

Bahía Rosario
Sebastián Vizcaíno
I. Cedros
Guerrero Negro
Punta
Eugenia
Bahía
Tortugas
Pta San
Hipólito

Tiburón

Puerto
Libertad

Hermosillo

Kino

Sahuaripa

La Junta

Las
Varas
San José
de Bavicora
Madera

Ciudad
Delicias

San
Juanito
Cuauhtémoc

Doctor J.
Domínguez

Camargo
Saucillo

Bolsón
de Mapimí

Múzquiz

Sierra
Mojada

Pta
Abreojos
Isla las
Tres
Vírgenes
Vol. las
Tres
Vírgenes
1908

Bahía
Kino

Tecoripa
Yécora

Creel

San Pablo
Baleza

Hidalgo
del Parral

Jiménez

El Oro
Escalón
Ceballos

Ocampo

Monclo
Buenaventu
Cuatro Ciénegas

Costan

San Ignacio
Sta
Rosalía
Mulegé

Empalme
Guaymas
Rosario
Esperanza
Ciudad
Obregón

Pía Obregón

Urvachic

Chinipas
Batopilas
Las Nieves
Inde
Bermejillo
Mapimí

Tlahualilo
San Pedro
de las Coloni

Las
Barbara
y Calvo

SIERRA

MADRE

Gómez Palacio

Matamoros

San José de Comondú

Loreto
Isla
del
Carmen

Huatabampo
Álamos
El Fuerte

Presa M.
Hidalgo

Choix
Presa
Guadalupe

Guanaceví
Santiago
Papasquiaro

Torreón

Viesca

Gerr
Cep

3150

Nazas
Cuencamé

2

Isla
Insurgentes
Ciudad Constitución
Isla
Santa
Magdalena
Puerto
Cortés

Topolobampo
Los Mochis
Guasave
Guamúchil
Mocorito

Ahome

Tepehuanes

Nuevo
Ideal

Canatlán

Cañitas de
Felipe Pescad

Río Grande

Concepci

DEL

Guadalupe
Victoria

Durango

Villa
Unión

Villa
Miguel
Auza

La Paz
Pichilingue
Isla Espíritu Santo
Isla Cerralvo
Pinacho de la Laguna

San Pedro

El Dorado

Navolato
Culiacán

Costa
Rica

Pericos

Cosalá
Co Huehueto

3150

El Salto
Sombrerete

Canelas

Villa
Nueva

Sain
Alto

Fresnillo

Jerez

Zacatecas
Villanueva

Salin

Todos Santos

Cabo San Lucas
San José del Cabo

Santiago

La Cruz

Rosario

MEX

Mezquital

Calvillo

Aguascalien

Mazatlán

Escuinapa
Teacapán
Tecuala

Acaponeta
Nayar

Rivas

Tuxpan
Santiago Ixcuintla

Islas
Marías

Tepic

San Martín
de Bolaños

Colotlán

Tepatitlán
Jalpa
Teocaltiche

Huejuquilla

Calvillo

2995

Encarnac

20°

Compostela
Las Varas

Ixtlán
Tequila

Ameca

Yahualica

León

Irapua

Puerto Vallarta
Bahía de Banderas
Cabo Corrientes

Guadalajara

Cocula

Zacoalco

La Piedad

La Barca
Sahuayo

Jiquilpan
 SLa
Chapala

Tomatlán

Sayula

Autlán

Nevado de Colima
4339

Cihuatlán

Ciudad
Guzmán

Ocotlán
Ciudad
Pénjamo

Zamora

Uruar
Apatzing

Colima

Tecalitpec
Tecomán

Manzanillo

Armería

3859

Coalcomán

Aguililla

Arteaga

PACIFIC

Islas Revillagigedo
(Mexico)

Isla San
Benedicto

Isla
Socorro

OCEAN

Lázaro Cárdenas

Zihuatane
Peta

3

Longitude 110° west of Greenwich

A B

144 Lambert Azimuthal Equal Area Projection 1 : 15 000 000 MILES 0 100 200 300

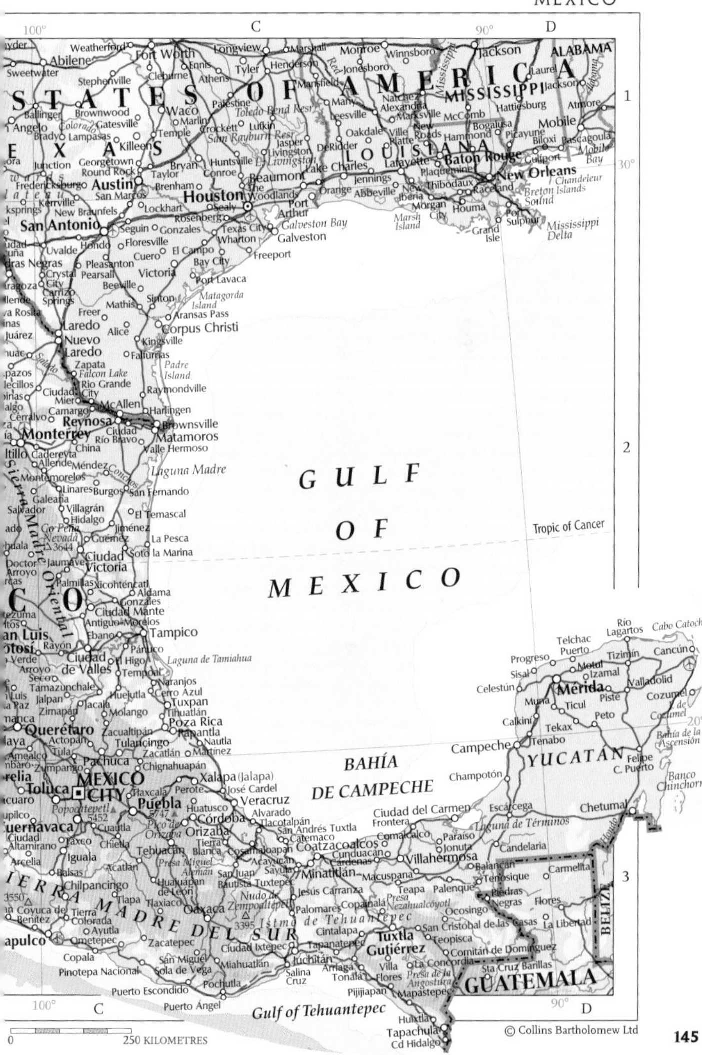
GULF OF MEXICO
BAHÍA DE CAMPECHE
Gulf of Tehuantepec
STATES OF AMERICA
LOUISIANA
MISSISSIPPI
ALABAMA
GUATEMALA
BELIZE
YUCATÁN
Tropic of Cancer
SIERRA MADRE DEL SUR
Houston
San Antonio
New Orleans
Baton Rouge
Monterrey
Tampico
Veracruz
MEXICO CITY
Puebla
Oaxaca
Mérida
Campeche
Villahermosa
Tuxtla Gutiérrez
250 KILOMETRES
© Collins Bartholomew Ltd

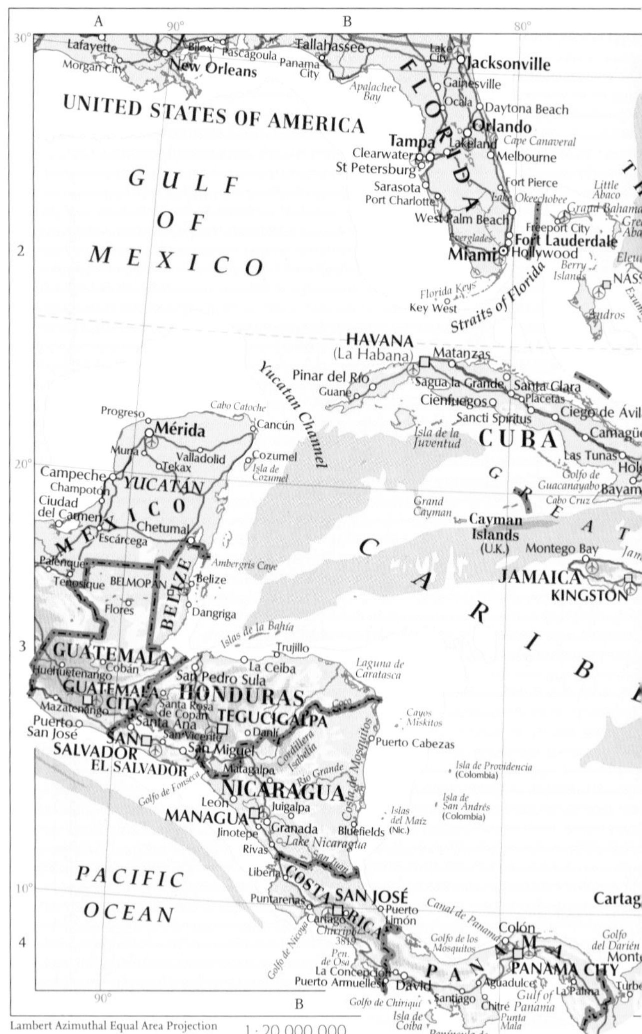

Lambert Azimuthal Equal Area Projection   1 : 20 000 000

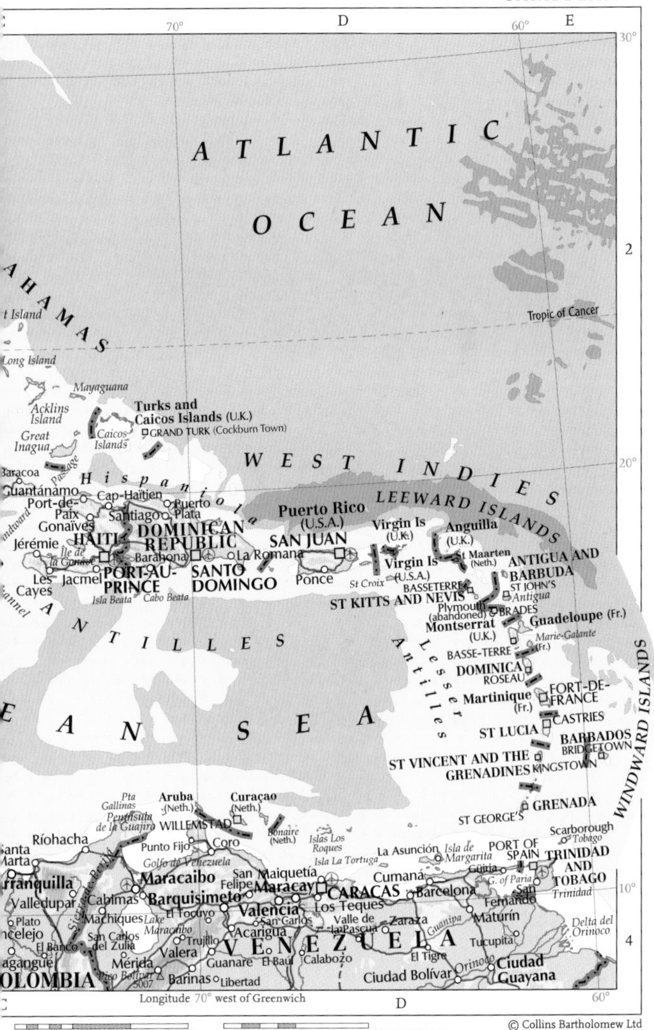

ATLANTIC

OCEAN

Tropic of Cancer

B A H A M A S

Cat Island

Long Island

Mayaguana

Acklins
Island

Great
Inagua

Caicos
Islands

Turks and
Caicos Islands (U.K.)
GRAND TURK (Cockburn Town)

W E S T   I N D I E S

Baracoa

Guantánamo

Port-de-
Paix

Cap-Haïtien

Santiago

Puerto
Plata

H i s p a n i o l a

Puerto Rico
(U.S.A.)

LEEWARD ISLANDS

Anguilla
(U.K.)

Gonaïves

Jérémie

Île de
la Gonâve

HAITI

DOMINICAN
REPUBLIC

SAN JUAN

Virgin Is
(U.K.)

St Maarten
(Neth.)

ANTIGUA AND
BARBUDA

Les
Cayes

Jacmel

PORT-AU-
PRINCE

SANTO
DOMINGO

Barahona

La Romana

Ponce

Virgin Is
(U.S.A.)

St Croix

BASSETERRE

Antigua

ST JOHN'S

Isla Beata   Cabo Beata

ST KITTS AND NEVIS

Plymouth
(abandoned)

BRADES

Guadeloupe (Fr.)

A N T I L L E S

Montserrat
(U.K.)

Marie-Galante

DOMINICA
ROSEAU

C A R I B B E A N   S E A

Martinique
(Fr.)

FORT-DE-
FRANCE

L e s s e r   A n t i l l e s

ST LUCIA

CASTRIES

BARBADOS
BRIDGETOWN

ST VINCENT AND THE
GRENADINES

KINGSTOWN

Pta
Gallinas

Aruba
(Neth.)

Curaçao
(Neth.)

ST GEORGE'S

GRENADA

WINDWARD ISLANDS

Ríohacha

Península
de la Guajira

Punto Fijo

Coro

WILLEMSTAD

Bonaire
(Neth.)

Islas Los
Roques

Scarborough
Tobago

PORT OF
SPAIN

Santa
Marta

Golfo de Venezuela

San
Felipe

Maiquetía

La Asunción

Isla de
Margarita

Isla La Tortuga

Cumaná

G. of Paria

TRINIDAD
AND
TOBAGO

Barranquilla

Valledupar

Cabimas

Barquisimeto

Maracay

Maracaibo

San Carlos
del Zulia

El Tocuyo

San
Carlos

Los Teques

CARACAS

Valencia

Valle de
La Pascua

Barcelona

Maturín

Trinidad

El Plato

Machiques

Lake
Maracaibo

Trujillo

Guanare

Zaraza

Guanipa

Delta del
Orinoco

Ocelejo

San Banco

Mérida

Valera

El Baúl

Calabozo

El Tigre

Tucupita

OLOMBIA

Arauca

Río Meta

Barinas

Libertad

VENEZUELA

Ciudad Bolívar

Orinoco

Ciudad
Guayana

S 0   100   200   300   0   200   400 KILOMETRES

© Collins Bartholomew Ltd

147

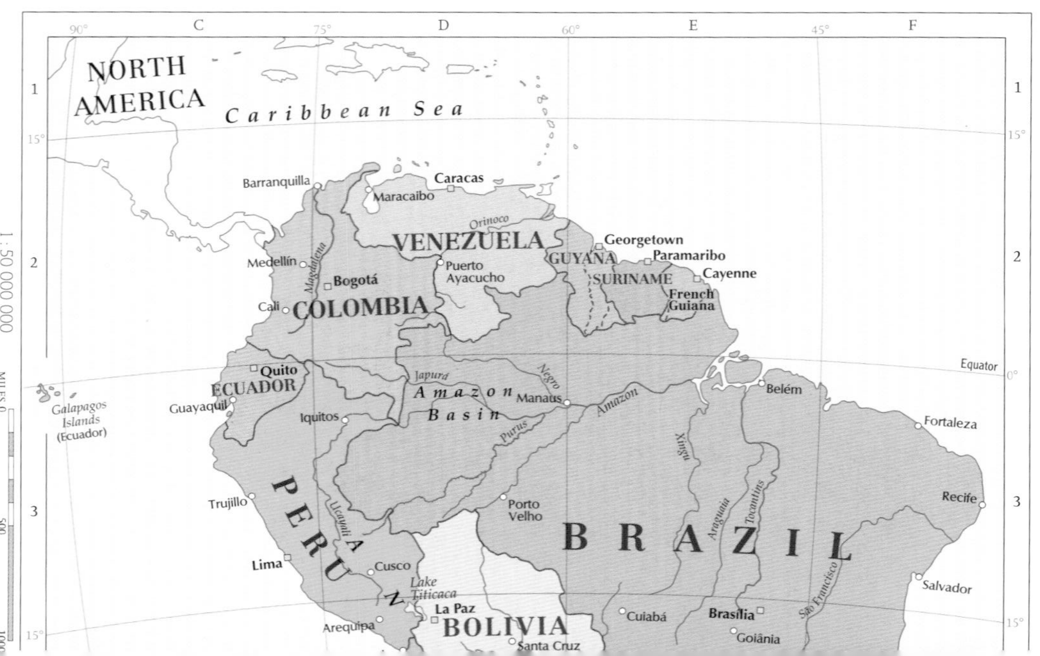

NORTH AMERICA

Caribbean Sea

Barranquilla
Maracaibo
Caracas
VENEZUELA
Puerto
Ayacucho
Orinoco
COLOMBIA
Bogotá
Medellín
Cali
Quito
ECUADOR
Guayaquil
Galápagos Islands
(Ecuador)
Trujillo
Iquitos
Lima
PERU
Cusco
Arequipa
Ucayali
Apurímac
Juruá
Japurá
Magdalena
Negro
Amazon Basin
Manaus
Purus
Porto
Velho
Lake
Titicaca
La Paz
BOLIVIA
Santa Cruz
GUYANA
Georgetown
Paramaribo
SURINAME
French
Guiana
Cayenne
Xingu
Amazon
Belém
BRAZIL
Tocantins
Araguaia
Cuiabá
Brasília
Goiânia
São Francisco
Fortaleza
Recife
Salvador

Equator

15°
45°
60°
75°
90°

0°

F
E
D
C

1
2
3

15°

148

1 : 50 000 000

MILES 0   500   1000

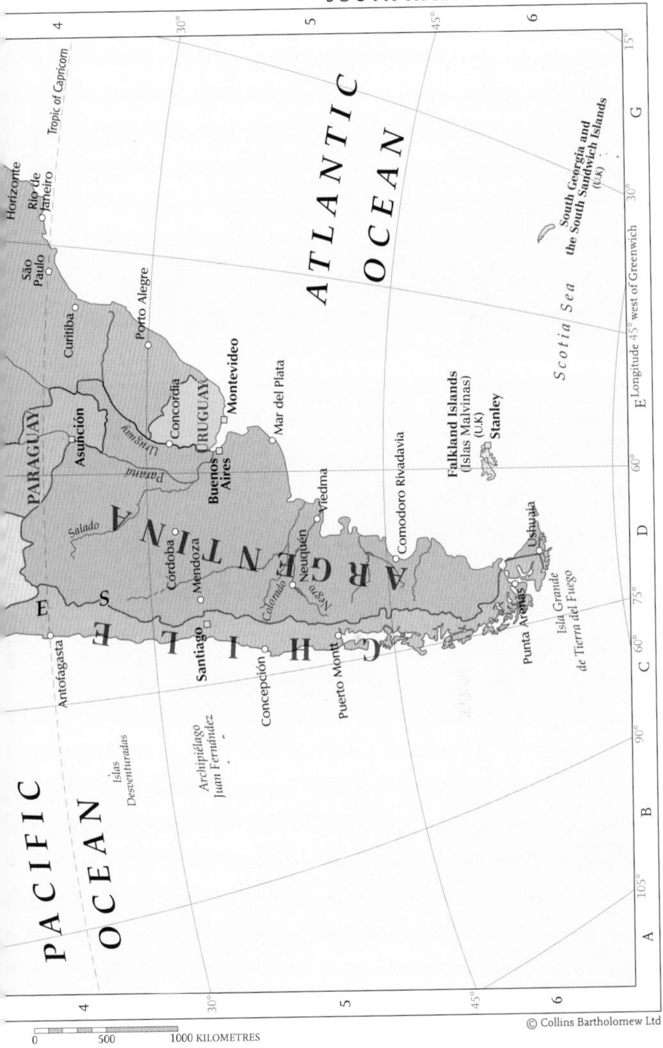

PACIFIC

OCEAN

ATLANTIC

OCEAN

Tropic of Capricorn

Horizonte

Río de Janeiro

São Paulo

Curitiba

Porto Alegre

PARAGUAY

Asunción

Paraná

Concordia

URUGUAY

Montevideo

Mar del Plata

Buenos Aires

Salado

ARGENTINA

Córdoba

Mendoza

Colorado

Neuquén

Negro

Viedma

Comodoro Rivadavia

Salado

CHILE

E

S

CHILE

Santiago

Antofagasta

Concepción

Puerto Montt

Islas Desventuradas

Archipiélago Juan Fernández

Isla Grande de Tierra del Fuego

Punta Arenas

Ushuaia

Falkland Islands
(Islas Malvinas)
(UK)
Stanley

Scotia Sea

South Georgia and
the South Sandwich Islands
(UK)

E Longitude 45° west of Greenwich

30°

45°

60°

75°

90°

105°

15°

30°

45°

60°

75°

90°

105°

4

30°

5

45°

6

15°

A

B

C

D

E

F

G

© Collins Bartholomew Ltd

0   500   1000 KILOMETRES

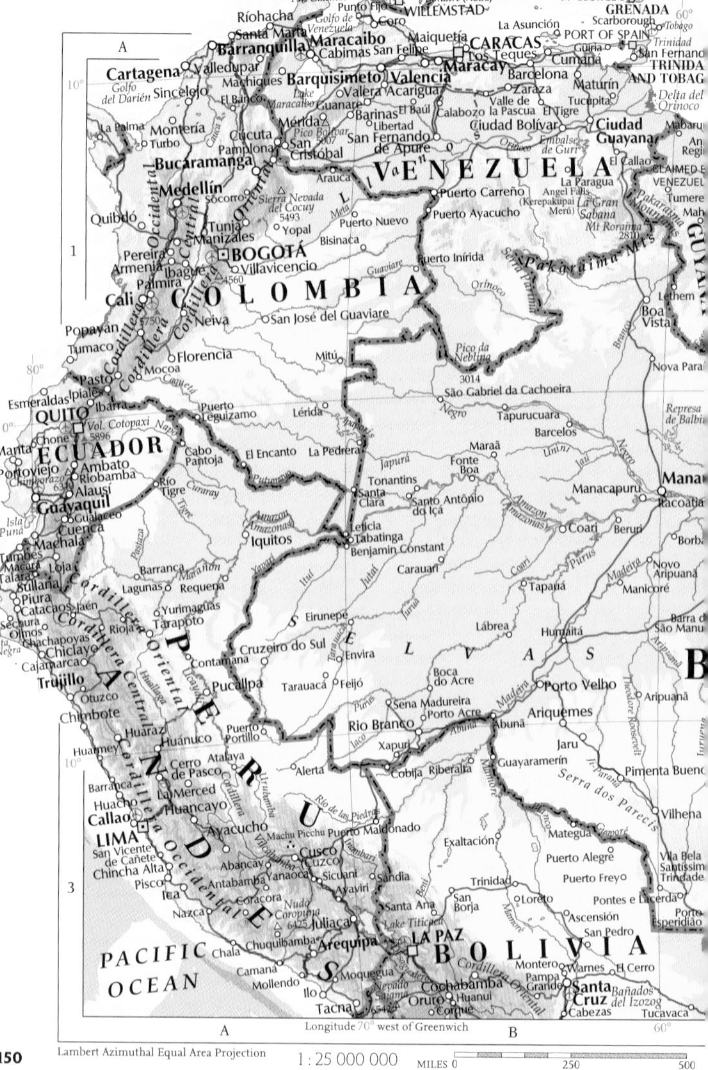

Aruba (Neth.) Curaçao (Neth.)
ST GEORGE'S
Pta Gallinas Bonaire (Neth.) GRENADA
Ríohacha Golfo de Pta Fijas WILLEMSTAD Scarborough
Santa Marta Coro La Asunción PORT OF SPAIN Trinidad
Cartagena Barranquilla Maracaibo Maiquetía CARACAS Cumaná TRINIDAD
Golfo del Darién Sincelejo Valledupar San Felipe Los Teques Barcelona AND TOBAGO
El Banco Cabimas Valera Acarigua Maturín Delta del
La Palma Montería Lake Maracaibo Valencia Calabozo El Tigre Ciudad Orinoco
La Turbo Cúcuta Mérida Barinas San Fernando Ciudad Guayana Maburu
Quibdó Bucaramanga Pico Bolívar de Apure Embalse An
Medellín Pamplona 5007 Libertad Ciudad Bolívar de Guri Regi
Socorro San Arauca El Callao CLAIMED BY
Sierra Nevada Cristóbal La Paragua VENEZUEL
Manizales de Cocuy Angel Falls Tumere
Pereira Tunja 5493 Puerto Carreño (Kerepakupai Mt Roraima GUY
Armenia Cordillera Oriental Puerto Nuevo Merú) La Gran 2810
Ibagué BOGOTÁ Sabana Lethem
Cali Palmira Villavicencio Puerto Ayacucho Boa
Popayán COLOMBIA Puerto Inírida Vista
Neiva San José del Guaviare Pakaraima
Tumaco Florencia Guaviare Orinoco Nova Para
Pasto Mocoa Mitú Pico da
Esmeraldas Ipiales Neblina
QUITO Ibarra Puerto 3014 São Gabriel da Cachoeira
Manta Leguízamo Lérida Tapurucuara
Portoviejo ECUADOR Ambato Cabo Negro Barcelos
Chone Riobamba Pantoja El Encanto La Pedrera Maraã Fonte Boa
Alausí Santa Santo Antônio Manacapuru Mana
Guayaquil Cuenca Clara da Iça Coari
Isla Puná Machala Iquitos Leticia Beruri Borb
Barranca Tabatinga Benjamín Constant
Tumbes Lagunas Requena Carauari Tapauá Manicoré
Talara Yurimaguas Eirunepé Lábrea Humaitá Barra
Piura Tarapoto SELVAS do São Manu
Catacaos Jaén Contamana Envira Boca Porto Velho
Olmos Chachapoyas Rioja Cruzeiro do Sul Feijó do Acre Porto Acre Ariquemes
Pta Negra Cajamarca PERU Tarauacá Sena Madureira Abunã Jaru Aripuanã
Chiclayo Pucallpa Rio Branco Guayaramerín Pimenta Buenc
Trujillo Otuzco Puerto Xapurí Cobija Riberalta Serra dos Parecis Vilhena
Chimbote Huánuco Portillo Alerta
Huaraz ANDES Cerro de Pasco Mategua
Huarmey Barranca La Merced Ayacucho Puerto Maldonado Exaltación Vila Bela
Huacho Huancayo Machu Picchu Cusco Puerto Alegre Santíssima
Callao LIMA Abancay CUZCO Sandía Trinidad Puerto Frey Trindade
San Vicente Ayaviri Sicuani Trinidad Ponces e Lacerda
Cañete Yanaoca Ascensión Porto
Chincha Alta Cordillera Occidental Coracora Juliaca Santa Ana San Pedro Esperidião
Pisco Abancay Chuquibamba Arequipa Loreto
Ica Nazca Coripata BOLIVIA
Nudo Lake Titicaca LA PAZ
Coropuna Montero
Chala Camaná 6425 Juliaca Pampa Santa
Mollendo Moquegua Oruro Warnes El Cerro Cruz
Ilo Nevado Cochabamba Grande
PACIFIC Tacna Huanuli Bañados
OCEAN Corque del Izozog
Cabezas Tucavaca

Longitude 70° west of Greenwich

A B

150 Lambert Azimuthal Equal Area Projection

1 : 25 000 000 MILES 0 250 500

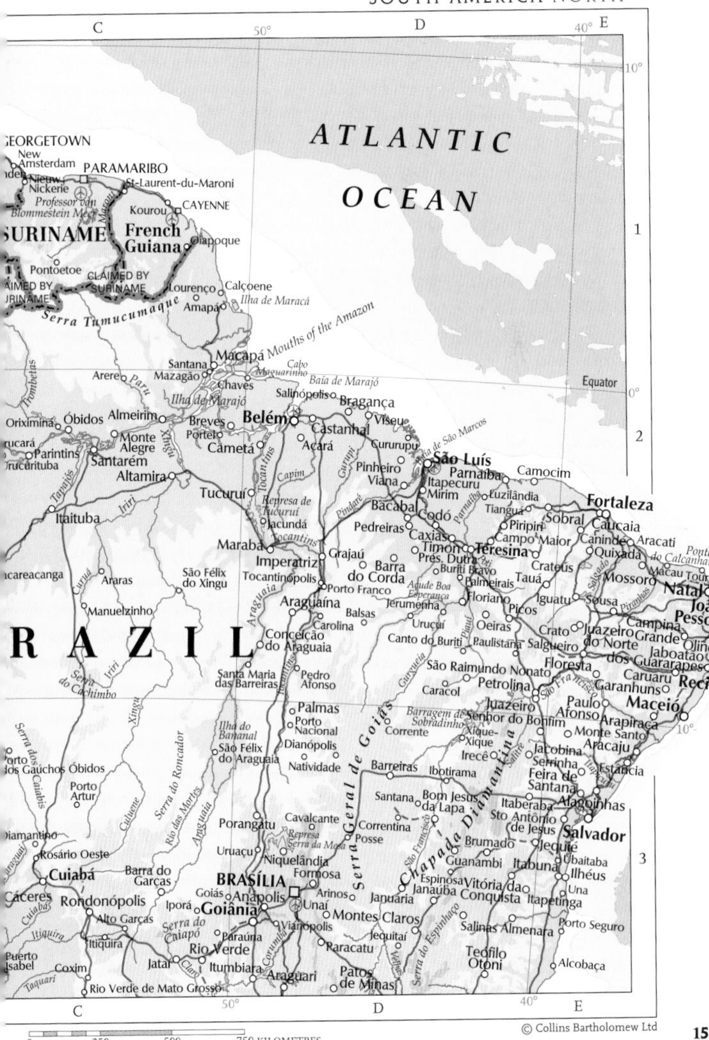

C   50°   D   40°   E

10°

ATLANTIC

OCEAN

GEORGETOWN
New
Amsterdam   PARAMARIBO
Nickerie   St-Laurent-du-Maroni
Professor van   Kourou   CAYENNE
Blommestein Meer
SURINAME   French   Oiapoque   1
Pontoetoe   Guiana
CLAIMED BY   Lourenço Calçoene
CLAIMED BY SURINAME   Amapá   Ilha de Maracá
Serra Tumucumaque
Macapá Mouths of the Amazon
Arere Paru   Santana   Cabo
Mazagão   Orange   Norte
Ilha do Marajó   Baía de Marajó   Equator   0°
Oriximiná Óbidos Almeirim   Chaves   Salinópolis Bragança
Breves   Belém   Viseu
Monte   Portel   Castanhal
Parintins Alegre Santarém Cametá Acará   Gurupi   Cururupu   São Luís   2
Itaituba Altamira   Pinheiro   Itapecuru   Camocim
Tucuruí   Viana Bacabal Mirim Tutóia   Fortaleza
Represa de   Capim   Parnaíba
Tucuruí   Pedreiras Caxias Timon   Sobral   Acaraú
Maraba Imperatriz   Grajaú Barra Prés. Dutra Teresina Crateús Canindé Aracati
Araras São Félix   do Corda   Campo Maior   Quixadá Ponta
do Xingu Tocantinópolis   Tauá   do Calcanhar
Manuelzinho   Porto Franco   Jerumenha Floriano Picos Iguatu Sousa Mossoró Natal
Araguaína   Balsas   Urucuí Paulistana Salgueiro do Norte Campina João
B R A Z I L   Conceição Carolina Canto do Buriti   Floresta Grande Olinda
do Araguaia   São Raimundo Nonato   Juazeiro Jaboatão Pessoa
Santa Maria Pedro Caracol Petrolina Garanhuns dos Guararapes
das Barreiras Afonso   Paulo Caruaru Recife
Palmas Barragem de   Juazeiro Afonso   Maceió
Ilha do Porto Sobradinho Senhor do Bonfim Arapiraca
Bananal Nacional Corrente Xique- Monte Santo
São Félix Dianópolis   Xique Jacobina Aracaju 10°
do Araguaia Natividade Barreiras Ibotirama Irecê Serrinha Estância
Porangatu Cavalcante   Feira de   Aragoinhas
Uruaçu Posse   Santana Sto Antônio
Niquelândia Correntina   Santana   de Jesus Salvador
Cuiabá Barra do Formosa   da Lapa Brumado Jequié
Garças Iporá Goiás Anápolis Arinos Januária Guanambi Itabuna
Rondonópolis   BRASÍLIA Januária Janaúba Vitória da Ilhéus 3
Alto Garças Goiânia Montes Claros Conquista Itapetinga Una
Vianópolis Jequitaí   Porto Seguro
Rio Verde Itumbiara Paracatu Salinas Almenara
Jataí   Araguari Patos Teófilo Alcobaça
Rio Verde de Mato Grosso de Minas Otoni

C   50°   D   40°   E

© Collins Bartholomew Ltd   151

0   250   500   750 KILOMETRES

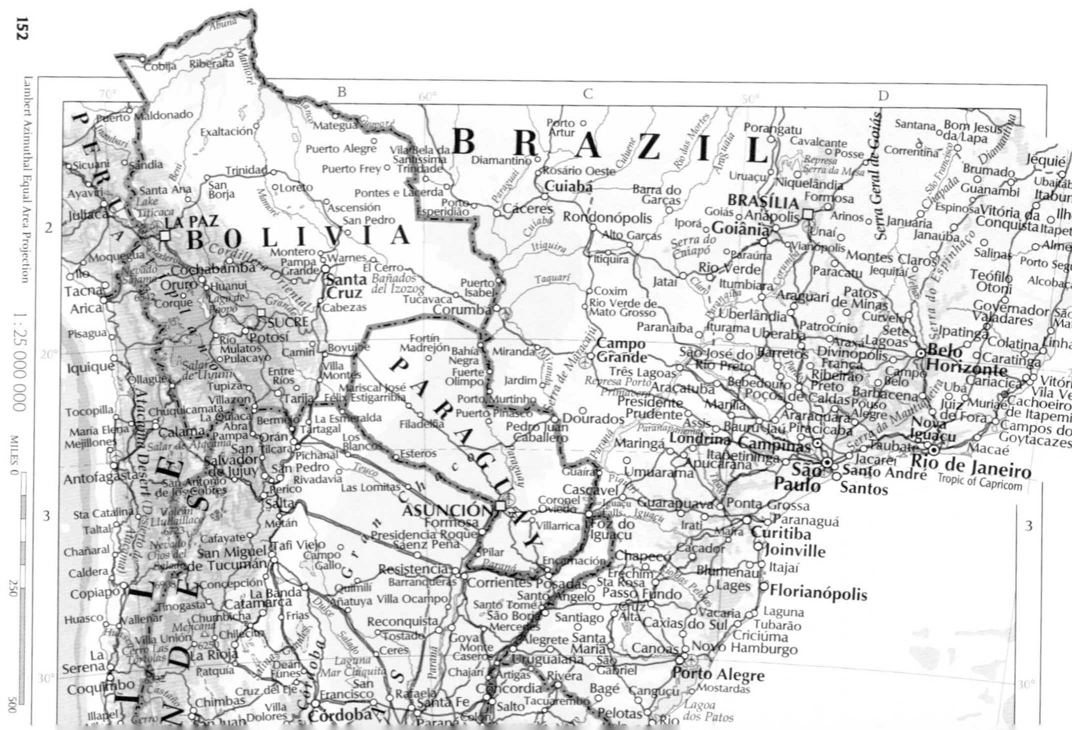

Major features and labels:

BRAZIL

BOLIVIA

PARAGUAY

PERU

ANDES

Tropic of Capricorn

Selected cities and places:
Rio de Janeiro, São Paulo, Belo Horizonte, Santos, Curitiba, Florianópolis, Porto Alegre, Pelotas, Campo Grande, Cuiabá, Goiânia, BRASÍLIA, Vitória, Santo André, Campinas, Londrina, Maringá, Cascavel, Rondonópolis, Porto Velho, LA PAZ, Cochabamba, SUCRE, Santa Cruz, Potosí, Oruro, ASUNCIÓN, Córdoba, Atacama Desert (Desierto de Atacama), Antofagasta, Iquique, Arica, Resistencia, Corrientes, Salta, Tucumán, Catamarca

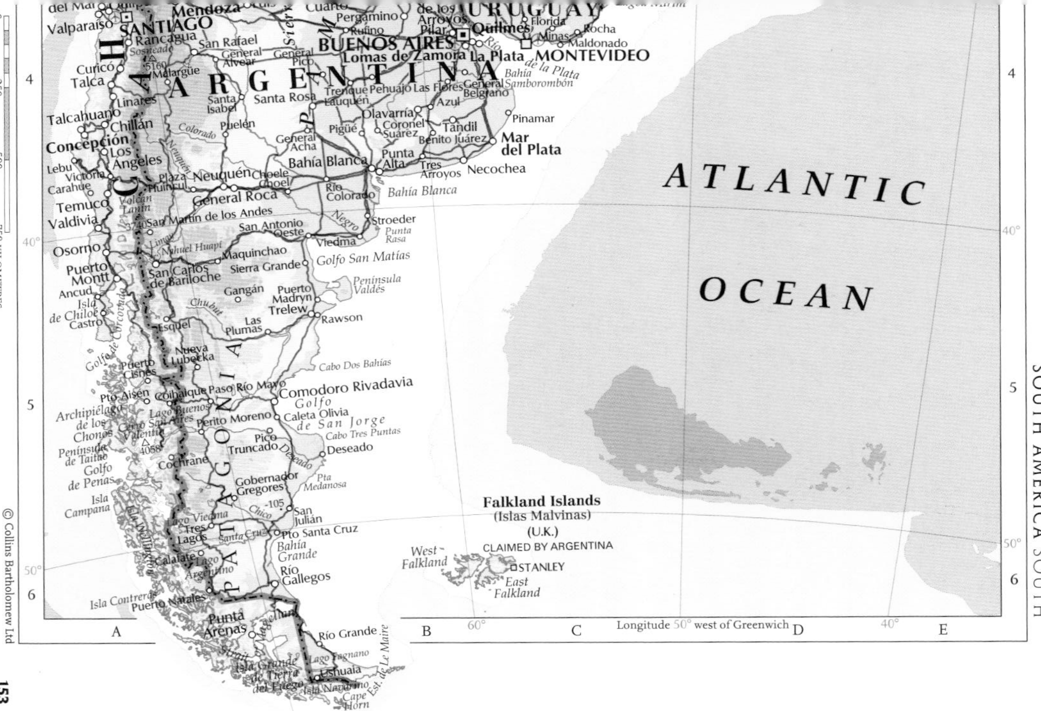

Falkland Islands
(Islas Malvinas)
(U.K.)
CLAIMED BY ARGENTINA
STANLEY
East
Falkland
West
Falkland

ATLANTIC

OCEAN

Longitude 50° west of Greenwich

0   250   500   750 KILOMETRES

© Collins Bartholomew Ltd

153

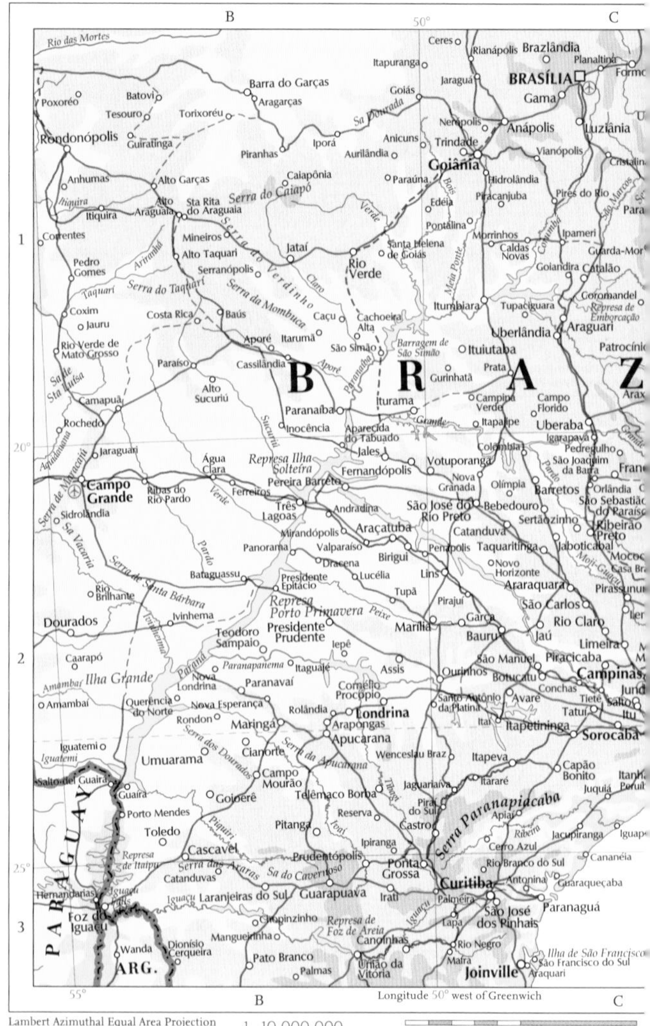

Rio das Mortes

Ceres o Rianápolis o Brazlândia
Itapuranga o   Planaltino   Formo
Poxoréo o   Batovi   o Jaraguá   BRASÍLIA
Tesouro o   Torixoréu o   Goiás o   Gama
Barra do Garças   Nerópolis
Rondonópolis o Guiratinga o   Aragarças   Anápolis   Luziânia
                               Anicuns   Trindade   Vianópolis
Piranhas o   Iporá o   o Goiânia
Anhumas o   Alto Garças o   Caiapônia o Aurilândia   Hidrolândia   Pires do Rio o Para
Itiquira o Sta Rita o Aragoiânia   Paraúna o Edéia   Pracajuba
Correntes o   do Araguaia   Mineiros o   Santa Helena   Morrinhos   Caldas   Goiandira Catalão
Pedro o   Alto Taquari o   Jataí o   de Goiás   Novas o
Gomes   Itumbiara   Tupaciguara   Araguari
Coxim o   Serranópolis o   Rio   Cachoeira   Prata o   Uberlândia   Ituiutaba
Jauru o Costa Rica o Baús o   Verde o   Alta   São Simão   Gurinhatã o   Campina   Uberaba
Rio Verde de o   Caçu o Itarumã   Barragem de   Iturama   Verde   Florido   Igarapava
Mato Grosso   Cassilândia o   São Simão   B R A Z
Camapuã o Paraíso o Alto o   Aporé   Inocência o   Aparecida   Jales o   Campinas   Ituverava
Rochedo o   Sucuriú   Paranaíba o   do Tabuado   Fernandópolis   Votuporanga   Pedregulho
                                                        Colômbia   São Joaquim   Fran
Jaraguari o   Água o   Represa Ilha   Três   Pereira Barreto   Olímpia   Barretos   Orlândia
Campo o   Clara   Solteira   Lagoas   Nova   o Bebedouro   Sertãozinho   São Sebastião
Grande   Ribas do o Ferreiros o   Andradina   Granada   São José do   Taquaritinga   Ribeirão
Sidrolândia o Rio Pardo   Mirandópolis o Araçatuba   Rio Preto   Catanduva   Jaboticabal   Preto
                 Panorama o   Valparaíso o   Birigui   Penápolis   Novo   Araraquara   Pirassununga
Bataguassu o Presidente o   Dracena   Lucélia o   Lins   Horizonte   São Carlos
Rio o   Epitácio   Represa   Tupã o   Pirajuí   Garça   Rio Claro   Limeira
Brilhante   Teodoro o Porto Primavera Peixe   Marília   Bauru   Jaú   Piracicaba
Dourados o Sampaio   Presidente   Iepê o   São Manuel   Campinas
Carapó o Ivinhema o Prudente   Paranapanema   Itaguisu   Assis   Ourinhos   Botucatu   Conchas   Tietê Salto
Amambai o Querência o Nova o   Paranavaí o   Cornélio   Santo Antônio   Avaré   Itu
          do Norte   Londrina   Procópio   da Platina   Itaí   Tatuí   Itapetininga
Iguatemi o Rondon o Nova Esperança o Rolândia   Londrina   Itapeva   Sorocaba
Salto do Guairá o   Maringá   Arapongas   Apucarana   Wenceslau Braz   Itararé   Capão   Itanh
Umuarama o   Cianorte o Serra da Apucarana   Jaguariaíva o Bonito   Juquiá Peruíb
Guaíra o   Campo o Telêmaco Borba   Piraí o Apiaí   Jacupiranga
Porto Mendes o   Goioerê   Mourão   Reserva   do Sul   Cerro Azul
Toledo o   Pitanga o   Ipiranga   Castro o   Ribeira   Iguap
Cascavel o Prudentópolis o   Ponta   Rio Branco do Sul   Cananéia
Catanduvas o Laranjeiras o   Guarapuava   Grossa   Antonina o Guaraqueçaba
Represa   do Sul   Irati o   Curitiba   Paranaguá
de Itaipu   Foz do o   Serra da o   São José o
Iguaçu   Hernandárias o Dionísio o Mangueirinha   Represa de   dos Pinhais
Wanda o Cerqueira   Chopinzinho o Foz do Areia   Tapa o Rio Negro   Ilha de São Francisco
ARG.   Pato Branco o   Canoinhas   Mafra   São Francisco do Sul
        Palmas o   União da o   Joinville
                   Vitória

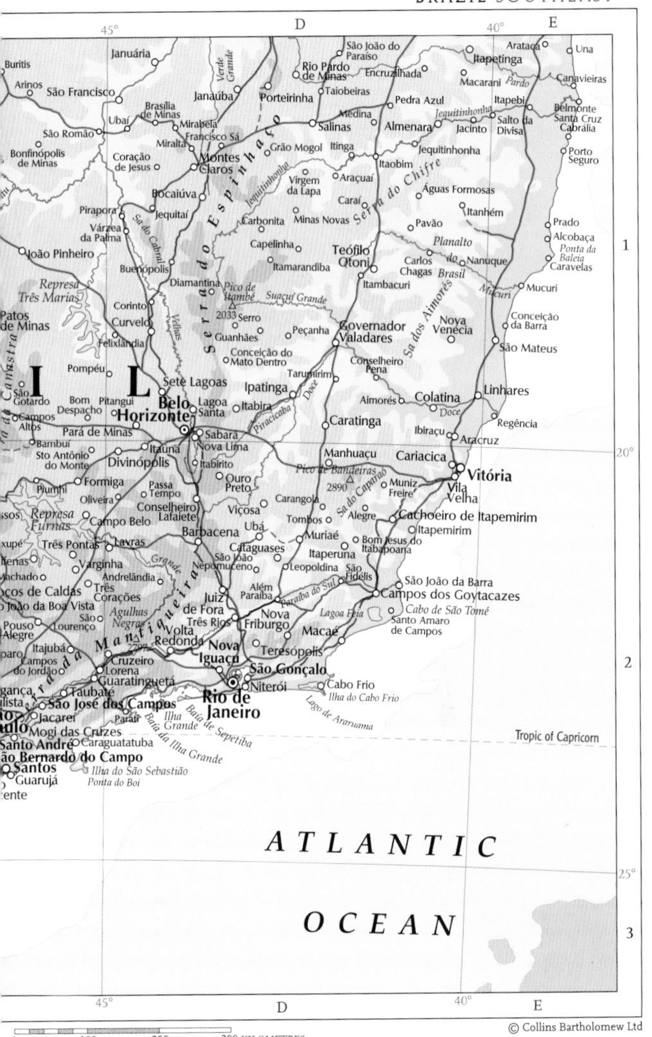

ATLANTIC

OCEAN

Tropic of Capricorn

© Collins Bartholomew Ltd

0   100   200   300 KILOMETRES

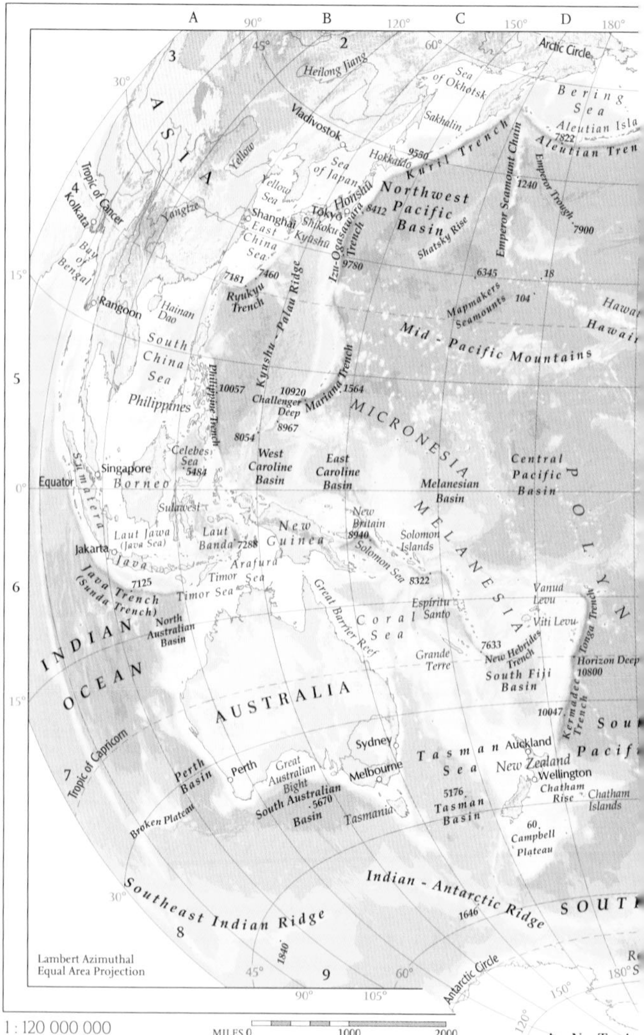

A   90°   B   120°   C   150°   D   180°

3   45°   2   60°   Arctic Circle

30°

A S I A   Heilong Jiang
                                    Vladivostok
Tropic of Cancer   Sea
                                    Yellow   of Okhotsk
Kolkata   Sakhalin   Bering
                          Yangtze   Sea of Japan   Hokkaido   Sea   Aleutian Isla
Bay   Honshu   Northwest   Aleutian Tren
of   Shanghai   Tokyo   Shikoku   9550   Pacific   Emperor Seamount Chain   7822
Bengal   Yellow   East   Kyushu   8412   Basin   1240
Rangoon   Sea   China   Izu Ogasawara Trench   Shatsky Rise   7900
                          Sea   9780
Hainan   7181   7460   6345   18
Dao   Ryukyu   Kyushu-Palau Ridge   Mapmakers   104   Hawai
                          Trench   Seamounts   Hawai
South   Mid - Pacific Mountains
China   Philippine Trench   10057   10920   Mariana Trench   1564
Sea   Challenger   8967   MICRONESIA
Philippines   Deep
                          8054   West   East   Central
                          Celebes   5484   Caroline   Caroline   Pacific
Singapore   Sea   Basin   Basin   Melanesian   Basin
Borneo   Basin
Equator   Sulawesi   P
Sumatra   Laut Jawa   New   Britain   8940   Solomon
              Jakarta   (Jawa Sea)   Banda   7288   Guinea   Solomon Sea   Islands   8322   O
Jawa   Laut   Timor   Arafura
              Java Trench   7125   Sea   Sea   L
(Sunda Trench)   North   Great Barrier Reef   Coral   Espiritu   7633   Vanua   Y
INDIAN   Australian   Sea   Santo   New Hebrides   Levu   N
              Basin   Grande   Trench   Viti Levu   E
OCEAN   Terre   South Fiji   10047   Horizon Deep   S
15°   Basin   10800
                                                            I
                                    AUSTRALIA   Tonga Trench   A
Tropic of Capricorn   Sydney   Tasman   Auckland   Kermadec   Sou
                          Perth   Great   Melbourne   Sea   New Zealand   Trench   Pacifi
                          Basin   Perth   Australian   5176   Wellington
                                    Bight   South Australian   Tasman   Chatham   Chatham
                                    Basin   5670   Basin   60   Rise   Islands
Broken Plateau   Tasmania   Campbell
7   Plateau
                          Southeast Indian Ridge   Indian - Antarctic Ridge   SOUT
30°   8   1646
                                    1340   9   Antarctic Circle   R
                          45°   60°   180°S
Lambert Azimuthal   90°   105°
Equal Area Projection   120°   150°

156   1 : 120 000 000   MILES 0   1000   2000   A N T A

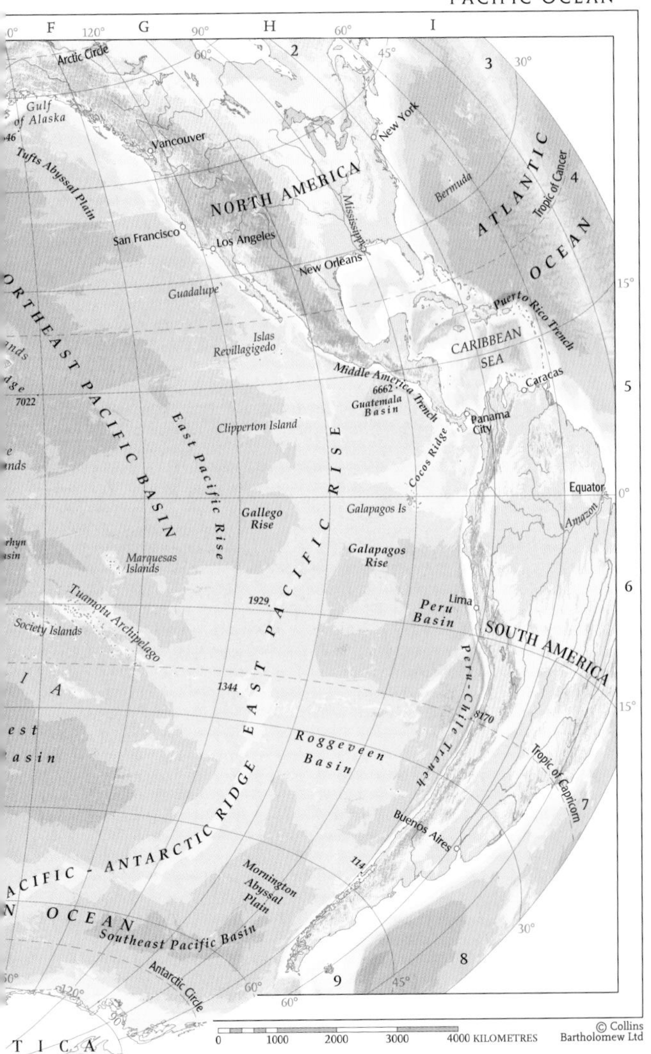

F 120° G 90° H 60° I

Arctic Circle

Gulf
of Alaska
46

Tufts Abyssal Plain

NORTH AMERICA

Vancouver

New York

ATLANTIC

Tropic of Cancer

San Francisco

Los Angeles

Bermuda

OCEAN

Mississippi

Guadalupe

New Orleans

Puerto Rico Trench

CARIBBEAN
SEA

Islas
Revillagigedo

Middle America Trench
6662
Guatemala
Basin

Caracas

Panama
City

ORTHEAST PACIFIC BASIN

Clipperton Island

Cocos Ridge

Equator

ands
ge
7022

EAST PACIFIC RISE

Gallego
Rise

Galapagos Is

Amazon

e
ands

Galapagos
Rise

rhyn
asin

Marquesas
Islands

Lima

Peru
Basin

SOUTH AMERICA

Tuamotu Archipelago

1929

Society Islands

I A

1344

EAST PACIFIC RISE

Peru-Chile Trench

Tropic of Capricorn

est
asin

Roggeveen
Basin

8170

7

PACIFIC - ANTARCTIC RIDGE

Mornington
Abyssal
Plain

Buenos Aires

114

N OCEAN

Southeast Pacific Basin

30°

CIFIC - ANTARCTIC RIDGE

Antarctic Circle

9

45°

120°

60°

T I C A

0   1000   2000   3000   4000 KILOMETRES

© Collins
Bartholomew Ltd   **157**

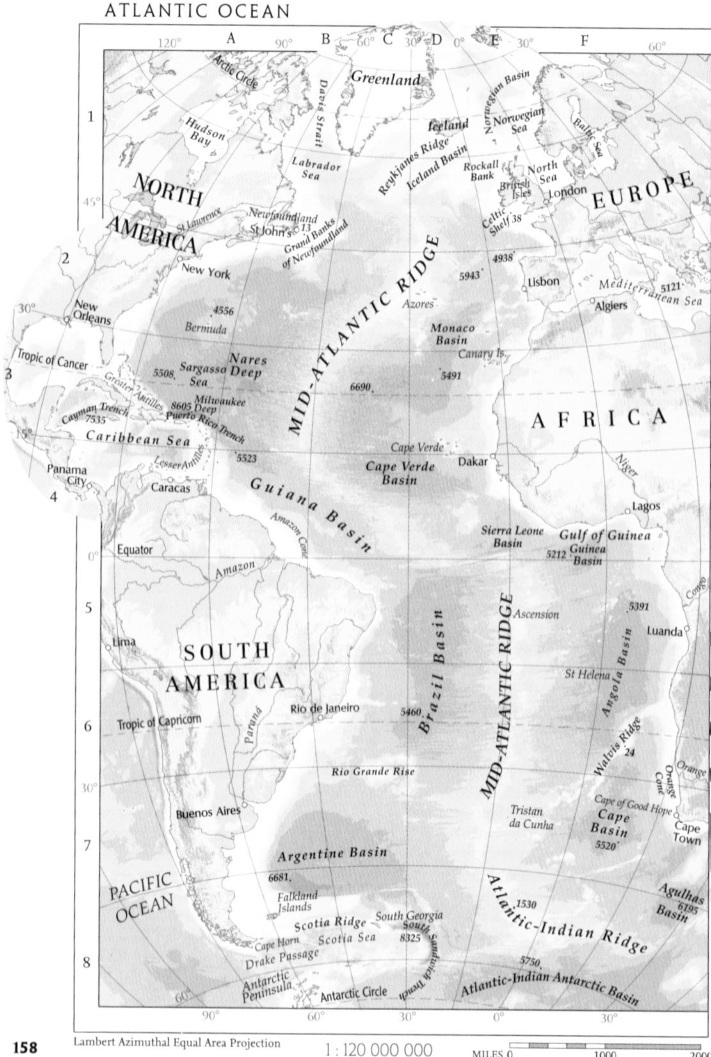

Lambert Azimuthal Equal Area Projection

1 : 120 000 000

MILES 0   1000   2000

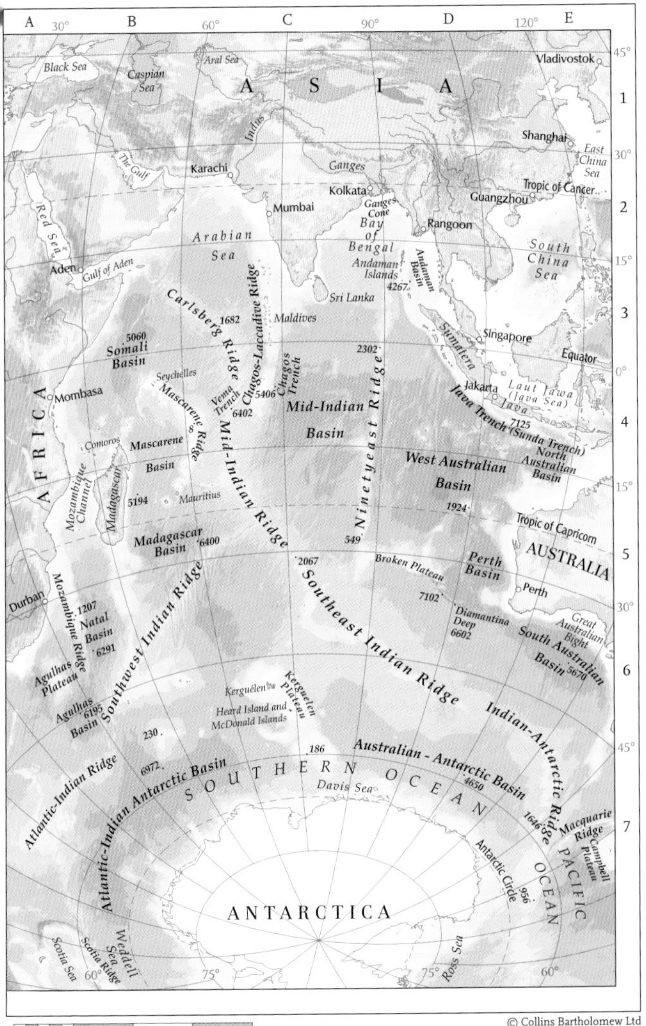

| A | 30° | B | 60° | C | 90° | D | 120° | E |

Black Sea
Caspian Sea
Aral Sea
Vladivostok
45°
1

A S I A

Indus
The Gulf
Karachi
Ganges
Kolkata
Shanghai
East China Sea
30°
Tropic of Cancer
2

Red Sea
Aden
Gulf of Aden
Mumbai
Ganges Cone
Bay of Bengal
Rangoon
Guangzhou
South China Sea
15°

Arabian Sea
Andaman Islands
4267
Andaman Basin
3

Carlsberg Ridge
1682
Maldives
Sri Lanka
2302
Sumatera
Singapore
Equator
0°

5060
Somali Basin
Seychelles
Mascarene Ridge
Vema Trench
Chagos-Laccadive Ridge
Chagos Trench
5406
6402
Mid-Indian Basin
Ninetyeast Ridge
Jakarta
Java Trench (Sunda Trench)
Laut Jawa (Java Sea)
North Australia Basin
7125
4

Mombasa
AFRICA
Comoros
Mascarene Basin
5194
Mauritius
Mid-Indian Ridge
West Australian Basin
1924
Java
15°

Mozambique Channel
Madagascar
Madagascar Basin
6400
2067
549
Broken Plateau
Tropic of Capricorn
AUSTRALIA
5

Durban
Mozambique Basin
1207
Natal Basin
6291
Agulhas Plateau
Southwest Indian Ridge
Southeast Indian Ridge
7102
Diamantina Deep 6602
Perth Basin
Perth
South Australian Basin
5670
Great Australian Bight
30°
6

Agulhas Basin
6195
Kerguélen
Kerguélen Plateau
Heard Island and McDonald Islands
Indian-Antarctic Ridge
1646
Macquarie Ridge
45°

Atlantic-Indian Ridge
Atlantic-Indian Antarctic Basin
230
6972
186
4650
Australian - Antarctic Basin
956
Campbell Plateau
PACIFIC
7

SOUTHERN OCEAN
Davis Sea
OCEAN
Antarctic Circle
Ross Sea
60°

ANTARCTICA

Scotia Sea
Scotia Ridge
75°
75°
60°

| 0 | 1000 | 2000 | 3000 | 4000 KILOMETRES |

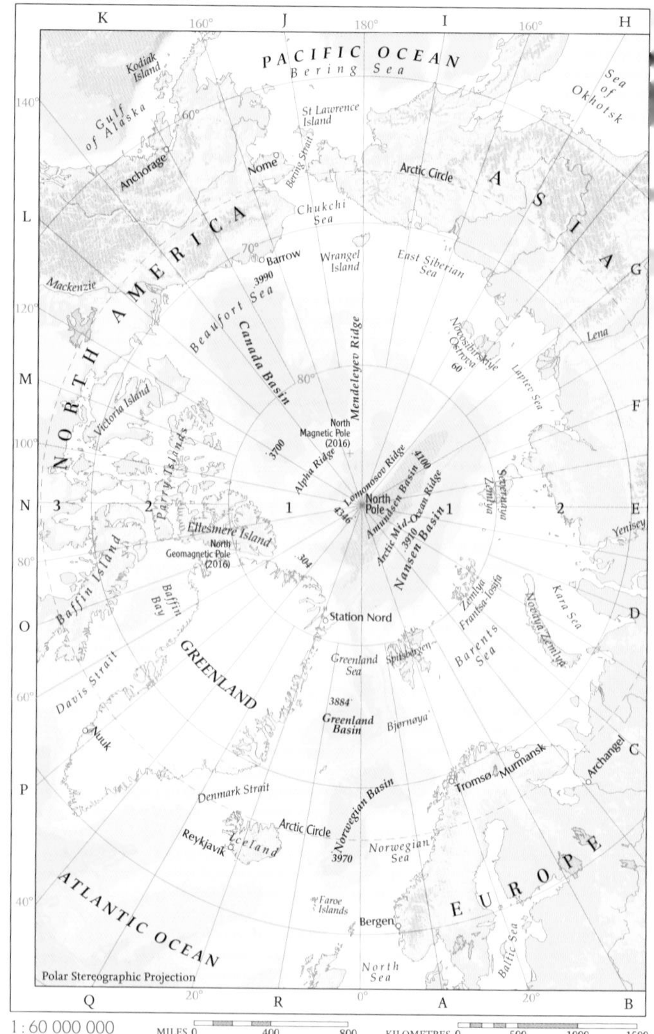

ARCTIC OCEAN

K   160°   J   180°   I   160°   H

PACIFIC OCEAN
Bering Sea

140°

Kodiak
Island

Gulf
of Alaska

St Lawrence
Island

Sea
of
Okhotsk

60°

Anchorage

Nome

Arctic Circle

A S I A

L

Bering Strait

Chukchi
Sea

Mackenzie

N O R T H   A M E R I C A

70°

Barrow
3990

Wrangel
Island

East Siberian
Sea

G

Beaufort Sea

Canada Basin

Lena

120°

Victoria Island

80°

Mendeleyev Ridge

Alpha Ridge-Chersky
60

Laptev Sea

M

3700

North
Magnetic Pole
(2016)

Lomonosov Ridge

Amundsen Basin
4100

F

Parry Islands

Alpha Ridge

North
Pole
4324

Arctic Mid-Ocean Ridge
3910

Khatanga

Olenëk

100°

3   2   1

N

1   2   E

Ellesmere Island

North
Geomagnetic Pole
(2016)

Nansen Basin

Zhelaniya

Yenisey

Baffin Island

80°

304

Zemlya
Frantsa-Iosifa

Kara Sea

Novaya Zemlya

O

Davis Strait

Baffin
Bay

Station Nord

D

Greenland
Sea

Spitsbergen

Barents
Sea

Zemlya

60°

Nuuk

G R E E N L A N D

3884
Greenland
Basin

Bjørnøya

Tromsø Murmansk

Archangel

C

P

Denmark Strait

Norwegian Basin

Norwegian
Sea

40°

Reykjavík

Iceland

Arctic Circle

3970

Bergen

E U R O P E

Baltic
Sea

Faroe
Islands

North
Sea

B

Polar Stereographic Projection

Q   20°   R   0°   A   20°   B

160   1 : 60 000 000   MILES 0   400   800   KILOMETRES 0   500   1000   1500

INTRODUCTION TO THE INDEX

The index includes all names shown on the maps in the Atlas of the World. Names are referenced by page number and by a grid reference. The grid reference correlates to the alphanumeric values which appear within each map frame. Each entry also includes the country or geographical area in which the feature is located. Entries relating to names appearing on insets are indicated by a small box symbol: □, followed by a grid reference if the inset has its own alphanumeric values.

Name forms are as they appear on the maps, with additional alternative names or name forms included as cross-references which refer the user to the entry for the map form of the name. Names beginning with Mc or Mac are alphabetized exactly as they appear. The terms Saint, Sainte, etc., are abbreviated to St, Ste, etc., but alphabetized as if in the full form.

Names of physical features beginning with generic, geographical terms are permuted – the descriptive term is placed after the main part of the name. For example, Lake Superior is indexed as Superior, Lake; Mount Everest as Everest, Mount. This policy is applied to all languages.

Entries, other than those for towns and cities, include a descriptor indicating the type of geographical feature. Descriptors are not included where the type of feature is implicit in the name itself.

Administrative divisions are included to differentiate entries of the same name and feature type within the one country. In such cases, duplicate names are alphabetized in order of administrative division. Additional qualifiers are also included for names within selected geographical areas.

INDEX ABBREVIATIONS

admin. div.	administrative division	Fin.	Finland	Phil.	Philippines
Afgh.	Afghanistan	for.	forest	plat.	plateau
Alg.	Algeria	Fr.	French	P.N.G.	Papua New Guinea
Arg.	Argentina	g.	gulf	Pol.	Poland
Austr.	Australia	Ger.	Germany	Port.	Portugal
aut. reg.	autonomous region	Guat.	Guatemala	prov.	province
Azer.	Azerbaijan	h.	hill	r.	river
b.	bay	hd	head	reg.	region
Bangl.	Bangladesh	Hond.	Honduras	resr.	reservoir
Bol.	Bolivia	imp. l.	impermanent lake	S.	South
Bos. & Herz.	Bosnia and Herzegovina	Indon.	Indonesia	str.	strait
		i.	island	Switz.	Switzerland
Bulg.	Bulgaria	is	Islands	Tajik.	Tajikistan
c.	cape	isth.	isthmus	Tanz.	Tanzania
Can.	Canada	Kazakh.	Kazakhstan	terr.	territory
C.A.R.	Central African Republic	Kyrg.	Kyrgyzstan	Thai.	Thailand
		lag.	lagoon	Trin. and Tob.	Trinidad and Tobago
chan.	channel	Lith.	Lithuania		
Col.	Colombia	Lux.	Luxembourg	Turkm.	Turkmenistan
Czech Rep.	Czech Republic	Madag.	Madagascar	U.A.E.	United Arab Emirates
Dem. Rep. Congo	Democratic Republic of the Congo	Maur.	Mauritania	U.K.	United Kingdom
		Mex.	Mexico	Ukr.	Ukraine
		Moz.	Mozambique	Uru.	Uruguay
depr.	depression	mt.	mountain	U.S.A.	United States of America
des.	desert	mun.	municipality		
disp. terr.	disputed territory	N.	North	Uzbek.	Uzbekistan
Dom. Rep.	Dominican Republic	Neth.	Netherlands	val.	valley
		Nic.	Nicaragua	Venez.	Venezuela
esc.	escarpment	N.Z.	New Zealand	vol.	volcano
est.	estuary	Pak.	Pakistan		
Eth.	Ethiopia	Para.	Paraguay		
		pen.	peninsula		

1

128 B2 **100 Mile House** Can.

A

93 E4 **Aabenraa** Denmark
100 C2 **Aachen** Ger.
93 E4 **Aalborg** Denmark
100 B2 **Aalst** Belgium
100 C2 **Aarschot** Belgium
93 E4 **Aarhus** Denmark
68 C2 **Aba** China
115 C4 **Aba** Nigeria
81 C2 **Ābādān** Iran
81 D2 **Ābādeh** Iran
114 B1 **Abadla** Alg.
115 C4 **Abakaliki** Nigeria
83 H3 **Abakan** Russia
150 A3 **Abancay** Peru
81 D2 **Abarkūh** Iran
66 D2 **Abashiri** Japan
117 B4 **Abaya, Lake** Eth.
Abay Wenz r. Eth./Sudan see
Blue Nile
82 G3 **Abaza** Russia
108 A2 **Abbasanta** Sardinia Italy
104 C1 **Abbeville** France
142 B3 **Abbeville** U.S.A.
55 O2 **Abbot Ice Shelf** Antarctica
74 B1 **Abbottabad** Pak.
115 E3 **Abéché** Chad
114 B4 **Abengourou** Côte d'Ivoire
114 C4 **Abeokuta** Nigeria
99 A2 **Aberaeron** U.K.
96 C2 **Aberchirder** U.K.
99 B3 **Aberdare** U.K.
99 A2 **Aberdaron** U.K.
122 B3 **Aberdeen** S. Africa
96 C2 **Aberdeen** U.K.
141 D3 **Aberdeen** MD U.S.A.
137 D1 **Aberdeen** SD U.S.A.
134 B1 **Aberdeen** WA U.S.A.
129 E1 **Aberdeen Lake** Can.
134 B2 **Abert, Lake** U.S.A.
99 A2 **Aberystwyth** U.K.
86 F2 **Abez'** Russia
78 B3 **Abhā** Saudi Arabia
Abiad, Bahr el r. Sudan/
Uganda see **White Nile**
114 B4 **Abidjan** Côte d'Ivoire
137 D3 **Abilene** KS U.S.A.
139 D2 **Abilene** TX U.S.A.
99 C3 **Abingdon** U.K.
91 D3 **Abinsk** Russia
130 B2 **Abitibi, Lake** Can.
81 C1 **Abkhazia** disp. terr. Georgia
Åbo Fin. see **Turku**
74 B1 **Abohar** India
114 C4 **Abomey** Benin
60 A1 **Abongabong, Gunung** mt.
Indon.
118 B2 **Abong Mbang** Cameroon
64 A2 **Aborlan** Phil.
115 D3 **Abou Déia** Chad
106 B2 **Abrantes** Port.
152 B3 **Abra Pampa** Arg.
136 A2 **Absaroka Range** mts U.S.A.
81 C1 **Abşeron Yarımadası** pen. Azer.
78 B3 **Abū 'Arīsh** Saudi Arabia
79 C2 **Abu Dhabi** U.A.E.
116 B3 **Abu Hamed** Sudan
115 C4 **Abuja** Nigeria
81 C2 **Abū Kamāl** Syria
152 B1 **Abunã** r. Bol./Brazil

150 B2 **Abunã** Brazil
74 B2 **Abu Road** India
116 B2 **Abū Sunbul** Egypt
117 A3 **Abu Zabad** Sudan
Abū Ẓaby U.A.E. see **Abu Dhabi**
117 A4 **Abyei** Sudan
145 B2 **Acambaro** Mex.
106 B1 **A Cañiza** Spain
144 B2 **Acaponeta** Mex.
145 C3 **Acapulco** Mex.
151 D2 **Acará** Brazil
150 B1 **Acarigua** Venez.
145 C3 **Acatlán** Mex.
145 C3 **Acayucán** Mex.
114 B4 **Accra** Ghana
98 B2 **Accrington** U.K.
74 B2 **Achalpur** India
97 A2 **Achill Island** Ireland
101 D1 **Achim** Ger.
96 B2 **Achnasheen** U.K.
91 D2 **Achuyevo** Russia
111 C3 **Acıpayam** Turkey
109 C3 **Acireale** Sicily Italy
147 C2 **Acklins Island** Bahamas
153 B4 **Aconcagua, Cerro** mt. Arg.
106 B1 **A Coruña** Spain
108 A2 **Acqui Terme** Italy
103 D2 **Acs** Hungary
145 C2 **Actopan** Mex.
139 D2 **Ada** U.S.A.
79 C2 **Adam** Oman
49 J4 **Adamstown** Pitcairn Is
'Adan Yemen see **Aden**
80 B2 **Adana** Turkey
111 D2 **Adapazarı** Turkey
Adapazari Turkey see
Adapazarı
108 A1 **Adda** r. Italy
78 B2 **Ad Dafinah** Saudi Arabia
78 B2 **Ad Dahnā'** des. Saudi Arabia
78 B2 **Ad Dahnā'** des. Saudi Arabia
Ad Dammām Saudi Arabia see
Dammam
78 A2 **Ad Dār al Ḥamrā'**
Saudi Arabia
78 B3 **Ad Darb** Saudi Arabia
78 B2 **Ad Dawādimī** Saudi Arabia
Ad Dawḥah Qatar see **Doha**
78 B2 **Ad Dilam** Saudi Arabia
116 C2 **Ad Dir'īyah** Saudi Arabia
117 B4 **Addis Ababa** Eth.
81 C2 **Ad Dīwānīyah** Iraq
52 A2 **Adelaide** Austr.
50 C1 **Adelaide River** Austr.
101 D2 **Adelebsen** Ger.
55 J2 **Adélie Land** Antarctica
78 B3 **Aden** Yemen
117 C3 **Aden, Gulf of** Somalia/Yemen
100 C2 **Adenau** Ger.
79 C2 **Adh Dhayd** U.A.E.
59 C3 **Adi** i. Indon.
78 A3 **Ādī Ārk'ay** Eth.
116 B3 **Adigrat** Eth.
75 B3 **Adilabad** India
141 E2 **Adirondack Mountains** U.S.A.
Ādīs Ābeba Eth. see
Addis Ababa
117 B4 **Ādīs Alem** Eth.
110 C1 **Adjud** Romania
50 B1 **Admiralty Gulf** Austr.
128 A2 **Admiralty Island** U.S.A.
104 B3 **Adour** r. France
106 C2 **Adra** Spain
114 B2 **Adrar** Alg.
140 C2 **Adrian** MI U.S.A.
139 C1 **Adrian** TX U.S.A.
108 B2 **Adriatic Sea** Europe
116 B3 **Ādwa** Eth.

83 K2 **Adycha** r. Russia
91 D3 **Adygeysk** Russia
114 B4 **Adzopé** Côte d'Ivoire
111 B3 **Aegean Sea** Greece/Turkey
101 D1 **Aerzen** Ger.
106 B1 **A Estrada** Spain
116 B3 **Afabet** Eritrea
76 C3 **Afghanistan** country Asia
78 B2 **'Afīf** Saudi Arabia
80 B2 **Afyon** Turkey
115 C3 **Agadez** Niger
114 B1 **Agadir** Morocco
74 B2 **Agar** India
75 D2 **Agartala** India
81 C1 **Ağdam** Azer.
81 C2 **Ağdam (abandoned)** Azer.
105 C3 **Agde** France
104 C3 **Agen** France
122 A2 **Aggeneys** S. Africa
111 C3 **Agia Varvara** Greece
111 B3 **Agios Dimitrios** Greece
111 C3 **Agios Efstratios** i. Greece
111 C3 **Agios Nikolaos** Greece
110 B1 **Agnita** Romania
75 B2 **Agra** India
81 C2 **Ağrı** Turkey
Ağrı Dağı mt. Turkey see
Ararat, Mount
108 B3 **Agrigento** Sicily Italy
111 B3 **Agrinio** Greece
109 B2 **Agropoli** Italy
154 B2 **Água Clara** Brazil
155 C3 **Agua Negras** mt. Brazil
146 B4 **Aguadulce** Panama
144 B2 **Aguanaval** r. Mex.
144 B1 **Agua Prieta** Mex.
144 B2 **Aguascalientes** Mex.
155 D1 **Águas Formosas** Brazil
106 B1 **Águeda** Port.
106 C1 **Aguilar de Campoo** Spain
107 C2 **Águilas** Spain
144 B3 **Aguililla** Mex.
122 B3 **Agulhas, Cape** S. Africa
155 D2 **Agulhas Negras** mt. Brazil
111 C2 **Ağva** Turkey
115 C2 **Ahaggar** plat. Alg.
115 C2 **Ahaggar, Tassili oua-n-** plat.
Alg.
81 C2 **Ahar** Iran
100 C1 **Ahaus** Ger.
81 C2 **Ahlat** Turkey
100 C2 **Ahlen** Ger.
74 B2 **Ahmadabad** India
73 B3 **Ahmadnagar** India
74 B1 **Ahmadpur East** Pak.
74 B1 **Ahmadpur Sial** Pak.
Ahmedabad India see
Ahmadabad
Ahmednagar India see
Ahmadnagar
144 B2 **Ahome** Mex.
79 C2 **Ahram** Iran
101 E1 **Ahrensburg** Ger.
104 C2 **Ahun** France
81 C2 **Ahvāz** Iran
122 A2 **Ai-Ais** Namibia
80 B2 **Aigialousa** Cyprus
111 B3 **Aigio** Greece
143 D2 **Aiken** U.S.A.
97 B1 **Ailt an Chorráin** Ireland
155 D1 **Aimorés** Brazil
155 D1 **Aimorés, Serra dos** hills Brazil
114 B2 **'Aïn Ben Tili** Maur.
107 D2 **Aïn Defla** Alg.
114 B1 **Aïn Sefra** Alg.
136 D2 **Ainsworth** U.S.A.
Aintab Turkey see **Gaziantep**
107 D2 **Aïn Taya** Alg.
107 D2 **Aïn Tédélès** Alg.

115 C3 Aïr, Massif de l' mts Niger
60 A1 Airbangis Indon.
128 C2 Airdrie Can.
104 B3 Aire-sur-l'Adour France
101 E1 Aisch r. Ger.
128 A1 Aishihik Lake Can.
100 A3 Aisne r. France
59 D3 Aitape P.N.G.
110 B1 Aiud Romania
105 D3 Aix-en-Provence France
105 D2 Aix-les-Bains France
62 A1 Aizawl India
88 C2 Aizkraukle Latvia
67 C3 Aizuwakamatsu Japan
105 D3 Ajaccio Corsica France
115 E1 Ajdābiyā Libya
115 C2 Ajjer, Tassili n' plat. Alg.
74 B2 Ajmer India
138 A2 Ajo U.S.A.
77 D2 Akadyr Kazakh.
87 E3 Akbulak Russia
80 B2 Akçakale Turkey
80 B2 Akdağmadeni Turkey
88 A2 Åkersberga Sweden
118 C2 Aketi Dem. Rep. Congo
87 D4 Akhalkalaki Georgia
79 C2 Akhdar, Jabal mts Oman
111 C3 Akhisar Turkey
87 D4 Akhtubinsk Russia
130 B1 Akimiski Island Can.
66 D3 Akita Japan
114 A3 Akjoujt Maur.
77 D1 Akkol' Kazakh.
88 B2 Akmenrags pt Latvia
      Akmola Kazakh. see Astana
117 B4 Akobo South Sudan
74 B2 Akola India
78 A3 Akordat Eritrea
127 G2 Akpatok Island Can.
92 □A3 Akranes Iceland
140 C2 Akron U.S.A.
75 B1 Aksai Chin terr. Asia
80 B2 Aksaray Turkey
76 B1 Aksay Kazakh.
91 D2 Aksay Russia
80 B2 Akşehir Turkey
76 C2 Akshiganak Kazakh.
77 E2 Aksu China
78 A3 Āksum Eth.
76 B2 Aktau Kazakh.
76 B1 Aktobe Kazakh.
77 D2 Aktogay Kazakh.
88 C3 Aktsyabrski Belarus
115 C4 Akure Nigeria
92 □B2 Akureyri Iceland
62 A1 Akyab Myanmar
142 C2 Alabama r. U.S.A.
142 C2 Alabama state U.S.A.
111 C3 Alaçatı Turkey
81 C1 Alagir Russia
151 E3 Alagoinhas Brazil
107 C2 Alagón Spain
79 B2 Al Aḥmadī Kuwait
77 C2 Alakol', Ozero salt l. Kazakh.
92 J2 Alakurtti Russia
78 B3 Al 'Alayyah Saudi Arabia
80 B2 Al 'Āmiriyah Egypt
135 C3 Alamo U.S.A.
138 B2 Alamogordo U.S.A.
144 A2 Alamos Sonora Mex.
144 B2 Alamos Sonora Mex.
144 B2 Alamos r. Mex.
136 B3 Alamosa U.S.A.
93 G3 Åland Islands Fin.
80 B2 Alanya Turkey
73 B4 Alappuzha India
80 B3 Al 'Aqabah Jordan

78 B2 Al 'Aqīq Saudi Arabia
107 C2 Alarcón, Embalse de resr Spain
80 B2 Al 'Arīsh Egypt
78 B2 Al Arţāwīyah Saudi Arabia
61 C2 Alas Indon.
111 C3 Alaşehir Turkey
128 A2 Alaska state U.S.A.
124 F3 Alaska, Gulf of U.S.A.
81 C2 Älät Azer.
87 D3 Alatyr' Russia
150 A2 Alausí Ecuador
93 H3 Alavus Fin.
52 B2 Alawoona Austr.
108 A2 Alba Italy
107 C2 Albacete Spain
110 B1 Alba Iulia Romania
109 C2 Albania country Europe
50 A3 Albany r. Can.
130 B1 Albany r. Can.
143 D2 Albany GA U.S.A.
141 E2 Albany NY U.S.A.
134 B2 Albany OR U.S.A.
      Al Başrah Iraq see Basra
51 D1 Albatross Bay Austr.
116 A2 Al Bawīti Egypt
115 E1 Al Baydā' Libya
78 B3 Al Baydā' Yemen
143 D1 Albemarle U.S.A.
143 E1 Albemarle Sound sea chan. U.S.A.
108 A2 Albenga Italy
51 C2 Alberga watercourse Austr.
119 D2 Albert, Lake Dem. Rep. Congo/Uganda
128 C2 Alberta prov. Can.
100 B2 Albert Kanaal canal Belgium
137 E2 Albert Lea U.S.A.
104 C3 Albi France
78 A2 Al Bi'r Saudi Arabia
78 B3 Al Birk Saudi Arabia
78 B2 Al Biyāḍh reg. Saudi Arabia
106 C2 Alboran Sea Europe
      Alborz, Reshteh-ye mts Iran see Elburz Mountains
106 B2 Albufeira Port.
138 B1 Albuquerque U.S.A.
79 C2 Al Buraymī Oman
53 C3 Albury Austr.
106 B2 Alcácer do Sal Port.
106 C1 Alcalá de Henares Spain
106 C2 Alcalá la Real Spain
108 B3 Alcamo Sicily Italy
107 C1 Alcañiz Spain
106 B2 Alcántara Spain
106 C2 Alcaraz Spain
106 C2 Alcaraz, Sierra de mts Spain
106 C2 Alcaudete Spain
106 C2 Alcázar de San Juan Spain
91 D2 Alchevs'k Ukr.
155 E1 Alcobaça Brazil
107 C2 Alcoy-Alcoi Spain
107 D2 Alcúdia Spain
145 C2 Aldama Mex.
83 J3 Aldan Russia
83 J2 Aldan r. Russia
95 C4 Alderney i. Channel Is
114 A3 Aleg Maur.
155 D2 Alegre Brazil
152 C3 Alegrete Brazil
83 K3 Aleksandrovsk-Sakhalinskiy Russia
91 D1 Alekseyevka Belgorodskaya Oblast' Russia
91 D1 Alekseyevka Belgorodskaya Oblast' Russia
89 E3 Aleksin Russia
109 D2 Aleksinac Serbia

118 B3 Alèmbé Gabon
155 D2 Além Paraíba Brazil
93 F3 Ålen Norway
104 C2 Alençon France
80 B2 Aleppo Syria
150 A3 Alerta Peru
128 B2 Alert Bay Can.
105 C3 Alès France
110 B1 Aleşd Romania
108 A2 Alessandria Italy
93 E3 Ålesund Norway
124 C3 Aleutian Islands U.S.A.
83 L3 Alevina, Mys c. Russia
128 A2 Alexander Archipelago is U.S.A.
122 A2 Alexander Bay S. Africa
142 C2 Alexander City U.S.A.
55 O2 Alexander Island Antarctica
53 C3 Alexandra Austr.
54 A3 Alexandra N.Z.
111 B2 Alexandreia Greece
      Alexandretta Turkey see İskenderun
116 A1 Alexandria Egypt
110 C2 Alexandria Romania
123 C3 Alexandria S. Africa
142 B2 Alexandria LA U.S.A.
137 D1 Alexandria MN U.S.A.
141 D3 Alexandria VA U.S.A.
52 A3 Alexandrina, Lake Austr.
111 C2 Alexandroupoli Greece
131 E1 Alexis r. Can.
128 B2 Alexis Creek Can.
77 E1 Aleysk Russia
107 C1 Alfaro Spain
81 C3 Al Fāw Iraq
101 D2 Alfeld (Leine) Ger.
155 C2 Alfenas Brazil
      Al Fujayrah U.A.E. see Fujairah
      Al Furāt r. Iraq/Syria see Euphrates
106 B2 Algeciras Spain
107 C2 Algemesí Spain
78 A3 Algena Eritrea
      Alger Alg. see Algiers
114 C2 Algeria country Africa
      Al Ghardaqah Egypt see Hurghada
79 B3 Al Ghaydah Yemen
108 A2 Alghero Sardinia Italy
79 B2 Al Ghwaybiyah Saudi Arabia
115 C1 Algiers Alg.
123 C3 Algoa Bay S. Africa
137 E2 Algona U.S.A.
106 C1 Algorta Spain
81 C2 Al Ḥadīthah Iraq
79 C2 Al Ḥajar al Gharbī mts Oman
107 C2 Alhama de Murcia Spain
80 A2 Al Ḥammām Egypt
78 B2 Al Ḥanākiyah Saudi Arabia
81 C2 Al Ḥasakah Syria
81 C2 Al Ḥayy Iraq
79 C3 Al Ḥibāk des. Saudi Arabia
78 B2 Al Ḥillah Saudi Arabia
79 B2 Al Ḥinnāh Saudi Arabia
      Al Ḥudaydah Yemen see Hodeidah
79 B2 Al Ḥufūf Saudi Arabia
115 D2 Al Ḥulayq al Kabīr hills Libya
79 C2 'Alīābād Iran
111 C3 Aliağa Turkey
111 B2 Aliakmonas r. Greece
107 C2 Alicante Spain
139 D3 Alice U.S.A.
109 C3 Alice, Punta pt Italy
51 C2 Alice Springs Austr.
75 B2 Aligarh India

81 C2 **Alīgūdarz** Iran
69 E1 **Alihe** China
118 B3 **Alima** *r.* Congo
111 C3 **Aliova** *r.* Turkey
117 C3 **Ali Sabieh** Djibouti
Al Iskandarīyah Egypt *see* **Alexandria**
116 B1 **Al Ismā'īlīyah** Egypt
123 C3 **Aliwal North** S. Africa
115 E2 **Al Jaghbūb** Libya
78 B2 **Al Jahrah** Kuwait
115 D1 **Al Jawsh** Libya
106 B2 **Aljezur** Port.
Al Jīzah Egypt *see* **Giza**
79 B2 **Al Jubayl** Saudi Arabia
79 C2 **Al Jumaylīyah** Qatar
78 B2 **Al Junaynah** Saudi Arabia
106 B2 **Aljustrel** Port.
78 B2 **Al Kahfah** Saudi Arabia
79 C2 **Al Kāmil** Oman
80 B2 **Al Karak** Jordan
79 C2 **Al Khābūrah** Oman
78 B2 **Al Khamāsīn** Saudi Arabia
116 B2 **Al Khārijah** Egypt
79 C2 **Al Khaşab** Oman
78 B3 **Al Khawkhah** Yemen
79 C2 **Al Khawr** Qatar
115 D1 **Al Khums** Libya
79 B2 **Al Khunn** Saudi Arabia
79 C2 **Al Kir'ānah** Qatar
100 B1 **Alkmaar** Neth.
115 E2 **Al Kufrah** Libya
81 C2 **Al Kūt** Iraq
Al Kuwayt Kuwait *see* **Kuwait**
Al Lādhiqīyah Syria *see* **Latakia**
75 C2 **Allahabad** India
83 K2 **Allakh-Yun'** Russia
141 D2 **Allegheny** *r.* U.S.A.
140 C3 **Allegheny Mountains** U.S.A.
97 B1 **Allen, Lough** *l.* Ireland
145 B2 **Allende** *Coahuila* Mex.
145 B2 **Allende** *Nuevo León* Mex.
141 D2 **Allentown** U.S.A.
101 D1 **Aller** *r.* Ger.
136 C2 **Alliance** *NE* U.S.A.
140 C2 **Alliance** *OH* U.S.A.
78 B2 **Al Līth** Saudi Arabia
96 C2 **Alloa** U.K.
131 C2 **Alma** Can.
Alma-Ata Kazakh. *see* **Almaty**
106 B2 **Almada** Port.
106 C2 **Almadén** Spain
Al Madīnah Saudi Arabia *see* **Medina**
116 B1 **Al Mafraq** Jordan
78 B3 **Al Maḩwīt** Yemen
78 B2 **Al Majma'ah** Saudi Arabia
135 B2 **Almanor, Lake** U.S.A.
107 C2 **Almansa** Spain
80 B2 **Al Manşūrah** Egypt
79 C2 **Al Mariyyah** U.A.E.
115 E1 **Al Marj** Libya
77 D2 **Almaty** Kazakh.
106 C1 **Almazán** Spain
151 C2 **Almeirim** Brazil
100 C1 **Almelo** Neth.
155 D1 **Almenara** Brazil
106 B1 **Almendra, Embalse de** *resr* Spain
106 B2 **Almendralejo** Spain
106 C2 **Almería** Spain
106 C2 **Almería, Golfo de** *b.* Spain
87 E3 **Al'met'yevsk** Russia
78 B2 **Al Mindak** Saudi Arabia
116 B2 **Al Minyā** Egypt
79 B2 **Al Mish'āb** Saudi Arabia
106 B2 **Almodôvar** Port.
106 B2 **Almonte** Spain
75 B2 **Almora** India
79 B2 **Al Mubarrez** Saudi Arabia
79 C2 **Al Muḑaibī** Oman
80 B3 **Al Mudawwarah** Jordan
Al Mukallā Yemen *see* **Mukalla**
Al Mukhā Yemen *see* **Mocha**
106 C2 **Almuñécar** Spain
78 A2 **Al Muwayliḩ** Saudi Arabia
111 B3 **Almyros** Greece
96 B2 **Alness** U.K.
98 C1 **Alnwick** U.K.
49 G4 **Alofi** Niue
111 B3 **Alonnisos** *i.* Greece
59 C3 **Alor** *i.* Indon.
59 C3 **Alor, Kepulauan** *is* Indon.
60 B1 **Alor Star** Malaysia
Alost Belgium *see* **Aalst**
86 C2 **Alozero (abandoned)** Russia
140 C1 **Alpena** U.S.A.
139 C2 **Alpine** U.S.A.
105 D2 **Alps** *mts* Europe
79 B3 **Al Qa'āmīyāt** *reg.* Saudi Arabia
115 D1 **Al Qaddāḩīyah** Libya
Al Qāhirah Egypt *see* **Cairo**
78 B2 **Al Qā'īyah** Saudi Arabia
81 C2 **Al Qāmishlī** Syria
80 B2 **Al Qaryatayn** Syria
79 B3 **Al Qaţn** Yemen
106 B2 **Alqueva, Barragem de** *resr* Port.
80 B2 **Al Qunayţirah (abandoned)** Syria
78 B3 **Al Qunfidhah** Saudi Arabia
116 B2 **Al Quşayr** Egypt
78 B2 **Al Quwayīyah** Saudi Arabia
101 D2 **Alsfeld** Ger.
92 H2 **Alta** Norway
92 H2 **Altaelva** *r.* Norway
68 B1 **Altai Mountains** Asia
143 D2 **Altamaha** *r.* U.S.A.
151 C2 **Altamira** Brazil
109 C2 **Altamura** Italy
68 B1 **Altay** China
68 C1 **Altay** Mongolia
105 D2 **Altdorf** Switz.
107 C2 **Altea** Spain
101 F2 **Altenburg** Ger.
100 C2 **Altenkirchen (Westerwald)** Ger.
111 C3 **Altınoluk** Turkey
111 D3 **Altıntaş** Turkey
152 B2 **Altiplano** *plain* Bol.
154 B1 **Alto Araguaia** Brazil
154 B1 **Alto Garças** Brazil
121 C2 **Alto Molócuè** Moz.
129 E3 **Altona** Can.
141 D2 **Altoona** U.S.A.
154 B1 **Alto Sucuriú** Brazil
154 B1 **Alto Taquari** Brazil
102 C2 **Altötting** Ger.
68 B2 **Altun Shan** *mts* China
134 B2 **Alturas** U.S.A.
139 D2 **Altus** U.S.A.
88 C2 **Alūksne** Latvia
78 A2 **Al 'Ulā** Saudi Arabia
115 D1 **Al 'Uqaylah** Libya
Al Uqşur Egypt *see* **Luxor**
91 C3 **Alushta** Ukr.
139 D1 **Alva** U.S.A.
145 C3 **Alvarado** Mex.
93 F3 **Älvdalen** Sweden
93 F3 **Älvdalen** *val.* Sweden
92 H2 **Älvsbyn** Sweden
78 A2 **Al Wajh** Saudi Arabia
74 B2 **Alwar** India
81 C2 **Al Widyān** *plat.* Iraq/Saudi Arabia
Alxa Youqi China *see* **Ehen Hudag**
Alxa Zuoqi China *see* **Bayan Hot**
51 C1 **Alyangula** Austr.
88 B3 **Alytus** Lith.
136 C1 **Alzada** U.S.A.
100 D3 **Alzey** Ger.
50 C2 **Amadeus, Lake** *imp. l.* Austr.
81 C2 **'Amādīyah/Amêdî** Iraq
127 G2 **Amadjuak Lake** Can.
106 B2 **Amadora** Port.
78 B2 **Amā'ir** Saudi Arabia
93 F4 **Åmål** Sweden
111 B3 **Amaliada** Greece
59 D3 **Amamapare** Indon.
154 A2 **Amambaí** Brazil
154 B2 **Amambaí** *r.* Brazil
69 E3 **Amami-Ō-shima** *i.* Japan
69 E3 **Amami-shotō** *is* Japan
77 C1 **Amankel'dy** Kazakh.
109 C3 **Amantea** Italy
151 C1 **Amapá** Brazil
106 B2 **Amareleja** Port.
139 C1 **Amarillo** U.S.A.
108 B2 **Amaro, Monte** *mt.* Italy
80 B1 **Amasya** Turkey
150 C1 **Amazon** *r.* S. America
151 D1 **Amazon, Mouths of the** Brazil
Amazonas *r.* S. America *see* **Amazon**
74 B1 **Ambala** India
121 □D3 **Ambalavao** Madag.
121 □D2 **Ambanja** Madag.
150 A2 **Ambato** Ecuador
121 □D2 **Ambato Boeny** Madag.
121 □D3 **Ambato Finandrahana** Madag.
121 □D2 **Ambatolampy** Madag.
121 □D2 **Ambatondrazaka** Madag.
101 E3 **Amberg** Ger.
146 B3 **Ambergris Caye** *i.* Belize
75 C2 **Ambikapur** India
121 □D2 **Ambilobe** Madag.
98 B1 **Ambleside** U.K.
121 □D3 **Amboasary** Madag.
121 □D3 **Ambohimahasoa** Madag.
59 C3 **Ambon** Indon.
59 C3 **Ambon** *i.* Indon.
121 □D3 **Ambositra** Madag.
121 □D3 **Ambovombe** Madag.
135 C4 **Amboy** U.S.A.
120 A1 **Ambriz** Angola
145 B2 **Amealco** Mex.
144 B2 **Ameca** Mex.
100 B1 **Ameland** *i.* Neth.
134 D2 **American Falls** U.S.A.
134 D2 **American Falls Reservoir** U.S.A.
135 D2 **American Fork** U.S.A.
49 G3 **American Samoa** *terr.* S. Pacific Ocean
143 D2 **Americus** U.S.A.
100 B1 **Amersfoort** Neth.
55 F2 **Amery Ice Shelf** Antarctica
137 E2 **Ames** U.S.A.
111 B3 **Amfissa** Greece
83 J2 **Amga** Russia
66 C1 **Amgu** Russia
115 C2 **Amguid** Alg.
83 K3 **Amgun'** *r.* Russia
131 D2 **Amherst** Can.
104 C2 **Amiens** France
73 B3 **Amindivi Islands** India
122 A1 **Aminuis** Namibia
74 A2 **Amir Chah** Pak.
129 D2 **Amisk Lake** Can.

139 C3 **Amistad Reservoir** Mex./U.S.A.
98 A2 **Amlwch** U.K.
80 B2 **'Ammān** Jordan
81 D2 **Āmol** Iran
111 C3 **Amorgos** *i.* Greece
142 C2 **Amory** U.S.A.
130 C2 **Amos** Can.
Amoy China *see* **Xiamen**
155 C2 **Amparo** Brazil
107 D1 **Amposta** Spain
75 B2 **Amravati** India
74 B1 **Amritsar** India
100 B1 **Amstelveen** Neth.
100 B1 **Amsterdam** Neth.
103 C2 **Amstetten** Austria
115 E3 **Am Timan** Chad
76 B2 **Amudar'ya** *r.* Asia
126 E1 **Amund Ringnes Island** Can.
126 C2 **Amundsen Gulf** Can.
55 M2 **Amundsen Sea** Antarctica
61 C2 **Amuntai** Indon.
Amur *r.* China *see* **Heilong Jiang**
78 A3 **'Amur, Wadi** *watercourse* Sudan
83 I2 **Anabar** *r.* Russia
83 I2 **Anabarskiy Zaliv** *b.* Russia
134 D1 **Anaconda** U.S.A.
139 D1 **Anadarko** U.S.A.
80 B1 **Anadolu Dağları** *mts* Turkey
83 M2 **Anadyr'** *r.* Russia
81 C2 **'Ānah** Iraq
145 B2 **Anáhuac** Mex.
60 B1 **Anambas, Kepulauan** *is* Indon.
137 E2 **Anamosa** U.S.A.
80 B2 **Anamur** Turkey
67 B4 **Anan** Japan
73 B3 **Anantapur** India
74 B1 **Anantnag** India
90 B2 **Anan'yiv** Ukr.
91 D3 **Anapa** Russia
154 C1 **Anápolis** Brazil
152 B3 **Añatuya** Arg.
97 B1 **An Baile Thiar** Ireland
65 B2 **Anbyon** N. Korea
104 B2 **Ancenis** France
108 B2 **Ancona** Italy
153 A5 **Ancud** Chile
Anda China *see* **Daqing**
93 E3 **Åndalsnes** Norway
142 C2 **Andalusia** U.S.A.
73 D3 **Andaman Islands** India
63 A2 **Andaman Sea** Indian Ocean
121 □D2 **Andapa** Madag.
100 B2 **Andelst** Neth.
92 G2 **Andenes** Norway
100 B2 **Andenne** Belgium
100 B2 **Anderlecht** Belgium
126 C2 **Anderson** *r.* Can.
126 B2 **Anderson** *AK* U.S.A.
140 B2 **Anderson** *IN* U.S.A.
143 D2 **Anderson** *SC* U.S.A.
148 D3 **Andes** *mts* S. America
77 D2 **Andijon** Uzbek.
121 □D2 **Andilamena** Madag.
121 □D2 **Andilanatoby** Madag.
121 □D2 **Andoany** Madag.
Andong China *see* **Dandong**
65 B2 **Andong** S. Korea
107 D1 **Andorra** *country* Europe
107 D1 **Andorra la Vella** Andorra
99 C3 **Andover** U.K.
154 B2 **Andradina** Brazil
89 D2 **Andreapol'** Russia
155 D2 **Andrelândia** Brazil
139 C2 **Andrews** U.S.A.
109 C2 **Andria** Italy
121 □D3 **Androka** Madag.
146 C2 **Andros** *i.* Bahamas
111 B3 **Andros** *i.* Greece
143 E4 **Andros Town** Bahamas
73 B3 **Andrott** *i.* India
90 B1 **Andrushivka** Ukr.
92 G2 **Andselv** Norway
106 C2 **Andújar** Spain
120 A2 **Andulo** Angola
114 C3 **Anéfis** Mali
115 D3 **Aney** Niger
83 H3 **Angara** *r.* Russia
69 C1 **Angarsk** Russia
93 G3 **Ånge** Sweden
144 A2 **Ángel de la Guarda, Isla** *i.* Mex.
64 B1 **Angeles** Phil.
150 B1 **Angel Falls** Venez.
93 F4 **Ängelholm** Sweden
92 G3 **Ångermanälven** *r.* Sweden
104 B2 **Angers** France
129 E1 **Angikuni Lake** Can.
98 A2 **Anglesey** *i.* U.K.
121 C2 **Angoche** Moz.
120 A2 **Angola** *country* Africa
140 C2 **Angola** U.S.A.
128 A2 **Angoon** U.S.A.
104 C2 **Angoulême** France
77 D2 **Angren** Uzbek.
147 D3 **Anguilla** *terr.* West Indies
75 C2 **Angul** India
93 F4 **Anholt** *i.* Denmark
71 B3 **Anhua** China
70 B2 **Anhui** *prov.* China
154 B1 **Anhumas** Brazil
154 C1 **Anicuns** Brazil
66 D1 **Aniva, Mys** *c.* Russia
65 B2 **Anjŭ** N. Korea
70 A2 **Ankang** China
80 B2 **Ankara** Turkey
70 B2 **Anlu** China
91 E1 **Anna** Russia
115 C1 **Annaba** Alg.
101 F2 **Annaberg-Buchholz** Ger.
78 B3 **An Nābiyah** Yemen
78 B2 **An Nafūd** *des.* Saudi Arabia
81 C2 **An Najaf** Iraq
96 C3 **Annan** U.K.
141 D3 **Annapolis** U.S.A.
75 C2 **Annapurna I** *mt.* Nepal
140 C2 **Ann Arbor** U.S.A.
150 C1 **Anna Regina** Guyana
81 C2 **An Nāşirīyah** Iraq
105 D2 **Annecy** France
78 B3 **An Nimāş** Saudi Arabia
62 B1 **Anning** China
142 C2 **Anniston** U.S.A.
105 C2 **Annonay** France
79 B2 **An Nu'ayrīyah** Saudi Arabia
121 □D2 **Anorontany, Tanjona** *hd* Madag.
71 B3 **Anpu** China
70 B2 **Anqing** China
102 C2 **Ansbach** Ger.
70 C1 **Anshan** China
71 A3 **Anshun** China
114 C3 **Ansongo** Mali
150 A3 **Antabamba** Peru
80 B2 **Antakya** Turkey
121 □E2 **Antalaha** Madag.
80 B2 **Antalya** Turkey
80 B2 **Antalya Körfezi** *g.* Turkey
121 □D2 **Antananarivo** Madag.
55 Q3 **Antarctic Peninsula** Antarctica
96 B2 **An Teallach** *mt.* U.K.
106 C2 **Antequera** Spain
138 B2 **Anthony** U.S.A.
114 B2 **Anti-Atlas** *mts* Morocco
105 D3 **Antibes** France
131 D2 **Anticosti, Île d'** *i.* Can.
131 D2 **Antigonish** Can.
147 D3 **Antigua** *i.* Antigua
147 D3 **Antigua and Barbuda** *country* West Indies
145 C2 **Antiguo-Morelos** Mex.
111 B3 **Antikythira** *i.* Greece
Antioch Turkey *see* **Antakya**
49 F6 **Antipodes Islands** N.Z.
152 A3 **Antofagasta** Chile
154 C3 **Antonina** Brazil
97 C1 **Antrim** U.K.
97 C1 **Antrim Hills** U.K.
121 □D2 **Antsalova** Madag.
121 □D2 **Antsirabe** Madag.
121 □D2 **Antsirañana** Madag.
121 □D2 **Antsohihy** Madag.
Antwerp Belgium *see* **Antwerpen**
100 B2 **Antwerpen** Belgium
An Uaimh Ireland *see* **Navan**
74 B2 **Anupgarh** India
73 C4 **Anuradhapura** Sri Lanka
51 C3 **Anxious Bay** Austr.
70 B2 **Anyang** China
65 B2 **Anyang** S. Korea
108 B2 **Anzio** Italy
Aomen China *see* **Macao**
66 D2 **Aomori** Japan
54 B2 **Aoraki/Mount Cook** *mt.* N.Z.
108 A1 **Aosta** Italy
143 D3 **Apalachee Bay** U.S.A.
150 B2 **Apaporis** *r.* Col.
154 B2 **Aparecida do Tabuado** Brazil
64 B1 **Aparri** Phil.
86 C2 **Apatity** Russia
144 B3 **Apatzingán** Mex.
100 B1 **Apeldoorn** Neth.
100 C1 **Apen** Ger.
108 A2 **Apennines** *mts* Italy
49 G3 **Apia** Samoa
154 C2 **Apiaí** Brazil
64 B2 **Apo, Mount** *vol.* Phil.
101 E2 **Apolda** Ger.
52 B3 **Apollo Bay** Austr.
143 D3 **Apopka, Lake** U.S.A.
154 B1 **Aporé** Brazil
154 B1 **Aporé** *r.* Brazil
80 B2 **Apostolos Andreas, Cape** Cyprus
133 E3 **Appalachian Mountains** U.S.A.
53 D2 **Appin** Austr.
140 B2 **Appleton** U.S.A.
108 B2 **Aprilia** Italy
91 D3 **Apsheronsk** Russia
154 B2 **Apucarana** Brazil
154 B2 **Apucarana, Serra da** *hills* Brazil
78 A2 **Aqaba, Gulf of** Asia
154 A1 **Aquidauana** *r.* Brazil
117 A4 **Arab, Bahr el** *watercourse* Sudan
Arabian Gulf Asia *see* **The Gulf**
78 B2 **Arabian Peninsula** Asia
56 G5 **Arabian Sea** Indian Ocean
151 E3 **Aracaju** Brazil
151 E2 **Aracati** Brazil
154 B2 **Araçatuba** Brazil
155 D1 **Aracruz** Brazil
155 D1 **Araçuaí** Brazil
110 B1 **Arad** Romania
115 E3 **Arada** Chad
156 C6 **Arafura Sea** Austr./Indon.
154 B1 **Aragarças** Brazil
107 C1 **Aragón** *r.* Spain
151 D2 **Araguaia** *r.* Brazil
151 D2 **Araguaína** Brazil

154 C1 **Araguari** Brazil
115 C2 **Arak** Alg.
81 C2 **Ārāk** Iran
62 A1 **Arakan Yoma** *mts* Myanmar
81 C1 **Arak's** *r.* Armenia
76 B2 **Aralkum** *des.* Uzbek.
76 C2 **Aral Sea** *salt l.* Kazakh./Uzbek.
76 C2 **Aral'sk** Kazakh.
Aral'skoye More *salt l.* Kazakh./Uzbek. *see* **Aral Sea**
106 C1 **Aranda de Duero** Spain
109 D2 **Aranđelovac** Serbia
97 B2 **Aran Islands** Ireland
106 C1 **Aranjuez** Spain
122 A1 **Aranos** Namibia
139 D3 **Aransas Pass** U.S.A.
67 B4 **Arao** Japan
114 B3 **Araouane** Mali
151 E2 **Arapiraca** Brazil
154 B2 **Arapongas** Brazil
154 C3 **Araquari** Brazil
78 B1 **'Ar'ar** Saudi Arabia
154 C2 **Araraquara** Brazil
151 C2 **Araras** Brazil
154 B3 **Araras, Serra das** *mts* Brazil
52 B3 **Ararat** Austr.
81 C2 **Ararat, Mount** Turkey
155 D2 **Araruama, Lago de** *lag.* Brazil
155 E1 **Arataca** Brazil
Aratürük China *see* **Yiwu**
150 A1 **Arauca** Col.
154 C1 **Araxá** Brazil
81 C2 **Arbīl/Hewlêr** Iraq
96 C2 **Arbroath** U.K.
74 A2 **Arbū-ye Shamālī, Dasht-e** *des.* Afgh.
104 B3 **Arcachon** France
143 D3 **Arcadia** U.S.A.
134 B2 **Arcata** U.S.A.
145 B3 **Arcelia** Mex.
86 D2 **Archangel** Russia
51 D1 **Archer** *r.* Austr.
134 D2 **Arco** U.S.A.
106 B2 **Arcos de la Frontera** Spain
127 F2 **Arctic Bay** Can.
160 **Arctic Ocean**
126 C2 **Arctic Red** *r.* Can.
81 C2 **Ardabīl** Iran
81 C1 **Ardahan** Turkey
93 E3 **Årdalstangen** Norway
100 B3 **Ardennes** *plat.* Belgium
81 D2 **Ardestān** Iran
53 C2 **Ardlethan** Austr.
139 D2 **Ardmore** U.S.A.
96 A2 **Ardnamurchan, Point of** U.K.
52 A2 **Ardrossan** Austr.
96 B3 **Ardrossan** U.K.
135 B3 **Arena, Point** U.S.A.
93 E4 **Arendal** Norway
101 E1 **Arendsee (Altmark)** Ger.
150 A3 **Arequipa** Peru
151 C2 **Arere** Brazil
106 C1 **Arévalo** Spain
108 B2 **Arezzo** Italy
104 B2 **Argentan** France
153 B4 **Argentina** *country* S. America
153 A6 **Argentino, Lago** *l.* Arg.
104 C2 **Argenton-sur-Creuse** France
110 C2 **Argeș** *r.* Romania
74 A1 **Arghandāb Rōd** *r.* Afgh.
111 B3 **Argolikos Kolpos** *b.* Greece
111 B3 **Argos** Greece
111 B3 **Argostoli** Greece
107 C1 **Arguis** Spain
69 E1 **Argun'** *r.* China/Russia
50 B1 **Argyle, Lake** Austr.
122 A2 **Ariamsvlei** Namibia
152 A2 **Arica** Chile
96 A2 **Arinagour** U.K.
155 C1 **Arinos** Brazil
150 C3 **Aripuanã** Brazil
150 B2 **Aripuanã** *r.* Brazil
150 B2 **Ariquemes** Brazil
154 B1 **Ariranhá** *r.* Brazil
138 A2 **Arizona** *state* U.S.A.
144 A1 **Arizpe** Mex.
78 B2 **'Arjah** Saudi Arabia
92 G2 **Arjeplog** Sweden
142 B2 **Arkadelphia** U.S.A.
77 C1 **Arkalyk** Kazakh.
142 B2 **Arkansas** *r.* U.S.A.
142 B1 **Arkansas** *state* U.S.A.
137 D3 **Arkansas City** U.S.A.
Arkhangel'sk Russia *see* **Archangel**
97 C2 **Arklow** Ireland
102 C1 **Arkona, Kap** *c.* Ger.
82 G1 **Arkticheskogo Instituta, Ostrova** *is* Russia
105 C3 **Arles** France
115 C3 **Arlit** Niger
100 B3 **Arlon** Belgium
97 C1 **Armagh** U.K.
116 B2 **Armant** Egypt
81 C1 **Armavir** Russia
81 C1 **Armenia** *country* Asia
150 A1 **Armenia** Col.
144 B3 **Armeria** Mex.
53 D2 **Armidale** Austr.
130 B1 **Armstrong** Can.
80 B1 **Armyans'k** Ukr.
80 B2 **Arnauti, Cape** Cyprus
100 B2 **Arnhem** Neth.
51 C1 **Arnhem, Cape** Austr.
51 C1 **Arnhem Bay** Austr.
51 C1 **Arnhem Land** *reg.* Austr.
108 B2 **Arno** *r.* Italy
52 A2 **Arno Bay** Austr.
130 C2 **Arnprior** Can.
100 D2 **Arnsberg** Ger.
101 E2 **Arnstadt** Ger.
122 A2 **Aroab** Namibia
101 D2 **Arolsen** Ger.
78 A3 **Aroma** Sudan
108 A1 **Arona** Italy
144 B2 **Aros** *r.* Mex.
75 C2 **Arrah** India
81 C2 **Ar Ramādī** Iraq
96 B3 **Arran** *i.* U.K.
97 B1 **Arranmore Island** Ireland
80 B2 **Ar Raqqah** Syria
104 C1 **Arras** France
78 B2 **Ar Rass** Saudi Arabia
145 C3 **Arriagá** Mex.
79 C2 **Ar Rimāl** *reg.* Saudi Arabia
Ar Riyāḍ Saudi Arabia *see* **Riyadh**
145 C2 **Arroyo Seco** Mex.
79 C2 **Ar Rustāq** Oman
80 C2 **Ar Ruṭbah** Iraq
81 D3 **Arsanajān** Iran
66 B2 **Arsen'yev** Russia
111 B3 **Arta** Greece
144 B3 **Arteaga** Mex.
66 B2 **Artem** Russia
91 D2 **Artemivs'k** Ukr.
104 C2 **Artenay** France
138 C2 **Artesia** U.S.A.
51 E2 **Arthur Point** Austr.
54 B2 **Arthur's Pass** N.Z.
152 C4 **Artigas** Uru.
129 D1 **Artillery Lake** Can.
90 B2 **Artsyz** Ukr.
77 D3 **Artux** China
81 C1 **Artvin** Turkey
59 C3 **Aru, Kepulauan** *is* Indon.
119 D2 **Arua** Uganda
147 D3 **Aruba** *terr.* West Indies
119 D3 **Arusha** Tanz.
69 C1 **Arvayheer** Mongolia
129 E1 **Arviat** Can.
92 G2 **Arvidsjaur** Sweden
93 F4 **Arvika** Sweden
87 D3 **Arzamas** Russia
107 C2 **Arzew** Alg.
100 C2 **Arzfeld** Ger.
101 F2 **Aš** Czech Rep.
115 C4 **Asaba** Nigeria
74 B1 **Asadābād** Afgh.
66 D2 **Asahi-dake** *vol.* Japan
66 D2 **Asahikawa** Japan
78 B3 **Āsalē** *l.* Eth.
75 C2 **Asansol** India
131 C2 **Asbestos** Can.
109 C2 **Ascea** Italy
152 B2 **Ascensión** Bol.
113 D7 **Ascension** *i.* S. Atlantic Ocean
145 D3 **Ascensión, Bahía de la** *b.* Mex.
101 D3 **Aschaffenburg** Ger.
100 C2 **Ascheberg** Ger.
101 E2 **Aschersleben** Ger.
108 B2 **Ascoli Piceno** Italy
92 G3 **Åsele** Sweden
110 B2 **Asenovgrad** Bulg.
76 B3 **Aşgabat** Turkm.
50 A2 **Ashburton** *watercourse* Austr.
54 B2 **Ashburton** N.Z.
142 B2 **Ashdown** U.S.A.
143 D1 **Asheville** U.S.A.
53 D1 **Ashford** Austr.
99 D3 **Ashford** U.K.
Ashgabat Turkm. *see* **Aşgabat**
98 C1 **Ashington** U.K.
67 B4 **Ashizuri-misaki** *pt* Japan
136 D3 **Ashland** *KS* U.S.A.
140 C3 **Ashland** *KY* U.S.A.
140 C2 **Ashland** *OH* U.S.A.
134 B2 **Ashland** *OR* U.S.A.
140 A1 **Ashland** *WI* U.S.A.
88 C3 **Ashmyany** Belarus
78 B3 **Ash Sharawrah** Saudi Arabia
Ash Shāriqah U.A.E. *see* **Sharjah**
81 C2 **Ash Sharqāṭ** Iraq
81 C2 **Ash Shaṭrah** Iraq
79 B3 **Ash Shiḥr** Yemen
79 C2 **Ash Şhināş** Oman
78 B2 **Ash Shu'bah** Saudi Arabia
78 B2 **Ash Shumlūl** Saudi Arabia
140 C2 **Ashtabula** U.S.A.
131 D1 **Ashuanipi Lake** Can.
106 B2 **Asilah** Morocco
108 A2 **Asinara, Golfo dell'** *b.* *Sardinia* Italy
82 G3 **Asino** Russia
88 C3 **Asipovichy** Belarus
78 B2 **'Asīr** *reg.* Saudi Arabia
93 F4 **Askim** Norway
68 C1 **Askiz** Russia
116 B3 **Asmara** Eritrea
93 F4 **Åsnen** *l.* Sweden
116 B2 **Asoteriba, Jebel** *mt.* Sudan
103 D2 **Aspang-Markt** Austria
136 B3 **Aspen** U.S.A.
54 A2 **Aspiring, Mount** N.Z.
117 C3 **Assab** Eritrea
Aş Şaḥrā' al Gharbīyah *des.* Egypt *see* **Western Desert**
Aş Şaḥrā' ash Sharqīyah *des.* Egypt *see* **Eastern Desert**
78 B2 **As Salamiyah** Saudi Arabia
81 C2 **As Samāwah** Iraq
79 C2 **Aş Şanām** *reg.* Saudi Arabia

As Sarīr reg. Libya

115 E2 As Sarīr reg. Libya
100 C1 Assen Neth.
100 B2 Assesse Belgium
115 D1 As Sidrah Libya
129 D3 Assiniboia Can.
128 C2 Assiniboine, Mount Can.
154 B2 Assis Brazil
78 B2 As Şubayḩīyah Kuwait
81 C2 As Sulaymānīyah/Slêmānî Iraq
78 B2 As Sulaymī Saudi Arabia
78 B2 As Sulayyil Saudi Arabia
78 B2 As Sūq Saudi Arabia
80 B2 As Suwaydā' Syria
79 C2 As Suwayq Oman
78 A2 As Suways Egypt see Suez
111 B3 Astakos Greece
77 D1 Astana Kazakh.
81 C2 Āstārā Iran
108 A2 Asti Italy
74 B1 Astor Pak.
106 B1 Astorga Spain
134 B1 Astoria U.S.A.
87 D4 Astrakhan' Russia
88 C3 Astravyets Belarus
111 C3 Astypalaia i. Greece
152 C3 Asunción Para.
116 B2 Aswān Egypt
116 B2 Asyūṭ Egypt
152 B3 Atacama, Desierto de des. Chile see Atacama Desert
152 B3 Atacama, Salar de salt flat Chile
152 B3 Atacama Desert Chile
114 C4 Atakpamé Togo
111 B3 Atalanti Greece
150 A3 Atalaya Peru
77 C3 Atamyrat Turkm.
78 B3 'Ataq Yemen
114 A2 Atâr Maur.
135 B3 Atascadero U.S.A.
77 D2 Atasu Kazakh.
111 C3 Atavyros mt. Greece
116 B3 Atbara Sudan
116 B3 Atbara r. Sudan
77 C1 Atbasar Kazakh.
137 D3 Atchison U.S.A.
108 B2 Aterno r. Italy
108 B2 Atessa Italy
100 A2 Ath Belgium
128 C2 Athabasca Can.
129 C2 Athabasca r. Can.
129 D2 Athabasca, Lake Can.
111 B3 Athens Greece
143 D2 Athens GA U.S.A.
140 C3 Athens OH U.S.A.
143 D1 Athens TN U.S.A.
139 D2 Athens TX U.S.A.
  Athina Greece see Athens
97 C2 Athlone Ireland
111 B2 Athos mt. Greece
97 C2 Athy Ireland
115 D3 Ati Chad
130 A2 Atikokan Can.
87 D3 Atkarsk Russia
143 D2 Atlanta U.S.A.
137 D2 Atlantic U.S.A.
141 E3 Atlantic City U.S.A.
158 Atlantic Ocean
122 A3 Atlantis S. Africa
114 B1 Atlas Mountains Africa
114 C1 Atlas Saharien mts Alg.
128 A2 Atlin Can.
128 A2 Atlin Lake Can.
142 C2 Atmore U.S.A.
139 D2 Atoka U.S.A.
75 C2 Atrai r. India
78 B2 Aṭ Ṭā'if Saudi Arabia

63 B2 Attapu Laos
130 B1 Attawapiskat Can.
130 B1 Attawapiskat r. Can.
130 B1 Attawapiskat Lake Can.
100 C2 Attendorn Ger.
116 B2 Aṭ Ṭūr Egypt
78 B3 At Turbah Yemen
76 B2 Atyrau Kazakh.
105 C3 Aubenas France
126 C2 Aubry Lake Can.
142 C2 Auburn AL U.S.A.
135 B3 Auburn CA U.S.A.
137 D2 Auburn NE U.S.A.
141 D2 Auburn NY U.S.A.
104 C2 Aubusson France
104 C3 Auch France
54 B1 Auckland N.Z.
48 F6 Auckland Islands is N.Z.
101 F2 Aue Ger.
102 C2 Augsburg Ger.
109 C3 Augusta Sicily Italy
143 D2 Augusta GA U.S.A.
137 D3 Augusta KS U.S.A.
141 F2 Augusta ME U.S.A.
50 A2 Augustus, Mount Austr.
100 A2 Aulnoye-Aymeries France
62 A2 Aunglan Myanmar
122 B2 Auob watercourse Namibia/S. Africa
74 B3 Aurangabad India
100 C1 Aurich Ger.
154 B1 Aurilândia Brazil
104 C3 Aurillac France
136 C3 Aurora CO U.S.A.
140 B3 Aurora IL U.S.A.
137 D2 Aurora NE U.S.A.
122 A2 Aus Namibia
137 E2 Austin MN U.S.A.
135 C3 Austin NV U.S.A.
139 D2 Austin TX U.S.A.
50 B2 Australia country Oceania
159 D7 Australian-Antarctic Basin Southern Ocean
53 C3 Australian Capital Territory admin. div. Austr.
102 C2 Austria country Europe
144 B3 Autlán Mex.
105 C2 Autun France
105 C2 Auxerre France
105 D2 Auxonne France
105 C2 Avallon France
131 E2 Avalon Peninsula Can.
74 B2 Avaré Brazil
49 H4 Avarua Cook Is.
91 D2 Avdiyivka Ukr.
106 B1 Aveiro Port.
108 B2 Avellino Italy
100 A2 Avesnes-sur-Helpe France
93 G3 Avesta Sweden
108 B2 Avezzano Italy
96 C2 Aviemore U.K.
109 C2 Avigliano Italy
105 C3 Avignon France
106 C1 Ávila Spain
106 B1 Avilés Spain
109 C3 Avola Sicily Italy
99 B3 Avon r. England U.K.
99 C3 Avon r. England U.K.
104 B2 Avranches France
54 B1 Awanui N.Z.
117 C4 Āwash Eth.
117 C4 Āwash r. Eth.
115 D2 Awbārī Libya
115 D2 Awbārī, Idhān des. Libya
117 C4 Aw Dheegle Somalia
96 B2 Awe, Loch l. U.K.
117 A4 Aweil South Sudan
126 E1 Axel Heiberg Island Can.

114 B4 Axim Ghana
150 A3 Ayacucho Peru
77 E2 Ayagoz Kazakh.
68 C2 Ayakkum Hu salt l. China
106 B2 Ayamonte Spain
83 K3 Ayan Russia
150 A3 Ayaviri Peru
76 A2 Aybas Kazakh.
91 D2 Aydar r. Ukr.
77 C2 Aydarko'l ko'li l. Uzbek.
111 C3 Aydın Turkey
99 C3 Aylesbury U.K.
106 C1 Ayllón Spain
129 D2 Aylmer Lake Can.
117 B4 Ayod South Sudan
83 M2 Ayon, Ostrov i. Russia
114 B3 'Ayoûn el 'Atroûs Maur.
51 D1 Ayr Austr.
96 B3 Ayr U.K.
98 A1 Ayre, Point of Isle of Man
76 C2 Ayteke Bi Kazakh.
110 C2 Aytos Bulg.
145 C3 Ayutla Mex.
63 B2 Ayutthaya Thai.
111 C3 Ayvacık Turkey
111 C3 Ayvalık Turkey
  Azaniba reg. Somalia see Jubaland
114 C3 Azaouagh, Vallée de watercourse Mali/Niger
77 C2 Azat, Gory h. Kazakh.
114 B3 Azawad reg. Mali
  Azbine mts Niger see Aïr, Massif de l'
81 C1 Azerbaijan country Asia
77 C1 Azhibeksor, Ozero salt l. Kazakh.
86 D2 Azopol'ye Russia
84 D5 Azores aut. reg. Port.
91 D2 Azov Russia
91 D2 Azov, Sea of Russia/Ukr.
  Azraq, Bahr el r. Eth./Sudan see Blue Nile
106 B2 Azuaga Spain
146 B4 Azuero, Península de pen. Panama
153 C4 Azul Arg.
80 B2 Az Zaqāzīq Egypt
80 B2 Az Zarqā' Jordan
78 B3 Az Zaydīyah Yemen
114 C2 Azzel Matti, Sebkha salt pan Alg.
78 B2 Az Zilfī Saudi Arabia
78 B3 Az Zuqur i. Yemen

B

63 B2 Ba, Sông r. Vietnam
117 C4 Baardheere Somalia
77 C3 Bābā, Kōh-e mts Afgh.
110 C2 Babadag Romania
111 C2 Babaeski Turkey
117 C3 Bāb al Mandab str. Africa/Asia
61 C2 Babana Indon.
59 C3 Babar i. Indon.
119 D3 Babati Tanz.
89 E2 Babayevo Russia
128 B2 Babine r. Can.
128 B2 Babine Lake Can.
59 C3 Babo Indon.
81 D2 Bābol Iran
122 A3 Baboon Point S. Africa
88 C3 Babruysk Belarus
64 B1 Babuyan i. Phil.
64 B1 Babuyan Islands Phil.

151	D2	Bacabal Brazil
59	C3	Bacan i. Indon.
110	C1	Bacău Romania
52	B3	Bacchus Marsh Austr.
77	D3	Bachu China
129	E1	Back r. Can.
109	C1	Bačka Palanka Serbia
63	B3	Bac Liêu Vietnam
64	B1	Bacolod Phil.
130	C1	Bacqueville, Lac l. Can.
106	B2	Badajoz Spain
62	A1	Badarpur India
101	F1	Bad Belzig Ger.
101	C2	Bad Berka Ger.
101	D1	Bad Berleburg Ger.
101	E1	Bad Bevensen Ger.
100	C2	Bad Ems Ger.
103	D2	Baden Austria
102	B2	Baden-Baden Ger.
101	E2	Bad Harzburg Ger.
101	D2	Bad Hersfeld Ger.
102	C2	Bad Hofgastein Austria
101	D2	Bad Homburg vor der Höhe Ger.
74	A2	Badin Pak.
		Bādiyat ash Shām des. Asia see Syrian Desert
101	E2	Bad Kissingen Ger.
100	C3	Bad Kreuznach Ger.
101	E2	Bad Lauterberg im Harz Ger.
101	D2	Bad Lippspringe Ger.
101	D3	Bad Mergentheim Ger.
101	D2	Bad Nauheim Ger.
100	C2	Bad Neuenahr-Ahrweiler Ger.
101	E2	Bad Neustadt an der Saale Ger.
101	E1	Bad Oldesloe Ger.
101	D2	Bad Pyrmont Ger.
78	A2	Badr Ḥunayn Saudi Arabia
101	D1	Bad Salzuflen Ger.
101	E2	Bad Salzungen Ger.
102	C1	Bad Schwartau Ger.
101	E1	Bad Segeberg Ger.
100	C3	Bad Sobernheim Ger.
101	E2	Bad Staffelstein Ger.
73	C4	Badulla Sri Lanka
100	D1	Bad Zwischenahn Ger.
65	A2	Baengnyeong-do i. S. Korea
106	C2	Baeza Spain
114	A3	Bafatá Guinea-Bissau
160	O2	Baffin Bay sea Can./Greenland
127	G2	Baffin Island Can.
118	B2	Bafia Cameroon
114	A3	Bafing r. Africa
114	A3	Bafoulabé Mali
118	B2	Bafoussam Cameroon
76	B3	Bāfq Iran
80	B1	Bafra Turkey
79	C2	Bāft Iran
119	C2	Bafwasende Dem. Rep. Congo
119	D3	Bagamoyo Tanz.
60	B1	Bagan Datuk Malaysia
120	B2	Bagani Namibia
60	B1	Bagansiapiapi Indon.
138	A2	Bagdad U.S.A.
62	B2	Bagé Brazil
152	C4	Bagé Brazil
97	C2	Bagenalstown Ireland
81	C2	Baghdad Iraq
77	C3	Baghlān Afgh.
104	C3	Bagnères-de-Luchon France
		Bago Myanmar see Pegu
88	B3	Bagrationovsk Russia
		Bagrax China see Bohu
64	B1	Baguio Phil.
115	C3	Bagzane, Monts mts Niger
		Bahamas country West Indies see The Bahamas

146	C2	Bahamas, The country West Indies
75	C2	Baharampur India
		Bahariya Oasis Egypt see Baḥrīyah, Wāḩāt al
76	B3	Baharly Turkm.
60	B1	Bahau Malaysia
72	B2	Bahawalnagar Pak.
74	B2	Bahawalpur Pak.
153	B4	Bahía Blanca Arg.
144	A2	Bahía Kino Mex.
152	C3	Bahía Negra Para.
144	A2	Bahia Tortugas Mex.
117	B3	Bahir Dar Eth.
75	C2	Bahraich India
79	C2	Bahrain country Asia
116	A2	Baḥrīyah, Wāḩāt al oasis Egypt
79	D2	Bāhū Kalāt Iran
110	B1	Baia Mare Romania
69	E1	Baicheng China
131	D2	Baie-Comeau Can.
		Baie-du-Poste Can. see Mistissini
131	C2	Baie-St-Paul Can.
65	B1	Baihe China
69	D1	Baikal, Lake Russia
110	B2	Băileşti Romania
68	C2	Baima China
143	D2	Bainbridge U.S.A.
48	F2	Bairiki Kiribati
		Bairin Youqi China see Daban
53	C3	Bairnsdale Austr.
71	A3	Baise China
65	B1	Baishan Jilin China
65	B1	Baishan Jilin China
65	B1	Baitou Shan mt. China/N. Korea
70	A2	Baiyin China
116	B3	Baiyuda Desert Sudan
103	D2	Baja Hungary
144	A1	Baja California pen. Mex.
78	B3	Bājil Yemen
114	A3	Bakel Senegal
135	C3	Baker CA U.S.A.
136	C1	Baker MT U.S.A.
134	C2	Baker OR U.S.A.
134	B1	Baker, Mount vol. U.S.A.
129	E1	Baker Foreland hd Can.
49	G2	Baker Island N. Pacific Ocean
129	E1	Baker Lake Can.
129	E1	Baker Lake Can.
135	C3	Bakersfield U.S.A.
91	C3	Bakhchysaray Ukr.
91	C1	Bakhmach Ukr.
		Bākhtarān Iran see Kermānshāh
		Baki Azer. see Baku
111	C2	Bakırköy Turkey
92	□C2	Bakkaflói b. Iceland
118	C2	Bakouma C.A.R.
81	C1	Baku Azer.
64	A2	Balabac Phil.
64	A2	Balabac i. Phil.
64	A2	Balabac Strait Malaysia/Phil.
61	C2	Balaiberkuak Indon.
52	A2	Balaklava Austr.
91	C3	Balaklava Ukr.
91	D2	Balakliya Ukr.
87	D3	Balakovo Russia
76	C3	Bālā Murghāb Afgh.
145	C3	Balancán Mex.
111	C3	Balan Dağı h. Turkey
64	B1	Balanga Phil.
75	C2	Balangir India
79	C2	Bālā Shahr Iran
87	D3	Balashov Russia

103	D2	Balaton, Lake Hungary
103	D2	Balatonboglár Hungary
150	C2	Balbina, Represa de resr Brazil
97	C2	Balbriggan Ireland
52	A2	Balcanoona Austr.
110	C2	Balchik Bulg.
54	A3	Balclutha N.Z.
129	E2	Baldock Lake Can.
129	D2	Baldy Mountain h. Can.
138	B2	Baldy Peak U.S.A.
		Baleares, Islas is Spain see Balearic Islands
107	D2	Balearic Islands Spain
107	D1	Balearic Islands Spain
155	E1	Baleia, Ponta da pt Brazil
130	C1	Baleine, Grande Rivière de la r. Can.
131	D1	Baleine, Rivière à la r. Can.
75	C2	Baleshwar India
108	A2	Balestrieri, Punta mt. Sardinia Italy
61	C2	Bali i. Indon.
115	D4	Bali Nigeria
60	A1	Balige Indon.
75	C2	Baligurha India
111	C3	Balıkesir Turkey
61	C2	Balikpapan Indon.
59	D3	Balimo P.N.G.
102	B2	Balingen Ger.
		Bali Sea Indon. see Laut Bali
76	B3	Balkanabat Turkm.
110	B2	Balkan Mountains Bulgaria/Serbia
77	D2	Balkash Kazakh.
77	D2	Balkhash, Lake Kazakh.
		Balkhash, Ozero l. Kazakh. see Balkhash, Lake
50	B3	Balladonia Austr.
97	B2	Ballaghaderreen Ireland
92	G2	Ballangen Norway
52	B3	Ballarat Austr.
50	B2	Ballard, Lake imp. l. Austr.
96	C2	Ballater U.K.
114	B3	Ballé Mali
53	D1	Ballina Austr.
97	B1	Ballina Ireland
97	B1	Ballinasloe Ireland
139	D2	Ballinger U.S.A.
97	B2	Ballinrobe Ireland
97	B1	Ballycastle Ireland
97	C1	Ballycastle U.K.
97	C1	Ballyclare U.K.
97	C1	Ballymena U.K.
97	C1	Ballymoney U.K.
97	D1	Ballynahinch U.K.
97	B1	Ballyshannon Ireland
95	B2	Ballyvoy U.K.
51	D2	Balonne r. Austr.
74	B2	Balotra India
75	C2	Balrampur India
52	B2	Balranald Austr.
110	B2	Balş Romania
151	D2	Balsas Brazil
145	C3	Balsas Mex.
90	B2	Balta Ukr.
90	B2	Bălți Moldova
93	G4	Baltic Sea g. Europe
80	B2	Baltim Egypt
123	C1	Baltimore S. Africa
141	D3	Baltimore U.S.A.
88	A3	Baltiysk Russia
62	A1	Balu India
88	C2	Balvi Latvia
77	D2	Balykchy Kyrg.
87	E4	Balykshi Kazakh.
79	C2	Bam Iran
51	D1	Bamaga Austr.
130	A1	Bamaji Lake Can.

114 B3 Bamako Mali
118 C2 Bambari C.A.R.
101 E3 Bamberg Ger.
119 C2 Bambili Dem. Rep. Congo
119 C2 Bambouti C.A.R.
155 C2 Bambuí Brazil
118 B2 Bamenda Cameroon
74 A1 Bāmyān Afgh.
119 C2 Banalia Dem. Rep. Congo
151 C3 Bananal, Ilha do i. Brazil
74 B2 Banas r. India
113 C3 Banaz Turkey
62 B2 Ban Ban Laos
97 C1 Banbridge U.K.
99 C2 Banbury U.K.
130 C2 Bancroft Can.
74 A2 Banda Dem. Rep. Congo
75 C2 Banda India
59 C3 Banda, Kepulauan is Indon.
59 C3 Banda, Laut sea Indon.
60 A1 Banda Aceh Indon.
79 C2 Bandar-e 'Abbās Iran
81 C2 Bandar-e Anzalī Iran
79 C2 Bandar-e Būshehr Iran
79 C2 Bandar-e Chārak Iran
81 C2 Bandar-e Emām Khomeynī Iran
81 D3 Bandar-e Ganāveh Iran
79 C2 Bandar-e Jāsk Iran
79 C2 Bandar-e Kangān Iran
79 C2 Bandar-e Lengeh Iran
79 C2 Bandar-e Moqām Iran
60 B2 Bandar Lampung Indon.
61 C1 Bandar Seri Begawan Brunei
Banda Sea Indon. see Banda, Laut
155 D2 Bandeiras, Pico de mt. Brazil
123 C1 Bandelierkop S. Africa
144 B2 Banderas, Bahía de b. Mex.
114 B3 Bandiagara Mali
111 C2 Bandırma Turkey
97 B3 Bandon Ireland
118 B3 Bandundu Dem. Rep. Congo
61 B2 Bandung Indon.
128 C2 Banff Can.
96 C2 Banff U.K.
114 B3 Banfora Burkina Faso
64 B2 Banga Phil.
Bangalore India see Bengaluru
118 C2 Bangassou C.A.R.
59 C3 Banggai Indon.
59 C3 Banggai, Kepulauan is Indon.
61 C1 Banggi i. Sabah Malaysia
60 B2 Bangka i. Indon.
60 B1 Bangkalan Indon.
60 B2 Bangkinang Indon.
60 B2 Bangko Indon.
63 B2 Bangkok Thai.
75 C2 Bangladesh country Asia
63 B2 Ba Ngoi Vietnam
97 D1 Bangor Northern Ireland U.K.
98 A2 Bangor Wales U.K.
141 F2 Bangor U.S.A.
63 A2 Bang Saphan Yai Thai.
64 B1 Bangued Phil.
118 B2 Bangui C.A.R.
121 B2 Bangweulu, Lake Zambia
63 B2 Ban Huai Khon Thai.
116 B2 Bani Suwayf Egypt
115 D1 Banī Walīd Libya
80 B2 Bāniyās Syria
109 C2 Banja Luka Bos. & Herz.
61 C2 Banjarmasin Indon.
114 A3 Banjul Gambia
128 A2 Banks Island B.C. Can.
126 F2 Banks Island N.W.T. Can.
48 F3 Banks Islands Vanuatu
129 E1 Banks Lake Can.

54 B2 Banks Peninsula N.Z.
75 C2 Bankura India
62 A1 Banmauk Myanmar
62 B2 Ban Mouang Laos
97 C1 Bann r. U.K.
62 B2 Ban Napè Laos
63 A3 Ban Na San Thai.
143 E4 Bannerman Town Bahamas
74 B1 Bannu Pak.
74 B2 Banswara India
63 A3 Ban Tha Kham Thai.
63 A2 Ban Tha Song Yang Thai.
62 A2 Ban Tôp Laos
97 B3 Bantry Ireland
97 B3 Bantry Bay Ireland
118 B2 Banyo Cameroon
107 D1 Banyoles Spain
61 C2 Banyuwangi Indon.
Bao'an China see Shenzhen
69 D2 Baochang China
70 B2 Baoding China
70 A2 Baoji China
62 B1 Bao Lac Vietnam
62 B1 Bao Lôc Vietnam
66 B1 Baoqing China
62 A1 Baoshan China
70 B1 Baotou China
81 C2 Ba'qūbah Iraq
109 C2 Bar Montenegro
117 C4 Baraawe Somalia
147 C2 Baracoa Cuba
53 C2 Baradine Austr.
147 C3 Barahona Dom. Rep.
116 B3 Baraka watercourse Eritrea/Sudan
61 C1 Baram r. Sarawak Malaysia
74 B1 Baramulla India
88 C3 Baranavichy Belarus
78 A2 Baranis Egypt
90 B1 Baranivka Ukr.
128 A2 Baranof Island U.S.A.
59 C3 Barat Daya, Kepulauan is Indon.
155 D2 Barbacena Brazil
147 E3 Barbados country West Indies
107 D1 Barbastro Spain
104 B2 Barbezieux-St-Hilaire France
51 D2 Barcaldine Austr.
107 D1 Barcelona Spain
150 B1 Barcelona Venez.
105 D3 Barcelonnette France
150 B2 Barcelos Brazil
Barcoo Creek watercourse Austr. see Cooper Creek
103 D2 Barcs Hungary
75 C2 Barddhaman India
103 E2 Bardejov Slovakia
79 C2 Bardsīr Iran
75 B2 Bareilly India
160 B2 Barents Sea Arctic Ocean
78 A3 Barentu Eritrea
75 C2 Barh India
141 F2 Bar Harbor U.S.A.
109 C2 Bari Italy
74 B1 Barī Kōt Afgh.
150 A1 Barinas Venez.
75 C2 Baripada India
75 D2 Barisal Bangl.
60 B2 Barisan, Pegunungan mts Indon.
61 C2 Barito r. Indon.
79 C2 Barkā Oman
88 C2 Barkava Latvia
51 C1 Barkly Tableland reg. Austr.
68 C2 Barkol China
110 C1 Bârlad Romania
105 D2 Bar-le-Duc France
50 A2 Barlee, Lake imp. l. Austr.

109 C2 Barletta Italy
53 C2 Barmedman Austr.
74 B2 Barmer India
99 A2 Barmouth U.K.
101 D1 Barmstedt Ger.
98 C1 Barnard Castle U.K.
53 B2 Barnato Austr.
82 G3 Barnaul Russia
127 G2 Barnes Icecap Can.
100 B1 Barneveld Neth.
98 C2 Barnsley U.K.
99 A3 Barnstaple U.K.
99 A3 Barnstaple Bay U.K.
143 D2 Barnwell U.S.A.
Baroda India see Vadodara
150 B1 Barquisimeto Venez.
96 A2 Barra i. U.K.
53 D2 Barraba Austr.
151 D2 Barra do Corda Brazil
154 B1 Barra do Garças Brazil
150 B2 Barra do São Manuel Brazil
150 A3 Barranca Lima Peru
150 A2 Barranca Loreto Peru
152 C3 Barranqueras Arg.
150 A1 Barranquilla Col.
151 D3 Barreiras Brazil
154 C2 Barretos Brazil
130 C2 Barrie Can.
128 B2 Barrière Can.
52 B2 Barrier Range hills Austr.
53 D2 Barrington, Mount Austr.
129 D2 Barrington Lake Can.
53 C1 Barringun Austr.
97 C2 Barrow r. Ireland
51 C2 Barrow Creek Austr.
98 B1 Barrow-in-Furness U.K.
50 A2 Barrow Island Austr.
126 E2 Barrow Strait Can.
99 B3 Barry U.K.
130 C2 Barrys Bay Can.
74 B2 Barsalpur India
135 C4 Barstow U.S.A.
105 C2 Bar-sur-Aube France
80 B1 Bartın Turkey
51 D1 Bartle Frere, Mount Austr.
137 D1 Bartlesville U.S.A.
103 E1 Bartoszyce Pol.
69 D1 Barung i. Indon.
69 D1 Baruun-Urt Mongolia
91 D2 Barvinkove Ukr.
53 C2 Barwon r. Austr.
88 C3 Barysaw Belarus
110 C2 Basarabi Romania
105 D2 Basel Switz.
91 C2 Bashtanka Ukr.
64 B2 Basilan i. Phil.
99 D3 Basildon U.K.
99 C3 Basingstoke U.K.
80 B2 Başkale Turkey
130 C2 Baskatong, Réservoir resr Can.
Basle Switz. see Basel
118 C2 Basoko Dem. Rep. Congo
81 C2 Basra Iraq
128 C2 Bassano Can.
114 C4 Bassar Togo
63 A2 Bassein Myanmar
147 D3 Basse-Terre Guadeloupe
147 D3 Basseterre St Kitts and Nevis
114 B3 Bassikounou Maur.
51 D3 Bass Strait Austr.
79 C2 Bastak Iran
101 E2 Bastheim Ger.
116 B2 Basti India
105 D3 Bastia Corsica France
100 B2 Bastogne Belgium
142 B2 Bastrop U.S.A.
Basuo China see Dongfang

Bata

118 A2 **Bata** Equat. Guinea
83 J2 **Batagay** Russia
154 B2 **Bataguassu** Brazil
106 C2 **Batalha** Port.
60 B1 **Batam** Indon.
71 C3 **Batan** i. Phil.
118 B2 **Batangafo** C.A.R.
64 B1 **Batangas** Phil.
60 B2 **Batanghari** r. Indon.
71 C3 **Batan Islands** Phil.
141 D2 **Batavia** U.S.A.
91 D2 **Bataysk** Russia
130 B2 **Batchawana Mountain** h. Can.
50 C1 **Batchelor** Austr.
63 B2 **Bătdâmbâng** Cambodia
53 D3 **Batemans Bay** Austr.
142 B1 **Batesville** U.S.A.
89 D2 **Batetskiy** Russia
99 B3 **Bath** U.K.
74 B1 **Bathinda** India
53 C2 **Bathurst** Austr.
131 D2 **Bathurst** Can.
126 C2 **Bathurst Inlet** Can.
126 D2 **Bathurst Inlet (abandoned)** Can.
50 C1 **Bathurst Island** Austr.
126 E1 **Bathurst Island** Can.
78 M1 **Bāṭin, Wādī al** watercourse Asia
81 C2 **Batman** Turkey
115 C1 **Batna** Alg.
142 B2 **Baton Rouge** U.S.A.
144 B2 **Batopilas** Mex.
118 B2 **Batouri** Cameroon
154 B1 **Batovi** Brazil
92 I1 **Båtsfjord** Norway
73 C4 **Batticaloa** Sri Lanka
109 B2 **Battipaglia** Italy
129 D2 **Battle** r. Can.
140 B2 **Battle Creek** U.S.A.
135 C2 **Battle Mountain** U.S.A.
74 B1 **Battura Glacier** Pak.
117 B4 **Batu** mt. Eth.
60 A2 **Batu, Pulau-pulau** is Indon.
81 C1 **Bat'umi** Georgia
60 B1 **Batu Pahat** Malaysia
59 C3 **Baubau** Indon.
115 C3 **Bauchi** Nigeria
104 B2 **Baugé-en-Anjou** France
105 D2 **Baume-les-Dames** France
154 B2 **Bauru** Brazil
154 B1 **Baús** Brazil
88 B2 **Bauska** Latvia
102 C1 **Bautzen** Ger.
144 B2 **Bavispe** r. Mex.
87 E3 **Bavly** Russia
62 A1 **Bawdwin** Myanmar
61 C2 **Bawean** i. Indon.
114 B3 **Bawku** Ghana
146 C2 **Bayamo** Cuba
Bayan Gol China see Dengkou
68 C2 **Bayanhongor** Mongolia
70 A2 **Bayan Hot** China
70 A1 **Bayannur** China
69 D2 **Bayan Shutu** China
69 D1 **Bayan-Uul** Mongolia
64 B2 **Bayawan** Phil.
80 C1 **Bayburt** Turkey
140 C2 **Bay City** MI U.S.A.
139 D3 **Bay City** TX U.S.A.
86 F2 **Baydaratskaya Guba** Russia
117 C4 **Baydhabo** Somalia
81 C2 **Bayjī** Iraq
Baykal, Ozero l. Russia see Baikal, Lake
83 I3 **Baykal'skiy Khrebet** mts Russia

76 C2 **Baykonyr** Kazakh.
87 E3 **Baymak** Russia
64 B1 **Bayombong** Phil.
104 B3 **Bayonne** France
111 C3 **Bayramiç** Turkey
101 E3 **Bayreuth** Ger.
78 B3 **Bayt al Faqīh** Yemen
106 C2 **Baza** Spain
106 C2 **Baza, Sierra de** mts Spain
74 A1 **Bāzārak** Afgh.
76 A2 **Bazardyuzyu, Gora** mt. Azer./ Russia
104 B3 **Bazas** France
74 A2 **Bazdar** Pak.
70 A2 **Bazhong** China
79 D2 **Bazmān** Iran
79 D2 **Bazmān, Kūh-e** mt. Iran
121 □D2 **Bé, Nosy** i. Madag.
99 D3 **Beachy Head** U.K.
123 C3 **Beacon Bay** S. Africa
50 B1 **Beagle Gulf** Austr.
121 □D2 **Bealanana** Madag.
97 B1 **Béal an Mhuirthead** Ireland
130 B2 **Beardmore** Can.
Bear Island Arctic Ocean see Bjørnøya
134 E1 **Bear Paw Mountain** U.S.A.
147 C3 **Beata, Cabo** c. Dom. Rep.
147 C3 **Beata, Isla** i. Dom. Rep.
137 D2 **Beatrice** U.S.A.
135 C3 **Beatty** U.S.A.
53 D1 **Beaudesert** Austr.
52 B3 **Beaufort** Austr.
61 C1 **Beaufort** Sabah Malaysia
143 D2 **Beaufort** U.S.A.
160 L2 **Beaufort Sea** Can./U.S.A.
122 B3 **Beaufort West** S. Africa
96 B2 **Beauly** r. U.K.
100 B2 **Beaumont** Belgium
54 A3 **Beaumont** N.Z.
139 E2 **Beaumont** U.S.A.
105 C2 **Beaune** France
100 B2 **Beauraing** Belgium
129 E2 **Beauséjour** Can.
104 C2 **Beauvais** France
129 D2 **Beauval** Can.
129 D2 **Beaver** r. Can.
135 D3 **Beaver** U.S.A.
126 B2 **Beaver Creek** Can.
140 B2 **Beaver Dam** U.S.A.
129 E2 **Beaver Hill Lake** Can.
140 B1 **Beaver Island** U.S.A.
128 C2 **Beaverlodge** Can.
74 B2 **Beawar** India
154 C2 **Bebedouro** Brazil
101 D2 **Bebra** Ger.
106 B1 **Becerreá** Spain
114 B1 **Béchar** Alg.
140 C3 **Beckley** U.S.A.
117 B4 **Bedelē** Eth.
99 C2 **Bedford** U.K.
140 B3 **Bedford** U.S.A.
100 C1 **Bedum** Neth.
53 D2 **Beecroft Peninsula** Austr.
101 F1 **Beelitz** Ger.
53 D1 **Beenleigh** Austr.
80 B2 **Beersheba** Israel
139 D3 **Beeville** U.S.A.
53 C3 **Bega** Austr.
107 D1 **Begur, Cap de** c. Spain
128 C1 **Behchokò** Can.
81 D2 **Behshahr** Iran
69 E1 **Bei'an** China
71 A3 **Beihai** China
70 B2 **Beijing** China
100 C1 **Beilen** Neth.
96 A2 **Beinn Mhòr** h. U.K.
121 C2 **Beira** Moz.

80 B2 **Beirut** Lebanon
123 C1 **Beitbridge** Zimbabwe
106 B2 **Beja** Port.
115 C1 **Bejaïa** Alg.
106 B1 **Béjar** Spain
74 A2 **Beji** r. Pak.
103 E2 **Békés** Hungary
103 E2 **Békéscsaba** Hungary
121 □D3 **Bekily** Madag.
74 A2 **Bela** Pak.
123 C1 **Bela-Bela** S. Africa
118 B2 **Bélabo** Cameroon
109 D2 **Bela Crkva** Serbia
61 C1 **Belaga** Sarawak Malaysia
73 B3 **Belagavi** India
88 C3 **Belarus** country Europe
Belau country N. Pacific Ocean see Palau
123 D2 **Bela Vista** Moz.
60 A1 **Belawan** Indon.
83 M2 **Belaya** r. Russia
103 D1 **Bełchatów** Pol.
130 C1 **Belcher Islands** Can.
117 C4 **Beledweyne** Somalia
151 D2 **Belém** Brazil
138 B2 **Belen** U.S.A.
89 E3 **Belev** Russia
97 D1 **Belfast** U.K.
141 F2 **Belfast** U.S.A.
105 D2 **Belfort** France
Belgaum India see Belagavi
100 B2 **Belgium** country Europe
91 D1 **Belgorod** Russia
109 D2 **Belgrade** Serbia
134 D1 **Belgrade** U.S.A.
60 B2 **Belinyu** Indon.
146 B3 **Belitung** i. Indon.
146 B3 **Belize** Belize
146 B3 **Belize** country Central America
83 K1 **Bel'kovskiy, Ostrov** i. Russia
128 B2 **Bella Bella** Can.
104 C2 **Bellac** France
128 B2 **Bella Coola** Can.
53 C1 **Bellata** Austr.
136 C2 **Belle Fourche** U.S.A.
136 C2 **Belle Fourche** r. U.S.A.
143 D3 **Belle Glade** U.S.A.
104 B2 **Belle-Île** i. France
131 E1 **Belle Isle** i. Can.
131 E1 **Belle Isle, Strait of** Can.
130 C2 **Belleville** Can.
140 B3 **Belleville** IL U.S.A.
137 D3 **Belleville** KS U.S.A.
134 B1 **Bellevue** U.S.A.
134 B1 **Bellingham** U.S.A.
55 O2 **Bellingshausen Sea** Antarctica
105 D2 **Bellinzona** Switz.
108 B1 **Belluno** Italy
122 A3 **Bellville** S. Africa
155 E1 **Belmonte** Brazil
146 B3 **Belmopan** Belize
69 E1 **Belogorsk** Russia
121 □D3 **Beloha** Madag.
155 D1 **Belo Horizonte** Brazil
140 B2 **Beloit** U.S.A.
86 C2 **Belomorsk** Russia
91 D3 **Belorechensk** Russia
87 E3 **Beloretsk** Russia
Belorussia country Europe see Belarus
86 F2 **Beloyarskiy** Russia
86 C2 **Beloye, Ozero** l. Russia
Beloye More sea Russia see White Sea
86 C2 **Belozersk** Russia
77 E2 **Belukha, Gora** mt. Kazakh./ Russia
86 D2 **Belush'ye** Russia

89 D2 **Belyy** Russia
82 F2 **Belyy, Ostrov** *i.* Russia
137 E1 **Bemidji** U.S.A.
118 C3 **Bena Dibele** Dem. Rep. Congo
53 C3 **Benalla** Austr.
106 B1 **Benavente** Spain
96 A2 **Benbecula** *i.* U.K.
134 B2 **Bend** U.S.A.
123 C3 **Bendearg** *mt.* S. Africa
90 B2 **Bender** Moldova
52 B3 **Bendigo** Austr.
121 C2 **Bene** Moz.
102 C2 **Benešov** Czech Rep.
109 B2 **Benevento** Italy
159 C2 **Bengal, Bay of** *sea* Indian Ocean
73 B3 **Bengaluru** India
70 B2 **Bengbu** China
115 E1 **Benghazi** Libya
61 B1 **Bengkayang** Indon.
60 B2 **Bengkulu** Indon.
120 A2 **Benguela** Angola
96 B1 **Ben Hope** *h.* U.K.
152 B2 **Beni** *r.* Bol.
119 C2 **Beni** Dem. Rep. Congo
114 B1 **Beni Abbès** Alg.
107 C2 **Benidorm** Spain
114 B1 **Beni Mellal** Morocco
114 C3 **Benin** *country* Africa
114 C4 **Benin, Bight of** *g.* Africa
115 C4 **Benin City** Nigeria
153 C4 **Benito Juárez** Arg.
150 B2 **Benjamin Constant** Brazil
144 A1 **Benjamín Hill** Mex.
59 C3 **Benjina** Indon.
96 B2 **Ben Lawers** *mt.* U.K.
96 B2 **Ben Lomond** *h.* U.K.
96 C2 **Ben Macdui** *mt.* U.K.
96 A2 **Ben More** *h.* U.K.
54 B2 **Benmore, Lake** N.Z.
96 B1 **Ben More Assynt** *h.* U.K.
128 A2 **Bennett (abandoned)** Can.
83 K1 **Bennetta, Ostrov** *i.* Russia
96 B2 **Ben Nevis** *mt.* U.K.
141 E2 **Bennington** U.S.A.
123 C2 **Benoni** S. Africa
101 D3 **Bensheim** Ger.
138 A2 **Benson** U.S.A.
58 C3 **Benteng** Indon.
140 B2 **Benton Harbor** U.S.A.
142 B1 **Bentonville** U.S.A.
115 C4 **Benue** *r.* Nigeria
97 B1 **Benwee Head** Ireland
96 B2 **Ben Wyvis** *mt.* U.K.
70 C1 **Benxi** China
Beograd Serbia *see* **Belgrade**
75 C2 **Beohari** India
67 B4 **Beppu** Japan
109 C2 **Berane** Montenegro
109 C2 **Berat** Albania
59 C3 **Berau, Teluk** *b.* Indon.
116 B3 **Berber** Sudan
117 C3 **Berbera** Somalia
118 B2 **Berbérati** C.A.R.
104 C1 **Berck** France
91 D2 **Berdyans'k** Ukr.
90 B2 **Berdychiv** Ukr.
90 A2 **Berehove** Ukr.
59 D3 **Bereina** P.N.G.
76 B3 **Bereket** Turkm.
129 E2 **Berens River** Can.
90 A2 **Berezhany** Ukr.
90 C2 **Berezivka** Ukr.
90 B1 **Berezne** Ukr.
86 D2 **Bereznik** Russia
86 E3 **Berezniki** Russia
86 F2 **Berezovo** Russia
107 D1 **Berga** Spain
111 C3 **Bergama** Turkey
108 A1 **Bergamo** Italy
101 D1 **Bergen** Ger.
93 E3 **Bergen** Norway
102 C1 **Bergen auf Rügen** Ger.
100 B2 **Bergen op Zoom** Neth.
104 C3 **Bergerac** France
100 C2 **Bergheim** Ger.
100 C2 **Bergisch Gladbach** Ger.
122 A1 **Bergland** Namibia
92 H2 **Bergsviken** Sweden
83 M3 **Beringa, Ostrov** *i.* Russia
100 B2 **Beringen** Belgium
124 C3 **Bering Sea** N. Pacific Ocean
83 N2 **Bering Strait** Russia/U.S.A.
135 B3 **Berkeley** U.S.A.
100 B1 **Berkhout** Neth.
55 Q2 **Berkner Sub-glacial Island** Antarctica
110 B2 **Berkovitsa** Bulg.
92 I1 **Berlevåg** Norway
101 F1 **Berlin** Ger.
141 E2 **Berlin** U.S.A.
101 E2 **Berlingerode** Ger.
53 D3 **Bermagui** Austr.
144 B2 **Bermejíllo** Mex.
152 B3 **Bermejo** Bol.
131 D1 **Bermen, Lac** *l.* Can.
125 K4 **Bermuda** *terr.* N. Atlantic Ocean
105 D2 **Bern** Switz.
101 E2 **Bernburg (Saale)** Ger.
127 F2 **Bernier Bay** Can.
100 C3 **Bernkastel-Kues** Ger.
121 □D3 **Beroroha** Madag.
52 B2 **Berri** Austr.
107 D2 **Berrouaghia** Alg.
146 C2 **Berry Islands** Bahamas
100 C1 **Bersenbrück** Ger.
90 B2 **Bershad'** Ukr.
131 D1 **Berté, Lac** *l.* Can.
118 B2 **Bertoua** Cameroon
150 B2 **Beruri** Brazil
98 B1 **Berwick-upon-Tweed** U.K.
91 C2 **Beryslav** Ukr.
121 □D2 **Besalampy** Madag.
105 D2 **Besançon** France
129 D2 **Besnard Lake** Can.
142 C2 **Bessemer** U.S.A.
76 B2 **Besshoky, Gora** *h.* Kazakh.
106 B1 **Betanzos** Spain
118 B2 **Bétaré Oya** Cameroon
122 A2 **Bethanie** Namibia
123 C2 **Bethlehem** S. Africa
141 D2 **Bethlehem** U.S.A.
121 □D3 **Betioky** Madag.
77 D2 **Betpakdala** *plain* Kazakh.
121 □D3 **Betroka** Madag.
131 D2 **Betsiamites** Can.
121 □D2 **Betsiboka** *r.* Madag.
137 E2 **Bettendorf** U.S.A.
75 C2 **Bettiah** India
75 B2 **Betul** India
75 B2 **Betwa** *r.* India
98 B2 **Betws-y-coed** U.K.
98 C2 **Beverley** U.K.
101 D2 **Beverungen** Ger.
100 B1 **Beverwijk** Neth.
99 D3 **Bexhill** U.K.
111 C2 **Beykoz** Turkey
114 B4 **Beyla** Guinea
76 B2 **Beyneu** Kazakh.
80 B1 **Beypazarı** Turkey
Beyrouth Lebanon *see* **Beirut**
80 B2 **Beyşehir** Turkey
80 B2 **Beyşehir Gölü** *l.* Turkey
91 D2 **Beysug** *r.* Russia
88 C2 **Bezhanitsy** Russia
89 E2 **Bezhetsk** Russia
105 C3 **Béziers** France
75 C2 **Bhadrak** India
73 B3 **Bhadravati** India
75 C2 **Bhagalpur** India
74 A2 **Bhairi Hol** *mt.* Pak.
74 B1 **Bhakkar** Pak.
62 A1 **Bhamo** Myanmar
75 C3 **Bhanjanagar** India
74 B2 **Bharatpur** India
74 B2 **Bharuch** India
74 B2 **Bhavnagar** India
75 C3 **Bhawanipatna** India
123 D2 **Bhekuzulu** S. Africa
74 B2 **Bhilwara** India
73 B3 **Bhima** *r.* India
123 C3 **Bhisho** S. Africa
74 B2 **Bhiwani** India
123 C3 **Bhongweni** S. Africa
74 B2 **Bhopal** India
75 C2 **Bhubaneshwar** India
74 A2 **Bhuj** India
74 B2 **Bhusawal** India
75 D2 **Bhutan** *country* Asia
59 D3 **Biak** Indon.
59 D3 **Biak** *i.* Indon.
103 E1 **Biała Podlaska** Pol.
103 D1 **Białogard** Pol.
103 E1 **Białystok** Pol.
109 C3 **Bianco** Italy
104 B3 **Biarritz** France
105 D2 **Biasca** Switz.
66 D2 **Bibai** Japan
120 A2 **Bibala** Angola
102 B2 **Biberach an der Riß** Ger.
115 C4 **Bida** Nigeria
141 E2 **Biddeford** U.S.A.
99 A3 **Bideford** U.K.
101 D2 **Biedenkopf** Ger.
105 D2 **Biel/Bienne** Switz.
101 D1 **Bielefeld** Ger.
108 A1 **Biella** Italy
103 D2 **Bielsko-Biała** Pol.
63 B2 **Biên Hoa** Vietnam
130 C1 **Bienville, Lac** *l.* Can.
100 B3 **Bièvre** Belgium
118 B3 **Bifoun** Gabon
111 C2 **Biga** Turkey
123 D2 **Big Bend** Swaziland
129 D2 **Biggar** Can.
96 C3 **Biggar** U.K.
134 D1 **Big Hole** *r.* U.S.A.
136 B1 **Bighorn** *r.* U.S.A.
136 B2 **Bighorn Mountains** U.S.A.
139 C2 **Big Lake** U.S.A.
140 B2 **Big Rapids** U.S.A.
129 D2 **Big River** Can.
129 E2 **Big Sand Lake** Can.
137 D2 **Big Sioux** *r.* U.S.A.
139 C2 **Big Spring** U.S.A.
134 E1 **Big Timber** U.S.A.
130 B1 **Big Trout Lake** Can.
130 A1 **Big Trout Lake** Can.
109 C2 **Bihać** Bos. & Herz.
75 C2 **Bihar Sharif** India
110 B1 **Bihor, Vârful** *mt.* Romania
114 A3 **Bijagós, Arquipélago dos** *is* Guinea-Bissau
81 C2 **Bījār** Iran
109 C2 **Bijeljina** Bos. & Herz.
109 C2 **Bijelo Polje** Montenegro
71 A3 **Bijie** China
74 B2 **Bikaner** India
69 E1 **Bikin** Russia
118 B3 **Bikoro** Dem. Rep. Congo
79 C2 **Bilād Banī Bū 'Alī** Oman
75 C2 **Bilaspur** India
90 C2 **Bila Tserkva** Ukr.

63 A2 **Bilauktaung Range** *mts* Myanmar/Thai.
106 C1 **Bilbao** Spain
111 C2 **Bilecik** Turkey
103 E1 **Biłgoraj** Pol.
90 C2 **Bilhorod-Dnistrovs'kyy** Ukr.
119 C2 **Bili** Dem. Rep. Congo
83 M2 **Bilibino** Russia
134 E1 **Billings** U.S.A.
99 B3 **Bill of Portland** *hd* U.K.
115 D3 **Bilma** Niger
115 D3 **Bilma, Grand Erg de** *des.* Niger
51 E2 **Biloela** Austr.
91 C2 **Bilohirs'k** Ukr.
90 B1 **Bilohir"ya** Ukr.
91 C1 **Bilopillya** Ukr.
91 D2 **Bilovods'k** Ukr.
142 C2 **Biloxi** U.S.A.
51 C2 **Bilpa Morea Claypan** *salt flat* Austr.
101 E2 **Bilshausen** Ger.
115 E3 **Biltine** Chad
90 C2 **Bilyayivka** Ukr.
143 E3 **Bimini Islands** Bahamas
75 B2 **Bina-Etawa** India
59 C3 **Binaija, Gunung** *mt.* Indon.
118 B3 **Bindu** Dem. Rep. Congo
121 C2 **Bindura** Zimbabwe
107 D1 **Binéfar** Spain
53 D1 **Bingara** Austr.
100 C3 **Bingen am Rhein** Ger.
141 F1 **Bingham** U.S.A.
141 D2 **Binghamton** U.S.A.
81 C2 **Bingöl** Turkey
60 A1 **Binjai** Indon.
60 B2 **Bintuhan** Indon.
61 C1 **Bintulu** *Sarawak* Malaysia
70 B2 **Binzhou** China
109 C2 **Biograd na Moru** Croatia
118 A2 **Bioko** *i.* Equat. Guinea
118 C1 **Birao** C.A.R.
75 C2 **Biratnagar** Nepal
128 C2 **Birch Mountains** Can.
51 C2 **Birdsville** Austr.
80 B2 **Birecik** Turkey
60 A1 **Bireun** Indon.
75 C2 **Birganj** Nepal
154 B2 **Birigui** Brazil
76 B3 **Bīrjand** Iran
98 B2 **Birkenhead** U.K.
114 B2 **Bir Lahlou** Western Sahara
99 C2 **Birmingham** U.K.
142 C2 **Birmingham** U.S.A.
114 A2 **Bîr Mogreïn** Maur.
115 C3 **Birnin-Kebbi** Nigeria
115 C3 **Birnin Konni** Niger
69 E1 **Birobidzhan** Russia
97 C2 **Birr** Ireland
96 C1 **Birsay** U.K.
78 A2 **Bi'r Shalatayn** Egypt
91 D1 **Biryuch** Russia
88 B2 **Biržai** Lith.
75 B2 **Bisalpur** India
138 B2 **Bisbee** U.S.A.
104 A2 **Biscay, Bay of** *sea* France/Spain
102 C2 **Bischofshofen** Austria
130 B2 **Biscotasi Lake** Can.
77 D2 **Bishkek** Kyrg.
135 C3 **Bishop** U.S.A.
69 E1 **Bishui** China
150 B1 **Bisinaca** Col.
115 C1 **Biskra** Alg.
136 C1 **Bismarck** U.S.A.
48 D3 **Bismarck Sea** *sea* P.N.G.
107 D2 **Bissa, Djebel** *mt.* Alg.
114 A3 **Bissau** Guinea-Bissau
129 E2 **Bissett** Can.
128 C2 **Bistcho Lake** Can.
110 B1 **Bistrița** Romania
110 C1 **Bistrița** *r.* Romania
100 C3 **Bitburg** Ger.
105 D2 **Bitche** France
115 D3 **Bitkine** Chad
109 D2 **Bitola** Macedonia
109 C2 **Bitonto** Italy
122 A3 **Bitterfontein** S. Africa
134 D1 **Bitterroot** *r.* U.S.A.
134 C1 **Bitterroot Range** *mts* U.S.A.
91 D1 **Bityug** *r.* Russia
115 D3 **Biu** Nigeria
67 C3 **Biwa-ko** *l.* Japan
68 B1 **Biysk** Russia
115 C1 **Bizerte** Tunisia
92 □A2 **Bjargtangar** *hd* Iceland
92 G3 **Bjästa** Sweden
92 G2 **Bjerkvik** Norway
82 C2 **Bjørnøya** *i.* Arctic Ocean
114 B3 **Bla** Mali
137 E3 **Black** *r.* U.S.A.
51 D2 **Blackall** Austr.
98 B2 **Blackburn** U.K.
134 D2 **Blackfoot** U.S.A.
102 B2 **Black Forest** *mts* Ger.
136 C2 **Black Hills** U.S.A.
96 B2 **Black Isle** *pen.* U.K.
129 D2 **Black Lake** Can.
129 D2 **Black Lake** Can.
99 B3 **Black Mountains** *hills* U.K.
98 B2 **Blackpool** U.K.
62 B1 **Black River** *r.* Vietnam
140 A2 **Black River Falls** U.S.A.
140 C3 **Blacksburg** U.S.A.
80 B1 **Black Sea** Asia/Europe
97 A1 **Blacksod Bay** Ireland
97 C2 **Blackstairs Mountains** *hills* Ireland
114 B4 **Black Volta** *r.* Africa
97 C2 **Blackwater** *r.* Ireland
128 B1 **Blackwater Lake** Can.
50 A3 **Blackwood** *r.* Austr.
76 A2 **Blagodarnyy** Russia
110 B2 **Blagoevgrad** Bulg.
69 E1 **Blagoveshchensk** Russia
129 D2 **Blaine Lake** Can.
137 D2 **Blair** U.S.A.
96 C2 **Blair Atholl** U.K.
96 C2 **Blairgowrie** U.K.
143 D2 **Blakely** U.S.A.
105 D2 **Blanc, Mont** *mt.* France/Italy
153 B4 **Blanca, Bahía** *b.* Arg.
52 A1 **Blanche, Lake** *imp. l.* Austr.
152 B2 **Blanco** *r.* Bol.
131 E1 **Blanc-Sablon** Can.
92 □A2 **Blanda** *r.* Iceland
99 B3 **Blandford Forum** U.K.
135 E3 **Blanding** U.S.A.
107 D1 **Blanes** Spain
60 A1 **Blangkejeren** Indon.
100 C2 **Blankenheim** Ger.
100 C2 **Blankenrath** Ger.
103 D2 **Blansko** Czech Rep.
121 C2 **Blantyre** Malawi
98 C1 **Blaydon** U.K.
53 C2 **Blayney** Austr.
54 B2 **Blenheim** N.Z.
115 C1 **Blida** Alg.
130 B2 **Blind River** Can.
123 C2 **Bloemfontein** S. Africa
123 C2 **Bloemhof** S. Africa
123 C2 **Bloemhof Dam** S. Africa
92 □A2 **Blönduós** Iceland
97 B1 **Bloody Foreland** *pt* Ireland
138 B1 **Bloomfield** U.S.A.
140 B2 **Bloomington** *IL* U.S.A.
140 B3 **Bloomington** *IN* U.S.A.
140 C3 **Bluefield** U.S.A.
146 B3 **Bluefields** Nic.
53 C2 **Blue Mountains** Austr.
134 C1 **Blue Mountains** U.S.A.
116 B3 **Blue Nile** *r.* Eth./Sudan
126 D2 **Bluenose Lake** Can.
140 C3 **Blue Ridge** *mts* U.S.A.
97 B1 **Blue Stack Mountains** *hills* Ireland
54 A3 **Bluff** N.Z.
135 E3 **Bluff** U.S.A.
152 D3 **Blumenau** Brazil
52 A2 **Blyth** Austr.
98 C1 **Blyth** U.K.
135 D4 **Blythe** U.S.A.
142 C1 **Blytheville** U.S.A.
114 A4 **Bo** Sierra Leone
64 B1 **Boac** Phil.
151 D2 **Boa Esperança, Açude** *resr* Brazil
150 B1 **Boa Vista** Brazil
53 C2 **Bobadah** Austr.
71 B3 **Bobai** China
121 □D2 **Bobaomby, Tanjona** *c.* Madag.
114 B3 **Bobo-Dioulasso** Burkina Faso
89 F3 **Bobrov** Russia
91 C1 **Bobrovytsya** Ukr.
91 C2 **Bobrynets'** Ukr.
121 □D3 **Boby** *mt.* Madag.
150 B2 **Boca do Acre** Brazil
155 D1 **Bocaiúva** Brazil
118 B2 **Bocaranga** C.A.R.
103 E2 **Bochnia** Pol.
100 C2 **Bocholt** Ger.
100 C2 **Bochum** Ger.
101 E1 **Bockenem** Ger.
118 B2 **Boda** C.A.R.
83 I3 **Bodaybo** Russia
115 D3 **Bodélé** *reg.* Chad
92 H2 **Boden** Sweden
99 A3 **Bodmin** U.K.
99 A3 **Bodmin Moor** *moorland* U.K.
92 F2 **Bodø** Norway
111 C3 **Bodrum** Turkey
118 C3 **Boende** Dem. Rep. Congo
142 C2 **Bogalusa** U.S.A.
114 B3 **Bogandé** Burkina Faso
68 B2 **Bogda Shan** *mts* China
53 D1 **Boggabilla** Austr.
97 B2 **Boggeragh Mountains** *hills* Ireland
100 B3 **Bogny-sur-Meuse** France
97 C2 **Bog of Allen** *reg.* Ireland
53 C3 **Bogong, Mount** Austr.
60 B2 **Bogor** Indon.
89 E3 **Bogoroditsk** Russia
150 A1 **Bogotá** Col.
82 G3 **Bogotol** Russia
83 H3 **Boguchany** Russia
91 E2 **Boguchar** Russia
70 B2 **Bo Hai** *g.* China
100 A3 **Bohain-en-Vermandois** France
70 B2 **Bohai Wan** *b.* China
123 C2 **Bohlokong** S. Africa
102 C2 **Böhmer Wald** *mts* Ger.
91 D1 **Bohodukhiv** Ukr.
64 B2 **Bohol** *i.* Phil.
64 B2 **Bohol Sea** Phil.
68 B2 **Bohu** China
155 C2 **Boi, Ponta do** *pt* Brazil
154 B1 **Bois** *r.* Brazil
126 C2 **Bois, Lac des** *l.* Can.
134 C2 **Boise** U.S.A.
139 C1 **Boise City** U.S.A.
123 C2 **Boitumelong** S. Africa

101 E1 **Boizenburg/Elbe** Ger.
76 B3 **Bojnūrd** Iran
118 B3 **Bokatola** Dem. Rep. Congo
114 A3 **Boké** Guinea
118 C3 **Bokele** Dem. Rep. Congo
93 E4 **Boknafjorden** *sea chan.* Norway
115 D3 **Bokoro** Chad
63 A2 **Bokpyin** Myanmar
89 D2 **Boksitogorsk** Russia
122 B2 **Bokspits** Botswana
114 A3 **Bolama** Guinea-Bissau
63 B2 **Bolavén, Phouphiang** *plat.* Laos
104 C2 **Bolbec** France
77 E2 **Bole** China
118 B3 **Boleko** Dem. Rep. Congo
114 B3 **Bolgatanga** Ghana
90 B2 **Bolhrad** Ukr.
66 B1 **Boli** China
62 B2 **Bolikhamxai** Laos
110 C2 **Bolintin-Vale** Romania
137 E3 **Bolivar** U.S.A.
150 A1 **Bolívar, Pico** *mt.* Venez.
152 B2 **Bolivia** *country* S. America
89 E3 **Bolkhov** Russia
105 C3 **Bollène** France
93 G3 **Bollnäs** Sweden
53 C1 **Bollon** Austr.
101 E2 **Bollstedt** Ger.
93 F4 **Bolmen** *l.* Sweden
118 B3 **Bolobo** Dem. Rep. Congo
108 B2 **Bologna** Italy
89 D2 **Bologovo** Russia
89 D2 **Bologoye** Russia
118 B2 **Bolomba** Dem. Rep. Congo
83 H1 **Bol'shevik, Ostrov** *i.* Russia
86 E2 **Bol'shezemel'skaya Tundra** *lowland* Russia
66 B2 **Bol'shoy Kamen'** Russia
Bol'shoy Kavkaz *mts* Asia/Europe *see* **Caucasus**
83 K2 **Bol'shoy Lyakhovskiy, Ostrov** *i.* Russia
100 B1 **Bolsward** Neth.
98 B2 **Bolton** U.K.
80 B1 **Bolu** Turkey
92 □A2 **Bolungarvík** Iceland
108 B1 **Bolzano** Italy
118 B3 **Boma** Dem. Rep. Congo
53 D2 **Bomaderry** Austr.
53 C3 **Bombala** Austr.
Bombay India *see* **Mumbai**
155 C1 **Bom Despacho** Brazil
75 D2 **Bomdila** India
151 D3 **Bom Jesus da Lapa** Brazil
155 D2 **Bom Jesus do Itabapoana** Brazil
115 D1 **Bon, Cap** *c.* Tunisia
147 D3 **Bonaire** *i.* West Indies
147 D3 **Bonaire** *mun.* West Indies
50 B1 **Bonaparte Archipelago** *is* Austr.
131 E2 **Bonavista** Can.
131 E2 **Bonavista Bay** Can.
118 C2 **Bondo** Dem. Rep. Congo
114 B4 **Bondoukou** Côte d'Ivoire
58 C3 **Bonerate, Kepulauan** *is* Indon.
155 C1 **Bonfinópolis de Minas** Brazil
117 B4 **Bonga** Eth.
75 D2 **Bongaigaon** India
118 C2 **Bongandanga** Dem. Rep. Congo
118 C2 **Bongo, Massif des** *mts* C.A.R.
115 D3 **Bongor** Chad
114 B4 **Bongouanou** Côte d'Ivoire
63 B2 **Bông Sơn** Vietnam
139 D2 **Bonham** U.S.A.
105 D3 **Bonifacio** *Corsica* France
108 A2 **Bonifacio, Strait of** France/Italy
100 C2 **Bonn** Ger.
134 C1 **Bonners Ferry** U.S.A.
50 A3 **Bonnie Rock** Austr.
129 C2 **Bonnyville** Can.
108 A2 **Bonorva** *Sardinia* Italy
61 C1 **Bontang** Indon.
64 B1 **Bontoc** Phil.
58 B3 **Bontosunggu** Indon.
123 C3 **Bontrug** S. Africa
52 B2 **Booligal** Austr.
53 C1 **Boomi** Austr.
53 D1 **Boonah** Austr.
137 E2 **Boone** U.S.A.
142 C2 **Booneville** U.S.A.
137 E3 **Boonville** U.S.A.
53 C2 **Boorowa** Austr.
126 F2 **Boothia, Gulf of** Can.
126 E2 **Boothia Peninsula** Can.
100 C2 **Boppard** Ger.
144 B2 **Boquilla, Presa de la** *resr* Mex.
109 D2 **Bor** Serbia
117 B4 **Bor** South Sudan
80 B2 **Bor** Turkey
121 □E2 **Boraha, Nosy** *i.* Madag.
76 B2 **Borankul** Kazakh.
93 F4 **Borås** Sweden
79 C2 **Borāzjān** Iran
150 C2 **Borba** Brazil
104 B3 **Bordeaux** France
127 F2 **Borden Peninsula** Can.
52 B3 **Bordertown** Austr.
107 D2 **Bordj Bou Arréridj** Alg.
107 D2 **Bordj Bounaama** Alg.
115 C1 **Bordj Messaouda** Alg.
115 C2 **Bordj Omer Driss** Alg.
94 B1 **Borðoy** *i.* Faroe Is
92 □A3 **Borgarnes** Iceland
108 A1 **Borgosesia** Italy
87 D3 **Borisoglebsk** Russia
89 E2 **Borisoglebskiy** Russia
91 D1 **Borisovka** Russia
100 C2 **Borken** Ger.
92 G2 **Borkenes** Norway
100 C1 **Borkum** Ger.
100 C1 **Borkum** *i.* Ger.
93 G3 **Borlänge** Sweden
101 F2 **Borna** Ger.
61 C1 **Borneo** *i.* Asia
93 F4 **Bornholm** *i.* Denmark
111 C3 **Bornova** Turkey
90 B1 **Borodyanka** Ukr.
89 D2 **Borovichi** Russia
89 E2 **Borovsk** Russia
107 C2 **Borriana** Spain
51 C1 **Borroloola** Austr.
110 B1 **Borşa** Romania
90 B2 **Borshchiv** Ukr.
69 D1 **Borshchovochnyy Khrebet** *mts* Russia
101 E1 **Börßum** Ger.
Bortala China *see* **Bole**
81 C2 **Borūjerd** Iran
65 B2 **Boryeong** S. Korea
90 A2 **Boryslav** Ukr.
90 C1 **Boryspil'** Ukr.
91 C1 **Borzna** Ukr.
69 D1 **Borzya** Russia
109 C1 **Bosanska Dubica** Bos. & Herz.
109 C1 **Bosanska Gradiška** Bos. & Herz.
109 C2 **Bosanska Krupa** Bos. & Herz.
109 C1 **Bosanski Novi** Bos. & Herz.
109 C2 **Bosansko Grahovo** Bos. & Herz.
123 C2 **Boshof** S. Africa
109 C2 **Bosnia and Herzegovina** *country* Europe
118 B2 **Bosobolo** Dem. Rep. Congo
110 C2 **Bosporus** *str.* Turkey
118 B2 **Bossangoa** C.A.R.
118 B2 **Bossembélé** C.A.R.
68 B2 **Bosten Hu** *l.* China
98 C2 **Boston** U.K.
141 E2 **Boston** U.S.A.
142 B1 **Boston Mountains** U.S.A.
53 D2 **Botany Bay** Austr.
110 B2 **Botev** *mt.* Bulg.
93 G3 **Bothnia, Gulf of** Fin./Sweden
110 C1 **Botoşani** Romania
123 C2 **Botshabelo** S. Africa
120 B3 **Botswana** *country* Africa
109 C3 **Botte Donato, Monte** *mt.* Italy
136 C1 **Bottineau** U.S.A.
100 C2 **Bottrop** Ger.
154 C2 **Botucatu** Brazil
114 B4 **Bouaké** Côte d'Ivoire
118 B2 **Bouar** C.A.R.
114 B1 **Bou Arfa** Morocco
131 D2 **Bouctouche** Can.
107 E2 **Bougaa** Alg.
114 B3 **Bougouni** Mali
100 B3 **Bouillon** Belgium
107 D2 **Bouira** Alg.
114 A2 **Boujdour** Western Sahara
136 B2 **Boulder** U.S.A.
135 D3 **Boulder City** U.S.A.
51 C2 **Boulia** Austr.
104 C2 **Boulogne-Billancourt** France
99 D3 **Boulogne-sur-Mer** France
118 B3 **Boumango** Gabon
118 B2 **Boumba** *r.* Cameroon
107 D2 **Boumerdès** Alg.
114 B4 **Bouna** Côte d'Ivoire
114 B4 **Boundiali** Côte d'Ivoire
134 D2 **Bountiful** U.S.A.
114 B3 **Bourem** Mali
104 C2 **Bourganeuf** France
105 D2 **Bourg-en-Bresse** France
104 C2 **Bourges** France
53 C2 **Bourke** Austr.
99 C3 **Bournemouth** U.K.
115 C1 **Bou Saâda** Alg.
115 D3 **Bousso** Chad
114 A3 **Boutilimit** Maur.
129 C3 **Bow** *r.* Can.
51 D2 **Bowen** Austr.
129 C3 **Bow Island** Can.
140 B3 **Bowling Green** *KY* U.S.A.
140 C2 **Bowling Green** *OH* U.S.A.
136 C1 **Bowman** U.S.A.
101 D3 **Boxberg** Ger.
100 B2 **Boxtel** Neth.
80 B1 **Boyabat** Turkey
Boyang China *see* **Poyang**
97 B2 **Boyle** Ireland
97 C2 **Boyne** *r.* Ireland
136 B2 **Boysen Reservoir** U.S.A.
152 B3 **Boyuibe** Bol.
111 C3 **Bozburun** Turkey
111 C3 **Bozcaada** *i.* Turkey
111 C3 **Bozdağ** *mt.* Turkey
111 C3 **Boz Dağları** *mts* Turkey
111 C3 **Bozdoğan** Turkey
134 D1 **Bozeman** U.S.A.
118 B2 **Bozoum** C.A.R.
111 D3 **Bozüyük** Turkey
109 C2 **Brač** *i.* Croatia
130 C2 **Bracebridge** Can.
99 C3 **Bracknell** U.K.
109 C2 **Bradano** *r.* Italy
143 D3 **Bradenton** U.S.A.

98 C2	Bradford U.K.
141 D2	Bradford U.S.A.
139 D2	Brady U.S.A.
96 C2	Braemar U.K.
106 B1	Braga Port.
151 D2	Bragança Brazil
106 B1	Bragança Port.
155 C2	Bragança Paulista Brazil
89 D3	Brahin Belarus
73 C3	Brahmapur India
62 A1	Brahmaputra r. China/India
110 C1	Brăila Romania
137 E1	Brainerd U.S.A.
99 D3	Braintree U.K.
100 B2	Braives Belgium
101 D1	Brake (Unterweser) Ger.
100 D1	Bramsche Ger.
150 B2	Branco r. Brazil
101 F1	Brandenburg an der Havel Ger.
129 E3	Brandon Can.
97 A2	Brandon Mountain h. Ireland
122 B3	Brandvlei S. Africa
103 D1	Braniewo Pol.
130 B2	Brantford Can.
131 D2	Bras d'Or Lake Can.
155 D1	Brasil, Planalto do plat. Brazil
154 C1	Brasília Brazil
155 D1	Brasília de Minas Brazil
88 C2	Braslaw Belarus
110 C1	Braşov Romania
103 D2	Bratislava Slovakia
83 H3	Bratsk Russia
102 C2	Braunau am Inn Austria
101 E1	Braunschweig Ger.
92 □A2	Brautarholt Iceland
	Bravo del Norte, Río r. Mex./U.S.A. see Rio Grande
135 C4	Brawley U.S.A.
97 B3	Bray Ireland
150 C2	Brazil country S. America
154 C1	Brazlândia Brazil
139 D3	Brazos r. U.S.A.
118 B3	Brazzaville Congo
109 C2	Brčko Bos. & Herz.
96 C2	Brechin U.K.
100 B2	Brecht Belgium
139 D2	Breckenridge U.S.A.
103 D2	Břeclav Czech Rep.
99 B3	Brecon U.K.
99 B3	Brecon Beacons reg. U.K.
100 B2	Breda Neth.
122 B3	Bredasdorp S. Africa
102 B2	Bregenz Austria
92 H1	Breivikbotn Norway
92 E3	Brekstad Norway
101 D1	Bremen Ger.
101 D1	Bremerhaven Ger.
134 B1	Bremerton U.S.A.
101 D1	Bremervörde Ger.
139 D2	Brenham U.S.A.
108 B1	Brennero Italy
102 C2	Brenner Pass Austria/Italy
99 D3	Brentwood U.K.
108 B1	Brescia Italy
108 B1	Bressanone Italy
96 □	Bressay i. U.K.
104 B2	Bressuire France
88 B3	Brest Belarus
104 B2	Brest France
142 C3	Breton Sound b. U.S.A.
151 C2	Breves Brazil
53 C1	Brewarrina Austr.
134 C1	Brewster U.S.A.
89 E2	Breytovo Russia
109 C1	Brezovo Polje plain Croatia
118 C2	Bria C.A.R.
105 D3	Briançon France
90 B2	Briceni Moldova
99 B3	Bridgend U.K.
141 E2	Bridgeport CT U.S.A.
136 C2	Bridgeport NE U.S.A.
147 E3	Bridgetown Barbados
131 D2	Bridgewater Can.
99 B3	Bridgwater U.K.
98 C1	Bridlington U.K.
98 C1	Bridlington Bay U.K.
105 D2	Brig Switz.
134 D2	Brigham City U.S.A.
54 B3	Brighton N.Z.
99 C3	Brighton U.K.
105 D3	Brignoles France
101 D2	Brilon Ger.
109 C2	Brindisi Italy
91 D2	Brin'kovskaya Russia
53 D1	Brisbane Austr.
99 B3	Bristol U.K.
143 D1	Bristol U.S.A.
99 A3	Bristol Channel est. U.K.
128 B2	British Columbia prov. Can.
56 G7	British Indian Ocean Territory terr. Indian Ocean
95 B2	British Isles is Europe
123 C2	Brits S. Africa
122 B3	Britstown S. Africa
104 C2	Brive-la-Gaillarde France
106 C1	Briviesca Spain
103 D2	Brno Czech Rep.
53 D2	Broad r. U.S.A.
130 C1	Broadback r. Can.
96 C3	Broad Law h. U.K.
136 B1	Broadus U.S.A.
129 D2	Brochet Can.
129 D2	Brochet, Lac l. Can.
131 D2	Brochet, Lac au l. Can.
101 E1	Bröckel Ger.
126 D1	Brock Island Can.
130 C2	Brockville Can.
127 F2	Brodeur Peninsula Can.
96 B3	Brodick U.K.
103 D1	Brodnica Pol.
97 B1	Brody Ukr.
139 D1	Broken Arrow U.S.A.
137 D2	Broken Bow U.S.A.
52 B2	Broken Hill Austr.
99 B2	Bromsgrove U.K.
93 E4	Brønderslev Denmark
92 F2	Brønnøysund Norway
64 A2	Brooke's Point Phil.
142 B2	Brookhaven U.S.A.
134 B2	Brookings OR U.S.A.
137 D2	Brookings SD U.S.A.
129 C2	Brooks Can.
126 B2	Brooks Range mts U.S.A.
143 D3	Brooksville U.S.A.
96 B2	Broom, Loch inlet U.K.
50 B1	Broome Austr.
134 B2	Brothers U.S.A.
	Broughton Island Can. see Qikiqtarjuaq
90 C1	Brovary Ukr.
139 C2	Brownfield U.S.A.
128 C3	Browning U.S.A.
142 C1	Brownsville TN U.S.A.
139 D3	Brownsville TX U.S.A.
139 D2	Brownwood U.S.A.
92 □A2	Brú Iceland
104 C1	Bruay-la-Buissière France
140 B1	Bruce Crossing U.S.A.
103 D2	Bruck an der Mur Austria
	Bruges Belgium see Brugge
100 A2	Brugge Belgium
128 C2	Brûlé Can.
151 D3	Brumado Brazil
93 F3	Brumunddal Norway
61 C1	Brunei country Asia
102 C2	Brunico Italy
101 D1	Brunsbüttel Ger.
143 D2	Brunswick GA U.S.A.
141 F2	Brunswick ME U.S.A.
53 D1	Brunswick Heads Austr.
136 C2	Brush U.S.A.
	Brussel Belgium see Brussels
100 B2	Brussels Belgium
	Bruxelles Belgium see Brussels
139 D2	Bryan U.S.A.
89 D3	Bryansk Russia
91 D2	Bryukhovetskaya Russia
103 D1	Brzeg Pol.
114 A3	Buba Guinea-Bissau
80 B2	Bucak Turkey
150 A1	Bucaramanga Col.
52 A3	Buchan Austr.
114 A4	Buchanan Liberia
110 C2	Bucharest Romania
65 B2	Bucheon S. Korea
101 D1	Buchholz in der Nordheide Ger.
110 C1	Bucin, Pasul pass Romania
101 D1	Bückeburg Ger.
138 A2	Buckeye U.S.A.
96 C2	Buckhaven U.K.
96 C2	Buckie U.K.
51 C1	Buckingham Bay Austr.
51 D2	Buckland Tableland reg. Austr.
52 A2	Buckleboo Austr.
141 F2	Bucksport U.S.A.
	Bucureşti Romania see Bucharest
89 D3	Buda-Kashalyova Belarus
103 D2	Budapest Hungary
75 B2	Budaun India
108 A2	Buddusò Sardinia Italy
99 A3	Bude U.K.
87 D4	Budennovsk Russia
89 D2	Budogoshch' Russia
108 A2	Budoni Sardinia Italy
118 A2	Buea Cameroon
144 B2	Buenaventura Mex.
106 C1	Buendia, Embalse de resr Spain
155 D1	Buenópolis Brazil
153 C4	Buenos Aires Arg.
153 A5	Buenos Aires, Lago l. Arg./Chile
141 D2	Buffalo NY U.S.A.
136 C1	Buffalo SD U.S.A.
136 B2	Buffalo WY U.S.A.
129 D2	Buffalo Narrows Can.
122 A2	Buffels watercourse S. Africa
110 C2	Buftea Romania
103 E1	Bug r. Pol.
61 C2	Bugel, Tanjung pt Indon.
109 C2	Bugojno Bos. & Herz.
64 A2	Bugsuk i. Phil.
87 E3	Buguruslan Russia
110 C1	Buhuşi Romania
99 B2	Builth Wells U.K.
120 A3	Buitepos Namibia
109 D2	Bujanovac Serbia
119 C3	Bujumbura Burundi
69 D1	Bukachacha Russia
119 C3	Bukavu Dem. Rep. Congo
60 B2	Bukittinggi Indon.
119 D3	Bukoba Tanz.
53 D2	Bulahdelah Austr.
121 B3	Bulawayo Zimbabwe
111 C3	Buldan Turkey
123 D2	Bulembu Swaziland
69 C1	Bulgan Mongolia
110 C2	Bulgaria country Europe
54 B2	Buller r. N.Z.

52 B1 Bulloo Downs Austr.
122 A1 Büllsport Namibia
58 C3 Bulukumba Indon.
118 B3 Bulungu Dem. Rep. Congo
118 C2 Bumba Dem. Rep. Congo
62 A1 Bumhkang Myanmar
118 B3 Buna Dem. Rep. Congo
50 A3 Bunbury Austr.
97 C1 Buncrana Ireland
119 D3 Bunda Tanz.
51 E2 Bundaberg Austr.
53 D2 Bundarra Austr.
74 B2 Bundi India
97 B1 Bundoran Ireland
53 C3 Bungendore Austr.
67 B4 Bungo-suidō sea chan. Japan
119 D2 Bunia Dem. Rep. Congo
118 C3 Bunianga Dem. Rep. Congo
63 B2 Buôn Ma Thuôt Vietnam
119 D3 Bura Kenya
78 B2 Buraydah Saudi Arabia
100 D2 Burbach Ger.
117 C4 Burco Somalia
100 B1 Burdaard Neth.
80 B2 Burdur Turkey
117 B3 Burē Eth.
99 D2 Bure r. U.K.
74 B1 Burewala Pak.
101 E1 Burg Ger.
110 C2 Burgas Bulg.
101 E1 Burgdorf Niedersachsen Ger.
101 E1 Burgdorf Niedersachsen Ger.
131 E2 Burgeo Can.
123 D1 Burgersfort S. Africa
100 A2 Burgh-Haamstede Neth.
145 C2 Burgos Mex.
106 C1 Burgos Spain
111 C3 Burhaniye Turkey
74 B2 Burhanpur India
101 D1 Burhave (Butjadingen) Ger.
131 C1 Burin Can.
151 D2 Buriti Bravo Brazil
155 C1 Buritis Brazil
51 C1 Burketown Austr.
114 B3 Burkina Faso country Africa
134 D2 Burley U.S.A.
136 C3 Burlington CO U.S.A.
137 E2 Burlington IA U.S.A.
143 E1 Burlington NC U.S.A.
141 E2 Burlington VT U.S.A.
Burma country Asia see
Myanmar
134 B2 Burney U.S.A.
51 D4 Burnie Austr.
98 B2 Burnley U.K.
134 C2 Burns U.S.A.
128 B2 Burns Lake Can.
77 C2 Burqin China
52 A2 Burra Austr.
109 D2 Burrel Albania
97 B2 Burren reg. Ireland
53 C2 Burrendong, Lake resr Austr.
53 C2 Burren Junction Austr.
Burriana Spain see Borriana
144 B2 Burrinjuck Reservoir Austr.
144 B2 Burro, Serranías del mts Mex.
111 C2 Bursa Turkey
116 B2 Bûr Safâjah Egypt
Bür Sa'îd Egypt see Port Said
130 C1 Burton, Lac l. Can.
99 C2 Burton upon Trent U.K.
59 C3 Buru i. Indon.
119 C3 Burundi country Africa
119 C3 Bururi Burundi
91 C1 Buryn' Ukr.
99 D2 Bury St Edmunds U.K.
108 B3 Busambra, Rocca mt. Sicily
Italy

65 B2 Busan S. Korea
118 C3 Busanga Dem. Rep. Congo
119 D2 Bushenyi Uganda
118 C2 Businga Dem. Rep. Congo
50 A3 Busselton Austr.
139 C3 Bustamante Mex.
118 C2 Buta Dem. Rep. Congo
119 C3 Butare Rwanda
123 C2 Butha-Buthe Lesotho
140 D2 Butler U.S.A.
59 C3 Buton i. Indon.
134 D1 Butte U.S.A.
60 B1 Butterworth Malaysia
96 A1 Butt of Lewis hd U.K.
129 E2 Button Bay Can.
64 B2 Butuan Phil.
91 E1 Buturlinovka Russia
75 C2 Butwal Nepal
101 D2 Butzbach Ger.
117 C4 Buulobarde Somalia
117 C5 Buur Gaabo Somalia
117 C4 Buurhabaka Somalia
76 C3 Buxoro Uzbek.
101 D1 Buxtehude Ger.
89 F2 Buy Russia
87 D4 Buynaksk Russia
69 D1 Buyr Nuur l. Mongolia
111 C3 Büyükmenderes r. Turkey
110 C1 Buzău Romania
121 C2 Búzi Moz.
87 E3 Buzuluk Russia
110 C2 Byala Bulg.
88 C3 Byalynichy Belarus
88 D3 Byarezina r. Belarus
88 B3 Byaroza Belarus
103 D1 Bydgoszcz Pol.
88 C3 Byerazino Belarus
88 C2 Byeshankovichy Belarus
89 D3 Bykhaw Belarus
127 F2 Bylot Island Can.
53 C2 Byrock Austr.
53 D1 Byron Bay Austr.
83 J2 Bytantay r. Russia
103 D1 Bytom Pol.
103 D1 Bytów Pol.

C

154 B2 Caarapó Brazil
64 B1 Cabanatuan Phil.
117 C3 Cabdul Qaadir Somalia
107 C2 Cabeza del Buey Spain
152 B2 Cabezas Bol.
150 A1 Cabimas Venez.
120 A1 Cabinda Angola
118 B3 Cabinda prov. Angola
155 D2 Cabo Frio Brazil
155 D2 Cabo Frio, Ilha do i. Brazil
130 C2 Cabonga, Réservoir resr Can.
51 E2 Caboolture Austr.
150 A2 Cabo Pantoja Peru
144 A1 Caborca Mex.
144 B2 Cabo San Lucas Mex.
131 D2 Cabot Strait Can.
155 D1 Cabral, Serra do mts Brazil
107 D2 Cabrera, Illa de i. Spain
106 B1 Cabrera, Sierra de la mts
Spain
129 D2 Cabri Can.
107 C2 Cabriel r. Spain
152 C3 Caçador Brazil
109 D2 Čačak Serbia
108 A2 Caccia, Capo c. Sardinia Italy
153 C3 Cáceres Brazil
106 B2 Cáceres Spain
128 B2 Cache Creek Can.

114 A3 Cacheu Guinea-Bissau
151 C2 Cachimbo, Serra do hills
Brazil
154 B1 Cachoeira Alta Brazil
155 D2 Cachoeiro de Itapemirim
Brazil
114 A3 Cacine Guinea-Bissau
120 A2 Cacolo Angola
154 B1 Caçu Brazil
103 D2 Čadca Slovakia
101 D1 Cadenberge Ger.
145 B2 Cadereyta Mex.
140 B2 Cadillac U.S.A.
106 B2 Cádiz Spain
106 B2 Cádiz, Golfo de g. Spain
128 C2 Cadotte Lake Can.
104 B2 Caen France
98 A2 Caernarfon U.K.
98 A2 Caernarfon Bay U.K.
152 B3 Cafayate Arg.
64 B2 Cagayan de Oro Phil.
64 A2 Cagayan de Tawi-Tawi i.
Phil.
108 B2 Cagli Italy
108 A3 Cagliari Sardinia Italy
108 A3 Cagliari, Golfo di b. Sardinia
Italy
76 B2 Çagyl Turkm.
97 B3 Caha Mountains hills Ireland
97 A3 Cahermore Ireland
97 C2 Cahir Ireland
97 A3 Cahirsiveen Ireland
97 C2 Cahore Point Ireland
104 C3 Cahors France
90 B2 Cahul Moldova
121 C2 Caia Moz.
151 C3 Caiabis, Serra dos hills Brazil
120 B2 Caianda Angola
154 B1 Caiapó, Serra do mts Brazil
154 B1 Caiapônia Brazil
147 C2 Caicos Islands
Turks and Caicos Is
96 C2 Cairngorm Mountains U.K.
98 A1 Cairnryan U.K.
51 D1 Cairns Austr.
116 B1 Cairo Egypt
98 C2 Caistor U.K.
120 A2 Caiundo Angola
150 A2 Cajamarca Peru
109 C1 Čakovec Croatia
123 C3 Cala S. Africa
150 B1 Calabozo Venez.
152 B3 Calafat Romania
153 A6 Calafate Arg.
107 C1 Calahorra Spain
104 C1 Calais France
141 F1 Calais U.S.A.
152 B3 Calama Chile
64 A1 Calamian Group is Phil.
107 C1 Calamocha Spain
120 A1 Calandula Angola
60 A1 Calang Indon.
64 B1 Calapan Phil.
110 C2 Călăraşi Romania
107 C1 Calatayud Spain
64 B1 Calayan i. Phil.
64 B1 Calbayog Phil.
151 E2 Calcanhar, Ponta do pt
Brazil
151 C1 Calçoene Brazil
Calcutta India see Kolkata
106 B2 Caldas da Rainha Port.
154 C1 Caldas Novas Brazil
152 A3 Caldera Chile
134 C2 Caldwell U.S.A.
123 C3 Caledon r. Lesotho/S. Africa
122 A3 Caledon S. Africa
153 B5 Caleta Olivia Arg.

98 A1 **Calf of Man** *i.* Isle of Man
128 C2 **Calgary** Can.
150 A1 **Cali** Col.
Calicut India *see* **Kozhikode**
135 D3 **Caliente** U.S.A.
135 B2 **California** *state* U.S.A.
144 A1 **California, Gulf of** Mex.
135 B3 **California Aqueduct** *canal* U.S.A.
122 B3 **Calitzdorp** S. Africa
145 C2 **Calkiní** Mex.
52 B1 **Callabonna, Lake** *imp. l.* Austr.
96 B2 **Callander** U.K.
150 A3 **Callao** Peru
108 B3 **Caltagirone** *Sicily* Italy
108 B3 **Caltanissetta** *Sicily* Italy
120 A2 **Caluquembe** Angola
117 D3 **Caluula** Somalia
105 D3 **Calvi** *Corsica* France
107 D2 **Calvià** Spain
144 B2 **Calvillo** Mex.
122 A3 **Calvinia** S. Africa
109 C2 **Calvo, Monte** *mt.* Italy
144 B2 **Camacho** Mex.
120 A2 **Camacupa** Angola
146 C2 **Camagüey** Cuba
150 A3 **Camaná** Peru
154 B1 **Camapuã** Brazil
145 C2 **Camargo** Mex.
63 B3 **Ca Mau** Vietnam
63 B3 **Ca Mau, Mui** *c.* Vietnam
63 B2 **Cambodia** *country* Asia
99 A3 **Camborne** U.K.
105 C1 **Cambrai** France
99 B2 **Cambrian Mountains** *hills* U.K.
54 C1 **Cambridge** N.Z.
99 D2 **Cambridge** U.K.
141 E2 **Cambridge** *MA* U.S.A.
141 D3 **Cambridge** *MD* U.S.A.
137 E1 **Cambridge** *MN* U.S.A.
140 C2 **Cambridge** *OH* U.S.A.
131 D1 **Cambrien, Lac** *l.* Can.
53 D2 **Camden** Austr.
142 B2 **Camden** *AR* U.S.A.
141 F2 **Camden** *ME* U.S.A.
118 B2 **Cameroon** *country* Africa
118 B2 **Cameroon Highlands** *slope* Cameroon/Nigeria
151 D2 **Cametá** Brazil
64 B1 **Camiguin** *i.* Phil.
152 B3 **Camiri** Bol.
151 D2 **Camocim** Brazil
51 C1 **Camooweal** Austr.
63 A3 **Camorta** *i.* India
153 A5 **Campana, Isla** *i.* Chile
122 B2 **Campbell** S. Africa
54 B2 **Campbell, Cape** N.Z.
48 F6 **Campbell Island** N.Z.
128 B2 **Campbell River** Can.
140 B3 **Campbellsville** U.S.A.
131 D2 **Campbellton** Can.
96 B3 **Campbeltown** U.K.
145 C3 **Campeche** Mex.
145 C3 **Campeche, Bahía de** *g.* Mex.
52 B3 **Camperdown** Austr.
110 C1 **Câmpina** Romania
151 E2 **Campina Grande** Brazil
154 C2 **Campinas** Brazil
154 C1 **Campina Verde** Brazil
108 B2 **Campobasso** Italy
155 C2 **Campo Belo** Brazil
154 C1 **Campo Florido** Brazil
152 B3 **Campo Gallo** Arg.
154 B2 **Campo Grande** Brazil
151 D2 **Campo Maior** Brazil
106 B2 **Campo Maior** Port.
154 B2 **Campo Mourão** Brazil
155 C1 **Campos Altos** Brazil
155 C2 **Campos do Jordão** Brazil
155 D2 **Campos dos Goytacazes** Brazil
110 C1 **Câmpulung** Romania
138 A2 **Camp Verde** U.S.A.
128 C2 **Camrose** Can.
129 D2 **Camsell Portage** Can.
111 C2 **Çan** Turkey
126 F2 **Canada** *country* N. America
139 C1 **Canadian** U.S.A.
139 D1 **Canadian** *r.* U.S.A.
111 C2 **Çanakkale** Turkey
144 A1 **Cananea** Mex.
154 C2 **Cananéia** Brazil
Canarias, Islas *terr.* N. Atlantic Ocean *see* **Canary Islands**
114 A2 **Canary Islands** *terr.* N. Atlantic Ocean
155 C1 **Canastra, Serra da** *mts* Brazil
144 B2 **Canatlán** Mex.
143 D3 **Canaveral, Cape** U.S.A.
155 E1 **Canavieiras** Brazil
53 C3 **Canberra** Austr.
145 D2 **Cancún** Mex.
111 C3 **Çandarlı** Turkey
145 C3 **Candelaria** Mex.
129 D2 **Candle Lake** Can.
120 A2 **Cangamba** Angola
106 B1 **Cangas del Narcea** Spain
152 C4 **Canguçu** Brazil
70 B2 **Cangzhou** China
131 D1 **Caniapiscau** Can.
131 D1 **Caniapiscau** *r.* Can.
131 C1 **Caniapiscau, Réservoir de** *resr* Can.
108 B3 **Canicattì** *Sicily* Italy
151 E2 **Canindé** Brazil
144 B2 **Cañitas de Felipe Pescador** Mex.
80 B1 **Çankırı** Turkey
128 C2 **Canmore** Can.
96 A2 **Canna** *i.* U.K.
Cannanore India *see* **Kannur**
105 D3 **Cannes** France
99 B2 **Cannock** U.K.
53 C3 **Cann River** Austr.
152 C3 **Canoas** Brazil
129 D2 **Canoe Lake** Can.
154 B3 **Canoinhas** Brazil
136 B3 **Canon City** U.S.A.
129 D2 **Canora** Can.
53 C2 **Canowindra** Austr.
106 C1 **Cantábrica, Cordillera** *mts* Spain
106 B1 **Cantábrico, Mar** *sea* Spain
99 D3 **Canterbury** U.K.
54 B2 **Canterbury Bight** *b.* N.Z.
54 B2 **Canterbury Plains** N.Z.
63 B2 **Cân Thơ** Vietnam
151 D2 **Canto do Buriti** Brazil
Canton China *see* **Guangzhou**
142 C2 **Canton** *MS* U.S.A.
140 C2 **Canton** *OH* U.S.A.
139 C1 **Canyon** U.S.A.
134 D1 **Canyon Ferry Lake** U.S.A.
62 B1 **Cao Bằng** Vietnam
154 C2 **Capão Bonito** Brazil
155 D2 **Caparaó, Serra do** *mts* Brazil
51 D4 **Cape Barren Island** Austr.
52 A3 **Cape Borda** Austr.
131 D2 **Cape Breton Island** Can.
114 B4 **Cape Coast** Ghana
141 E2 **Cape Cod Bay** U.S.A.
127 F2 **Cape Dorset** Can.
143 E2 **Cape Fear** *r.* U.S.A.
137 F3 **Cape Girardeau** U.S.A.
155 D1 **Capelinha** Brazil
100 B2 **Capelle aan den IJssel** Neth.
120 A1 **Capenda-Camulemba** Angola
122 A3 **Cape Town** S. Africa
112 C5 **Cape Verde** *country* Africa
51 D1 **Cape York Peninsula** Austr.
147 C3 **Cap-Haïtien** Haiti
151 D2 **Capim** *r.* Brazil
58 D1 **Capitol Hill** N. Mariana Is
109 C2 **Čapljina** Bos. & Herz.
109 B3 **Capo d'Orlando** *Sicily* Italy
108 A2 **Capraia, Isola di** *i.* Italy
108 A2 **Caprara, Punta** *pt Sardinia* Italy
108 B2 **Capri, Isola di** *i.* Italy
120 B2 **Caprivi Strip** *reg.* Namibia
150 B2 **Caquetá** *r.* Col.
110 B2 **Caracal** Romania
150 B1 **Caracas** Venez.
151 D2 **Caracol** Brazil
155 C2 **Caraguatatuba** Brazil
153 A4 **Carahue** Chile
155 D1 **Caraí** Brazil
155 D2 **Carangola** Brazil
110 B1 **Caransebeş** Romania
131 D2 **Caraquet** Can.
146 B3 **Caratasca, Laguna de** *lag.* Hond.
155 D1 **Caratinga** Brazil
150 B2 **Carauari** Brazil
107 C2 **Caravaca de la Cruz** Spain
155 E1 **Caravelas** Brazil
129 E3 **Carberry** Can.
144 A2 **Carbó** Mex.
107 C2 **Carbon, Cap** *c.* Alg.
153 B5 **Carbón, Laguna del** *l.* Arg.
108 A3 **Carbonara, Capo** *c. Sardinia* Italy
136 B3 **Carbondale** *CO* U.S.A.
140 B3 **Carbondale** *IL* U.S.A.
131 E2 **Carbonear** Can.
155 D1 **Carbonita** Brazil
107 C2 **Carcaixent** Spain
104 C3 **Carcassonne** France
128 A1 **Carcross** Can.
145 C3 **Cárdenas** Mex.
99 B3 **Cardiff** U.K.
99 A2 **Cardigan** U.K.
99 A2 **Cardigan Bay** U.K.
128 C3 **Cardston** Can.
110 B1 **Carei** Romania
104 B2 **Carentan** France
50 B2 **Carey, Lake** *imp. l.* Austr.
155 D2 **Cariacica** Brazil
146 B3 **Caribbean Sea** N. Atlantic Ocean
141 F1 **Caribou** U.S.A.
130 B1 **Caribou Lake** Can.
128 C2 **Caribou Mountains** Can.
144 B2 **Carichic** Mex.
100 B3 **Carignan** France
53 C2 **Carinda** Austr.
107 C1 **Cariñena** Spain
130 C2 **Carleton Place** Can.
123 C2 **Carletonville** S. Africa
97 C1 **Carlingford Lough** *inlet* Ireland/U.K.
98 B1 **Carlisle** U.K.
141 D2 **Carlisle** U.S.A.
155 D1 **Carlos Chagas** Brazil
97 C2 **Carlow** Ireland
135 C4 **Carlsbad** *CA* U.S.A.
138 C2 **Carlsbad** *NM* U.S.A.
129 D3 **Carlyle** Can.
128 A1 **Carmacks** Can.
129 E3 **Carman** Can.
99 A3 **Carmarthen** U.K.
99 A3 **Carmarthen Bay** U.K.

104 C3 **Carmaux** France
145 C3 **Carmelita** Guat.
144 A2 **Carmen, Isla** *i.* Mex.
104 B2 **Carnac** France
122 B3 **Carnarvon** S. Africa
97 C1 **Carndonagh** Ireland
50 B2 **Carnegie, Lake** *imp. l.* Austr.
96 B2 **Carn Eige** *mt.* U.K.
63 A3 **Car Nicobar** *i.* India
118 B2 **Carnot** C.A.R.
52 A2 **Carnot, Cape** Austr.
97 C2 **Carnsore Point** Ireland
151 D2 **Carolina** Brazil
48 D2 **Caroline Islands** N. Pacific Ocean
103 D2 **Carpathian Mountains** Europe
Carpaţii Meridionali *mts* Romania *see* **Transylvanian Alps**
51 C1 **Carpentaria, Gulf of** Austr.
105 D3 **Carpentras** France
97 B3 **Carrantuohill** *mt.* Ireland
105 E3 **Carrara** Italy
97 C2 **Carrickmacross** Ireland
97 B2 **Carrick-on-Shannon** Ireland
97 C2 **Carrick-on-Suir** Ireland
137 D1 **Carrington** U.S.A.
139 D3 **Carrizo Springs** U.S.A.
138 B2 **Carrizozo** U.S.A.
137 E2 **Carroll** U.S.A.
143 C2 **Carrollton** U.S.A.
129 D2 **Carrot River** Can.
135 C3 **Carson City** U.S.A.
150 A1 **Cartagena** Col.
107 C2 **Cartagena** Spain
146 B4 **Cartago** Costa Rica
137 E3 **Carthage** *MO* U.S.A.
139 E2 **Carthage** *TX* U.S.A.
131 E1 **Cartwright** Can.
151 E2 **Caruaru** Brazil
114 B1 **Casablanca** Morocco
154 C2 **Casa Branca** Brazil
144 B1 **Casa de Janos** Mex.
138 A2 **Casa Grande** U.S.A.
108 A1 **Casale Monferrato** Italy
109 C2 **Casarano** Italy
134 C2 **Cascade** U.S.A.
134 B2 **Cascade Range** *mts* Can./U.S.A.
106 B2 **Cascais** Port.
154 B2 **Cascavel** Brazil
108 B2 **Caserta** Italy
97 C2 **Cashel** Ireland
53 D1 **Casino** Austr.
107 C1 **Caspe** Spain
136 B2 **Casper** U.S.A.
76 A2 **Caspian Lowland** Kazakh./Russia
81 C1 **Caspian Sea** Asia/Europe
154 C2 **Cássia** Brazil
128 B2 **Cassiar (abandoned)** Can.
128 A2 **Cassiar Mountains** Can.
154 B1 **Cassilândia** Brazil
108 B2 **Cassino** Italy
96 B2 **Cassley** *r.* U.K.
151 D2 **Castanhal** Brazil
152 B4 **Castaño** *r.* Arg.
144 B2 **Castaños** Mex.
104 C3 **Casteljaloux** France
107 C2 **Castellón de la Plana** Spain
106 B2 **Castelo Branco** Port.
108 B3 **Castelvetrano** *Sicily* Italy
52 B3 **Casterton** Austr.
108 B2 **Castiglione della Pescaia** Italy
97 B2 **Castlebar** Ireland
96 A2 **Castlebay** U.K.
97 C1 **Castleblayney** Ireland
97 C1 **Castlederg** U.K.
96 C3 **Castle Douglas** U.K.
128 C3 **Castlegar** Can.
97 B2 **Castleisland** Ireland
52 B3 **Castlemaine** Austr.
97 B2 **Castlerea** Ireland
53 C2 **Castlereagh** *r.* Austr.
136 C3 **Castle Rock** U.S.A.
129 C2 **Castor** Can.
104 C3 **Castres** France
100 B1 **Castricum** Neth.
147 D3 **Castries** St Lucia
154 C2 **Castro** Brazil
153 A5 **Castro** Chile
106 B2 **Castro Verde** Port.
109 C3 **Castrovillari** Italy
150 A2 **Catacaos** Peru
155 D2 **Cataguases** Brazil
154 C1 **Catalão** Brazil
152 B3 **Catamarca** Arg.
64 B1 **Catanduanes** *i.* Phil.
154 C2 **Catanduva** Brazil
154 B3 **Catanduvas** Brazil
109 C3 **Catania** *Sicily* Italy
109 C3 **Catanzaro** Italy
64 B1 **Catarman** Phil.
64 B1 **Catbalogan** Phil.
145 C3 **Catemaco** Mex.
147 C2 **Cat Island** Bahamas
130 A1 **Cat Lake** Can.
145 D2 **Catoche, Cabo** *c.* Mex.
141 E2 **Catskill Mountains** U.S.A.
64 B2 **Cauayan** Phil.
150 A1 **Cauca** *r.* Col.
151 E2 **Caucaia** Brazil
81 C1 **Caucasus** *mts* Asia/Europe
100 A2 **Caudry** France
109 C3 **Caulonia** Italy
131 D2 **Causapscal** Can.
105 D3 **Cavaillon** France
151 D3 **Cavalcante** Brazil
97 C2 **Cavan** Ireland
154 B3 **Cavernoso, Serra do** *mts* Brazil
151 D2 **Caxias** Brazil
152 C3 **Caxias do Sul** Brazil
120 A1 **Caxito** Angola
151 C1 **Cayenne** Fr. Guiana
146 B3 **Cayman Islands** *terr.* West Indies
117 C4 **Caynaba** Somalia
120 B2 **Cazombo** Angola
144 B2 **Ceballos** Mex.
64 B1 **Cebu** Phil.
64 B1 **Cebu** *i.* Phil.
108 B2 **Cecina** Italy
137 F2 **Cedar** *r.* U.S.A.
135 D3 **Cedar City** U.S.A.
137 E2 **Cedar Falls** U.S.A.
129 D2 **Cedar Lake** Can.
137 E2 **Cedar Rapids** U.S.A.
144 A2 **Cedros, Isla** *i.* Mex.
51 C3 **Ceduna** Austr.
117 C4 **Ceeldheere** Somalia
117 C3 **Ceerigaabo** Somalia
108 B3 **Cefalù** *Sicily* Italy
145 B2 **Celaya** Mex.
58 C3 **Celebes** *i.* Indon.
156 B5 **Celebes Sea** Indon./Phil.
145 C2 **Celestún** Mex.
101 E1 **Celle** Ger.
95 B3 **Celtic Sea** Ireland/U.K.
59 D3 **Cenderawasih, Teluk** *b.* Indon.
150 A1 **Central, Cordillera** *mts* Col.
150 A3 **Central, Cordillera** *mts* Peru
64 B1 **Central, Cordillera** *mts* Phil.
118 C2 **Central African Republic** *country* Africa
74 A2 **Central Brahui Range** *mts* Pak.
137 D2 **Central City** U.S.A.
140 B3 **Centralia** *IL* U.S.A.
134 B1 **Centralia** *WA* U.S.A.
74 A2 **Central Makran Range** *mts* Pak.
59 D3 **Central Range** *mts* P.N.G.
89 E3 **Central Russian Upland** *hills* Russia
83 I2 **Central Siberian Plateau** Russia
111 B3 **Cephalonia** *i.* Greece
Ceram Sea Indon. *see* **Seram, Laut**
152 B3 **Ceres** Arg.
154 C1 **Ceres** Brazil
122 A3 **Ceres** S. Africa
104 C3 **Céret** France
106 C1 **Cerezo de Abajo** Spain
109 C2 **Cerignola** Italy
110 C2 **Cernavodă** Romania
145 C2 **Cerralvo** Mex.
144 B2 **Cerralvo, Isla** *i.* Mex.
145 B2 **Cerritos** Mex.
154 C2 **Cerro Azul** Brazil
145 C2 **Cerro Azul** Mex.
150 A3 **Cerro de Pasco** Peru
105 D3 **Cervione** *Corsica* France
106 B1 **Cervo** Spain
108 B2 **Cesena** Italy
88 C2 **Cēsis** Latvia
102 C2 **České Budějovice** Czech Rep.
101 F3 **Český les** *mts* Czech Rep.
111 C3 **Çeşme** Turkey
53 D2 **Cessnock** Austr.
109 C2 **Cetinje** Montenegro
109 C3 **Cetraro** Italy
106 B2 **Ceuta** N. Africa
105 C3 **Cévennes** *mts* France
Ceylon *country* Asia *see* **Sri Lanka**
79 D2 **Chābahār** Iran
150 A2 **Chachapoyas** Peru
89 D3 **Chachersk** Belarus
63 B2 **Chachoengsao** Thai.
115 D3 **Chad** *country* Africa
115 D3 **Chad, Lake** Africa
69 C1 **Chadaasan** Mongolia
68 C1 **Chadan** Russia
123 C1 **Chadibe** Botswana
136 C2 **Chadron** U.S.A.
65 B2 **Chaeryŏng** N. Korea
74 A2 **Chagai** Pak.
77 C3 **Chaghcharān** Afgh.
89 E2 **Chagoda** Russia
75 C2 **Chaibasa** India
63 B2 **Chainat** Thai.
63 B2 **Chaiyaphum** Thai.
152 C4 **Chajarí** Arg.
131 D1 **Chakonipau, Lac** *l.* Can.
150 A3 **Chala** Peru
131 D2 **Chaleur Bay** *inlet* Can.
74 B2 **Chalisgaon** India
111 C3 **Chalki** *i.* Greece
111 B3 **Chalkida** Greece
104 B2 **Challans** France
134 D2 **Challis** U.S.A.
105 C2 **Châlons-en-Champagne** France
105 C2 **Chalon-sur-Saône** France
138 B1 **Chama** U.S.A.
121 C2 **Chama** Zambia
74 A1 **Chaman** Pak.
74 B1 **Chamba** India
74 B2 **Chambal** *r.* India

137 D2 **Chamberlain** U.S.A.
141 D3 **Chambersburg** U.S.A.
105 D2 **Chambéry** France
121 C2 **Chambeshi** Zambia
140 B2 **Champaign** U.S.A.
141 E2 **Champlain, Lake** Can./U.S.A.
145 C3 **Champotón** Mex.
152 A3 **Chañaral** Chile
126 B2 **Chandalar** *r.* U.S.A.
142 C3 **Chandeleur Islands** U.S.A.
74 B1 **Chandigarh** India
138 A2 **Chandler** U.S.A.
75 B3 **Chandrapur** India
63 B2 **Chang, Ko** *i.* Thai.
Chang'an China *see* **Rong'an**
121 C3 **Changane** *r.* Moz.
121 C2 **Changara** Moz.
65 B1 **Changbai** China
65 B1 **Changbai Shan** *mts* China/N. Korea
69 E2 **Changchun** China
71 B3 **Changde** China
65 B2 **Ch'angdo** N. Korea
Chang Jiang *r.* China *see* **Yangtze**
65 B1 **Changjin** N. Korea
65 B1 **Changjin-gang** *r.* N. Korea
71 B3 **Changsha** China
71 B3 **Changting** China
65 B2 **Changwon** S. Korea
70 B2 **Changyuan** China
70 B2 **Changzhi** China
70 B2 **Changzhou** China
111 B3 **Chania** Greece
95 C4 **Channel Islands** English Chan.
135 C4 **Channel Islands** U.S.A.
131 E2 **Channel-Port-aux-Basques** Can.
63 B2 **Chanthaburi** Thai.
104 C2 **Chantilly** France
137 D3 **Chanute** U.S.A.
82 G3 **Chany, Ozero** *salt l.* Russia
71 B3 **Chaoyang** *Guangdong* China
Chaoyang China *see* **Huinan**
71 B3 **Chaozhou** China
144 B2 **Chapala, Laguna de** *l.* Mex.
76 B1 **Chapayevo** Kazakh.
152 C3 **Chapecó** Brazil
143 E1 **Chapel Hill** U.S.A.
130 B2 **Chapleau** Can.
89 E3 **Chaplygin** Russia
91 C2 **Chaplynka** Ukr.
75 C2 **Chapra** India
145 B2 **Charcas** Mex.
99 B3 **Chard** U.K.
104 B2 **Charente** *r.* France
77 C3 **Chārīkār** Afgh.
86 E2 **Charkayuvom** Russia
100 B2 **Charleroi** Belgium
141 D3 **Charles, Cape** U.S.A.
137 E2 **Charles City** U.S.A.
140 B3 **Charleston** *IL* U.S.A.
143 E2 **Charleston** *SC* U.S.A.
140 C3 **Charleston** *WV* U.S.A.
135 C3 **Charleston Peak** U.S.A.
51 D2 **Charleville** Austr.
105 C2 **Charleville-Mézières** France
143 D1 **Charlotte** U.S.A.
143 D3 **Charlotte Harbor** *b.* U.S.A.
141 D3 **Charlottesville** U.S.A.
131 D2 **Charlottetown** Can.
52 B3 **Charlton** Austr.
130 C1 **Charlton Island** Can.
51 D2 **Charters Towers** Austr.
104 C2 **Chartres** France
128 C2 **Chase** Can.
88 C3 **Chashniki** Belarus
54 A3 **Chaslands Mistake** *c.* N.Z.
65 B1 **Chasŏng** N. Korea
104 B2 **Chassiron, Pointe de** *pt* France
104 B2 **Châteaubriant** France
104 C2 **Château-du-Loir** France
104 C2 **Châteaudun** France
104 B2 **Châteaulin** France
105 D3 **Châteauneuf-les-Martigues** France
104 C2 **Châteauneuf-sur-Loire** France
105 C2 **Château-Thierry** France
128 C2 **Chateh** Can.
100 B2 **Châtelet** Belgium
104 C2 **Châtellerault** France
140 C2 **Chatham** Can.
49 G5 **Chatham Islands** *is* N.Z.
105 C2 **Châtillon-sur-Seine** France
143 D2 **Chattahoochee** *r.* U.S.A.
143 C1 **Chattanooga** U.S.A.
63 B2 **Châu Đôc** Vietnam
62 A1 **Chauk** Myanmar
105 D2 **Chaumont** France
105 C2 **Chauny** France
151 D2 **Chaves** Brazil
106 B1 **Chaves** Port.
130 C1 **Chavigny, Lac** *l.* Can.
89 D3 **Chavusy** Belarus
89 E2 **Chayevo** Russia
86 E3 **Chaykovskiy** Russia
102 C1 **Cheb** Czech Rep.
87 D3 **Cheboksary** Russia
140 C1 **Cheboygan** U.S.A.
114 B2 **Chegga** Maur.
134 B1 **Chehalis** U.S.A.
Cheju S. Korea *see* **Jeju**
Cheju-do *i.* S. Korea *see* **Jeju-do**
89 E2 **Chekhov** Russia
134 B1 **Chelan, Lake** U.S.A.
103 E1 **Chełm** Pol.
99 D3 **Chelmer** *r.* U.K.
103 D1 **Chełmno** Pol.
99 D3 **Chelmsford** U.K.
99 B3 **Cheltenham** U.K.
87 F3 **Chelyabinsk** Russia
101 F2 **Chemnitz** Ger.
114 B2 **Chenachane** Alg.
70 B1 **Chengde** China
70 A2 **Chengdu** China
71 A3 **Chengguan** China
71 B4 **Chengmai** China
Chengshou China *see* **Yingshan**
70 A2 **Chengxian** China
Chengyang China *see* **Juxian**
73 C3 **Chennai** India
71 B3 **Chenzhou** China
65 B2 **Cheonan** S. Korea
65 B2 **Cheorwon** S. Korea
99 B3 **Chepstow** U.K.
104 B2 **Cherbourg-Octeville** France
89 E3 **Cheremisinovo** Russia
69 C1 **Cheremkhovo** Russia
89 E2 **Cherepovets** Russia
91 C2 **Cherkasy** Ukr.
87 D4 **Cherkessk** Russia
91 C1 **Chernihiv** Ukr.
91 D2 **Cherninivka** Ukr.
90 B2 **Chernivtsi** Ukr.
90 B1 **Chernyakhiv** Ukr.
88 B3 **Chernyakhovsk** Russia
89 E3 **Chernyanka** Russia
83 I2 **Chernyshevskiy** Russia
137 D2 **Cherokee** U.S.A.
83 K2 **Cherskogo, Khrebet** *mts* Russia
91 E2 **Chertkovo** Russia
90 A1 **Chervonohrad** Ukr.
88 C3 **Chervyen'** Belarus
89 D3 **Cherykaw** Belarus
141 D3 **Chesapeake Bay** U.S.A.
86 D2 **Cheshskaya Guba** *b.* Russia
98 B2 **Chester** U.K.
140 B3 **Chester** *IL* U.S.A.
143 D2 **Chester** *SC* U.S.A.
98 C2 **Chesterfield** U.K.
129 E1 **Chesterfield Inlet** Can.
129 E1 **Chesterfield Inlet** Can.
141 F1 **Chesuncook Lake** U.S.A.
131 D2 **Chéticamp** Can.
145 D3 **Chetumal** Mex.
128 B2 **Chetwynd** Can.
98 B1 **Cheviot Hills** U.K.
136 C2 **Cheyenne** U.S.A.
136 C2 **Cheyenne** *r.* U.S.A.
136 C3 **Cheyenne Wells** U.S.A.
75 B2 **Chhatarpur** India
62 A2 **Chiang Dao** Thai.
62 A2 **Chiang Mai** Thai.
62 A2 **Chiang Rai** Thai.
108 A1 **Chiavenna** Italy
70 B3 **Chibi** China
121 C3 **Chiboma** Moz.
130 C2 **Chibougamau** Can.
123 D1 **Chibuto** Moz.
75 D1 **Chibuzhang Co** *l.* China
140 B2 **Chicago** U.S.A.
128 A2 **Chichagof Island** U.S.A.
99 C3 **Chichester** U.K.
50 A2 **Chichester Range** *mts* Austr.
139 D1 **Chickasha** U.S.A.
150 A2 **Chiclayo** Peru
153 B5 **Chico** *r.* Arg.
135 B3 **Chico** U.S.A.
131 C2 **Chicoutimi** Can.
108 B2 **Chieti** Italy
145 C3 **Chietla** Mex.
69 D2 **Chifeng** China
155 D1 **Chifre, Serra do** *mts* Brazil
145 C3 **Chignahuapán** Mex.
121 C3 **Chigubo** Moz.
74 A1 **Chihil Abdālān, Kōh-e** *mts* Afgh.
144 B2 **Chihuahua** Mex.
88 C2 **Chikhachevo** Russia
67 C3 **Chikuma-gawa** *r.* Japan
128 B2 **Chilanko** *r.* Can.
74 B1 **Chilas** Pak.
139 C2 **Childress** U.S.A.
153 A4 **Chile** *country* S. America
152 B3 **Chilecito** Arg.
75 C3 **Chilika Lake** India
121 B2 **Chililabombwe** Zambia
128 B2 **Chilko** *r.* Can.
128 B2 **Chilko Lake** Can.
153 A4 **Chillán** Chile
137 E3 **Chillicothe** *MO* U.S.A.
140 C3 **Chillicothe** *OH* U.S.A.
128 B3 **Chilliwack** Can.
153 A5 **Chiloé, Isla de** *i.* Chile
145 C3 **Chilpancingo** Mex.
53 C3 **Chiltern** Austr.
71 C3 **Chilung** Taiwan
119 D3 **Chimala** Tanz.
152 B4 **Chimbas** Arg.
150 A2 **Chimborazo** *mt.* Ecuador
150 A2 **Chimbote** Peru
87 E4 **Chimboy** Uzbek.
Chimkent Kazakh. *see* **Shymkent**
121 C2 **Chimoio** Moz.
77 C3 **Chimtargha, Qullai** *mt.* Tajik.
68 C2 **China** *country* Asia
145 C2 **China** Mex.

150 A3 Chincha Alta Peru
128 C2 Chinchaga r. Can.
145 D3 Chinchorro, Banco Mex.
121 C2 Chinde Moz.
65 B3 Chindo S. Korea
68 C2 Chindu China
62 A1 Chindwin r. Myanmar
65 B2 Chinghwa N. Korea
120 B2 Chingola Zambia
120 A2 Chinguar Angola
121 C2 Chinhoyi Zimbabwe
74 B1 Chiniot Pak.
144 B2 Chinipas Mex.
65 B2 Chinju S. Korea
118 C2 Chinko r. C.A.R.
138 B1 Chinle U.S.A.
67 C3 Chino Japan
104 C2 Chinon France
138 A2 Chino Valley U.S.A.
121 C2 Chinsali Zambia
108 B1 Chioggia Italy
111 C3 Chios Greece
111 C3 Chios i. Greece
121 C2 Chipata Zambia
120 A2 Chipindo Angola
121 C3 Chipinge Zimbabwe
73 B3 Chiplun India
99 B3 Chippenham U.K.
99 C3 Chipping Norton U.K.
77 C2 Chirchiq Uzbek.
121 C3 Chiredzi Zimbabwe
138 B2 Chiricahua Peak U.S.A.
146 B4 Chiriquí, Golfo de b. Panama
146 B4 Chirripó mt. Costa Rica
121 B2 Chirundu Zimbabwe
130 C1 Chisasibi Can.
137 E1 Chisholm U.S.A.
90 B2 Chișinău Moldova
87 E3 Chistopol' Russia
69 D1 Chita Russia
120 A2 Chitado Angola
121 C2 Chitambo Zambia
120 B1 Chitato Angola
121 C1 Chitipa Malawi
73 B3 Chitradurga India
74 B1 Chitral Pak.
146 B4 Chitré Panama
75 D2 Chittagong Bangl.
74 B2 Chittaurgarh India
121 C2 Chitungwiza Zimbabwe
120 B2 Chiume Angola
121 C2 Chivhu Zimbabwe
70 B2 Chizhou China
114 C1 Chlef Alg.
107 D2 Chlef, Oued r. Alg.
153 B4 Choele Choel Arg.
144 B2 Choix Mex.
103 D1 Chojnice Pol.
117 B3 Ch'ok'ē Mountains Eth.
117 B3 Ch'ok'ē Terara mt. Eth.
83 K2 Chokurdakh Russia
121 C3 Chókwè Moz.
104 B2 Cholet France
102 C1 Chomutov Czech Rep.
83 I2 Chona r. Russia
150 A2 Chone Ecuador
65 B1 Ch'ŏngjin N. Korea
65 B2 Chŏngju N. Korea
65 B2 Chŏngp'yŏng N. Korea
70 A3 Chongqing China
70 A2 Chongqing mun. China
71 A3 Chongzuo China
Chŏnju S. Korea see Jeonju
153 A5 Chonos, Archipiélago de los is Chile
154 B3 Chopinzinho Brazil
111 B3 Chora Sfakion Greece
98 B2 Chorley U.K.

91 C2 Chornomors'ke Ukr.
90 B2 Chortkiv Ukr.
65 B1 Ch'osan N. Korea
67 D3 Chōshi Japan
103 D1 Choszczno Pol.
114 A2 Choûm Maur.
69 D1 Choybalsan Mongolia
69 D1 Choyr Mongolia
54 B2 Christchurch N.Z.
99 C3 Christchurch U.K.
127 G2 Christian, Cape Can.
123 C2 Christiana S. Africa
54 A2 Christina, Mount N.Z.
153 B5 Chubut r. Arg.
90 B1 Chudniv Ukr.
89 D2 Chudovo Russia
    Chudskoye Ozero l. Estonia/Russia see Peipus, Lake
126 B2 Chugach Mountains U.S.A.
67 B4 Chūgoku-sanchi mts Japan
66 B2 Chuguyevka Russia
91 D2 Chuhuyiv Ukr.
160 J3 Chukchi Sea Russia/U.S.A.
83 N2 Chukotskiy Poluostrov pen. Russia
135 C4 Chula Vista U.S.A.
82 G3 Chulym Russia
152 B3 Chumbicha Arg.
83 K3 Chumikan Russia
63 A2 Chumphon Thai.
65 B2 Chuncheon S. Korea
    Chungking China see Chongqing
83 H2 Chunya r. Russia
150 A3 Chuquibamba Peru
152 B3 Chuquicamata Chile
105 D2 Chur Switz.
62 A1 Churachandpur India
129 E2 Churchill Can.
129 E2 Churchill r. Man. Can.
131 D1 Churchill r. Nfld. and Lab. Can.
129 E2 Churchill, Cape Can.
131 D1 Churchill Falls Can.
129 D2 Churchill Lake Can.
74 B2 Churu India
131 C2 Chute-des-Passes Can.
62 B1 Chuxiong China
90 B2 Ciadîr-Lunga Moldova
61 B2 Ciamis Indon.
60 B2 Cianjur Indon.
154 B2 Cianorte Brazil
103 E1 Ciechanów Pol.
146 C2 Ciego de Ávila Cuba
146 B2 Cienfuegos Cuba
107 C2 Cieza Spain
106 C2 Cigüela r. Spain
80 B2 Cihanbeyli Turkey
144 B3 Cihuatlán Mex.
106 C2 Cíjara, Embalse de resr Spain
61 B2 Cilacap Indon.
139 C1 Cimarron r. U.S.A.
90 B2 Cimişlia Moldova
108 B2 Cimone, Monte mt. Italy
140 C3 Cincinnati U.S.A.
111 C3 Çine Turkey
100 B2 Ciney Belgium
145 C3 Cintalapa Mex.
71 B3 Ciping China
126 B2 Circle AK U.S.A.
136 B1 Circle MT U.S.A.
58 B3 Cirebon Indon.
99 C3 Cirencester U.K.
108 A1 Ciriè Italy
109 C3 Cirò Marina Italy
109 C2 Čitluk Bos. & Herz.
122 A3 Citrusdal S. Africa
145 B2 Ciudad Acuña Mex.

145 B3 Ciudad Altamirano Mex.
150 B1 Ciudad Bolívar Venez.
144 B2 Ciudad Camargo Mex.
144 A2 Ciudad Constitución Mex.
145 C3 Ciudad del Carmen Mex.
144 B2 Ciudad Delicias Mex.
145 C2 Ciudad de Valles Mex.
150 B1 Ciudad Guayana Venez.
138 B3 Ciudad Guerrero Mex.
144 B3 Ciudad Guzmán Mex.
145 C3 Ciudad Hidalgo Mex.
145 C3 Ciudad Ixtepec Mex.
144 B1 Ciudad Juárez Mex.
145 C2 Ciudad Mante Mex.
145 C2 Ciudad Mier Mex.
144 B2 Ciudad Obregón Mex.
106 C2 Ciudad Real Spain
145 C2 Ciudad Río Bravo Mex.
106 B1 Ciudad Rodrigo Spain
145 C2 Ciudad Victoria Mex.
107 D1 Ciutadella Spain
111 C3 Civan Dağ mt. Turkey
108 B1 Cividale del Friuli Italy
108 B2 Civitanova Marche Italy
108 B2 Civitavecchia Italy
104 C2 Civray France
111 C3 Çivril Turkey
70 C2 Cixi China
99 D3 Clacton-on-Sea U.K.
128 C2 Claire, Lake Can.
105 C2 Clamecy France
122 A3 Clanwilliam S. Africa
52 A2 Clare Austr.
97 A2 Clare Island Ireland
141 E2 Claremont U.S.A.
97 B2 Claremorris Ireland
54 B2 Clarence r. N.Z.
131 E2 Clarenville Can.
128 C2 Claresholm Can.
137 D2 Clarinda U.S.A.
123 C3 Clarkebury S. Africa
143 D2 Clark Hill Reservoir U.S.A.
140 C3 Clarksburg U.S.A.
142 B2 Clarksdale U.S.A.
134 C1 Clarks Fork r. U.S.A.
142 B1 Clarksville AR U.S.A.
142 C1 Clarksville TN U.S.A.
154 B1 Claro r. Brazil
139 C1 Clayton U.S.A.
97 B3 Clear, Cape Ireland
137 E2 Clear Lake U.S.A.
135 B3 Clear Lake U.S.A.
128 C2 Clearwater r. Can.
129 C2 Clearwater r. Can.
143 D3 Clearwater U.S.A.
134 C1 Clearwater r. U.S.A.
139 D2 Cleburne U.S.A.
51 D2 Clermont Austr.
105 C2 Clermont-Ferrand France
52 A2 Cleve Austr.
142 C2 Cleveland MS U.S.A.
140 C2 Cleveland OH U.S.A.
143 D1 Cleveland TN U.S.A.
134 D1 Cleveland, Mount U.S.A.
143 D3 Clewiston U.S.A.
97 A2 Clifden Ireland
53 D1 Clifton Austr.
138 B2 Clifton U.S.A.
128 B2 Clinton Can.
137 E2 Clinton IA U.S.A.
137 E3 Clinton MO U.S.A.
139 D1 Clinton OK U.S.A.
96 A2 Clisham h. U.K.
98 B2 Clitheroe U.K.
97 B3 Clonakilty Ireland
51 D2 Cloncurry Austr.
97 C1 Clones Ireland
97 C2 Clonmel Ireland

179

100 D1 Cloppenburg Ger.
50 A2 Cloud Break Austr.
136 B2 Cloud Peak U.S.A.
139 C2 Clovis U.S.A.
129 D2 Cluff Lake Mine Can.
110 B1 Cluj-Napoca Romania
51 C2 Cluny Austr.
105 D2 Cluses France
54 A3 Clutha r. N.Z.
96 B3 Clyde r. U.K.
96 B3 Clyde, Firth of est. U.K.
96 B3 Clydebank U.K.
127 G2 Clyde River Can.
144 B3 Coalcomán Mex.
135 C3 Coaldale (abandoned) U.S.A.
128 B2 Coal River Can.
150 B2 Coari Brazil
150 B2 Coari r. Brazil
142 B2 Coastal Plain U.S.A.
128 B2 Coast Mountains Can.
135 B2 Coast Ranges mts U.S.A.
96 B3 Coatbridge U.K.
127 F2 Coats Island Can.
55 R2 Coats Land reg. Antarctica
145 C3 Coatzacoalcos Mex.
146 A3 Cobán Guat.
53 C2 Cobar Austr.
97 B3 Cobh Ireland
152 B2 Cobija Bol.
141 D2 Cobourg Can.
50 C1 Cobourg Peninsula Austr.
53 C3 Cobram Austr.
101 E2 Coburg Ger.
152 B2 Cochabamba Bol.
100 C2 Cochem Ger.
Cochin India see Kochi
128 C2 Cochrane Alta Can.
130 B2 Cochrane Ont. Can.
153 A5 Cochrane Chile
52 B2 Cockburn Austr.
Cockburn Town Turks and
Caicos Is see Grand Turk
98 B1 Cockermouth U.K.
122 B3 Cockscomb mt. S. Africa
146 B3 Coco r. Hond./Nic.
144 B2 Cocula Mex.
150 A1 Cocuy, Sierra Nevada del mt. Col.
141 E2 Cod, Cape U.S.A.
108 B2 Codigoro Italy
131 D1 Cod Island Can.
151 D2 Codó Brazil
136 B2 Cody U.S.A.
51 D1 Coen Austr.
100 C2 Coesfeld Ger.
134 C1 Coeur d'Alene U.S.A.
123 C3 Coffee Bay S. Africa
137 D3 Coffeyville U.S.A.
53 D2 Coffs Harbour Austr.
104 B2 Cognac France
118 A2 Cogo Equat. Guinea
52 A3 Cohuna Austr.
146 B4 Coiba, Isla de i. Panama
153 A5 Coihaique Chile
73 B3 Coimbatore India
106 B1 Coimbra Port.
52 B3 Colac Austr.
155 D1 Colatina Brazil
136 C3 Colby U.S.A.
99 D3 Colchester U.K.
129 C2 Cold Lake Can.
96 C3 Coldstream U.K.
139 D2 Coleman U.S.A.
52 B3 Coleraine Austr.
97 C1 Coleraine U.K.
123 C3 Colesberg S. Africa
144 B3 Colima Mex.
144 B3 Colima, Nevado de vol. Mex.

96 C1 Coll i. U.K.
53 C1 Collarenebri Austr.
50 B1 Collier Bay Austr.
54 B2 Collingwood N.Z.
97 B1 Collooney Ireland
105 D2 Colmar France
100 C2 Cologne Ger.
154 C2 Colômbia Brazil
150 A1 Colombia country S. America
73 B4 Colombo Sri Lanka
104 C3 Colomiers France
152 C4 Colón Arg.
146 C4 Colón Panama
109 C3 Colonna, Capo c. Italy
96 A2 Colonsay i. U.K.
153 B4 Colorado r. Arg.
138 A2 Colorado r. Mex./U.S.A.
139 D3 Colorado r. U.S.A.
136 B3 Colorado state U.S.A.
135 E3 Colorado Plateau U.S.A.
136 C3 Colorado Springs U.S.A.
144 B2 Cotolán Mex.
136 B1 Colstrip U.S.A.
137 E3 Columbia MO U.S.A.
143 D2 Columbia SC U.S.A.
142 C1 Columbia TN U.S.A.
134 B1 Columbia r. U.S.A.
128 C2 Columbia, Mount Can.
134 D1 Columbia Falls U.S.A.
128 B2 Columbia Mountains Can.
134 C1 Columbia Plateau U.S.A.
143 D2 Columbus GA U.S.A.
140 B3 Columbus IN U.S.A.
142 C2 Columbus MS U.S.A.
137 D2 Columbus NE U.S.A.
138 B2 Columbus NM U.S.A.
140 C3 Columbus OH U.S.A.
134 C1 Colville U.S.A.
126 A2 Colville r. U.S.A.
126 C2 Colville Lake Can.
98 B2 Colwyn Bay U.K.
108 B2 Comacchio Italy
145 C3 Comalcalco Mex.
110 C1 Comănești Romania
130 C1 Comencho, Lac l. Can.
97 C2 Comeragh Mountains hills Ireland
75 D2 Comilla Bangl.
108 A2 Comino, Capo c. Sardinia Italy
145 C3 Comitán de Domínguez Mex.
104 C2 Commentry France
139 D2 Commerce U.S.A.
127 F2 Committee Bay Can.
108 A1 Como Italy
153 B5 Comodoro Rivadavia Arg.
121 D2 Comoros country Africa
104 C2 Compiègne France
144 B2 Compostela Mex.
90 B2 Comrat Moldova
114 A4 Conakry Guinea
155 E1 Conceição da Barra Brazil
151 D2 Conceição do Araguaia Brazil
155 D1 Conceição do Mato Dentro Brazil
152 B3 Concepción Arg.
153 A4 Concepción Chile
144 B2 Concepción Mex.
135 B4 Conception, Point U.S.A.
154 C2 Conchas Brazil
138 C1 Conchas Lake U.S.A.
144 B2 Conchos r. Chihuahua Mex.
145 C2 Conchos r. Nuevo León/ Tamaulipas Mex.
135 B3 Concord CA U.S.A.
141 E2 Concord NH U.S.A.
152 C4 Concordia Arg.
122 A2 Concordia S. Africa

137 D3 Concordia U.S.A.
53 C2 Condobolin Austr.
104 C3 Condom France
134 B1 Condon U.S.A.
108 B1 Conegliano Italy
104 C2 Confolens France
75 C2 Congdü China
118 B3 Congo country Africa
118 B3 Congo r. Congo/Dem. Rep. Congo
118 C3 Congo, Democratic Republic of the country Africa
129 C2 Conklin Can.
97 B1 Conn, Lough l. Ireland
97 B2 Connacht reg. Ireland
141 E2 Connecticut r. U.S.A.
141 E2 Connecticut state U.S.A.
97 B2 Connemara reg. Ireland
134 D1 Conrad U.S.A.
139 D2 Conroe U.S.A.
155 D2 Conselheiro Lafaiete Brazil
155 D1 Conselheiro Pena Brazil
98 C1 Consett U.K.
63 B3 Côn Son, Đao i. Vietnam
110 C2 Constanța Romania
106 B2 Constantina Spain
115 C1 Constantine Alg.
134 D2 Contact U.S.A.
150 A2 Contamana Peru
153 A6 Contreras, Isla i. Chile
126 D2 Contwoyto Lake Can.
142 B1 Conway AR U.S.A.
141 E2 Conway NH U.S.A.
51 C2 Coober Pedy Austr.
Cook, Mount mt. N.Z. see Aoraki/Mount Cook
143 C1 Cookeville U.S.A.
49 H4 Cook Islands S. Pacific Ocean
131 E1 Cook's Harbour Can.
97 C1 Cookstown U.K.
54 B2 Cook Strait N.Z.
51 D1 Cooktown Austr.
53 C2 Coolabah Austr.
53 C2 Coolamon Austr.
50 B3 Coolangatta Austr.
50 B3 Coolgardie Austr.
53 C3 Cooma Austr.
52 B2 Coombah Austr.
53 C2 Coonabarabran Austr.
52 A3 Coonalpyn Austr.
53 C2 Coonamble Austr.
52 A1 Cooper Creek watercourse Austr.
134 B2 Coos Bay U.S.A.
53 C2 Cootamundra Austr.
145 C3 Copainalá Mex.
145 C3 Copala Mex.
93 F4 Copenhagen Denmark
109 C2 Copertino Italy
152 A3 Copiapó Chile
140 B1 Copper Harbor U.S.A.
Coppermine Can. see Kugluktuk
126 D2 Coppermine r. Can.
122 B2 Copperton S. Africa
152 A3 Coquimbo Chile
110 B2 Corabia Romania
155 D1 Coração de Jesus Brazil
150 A3 Coracora Peru
53 D1 Coraki Austr.
50 A2 Coral Bay Austr.
127 F2 Coral Harbour Can.
156 D7 Coral Sea S. Pacific Ocean
48 D4 Coral Sea Islands Territory Austr.
52 B2 Corangamite, Lake Austr.
99 C2 Corby U.K.

153 A5 Corcovado, Golfo de *sea chan.* Chile
143 D2 Cordele U.S.A.
64 B1 Cordilleras Range *mts* Phil.
152 B4 Córdoba Arg.
145 C3 Córdoba Mex.
106 C2 Córdoba Spain
153 B4 Córdoba, Sierras de *mts* Arg.
111 A3 Corfu *i.* Greece
106 B2 Coria Spain
111 B3 Corinth Greece
142 C2 Corinth U.S.A.
155 D1 Corinto Brazil
97 B3 Cork Ireland
111 C2 Çorlu Turkey
154 B2 Cornélio Procópio Brazil
131 E2 Corner Brook Can.
53 C3 Corner Inlet *b.* Austr.
135 B3 Corning CA U.S.A.
141 D2 Corning NY U.S.A.
 Corn Islands *is* Nic. *see* Maíz, Islas del
108 B2 Corno Grande *mt.* Italy
130 C2 Cornwall Can.
126 E1 Cornwallis Island Can.
150 B1 Coro Venez.
154 C1 Coromandel Brazil
54 C1 Coromandel Peninsula N.Z.
129 C2 Coronation Can.
126 D2 Coronation Gulf Can.
152 C3 Coronel Oviedo Para.
153 B4 Coronel Suárez Arg.
150 A3 Coropuna, Nudo *mt.* Peru
109 D2 Çorovodë Albania
139 D3 Corpus Christi U.S.A.
152 B2 Corque Bol.
151 D3 Corrente Brazil
154 B1 Correntes Brazil
151 D3 Correntina Brazil
97 B2 Corrib, Lough *l.* Ireland
152 C3 Corrientes Arg.
144 B2 Corrientes, Cabo *c.* Mex.
53 C3 Corryong Austr.
 Corse *i.* France *see* Corsica
105 D3 Corse, Cap *c.* Corsica France
105 D3 Corsica *i.* France
139 D2 Corsicana U.S.A.
105 D3 Corte *Corsica* France
106 B2 Cortegana Spain
136 B3 Cortez U.S.A.
108 B1 Cortina d'Ampezzo Italy
141 D2 Cortland U.S.A.
108 B2 Cortona Italy
106 B2 Coruche Port.
 Çoruh Turkey *see* Artvin
80 B1 Çorum Turkey
152 C2 Corumbá Brazil
154 C1 Corumbá *r.* Brazil
134 B2 Corvallis U.S.A.
98 B2 Corwen U.K.
144 B2 Cosalá Mex.
145 C3 Cosamaloapan Mex.
109 C3 Cosenza Italy
105 C2 Cosne-Cours-sur-Loire France
107 C2 Costa Blanca *coastal area* Spain
107 D1 Costa Brava *coastal area* Spain
106 B2 Costa del Sol *coastal area* Spain
154 B1 Costa Rica Brazil
146 B3 Costa Rica *country* Central America
144 B2 Costa Rica Mex.
110 C1 Costeşti Romania
64 B2 Cotabato Phil.
114 B4 Côte d'Ivoire *country* Africa

150 A2 Cotopaxi, Volcán *vol.* Ecuador
99 B3 Cotswold Hills U.K.
134 B2 Cottage Grove U.S.A.
102 C1 Cottbus Ger.
104 B2 Coubre, Pointe de la *pt* France
52 A3 Couedic, Cape du Austr.
137 D2 Council Bluffs U.S.A.
88 B2 Courland Lagoon *b.* Lith./ Russia
128 B3 Courtenay Can.
104 B2 Coutances France
104 B2 Coutras France
100 B2 Couvin Belgium
99 C2 Coventry U.K.
140 C3 Covington U.S.A.
50 B3 Cowan, Lake *imp. l.* Austr.
96 C2 Cowdenbeath U.K.
53 C3 Cowes Austr.
134 B1 Cowlitz *r.* U.S.A.
53 C2 Cowra Austr.
154 B1 Coxim Brazil
75 D2 Cox's Bazar Bangl.
144 B3 Coyuca de Benítez Mex.
75 C1 Cozhê China
145 D2 Cozumel Mex.
145 D2 Cozumel, Isla de *i.* Mex.
123 C3 Cradock S. Africa
136 B2 Craig U.S.A.
102 C2 Crailsheim Ger.
110 B2 Craiova Romania
129 D2 Cranberry Portage Can.
53 C3 Cranbourne Austr.
128 C3 Cranbrook Can.
151 D2 Crateús Brazil
151 E2 Crato Brazil
136 C2 Crawford U.S.A.
140 B2 Crawfordsville U.S.A.
99 C3 Crawley U.K.
134 D1 Crazy Mountains U.S.A.
129 D2 Cree *r.* Can.
144 B2 Creel Mex.
129 D2 Cree Lake Can.
100 B1 Creil Neth.
105 D2 Crema Italy
108 B1 Cremona Italy
108 B2 Cres *i.* Croatia
134 B2 Crescent City U.S.A.
128 C3 Creston Can.
137 E2 Creston U.S.A.
142 C2 Crestview U.S.A.
111 B3 Crete *i.* Greece
107 D1 Creus, Cap de *c.* Spain
98 B2 Crewe U.K.
96 B2 Crianlarich U.K.
152 D3 Criciúma Brazil
96 C2 Crieff U.K.
108 B1 Crikvenica Croatia
91 C2 Crimea *disp. terr.* Ukr.
91 C2 Crimea *pen.* Ukr.
101 F2 Crimmitschau Ger.
154 C1 Cristalina Brazil
101 E1 Crivitz Ger.
 Crna Gora *country* Europe *see* Montenegro
109 D2 Crni Vrh *h.* Serbia
109 C1 Črnomelj Slovenia
97 B2 Croagh Patrick *h.* Ireland
109 C1 Croatia *country* Europe
61 C1 Crocker, Banjaran *mts* Malaysia
139 D2 Crockett U.S.A.
59 C3 Croker Island Austr.
99 D2 Cromer U.K.
54 A3 Cromwell N.Z.
137 D1 Crookston U.S.A.
53 C2 Crookwell Austr.
136 C1 Crosby U.S.A.

143 D3 Cross City U.S.A.
142 B2 Crossett U.S.A.
98 B1 Cross Fell *h.* U.K.
129 E2 Cross Lake Can.
143 C1 Crossville U.S.A.
109 C3 Crotone Italy
99 D3 Crowborough U.K.
142 B2 Crowley U.S.A.
128 C3 Crowsnest Pass Can.
146 C3 Cruz, Cabo *c.* Cuba
152 C3 Cruz Alta Brazil
155 D2 Cruz del Eje Arg.
150 A2 Cruzeiro Brazil
52 A2 Cruzeiro do Sul Brazil
139 D3 Crystal City U.S.A.
140 B1 Crystal Falls U.S.A.
103 E2 Csongrád Hungary
120 B2 Cuando *r.* Angola/Zambia
120 A2 Cuangar Angola
118 B3 Cuango *r.* Angola/Dem. Rep. Congo
120 A1 Cuanza *r.* Angola
139 C3 Cuatro Ciénegas Mex.
144 B2 Cuauhtémoc Mex.
145 C3 Cuautla Mex.
146 B2 Cuba *country* West Indies
120 A2 Cubal Angola
120 B2 Cubango *r.* Angola/Namibia
150 A1 Cúcuta Col.
73 B3 Cuddalore India
 Cuddapah. India *see* Kadapa
106 C1 Cuéllar Spain
120 A2 Cuemba Angola
150 A2 Cuenca Ecuador
107 C1 Cuenca Spain
107 C1 Cuenca, Serranía de *mts* Spain
145 C3 Cuernavaca Mex.
139 D3 Cuero U.S.A.
151 C3 Cuiabá Brazil
151 C3 Cuiabá *r.* Brazil
96 A2 Cuillin Sound *sea chan.* U.K.
120 A1 Cuilo Angola
120 B2 Cuito *r.* Angola
120 A2 Cuito Cuanavale Angola
60 B1 Cukai Malaysia
53 C3 Culcairn Austr.
53 C1 Culgoa *r.* Austr.
144 B2 Culiacán Mex.
64 A1 Culion *i.* Phil.
107 C2 Cullera Spain
142 C2 Cullman U.S.A.
97 C1 Cullybackey U.K.
150 B1 Cumaná Venez.
141 D3 Cumberland U.S.A.
140 B3 Cumberland *r.* U.S.A.
129 D2 Cumberland Lake Can.
127 G2 Cumberland Peninsula Can.
142 C1 Cumberland Plateau U.S.A.
127 G2 Cumberland Sound *sea chan.* Can.
96 C3 Cumbernauld U.K.
135 B3 Cummings U.S.A.
96 B3 Cumnock U.K.
144 B1 Cumpas Mex.
145 C3 Cunduacán Mex.
120 A2 Cunene *r.* Angola
108 A2 Cuneo Italy
53 C1 Cunnamulla Austr.
108 A1 Cuorgnè Italy
96 C2 Cupar U.K.
147 D3 Curaçao *i.* West Indies
147 D3 Curaçao *terr.* West Indies
150 A2 Curaray *r.* Ecuador
153 A4 Curicó Chile
154 C3 Curitiba Brazil

52 A2 **Curnamona** Austr.
51 D3 **Currie** Austr.
51 E2 **Curtis Island** Austr.
151 C1 **Curuá** r. Brazil
60 B2 **Curup** Indon.
151 D2 **Cururupu** Brazil
155 D1 **Curvelo** Brazil
150 A3 **Cusco** Peru
139 D1 **Cushing** U.S.A.
134 D1 **Cut Bank** U.S.A.
75 C2 **Cuttack** India
101 D1 **Cuxhaven** Ger.
64 B1 **Cuyo Islands** Phil.
Cuzco Peru see **Cusco**
119 C3 **Cyangugu** Rwanda
111 B3 **Cyclades** is Greece
129 C3 **Cypress Hills** Can.
80 B2 **Cyprus** country Asia
102 C2 **Czech Republic** country Europe
103 D1 **Czersk** Pol.
103 D1 **Częstochowa** Pol.

D

Đa, Sông r. Vietnam see **Black River**
69 D2 **Daban** China
114 A3 **Dabola** Guinea
Dacca Bangl. see **Dhaka**
102 C2 **Dachau** Ger.
117 C3 **Dadaab** Kenya
74 A2 **Dadu** Pak.
65 B2 **Daegu** S. Korea
65 B2 **Daejeon** S. Korea
65 B3 **Daejeong** S. Korea
64 B1 **Daet** Phil.
114 A3 **Dagana** Senegal
64 B1 **Dagupan** Phil.
74 B3 **Dahanu** India
69 D2 **Da Hinggan Ling** mts China
116 C3 **Dahlak Archipelago** is Eritrea
100 C2 **Dahlem** Ger.
78 B3 **Dahm, Ramlat** des. Saudi Arabia /Yemen
60 B2 **Daik** Indon.
106 C2 **Daimiel** Spain
97 A2 **Daingean Uí Chúis** Ireland
51 C2 **Dajarra** Austr.
114 A3 **Dakar** Senegal
116 A2 **Dākhilah, Wāḩāt ad** oasis Egypt
114 A2 **Dakhla** Western Sahara
Dakhla Oasis Egypt see **Dākhilah, Wāḩāt ad**
63 A3 **Dakoank** India
88 C3 **Dakol'ka** r. Belarus
Đakovica Kosovo see **Gjakovë**
109 C1 **Đakovo** Croatia
120 B2 **Dala** Angola
68 C2 **Dalain Hob** China
93 G3 **Dalälven** r. Sweden
111 C3 **Dalaman** Turkey
111 C3 **Dalaman** r. Turkey
69 C2 **Dalandzadgad** Mongolia
63 B2 **Đa Lat** Vietnam
74 A2 **Dalbandin** Pak.
96 C3 **Dalbeattie** U.K.
51 E2 **Dalby** Austr.
143 C1 **Dale Hollow Lake** U.S.A.
53 C3 **Dalgety** Austr.
139 C1 **Dalhart** U.S.A.
131 D2 **Dalhousie** Can.
62 B1 **Dali** China
70 C2 **Dalian** China
96 C3 **Dalkeith** U.K.

139 D2 **Dallas** U.S.A.
128 A2 **Dall Island** U.S.A.
109 C2 **Dalmatia** reg. Bos. & Herz./ Croatia
66 C2 **Dal'negorsk** Russia
66 B1 **Dal'nerechensk** Russia
114 B4 **Daloa** Côte d'Ivoire
51 D2 **Dalrymple, Mount** Austr.
92 □A3 **Dalsmynni** Iceland
143 D2 **Dalton** U.S.A.
75 C2 **Daltonganj** India
60 B1 **Daludalu** Indon.
92 □B2 **Dalvík** Iceland
50 C1 **Daly** r. Austr.
51 C1 **Daly Waters** Austr.
74 B2 **Daman** India
80 B2 **Damanhûr** Egypt
59 C3 **Damar** i. Indon.
80 B2 **Damascus** Syria
115 D3 **Damaturu** Nigeria
76 B3 **Damāvand, Qolleh-ye** mt. Iran
81 D2 **Dāmghān** Iran
79 C2 **Dammam** Saudi Arabia
101 D1 **Damme** Ger.
75 B2 **Damoh** India
114 B4 **Damongo** Ghana
75 C2 **Dampir, Selat** sea chan. Indon.
72 C2 **Damqoq Zangbo** r. China
117 C3 **Danakil** reg. Africa
114 B4 **Danané** Côte d'Ivoire
63 B2 **Đa Nẵng** Vietnam
141 E2 **Danbury** U.S.A.
65 A1 **Dandong** China
146 B3 **Dangriga** Belize
70 B2 **Dangshan** China
89 F2 **Danilov** Russia
89 E2 **Danilovskaya Vozvyshennost'** hills Russia
70 B2 **Danjiangkou** China
89 E3 **Dankov** Russia
146 B3 **Danlí** Hond.
101 E1 **Dannenberg (Elbe)** Ger.
54 C2 **Dannevirke** N.Z.
62 B2 **Dan Sai** Thai.
Dantu China see **Zhenjiang**
110 A1 **Danube** r. Europe
119 D3 **Danube Delta** Romania/Ukr.
140 B2 **Danville** IL U.S.A.
140 C3 **Danville** KY U.S.A.
141 D3 **Danville** VA U.S.A.
71 A4 **Danzhou** China
71 B3 **Daoxian** China
114 C3 **Dapaong** Togo
64 B2 **Dapitan** Phil.
68 C2 **Da Qaidam** China
69 E1 **Daqing** China
80 B2 **Dar'ā** Syria
79 C2 **Dārāb** Iran
81 D2 **Dārān** Iran
75 C2 **Darbhanga** India
119 D3 **Dar es Salaam** Tanz.
117 A3 **Darfur** reg. Sudan
74 B1 **Dargai** Pak.
54 B1 **Dargaville** N.Z.
53 C3 **Dargo** Austr.
69 D1 **Darhan** Mongolia
150 A1 **Darién, Golfo del** g. Col.
75 C2 **Darjiling** India
52 B2 **Darling** r. Austr.
53 C1 **Darling Downs** hills Austr.
50 A3 **Darling Range** hills Austr.
98 C1 **Darlington** U.K.
53 C2 **Darlington Point** Austr.
103 D1 **Darłowo** Pol.
101 D1 **Darmstadt** Ger.
115 E1 **Darnah** Libya
52 B2 **Darnick** Austr.
107 C1 **Daroca** Spain

99 D3 **Dartford** U.K.
99 A3 **Dartmoor** hills U.K.
131 D2 **Dartmouth** Can.
99 B3 **Dartmouth** U.K.
59 D3 **Daru** P.N.G.
50 C1 **Darwin** Austr.
74 A2 **Dasht** r. Pak.
76 B2 **Daşoguz** Turkm.
61 C1 **Datadian** Indon.
111 C3 **Datça** Turkey
70 B1 **Datong** China
64 B2 **Datu Piang** Phil.
74 B1 **Daud Khel** Pak.
88 B2 **Daugava** r. Latvia
88 C2 **Daugavpils** Latvia
100 C2 **Daun** Ger.
129 D2 **Dauphin** Can.
129 E2 **Dauphin Lake** Can.
73 B3 **Davangere** India
64 B2 **Davao** Phil.
64 B2 **Davao Gulf** Phil.
137 E2 **Davenport** U.S.A.
99 C2 **Daventry** U.K.
123 C2 **Daveyton** S. Africa
146 B4 **David** Panama
129 D2 **Davidson** Can.
126 E3 **Davidson Lake** Can.
135 B3 **Davis** U.S.A.
131 D1 **Davis Inlet (abandoned)** Can.
159 F3 **Davis Sea** Antarctica
160 P3 **Davis Strait** Can./Greenland
105 D2 **Davos** Switz.
Dawei Myanmar see **Tavoy**
78 A2 **Dawmat al Jandal** Saudi Arabia
79 C3 **Dawqah** Oman
126 B2 **Dawson** Can.
143 D2 **Dawson** U.S.A.
128 B2 **Dawson Creek** Can.
126 C2 **Dawsons Landing** Can.
68 C2 **Dawu** China
Dawukou China see **Shizuishan**
104 B3 **Dax** France
68 C2 **Da Xueshan** mts China
80 C2 **Dayr az Zawr** Syria
140 C3 **Dayton** U.S.A.
143 D3 **Daytona Beach** U.S.A.
70 A2 **Dazhou** China
122 B3 **De Aar** S. Africa
80 B2 **Dead Sea** salt l. Asia
71 B3 **De'an** China
152 B4 **Deán Funes** Arg.
128 B2 **Dease Lake** Can.
126 D2 **Dease Strait** Can.
135 C3 **Death Valley** depr. U.S.A.
104 C2 **Deauville** France
61 C1 **Debak** Sarawak Malaysia
109 D2 **Debar** Macedonia
103 E2 **Debrecen** Hungary
117 B3 **Debre Markos** Eth.
117 B3 **Debre Tabor** Eth.
117 B4 **Debre Zeyit** Eth.
142 C2 **Decatur** AL U.S.A.
140 B3 **Decatur** IL U.S.A.
73 B3 **Deccan** plat. India
102 C1 **Děčín** Czech Rep.
137 E2 **Decorah** U.S.A.
88 C2 **Dedovichi** Russia
121 C2 **Dedza** Malawi
98 B2 **Dee** r. England/Wales U.K.
96 C2 **Dee** r. Scotland U.K.
53 D1 **Deepwater** Austr.
131 E2 **Deer Lake** Can.
134 D1 **Deer Lodge** U.S.A.
140 C3 **Defiance** U.S.A.
68 C2 **Dêgê** China

117 C4 Degeh Bur Eth.
102 C2 Deggendorf Ger.
91 E2 Degtevo Russia
75 B1 Dehra Dun India
75 C2 Dehri India
69 E2 Dehui China
100 A2 Deinze Belgium
110 B1 Dej Romania
140 B2 De Kalb U.S.A.
78 A3 Dekemhare Eritrea
118 C3 Dekese Dem. Rep. Congo
135 C3 Delano U.S.A.
135 D3 Delano Peak U.S.A.
123 C2 Delareyville S. Africa
129 D2 Delaronde Lake Can.
140 C2 Delaware U.S.A.
141 D3 Delaware r. U.S.A.
141 D3 Delaware state U.S.A.
141 D3 Delaware Bay U.S.A.
53 C3 Delegate Austr.
105 D2 Delémont Switz.
100 B1 Delft Neth.
100 C1 Delfzijl Neth.
121 D2 Delgado, Cabo c. Moz.
69 C1 Delgerhaan Mongolia
75 B2 Delhi India
60 B2 Deli i. Indon.
126 C2 Déline Can.
101 F2 Delitzsch Ger.
107 D2 Dellys Alg.
101 D1 Delmenhorst Ger.
109 B1 Delnice Croatia
83 L1 De-Longa, Ostrova is Russia
129 D3 Deloraine Can.
111 B3 Delphi tourist site Greece
135 C3 Del Rio U.S.A.
136 B3 Delta CO U.S.A.
135 D3 Delta UT U.S.A.
126 B2 Delta Junction U.S.A.
109 D3 Delvinë Albania
106 C1 Demanda, Sierra de la mts Spain
118 C3 Demba Dem. Rep. Congo
117 B4 Dembī Dolo Eth.
89 D2 Demidov Russia
138 B2 Deming U.S.A.
111 C3 Demirci Turkey
110 C2 Demirköy Turkey
102 C1 Demmin Ger.
142 C2 Demopolis U.S.A.
60 B2 Dempo, Gunung vol. Indon.
89 D2 Demyansk Russia
122 B3 De Naawte S. Africa
124 E2 Denali mt U.S.A.
100 B1 Den Burg Neth.
100 B2 Dendermonde Belgium
70 A1 Dengkou China
70 B2 Dengzhou China
Den Haag Neth. see The Hague
50 A2 Denham Austr.
100 B1 Den Helder Neth.
52 B3 Deniliquin Austr.
134 C2 Denio U.S.A.
137 D2 Denison IA U.S.A.
139 D2 Denison TX U.S.A.
111 C3 Denizli Turkey
53 D2 Denman Austr.
50 A3 Denmark Austr.
93 E4 Denmark country Europe
160 Q3 Denmark Strait Greenland/ Iceland
61 C2 Denpasar Indon.
139 D2 Denton U.S.A.
50 A3 D'Entrecasteaux, Point Austr.
136 B3 Denver U.S.A.
75 C2 Deogarh Odisha India
74 B2 Deogarh Rajasthan India

75 C2 Deoghar India
83 K2 Deputatskiy Russia
68 C3 Dêqên China
142 B2 De Queen U.S.A.
74 A2 Dera Bugti Pak.
74 B1 Dera Ghazi Khan Pak.
74 B1 Dera Ismail Khan Pak.
87 D4 Derbent Russia
50 B1 Derby Austr.
99 C2 Derby U.K.
99 D2 Dereham U.K.
97 B2 Derg, Lough l. Ireland
91 D1 Derhachi Ukr.
142 B2 DeRidder U.S.A.
91 D2 Derkul r. Russia/Ukr. Derry U.K. see Londonderry
75 B1 Dêrub China
116 B3 Derudeb Sudan
122 B3 De Rust S. Africa
109 C2 Derventa Bos. & Herz.
98 C2 Derwent r. U.K.
98 B1 Derwent Water l. U.K.
77 C1 Derzhavinsk Kazakh.
152 B2 Desaguadero r. Bol.
129 D2 Deschambault Lake Can.
134 B1 Deschutes r. U.S.A.
117 B3 Desē Eth.
153 B5 Deseado Arg.
153 B5 Deseado r. Arg.
137 E2 Des Moines U.S.A.
137 E2 Des Moines r. U.S.A.
91 C1 Desna r. Russia/Ukr.
89 D3 Desnogorsk Russia
101 F2 Dessau-Roßlau Ger.
126 B2 Destruction Bay Can.
149 C3 Desventuradas, Islas is S. Pacific Ocean
101 D2 Detah Can.
101 D2 Detmold Ger.
140 C2 Detroit U.S.A.
137 D1 Detroit Lakes U.S.A.
100 B2 Deurne Neth.
110 B1 Deva Romania
100 C1 Deventer Neth.
96 C2 Deveron r. U.K.
103 D2 Devét skal h. Czech Rep.
137 D1 Devils Lake U.S.A.
128 A2 Devils Paw mt. U.S.A.
99 C3 Devizes U.K.
74 B2 Devli India
110 C2 Devnya Bulg.
128 C2 Devon r. U.K.
126 E1 Devon Island Can.
51 D4 Devonport Austr.
74 B2 Dewas India
137 F3 Dexter U.S.A.
70 A2 Deyang China
59 D3 Deyong, Tanjung pt Indon.
81 C2 Dezful Iran
70 B2 Dezhou China
79 C2 Dhahran Saudi Arabia
75 D2 Dhaka Bangl.
78 B3 Dhamār Yemen
75 C2 Dhamtari India
75 C2 Dhanbad India
75 C2 Dhankuta Nepal
62 A1 Dharmanagar India
75 C2 Dharmjaygarh India
73 B3 Dharwad India
74 B2 Dhasa India
78 B3 Dhubāb Yemen
74 B2 Dhule India
144 A1 Diablo, Picacho del mt. Mex.
51 C2 Diamantina watercourse Austr.
155 D1 Diamantina Brazil
151 D3 Diamantina, Chapada plat. Brazil
151 C3 Diamantino Brazil

71 B3 Dianbai China
151 D3 Dianópolis Brazil
114 B4 Dianra Côte d'Ivoire
114 C3 Diapaga Burkina Faso
79 C2 Dibā al Ḥiṣn U.A.E.
118 C3 Dibaya Dem. Rep. Congo
62 A1 Dibrugarh India
136 C1 Dickinson U.S.A.
142 C1 Dickson U.S.A.
Dicle r. Turkey see Tigris
105 D3 Die France
129 D2 Diefenbaker, Lake Can.
114 B3 Diéma Mali
62 B2 Điện Châu Vietnam
101 D1 Diepholz Ger.
104 C2 Dieppe France
115 D3 Diffa Niger
131 D2 Digby Can.
105 D3 Digne-les-Bains France
105 C2 Digoin France
64 B2 Digos Phil.
59 C3 Digul r. Indon.
Dihang r. China/India see Brahmaputra
Dihang r. China/India see Yarlung Zangbo
105 D2 Dijon France
117 C3 Dikhil Djibouti
111 C3 Dikili Turkey
100 A2 Diksmuide Belgium
115 D3 Dikwa Nigeria
117 B4 Dīla Eth.
74 A1 Dilārām Afgh.
59 C3 Dili East Timor
101 D2 Dillenburg Ger.
134 D1 Dillon U.S.A.
118 C4 Dilolo Dem. Rep. Congo
72 D2 Dimapur India
Dimashq Syria see Damascus
52 B3 Dimboola Austr.
110 C2 Dimitrovgrad Bulg.
87 D3 Dimitrovgrad Russia
64 B1 Dinagat i. Phil.
104 B2 Dinan France
100 B2 Dinant Belgium
111 D3 Dinar Turkey
81 D2 Dīnār, Kūh-e mt. Iran
73 B3 Dindigul India
123 D2 Dindiza Moz.
101 E2 Dingelstädt Ger.
75 C2 Dinggyê China
Dingle Ireland see Daingean Uí Chúis
97 A2 Dingle Bay Ireland
96 B2 Dingwall U.K.
70 A2 Dingxi China
154 B3 Dionísio Cerqueira Brazil
114 A3 Diourbel Senegal
74 B1 Dir Pak.
51 D1 Direction, Cape Austr.
117 C4 Dire Dawa Eth.
120 B2 Dirico Angola
115 D1 Dirj Libya
50 A2 Dirk Hartog Island Austr.
53 C1 Dirranbandi Austr.
78 B3 Dirs Saudi Arabia
50 B2 Disappointment, Lake imp. l. Austr.
52 B3 Discovery Bay Austr.
143 E1 Dismal Swamp U.S.A.
99 D2 Diss U.K.
108 B3 Dittaino r. Sicily Italy
74 B2 Diu India
155 D2 Divinópolis Brazil
87 D4 Divnoye Russia
114 B4 Divo Côte d'Ivoire
80 B2 Divriği Turkey

Dixon

140	B2	Dixon U.S.A.
128	A2	Dixon Entrance sea chan. Can./U.S.A.
80	C2	Diyarbakır Turkey
74	A2	Diz Pak.
115	D2	Djado Niger
115	D2	Djado, Plateau du Niger
118	B3	Djambala Congo
115	C2	Djanet Alg.
115	C1	Djelfa Alg.
119	C2	Djéma C.A.R.
114	B3	Djenné Mali
118	B2	Djibloho Equat. Guinea
114	B3	Djibo Burkina Faso
117	C3	Djibouti country Africa
117	C3	Djibouti Djibouti
114	C4	Djougou Benin
92	☐C3	Djúpivogur Iceland
91	E1	Dmitriyevka Russia
89	E3	Dmitriyev-L'govskiy Russia
89	E2	Dmitrov Russia
		Dnepr r. Ukr. see Dnieper
91	C2	Dnieper r. Ukr.
90	B2	Dniester r. Ukr.
		Dnipro r. Ukr. see Dnieper
91	C2	Dniprodzerzhyns'k Ukr.
91	D2	Dnipropetrovs'k Ukr.
91	C2	Dniprorudne Ukr.
		Dnister r. Ukr. see Dniester
88	C2	Dno Russia
115	D4	Doba Chad
88	B2	Dobele Latvia
101	F2	Döbeln Ger.
59	C3	Doberai, Jazirah pen. Indon.
59	C3	Dobo Indon.
109	C2	Doboj Bos. & Herz.
110	C2	Dobrich Bulg.
89	F3	Dobrinka Russia
89	E3	Dobroye Russia
89	D3	Dobrush Belarus
155	E1	Doce r. Brazil
145	B2	Doctor Arroyo Mex.
144	B2	Doctor Belisario Domínguez Mex.
111	C3	Dodecanese is Greece see Dodecanese
		Dodekanisos is Greece see Dodecanese
136	C3	Dodge City U.S.A.
119	D3	Dodoma Tanz.
100	C2	Doetinchem Neth.
59	C3	Dofa Indon.
75	C1	Dogai Coring salt l. China
128	B2	Dog Creek Can.
67	B3	Dōgo i. Japan
115	C3	Dogondoutchi Niger
81	C2	Doğubeyazıt Turkey
79	C2	Doha Qatar
62	A2	Doi Saket Thai.
100	B1	Dokkum Neth.
88	C3	Dokshytsy Belarus
91	D2	Dokuchayevs'k Ukr.
131	C2	Dolbeau-Mistassini Can.
104	B2	Dol-de-Bretagne France
105	D2	Dole France
99	B2	Dolgellau U.K.
89	E3	Dolgorukovo Russia
89	E3	Dolgoye Russia
		Dolisie Congo see Loubomo
59	D3	Dolok, Pulau i. Indon.
108	B1	Dolomites mts Italy
117	C4	Dolo Odo Eth.
126	D2	Dolphin and Union Strait Can.
90	A2	Dolyna Ukr.
102	C2	Domažlice Czech Rep.
93	E3	Dombås Norway
103	D2	Dombóvár Hungary
128	B2	Dome Creek Can.
147	D3	Dominica country West Indies
147	C3	Dominican Republic country West Indies
89	E2	Domodedovo Russia
111	B3	Domokos Greece
61	C2	Dompu Indon.
89	E3	Don r. Russia
96	C2	Don r. U.K.
97	D1	Donaghadee U.K.
52	B3	Donald Austr.
		Donau r. Austria/Ger. see Danube
102	C2	Donauwörth Ger.
106	B2	Don Benito Spain
98	C2	Doncaster U.K.
120	A1	Dondo Angola
121	C2	Dondo Moz.
73	C4	Dondra Head Sri Lanka
97	B1	Donegal Ireland
97	B1	Donegal Bay Ireland
91	D2	Donets'k Ukr.
91	D2	Donets'kyy Kryazh hills Russia/Ukr.
50	A2	Dongara Austr.
62	B1	Dongchuan China
65	B2	Dongducheon S. Korea
71	A4	Dongfang China
66	B1	Dongfanghong China
58	B3	Donggala Indon.
65	A2	Donggang China
71	B3	Dongguan China
62	B2	Đông Ha Vietnam
65	B2	Donghae S. Korea
		Dong Hai sea N. Pacific Ocean see East China Sea
62	B2	Đông Hoi Vietnam
118	B2	Dongou Congo
71	B3	Dongshan China
70	B2	Dongsheng China
70	C2	Dongtai China
71	B3	Dongting Hu l. China
		Dong Ujimqin Qi China see Uliastai
70	B2	Dongying China
63	B2	Đôn Kêv Cambodia
54	B1	Donnellys Crossing N.Z.
99	B3	Dorchester U.K.
122	A1	Dordabis Namibia
104	B2	Dordogne r. France
100	B2	Dordrecht Neth.
123	C3	Dordrecht S. Africa
129	D2	Doré Lake Can.
101	D1	Dorfmark Ger.
68	C1	Dörgön Nuur salt l. Mongolia
114	B3	Dori Burkina Faso
122	A3	Doring r. S. Africa
96	B2	Dornoch U.K.
96	B2	Dornoch Firth est. U.K.
89	D3	Dorogobuzh Russia
90	B2	Dorohoi Romania
92	G3	Dorotea Sweden
50	A2	Dorre Island Austr.
53	D2	Dorrigo Austr.
100	C2	Dortmund Ger.
100	C2	Dortmund-Ems-Kanal canal Ger.
153	B5	Dos Bahías, Cabo c. Arg.
77	D3	Dōshī Afgh.
101	F1	Dosse r. Ger.
115	C3	Dosso Niger
143	C2	Dothan U.S.A.
101	D1	Dötlingen Ger.
105	C1	Douai France
118	A2	Douala Cameroon
104	B2	Douarnenez France
114	B3	Douentza Mali
98	A1	Douglas Isle of Man
122	B2	Douglas S. Africa
128	A2	Douglas AK U.S.A.
138	B2	Douglas AZ U.S.A.
143	D2	Douglas GA U.S.A.
136	B2	Douglas WY U.S.A.
71	C3	Douliu Taiwan
104	C1	Doullens France
154	B1	Dourada, Serra hills Brazil
154	B2	Dourados Brazil
154	B2	Dourados, Serra dos hills Brazil
106	B1	Douro r. Port.
99	D3	Dover U.K.
141	D3	Dover U.S.A.
99	D3	Dover, Strait of France/U.K.
141	F1	Dover-Foxcroft U.S.A.
79	C2	Dowlatābād Būshehr Iran
79	C2	Dowlatābād Kermān Iran
97	D1	Downpatrick U.K.
67	B3	Dōzen is Japan
130	C2	Dozois, Réservoir resr Can.
114	B2	Drâa, Hamada du plat. Alg.
154	B2	Dracena Brazil
100	C1	Drachten Neth.
110	B2	Drăgănești-Olt Romania
110	B2	Drăgășani Romania
88	C3	Drahichyn Belarus
123	C2	Drakensberg mts Lesotho/S. Africa
123	C2	Drakensberg mts S. Africa
158	B8	Drake Passage S. Atlantic Ocean
111	B2	Drama Greece
93	F4	Drammen Norway
109	C1	Drava r. Europe
128	C2	Drayton Valley Can.
101	D2	Dreieich Ger.
102	C1	Dresden Ger.
104	C2	Dreux France
100	B1	Driemond Neth.
109	C2	Drina r. Bos. & Herz./Serbia
109	C2	Drniš Croatia
110	B2	Drobeta-Turnu Severin Romania
101	D1	Drochtersen Ger.
97	C2	Drogheda Ireland
90	A2	Drohobych Ukr.
97	C1	Dromore U.K.
74	B1	Drosh Pak.
53	C3	Drouin Austr.
128	C2	Drumheller Can.
140	C1	Drummond Island U.S.A.
131	C2	Drummondville Can.
88	B3	Druskininkai Lith.
91	D2	Druzhkivka Ukr.
88	D2	Druzhnaya Gorka Russia
130	A2	Dryden Can.
50	B1	Drysdale r. Austr.
78	A2	Dubā Saudi Arabia
79	C2	Dubai U.A.E.
129	D1	Dubawnt Lake Can.
		Dubayy U.A.E. see Dubai
78	A2	Dubbagh, Jabal ad mt. Saudi Arabia
53	C2	Dubbo Austr.
97	C2	Dublin Ireland
143	D2	Dublin U.S.A.
90	B1	Dubno Ukr.
141	D2	Du Bois U.S.A.
114	A4	Dubréka Guinea
109	C2	Dubrovnik Croatia
90	B1	Dubrovytsya Ukr.
89	D3	Dubrowna Belarus
137	E2	Dubuque U.S.A.
129	D2	Duck Bay Can.
101	E2	Duderstadt Ger.
82	G2	Dudinka Russia
99	B2	Dudley U.K.
106	B1	Duero r. Spain

131 C1 Duffreboy, Lac l. Can.
96 C2 Dufftown U.K.
109 C2 Dugi Rat Croatia
100 C2 Duisburg Ger.
123 C3 Dukathole S. Africa
79 C2 Dukhān Qatar
89 D2 Dukhovshchina Russia
Dukou China see Panzhihua
88 C2 Dūkštas Lith.
68 C2 Dulan China
152 B4 Dulce r. Arg.
100 C2 Dülmen Ger.
110 C2 Dulovo Bulg.
137 E1 Duluth U.S.A.
64 B2 Dumaguete Phil.
60 B1 Dumai Indon.
64 B1 Dumaran i. Phil.
142 B2 Dumas AR U.S.A.
139 C1 Dumas TX U.S.A.
96 B3 Dumbarton U.K.
103 D2 Ďumbier mt. Slovakia
96 C3 Dumfries U.K.
55 J3 Dumont d'Urville Sea
        Antarctica
116 B1 Dumyāṭ Egypt
        Duna r. Hungary see Danube
        Dunaj r. Slovakia see Danube
103 D2 Dunakeszi Hungary
        Dunărea r. Romania see
        Danube
103 D2 Dunaújváros Hungary
        Dunav r. Serbia see Danube
90 B2 Dunayivtsi Ukr.
96 C2 Dunbar U.K.
96 C1 Dunbeath U.K.
128 A2 Duncan Can.
139 D2 Duncan U.S.A.
96 C1 Duncansby Head U.K.
97 C1 Dundalk Ireland
97 C2 Dundalk Bay Ireland
123 D2 Dundee S. Africa
96 C2 Dundee U.K.
97 D1 Dundrum Bay U.K.
54 B3 Dunedin N.Z.
96 C2 Dunfermline U.K.
97 C1 Dungannon U.K.
74 B2 Dungarpur India
97 C2 Dungarvan Ireland
99 D3 Dungeness hd U.K.
97 C1 Dungiven U.K.
53 D2 Dungog Austr.
119 C2 Dungu Dem. Rep. Congo
60 B1 Dungun Malaysia
116 B2 Dungunab Sudan
69 E2 Dunhua China
68 C2 Dunhuang China
        Dunkerque France see
        Dunkirk
104 C1 Dunkirk France
141 D2 Dunkirk U.S.A.
97 C2 Dún Laoghaire Ireland
97 D1 Dunmurry U.K.
97 C2 Dunnet Head U.K.
96 C3 Duns U.K.
99 C3 Dunstable U.K.
110 B2 Dupnitsa Bulg.
136 C1 Dupree U.S.A.
50 B1 Durack r. Austr.
144 B2 Durango Mex.
106 C1 Durango Spain
136 B3 Durango U.S.A.
139 D2 Durant U.S.A.
153 C4 Durazno Uru.
123 D2 Durban S. Africa
104 C3 Durban-Corbières France
122 A3 Durbanville S. Africa
100 B2 Durbuy Belgium
100 C2 Düren Ger.

73 C2 Durg India
98 C1 Durham U.K.
143 E1 Durham U.S.A.
60 B1 Duri Indon.
109 C2 Durmitor mt. Montenegro
96 B1 Durness U.K.
109 C2 Durrës Albania
97 A3 Dursey Island Ireland
111 C3 Dursunbey Turkey
59 D3 D'Urville, Tanjung pt Indon.
54 B2 D'Urville Island N.Z.
71 A3 Dushan China
77 C3 Dushanbe Tajik.
100 C2 Düsseldorf Ger.
71 A3 Duyun China
91 D2 Dvorichna Ukr.
74 A2 Dwarka India
123 C1 Dwarsberg S. Africa
134 C1 Dworshak Reservoir U.S.A.
89 D3 Dyat'kovo Russia
96 C2 Dyce U.K.
127 G2 Dyer, Cape Can.
142 C1 Dyersburg U.S.A.
103 D2 Dyje r. Austria/Czech Rep.
103 D1 Dylewska Góra h. Pol.
91 D2 Dymytrov Ukr.
123 C3 Dyoki S. Africa
87 E3 Dyurtyuli Russia
69 D2 Dzamïn Üüd Mongolia
120 D2 Dzaoudzi Mayotte
        Dzhambul Kazakh. see Taraz
91 C2 Dzhankoy Ukr.
91 D3 Dzhubga Russia
83 K3 Dzhugdzhur, Khrebet mts
        Russia
103 E1 Działdowo Pol.
69 D1 Dzuunmod Mongolia
88 C3 Dzyarzhynsk Belarus
88 C3 Dzyatlavichy Belarus

E

131 E1 Eagle r. Can.
134 C1 Eagle Cap mt. U.S.A.
130 A2 Eagle Lake Can.
134 B2 Eagle Lake U.S.A.
139 C3 Eagle Pass U.S.A.
126 B2 Eagle Plain Can.
130 A1 Ear Falls Can.
99 D3 Eastbourne U.K.
156 C3 East China Sea
        N. Pacific Ocean
54 B1 East Coast Bays N.Z.
129 D2 Eastend Can.
123 C3 Eastern Cape prov. S. Africa
116 B2 Eastern Desert Egypt
73 B3 Eastern Ghats mts India
129 E2 Easterville Can.
153 C6 East Falkland i. Falkland Is
100 C1 East Frisian Islands Ger.
96 B3 East Kilbride U.K.
99 C3 Eastleigh U.K.
140 C2 East Liverpool U.S.A.
123 C3 East London S. Africa
130 C1 Eastmain Can.
130 C1 Eastmain r. Can.
143 D2 Eastman U.S.A.
140 A3 East St Louis U.S.A.
        East Sea N. Pacific Ocean see
        Japan, Sea of
83 K2 East Siberian Sea Russia
59 C3 East Timor country Asia
140 A2 Eau Claire U.S.A.
130 C1 Eau Claire, Lac à l' l. Can.
59 D2 Eauripik atoll Micronesia
145 C2 Ebano Mex.

99 B3 Ebbw Vale U.K.
102 C1 Eberswalde Ger.
109 C2 Eboli Italy
118 B2 Ebolowa Cameroon
107 D1 Ebro r. Spain
144 A2 Echeverria, Pico mt. Mex.
67 C3 Echizen Japan
129 E2 Echoing r. Can.
100 C3 Echternach Lux.
53 B3 Echuca Austr.
106 B2 Écija Spain
102 B1 Eckernförde Ger.
127 F2 Eclipse Sound sea chan.
        Can.

150 A2 Ecuador country S. America
116 C3 Ed Eritrea
117 A3 Ed Da'ein Sudan
117 B3 Ed Damazin Sudan
116 B3 Ed Damer Sudan
116 B3 Ed Debba Sudan
116 B3 Ed Dueim Sudan
51 D4 Eddystone Point Austr.
100 B1 Ede Neth.
118 B2 Edéa Cameroon
154 C1 Edéia Brazil
53 C3 Eden Austr.
98 B1 Eden r. U.K.
123 C2 Edenburg S. Africa
97 C2 Edenderry Ireland
52 B3 Edenhope Austr.
111 B2 Edessa Greece
82 C1 Edgeøya i. Svalbard
139 D3 Edinburg U.S.A.
96 C3 Edinburgh U.K.
110 C2 Edirne Turkey
128 C2 Edmonton Can.
131 D2 Edmundston Can.
111 C3 Edremit Turkey
111 C3 Edremit Körfezi b. Turkey
128 C2 Edson Can.
119 C3 Edward, Lake Dem. Rep.
        Congo/Uganda
139 C2 Edwards Plateau U.S.A.
100 C1 Eenrum Neth.
48 F4 Éfaté i. Vanuatu
140 B3 Effingham U.S.A.
135 C3 Egan Range mts U.S.A.
103 E2 Eger Hungary
93 E4 Egersund Norway
92 □C2 Egilsstaðir Iceland
80 B2 Eğirdir Turkey
80 B2 Eğirdir Gölü l. Turkey
104 C2 Égletons France
        Egmont, Mount vol. N.Z. see
        Taranaki, Mount
83 M2 Egvekinot Russia
116 A2 Egypt country Africa
68 C2 Ehen Hudag China
100 C1 Eibergen Neth.
100 C1 Eifel hills Ger.
96 A2 Eigg i. U.K.
73 B4 Eight Degree Channel India/
        Maldives
50 B1 Eighty Mile Beach Austr.
80 B1 Eilat Israel
101 F2 Eilenburg Ger.
101 D2 Einbeck Ger.
100 B2 Eindhoven Neth.
150 B2 Eirunepé Brazil
120 B2 Eiseb watercourse Namibia
101 E2 Eisenach Ger.
102 C1 Eisenhüttenstadt Ger.
103 D2 Eisenstadt Austria
101 E2 Eisleben, Lutherstadt Ger.
        Eivissa Spain see Ibiza
        Eivissa i. Spain see Ibiza
107 C2 Ejea de los Caballeros Spain
121 □D3 Ejeda Madag.

Ejin Qi

		Ejin Qi China *see*
		Dalain Hob
93	H4	Ekenäs Fin.
92	J2	Ekostrovskaya Imandra,
		Ozero *l.* Russia
93	F4	Eksjö Sweden
122	A2	Eksteenfontein S. Africa
130	B1	Ekwan *r.* Can.
62	A2	Ela Myanmar
123	C2	Elandsdoorn S. Africa
111	B3	Elassona Greece
80	B2	Elazığ Turkey
108	B2	Elba, Isola d' *i.* Italy
150	A1	El Banco Col.
138	B2	El Barreal *salt l.* Mex.
109	C2	Elbasan Albania
150	B1	El Baúl Venez.
114	C1	El Bayadh Alg.
101	D1	Elbe *r.* Ger.
136	B3	Elbert, Mount U.S.A.
143	D2	Elberton U.S.A.
104	C2	Elbeuf France
80	B2	Elbistan Turkey
103	D1	Elbląg Pol.
87	D4	El'brus *mt.* Russia
81	C2	Elburz Mountains Iran
150	B1	El Callao Venez.
139	D3	El Campo U.S.A.
135	C4	El Centro U.S.A.
152	B2	El Cerro Bol.
107	C2	Elche-Elx Spain
107	C2	Elda Spain
137	E3	Eldon U.S.A.
144	B2	El Dorado Mex.
142	B2	El Dorado *AR* U.S.A.
137	D3	El Dorado *KS* U.S.A.
114	B2	El Eglab *plat.* Alg.
106	C2	El Ejido Spain
89	E2	Elektrostal' Russia
		Elemi Triangle *disp. terr.*
		Africa *see* Ilemi Triangle
150	A2	El Encanto Col.
146	C2	Eleuthera *i.* Bahamas
117	A3	El Fasher Sudan
144	B2	El Fuerte Mex.
117	A3	El Geneina Sudan
116	B3	El Geteina Sudan
96	C2	Elgin U.K.
140	B2	Elgin U.S.A.
115	C1	El Goléa Alg.
144	A1	El Golfo de Santa Clara Mex.
119	D2	Elgon, Mount Kenya/Uganda
114	A2	El Hammâmi *reg.* Maur.
114	A2	El Hierro *i.* Canary Islands
145	C2	El Higo Mex.
114	C2	El Homr Alg.
110	C2	Elhovo Bulg.
87	D4	Elista Russia
141	E2	Elizabeth U.S.A.
143	E1	Elizabeth City U.S.A.
140	B3	Elizabethtown U.S.A.
114	B1	El Jadida Morocco
103	E1	Ełk Pol.
139	D1	Elk City U.S.A.
128	C2	Elkford Can.
140	B2	Elkhart U.S.A.
		El Khartum Sudan *see*
		Khartoum
140	D3	Elkins U.S.A.
128	C3	Elko Can.
134	C2	Elko U.S.A.
129	C2	Elk Point Can.
126	E1	Ellef Ringnes Island Can.
137	D1	Ellendale U.S.A.
134	B1	Ellensburg U.S.A.
54	B2	Ellesmere, Lake N.Z.
127	F1	Ellesmere Island Can.
98	B2	Ellesmere Port U.K.
126	E2	Ellice *r.* Can.
		Ellice Islands *country*
		S. Pacific Ocean *see* Tuvalu
123	C3	Elliotdale S. Africa
96	C2	Ellon U.K.
141	F2	Ellsworth U.S.A.
55	O2	Ellsworth Mountains
		Antarctica
111	C3	Elmalı Turkey
115	C1	El Meghaïer Alg.
141	D2	Elmira U.S.A.
107	C2	El Moral Spain
101	D1	Elmshorn Ger.
117	A3	El Muglad Sudan
64	A1	El Nido Phil.
117	B3	El Obeid Sudan
144	B2	El Oro Mex.
115	C1	El Oued Alg.
138	A2	Eloy U.S.A.
138	B2	El Paso U.S.A.
144	B1	El Porvenir Mex.
107	D1	El Prat de Llobregat Spain
139	D1	El Reno U.S.A.
144	B2	El Salado Mex.
144	B2	El Salto Mex.
146	B3	El Salvador *country*
		Central America
145	B2	El Salvador Mex.
138	B3	El Sauz Mex.
144	A1	El Socorro Mex.
145	C2	El Temascal Mex.
150	B1	El Tigre Venez.
147	D4	El Tocuyo Venez.
88	C2	Elva Estonia
106	B2	Elvas Port.
93	F3	Elverum Norway
119	E2	El Wak Kenya
99	D2	Ely U.K.
137	E1	Ely *MN* U.S.A.
135	D3	Ely *NV* U.S.A.
123	C2	eMalahleni S. Africa
93	G4	Emån *r.* Sweden
123	D3	eManzimtoti S. Africa
76	B2	Emba Kazakh.
123	C2	Embalenhle S. Africa
154	C1	Emborcação, Represa de *resr*
		Brazil
119	D3	Embu Kenya
100	B1	Emden Ger.
51	D2	Emerald Austr.
129	E3	Emerson Can.
111	C3	Emet Turkey
123	D2	eMgwenya S. Africa
115	D3	Emi Koussi *mt.* Chad
110	C2	Emine, Nos *pt* Bulg.
80	B2	Emirdağ Turkey
123	D2	eMjindini S. Africa
88	B2	Emmaste Estonia
100	B1	Emmeloord Neth.
100	C1	Emmelshausen Ger.
100	C1	Emmen Neth.
123	D2	eMondlo S. Africa
139	C3	Emory Peak U.S.A.
144	A2	Empalme Mex.
123	D2	Empangeni S. Africa
108	B2	Empoli Italy
137	D3	Emporia *KS* U.S.A.
141	D3	Emporia *VA* U.S.A.
		Empty Quarter *des.*
		Saudi Arabia *see* Rub' al Khālī
100	C1	Ems *r.* Ger.
100	C1	Emsdetten Ger.
123	C2	eMzinoni S. Africa
59	D3	Enarotali Indon.
144	B3	Encarnación Mex.
152	C3	Encarnación Para.
155	D1	Encruzilhada Brazil
58	C3	Ende Indon.
126	A2	Endicott Mountains U.S.A.
91	C2	Enerhodar Ukr.
87	D3	Engel's Russia
60	B2	Enggano *i.* Indon.
98	C2	England *admin. div.* U.K.
130	A1	English *r.* Can.
95	C4	English Channel France/U.K.
139	D1	Enid U.S.A.
100	B1	Enkhuizen Neth.
93	G4	Enköping Sweden
108	B3	Enna *Sicily* Italy
129	D1	Ennadai Lake Can.
117	A3	En Nahud Sudan
115	E3	Ennedi, Massif *mts* Chad
53	C1	Enngonia Austr.
97	B2	Ennis Ireland
139	D2	Ennis U.S.A.
97	C2	Enniscorthy Ireland
97	C1	Enniskillen Ireland
97	B2	Ennistymon Ireland
102	C2	Enns *r.* Austria
92	H2	Enontekiö Fin.
53	C3	Ensay Austr.
100	C1	Enschede Neth.
144	A1	Ensenada Mex.
70	A2	Enshi China
128	C1	Enterprise Can.
142	C2	Enterprise *AL* U.S.A.
134	C1	Enterprise *OR* U.S.A.
152	B3	Entre Ríos Bol.
106	B2	Entroncamento Port.
115	C4	Enugu Nigeria
150	A2	Envira Brazil
135	D3	Ephraim U.S.A.
134	C1	Ephrata U.S.A.
105	D2	Épinal France
99	C3	Epsom U.K.
118	A2	Equatorial Guinea *country*
		Africa
101	F3	Erbendorf Ger.
100	C3	Erbeskopf *h.* Ger.
81	C2	Erciş Turkey
65	B1	Erdao Jiang *r.* China
111	C2	Erdek Turkey
80	B2	Erdemli Turkey
152	C3	Erechim Brazil
69	D1	Ereentsav Mongolia
80	B2	Ereğli *Konya* Turkey
80	B1	Ereğli *Zonguldak* Turkey
69	D2	Erenhot China
		Erevan Armenia *see* Yerevan
101	E2	Erfurt Ger.
80	B2	Ergani Turkey
114	B2	'Erg Chech *des.* Alg./Mali
111	C2	Ergene *r.* Turkey
140	C2	Erie U.S.A.
140	C2	Erie, Lake Can./U.S.A.
66	D2	Erimo-misaki *c.* Japan
116	B3	Eritrea *country* Africa
101	E3	Erlangen Ger.
50	C2	Erldunda Austr.
123	C2	Ermelo S. Africa
80	B2	Ermenek Turkey
111	B3	Ermoupoli Greece
73	B4	Ernakulam India
73	B3	Erode India
100	B2	Erp Neth.
114	B1	Er Rachidia Morocco
117	B3	Er Rahad Sudan
97	B1	Errigal *h.* Ireland
97	A1	Erris Head Ireland
109	D2	Erseke Albania
91	E1	Ertil' Russia
101	D2	Erwitte Ger.
101	F2	Erzgebirge *mts* Czech Rep./
		Ger.
80	B2	Erzincan Turkey
81	C2	Erzurum Turkey

93 E4 **Esbjerg** Denmark
135 D3 **Escalante** U.S.A.
144 B2 **Escalón** Mex.
140 B1 **Escanaba** U.S.A.
145 C3 **Escárcega** Mex.
107 C1 **Escatrón** Spain
100 A2 **Escaut** *r.* Belgium/France
101 E1 **Eschede** Ger.
100 B3 **Esch-sur-Alzette** Lux.
101 E2 **Eschwege** Ger.
100 C2 **Eschweiler** Ger.
135 C4 **Escondido** U.S.A.
144 B2 **Escuinapa** Mex.
111 C3 **Eşen** Turkey
81 D2 **Eşfahān** Iran
123 D2 **eSikhaleni** S. Africa
98 B1 **Esk** *r.* U.K.
131 D1 **Esker** Can.
92 □C2 **Eskifjörður** Iceland
93 G4 **Eskilstuna** Sweden
Eskimo Point Can. *see* **Arviat**
80 B2 **Eskişehir** Turkey
81 C2 **Eslāmābād-e Gharb** Iran
111 C3 **Esler Dağı** *mt.* Turkey
111 C3 **Eşme** Turkey
150 A1 **Esmeraldas** Ecuador
79 D2 **Espakeh** Iran
104 C3 **Espalion** France
130 B2 **Espanola** Can.
138 B1 **Espanola** U.S.A.
50 B3 **Esperance** Austr.
144 B2 **Esperanza** Mex.
106 B2 **Espichel, Cabo** *c.* Port.
155 D1 **Espinhaço, Serra do** *mts* Brazil
151 D3 **Espinosa** Brazil
48 F4 **Espiritu Santo** *i.* Vanuatu
144 A2 **Espíritu Santo, Isla** *i.* Mex.
93 H3 **Espoo** Fin.
153 A5 **Esquel** Arg.
114 B1 **Essaouira** Morocco
100 C2 **Essen** Ger.
150 C1 **Essequibo** *r.* Guyana
114 A2 **Es-Smara** Western Sahara
83 L3 **Esso** Russia
79 C2 **Estahbān** Iran
151 E3 **Estância** Brazil
123 C2 **Estcourt** S. Africa
107 C1 **Estella** Spain
106 B2 **Estepona** Spain
106 C1 **Esteras de Medinaceli** Spain
129 D2 **Esterhazy** Can.
152 B3 **Esteros** Para.
136 B2 **Estes Park** U.S.A.
129 D3 **Estevan** Can.
137 E2 **Estherville** U.S.A.
129 D2 **Eston** Can.
88 C2 **Estonia** *country* Europe
106 B1 **Estrela, Serra da** *mts* Port.
106 B2 **Estremoz** Port.
52 A1 **Etadunna** Austr.
104 C2 **Étampes** France
104 C1 **Étaples** France
75 B2 **Etawah** India
123 D2 **Ethandakukhanya** S. Africa
117 B4 **Ethiopia** *country* Africa
109 C3 **Etna, Mount** *vol. Sicily* Italy
128 A2 **Etolin Island** U.S.A.
120 A2 **Etosha Pan** *salt pan* Namibia
100 C3 **Ettelbruck** Lux.
100 B2 **Etten-Leur** Neth.
107 C1 **Etxarri-Aranatz** Spain
99 D3 **Eu** France
53 C2 **Euabalong** Austr.
Euboea *i.* Greece *see* **Evvoia**
50 B3 **Eucla** Austr.
143 C2 **Eufaula** U.S.A.
139 D1 **Eufaula Lake** *resr* U.S.A.
134 B2 **Eugene** U.S.A.
144 A2 **Eugenia, Punta** *pt* Mex.
53 C1 **Eulo** Austr.
53 C2 **Eumungerie** Austr.
139 C2 **Eunice** U.S.A.
80 C2 **Euphrates** *r.* Asia
134 B2 **Eureka** *CA* U.S.A.
134 C1 **Eureka** *MT* U.S.A.
135 C3 **Eureka** *NV* U.S.A.
52 B2 **Euriowie** Austr.
53 C3 **Euroa** Austr.
106 B2 **Europa Point** Gibraltar
128 B2 **Eutsuk Lake** Can.
130 C1 **Evans, Lac** *l.* Can.
53 D1 **Evans Head** Austr.
127 F2 **Evans Strait** Can.
136 A2 **Evanston** U.S.A.
140 B3 **Evansville** U.S.A.
123 C2 **Evaton** S. Africa
79 C2 **Evaz** Iran
83 L2 **Evensk** Russia
50 C2 **Everard Range** *hills* Austr.
75 C2 **Everest, Mount** China/Nepal
134 B1 **Everett** U.S.A.
100 A2 **Evergem** Belgium
143 D3 **Everglades** *swamp* U.S.A.
118 B2 **Evinayong** Equat. Guinea
93 E4 **Evje** Norway
106 B2 **Évora** Port.
104 C2 **Évreux** France
111 C2 **Evros** *r.* Greece/Turkey
111 B3 **Evrotas** *r.* Greece
80 B2 **Evrychou** Cyprus
111 B3 **Evvoia** *i.* Greece
119 E2 **Ewaso Ngiro** *r.* Kenya
152 B2 **Exaltación** Bol.
99 B3 **Exe** *r.* U.K.
99 B3 **Exeter** U.K.
99 B3 **Exmoor** *hills* U.K.
99 B3 **Exmouth** U.K.
50 A2 **Exmouth Gulf** Austr.
146 C2 **Exuma Cays** *is* Bahamas
117 C4 **Eyl** Somalia
51 C3 **Eyre Peninsula** Austr.
94 B1 **Eysturoy** *i.* Faroe Is
123 D2 **Ezakheni** S. Africa
123 C2 **Ezenzeleni** S. Africa
70 B2 **Ezhou** China
86 E2 **Ezhva** Russia
111 C3 **Ezine** Turkey

F

138 B2 **Fabens** U.S.A.
108 B2 **Fabriano** Italy
115 D3 **Fachi** Niger
114 C3 **Fada-N'Gourma** Burkina Faso
108 B2 **Faenza** Italy
59 C3 **Fafanlap** Indon.
110 B1 **Făgăraş** Romania
49 G3 **Fagatogo** American Samoa
93 E3 **Fagernes** Norway
93 G4 **Fagersta** Sweden
153 B6 **Fagnano, Lago** *l.* Arg./Chile
114 B3 **Faguibine, Lac** *l.* Mali
92 □B3 **Fagurhólsmýri** Iceland
126 B2 **Fairbanks** U.S.A.
137 D2 **Fairbury** U.S.A.
135 B3 **Fairfield** U.S.A.
96 □ **Fair Isle** *i.* U.K.
137 E2 **Fairmont** *MN* U.S.A.
140 C3 **Fairmont** *WV* U.S.A.
128 C2 **Fairview** Can.
59 D2 **Fais** *i.* Micronesia
74 B1 **Faisalabad** Pak.
136 C1 **Faith** U.S.A.
77 D3 **Faīẕābād** Afgh.
75 C2 **Faizabad** India
59 C3 **Fakfak** Indon.
65 A1 **Faku** China
114 A4 **Falaba** Sierra Leone
139 D3 **Falcon Lake** Mex./U.S.A.
139 D3 **Falfurrias** U.S.A.
128 C2 **Falher** Can.
93 F4 **Falkenberg** Sweden
101 F2 **Falkenberg/Elster** Ger.
101 F1 **Falkensee** Ger.
96 C3 **Falkirk** U.K.
153 C6 **Falkland Islands** *terr.* S. Atlantic Ocean
93 F4 **Falköping** Sweden
135 C3 **Fallon** U.S.A.
141 E2 **Fall River** U.S.A.
137 D2 **Falls City** U.S.A.
99 A3 **Falmouth** U.K.
122 A3 **False Bay** S. Africa
93 F4 **Falster** *i.* Denmark
110 C1 **Fălticeni** Romania
93 G3 **Falun** Sweden
71 A3 **Fangcheng** China
71 C3 **Fangshan** Taiwan
69 E1 **Fangzheng** China
108 B2 **Fano** Italy
119 C2 **Faradje** Dem. Rep. Congo
121 □D3 **Farafangana** Madag.
116 A2 **Farāfirah, Wāḩāt al** *oasis* Egypt
76 C3 **Farāh** Afgh.
114 A3 **Faranah** Guinea
78 B3 **Farasān, Jazā'ir** *is* Saudi Arabia
127 J3 **Farewell, Cape** Greenland
54 B2 **Farewell, Cape** N.Z.
137 D1 **Fargo** U.S.A.
77 D2 **Farg'ona** Uzbek.
137 E2 **Faribault** U.S.A.
141 E2 **Farmington** *ME* U.S.A.
138 B1 **Farmington** *NM* U.S.A.
141 D3 **Farmville** U.S.A.
99 C3 **Farnborough** U.K.
128 C2 **Farnham, Mount** Can.
128 A1 **Faro** Can.
106 B2 **Faro** Port.
88 A2 **Fårö** *i.* Sweden
94 B1 **Faroe Islands** *terr.* N. Atlantic Ocean
79 C2 **Farrāshband** Iran
139 C2 **Farwell** U.S.A.
79 C2 **Fāryāb** Iran
79 C2 **Fasā** Iran
109 C2 **Fasano** Italy
90 B1 **Fastiv** Ukr.
75 B2 **Fatehgarh** India
75 C2 **Fatehpur** India
92 G2 **Fauske** Norway
92 □A3 **Faxaflói** *b.* Iceland
92 G3 **Faxälven** *r.* Sweden
115 D3 **Faya** Chad
142 B1 **Fayetteville** *AR* U.S.A.
143 E1 **Fayetteville** *NC* U.S.A.
142 C1 **Fayetteville** *TN* U.S.A.
74 B1 **Fazilka** India
114 A2 **Fdérik** Maur.
143 E2 **Fear, Cape** U.S.A.
54 C2 **Featherston** N.Z.
104 C2 **Fécamp** France
102 C1 **Fehmarn** *i.* Ger.
101 F1 **Fehrbellin** Ger.
155 D2 **Feia, Lagoa** *lag.* Brazil
150 A2 **Feijó** Brazil
54 C2 **Feilding** N.Z.
151 E3 **Feira de Santana** Brazil
107 D2 **Felanitx** Spain
145 D3 **Felipe C. Puerto** Mex.
155 D1 **Felixlândia** Brazil

99 D3 Felixstowe U.K.
101 D2 Felsberg Ger.
108 B1 Feltre Italy
93 F3 Femunden l. Norway
71 B3 Fengcheng Jiangxi China
65 A1 Fengcheng Liaoning China
62 A1 Fengqing China
70 B2 Fengxian China
Fengxiang China see Lincang
71 C3 Fengyuan Taiwan
70 B1 Fengzhen China
105 D3 Feno, Capo di c. Corsica France
121 □D2 Fenoarivo Atsinanana Madag.
91 D2 Feodosiya Ukr.
108 A3 Fer, Cap de c. Alg.
137 D1 Fergus Falls U.S.A.
109 D2 Ferizaj Kosovo
114 B4 Ferkessédougou Côte d'Ivoire
108 B2 Fermo Italy
131 C1 Fermont Can.
106 B1 Fermoselle Spain
97 B2 Fermoy Ireland
143 D2 Fernandina Beach U.S.A.
154 B2 Fernandópolis Brazil
128 C3 Fernie Can.
108 B2 Ferrara Italy
154 B2 Ferreiros Brazil
108 A2 Ferro, Capo c. Sardinia Italy
106 B1 Ferrol Spain
100 B1 Ferwerd Neth.
114 B1 Fès Morocco
118 B3 Feshi Dem. Rep. Congo
137 E3 Festus U.S.A.
111 C3 Fethiye Turkey
96 □ Fetlar i. U.K.
130 C1 Feuilles, Rivière aux r. Can.
Fez Morocco see Fès
121 □D3 Fianarantsoa Madag.
117 B4 Fiché Eth.
109 C2 Fier Albania
96 C2 Fife Ness pt U.K.
104 C3 Figeac France
106 B1 Figueira da Foz Port.
107 D1 Figueres Spain
114 B1 Figuig Morocco
48 F3 Fiji country S. Pacific Ocean
152 B3 Filadelfia Para.
55 Q2 Filchner Ice Shelf Antarctica
98 C1 Filey U.K.
111 B3 Filippiada Greece
93 F4 Filipstad Sweden
96 C2 Findhorn r. U.K.
140 C2 Findlay U.S.A.
51 D4 Fingal Austr.
141 D2 Finger Lakes U.S.A.
106 B1 Finisterre, Cape Spain
92 I3 Finland country Europe
93 H4 Finland, Gulf of Europe
128 B2 Finlay r. Can.
53 C3 Finley Austr.
101 E2 Finne ridge Ger.
92 H2 Finnmarksvidda reg. Norway
92 G2 Finnsnes Norway
93 G4 Finspång Sweden
96 A2 Fionnphort U.K.
Firat r. Turkey see Euphrates
Firenze Italy see Florence
105 C2 Firminy France
75 B2 Firozabad India
74 B1 Firozpur India
79 C2 Fīrūzābād Iran
122 A2 Fish watercourse Namibia
122 B3 Fish r. S. Africa
99 A3 Fishguard U.K.
105 C2 Fismes France
Fisterra, Cabo c. Spain see Finisterre, Cape

141 E2 Fitchburg U.S.A.
129 C2 Fitzgerald Can.
50 B1 Fitzroy Crossing Austr.
108 B2 Fivizzano Italy
119 C3 Fizi Dem. Rep. Congo
92 G3 Fjällsjöälven r. Sweden
123 C3 Flagstaff S. Africa
138 A1 Flagstaff U.S.A.
130 C1 Flaherty Island Can.
98 C1 Flamborough Head U.K.
101 F1 Fläming hills Ger.
136 B2 Flaming Gorge Reservoir U.S.A.
134 D1 Flathead r. U.S.A.
134 D1 Flathead Lake U.S.A.
51 D1 Flattery, Cape Austr.
134 B1 Flattery, Cape U.S.A.
98 B2 Fleetwood U.K.
93 E4 Flekkefjord Norway
102 B1 Flensburg Ger.
104 B2 Flers France
51 D1 Flinders r. Austr.
50 A3 Flinders Bay Austr.
51 D3 Flinders Island Austr.
52 A2 Flinders Ranges mts Austr.
129 D2 Flin Flon Can.
140 C2 Flint U.S.A.
107 D1 Florac France
108 B2 Florence Italy
142 C2 Florence AL U.S.A.
138 A2 Florence AZ U.S.A.
134 B2 Florence OR U.S.A.
143 E2 Florence SC U.S.A.
150 A1 Florencia Col.
146 B3 Flores Guat.
58 C3 Flores i. Indon.
58 B3 Flores, Laut sea Indon.
Flores Sea Indon. see Flores, Laut
151 E2 Floresta Brazil
139 D3 Floresville U.S.A.
151 D2 Floriano Brazil
152 D3 Florianópolis Brazil
153 C4 Florida Uru.
143 D2 Florida state U.S.A.
143 D4 Florida, Straits of N. Atlantic Ocean
143 D4 Florida Keys is U.S.A.
111 B2 Florina Greece
93 E3 Florø Norway
129 D2 Foam Lake Can.
109 C2 Foča Bos. & Herz.
110 C1 Focşani Romania
71 B3 Fogang China
109 C2 Foggia Italy
131 E2 Fogo Island Can.
104 C3 Foix France
89 D3 Fokino Russia
130 B2 Foleyet Can.
108 B2 Foligno Italy
99 D3 Folkestone U.K.
143 D2 Folkston U.S.A.
108 B2 Follonica Italy
129 D2 Fond-du-Lac Can.
129 D2 Fond du Lac r. Can.
140 B2 Fond du Lac U.S.A.
106 B1 Fondevila Spain
108 B2 Fondi Italy
146 B3 Fonseca, Golfo de b. Central America
150 B2 Fonte Boa Brazil
104 B2 Fontenay-le-Comte France
92 □C2 Fontur pt Iceland
53 C2 Forbes Austr.
101 E2 Forchheim Ger.
93 E3 Førde Norway
53 C1 Fords Bridge Austr.
142 B2 Fordyce U.S.A.

142 C2 Forest U.S.A.
53 C3 Forest Hill Austr.
131 D2 Forestville Can.
96 C2 Forfar U.K.
134 B1 Forks U.S.A.
108 B2 Forlì Italy
107 D2 Formentera i. Spain
107 D2 Formentor, Cap de c. Spain
155 C2 Formiga Brazil
152 C3 Formosa Arg.
Formosa country Asia see Taiwan
154 C1 Formosa Brazil
96 C2 Forres U.K.
50 B3 Forrest Austr.
142 B1 Forrest City U.S.A.
51 D1 Forsayth Austr.
93 H3 Forssa Fin.
53 D2 Forster Austr.
136 B1 Forsyth U.S.A.
74 B2 Fort Abbas Pak.
130 B1 Fort Albany Can.
151 E2 Fortaleza Brazil
128 C2 Fort Assiniboine Can.
96 B2 Fort Augustus U.K.
134 D1 Fort Benton U.S.A.
135 B3 Fort Bragg U.S.A.
Fort Chimo Can. see Kuujjuaq
129 C2 Fort Chipewyan Can.
136 B2 Fort Collins U.S.A.
147 D3 Fort-de-France Martinique
137 E2 Fort Dodge U.S.A.
130 A2 Fort Frances Can.
Fort Franklin Can. see Déline
Fort George Can. see Chisasibi
126 C2 Fort Good Hope Can.
96 C2 Forth r. U.K.
96 C2 Forth, Firth of est. U.K.
152 C3 Fortín Madrejón Para.
143 D3 Fort Lauderdale U.S.A.
128 B1 Fort Liard Can.
129 C2 Fort Mackay Can.
129 C2 Fort McMurray Can.
126 C2 Fort McPherson Can.
136 C2 Fort Morgan U.S.A.
143 D3 Fort Myers U.S.A.
128 B2 Fort Nelson Can.
128 B2 Fort Nelson r. Can.
142 C2 Fort Payne U.S.A.
136 B1 Fort Peck U.S.A.
136 B1 Fort Peck Reservoir U.S.A.
128 C1 Fort Pierce U.S.A.
128 C1 Fort Providence Can.
129 D2 Fort Qu'Appelle Can.
128 C1 Fort Resolution Can.
Fort Rupert Can. see Waskaganish
128 B2 Fort St James Can.
128 B2 Fort St John Can.
128 C2 Fort Saskatchewan Can.
137 E3 Fort Scott U.S.A.
130 B1 Fort Severn Can.
76 B2 Fort-Shevchenko Kazakh.
128 B1 Fort Simpson Can.
129 C1 Fort Smith Can.
142 B1 Fort Smith U.S.A.
139 C2 Fort Stockton U.S.A.
138 C2 Fort Sumner U.S.A.
128 C2 Fort Vermilion Can.
142 C2 Fort Walton Beach U.S.A.
140 B2 Fort Wayne U.S.A.
96 B2 Fort William U.K.
139 D2 Fort Worth U.S.A.
126 B2 Fort Yukon U.S.A.
71 B3 Foshan China
92 F3 Fosna pen. Norway
93 E3 Fosnavåg Norway
92 □B3 Foss Iceland

92 □A2 Fossá Iceland
108 A2 Fossano Italy
53 C3 Foster Austr.
104 B2 Fougères France
96 □ Foulá i. U.K.
111 C3 Fournoi i. Greece
114 A3 Fouta Djallon reg. Guinea
54 A3 Foveaux Strait N.Z.
136 C3 Fowler U.S.A.
50 C3 Fowlers Bay Austr.
54 C1 Fox Creek Can.
127 F2 Foxe Basin g. Can.
127 F2 Foxe Channel Can.
127 F2 Foxe Peninsula Can.
54 B2 Fox Glacier N.Z.
128 C2 Fox Lake Can.
128 A1 Fox Mountain Can.
129 D2 Foxton N.Z.
129 D2 Fox Valley Can.
97 C1 Foyle, Lough b. Ireland/U.K.
154 B3 Foz de Areia, Represa de resr
Brazil
120 A2 Foz do Cunene Angola
154 B3 Foz do Iguaçu Brazil
107 D1 Fraga Spain
154 C2 Franca Brazil
108 A2 Francavilla Fontana Italy
118 B3 Franceville Gabon
104 C2 France country Europe
137 D2 Francis Case, Lake U.S.A.
155 D1 Francisco Sá Brazil
120 B3 Francistown Botswana
108 A2 François Lake Can.
101 D2 Frankenberg (Eder) Ger.
101 D3 Frankenthal (Pfalz) Ger.
101 E2 Frankenwald mts Ger.
140 C1 Frankfort U.S.A.
101 D2 Frankfurt am Main Ger.
102 C2 Frankfurt (Oder) Ger.
101 E3 Fränkische Alb hills Ger.
101 E3 Fränkische Schweiz reg.
Ger.
141 D2 Franklin U.S.A.
126 C2 Franklin Bay Can.
134 C1 Franklin D. Roosevelt Lake
U.S.A.
128 B1 Franklin Mountains Can.
131 D3 Franklin Strait Can.
82 E1 Frantsa-Iosifa, Zemlya is
Russia
54 B2 Franz Josef Glacier N.Z.
Franz Josef Land is Russia see
Frantsa-Iosifa, Zemlya
108 A3 Frasca, Capo della c. Sardinia
Italy
128 B3 Fraser r. B.C. Can.
131 D1 Fraser r. Nfld. and Lab. Can.
122 B3 Fraserburg S. Africa
96 C2 Fraserburgh U.K.
130 B2 Fraserdale Can.
51 E2 Fraser Island Austr.
128 B2 Fraser Lake Can.
153 C4 Fray Bentos Uru.
93 E4 Fredericia Denmark
139 D2 Fredericksburg TX U.S.A.
141 D3 Fredericksburg VA U.S.A.
128 A2 Frederick Sound sea chan.
U.S.A.
131 D2 Fredericton Can.
93 F4 Frederikshavn Denmark
Frederikshamn Fin. see
Hamina
93 F4 Fredrikstad Norway
140 B2 Freeport IL U.S.A.
139 D3 Freeport TX U.S.A.
146 C2 Freeport City Bahamas
139 D3 Freer U.S.A.

123 C2 Free State prov. S. Africa
114 A4 Freetown Sierra Leone
106 B2 Fregenal de la Sierra Spain
104 B2 Fréhel, Cap c. France
102 B2 Freiburg im Breisgau Ger.
102 C2 Freising Ger.
102 C2 Freistadt Austria
105 D3 Fréjus France
50 A3 Fremantle Austr.
137 D2 Fremont NE U.S.A.
140 C2 Fremont OH U.S.A.
151 C1 French Guiana terr.
S. America
134 C1 Frenchman r. U.S.A.
49 I4 French Polynesia terr.
S. Pacific Ocean
144 B2 Fresnillo Mex.
135 C3 Fresno U.S.A.
107 D2 Freu, Cap des c. Spain
105 D2 Freyming-Merlebach
France
114 A3 Fria Guinea
152 B3 Frías Arg.
102 B2 Friedrichshafen Ger.
101 D1 Friesack Ger.
100 C1 Friesoythe Ger.
Frobisher Bay Nunavut Can.
see Iqaluit
127 G2 Frobisher Bay Can.
101 F2 Frohburg Ger.
87 D4 Frolovo Russia
52 A2 Frome, Lake imp. l. Austr.
52 A2 Frome Downs Austr.
100 C2 Fröndenberg/Ruhr Ger.
145 C3 Frontera Mex.
144 B1 Fronteras Mex.
108 B2 Frosinone Italy
92 E3 Frøya i. Norway
Frunze Kyrg. see Bishkek
105 D2 Frutigen Switz.
103 D2 Frýdek-Místek Czech Rep.
71 B3 Fu'an China
106 C1 Fuenlabrada Spain
152 C3 Fuerte Olimpo Para.
114 A2 Fuerteventura i.
Canary Islands
64 B1 Fuga i. Phil.
79 C2 Fujairah U.A.E.
67 C3 Fuji Japan
71 B3 Fujian prov. China
67 C3 Fujinomiya Japan
67 C3 Fuji-san vol. Japan
67 B4 Fukui Japan
67 B4 Fukuoka Japan
67 D3 Fukushima Japan
101 D2 Fulda Ger.
101 D2 Fulda r. Ger.
70 A3 Fuling China
137 E3 Fulton U.S.A.
105 C2 Fumay France
49 F3 Funafuti atoll Tuvalu
114 A1 Funchal Arquipélago da
Madeira
106 B1 Fundão Port.
131 D2 Fundy, Bay of g. Can.
70 B2 Funing Jiangsu China
71 A3 Funing Yunnan China
115 C3 Funtua Nigeria
79 C2 Fürgun, Küh-e mt. Iran
89 F2 Furmanov Russia
155 D1 Furnas, Represa resr Brazil
51 D4 Furneaux Group is Austr.
100 C1 Fürstenau Ger.
101 E3 Fürth Ger.
127 F2 Fury and Hecla Strait Can.
65 A1 Fushun China
65 B1 Fusong China
79 C2 Fuwayriṭ Qatar

70 B2 Fuyang China
69 E1 Fuyu China
68 B1 Fuyun China
71 B3 Fuzhou Fujian China
71 B3 Fuzhou Jiangxi China
93 F4 Fyn i. Denmark
F.Y.R.O.M. country Europe see
Macedonia

G

117 C4 Gaalkacyo Somalia
120 A2 Gabela Angola
115 D1 Gabès Tunisia
115 D1 Gabès, Golfe de g. Tunisia
118 B3 Gabon country Africa
123 C1 Gaborone Botswana
110 C2 Gabrovo Bulg.
114 A3 Gabú Guinea-Bissau
73 B3 Gadag-Betigeri India
75 C2 Gadchiroli India
101 E1 Gadebusch Ger.
142 C2 Gadsden U.S.A.
110 C2 Găeşti Romania
108 B2 Gaeta Italy
143 D1 Gaffney U.S.A.
115 C1 Gafsa Tunisia
89 E2 Gagarin Russia
114 B4 Gagnoa Côte d'Ivoire
131 D1 Gagnon Can.
81 C1 Gagra Georgia
122 A2 Gaiab watercourse Namibia
111 C3 Gaidouronisi i. Greece
104 C3 Gaillac France
143 D3 Gainesville FL U.S.A.
143 D2 Gainesville GA U.S.A.
139 D2 Gainesville TX U.S.A.
98 C2 Gainsborough U.K.
52 A2 Gairdner, Lake imp. l. Austr.
96 B2 Gairloch U.K.
119 E3 Galana r. Kenya
103 D2 Galanta Slovakia
148 B3 Galapagos Islands Ecuador
96 C3 Galashiels U.K.
110 C1 Galaţi Romania
93 E3 Galdhøpiggen mt. Norway
145 B2 Galeana Mex.
128 C2 Galena Bay Can.
140 A2 Galesburg U.S.A.
122 B2 Galeshewe S. Africa
86 D3 Galich Russia
116 B1 Galilee, Sea of l. Israel
142 C1 Gallatin U.S.A.
73 C4 Galle Sri Lanka
150 A1 Gallinas, Punta pt Col.
109 C2 Gallipoli Italy
111 C2 Gallipoli Turkey
92 H2 Gällivare Sweden
138 B1 Gallup U.S.A.
117 C4 Galmudug reg. Somalia
114 A2 Galtat-Zemmour
Western Sahara
97 B2 Galtymore h. Ireland
139 E3 Galveston U.S.A.
139 E3 Galveston Bay U.S.A.
97 B2 Galway Ireland
97 B2 Galway Bay Ireland
154 C1 Gama Brazil
123 D3 Gamalakhe S. Africa
114 A3 Gambia, The country Africa
52 A3 Gambier Islands Austr.
131 E2 Gambo Can.
118 B3 Gamboma Congo
128 C1 Gamêtî Can.
138 B1 Ganado U.S.A.
81 C1 Gäncä Azer.

		Gand Belgium see Ghent
61	C2	Gandadiwata, Bukit mt. Indon.
118	C3	Gandajika Dem. Rep. Congo
131	E2	Gander Can.
131	E2	Gander r. Can.
101	D1	Ganderkesee Ger.
107	D1	Gandesa Spain
74	B2	Gandhidham India
74	B2	Gandhinagar India
74	B2	Gandhi Sagar resr India
107	C2	Gandia Spain
		Ganga r. Bangl./India see Ganges
153	B5	Gangán Arg.
74	B2	Ganganagar India
68	C2	Gangca China
75	C1	Gangdisê Shan mts China
75	D2	Ganges r. Bangl./India
105	C3	Ganges France
75	C2	Ganges, Mouths of the Bangl./India
65	B2	Gangneung S. Korea
75	C2	Gangtok India
105	C2	Gannat France
136	B2	Gannett Peak U.S.A.
122	A3	Gansbaai S. Africa
70	A1	Gansu prov. China
71	B3	Ganzhou China
114	B3	Gao Mali
97	B1	Gaoth Dobhair Ireland
114	A3	Gaoual Guinea
71	C3	Gaoxiong Taiwan
70	B2	Gaoyou China
70	B2	Gaoyou Hu l. China
105	D3	Gap France
75	C1	Gar China
76	B2	Garabogaz Turkm.
76	B2	Garabogazköl Turkm.
76	B2	Garabogazköl Aylagy b. Turkm.
53	C1	Garah Austr.
151	E2	Garanhuns Brazil
135	B2	Garberville U.S.A.
101	D1	Garbsen Ger.
154	C2	Garça Brazil
101	E1	Gardelegen Ger.
136	C3	Garden City U.S.A.
129	E2	Garden Hill Can.
77	C3	Gardēz Afgh.
88	B2	Gargždai Lith.
123	C3	Gariep Dam dam S. Africa
122	A3	Garies S. Africa
119	D3	Garissa Kenya
102	C2	Garmisch-Partenkirchen Ger.
52	B2	Garnpung Lake imp. l. Austr.
104	B3	Garonne r. France
117	C4	Garoowe Somalia
74	B2	Garoth India
118	B2	Garoua Cameroon
96	B2	Garry r. U.K.
126	E2	Garry Lake Can.
119	E3	Garsen Kenya
61	B2	Garut Indon.
140	B2	Gary U.S.A.
145	B2	Garza García Mex.
68	C2	Garzê China
104	B2	Gascony, Gulf of France
50	A2	Gascoyne r. Austr.
115	D3	Gashua Nigeria
131	D2	Gaspé Can.
131	D2	Gaspésie, Péninsule de la pen. Can.
143	E1	Gaston, Lake U.S.A.
143	D1	Gastonia U.S.A.
107	C2	Gata, Cabo de c. Spain
88	D2	Gatchina Russia
98	C1	Gateshead U.K.
139	D2	Gatesville U.S.A.
130	C2	Gatineau r. Can.
53	D1	Gatton Austr.
129	E2	Gauer Lake Can.
93	E4	Gausta mt. Norway
123	C2	Gauteng prov. S. Africa
111	B3	Gavdos i. Greece
93	G3	Gävle Sweden
89	F2	Gavrilov Posad Russia
89	E2	Gavrilov-Yam Russia
62	A1	Gawai Myanmar
52	A2	Gawler Austr.
52	A2	Gawler Ranges hills Austr.
114	C3	Gaya Niger
75	C2	Gaya India
86	E2	Gayny Russia
80	B2	Gaza disp. terr. Asia
80	B2	Gaziantep Turkey
76	C2	Gazojak Turkm.
114	B4	Gbarnga Liberia
103	D1	Gdańsk Pol.
88	A3	Gdańsk, Gulf of Pol./Russia
88	C2	Gdov Russia
103	D1	Gdynia Pol.
116	B3	Gedaref Sudan
101	D2	Gedern Ger.
111	C3	Gediz r. Turkey
102	C1	Gedser Denmark
100	B2	Geel Belgium
52	B3	Geelong Austr.
101	E1	Geesthacht Ger.
75	C1	Gê'gyai China
129	D2	Geikie r. Can.
93	E3	Geilo Norway
62	B1	Gejiu China
108	B3	Gela Sicily Italy
91	D3	Gelendzhik Russia
		Gelibolu Turkey see Gallipoli
100	C2	Gelsenkirchen Ger.
118	B2	Gemena Dem. Rep. Congo
111	C2	Gemlik Turkey
117	C4	Genalē Wenz r. Eth.
153	B4	General Acha Arg.
153	B4	General Alvear Arg.
153	C4	General Belgrano Arg.
144	B2	General Cepeda Mex.
153	B4	General Pico Arg.
153	B4	General Roca Arg.
64	B2	General Santos Phil.
141	D2	Genesee r. U.S.A.
141	D2	Geneseo U.S.A.
105	D2	Geneva Switz.
141	D2	Geneva U.S.A.
105	D2	Geneva, Lake France/Switz.
		Genève Switz. see Geneva
106	B2	Genil r. Spain
100	B2	Genk Belgium
108	A2	Genoa Italy
		Genova Italy see Genoa
101	F1	Genthin Ger.
50	A3	Geographe Bay Austr.
65	B2	Geongju S. Korea
131	D1	George r. Can.
122	B3	George S. Africa
143	D3	George, Lake FL U.S.A.
141	E2	George, Lake NY U.S.A.
151	C1	Georgetown Guyana
60	B1	George Town Malaysia
143	E2	Georgetown SC U.S.A.
139	D2	Georgetown TX U.S.A.
55	I2	George V Land reg. Antarctica
81	C1	Georgia country Asia
143	D2	Georgia state U.S.A.
130	B2	Georgian Bay Can.
51	C2	Georgina watercourse Austr.
77	E2	Georgiyevka Kazakh.
87	D4	Georgiyevsk Russia
101	F2	Gera Ger.
151	D3	Geral de Goiás, Serra hills Brazil
54	B2	Geraldine N.Z.
50	A2	Geraldton Austr.
80	B1	Gerede Turkey
135	C2	Gerlach U.S.A.
103	E2	Gerlachovský štít mt. Slovakia
102	C1	Germany country Europe
100	C2	Gerolstein Ger.
101	E3	Gerolzhofen Ger.
101	D2	Gersfeld (Rhön) Ger.
75	C1	Gêrzê China
117	C4	Gestro Wenz, Wabē r. Eth.
141	D3	Gettysburg PA U.S.A.
136	D1	Gettysburg SD U.S.A.
109	D2	Gevgelija Macedonia
111	C3	Geyikli Turkey
122	B2	Ghaap Plateau S. Africa
115	C1	Ghadāmis Libya
75	C2	Ghaghara r. India
114	B4	Ghana country Africa
120	B3	Ghanzi Botswana
115	C1	Ghardaïa Alg.
115	D1	Gharyān Libya
75	C2	Ghatal India
75	B2	Ghaziabad India
75	C2	Ghazipur India
77	C3	Ghaznī Afgh.
100	A2	Ghent Belgium
110	B1	Gherla Romania
105	D3	Ghisonaccia Corsica France
74	B2	Ghotaru India
74	A2	Ghotki Pak.
91	E3	Giaginskaya Russia
97	C1	Giant's Causeway lava field U.K.
61	C2	Gianyar Indon.
109	C3	Giarre Sicily Italy
108	A1	Giaveno Italy
122	A2	Gibeon Namibia
106	B2	Gibraltar Gibraltar
106	B2	Gibraltar, Strait of Morocco/Spain
50	B2	Gibson Desert Austr.
68	C1	Gichgeniyn Nuruu mts Mongolia
117	B4	Gīdolē Eth.
104	C2	Gien France
101	D2	Gießen Ger.
101	E1	Gifhorn Ger.
128	C2	Gift Lake Can.
67	C3	Gifu Japan
96	B3	Gigha i. U.K.
106	B1	Gijón/Xixón Spain
138	A2	Gila r. U.S.A.
138	A2	Gila Bend U.S.A.
51	D1	Gilbert r. Austr.
49	F2	Gilbert Islands is Kiribati
134	D1	Gildford U.S.A.
53	C2	Gilgandra Austr.
74	B1	Gilgit Pak.
74	B1	Gilgit r. Pak.
53	C2	Gilgunnia Austr.
129	E2	Gillam Can.
136	B2	Gillette U.S.A.
99	D3	Gillingham U.K.
65	B2	Gimcheon S. Korea
129	E2	Gimli Can.
117	C4	Gīnīr Eth.
109	C2	Ginosa Italy
53	C3	Gippsland reg. Austr.
74	A2	Girdar Dhor r. Pak.
80	B1	Giresun Turkey
74	A1	Girishk Afgh.
107	D1	Girona Spain
96	B3	Girvan U.K.
54	C1	Gisborne N.Z.

93 F4 Gislaved Sweden
119 C3 Gitarama Rwanda
108 B2 Giulianova Italy
110 C2 Giurgiu Romania
110 C1 Giuvala, Pasul pass Romania
105 C2 Givors France
123 D1 Giyani S. Africa
116 B2 Giza Egypt
109 D2 Gjakovë Kosovo
109 D2 Gjilan Kosovo
109 D2 Gjirokastër Albania
126 E2 Gjoa Haven Can.
93 F3 Gjøvik Norway
131 E2 Glace Bay Can.
134 B1 Glacier Peak vol. U.S.A.
51 E2 Gladstone Austr.
92 □A2 Gláma mts Iceland
109 C2 Glamoč Bos. & Herz.
100 C3 Glan r. Ger.
97 B2 Glanaruddery Mountains hills Ireland
96 C3 Glasgow U.K.
140 B3 Glasgow KY U.S.A.
136 B1 Glasgow MT U.S.A.
99 B3 Glastonbury U.K.
101 F2 Glauchau Ger.
86 E3 Glazov Russia
89 E3 Glazunovka Russia
96 B2 Glen Coe val. U.K.
138 A2 Glendale U.S.A.
53 D2 Glen Davis Austr.
136 C1 Glendive U.S.A.
52 B3 Glenelg r. Austr.
53 D1 Glen Innes Austr.
126 B2 Glennallen U.S.A.
96 C2 Glenrothes U.K.
141 E2 Glens Falls U.S.A.
96 C2 Glen Shee val. U.K.
97 B1 Glenties Ireland
138 B2 Glenwood U.S.A.
136 B3 Glenwood Springs U.S.A.
103 D1 Gliwice Pol.
138 A2 Globe U.S.A.
103 D1 Głogów Pol.
92 F2 Glomfjord Norway
93 F4 Glomma r. Norway
53 D2 Gloucester Austr.
99 B3 Gloucester U.K.
101 F1 Glöwen Ger.
77 E1 Glubokoye Kazakh.
101 D1 Glückstadt Ger.
103 C2 Gmünd Austria
102 C2 Gmunden Austria
101 D1 Gnarrenburg Ger.
103 D1 Gniezno Pol.
75 D2 Goalpara India
96 B3 Goat Fell h. U.K.
117 C4 Goba Eth.
120 A3 Gobabis Namibia
153 A5 Gobernador Gregores Arg.
69 D2 Gobi des. China/Mongolia
100 C2 Goch Ger.
122 A1 Gochas Namibia
74 B3 Godavari r. India
73 C3 Godavari, Mouths of the India
130 B2 Goderich Can.
74 B2 Godhra India
129 E2 Gods r. Can.
129 E2 Gods Lake Can.
  Godthåb Greenland see Nuuk
  Godwin-Austen, Mount China/Pak. see K2
130 C2 Goéland, Lac au l. Can.
131 D1 Goélands, Lac aux l. Can.
100 A2 Goes Neth.
154 C1 Goiandira Brazil
154 C1 Goiânia Brazil

154 B1 Goiás Brazil
154 B2 Goioerê Brazil
111 C2 Gökçeada i. Turkey
111 C3 Gökçedağ Turkey
121 B2 Gokwe Zimbabwe
93 E3 Gol Norway
62 A1 Golaghat India
111 C2 Gölcük Turkey
103 E1 Gołdap Pol.
101 F1 Goldberg Ger.
53 D1 Gold Coast Austr.
114 B4 Gold Coast Ghana
128 C2 Golden Can.
54 B2 Golden Bay N.Z.
128 B3 Golden Hinde mt. Can.
97 B2 Golden Vale lowland Ireland
135 C3 Goldfield U.S.A.
128 B3 Gold River Can.
143 E1 Goldsboro U.S.A.
135 C4 Goleta U.S.A.
68 C2 Golmud China
81 D2 Golpāyegān Iran
96 C2 Golspie U.K.
119 C3 Goma Dem. Rep. Congo
75 C2 Gomati r. India
115 D3 Gombe Nigeria
115 D3 Gombi Nigeria
  Gomel' Belarus see Homyel'
144 B2 Gómez Palacio Mex.
147 C3 Gonaïves Haiti
147 C3 Gonâve, Île de la i. Haiti
81 D2 Gonbad-e Kāvūs Iran
117 B3 Gonder Eth.
75 C2 Gondiya India
111 C2 Gönen Turkey
65 B2 Gongju S. Korea
115 D4 Gongola r. Nigeria
53 C2 Gongolgon Austr.
75 D1 Gongtang China
145 C2 Gonzáles Mex.
139 D3 Gonzales U.S.A.
122 A3 Good Hope, Cape of S. Africa
134 D2 Gooding U.S.A.
136 D2 Goodland U.S.A.
53 C1 Goodooga Austr.
98 C2 Goole U.K.
53 C2 Goolgowi Austr.
52 A3 Goolwa Austr.
53 D1 Goondiwindi Austr.
134 B2 Goose Lake U.S.A.
102 B2 Göppingen Ger.
75 C2 Gorakhpur India
109 C2 Goražde Bos. & Herz.
111 C3 Gördes Turkey
89 D3 Gordeyevka Russia
128 C1 Gordon, Lake Austr.
115 D4 Goré Chad
117 B4 Goré Eth.
54 A3 Gore N.Z.
97 C2 Gorey Ireland
81 D2 Gorgān Iran
81 C1 Gori Georgia
108 B1 Gorizia Italy
  Gor'kiy Russia see Nizhniy Novgorod
103 D1 Gorlice Pol.
103 C1 Görlitz Ger.
109 D2 Gornji Milanovac Serbia
109 C2 Gornji Vakuf Bos. & Herz.
77 E1 Gorno-Altaysk Russia
110 C2 Gornotrakiyska Nizina lowland Bulg.
77 E1 Gornyak Russia
59 D3 Goroka P.N.G.
114 B3 Gorom Gorom Burkina Faso
59 C2 Gorontalo Indon.
89 E3 Gorshechnoye Russia

97 B2 Gorumna Island Ireland
91 D3 Goryachiy Klyuch Russia
65 B2 Goryeong S. Korea
103 D1 Gorzów Wielkopolski Pol.
53 D2 Gosford Austr.
66 D2 Goshogawara Japan
101 E2 Goslar Ger.
109 C2 Gospić Croatia
99 C3 Gosport U.K.
109 D2 Gostivar Macedonia
  Göteborg Sweden see Gothenburg
101 E2 Gotha Ger.
93 F4 Gothenburg Sweden
136 C2 Gothenburg U.S.A.
93 G4 Gotland i. Sweden
111 B2 Gotse Delchev Bulg.
93 G4 Gotska Sandön i. Sweden
67 B4 Götsu Japan
101 D2 Göttingen Ger.
128 B2 Gott Peak Can.
100 B1 Gouda Neth.
114 A3 Goudiri Senegal
115 D3 Goudoumaria Niger
130 C2 Gouin, Réservoir resr Can.
53 C2 Goulburn r. N.S.W. Austr.
53 B3 Goulburn r. Vic. Austr.
114 B3 Goundam Mali
107 D2 Gouraya Alg.
104 C3 Gourdon France
115 D3 Gouré Niger
67 B4 Gourits r. S. Africa
114 B3 Gourma-Rharous Mali
53□ C3 Gourock Range mts Austr.
155 D1 Governador Valadares Brazil
143 E3 Governor's Harbour Bahamas
68 C2 Govĭ Altayn Nuruu mts Mongolia
75 C2 Govind Ballash Pant Sagar resr India
99 A3 Gower pen. U.K.
152 C3 Goya Arg.
81 C1 Göyçay Azer.
75 C1 Gozha Co salt l. China
122 B3 Graaff-Reinet S. Africa
101 E1 Grabow Ger.
109 C2 Gračac Croatia
87 E3 Grachevka Russia
101 F2 Gräfenhainichen Ger.
53 D1 Grafton Austr.
137 D1 Grafton U.S.A.
139 D2 Graham U.S.A.
128 A2 Graham Island Can.
55 P3 Graham Land pen. Antarctica
123 C3 Grahamstown S. Africa
151 D2 Grajaú Brazil
111 B2 Grammos mt. Greece
96 B2 Grampian Mountains U.K.
146 B3 Granada Nic.
106 C2 Granada Spain
141 E1 Granby Can.
114 A2 Gran Canaria i. Canary Islands
152 B3 Gran Chaco reg. Arg./Para.
136 C1 Grand r. U.S.A.
146 C2 Grand Bahama i. Bahamas
131 E2 Grand Bank Can.
158 C2 Grand Banks of Newfoundland N. Atlantic Ocean
  Grand Canal canal China see Jinghang Yunhe
138 A1 Grand Canyon U.S.A.
138 A1 Grand Canyon gorge U.S.A.
146 B3 Grand Cayman i. Cayman Is
129 C2 Grand Centre Can.
134 C1 Grand Coulee U.S.A.
152 B2 Grande r. Bol.

154 B2	Grande r. Brazil	
153 B6	Grande, Bahía b. Arg.	
155 D2	Grande, Ilha i. Brazil	
128 C2	Grande Cache Can.	
128 C2	Grande Prairie Can.	
114 B1	Grand Erg Occidental des. Alg.	
115 C2	Grand Erg Oriental des. Alg.	
131 D2	Grande-Rivière Can.	
152 B4	Grandes, Salinas salt flat Arg.	
156 D7	Grande Terre i. S. Pacific Ocean	
131 D2	Grand Falls Can.	
131 E2	Grand Falls-Windsor Can.	
128 C3	Grand Forks Can.	
137 D1	Grand Forks U.S.A.	
128 C1	Grandin, Lac l. Can.	
137 D2	Grand Island U.S.A.	
142 B3	Grand Isle U.S.A.	
136 B3	Grand Junction U.S.A.	
114 B4	Grand-Lahou Côte d'Ivoire	
131 D2	Grand Lake N.B. Can.	
131 E2	Grand Lake Nfld. and Lab. Can.	
137 E1	Grand Marais U.S.A.	
106 B2	Grândola Port.	
129 E2	Grand Rapids Can.	
140 B2	Grand Rapids MI U.S.A.	
137 E1	Grand Rapids MN U.S.A.	
136 A2	Grand Teton mt. U.S.A.	
147 C2	Grand Turk Turks and Caicos Is	
134 C1	Grangeville U.S.A.	
128 B2	Granisle Can.	
134 E1	Granite Peak U.S.A.	
108 B3	Granitola, Capo c. Sicily Italy	
93 F4	Gränna Sweden	
101 F1	Gransee Ger.	
99 C2	Grantham U.K.	
96 C2	Grantown-on-Spey U.K.	
138 B1	Grants U.S.A.	
134 B2	Grants Pass U.S.A.	
104 B2	Granville France	
129 D3	Granville Lake Can.	
155 D1	Grão Mogol Brazil	
123 D1	Graskop S. Africa	
105 D3	Grasse France	
107 D1	Graus Spain	
92 F2	Gravdal Norway	
104 B2	Grave, Pointe de pt France	
129 D3	Gravelbourg Can.	
130 C2	Gravenhurst Can.	
53 D1	Gravesend Austr.	
99 D3	Gravesend U.K.	
105 D2	Gray France	
103 D2	Graz Austria	
146 C2	Great Abaco i. Bahamas	
50 B3	Great Australian Bight g. Austr.	
54 C1	Great Barrier Island N.Z.	
51 D1	Great Barrier Reef Austr.	
135 C3	Great Basin U.S.A.	
126 D2	Great Bear Lake Can.	
93 F4	Great Belt sea chan. Denmark	
137 D3	Great Bend U.S.A.	
63 A2	Great Coco Island Cocos Is	
53 B3	Great Dividing Range mts Austr.	
146 B2	Greater Antilles is Caribbean Sea	
60 B2	Greater Sunda Islands is Indon.	
134 D1	Great Falls U.S.A.	
123 C3	Great Fish r. S. Africa	
123 C3	Great Fish Point S. Africa	
147 C2	Great Inagua i. Bahamas	
122 B3	Great Karoo plat. S. Africa	
123 C3	Great Kei r. S. Africa	
99 B2	Great Malvern U.K.	
122 A2	Great Namaqualand reg. Namibia	
63 A3	Great Nicobar i. India	
99 D2	Great Ouse r. U.K.	
119 D3	Great Rift Valley Africa	
119 D3	Great Ruaha r. Tanz.	
134 D2	Great Salt Lake U.S.A.	
135 D2	Great Salt Lake Desert U.S.A.	
116 A2	Great Sand Sea des. Egypt/Libya	
50 B2	Great Sandy Desert Austr.	
128 C1	Great Slave Lake Can.	
143 D1	Great Smoky Mountains U.S.A.	
50 B2	Great Victoria Desert Austr.	
70 B1	Great Wall tourist site China	
99 D2	Great Yarmouth U.K.	
106 B1	Gredos, Sierra de mts Spain	
111 B3	Greece country Europe	
136 C2	Greeley U.S.A.	
82 F1	Greem-Bell, Ostrov i. Russia	
140 B3	Green r. KY U.S.A.	
136 B3	Green r. WY U.S.A.	
140 B2	Green Bay U.S.A.	
140 B1	Green Bay U.S.A.	
140 C3	Greenbrier r. U.S.A.	
140 B3	Greencastle U.S.A.	
143 D1	Greeneville U.S.A.	
141 E2	Greenfield U.S.A.	
129 D2	Green Lake Can.	
127 I2	Greenland terr. N. America	
160 R2	Greenland Sea Greenland/Svalbard	
96 B3	Greenock U.K.	
135 D3	Green River UT U.S.A.	
136 B2	Green River WY U.S.A.	
140 B3	Greensburg IN U.S.A.	
141 D2	Greensburg PA U.S.A.	
143 E2	Green Swamp U.S.A.	
138 A2	Green Valley U.S.A.	
114 B4	Greenville Liberia	
142 C2	Greenville AL U.S.A.	
142 B2	Greenville MS U.S.A.	
143 E1	Greenville NC U.S.A.	
143 D2	Greenville SC U.S.A.	
139 D2	Greenville TX U.S.A.	
53 D2	Greenwell Point Austr.	
143 D2	Greenwood U.S.A.	
50 B2	Gregory, Lake imp. l. Austr.	
51 D1	Gregory Range hills Austr.	
102 C1	Greifswald Ger.	
101 F2	Greiz Ger.	
93 F4	Grenaa Denmark	
142 C2	Grenada U.S.A.	
147 D3	Grenada country West Indies	
104 C3	Grenade France	
53 C2	Grenfell Austr.	
129 D2	Grenfell Can.	
105 D2	Grenoble France	
51 D1	Grenville, Cape Austr.	
134 B1	Gresham U.S.A.	
100 C1	Greven Ger.	
111 B2	Grevena Greece	
100 C2	Grevenbroich Ger.	
101 E1	Grevesmühlen Ger.	
136 B2	Greybull U.S.A.	
128 A1	Grey Hunter Peak Can.	
131 E1	Grey Islands Can.	
54 B2	Greymouth N.Z.	
52 B1	Grey Range hills Austr.	
97 C2	Greystones Ireland	
143 D2	Griffin U.S.A.	
53 C2	Griffith Austr.	
101 F2	Grimma Ger.	
102 C1	Grimmen Ger.	
98 C2	Grimsby U.K.	
128 C2	Grimshaw Can.	
92 □B2	Grímsstaðir Iceland	
93 E4	Grimstad Norway	
137 E2	Grinnell U.S.A.	
123 C3	Griqualand East reg. S. Africa	
122 B2	Griqualand West reg. S. Africa	
127 F1	Grise Fiord Can.	
96 C1	Gritley U.K.	
123 C2	Groblersdal S. Africa	
122 B2	Groblershoop S. Africa	
	Grodno Belarus see Hrodna	
104 B2	Groix, Île de i. France	
100 C1	Gronau (Westfalen) Ger.	
92 F3	Grong Norway	
100 C1	Groningen Neth.	
122 B2	Grootdrink S. Africa	
51 C1	Groote Eylandt i. Austr.	
120 A2	Grootfontein Namibia	
122 A2	Groot Karas Berg plat. Namibia	
122 B3	Groot Swartberge mts S. Africa	
123 C3	Groot Winterberg mt. S. Africa	
101 D2	Großenlüder Ger.	
102 C2	Großer Rachel mt. Ger.	
103 C2	Grosser Speikkogel mt. Austria	
108 B2	Grosseto Italy	
101 D3	Groß-Gerau Ger.	
102 C2	Großglockner mt. Austria	
100 C1	Groß Hesepe Ger.	
101 E2	Großlohra Ger.	
122 A1	Gross Ums Namibia	
131 E1	Groswater Bay Can.	
130 B2	Groundhog r. Can.	
49 I4	Groupe Actéon is Fr. Polynesia	
135 B3	Grover Beach U.S.A.	
141 E2	Groveton U.S.A.	
87 D4	Groznyy Russia	
109 C1	Grubišno Polje Croatia	
103 D1	Grudziądz Pol.	
122 A2	Grünau Namibia	
92 □A3	Grundarfjörður Iceland	
89 E3	Gryazi Russia	
89 F2	Gryazovets Russia	
103 D1	Gryfice Pol.	
102 C1	Gryfino Pol.	
146 C2	Guacanayabo, Golfo de b. Cuba	
144 B2	Guadalajara Mex.	
106 C1	Guadalajara prov. Spain	
49 E3	Guadalcanal i. Solomon Is	
107 C1	Guadalope r. Spain	
106 B2	Guadalquivir r. Spain	
132 B4	Guadalupe i. Mex.	
106 B2	Guadalupe, Sierra de mts Spain	
138 C2	Guadalupe Peak U.S.A.	
144 B2	Guadalupe Victoria Mex.	
144 B2	Guadalupe y Calvo Mex.	
106 C1	Guadarrama, Sierra de mts Spain	
147 D3	Guadeloupe terr. West Indies	
106 B2	Guadiana r. Port./Spain	
106 C2	Guadix Spain	
154 B2	Guaíra Brazil	
147 C3	Guajira, Península de la pen. Col.	
150 A2	Gualaceo Ecuador	
59 D2	Guam terr. N. Pacific Ocean	
144 B2	Guamúchil Mex.	
144 B2	Guanaceví Mex.	
151 D3	Guanambi Brazil	
150 B1	Guanare Venez.	
146 B2	Guane Cuba	
70 A2	Guang'an China	
71 B3	Guangchang China	
71 B3	Guangdong prov. China	

71 A3 **Guangxi Zhuangzu Zizhiqu** *aut. reg.* China
70 A2 **Guangyuan** China
71 B3 **Guangzhou** China
155 D1 **Guanhães** Brazil
147 D4 **Guanipa** *r.* Venez.
71 A3 **Guanling** China
65 A1 **Guanshui** China
Guansuo China *see* **Guanling**
147 C2 **Guantánamo** Cuba
150 B3 **Guaporé** *r.* Bol./Brazil
154 B3 **Guarapuava** Brazil
154 C3 **Guaraqueçaba** Brazil
155 C2 **Guaratinguetá** Brazil
106 B1 **Guarda** Port.
154 C1 **Guarda-Mor** Brazil
106 C1 **Guardo** Spain
155 C2 **Guarujá** Brazil
144 B2 **Guasave** Mex.
146 A3 **Guatemala** *country* Central America
146 A3 **Guatemala City** Guat.
150 B1 **Guaviare** *r.* Col.
155 C2 **Guaxupé** Brazil
150 A2 **Guayaquil** Ecuador
150 B3 **Guayaramerín** Bol.
144 A2 **Guaymas** Mex.
68 C2 **Guazhou** China
117 B3 **Guba** Eth.
86 E1 **Guba Dolgaya** Russia
89 E3 **Gubkin** Russia
115 C1 **Guelma** Alg.
114 A2 **Guelmim** Morocco
130 B2 **Guelph** Can.
145 C2 **Guémez** Mex.
104 C2 **Guéret** France
95 C4 **Guernsey** *terr.* Channel Is
144 A2 **Guerrero Negro** Mex.
131 D1 **Guers, Lac** *l.* Can.
79 C2 **Gūhrān** Iran
118 B2 **Guider** Cameroon
108 B2 **Guidonia Montecelio** Italy
71 A3 **Guigang** China
100 A3 **Guignicourt** France
123 D1 **Guija** Moz.
99 C3 **Guildford** U.K.
71 B3 **Guilin** China
130 C1 **Guillaume-Delisle, Lac** *l.* Can.
106 B1 **Guimarães** Port.
114 A3 **Guinea** *country* Africa
113 F6 **Guinea, Gulf of** Africa
114 A3 **Guinea-Bissau** *country* Africa
104 B2 **Guingamp** France
104 B2 **Guipavas** France
154 B1 **Guiratinga** Brazil
150 B1 **Güiria** Venez.
100 A3 **Guise** France
64 B1 **Guiuan** Phil.
71 A3 **Guiyang** China
71 A3 **Guizhou** *prov.* China
74 B1 **Gujranwala** Pak.
74 B1 **Gujrat** Pak.
91 D2 **Gukovo** Russia
53 C2 **Gulargambone** Austr.
Gulbarga India *see* Kalaburagi
88 C2 **Gulbene** Latvia
79 C2 **Gulf, the** Asia
111 B3 **Gulf of Corinth** *sea chan.* Greece
142 C2 **Gulfport** U.S.A.
69 E1 **Gulian** China
77 C2 **Guliston** Uzbek.
Gulja China *see* **Yining**
129 D2 **Gull Lake** Can.
111 C3 **Güllük** Turkey
119 D2 **Gulu** Uganda
120 B2 **Gumare** Botswana
76 B3 **Gumdag** Turkm.
65 B2 **Gumi** S. Korea
75 C2 **Gumla** India
100 C2 **Gummersbach** Ger.
74 B2 **Guna** India
53 C3 **Gundagai** Austr.
111 C3 **Güney** Turkey
118 B3 **Gungu** Dem. Rep. Congo
129 E2 **Gunisao** *r.* Can.
53 D2 **Gunnedah** Austr.
136 B3 **Gunnison** *CO* U.S.A.
135 D3 **Gunnison** *UT* U.S.A.
136 B3 **Gunnison** *r.* U.S.A.
65 B2 **Gunsan** S. Korea
73 B3 **Guntakal** India
60 A1 **Gunungsitoli** Indon.
60 A1 **Gunungtua** Indon.
102 C2 **Günzburg** Ger.
102 C2 **Gunzenhausen** Ger.
70 B2 **Guojiaba** China
74 B2 **Gurgaon** India
151 D2 **Gurgueia** *r.* Brazil
150 B1 **Guri, Embalse de** *resr* Venez.
154 C1 **Gurinhatã** Brazil
151 D2 **Gurupi** *r.* Brazil
74 B2 **Guru Sikhar** *mt.* India
Gur'yev Kazakh. *see* **Atyrau**
115 C3 **Gusau** Nigeria
65 A2 **Gushan** China
70 B2 **Gushi** China
83 I3 **Gusinoozersk** Russia
89 F2 **Gus'-Khrustal'nyy** Russia
108 A3 **Guspini** *Sardinia* Italy
128 A2 **Gustavus** U.S.A.
101 F1 **Güstrow** Ger.
101 D2 **Gütersloh** Ger.
121 C2 **Gutu Mupandawana** Zimbabwe
75 D2 **Guwahati** India
150 C1 **Guyana** *country* S. America
Guyi China *see* **Sanjiang**
139 C1 **Guymon** U.S.A.
53 D2 **Guyra** Austr.
70 A2 **Guyuan** China
144 B1 **Guzmán** Mex.
74 A2 **Gwadar** Pak.
128 A2 **Gwaii Haanas** Can.
75 B2 **Gwalior** India
121 B3 **Gwanda** Zimbabwe
65 B2 **Gwangju** S. Korea
117 D3 **Gwardafuy, Gees** *c.* Somalia
97 B1 **Gweebarra Bay** Ireland
121 B2 **Gweru** Zimbabwe
115 D3 **Gwoza** Nigeria
53 D2 **Gwydir** *r.* Austr.
75 C2 **Gyangzê** China
75 C1 **Gyaring Co** *l.* China
68 C2 **Gyaring Hu** *l.* China
86 G1 **Gydan Peninsula** Russia
Gydanskiy Poluostrov *pen.* Russia *see* **Gydan Peninsula**
Gyêgu China *see* **Yushu**
65 B2 **Gyeonggi-man** *b.* S. Korea
51 E2 **Gympie** Austr.
103 D2 **Gyöngyös** Hungary
103 D2 **Gyr** Hungary
129 E2 **Gypsumville** Can.
103 E2 **Gyula** Hungary
81 C1 **Gyumri** Armenia

H

88 B2 **Haapsalu** Estonia
100 B1 **Haarlem** Neth.
101 C2 **Haarstrang** *ridge* Ger.
54 A2 **Haast** N.Z.
78 B3 **Ḩabbān** Yemen
81 C2 **Ḩabbānīyah, Hawr al** *l.* Iraq
67 C4 **Hachijō-jima** *i.* Japan
66 D2 **Hachinohe** Japan
81 C1 **Hacıqabul** Azer.
121 C3 **Hacufera** Moz.
79 C2 **Ḩadd, Ra's al** *pt* Oman
96 C3 **Haddington** U.K.
115 D3 **Hadejia** Nigeria
93 E4 **Haderslev** Denmark
91 C1 **Hadyach** Ukr.
65 B2 **Haeju** N. Korea
65 B2 **Haeju-man** *b.* N. Korea
65 B3 **Haenam** S. Korea
78 B2 **Ḩafar al Bāţin** Saudi Arabia
62 A1 **Haflong** India
92 □A3 **Hafnarfjörður** Iceland
78 A3 **Hagar Nish Plateau** Eritrea/Sudan
48 D2 **Hagåtña** Guam
100 C2 **Hagen** Ger.
101 E1 **Hagenow** Ger.
128 B2 **Hagensborg** Can.
141 D3 **Hagerstown** U.S.A.
93 F3 **Hagfors** Sweden
67 B4 **Hagi** Japan
62 B1 **Ha Giang** Vietnam
97 B2 **Hag's Head** Ireland
104 B2 **Hague, Cap de la** *c.* France
119 D3 **Hai** Tanz.
128 A2 **Haida Gwaii** Can.
62 B1 **Hai Dương** Vietnam
80 B2 **Haifa** Israel
71 B3 **Haifeng** China
71 B3 **Haikou** China
78 B2 **Ḩā'īl** Saudi Arabia
92 H2 **Hailuoto** *i.* Fin.
71 A4 **Hainan** *prov.* China
69 D3 **Hainan Dao** *i.* China
128 A2 **Haines** U.S.A.
128 A1 **Haines Junction** Can.
101 E2 **Hainich** *ridge* Ger.
101 E2 **Hainleite** *ridge* Ger.
62 B1 **Hai Phong** Vietnam
147 C3 **Haiti** *country* West Indies
116 B3 **Haiya** Sudan
103 E2 **Hajdúböszörmény** Hungary
78 B3 **Ḩajjah** Yemen
79 C2 **Ḩājjīābād** Iran
62 A1 **Hakha** Myanmar
81 C2 **Hakkâri** Turkey
66 D2 **Hakodate** Japan
Ḩalab Syria *see* **Aleppo**
78 B2 **Ḩalabān** Saudi Arabia
81 C2 **Ḩalabjah/Hełebce** Iraq
116 B2 **Ḩalā'ib** Sudan
78 A2 **Halaib Triangle** *terr.* Egypt/Sudan
79 C3 **Ḩalāniyāt, Juzur al** *is* Oman
78 A2 **Ḩālat 'Ammār** Saudi Arabia
101 E2 **Halberstadt** Ger.
64 B1 **Halcon, Mount** Phil.
93 F4 **Halden** Norway
101 E1 **Haldensleben** Ger.
75 B2 **Haldwani** India
79 C2 **Hāleh** Iran
54 A3 **Halfmoon Bay** N.Z.
131 D2 **Halifax** Can.
98 C2 **Halifax** U.K.
141 D3 **Halifax** U.S.A.
65 B3 **Halla-san** *mt.* S. Korea
127 F2 **Hall Beach** Can.
100 B2 **Halle** Belgium
101 E2 **Halle (Saale)** Ger.
102 C2 **Hallein** Austria
137 D1 **Hallock** U.S.A.
127 G2 **Hall Peninsula** Can.
50 B1 **Halls Creek** Austr.

Halmahera

59 B2 Halmahera *i.* Indon.
93 F4 Halmstad Sweden
62 B1 Ha Long Vietnam
67 B4 Hamada Japan
81 C2 Hamadān Iran
80 B2 Ḥamāh Syria
67 C4 Hamamatsu Japan
93 F3 Hamar Norway
116 B2 Ḥamāṭah, Jabal *mt.* Egypt
73 C4 Hambantota Sri Lanka
101 D1 Hamburg Ger.
78 A2 Ḥamd, Wādī al *watercourse*
   Saudi Arabia
78 B3 Ḥamḍah Saudi Arabia
93 H3 Hämeenlinna Fin.
101 D1 Hameln Ger.
50 A2 Hamersley Range *mts* Austr.
65 B2 Hamhŭng N. Korea
68 C2 Hami China
116 B2 Hamid Sudan
52 B3 Hamilton Austr.
130 C2 Hamilton Can.
54 C1 Hamilton N.Z.
96 B3 Hamilton U.K.
142 C2 Hamilton *AL* U.S.A.
134 D1 Hamilton *MT* U.S.A.
140 C3 Hamilton *OH* U.S.A.
93 I3 Hamina Fin.
100 C2 Hamm Ger.
81 C2 Ḥammār, Hawr al *imp. l.* Iraq
101 D2 Hammelburg Ger.
92 G3 Hammerdal Sweden
92 H1 Hammerfest Norway
142 B2 Hammond U.S.A.
141 E3 Hammonton U.S.A.
115 D2 Ḥamrā', Al Ḥamādah al *plat.*
   Libya
78 A2 Ḥanak Saudi Arabia
66 D3 Hanamaki Japan
101 D2 Hanau Ger.
69 D2 Hanbogd Mongolia
70 B2 Hancheng China
140 B1 Hancock U.S.A.
70 B2 Handan China
135 C3 Hanford U.S.A.
68 C1 Hangayn Nuruu *mts*
   Mongolia
   Hanggin Houqi China see
   Xamba
   Hangö Fin. see Hanko
70 C2 Hangzhou China
70 C2 Hangzhou Wan *b.* China
   Hanjia China see Pengshui
   Hanjiang China see
   Yangzhou
93 H4 Hanko Fin.
135 D3 Hanksville U.S.A.
54 B2 Hanmer Springs N.Z.
129 C2 Hanna Can.
137 E3 Hannibal U.S.A.
101 D1 Hannover Ger.
101 D2 Hannoversch Münden Ger.
93 F4 Hanöbukten *b.* Sweden
62 B1 Ha Nôi Vietnam
   Hanoi Vietnam see Ha Nôi
130 B2 Hanover Can.
122 B3 Hanover S. Africa
93 E4 Hanstholm Denmark
88 C2 Hantsavichy Belarus
75 C2 Hanumana India
74 B2 Hanumangarh India
70 A2 Hanzhong China
92 H2 Haparanda Sweden
100 B2 Hapert Neth.
131 D1 Happy Valley-Goose Bay Can.
78 A2 Ḥaql Saudi Arabia
79 B2 Ḥaraḍh Saudi Arabia
88 C2 Haradok Belarus

78 B3 Ḥarajā Saudi Arabia
121 C2 Harare Zimbabwe
79 C3 Ḥarāsīs, Jiddat al *des.* Oman
69 E1 Harbin China
131 E2 Harbour Breton Can.
74 B2 Harda India
   Hardangerfjorden *sea chan.*
   Norway
100 C1 Hardenberg Neth.
100 B1 Harderwijk Neth.
122 A3 Hardeveld *mts* S. Africa
134 C1 Hardin U.S.A.
128 C1 Hardisty Lake Can.
100 C1 Haren (Ems) Ger.
117 C4 Härer Eth.
117 C4 Hargeysa Somalia
110 C1 Harghita-Mădăraş, Vârful *mt.*
   Romania
68 C2 Har Hu *l.* China
74 B1 Haripur Pak.
74 A1 Hari Röd *r.* Afgh./Iran
100 B1 Harlingen Neth.
139 D3 Harlingen U.S.A.
99 D3 Harlow U.K.
134 E1 Harlowton U.S.A.
110 C2 Harmanli Bulg.
134 C2 Harney Basin U.S.A.
134 C2 Harney Lake U.S.A.
93 G3 Härnösand Sweden
69 E1 Har Nur China
68 C1 Har Nuur *l.* Mongolia
114 B4 Harper Liberia
101 D1 Harpstedt Ger.
130 C1 Harricana, Rivière d' *r.* Can.
53 D2 Harrington Austr.
131 E1 Harrington Harbour Can.
96 A2 Harris, Sound of *sea chan.*
   U.K.
140 B3 Harrisburg *IL* U.S.A.
141 D2 Harrisburg *PA* U.S.A.
123 C2 Harrismith S. Africa
142 B1 Harrison U.S.A.
131 E1 Harrison, Cape Can.
126 A2 Harrison Bay U.S.A.
141 D3 Harrisonburg U.S.A.
137 E3 Harrisonville U.S.A.
98 C2 Harrogate U.K.
110 C2 Hârşova Romania
92 G2 Harstad Norway
122 B2 Hartbees *watercourse* S. Africa
103 D2 Hartberg Austria
141 E2 Hartford U.S.A.
99 A3 Hartland Point U.K.
98 C1 Hartlepool U.K.
128 B2 Hartley Bay Can.
123 B2 Harts *r.* S. Africa
143 D2 Hartwell Reservoir U.S.A.
68 C1 Har Us Nuur *l.* Mongolia
136 C1 Harvey U.S.A.
99 D3 Harwich U.K.
101 E2 Harz *hills* Ger.
110 C2 Haskovo Bulg.
73 B3 Hassan India
100 B2 Hasselt Belgium
115 C1 Hassi Messaoud Alg.
93 F4 Hässleholm Sweden
100 B2 Hastière-Lavaux Belgium
54 C1 Hastings Austr.
54 C1 Hastings N.Z.
99 D3 Hastings U.K.
137 E2 Hastings *MN* U.S.A.
137 D2 Hastings *NE* U.S.A.
   Hatay Turkey see Antakya
129 D2 Hatchet Lake Can.
52 B2 Hatfield Austr.
68 C1 Hatgal Mongolia
62 B2 Ha Tinh Vietnam
143 E1 Hatteras, Cape U.S.A.

142 C2 Hattiesburg U.S.A.
100 C2 Hattingen Ger.
63 B3 Hat Yai Thai.
117 C4 Haud *reg.* Eth.
93 E4 Haugesund Norway
93 E4 Haukeligrend Norway
92 I2 Haukipudas Fin.
54 C1 Hauraki Gulf N.Z.
114 B1 Haut Atlas *mts* Morocco
131 D2 Hauterive Can.
114 B1 Hauts Plateaux Alg.
146 B2 Havana Cuba
99 C3 Havant U.K.
101 F1 Havel *r.* Ger.
54 B2 Havelberg Ger.
54 B2 Havelock N.Z.
54 C1 Havelock North N.Z.
99 A3 Haverfordwest U.K.
103 D2 Havlíčkův Brod Czech Rep.
92 H1 Havøysund Norway
111 C3 Havran Turkey
134 E1 Havre U.S.A.
131 D2 Havre-Aubert Can.
131 D2 Havre-St-Pierre Can.
124 E5 Hawai'i *i.* U.S.A.
124 E5 Hawai'ian Islands
   N. Pacific Ocean
98 B2 Hawarden U.K.
54 A2 Hawea, Lake N.Z.
54 B1 Hawera N.Z.
98 B1 Hawes U.K.
96 C3 Hawick U.K.
54 C1 Hawke Bay N.Z.
52 A2 Hawker Austr.
52 B1 Hawkers Gate Austr.
135 C3 Hawthorne U.S.A.
52 B2 Hay Austr.
128 C1 Hay *r.* Can.
134 C1 Hayden U.S.A.
129 E2 Hayes *r.* Man. Can.
126 E2 Hayes *r. Nunavut* Can.
79 C3 Haymā' Oman
77 C2 Hayotboshi tog'i *mt.* Uzbek.
111 C2 Hayrabolu Turkey
128 C1 Hay River Can.
137 D3 Hays U.S.A.
78 B3 Ḥays Yemen
90 B2 Haysyn Ukr.
99 C3 Haywards Heath U.K.
81 D2 Hazar Turkm.
74 A1 Hazārah Jāt *reg.* Afgh.
140 D3 Hazard U.S.A.
75 C2 Hazaribagh India
75 C2 Hazaribagh Range *mts* India
128 B2 Hazelton Can.
141 D2 Hazleton U.S.A.
78 B3 Ḥazm al Jawf Yemen
53 C3 Healesville Austr.
130 B2 Hearst Can.
70 B2 Hebei *prov.* China
53 C1 Hebel Austr.
142 B1 Heber Springs U.S.A.
131 D1 Hebron Can.
128 A2 Hecate Strait Can.
71 A3 Hechi China
93 F3 Hede Sweden
100 B1 Heerenveen Neth.
100 B1 Heerhugowaard Neth.
100 B2 Heerlen Neth.
   Hefa Israel *see* Haifa
70 B2 Hefei China
70 B3 Hefeng China
69 E1 Hegang China
122 A1 Heide Namibia
101 D1 Heidelberg Ger.
122 B3 Heidelberg S. Africa
102 B2 Heilbronn Ger.

69 E1 Heilong Jiang r. China
93 I3 Heinola Fin.
92 F3 Helagsfjället mt. Sweden
142 B2 Helena AR U.S.A.
134 D1 Helena MT U.S.A.
96 B2 Helensburgh U.K.
102 B1 Helgoland i. Ger.
102 B1 Helgoländer Bucht g. Ger.
Helixi China see Ningguo
100 □A3 Hella Iceland
100 B2 Hellevoetsluis Neth.
107 C2 Hellín Spain
76 C3 Helmand r. Afgh.
101 E2 Helmbrechts Ger.
122 A2 Helmeringhausen Namibia
100 B2 Helmond Neth.
96 C1 Helmsdale U.K.
96 C1 Helmsdale r. U.K.
101 E1 Helmstedt Ger.
65 B1 Helong China
93 F4 Helsingborg Sweden
Helsingfors Fin. see Helsinki
93 F4 Helsingør Denmark
93 H3 Helsinki Fin.
97 C2 Helvick Head Ireland
99 C3 Hemel Hempstead U.K.
101 D1 Hemmoor Ger.
92 F2 Hemnesberget Norway
70 B2 Henan prov. China
140 B3 Henderson KY U.S.A.
143 E1 Henderson NC U.S.A.
135 D3 Henderson NV U.S.A.
139 E2 Henderson TX U.S.A.
143 D1 Hendersonville U.S.A.
99 C3 Hendon U.K.
62 A1 Hengduan Shan mts China
100 C1 Hengelo Neth.
Hengnan China see Hengyang
70 B2 Hengshui China
71 A3 Hengxian China
71 B3 Hengyang China
Hengzhou China see Hengxian
91 C2 Heniches'k Ukr.
100 C2 Hennef (Sieg) Ger.
130 B1 Henrietta Maria, Cape Can.
139 D1 Henryetta U.S.A.
127 G2 Henry Kater, Cape Can.
101 D1 Henstedt-Ulzburg Ger.
120 A3 Hentiesbaai Namibia
71 A3 Hepu China
76 C3 Herāt Afgh.
129 D2 Herbert Can.
101 D2 Herbstein Ger.
99 B2 Hereford U.K.
139 C2 Hereford U.S.A.
101 D1 Herford Ger.
100 C2 Herkenbosch Neth.
96 □ Herma Ness hd U.K.
122 A3 Hermanus S. Africa
53 C2 Hermidale Austr.
134 C1 Hermiston U.S.A.
59 D3 Hermit Islands P.N.G.
144 A2 Hermosillo Mex.
154 B3 Hernandarias Para.
100 C2 Herne Ger.
93 E4 Herning Denmark
99 C3 Hertford U.K.
123 C2 Hertzogville S. Africa
51 E2 Hervey Bay Austr.
101 F2 Herzberg (Elster) Ger.
101 E3 Herzogenaurach Ger.
71 A3 Heshan China
128 A1 Hess r. Can.
101 E2 Hessisch Lichtenau Ger.
136 C1 Hettinger U.S.A.
101 E2 Hettstedt Ger.
98 B1 Hexham U.K.

71 B3 Heyuan China
52 B3 Heywood Austr.
70 B2 Heze China
71 B3 Hezhou China
137 D3 Hiawatha U.S.A.
137 E1 Hibbing U.S.A.
54 C1 Hicks Bay N.Z.
66 D2 Hidaka-sanmyaku mts Japan
145 C2 Hidalgo Mex.
144 B2 Hidalgo del Parral Mex.
154 C1 Hidrolândia Brazil
High Atlas mts Morocco see
Haut Atlas
134 B2 High Desert U.S.A.
128 C2 High Level Can.
143 E1 High Point U.S.A.
128 C2 High Prairie Can.
128 C2 High River Can.
129 D2 Highrock Lake Can.
99 C3 High Wycombe U.K.
88 B2 Hiiumaa i. Estonia
78 A2 Hijaz reg. Saudi Arabia
54 C1 Hikurangi mt. N.Z.
101 E2 Hildburghausen Ger.
101 E2 Hilders Ger.
101 D1 Hildesheim Ger.
81 C2 Hillah Iraq
100 C2 Hillesheim Ger.
140 C3 Hillsboro OH U.S.A.
139 D2 Hillsboro TX U.S.A.
53 C2 Hillston Austr.
143 D2 Hilton Head Island U.S.A.
100 B1 Hilversum Neth.
68 B2 Himalaya mts Asia
67 B4 Himeji Japan
123 C2 Himeville S. Africa
51 D1 Hinchinbrook Island Austr.
74 A1 Hindu Kush mts Afgh./Pak.
143 D2 Hinesville U.S.A.
75 B2 Hinganghat India
81 C2 Hınıs Turkey
92 G2 Hinnøya i. Norway
106 B2 Hinojosa del Duque Spain
62 A2 Hinthada Myanmar
128 C2 Hinton Can.
75 C2 Hirakud Reservoir India
66 D2 Hirosaki Japan
67 B4 Hiroshima Japan
101 E3 Hirschaid Ger.
101 E2 Hirschberg Ger.
105 C2 Hirson France
93 E4 Hirtshals Denmark
74 B2 Hisar India
147 C2 Hispaniola i. Caribbean Sea
81 C2 Hīt Iraq
67 D3 Hitachi Japan
67 D3 Hitachinaka Japan
92 E3 Hitra i. Norway
49 I3 Hiva Oa i. Fr. Polynesia
93 G4 Hjälmaren l. Sweden
129 D1 Hjalmar Lake Can.
93 F4 Hjørring Denmark
123 D2 Hlabisa S. Africa
92 □B2 Hlíð Iceland
91 C2 Hlobyne Ukr.
123 C2 Hlohlowane S. Africa
123 C2 Hlotse Lesotho
91 C1 Hlukhiv Ukr.
88 C2 Hlybokaye Belarus
114 C4 Ho Ghana
62 B2 Hoa Binh Vietnam
122 A1 Hoachanas Namibia
51 D4 Hobart Austr.
139 D1 Hobart U.S.A.
139 C2 Hobbs U.S.A.
93 E4 Hobro Denmark
117 C4 Hobyo Somalia
63 B2 Ho Chi Minh City Vietnam

114 B3 Hôd reg. Maur.
78 B3 Hodeidah Yemen
103 E2 Hódmezővásárhely Hungary
Hoek van Holland Neth. see
Hook of Holland
65 B2 Hoeyang N. Korea
101 E2 Hof Ger.
101 E2 Hofheim in Unterfranken
Ger.
92 □B3 Höfn Austurland Iceland
92 □A2 Höfn Vestfirðir Iceland
92 □B3 Hofsjökull Iceland
67 B4 Hōfu Japan
93 G4 Högsby Sweden
101 D2 Hohe Rhön mts Ger.
100 C2 Hohe Venn moorland
Belgium
70 B1 Hohhot China
69 Xil Shan mts China
63 B2 Hôi An Vietnam
62 A1 Hojai India
54 B2 Hokitika N.Z.
66 D2 Hokkaidō i. Japan
128 B2 Holberg Can.
138 A2 Holbrook U.S.A.
137 D2 Holdrege U.S.A.
146 C2 Holguín Cuba
92 □B2 Hóll Iceland
Holland country Europe see
Netherlands
140 B2 Holland U.S.A.
100 B1 Hollum Neth.
142 C2 Holly Springs U.S.A.
134 C4 Hollywood CA U.S.A.
143 D3 Hollywood FL U.S.A.
92 F2 Holm Norway
92 H3 Holmsund Sweden
122 A2 Holoog Namibia
93 E4 Holstebro Denmark
143 D1 Holston r. U.S.A.
98 A2 Holyhead U.K.
98 C1 Holy Island England U.K.
98 A2 Holy Island Wales U.K.
136 C2 Holyoke U.S.A.
101 D2 Holzminden Ger.
62 A1 Homalin Myanmar
101 D2 Homberg (Efze) Ger.
114 B3 Hombori Mali
127 G2 Home Bay Can.
143 D3 Homestead U.S.A.
92 F3 Hommelvik Norway
80 B2 Homs Syria
89 D3 Homyel' Belarus
122 A3 Hondeklipbaai S. Africa
145 C3 Hondo r. Belize/Mex.
139 D3 Hondo U.S.A.
146 B3 Honduras country
Central America
93 F3 Hønefoss Norway
135 B2 Honey Lake salt l. U.S.A.
104 C2 Honfleur France
70 B2 Honghu China
71 A3 Hongjiang China
71 B3 Hong Kong China
71 B3 Hong Kong aut. reg. China
65 B1 Hongwŏn N. Korea
70 B2 Hongze Hu l. China
49 E3 Honiara Solomon Is
92 I1 Honningsvåg Norway
67 B3 Honshū i. Japan
134 B1 Hood, Mount vol. U.S.A.
50 A3 Hood Point Austr.
134 B1 Hood River U.S.A.
100 C1 Hoogeveen Neth.
100 C1 Hoogezand-Sappemeer Neth.
100 C2 Hoog-Keppel Neth.
100 B2 Hook of Holland Neth.
128 A2 Hoonah U.S.A.

100 B1 **Hoorn** Neth.
128 B3 **Hope** Can.
142 B2 **Hope** U.S.A.
83 N2 **Hope, Point** U.S.A.
131 D1 **Hopedale** Can.
131 D1 **Hope Mountains** Can.
52 B3 **Hopetoun** Austr.
122 B2 **Hopetown** S. Africa
141 D3 **Hopewell** U.S.A.
130 C1 **Hopewell Islands** Can.
50 B2 **Hopkins, Lake** *imp. l.* Austr.
140 B3 **Hopkinsville** U.S.A.
134 B1 **Hoquiam** U.S.A.
81 C1 **Horasan** Turkey
93 F4 **Hörby** Sweden
89 D3 **Horki** Belarus
91 D2 **Horlivka** Ukr.
79 D2 **Hormak** Iran
79 C2 **Hormuz, Strait of** Iran/Oman
103 D2 **Horn** Austria
92 □A2 **Horn** *c.* Iceland
153 B6 **Horn, Cape** Chile
141 D2 **Hornell** U.S.A.
130 B2 **Hornepayne** Can.
98 C2 **Hornsea** U.K.
90 B2 **Horodenka** Ukr.
91 C1 **Horodnya** Ukr.
90 B2 **Horodok** *Khmel'nyts'ka Oblast'* Ukr.
90 A2 **Horodok** *L'vivs'ka Oblast'* Ukr.
90 A1 **Horokhiv** Ukr.
Horqin Youyi Qianqi China *see* **Ulanhot**
131 E1 **Horse Islands** Can.
52 B3 **Horsham** Austr.
126 C2 **Horton** *r.* Can.
117 B4 **Hosa'ina** Eth.
74 A2 **Hoshab** Pak.
74 B1 **Hoshiarpur** India
77 E3 **Hotan** China
122 B2 **Hotazel** S. Africa
142 B2 **Hot Springs** *AR* U.S.A.
136 C2 **Hot Springs** *SD* U.S.A.
128 C1 **Hottah Lake** Can.
62 B1 **Houayxay** Laos
100 B2 **Houffalize** Belgium
70 B2 **Houma** China
142 B3 **Houma** U.S.A.
128 B2 **Houston** Can.
139 D3 **Houston** U.S.A.
122 B3 **Houwater** S. Africa
68 C1 **Hovd** Mongolia
99 C3 **Hove** U.K.
68 C1 **Hövsgöl Nuur** *l.* Mongolia
116 A3 **Howar, Wadi** *watercourse* Sudan
53 C3 **Howe, Cape** Austr.
49 G2 **Howland Island** N. Pacific Ocean
53 C3 **Howlong** Austr.
101 D2 **Höxter** Ger.
96 C1 **Hoy** *i.* U.K.
93 E3 **Høyanger** Norway
102 C1 **Hoyerswerda** Ger.
62 A2 **Hpapun** Myanmar
103 D1 **Hradec Králové** Czech Rep.
109 C2 **Hrasnica** Bos. & Herz.
91 C1 **Hrebinka** Ukr.
88 B3 **Hrodna** Belarus
62 A1 **Hsi-hseng** Myanmar
62 A1 **Hsipaw** Myanmar
70 A2 **Huachi** China
150 A3 **Huacho** Peru
69 D2 **Huade** China
65 B1 **Huadian** China
70 B2 **Huai'an** China
70 B2 **Huaibei** China
71 A3 **Huaihua** China
70 B2 **Huainan** China
70 B2 **Huaiyang** China
145 C3 **Huajuápan de León** Mex.
59 C3 **Huaki** Indon.
71 C3 **Hualian** Taiwan
150 A2 **Huallaga** *r.* Peru
120 A2 **Huambo** Angola
150 A3 **Huancayo** Peru
Huangcaoba China *see* **Xingyi**
70 B2 **Huangchuan** China
Huang Hai *sea* N. Pacific Ocean *see* **Yellow Sea**
Huang He *r.* China *see* **Yellow River**
71 A4 **Huangliu** China
70 B3 **Huangshan** China
70 B2 **Huangshi** China
70 A2 **Huangtu Gaoyuan** *plat.* China
71 C3 **Huangyan** China
65 B1 **Huanren** China
150 A2 **Huánuco** Peru
152 B2 **Huanuni** Bol.
150 A2 **Huaraz** Peru
150 A3 **Huarmey** Peru
152 A3 **Huasco** Chile
152 A3 **Huasco** *r.* Chile
144 B2 **Huatabampo** Mex.
145 C3 **Huatusco** Mex.
71 A3 **Huayuan** China
73 B3 **Hubballi** India
70 B2 **Hubei** *prov.* China
Hubli India *see* **Hubballi**
100 C2 **Hückelhoven** Ger.
98 C2 **Hucknall** U.K.
98 C2 **Huddersfield** U.K.
93 G3 **Hudiksvall** Sweden
141 E2 **Hudson** *r.* U.S.A.
129 D2 **Hudson Bay** Can.
127 F3 **Hudson Bay** *sea* Can.
128 B2 **Hudson's Hope** Can.
127 G2 **Hudson Strait** Can.
63 B2 **Huê** Vietnam
146 A3 **Huehuetenango** Guat.
144 B2 **Huehueto, Cerro** *mt.* Mex.
145 C2 **Huejutla** Mex.
106 B2 **Huelva** Spain
107 C2 **Huércal-Overa** Spain
107 C1 **Huesca** Spain
106 C2 **Huéscar** Spain
50 B3 **Hughes (abandoned)** Austr.
139 D2 **Hugo** U.S.A.
122 B2 **Huhudi** S. Africa
122 A2 **Huib-Hoch Plateau** Namibia
71 B3 **Huichang** China
65 B1 **Huich'ŏn** N. Korea
120 A2 **Huíla, Planalto da** Angola
71 B3 **Huilai** China
62 B1 **Huili** China
65 B1 **Huinan** China
93 H3 **Huittinen** Fin.
145 C3 **Huixtla** Mex.
Huiyang China *see* **Huizhou**
62 B1 **Huize** China
71 B3 **Huizhou** China
78 B2 **Hujr** Saudi Arabia
122 B1 **Hukuntsi** Botswana
78 B2 **Ḥulayfah** Saudi Arabia
66 B1 **Hulin** China
130 C2 **Hull** Can.
Hulun China *see* **Hulun Buir**
69 D1 **Hulun Buir** China
69 D1 **Hulun Nur** *l.* China
91 D2 **Hulyaypole** Ukr.
69 E1 **Huma** China
150 B2 **Humaitá** Brazil
122 B3 **Humansdorp** S. Africa
98 C2 **Humber** *est.* U.K.
126 D3 **Humboldt** Can.
142 C1 **Humboldt** U.S.A.
135 C2 **Humboldt** *r.* U.S.A.
103 E2 **Humenné** Slovakia
53 C3 **Hume Reservoir** Austr.
138 A1 **Humphreys Peak** U.S.A.
92 □A2 **Húnaflói** *b.* Iceland
71 B3 **Hunan** *prov.* China
65 C1 **Hunchun** China
110 B1 **Hunedoara** Romania
101 D2 **Hünfeld** Ger.
103 D2 **Hungary** *country* Europe
52 B1 **Hungerford** Austr.
65 B2 **Hŭngnam** N. Korea
65 A1 **Hun He** *r.* China
99 D2 **Hunstanton** U.K.
101 D1 **Hunte** *r.* Ger.
51 D4 **Hunter Islands** Austr.
99 C2 **Huntingdon** U.K.
140 B2 **Huntington** *IN* U.S.A.
140 C3 **Huntington** *WV* U.S.A.
54 C1 **Huntly** N.Z.
96 C2 **Huntly** U.K.
130 C2 **Huntsville** Can.
142 C2 **Huntsville** *AL* U.S.A.
139 D2 **Huntsville** *TX* U.S.A.
59 D3 **Huon Peninsula** P.N.G.
70 B2 **Huozhou** China
116 B1 **Hurghada** Egypt
137 D2 **Huron** U.S.A.
140 C2 **Huron, Lake** Can./U.S.A.
135 D3 **Hurricane** U.S.A.
92 □B2 **Húsavík** Iceland
110 C1 **Huşi** Romania
126 A2 **Huslia** U.S.A.
78 B3 **Ḥusn Āl 'Abr** Yemen
102 B1 **Husum** Ger.
69 C1 **Hutag-Öndör** Mongolia
60 A1 **Hutanopan** Indon.
137 D3 **Hutchinson** U.S.A.
70 C2 **Huzhou** China
92 □C3 **Hvalnes** Iceland
92 □B3 **Hvannadalshnúkur** *vol.* Iceland
109 C2 **Hvar** *i.* Croatia
120 B2 **Hwange** Zimbabwe
136 C2 **Hyannis** U.S.A.
68 C1 **Hyargas Nuur** *salt l.* Mongolia
50 A3 **Hyden** Austr.
73 B3 **Hyderabad** India
74 A2 **Hyderabad** Pak.
105 D3 **Hyères** France
105 D3 **Hyères, Îles d'** *is* France
65 B1 **Hyesan** N. Korea
128 B2 **Hyland Post** Can.
67 B3 **Hyōno-sen** *mt.* Japan
99 D3 **Hythe** U.K.
93 H3 **Hyvinkää** Fin.

I

150 B2 **Iaco** *r.* Brazil
110 C2 **Ialomiţa** *r.* Romania
110 C1 **Ianca** Romania
110 C1 **Iaşi** Romania
64 A1 **Iba** Phil.
115 C4 **Ibadan** Nigeria
150 A1 **Ibagué** Col.
150 A1 **Ibarra** Ecuador
78 B3 **Ibb** Yemen
100 C1 **Ibbenbüren** Ger.
115 C4 **Ibi** Nigeria
155 C1 **Ibiá** Brazil
155 D1 **Ibiraçu** Brazil
107 D2 **Ibiza** Spain

107 D2 **Ibiza** *i.* Spain
151 D3 **Ibotirama** Brazil
79 C2 **Ibrā'** Oman
79 C2 **Ibrī** Oman
150 A3 **Ica** Peru
92 □B2 **Iceland** *country* Europe
66 D3 **Ichinoseki** Japan
91 C1 **Ichnya** Ukr.
65 B2 **Ich'ŏn** N. Korea
139 E2 **Idabel** U.S.A.
134 D2 **Idaho** *state* U.S.A.
134 D2 **Idaho Falls** U.S.A.
100 C3 **Idar-Oberstein** Ger.
116 B2 **Idfū** Egypt
118 B3 **Idiofa** Dem. Rep. Congo
80 B2 **Idlib** Syria
154 B2 **Iepê** Brazil
100 A2 **Ieper** Belgium
119 D3 **Ifakara** Tanz.
121 □D3 **Ifanadiana** Madag.
115 C4 **Ife** Nigeria
114 C3 **Ifôghas, Adrar des** *hills* Mali
61 C1 **Igan** *Sarawak* Malaysia
154 C2 **Igarapava** Brazil
82 G2 **Igarka** Russia
74 B3 **Igatpuri** India
81 C2 **Iğdır** Turkey
108 A3 **Iglesias** *Sardinia* Italy
127 F2 **Igloolik** Can.
Igluligaarjuk Can. *see* **Chesterfield Inlet**
130 A2 **Ignace** Can.
88 C2 **Ignalina** Lith.
110 C2 **İğneada** Turkey
111 B3 **Igoumenitsa** Greece
86 E3 **Igra** Russia
86 F2 **Igrim** Russia
154 B3 **Iguaçu** *r.* Brazil
154 B3 **Iguaçu Falls** Arg./Brazil
145 C3 **Iguala** Mex.
107 D1 **Igualada** Spain
154 C2 **Iguape** Brazil
154 B2 **Iguatemi** Brazil
154 B2 **Iguatemi** *r.* Brazil
151 E2 **Iguatu** Brazil
118 A3 **Iguéla** Gabon
119 D3 **Igunga** Tanz.
121 □D3 **Ihosy** Madag.
110 B2 **Ihtiman** Bulg.
92 I3 **Iisalmi** Fin.
115 C4 **Ijebu-Ode** Nigeria
100 B1 **IJmuiden** Neth.
100 B1 **IJssel** *r.* Neth.
100 B1 **IJsselmeer** *l.* Neth.
123 C2 **Ikageng** S. Africa
111 C3 **Ikaria** *i.* Greece
118 C3 **Ikela** Dem. Rep. Congo
67 A4 **Iki-shima** *i.* Japan
121 □D3 **Ikongo** Madag.
65 B2 **Iksan** S. Korea
64 B1 **Ilagan** Phil.
81 C2 **Īlām** Iran
75 C2 **Ilam** Nepal
103 D1 **Iława** Pol.
79 C2 **Ilazārān, Kūh-e** *mt.* Iran
129 D2 **Île-à-la-Crosse** Can.
129 D2 **Île-à-la-Crosse, Lac** *l.* Can.
118 C3 **Ilebo** Dem. Rep. Congo
124 H6 **Île Clipperton** *terr.* N. Pacific Ocean
119 D2 **Ilemi Triangle** *disp. terr.* Africa
119 D2 **Ileret** Kenya
113 K11 **Îles Crozet** *is* Indian Ocean
49 I3 **Îles du Désappointement** *is* Fr. Polynesia
49 I4 **Îles Gambier** *is* Fr. Polynesia
99 D3 **Ilford** U.K.
99 A3 **Ilfracombe** U.K.
154 B2 **Ilha Grande** *resr* Brazil
155 D2 **Ilha Grande, Baía da** *b.* Brazil
154 B2 **Ilha Solteíra, Represa** *resr* Brazil
106 B1 **Ílhavo** Port.
151 E3 **Ilhéus** Brazil
64 B2 **Iligan** Phil.
152 A4 **Illapel** Chile
90 C2 **Illichivs'k** Ukr.
140 A3 **Illinois** *r.* U.S.A.
140 B3 **Illinois** *state* U.S.A.
90 B2 **Illintsi** Ukr.
115 C2 **Illizi** Alg.
89 D2 **Il'men', Ozero** *l.* Russia
101 E2 **Ilmenau** Ger.
150 A3 **Ilo** Peru
64 B1 **Iloilo** Phil.
92 J3 **Ilomantsi** Fin.
115 C4 **Ilorin** Nigeria
53 D1 **Iluka** Austr.
127 H2 **Ilulissat** Greenland
67 A4 **Imari** Japan
117 C4 **Īmī** Eth.
108 B2 **Imola** Italy
151 D2 **Imperatriz** Brazil
136 C2 **Imperial** U.S.A.
118 B2 **Impfondo** Congo
62 A1 **Imphal** India
111 C2 **İmroz** Turkey
150 B3 **Inambari** *r.* Peru
115 C2 **In Aménas** Alg.
59 C3 **Inanwatan** Indon.
92 I2 **Inari** Fin.
92 I2 **Inarijärvi** *l.* Fin.
67 D3 **Inawashiro-ko** *l.* Japan
80 B1 **İnce Burun** *pt* Turkey
65 B2 **Incheon** S. Korea
123 D2 **Incomati** *r.* Moz.
78 A3 **Inda Silasē** Eth.
144 B2 **Indé** Mex.
135 C3 **Independence** *CA* U.S.A.
137 E2 **Independence** *IA* U.S.A.
137 D3 **Independence** *KS* U.S.A.
137 E3 **Independence** *MO* U.S.A.
134 C2 **Independence Mountains** U.S.A.
76 B2 **Inderbor** Kazakh.
72 B2 **India** *country* Asia
141 D2 **Indiana** U.S.A.
140 B2 **Indiana** *state* U.S.A.
140 B3 **Indianapolis** U.S.A.
129 D2 **Indian Head** Can.
159 **Indian Ocean**
137 E2 **Indianola** *IA* U.S.A.
142 B2 **Indianola** *MS* U.S.A.
135 C3 **Indian Springs** U.S.A.
86 D2 **Indiga** Russia
83 K2 **Indigirka** *r.* Russia
109 D1 **Inđija** Serbia
135 C4 **Indio** U.S.A.
58 B3 **Indonesia** *country* Asia
74 B2 **Indore** India
61 B2 **Indramayu, Tanjung** *pt* Indon.
104 C2 **Indre** *r.* France
74 A2 **Indus** *r.* China/Pak.
74 A2 **Indus, Mouths of the** Pak.
80 B1 **İnebolu** Turkey
111 C2 **İnegöl** Turkey
144 B3 **Infiernillo, Presa** *resr* Mex.
53 D1 **Inglewood** Austr.
102 C2 **Ingolstadt** Ger.
75 C2 **Ingraj Bazar** India
123 D2 **Inhaca** Moz.
121 C3 **Inhambane** Moz.
97 A2 **Inishbofin** *i.* Ireland
97 B2 **Inishmore** *i.* Ireland
97 C1 **Inishowen** *pen.* Ireland
54 B2 **Inland Kaikoura Range** *mts* N.Z.
102 C2 **Inn** *r.* Europe
127 G1 **Innaanganeq** *c.* Greenland
96 B2 **Inner Sound** *sea chan.* U.K.
51 D1 **Innisfail** Austr.
102 C2 **Innsbruck** Austria
154 B1 **Inocência** Brazil
118 B3 **Inongo** Dem. Rep. Congo
103 D1 **Inowrocław** Pol.
114 C2 **In Salah** Alg.
62 A2 **Insein** Myanmar
86 F2 **Inta** Russia
137 E1 **International Falls** U.S.A.
130 C1 **Inukjuak** Can.
126 C2 **Inuvik** Can.
96 B2 **Inveraray** U.K.
54 A3 **Invercargill** N.Z.
53 D1 **Inverell** Austr.
96 B2 **Invergordon** U.K.
128 C2 **Invermere** Can.
131 D2 **Inverness** Can.
96 B2 **Inverness** U.K.
96 C2 **Inverurie** U.K.
52 A3 **Investigator Strait** Austr.
77 E1 **Inya** Russia
119 D3 **Inyonga** Tanz.
87 D3 **Inza** Russia
111 B3 **Ioannina** Greece
137 D3 **Iola** U.S.A.
96 A2 **Iona** *i.* U.K.
111 B3 **Ionian Islands** Greece
109 C3 **Ionian Sea** Greece/Italy
Ionioi Nisoi *is* Greece *see* **Ionian Islands**
111 C3 **Ios** *i.* Greece
137 E2 **Iowa** *state* U.S.A.
137 E2 **Iowa City** U.S.A.
154 C1 **Ipameri** Brazil
155 D1 **Ipatinga** Brazil
81 C1 **Ipatovo** Russia
123 C2 **Ipelegeng** S. Africa
150 A1 **Ipiales** Col.
154 B3 **Ipiranga** Brazil
60 B1 **Ipoh** Malaysia
154 B1 **Iporá** Brazil
118 C2 **Ippy** C.A.R.
111 C2 **İpsala** Turkey
53 D1 **Ipswich** Austr.
99 D2 **Ipswich** U.K.
127 G2 **Iqaluit** Can.
152 A3 **Iquique** Chile
150 A2 **Iquitos** Peru
Irakleio Greece *see* **Iraklion**
111 C3 **Iraklion** Greece
76 B3 **Iran** *country* Asia
61 C1 **Iran, Pegunungan** *mts* Indon.
79 D2 **Īrānshahr** Iran
144 B2 **Irapuato** Mex.
81 C2 **Iraq** *country* Asia
154 B3 **Irati** Brazil
80 B2 **Irbid** Jordan
86 F3 **Irbit** Russia
151 D3 **Irecê** Brazil
97 C2 **Ireland** *country* Europe
118 C3 **Irema** Dem. Rep. Congo
114 B3 **Irîgui** *reg.* Mali/Maur.
119 D3 **Iringa** Tanz.
151 C2 **Iriri** *r.* Brazil
95 B3 **Irish Sea** Ireland/U.K.
69 C1 **Irkutsk** Russia
52 A2 **Iron Knob** Austr.
140 B1 **Iron Mountain** U.S.A.
140 A1 **Ironwood** U.S.A.
64 B1 **Irosin** Phil.
67 C4 **Irō-zaki** *pt* Japan
90 C1 **Irpin'** Ukr.

Irrawaddy

62 A2 Irrawaddy *r.* Myanmar
63 A2 Irrawaddy, Mouths of the Myanmar
86 F2 Irtysh *r.* Kazakh./Russia
107 C1 Irun Spain
96 B3 Irvine U.K.
64 B2 Isabela Phil.
146 B3 Isabelia, Cordillera *mts* Nic.
92 ☐A2 Ísafjörður Iceland
67 B4 Isahaya Japan
105 E2 Isar *r.* Ger.
96 ☐ Isbister U.K.
108 B2 Ischia, Isola d' *i.* Italy
67 C4 Ise Japan
118 C2 Isengi Dem. Rep. Congo
100 C2 Iserlohn Ger.
101 D1 Isernhagen Ger.
67 C4 Ise-wan *b.* Japan
114 C4 Iseyin Nigeria
Isfahan Iran *see* Eşfahān
66 D2 Ishikari-wan *b.* Japan
66 D3 Ishinomaki Japan
67 D3 Ishioka Japan
140 B1 Ishpeming U.S.A.
111 C2 Işıklar Dağı *mts* Turkey
111 C3 Işıklı Turkey
123 D2 Isipingo S. Africa
119 C2 Isiro Dem. Rep. Congo
110 B2 Iskar *r.* Bulg.
80 B2 İskenderun Turkey
82 G3 Iskitim Russia
128 A2 Iskut *r.* Can.
74 B1 Islamabad Pak.
52 A2 Island Lagoon *imp. l.* Austr.
129 E2 Island Lake Can.
54 B1 Islands, Bay of N.Z.
Islas Malvinas *terr.* S. Atlantic Ocean *see* Falkland Islands
96 A3 Islay *i.* U.K.
98 A1 Isle of Man *i.* Irish Sea
77 D3 Ismoili Somoní, Qullai *mt.* Tajik.
109 C3 Isola di Capo Rizzuto Italy
110 C2 Isperih Bulg.
80 B2 Israel *country* Asia
105 C2 Issoire France
111 C2 İstanbul Turkey
İstanbul Boğazı *str.* Turkey *see* Bosporus
111 B3 Istiaia Greece
105 C3 Istres France
108 B1 Istria *pen.* Croatia
151 D3 Itaberaba Brazil
155 D1 Itabira Brazil
155 D2 Itabirito Brazil
151 E3 Itabuna Brazil
150 C2 Itacoatiara Brazil
154 B2 Itaguajé Brazil
154 C2 Itaí Brazil
154 B3 Itaipu, Represa de *resr* Brazil
151 C2 Itaituba Brazil
152 D3 Itajaí Brazil
155 C2 Itajubá Brazil
108 B2 Italy *country* Europe
155 D1 Itamarandiba Brazil
155 D1 Itambacuri Brazil
155 D1 Itambé, Pico de *mt.* Brazil
62 A1 Itanagar India
154 C2 Itanhaém Brazil
155 D1 Itanhém Brazil
155 D1 Itaobim Brazil
154 C1 Itapajipe Brazil
155 E1 Itapebi Brazil
151 D2 Itapecuru Mirim Brazil
155 D2 Itapemirim Brazil
155 D2 Itaperuna Brazil
155 D1 Itapetinga Brazil
154 C2 Itapetininga Brazil

154 C2 Itapeva Brazil
151 E3 Itapicuru *r.* Brazil
154 C1 Itapuranga Brazil
154 C2 Itararé Brazil
75 B2 Itarsi India
154 B1 Itarumã Brazil
155 D2 Itaúna Brazil
71 C3 Itbayat *i.* Phil.
141 D2 Ithaca U.S.A.
101 D1 Ith Hils *ridge* Ger.
118 C2 Itimbiri *r.* Dem. Rep. Congo
155 D1 Itinga Brazil
154 B1 Itiquira Brazil
154 A1 Itiquira *r.* Brazil
67 C4 Itō Japan
154 C2 Itu Brazil
150 A2 Itui *r.* Brazil
154 C1 Ituiutaba Brazil
119 C3 Itula Dem. Rep. Congo
154 C1 Itumbiara Brazil
154 B1 Iturama Brazil
101 D1 Itzehoe Ger.
62 A2 Iul'tin Russia
154 B2 Ivaí *r.* Brazil
92 I2 Ivalo Fin.
88 C3 Ivanava Belarus
52 B2 Ivanhoe Austr.
90 B1 Ivankiv Ukr.
90 A2 Ivano-Frankivs'k Ukr.
89 F2 Ivanovo Russia
88 C3 Ivatsevichy Belarus
111 C2 Ivaylovgrad Bulg.
86 F2 Ivdel' Russia
154 B2 Ivinheima *r.* Brazil
127 H2 Ivittuut Greenland
Ivory Coast *country* Africa *see* Côte d'Ivoire
108 A1 Ivrea Italy
111 C3 Ivrindi Turkey
127 F2 Ivujivik Can.
67 D3 Iwaki Japan
67 B4 Iwakuni Japan
66 D2 Iwamizawa Japan
66 C2 Iwanai Japan
88 C3 Iwye Belarus
123 D3 Ixopo S. Africa
144 B2 Ixtlán Mex.
145 D2 Izamal Mex.
81 C1 Izberbash Russia
86 F3 Izhevsk Russia
86 E2 Izhma Russia
89 E3 Izmalkovo Russia
90 B2 Izmayil Ukr.
111 C3 İzmir Turkey
111 C2 İznik Gölü *l.* Turkey
152 B2 Izozog, Bañados del *swamp* Bol.
67 B3 Izumo Japan
90 B1 Izyaslav Ukr.
91 D2 Izyum Ukr.

155 C2 Jacareí Brazil
155 D1 Jacinto Brazil
141 E1 Jackman U.S.A.
142 C2 Jackson *AL* U.S.A.
140 C2 Jackson *MI* U.S.A.
142 B2 Jackson *MS* U.S.A.
142 C1 Jackson *TN* U.S.A.
136 A2 Jackson *WY* U.S.A.
54 A2 Jackson Head N.Z.
142 B2 Jacksonville *AR* U.S.A.
143 D2 Jacksonville *FL* U.S.A.
140 A3 Jacksonville *IL* U.S.A.
143 E2 Jacksonville *NC* U.S.A.
139 D2 Jacksonville *TX* U.S.A.
147 C3 Jacmel Haiti
74 A2 Jacobabad Pak.
151 D3 Jacobina Brazil
131 D2 Jacques-Cartier, Mont *mt.* Can.
151 D2 Jacundá Brazil
154 C2 Jacupiranga Brazil
109 C2 Jadovnik *mt.* Bos. & Herz.
150 A2 Jaén Peru
106 C2 Jaén Spain
52 A3 Jaffa, Cape Austr.
73 B4 Jaffna Sri Lanka
73 C3 Jagdalpur India
123 C2 Jagersfontein S. Africa
154 C2 Jaguariaíva Brazil
79 C2 Jahrom Iran
74 B2 Jaipur India
74 B2 Jaisalmer India
75 C2 Jajarkot Nepal
109 C2 Jajce Bos. & Herz.
60 B2 Jakarta Indon.
128 A1 Jakes Corner Can.
92 G2 Jäkkvik Sweden
92 H3 Jakobstad Fin.
77 D3 Jalālābād Afgh.
77 D2 Jalal-Abad Kyrg.
74 B1 Jalandhar India
Jalapa Mex. *see* Xalapa
154 B2 Jales Brazil
74 B2 Jalgaon India
115 D4 Jalingo Nigeria
74 B3 Jalna India
144 B2 Jalpa Mex.
75 C2 Jalpaiguri India
145 C2 Jalpan Mex.
115 E2 Jālū Libya
146 C3 Jamaica *country* West Indies
146 C3 Jamaica Channel Haiti/Jamaica
75 C2 Jamalpur Bangl.
60 B2 Jambi Indon.
137 D2 James *r. ND/SD* U.S.A.
141 D3 James *r. VA* U.S.A.
130 B1 James Bay Can.
52 A2 Jamestown Austr.
137 D1 Jamestown *ND* U.S.A.
141 D2 Jamestown *NY* U.S.A.
74 B1 Jammu India
74 B1 Jammu and Kashmir *state* India
74 B2 Jamnagar India
93 I3 Jämsä Fin.
75 C2 Jamshedpur India
74 A2 Jamuna *r.* Bangl.
75 C2 Janakpur Nepal
155 D1 Janaúba Brazil
81 D2 Jandaq Iran
140 B2 Janesville U.S.A.
65 B3 Jangheung S. Korea
65 B2 Jangseong S. Korea
80 B2 Janin West Bank
114 A3 Janjanbureh Gambia
84 F1 Jan Mayen *terr.* Arctic Ocean
81 D1 Jañña Turkm.

J

Jabal, Bahr el *r.* South Sudan/Uganda *see* White Nile
106 C2 Jabalón *r.* Spain
75 B2 Jabalpur India
50 C1 Jabiru Austr.
109 C2 Jablanica Bos. & Herz.
151 E2 Jaboatão dos Guararapes Brazil
154 C2 Jaboticabal Brazil
107 C1 Jaca Spain
145 C2 Jacala Mex.
151 C2 Jacareacanga Brazil

122 B3 **Jansenville** S. Africa
155 D1 **Januária** Brazil
74 B2 **Jaora** India
67 C3 **Japan** *country* Asia
156 C3 **Japan, Sea of** N. Pacific Ocean
150 B2 **Japurá** *r.* Brazil
154 C1 **Jaraguá** Brazil
154 B2 **Jaraguari** Brazil
70 A2 **Jarantai** China
152 C3 **Jardim** Brazil
103 D1 **Jarocin** Pol.
103 E1 **Jarosław** Pol.
92 F3 **Järpen** Sweden
150 B3 **Jaru** Brazil
Jarud China *see* **Lubei**
49 H3 **Jarvis Island** S. Pacific Ocean
103 E2 **Jasło** Pol.
128 C2 **Jasper** Can.
140 B3 **Jasper** *IN* U.S.A.
139 E2 **Jasper** *TX* U.S.A.
103 D2 **Jastrzębie-Zdrój** Pol.
103 D2 **Jászberény** Hungary
154 B1 **Jataí** Brazil
74 A2 **Jati** Pak.
154 C2 **Jaú** Brazil
150 B2 **Jaú** *r.* Brazil
145 C2 **Jaumave** Mex.
75 C2 **Jaunpur** India
154 B1 **Jauru** Brazil
61 B2 **Java** *i.* Indon.
Java Sea Indon. *see* **Jawa, Laut**
Jawa *i.* Indon. *see* **Java**
159 D4 **Jawa, Laut** *sea* Indon.
117 C4 **Jawhar** Somalia
103 D1 **Jawor** Pol.
103 D1 **Jaworzno** Pol.
59 D3 **Jaya, Puncak** *mt.* Indon.
59 D3 **Jayapura** Indon.
78 B3 **Jāzān** Saudi Arabia
79 C2 **Jaz Mūrīān, Hāmūn-e** *imp. l.* Iran
128 B1 **Jean Marie River** Can.
131 D1 **Jeannin, Lac** *l.* Can.
116 A3 **Jebel Abyad Plateau** Sudan
65 B2 **Jecheon** S. Korea
96 C3 **Jedburgh** U.K.
78 A2 **Jeddah** Saudi Arabia
101 E1 **Jeetze** *r.* Ger.
135 C3 **Jefferson, Mount** U.S.A.
137 E3 **Jefferson City** U.S.A.
65 B3 **Jeju** S. Korea
65 B3 **Jeju-do** *i.* S. Korea
65 B3 **Jeju-haehyeop** *sea chan.* S. Korea
88 C2 **Jēkabpils** Latvia
103 D1 **Jelenia Góra** Pol.
88 B2 **Jelgava** Latvia
61 C2 **Jember** Indon.
101 E2 **Jena** Ger.
Jengish Chokusu *mt.* China/Kyrg. *see* **Pobeda Peak**
142 B2 **Jennings** U.S.A.
65 B2 **Jeonju** S. Korea
151 D3 **Jequié** Brazil
155 D1 **Jequitaí** Brazil
155 D1 **Jequitinhonha** Brazil
155 E1 **Jequitinhonha** *r.* Brazil
147 C3 **Jérémie** Haiti
144 B2 **Jerez** Mex.
106 B2 **Jerez de la Frontera** Spain
109 D3 **Jergucat** Albania
115 C1 **Jerid, Chott el** *salt l.* Tunisia
134 D2 **Jerome** U.S.A.
95 C4 **Jersey** *terr.* Channel Is
151 D2 **Jerumenha** Brazil
80 B2 **Jerusalem** Israel/West Bank
53 D3 **Jervis Bay Territory** *admin. div.* Austr.
108 B1 **Jesenice** Slovenia
108 B2 **Jesi** Italy
101 F2 **Jessen (Elster)** Ger.
75 C2 **Jessore** Bangl.
143 D2 **Jesup** U.S.A.
145 C3 **Jesús Carranza** Mex.
109 C2 **Jezercë, Maja** *mt.* Albania
74 B2 **Jhalawar** India
74 B1 **Jhang** Pak.
75 B2 **Jhansi** India
75 C2 **Jharsuguda** India
74 B1 **Jhelum** Pak.
70 C2 **Jiading** China
69 E1 **Jiamusi** China
71 B3 **Ji'an** *Jiangxi* China
65 B1 **Ji'an** *Jilin* China
62 A1 **Jianchuan** China
Jiandaoyu China *see* **Guojiaba**
70 B2 **Jiangsu** *prov.* China
71 B3 **Jiangxi** *prov.* China
70 A2 **Jiangyou** China
70 B3 **Jianli** China
70 B2 **Jianqiao** China
71 B3 **Jianyang** *Fujian* China
70 A2 **Jianyang** *Sichuan* China
70 C2 **Jiaozhou** China
70 B2 **Jiaozuo** China
70 C2 **Jiaxing** China
71 C3 **Jiayi** Taiwan
68 C2 **Jiayuguan** China
Jiddah Saudi Arabia *see* **Jeddah**
92 G2 **Jiehkkevárri** *mt.* Norway
70 B2 **Jiexiu** China
68 C2 **Jigzhi** China
103 D2 **Jihlava** Czech Rep.
117 C4 **Jijiga** Eth.
116 A2 **Jilf al Kabīr, Haḍabat al** *plat.* Egypt
117 C4 **Jilib** Somalia
69 E2 **Jilin** China
65 B1 **Jilin** *prov.* China
65 A1 **Jilin Hada Ling** *mts* China
117 B4 **Jīma** Eth.
144 B2 **Jiménez** *Chihuahua* Mex.
145 C2 **Jiménez** *Tamaulipas* Mex.
70 B2 **Jinan** China
70 B2 **Jincheng** China
53 C3 **Jindabyne** Austr.
65 B3 **Jin-do** *i.* S. Korea
103 D2 **Jindřichův Hradec** Czech Rep.
71 B3 **Jingdezhen** China
70 B2 **Jinghang Yunhe** *canal* China
62 B1 **Jinghong** China
70 B2 **Jingmen** China
70 A2 **Jingning** China
70 A2 **Jingtai** China
71 A3 **Jingxi** China
65 B1 **Jingyu** China
70 A2 **Jingyuan** China
70 B2 **Jingzhou** China
65 B2 **Jinhae** S. Korea
71 B3 **Jinhua** China
70 B2 **Jining** China
119 D2 **Jinja** Uganda
117 B4 **Jinka** Eth.
71 B3 **Jinmen** Taiwan
146 B3 **Jinotepe** Nic.
71 A3 **Jinping** China
Jinsha Jiang *r.* China *see* **Yangtze**
70 B3 **Jinshi** China
70 B2 **Jinzhong** China
70 C1 **Jinzhou** China
150 B2 **Ji-Paraná** *r.* Brazil
75 C1 **Jirang** China
65 B2 **Jiri-san** *mt.* S. Korea
79 C2 **Jīroft** Iran
71 A3 **Jishou** China
110 B2 **Jiu** *r.* Romania
70 A2 **Jiuding Shan** *mt.* China
70 B3 **Jiujiang** China
66 B1 **Jixi** China
77 C2 **Jizzax** Uzbek.
151 E2 **João Pessoa** Brazil
155 C1 **João Pinheiro** Brazil
74 B2 **Jodhpur** India
92 I3 **Joensuu** Fin.
67 C3 **Jōetsu** Japan
121 C3 **Jofane** Moz.
88 C2 **Jõgeva** Estonia
123 C2 **Johannesburg** S. Africa
134 C2 **John Day** U.S.A.
134 B1 **John Day** *r.* U.S.A.
128 C2 **John D'Or Prairie** Can.
143 E1 **John H. Kerr Reservoir** U.S.A.
96 C1 **John o' Groats** U.K.
143 D1 **Johnson City** U.S.A.
128 A1 **Johnson's Crossing** Can.
49 H1 **Johnston Atoll** N. Pacific Ocean
96 B3 **Johnstone** U.K.
141 D2 **Johnstown** U.S.A.
60 B1 **Johor Bahru** Malaysia
88 C2 **Jõhvi** Estonia
154 C3 **Joinville** Brazil
105 D2 **Joinville** France
92 G2 **Jokkmokk** Sweden
92 □B2 **Jökulsá á Fjöllum** *r.* Iceland
140 B2 **Joliet** U.S.A.
130 C2 **Joliette** Can.
64 B2 **Jolo** Phil.
64 B2 **Jolo** *i.* Phil.
61 C2 **Jombang** Indon.
75 C2 **Jomsom** Nepal
88 B2 **Jonava** Lith.
142 B1 **Jonesboro** *AR* U.S.A.
142 B2 **Jonesboro** *LA* U.S.A.
127 F1 **Jones Sound** *sea chan.* Can.
93 F4 **Jönköping** Sweden
131 C2 **Jonquière** Can.
145 C3 **Jonuta** Mex.
137 E3 **Joplin** U.S.A.
80 B2 **Jordan** *country* Asia
80 B2 **Jordan** *r.* Asia
136 B1 **Jordan** U.S.A.
134 C2 **Jordan Valley** U.S.A.
62 A1 **Jorhat** India
93 E4 **Jørpeland** Norway
115 C4 **Jos** Nigeria
145 C3 **José Cardel** Mex.
131 D1 **Joseph, Lac** *l.* Can.
50 B1 **Joseph Bonaparte Gulf** Austr.
115 C4 **Jos Plateau** Nigeria
93 E3 **Jotunheimen** *mts* Norway
122 B3 **Joubertina** S. Africa
123 C2 **Jouberton** S. Africa
93 I3 **Joutseno** Fin.
134 B1 **Juan de Fuca Strait** Can./U.S.A.
Juanshui China *see* **Tongcheng**
145 B2 **Juárez** Mex.
151 D2 **Juazeiro** Brazil
151 E2 **Juazeiro do Norte** Brazil
117 B4 **Juba** South Sudan
117 C4 **Jubaland** *reg.* Somalia
117 C5 **Jubba** *r.* Somalia
78 B2 **Jubbah** Saudi Arabia
145 C3 **Juchitán** Mex.
102 C2 **Judenburg** Austria
101 D2 **Jühnde** Ger.

146 B3 Juigalpa Nic.
100 C1 Juist i. Ger.
155 D2 Juiz de Fora Brazil
150 A3 Juliaca Peru
75 C2 Jumla Nepal
74 B2 Junagadh India
139 D2 Junction U.S.A.
137 D3 Junction City U.S.A.
154 C2 Jundiaí Brazil
128 A2 Juneau U.S.A.
53 C2 Junee Austr.
105 D2 Jungfrau mt. Switz.
141 D2 Juniata r. U.S.A.
92 G3 Junsele Sweden
134 C2 Juntura U.S.A.
154 C2 Juquiá Brazil
117 A4 Jur r. South Sudan
105 D2 Jura mts France/Switz.
96 B2 Jura i. U.K.
96 B3 Jura, Sound of sea chan. U.K.
88 B2 Jurbarkas Lith.
88 B2 Jūrmala Latvia
150 B2 Juruá r. Brazil
150 C2 Juruena r. Brazil
150 B2 Jutai r. Brazil
101 F2 Jüterbog Ger.
146 B2 Juventud, Isla de la i. Cuba
70 B2 Juxian China
79 C2 Jüyom Iran
122 B1 Jwaneng Botswana
93 I3 Jyväskylä Fin.

K

74 B1 K2 mt. China/Pak.
119 C3 Kabalo Dem. Rep. Congo
119 C3 Kabare Dem. Rep. Congo
130 B2 Kabinakagami Lake Can.
118 C3 Kabinda Dem. Rep. Congo
118 B2 Kabo C.A.R.
120 B2 Kabompo Zambia
119 C3 Kabongo Dem. Rep. Congo
77 C3 Kābul Afgh.
64 B2 Kaburuang i. Indon.
121 B2 Kabwe Zambia
74 A2 Kachchh, Gulf of India
74 B2 Kachchh, Rann of marsh India
83 I3 Kachug Russia
81 C1 Kaçkar Dağı mt. Turkey
73 B3 Kadapa India
111 C2 Kadıköy Turkey
114 B3 Kadiolo Mali
73 B3 Kadmat atoll India
121 B2 Kadoma Zimbabwe
63 A2 Kadonkani Myanmar
117 A3 Kadugli Sudan
115 C3 Kaduna Nigeria
89 E2 Kaduy Russia
86 E2 Kadzherom Russia
114 A3 Kaédi Maur.
118 B1 Kaélé Cameroon
65 B2 Kaesŏng N. Korea
114 A3 Kaffrine Senegal
121 B2 Kafue Zambia
120 B2 Kafue r. Zambia
118 B2 Kaga Bandoro C.A.R.
91 E2 Kagal'nitskaya Russia
67 B4 Kagoshima Japan
91 C2 Kaharlyk Ukr.
61 C2 Kahayan r. Indon.
118 B3 Kahemba Dem. Rep. Congo
101 E2 Kahla Ger.
79 C2 Kahnūj Iran
92 H2 Kahperusvaarat mts Fin.
80 B2 Kahramanmaraş Turkey
79 C2 Kahūrak Iran

59 C3 Kai, Kepulauan is Indon.
115 C4 Kaiama Nigeria
54 B2 Kaiapoi N.Z.
59 C3 Kai Besar i. Indon.
70 B2 Kaifeng China
Kaihua China see Wenshan
122 B2 Kaiingveld reg. S. Africa
59 C3 Kai Kecil i. Indon.
54 B2 Kaikoura N.Z.
114 A4 Kailahun Sierra Leone
71 A3 Kaili China
59 C3 Kaimana Indon.
54 C1 Kaimanawa Mountains N.Z.
67 C4 Kainan Japan
115 C3 Kainji Reservoir Nigeria
54 B1 Kaipara Harbour N.Z.
74 B2 Kairana India
115 D1 Kairouan Tunisia
54 B1 Kaitaia N.Z.
54 C1 Kaitawa N.Z.
Kaitong China see Tongyu
59 C3 Kaiwatu Indon.
65 A1 Kaiyuan Liaoning China
62 B1 Kaiyuan Yunnan China
92 I3 Kajaani Fin.
51 D2 Kajabbi Austr.
122 B2 Kakamas S. Africa
119 D2 Kakamega Kenya
91 C2 Kakhovka Ukr.
91 C2 Kakhovs'ke Vodoskhovyshche resr Ukr.
73 C3 Kakinada India
128 C1 Kakisa Can.
119 C3 Kakoswa Dem. Rep. Congo
126 B2 Kaktovik U.S.A.
Kalaallit Nunaat terr. N. America see Greenland
59 C3 Kalabahi Indon.
120 B2 Kalabo Zambia
73 B3 Kalaburagi India
91 E1 Kalach Russia
119 D2 Kalacha Dida Kenya
62 A1 Kaladan r. India/Myanmar
120 B3 Kalahari Desert Africa
92 H3 Kalajoki Fin.
111 B2 Kalamaria Greece
111 B3 Kalamata Greece
140 B2 Kalamazoo U.S.A.
111 B3 Kalampaka Greece
91 C2 Kalanchak Ukr.
115 E1 Kalanshiyū ar Ramli al Kabīr, Sarīr des. Libya
63 B2 Kalasin Thai.
79 C2 Kalāt Iran
74 A2 Kalat Pak.
50 A2 Kalbarri Austr.
Kalburgi India see Gulbarga
111 C3 Kale Turkey
80 B1 Kalecik Turkey
118 C3 Kalema Dem. Rep. Congo
119 C3 Kalemie Dem. Rep. Congo
62 A1 Kalemyo Myanmar
Kalgan China see Zhangjiakou
50 B3 Kalgoorlie Austr.
109 C2 Kali Croatia
110 C2 Kaliakra, Nos pt Bulg.
119 C3 Kalima Dem. Rep. Congo
61 C2 Kalimantan reg. Indon.
88 B3 Kaliningrad Russia
91 D2 Kalininskaya Russia
88 C3 Kalinkavichy Belarus
134 D1 Kalispell U.S.A.
103 D1 Kalisz Pol.
91 E2 Kalitva r. Russia
92 H2 Kalix Sweden
92 H2 Kalixälven r. Sweden
111 C3 Kalkan Turkey
120 A3 Kalkfeld Namibia

92 I3 Kallavesi l. Fin.
92 F3 Kallsjön l. Sweden
93 G4 Kalmar Sweden
93 G4 Kalmarsund sea chan. Sweden
120 B2 Kalomo Zambia
128 B2 Kalone Peak Can.
75 B1 Kalpa India
73 B3 Kalpeni atoll India
75 B2 Kalpi India
101 D1 Kaltenkirchen Ger.
89 E3 Kaluga Russia
93 F4 Kalundborg Denmark
90 A2 Kalush Ukr.
89 E2 Kalyazin Russia
111 C3 Kalymnos i. Greece
119 C3 Kama Dem. Rep. Congo
62 A2 Kama Myanmar
86 E3 Kama r. Russia
66 D3 Kamaishi Japan
120 A2 Kaman Turkey
120 A2 Kamanjab Namibia
78 B3 Kamarān i. Yemen
74 A2 Kamarod Pak.
50 B3 Kambalda Austr.
119 C4 Kambove Dem. Rep. Congo
183 L3 Kamchatka Peninsula Russia
110 C2 Kamchia r. Bulg.
110 B2 Kamenitsa mt. Bulg.
108 B2 Kamenjak, Rt pt Croatia
91 D1 Kamenka Russia
91 E2 Kamenolomni Russia
83 M2 Kamenskoye Russia
91 E2 Kamensk-Shakhtinskiy Russia
86 F3 Kamensk-Ural'skiy Russia
122 A3 Kamiesberg mts S. Africa
122 A3 Kamieskroon S. Africa
129 D1 Kamilukuak Lake Can.
119 C3 Kamina Dem. Rep. Congo
129 E1 Kaminak Lake Can.
90 A1 Kamin'-Kashyrs'kyy Ukr.
128 B2 Kamloops Can.
118 C3 Kamonia Dem. Rep. Congo
119 D2 Kampala Uganda
60 B1 Kampar r. Indon.
60 B1 Kampar Malaysia
100 B1 Kampen Neth.
119 C3 Kampene Dem. Rep. Congo
63 A2 Kamphaeng Phet Thai.
63 B2 Kâmpóng Cham Cambodia
63 B2 Kâmpóng Chhnang Cambodia
Kâmpóng Saôm Cambodia see Sihanoukville
63 B2 Kâmpóng Spœ Cambodia
63 B2 Kâmpôt Cambodia
129 D2 Kamsack Can.
86 E3 Kamskoye Vodokhranilishche resr Russia
117 C4 Kamsuuma Somalia
90 B2 Kam"yanets'-Podil's'kyy Ukr.
90 A1 Kam"yanka-Buz'ka Ukr.
88 B3 Kamyanyets Belarus
91 D2 Kamyshevatskaya Russia
87 D3 Kamyshin Russia
135 D3 Kanab U.S.A.
118 C3 Kananga Dem. Rep. Congo
87 D3 Kanash Russia
140 C3 Kanawha r. U.S.A.
67 C3 Kanazawa Japan
62 A1 Kanbalu Myanmar
63 A2 Kanchanaburi Thai.
73 B3 Kanchipuram India
77 C3 Kandahār Afgh.
86 C2 Kandalaksha Russia
61 C2 Kandangan Indon.
74 A2 Kandh Kot Pak.
114 C3 Kandi Benin
74 B2 Kandla India

53 C2 **Kandos** Austr.
121 □D2 **Kandreho** Madag.
73 C4 **Kandy** Sri Lanka
76 B2 **Kandyagash** Kazakh.
127 G1 **Kane Bassin** *b.* Greenland
91 D2 **Kanevskaya** Russia
122 B1 **Kang** Botswana
127 H2 **Kangaatsiaq** Greenland
114 B3 **Kangaba** Mali
80 B2 **Kangal** Turkey
60 B1 **Kangar** Malaysia
52 A3 **Kangaroo Island** Austr.
75 C2 **Kangchenjunga** *mt.* India/Nepal
65 B2 **Kangdong** N. Korea
61 C2 **Kangean, Kepulauan** *is* Indon.
127 I2 **Kangeq** *c.* Greenland
127 H2 **Kangerlussuaq** *inlet* Greenland
127 I2 **Kangerlussuaq** *inlet* Greenland
127 H2 **Kangersuatsiaq** Greenland
65 B1 **Kanggye** N. Korea
131 D1 **Kangiqsualujjuaq** Can.
127 G2 **Kangiqsujuaq** Can.
127 G2 **Kangirsuk** Can.
75 C2 **Kangmar** China
65 A1 **Kangping** China
72 D2 **Kangto** *mt.* China/India
62 A1 **Kani** Myanmar
86 D2 **Kanin, Poluostrov** *pen.* Russia
86 D2 **Kanin Nos** Russia
91 C2 **Kaniv** Ukr.
93 H3 **Kankaanpää** Fin.
140 B2 **Kankakee** U.S.A.
114 B3 **Kankan** Guinea
75 C2 **Kanker** India
73 B3 **Kannur** India
115 C3 **Kano** Nigeria
122 B3 **Kanonpunt** *pt* S. Africa
67 B4 **Kanoya** Japan
75 C2 **Kanpur** India
136 C3 **Kansas** *r.* U.S.A.
137 D3 **Kansas** *state* U.S.A.
137 E3 **Kansas City** U.S.A.
83 H3 **Kansk** Russia
114 C3 **Kantchari** Burkina Faso
91 D2 **Kantemirovka** Russia
97 B2 **Kanturk** Ireland
123 D2 **Kanyamazane** S. Africa
123 C1 **Kanye** Botswana
120 A2 **Kaokoveld** *plat.* Namibia
114 A3 **Kaolack** Senegal
120 B2 **Kaoma** Zambia
118 C3 **Kapanga** Dem. Rep. Congo
100 B2 **Kapellen** Belgium
121 B2 **Kapiri Mposhi** Zambia
127 H2 **Kapisillit** Greenland
130 B1 **Kapiskau** *r.* Can.
61 C1 **Kapit** *Sarawak* Malaysia
63 A3 **Kapoe** Thai.
117 B4 **Kapoeta** South Sudan
103 D2 **Kaposvár** Hungary
77 D2 **Kapshagay** Kazakh.
77 D2 **Kapshagay, Vodokhranilishche** *resr* Kazakh.
61 B2 **Kapuas** *r.* Indon.
52 A2 **Kapunda** Austr.
130 B2 **Kapuskasing** Can.
103 D2 **Kapuvár** Hungary
88 C3 **Kapyl'** Belarus
114 C4 **Kara** Togo
111 C3 **Kara Ada** *i.* Turkey
76 C1 **Karabalyk** Kazakh.
80 B1 **Karabük** Turkey
76 C2 **Karabutak** Kazakh.
110 C2 **Karacaköy** Turkey
89 D3 **Karachev** Russia
74 A2 **Karachi** Pak.
Kara Deniz *sea* Asia/Europe *see* **Black Sea**
77 D2 **Karagandy** Kazakh.
77 D2 **Karagayly** Kazakh.
83 L3 **Karaginskiy Zaliv** *b.* Russia
81 D2 **Karaj** Iran
64 B2 **Karakelong** *i.* Indon.
77 D2 **Kara-Köl** Kyrg.
77 D2 **Karakol** Kyrg.
74 B1 **Karakoram Range** *mts* Asia
Karakum, Peski *des.* Kazakh. *see* **Karakum Desert**
76 B2 **Karakum Desert** Kazakh.
76 C3 **Karakum Desert** Turkm.
Karakumy, Peski *des.* Turkm. *see* **Karakum Desert**
80 B2 **Karaman** Turkey
77 E2 **Karamay** China
54 B2 **Karamea** N.Z.
54 B2 **Karamea Bight** *b.* N.Z.
80 B2 **Karapınar** Turkey
122 A2 **Karasburg** Namibia
86 F1 **Kara Sea** Russia
92 I2 **Karasjok** Norway
82 G3 **Karasuk** Russia
77 D2 **Karatau** Kazakh.
77 C2 **Karatau, Khrebet** *mts* Kazakh.
86 F2 **Karatayka** Russia
67 A4 **Karatsu** Japan
60 B2 **Karawang** Indon.
81 C2 **Karbalā'** Iraq
103 E2 **Karcag** Hungary
111 B3 **Karditsa** Greece
88 B2 **Kärdla** Estonia
110 C2 **Kardzhali** Bulg.
122 B3 **Kareeberge** *mts* S. Africa
75 B2 **Kareli** India
74 B1 **Kargil** India
121 B2 **Kariba** Zimbabwe
121 B2 **Kariba, Lake** *resr* Zambia/Zimbabwe
61 B2 **Karimata, Pulau-pulau** *is* Indon.
61 B2 **Karimata, Selat** *str.* Indon.
73 B3 **Karimnagar** India
61 C2 **Karimunjawa, Pulau-pulau** *is* Indon.
91 C2 **Karkinits'ka Zatoka** *g.* Ukr.
91 D2 **Karlivka** Ukr.
109 C1 **Karlovac** Croatia
102 C1 **Karlovy Vary** Czech Rep.
93 F4 **Karlshamn** Sweden
93 G4 **Karlskrona** Sweden
102 B2 **Karlsruhe** Ger.
93 F4 **Karlstad** Sweden
101 D3 **Karlstadt** Ger.
89 D3 **Karma** Belarus
93 E4 **Karmøy** *i.* Norway
74 B2 **Karnal** India
75 D2 **Karnaphuli Reservoir** Bangl.
110 C2 **Karnobat** Bulg.
74 A2 **Karodi** Pak.
121 B2 **Karoi** Zimbabwe
121 C1 **Karonga** Malawi
116 B3 **Karora** Eritrea
111 C3 **Karpathos** *i.* Greece
111 B3 **Karpenisi** Greece
86 D2 **Karpogory** Russia
50 A2 **Karratha** Austr.
81 C1 **Kars** Turkey
88 C2 **Kārsava** Latvia
86 E2 **Karskiye Vorota, Proliv** *str.* Russia
Karskoye More *sea* Russia *see* **Kara Sea**
101 E1 **Karstädt** Ger.
111 C2 **Kartal** Turkey
87 F3 **Kartaly** Russia
73 B3 **Karwar** India
83 I3 **Karymskoye** Russia
111 B3 **Karystos** Greece
80 A2 **Kaş** Turkey
130 B1 **Kasabonika Lake** Can.
118 C4 **Kasaji** Dem. Rep. Congo
121 C2 **Kasama** Zambia
120 B2 **Kasane** Botswana
118 B3 **Kasangulu** Dem. Rep. Congo
73 B3 **Kasaragod** India
129 D1 **Kasba Lake** Can.
120 B2 **Kasempa** Zambia
119 C4 **Kasenga** Dem. Rep. Congo
119 C3 **Kasese** Dem. Rep. Congo
119 D2 **Kasese** Uganda
81 D2 **Kāshān** Iran
Kashgar China *see* **Kashi**
77 D3 **Kashi** China
67 D3 **Kashima-nada** *b.* Japan
89 E2 **Kashin** Russia
89 E3 **Kashira** Russia
89 E3 **Kashirskoye** Russia
67 C3 **Kashiwazaki** Japan
76 B3 **Kāshmar** Iran
74 B1 **Kashmir** *reg.* Asia
74 A2 **Kashmore** Pak.
119 C3 **Kashyukulu** Dem. Rep. Congo
87 D3 **Kasimov** Russia
93 H3 **Kaskinen** Fin.
119 C3 **Kasongo** Dem. Rep. Congo
118 B3 **Kasongo-Lunda** Dem. Rep. Congo
111 C3 **Kasos** *i.* Greece
Kaspiyskoye More *l.* Asia/Europe *see* **Caspian Sea**
116 B3 **Kassala** Sudan
101 D2 **Kassel** Ger.
80 B1 **Kastamonu** Turkey
111 B2 **Kastoria** Greece
89 D3 **Kastsyukovichy** Belarus
119 D3 **Kasulu** Tanz.
121 C2 **Kasungu** Malawi
141 F1 **Katahdin, Mount** U.S.A.
118 C3 **Katako-Kombe** Dem. Rep. Congo
50 A3 **Katanning** Austr.
63 A3 **Katchall** *i.* India
111 B2 **Katerini** Greece
128 A2 **Kate's Needle** *mt.* Can./U.S.A.
121 C2 **Katete** Zambia
62 A1 **Katha** Myanmar
50 C1 **Katherine** *r.* Austr.
74 B2 **Kathiawar** *pen.* India
75 C2 **Kathmandu** Nepal
122 B2 **Kathu** S. Africa
74 B1 **Kathua** India
114 B3 **Kati** Mali
75 C2 **Katihar** India
54 C1 **Katikati** N.Z.
123 C3 **Katikati** S. Africa
120 B2 **Katima Mulilo** Namibia
52 A1 **Kati Thanda-Lake Eyre (North)** *imp. l.* Austr.
52 A1 **Kati Thanda-Lake Eyre (South)** *imp. l.* Austr.
123 C2 **Katlehong** S. Africa
75 C2 **Katni** India
111 B3 **Kato Achaïa** Greece
53 D2 **Katoomba** Austr.
103 D1 **Katowice** Pol.
78 A2 **Kātrīnā, Jabal** *mt.* Egypt
93 G4 **Katrineholm** Sweden
115 C3 **Katsina** Nigeria
115 C4 **Katsina-Ala** Nigeria
77 C3 **Kattaqo'rg'on** Uzbek.
93 F4 **Kattegat** *str.* Denmark/Sweden
100 B1 **Katwijk aan Zee** Neth.

124 E5 **Kaua'i** *i.* U.S.A.
93 H3 **Kauhajoki** Fin.
88 B3 **Kaunas** Lith.
115 C3 **Kaura-Namoda** Nigeria
92 H2 **Kautokeino** Norway
111 B2 **Kavala** Greece
66 C2 **Kavalerovo** Russia
73 C3 **Kavali** India
73 B3 **Kavaratti** *atoll* India
110 C2 **Kavarna** Bulg.
81 D2 **Kavīr, Dasht-e** *des.* Iran
67 C3 **Kawagoe** Japan
54 B1 **Kawakawa** N.Z.
67 C3 **Kawanishi** Japan
130 C2 **Kawartha Lakes** Can.
67 C3 **Kawasaki** Japan
54 C1 **Kawerau** N.Z.
63 A2 **Kawkareik** Myanmar
62 A1 **Kawlin** Myanmar
63 A2 **Kawmapyin** Myanmar
63 A2 **Kawthaung** Myanmar
77 D3 **Kaxgar He** *r.* China
114 B3 **Kaya** Burkina Faso
61 C1 **Kayan** *r.* Indon.
136 B2 **Kaycee** U.S.A.
138 A1 **Kayenta** U.S.A.
114 A3 **Kayes** Mali
77 D2 **Kaynar** Kazakh.
80 B2 **Kayseri** Turkey
81 D1 **Kazakhskiy Zaliv** *b.* Kazakh.
76 C2 **Kazakhstan** *country* Asia
87 D3 **Kazan'** Russia
80 A1 **Kazanlak** Bulg.
76 A2 **Kazbek** *mt.* Georgia/Russia
81 D3 **Kāzerūn** Iran
103 E2 **Kazincbarcika** Hungary
86 F2 **Kazym-Mys** Russia
111 B3 **Kea** *i.* Greece
97 C1 **Keady** U.K.
137 D2 **Kearney** U.S.A.
138 A2 **Kearny** U.S.A.
116 A3 **Kebkabiya** Sudan
92 G2 **Kebnekaise** *mt.* Sweden
117 C4 **K'ebrī Dehar** Eth.
61 B2 **Kebumen** Indon.
128 B2 **Kechika** *r.* Can.
103 D2 **Kecskemét** Hungary
88 B2 **Kdainiai** Lith.
114 A3 **Kédougou** Senegal
103 D1 **Kędzierzyn-Koźle** Pol.
128 B1 **Keele** *r.* Can.
128 A1 **Keele Peak** Can.
Keelung Taiwan *see* **Chilung**
141 E2 **Keene** U.S.A.
122 A2 **Keetmanshoop** Namibia
129 E3 **Keewatin** Can.
Kefallonia *i.* Greece *see* **Cephalonia**
59 C3 **Kefamenanu** Indon.
92 □A3 **Keflavík** Iceland
77 D2 **Kegen** Kazakh.
128 C2 **Keg River** Can.
62 A1 **Kehsi Mansam** Myanmar
98 C2 **Keighley** U.K.
88 B2 **Keila** Estonia
122 B2 **Keimoes** S. Africa
92 I3 **Keitele** *l.* Fin.
52 B3 **Keith** Austr.
103 E2 **Kékes** *mt.* Hungary
92 J2 **Kelesuayv, Gora** *h.* Russia
102 C2 **Kelheim** Ger.
80 B1 **Kelkit** *r.* Turkey
128 B1 **Keller Lake** Can.
134 C1 **Kellogg** U.S.A.
92 I2 **Kelloselkä** Fin.
97 C2 **Kells** Ireland
88 B2 **Kelm** Lith.
115 D4 **Kélo** Chad
128 C3 **Kelowna** Can.
96 C3 **Kelso** U.K.
134 B1 **Kelso** U.S.A.
60 B1 **Keluang** Malaysia
129 D2 **Kelvington** Can.
86 C2 **Kem'** Russia
128 B2 **Kemano (abandoned)** Can.
111 C3 **Kemer** Turkey
82 G3 **Kemerovo** Russia
92 H2 **Kemi** Fin.
92 I2 **Kemijärvi** Fin.
92 I2 **Kemijoki** *r.* Fin.
136 A2 **Kemmerer** U.S.A.
92 I3 **Kempele** Fin.
53 D2 **Kempsey** Austr.
130 C2 **Kempt, Lac** *l.* Can.
102 C2 **Kempten (Allgäu)** Ger.
123 C2 **Kempton Park** S. Africa
61 C2 **Kemujan** *i.* Indon.
129 D2 **Kenaston** Can.
98 B1 **Kendal** U.K.
59 C3 **Kendari** Indon.
61 C2 **Kendawangan** Indon.
115 D3 **Kendégué** Chad
75 C2 **Kendujhargarh** India
114 A4 **Kenema** Sierra Leone
118 B3 **Kenge** Dem. Rep. Congo
62 A1 **Kengtung** Myanmar
122 B2 **Kenhardt** S. Africa
114 B1 **Kenitra** Morocco
97 B3 **Kenmare** Ireland
136 C1 **Kenmare** U.S.A.
97 A3 **Kenmare River** *inlet* Ireland
100 C3 **Kenn** Ger.
137 E3 **Kennett** U.S.A.
134 C1 **Kennewick** U.S.A.
129 E3 **Kenora** Can.
140 B2 **Kenosha** U.S.A.
138 C2 **Kent** U.S.A.
77 C2 **Kentau** Kazakh.
140 B3 **Kentucky** *r.* U.S.A.
140 C3 **Kentucky** *state* U.S.A.
140 B3 **Kentucky Lake** U.S.A.
119 D2 **Kenya** *country* Africa
119 D3 **Kenya, Mount** Kenya
137 E2 **Keokuk** U.S.A.
111 C3 **Kepsut** Turkey
52 B3 **Kerang** Austr.
91 D2 **Kerch** Ukr.
59 D3 **Kerema** P.N.G.
128 C3 **Keremeos** Can.
116 B3 **Keren** Eritrea
81 C2 **Kerend-e Gharb** Iran
Kerepakupai Merú Venez. *see* **Angel Falls**
159 C7 **Kerguelen Plateau** Indian Ocean
119 D3 **Kericho** Kenya
54 B1 **Kerikeri** N.Z.
60 B2 **Kerinci, Gunung** *vol.* Indon.
111 A3 **Kerkyra** Greece
Kerkyra *i.* Greece *see* **Corfu**
116 B3 **Kerma** Sudan
49 G4 **Kermadec Islands** S. Pacific Ocean
79 C1 **Kermān** Iran
81 C2 **Kermānshāh** Iran
139 C2 **Kermit** U.S.A.
135 C3 **Kern** *r.* U.S.A.
100 C2 **Kerpen** Ger.
129 D2 **Kerrobert** Can.
139 D2 **Kerrville** U.S.A.
Keryneia Cyprus *see* **Kyrenia**
130 B1 **Kesagami Lake** Can.
111 C2 **Keşan** Turkey
66 D3 **Kesennuma** Japan
74 B2 **Keshod** India
100 C2 **Kessel** Neth.
98 B1 **Keswick** U.K.
103 D2 **Keszthely** Hungary
82 G3 **Ket'** *r.* Russia
61 C2 **Ketapang** Indon.
128 A2 **Ketchikan** U.S.A.
134 D2 **Ketchum** U.S.A.
99 C2 **Kettering** U.K.
93 H3 **Keuruu** Fin.
100 C2 **Kevelaer** Ger.
140 B2 **Kewanee** U.S.A.
140 B1 **Keweenaw Bay** U.S.A.
140 B1 **Keweenaw Peninsula** U.S.A.
143 D3 **Key Largo** U.S.A.
141 D3 **Keyser** U.S.A.
143 D4 **Key West** U.S.A.
123 C2 **Kgotsong** S. Africa
69 E1 **Khabarovsk** Russia
80 B1 **Khadyzhensk** Russia
62 A1 **Khagrachari** Bangl.
74 A2 **Khairpur** Pak.
122 B1 **Khakhea** Botswana
68 C1 **Khamar-Daban, Khrebet** *mts* Russia
74 B2 **Khambhat** India
73 B3 **Khambhat, Gulf of** India
74 B2 **Khamgaon** India
78 B3 **Khamis Mushayţ** Saudi Arabia
78 B3 **Khamr** Yemen
77 C3 **Khānābād** Afgh.
74 B2 **Khandwa** India
83 K2 **Khandyga** Russia
74 B1 **Khanewal** Pak.
66 B2 **Khanka, Lake** China/Russia
74 B2 **Khanpur** Pak.
77 D2 **Khantau** Kazakh.
83 H2 **Khantayskoye, Ozero** *l.* Russia
86 F2 **Khanty-Mansiysk** Russia
63 A3 **Khao Chum Thong** Thai.
63 A2 **Khao Laem, Ang Kep Nam** Thai.
87 D4 **Kharabali** Russia
75 C2 **Kharagpur** India
81 D3 **Kharāmeh** Iran
79 C2 **Khārān** *r.* Iran
116 B2 **Khārijah, Wāḥāt al** *oasis* Egypt
91 D2 **Kharkiv** Ukr.
Khar'kov Ukr. *see* **Kharkiv**
86 D3 **Kharovsk** Russia
116 B3 **Khartoum** Sudan
87 D4 **Khasavyurt** Russia
79 D2 **Khāsh** Iran
78 A3 **Khashm el Girba** Sudan
78 A3 **Khashm el Girba Dam** Sudan
74 D2 **Khasi Hills** India
123 C3 **Khayamnandi** S. Africa
78 A2 **Khaybar** Saudi Arabia
122 A3 **Khayelitsha** S. Africa
107 D2 **Khemis Miliana** Alg.
63 B2 **Khemmarat** Thai.
115 C1 **Khenchela** Alg.
91 C2 **Kherson** Ukr.
83 H2 **Kheta** *r.* Russia
69 D1 **Khilok** Russia
89 E2 **Khimki** Russia
74 A2 **Khipro** Pak.
89 E3 **Khlevnoye** Russia
90 B2 **Khmel'nyts'kyy** Ukr.
89 E3 **Khokhol'skiy** Russia
74 B2 **Khokhropar** Pak.
89 D2 **Kholm** Russia
89 D2 **Kholm-Zhirkovskiy** Russia
79 C2 **Khonj** Iran
63 B2 **Khon Kaen** Thai.
62 A1 **Khonsa** India
83 K2 **Khonuu** Russia

86 E2	Khorey-Ver Russia
69 D1	Khorinsk Russia
91 C2	Khorol Ukr.
81 C2	Khorramābād Iran
81 C2	Khorramshahr Iran
77 D3	Khorugh Tajik.
74 A1	Khōst Afgh.
62 A1	Khreum Myanmar
76 B1	Khromtau Kazakh.
90 B2	Khrystynivka Ukr.
77 C2	Khŭjand Tajik.
63 B2	Khu Khan Thai.
78 A2	Khulays Saudi Arabia
75 C2	Khulna Bangl.
79 B2	Khurays Saudi Arabia
74 B1	Khushab Pak.
90 A2	Khust Ukr.
123 C2	Khutsong S. Africa
74 A2	Khuzdar Pak.
81 D2	Khvānsār Iran
81 C2	Khvormūj Iran
81 C2	Khvoy Iran
77 D3	Khvoynaya Russia
74 B1	Khyber Pass Afgh./Pak.
53 D2	Kiama Austr.
119 C3	Kiambi Dem. Rep. Congo
119 D3	Kibiti Tanz.
109 D2	Kičevo Macedonia
114 C3	Kidal Mali
99 B2	Kidderminster U.K.
114 A3	Kidira Senegal
54 C1	Kidnappers, Cape N.Z.
102 C1	Kiel Ger.
103 E1	Kielce Pol.
98 B1	Kielder Water U.K.
90 C1	Kiev Ukr.
114 A3	Kiffa Maur.
119 D3	Kigali Rwanda
119 C3	Kigoma Tanz.
88 B2	Kihnu i. Estonia
92 I2	Kiiminki Fin.
67 B4	Kii-suidō sea chan. Japan
109 D1	Kikinda Serbia
119 C3	Kikondja Dem. Rep. Congo
59 D3	Kikori P.N.G.
59 D3	Kikori r. P.N.G.
118 B3	Kikwit Dem. Rep. Congo
65 B1	Kilchu N. Korea
118 B3	Kilembe Dem. Rep. Congo
119 E2	Kilgore U.S.A.
119 D3	Kilimanjaro vol. Tanz.
80 B2	Kilis Turkey
90 B2	Kiliya Ukr.
97 B2	Kilkee Ireland
97 D1	Kilkeel U.K.
97 C2	Kilkenny Ireland
111 B2	Kilkis Greece
97 B1	Killala Bay Ireland
97 B2	Killaloe Ireland
129 C2	Killam Can.
97 B2	Killarney Ireland
111 E3	Killeen U.S.A.
96 B2	Killin U.K.
97 B1	Killybegs Ireland
96 B3	Kilmarnock U.K.
53 B3	Kilmore Austr.
119 D3	Kilosa Tanz.
97 B2	Kilrush Ireland
119 C3	Kilwa Dem. Rep. Congo
119 D3	Kilwa Masoko Tanz.
119 D3	Kimambi Tanz.
52 A2	Kimba Austr.
136 C2	Kimball U.S.A.
128 C3	Kimberley Can.
122 B2	Kimberley S. Africa
50 B1	Kimberley Plateau Austr.
65 B1	Kimch'aek N. Korea
127 G2	Kimmirut Can.

89 E3	Kimovsk Russia
118 B3	Kimpese Dem. Rep. Congo
89 E2	Kimry Russia
61 C1	Kinabalu, Gunung mt. Sabah Malaysia
128 C2	Kinbasket Lake Can.
130 B2	Kincardine Can.
62 A1	Kinchang Myanmar
119 C3	Kinda Dem. Rep. Congo
98 C2	Kinder Scout h. U.K.
129 D2	Kindersley Can.
114 A3	Kindia Guinea
119 C3	Kindu Dem. Rep. Congo
86 D3	Kineshma Russia
78 A2	King Abdullah Economic City Saudi Arabia
51 E2	Kingaroy Austr.
135 B3	King City U.S.A.
130 C1	King George Islands Can.
88 C2	Kingisepp Russia
51 D3	King Island Austr.
50 B1	King Leopold Ranges hills Austr.
138 A1	Kingman U.S.A.
135 B3	Kings r. U.S.A.
52 A3	Kingscote Austr.
99 D2	King's Lynn U.K.
48 F3	Kingsmill Group is Kiribati
50 B1	King Sound b. Austr.
134 D2	Kings Peak U.S.A.
143 D1	Kingsport U.S.A.
130 C2	Kingston Can.
146 C3	Kingston Jamaica
141 E2	Kingston U.S.A.
52 A3	Kingston South East Austr.
98 C2	Kingston upon Hull U.K.
147 D3	Kingstown St Vincent
139 D3	Kingsville U.S.A.
99 B3	Kingswood U.K.
96 B2	Kingussie U.K.
126 E2	King William Island Can.
123 C3	King William's Town S. Africa
67 D3	Kinka-san i. Japan
93 F4	Kinna Sweden
97 B2	Kinsale Ireland
118 B3	Kinshasa Dem. Rep. Congo
143 E1	Kinston U.S.A.
88 B2	Kintai Lith.
114 B4	Kintampo Ghana
96 B3	Kintyre pen. U.K.
62 A1	Kin-U Myanmar
130 C2	Kipawa, Lac l. Can.
83 I3	Kirensk Russia
89 E3	Kireyevsk Russia
	Kirghizia country Asia see Kyrgyzstan
49 G3	Kiribati country Pacific Ocean
80 B2	Kırıkkale Turkey
89 E2	Kirillov Russia
	Kirin China see Jilin
	Kirinyaga mt. Kenya see Kenya, Mount
89 D2	Kirishi Russia
49 H2	Kiritimati atoll Kiribati
111 C3	Kırkağaç Turkey
96 C2	Kirkcaldy U.K.
96 B3	Kirkcudbright U.K.
92 J2	Kirkenes Norway
130 B2	Kirkland Lake Can.
137 E2	Kirksville U.S.A.
81 C2	Kirkūk Iraq
96 C1	Kirkwall U.K.
89 D3	Kirov Kaluzhskaya Oblast' Russia
86 D3	Kirov Kirovskaya Oblast' Russia
	Kirovabad Azer. see Gäncä
86 E3	Kirovo-Chepetsk Russia

91 C2	Kirovohrad Ukr.
86 C2	Kirovsk Russia
91 D2	Kirovs'ke Ukr.
96 C2	Kirriemuir U.K.
86 E3	Kirs Russia
74 A2	Kirthar Range mts Pak.
92 H2	Kiruna Sweden
67 C3	Kiryū Japan
89 E2	Kirzhach Russia
119 C2	Kisangani Dem. Rep. Congo
118 B3	Kisantu Dem. Rep. Congo
60 A1	Kisaran Indon.
82 G3	Kiselevsk Russia
75 C2	Kishanganj India
115 C4	Kishi Nigeria
	Kishinev Moldova see Chişinău
77 D1	Kishkenekol' Kazakh.
74 B1	Kishtwar India
119 D3	Kisii Kenya
103 D2	Kiskunfélegyháza Hungary
103 D2	Kiskunhalas Hungary
87 D4	Kislovodsk Russia
117 C5	Kismaayo Somalia
119 C3	Kisoro Uganda
111 B3	Kissamos Greece
114 A4	Kissidougou Guinea
143 D3	Kissimmee U.S.A.
143 D3	Kissimmee, Lake U.S.A.
129 C2	Kississing Lake Can.
119 D3	Kisumu Kenya
114 B3	Kita Mali
66 D3	Kitakami Japan
66 D3	Kitakami-gawa r. Japan
67 B4	Kita-Kyūshū Japan
119 D2	Kitale Kenya
66 D2	Kitami Japan
130 B2	Kitchener Can.
93 J3	Kitee Fin.
119 D2	Kitgum Uganda
128 B2	Kitimat Can.
118 B3	Kitona Dem. Rep. Congo
119 D3	Kitunda Tanz.
128 B2	Kitwanga Can.
121 B2	Kitwe Zambia
101 E3	Kitzingen Ger.
92 I3	Kiuruvesi Fin.
119 C3	Kivu, Lac Dem. Rep. Congo/ Rwanda
110 C2	Kıyıköy Turkey
86 E3	Kizel Russia
111 C3	Kızılca Dağ mt. Turkey
87 D4	Kizlyar Russia
92 I1	Kjøllefjord Norway
92 G2	Kjøpsvik Norway
102 C1	Kladno Czech Rep.
102 C2	Klagenfurt am Wörthersee Austria
88 B2	Klaipėda Lith.
94 B1	Klaksvík Faroe Is
134 B2	Klamath r. U.S.A.
134 B2	Klamath Falls U.S.A.
134 B2	Klamath Mountains U.S.A.
60 B1	Klang Malaysia
102 C2	Klatovy Czech Rep.
122 A3	Klawer S. Africa
128 A2	Klawock U.S.A.
128 B2	Kleena Kleene Can.
122 B2	Kleinbegin S. Africa
122 A2	Kleinsee S. Africa
123 C2	Klerksdorp S. Africa
89 D3	Kletnya Russia
100 C2	Kleve Ger.
89 D3	Klimavichy Belarus
89 E3	Klimovo Russia
89 E2	Klimovsk Russia
89 E2	Klin Russia
101 F2	Klínovec mt. Czech Rep.

93 G4 **Klintehamn** Sweden
89 D3 **Klintsy** Russia
109 C2 **Ključ** Bos. & Herz.
103 D1 **Kłodzko** Pol.
100 C1 **Kloosterhaar** Neth.
103 D2 **Klosterneuburg** Austria
101 E1 **Klötze (Altmark)** Ger.
103 D1 **Kluczbork** Pol.
128 A2 **Klukwan** U.S.A.
88 C3 **Klyetsk** Belarus
98 C1 **Knaresborough** U.K.
93 F3 **Knästen** *h.* Sweden
129 E2 **Knee Lake** Can.
101 E1 **Knesebeck** Ger.
101 E3 **Knetzgau** Ger.
109 C2 **Knin** Croatia
103 C2 **Knittelfeld** Austria
109 D2 **Knjaževac** Serbia
100 A2 **Knokke-Heist** Belgium
143 D1 **Knoxville** U.S.A.
122 B3 **Knysna** S. Africa
76 B1 **Kobda** Kazakh.
67 C4 **Kōbe** Japan
København Denmark *see* **Copenhagen**
100 C2 **Koblenz** Ger.
59 C3 **Kobroör** *i.* Indon.
88 B3 **Kobryn** Belarus
109 D2 **Kočani** Macedonia
111 C2 **Kocasu** *r.* Turkey
75 C2 **Koch Bihar** India
73 B4 **Kochi** India
67 B4 **Kōchi** Japan
87 D4 **Kochubey** Russia
75 C2 **Kodarma** India
117 B4 **Kodok** South Sudan
90 B2 **Kodyma** Ukr.
111 C2 **Kodzhaele** *mt.* Bulg./Greece
122 A2 **Koës** Namibia
122 C2 **Koffiefontein** S. Africa
114 B4 **Koforidua** Ghana
67 C3 **Kōfu** Japan
131 D1 **Kogaluk** *r.* Can.
117 B5 **Kogelo** Kenya
74 B1 **Kohat** Pak.
62 A1 **Kohima** India
88 C2 **Kohtla-Järve** Estonia
114 A4 **Koidu-Sefadu** Sierra Leone
92 H3 **Kokkola** Fin.
140 B2 **Kokomo** U.S.A.
77 E2 **Kokpekty** Kazakh.
77 C1 **Kokshetau** Kazakh.
131 D1 **Koksoak** *r.* Can.
123 C3 **Kokstad** S. Africa
Koktokay China *see* **Fuyun**
58 C3 **Kolaka** Indon.
86 C2 **Kola Peninsula** Russia
92 H2 **Kolari** Fin.
114 A3 **Kolda** Senegal
93 E4 **Kolding** Denmark
107 D2 **Koléa** Alg.
86 D2 **Kolguyev, Ostrov** *i.* Russia
73 B3 **Kolhapur** India
88 B2 **Kolkasrags** *pt* Latvia
75 C2 **Kolkata** India
73 B4 **Kollam** India
Köln Ger. *see* **Cologne**
103 D1 **Kołobrzeg** Pol.
114 B3 **Kolokani** Mali
89 E2 **Kolomna** Russia
90 B2 **Kolomyya** Ukr.
122 B2 **Kolonkwaneng** Botswana
82 G3 **Kolpashevo** Russia
89 E3 **Kolpny** Russia
Kol'skiy Poluostrov *pen.* Russia *see* **Kola Peninsula**
78 B3 **Koluli** Eritrea
119 C4 **Kolwezi** Dem. Rep. Congo
83 L2 **Kolyma** *r.* Russia
83 L2 **Kolymskaya Nizmennost'** *lowland* Russia
83 M2 **Kolymskiy, Khrebet** *mts* Russia
67 C3 **Komaki** Japan
83 M3 **Komandorskiye Ostrova** *is* Russia
103 D2 **Komárno** Slovakia
123 D2 **Komati** *r.* S. Africa/Swaziland
67 C3 **Komatsu** Japan
119 C3 **Kombe** Dem. Rep. Congo
90 C2 **Kominternivs'ke** Ukr.
109 C2 **Komiža** Croatia
103 D2 **Komló** Hungary
118 B3 **Komono** Congo
111 C2 **Komotini** Greece
122 B3 **Komsberg** *mts* S. Africa
83 H1 **Komsomolets, Ostrov** *i.* Russia
89 F2 **Komsomol'sk** Russia
91 C2 **Komsomol's'k** Ukr.
87 D4 **Komsomol'skiy** Russia
69 E1 **Komsomol'sk-na-Amure** Russia
89 E2 **Konakovo** Russia
75 C3 **Kondagaon** India
86 F2 **Kondinskoye** Russia
119 D3 **Kondoa** Tanz.
86 C2 **Kondopoga** Russia
89 E3 **Kondrovo** Russia
127 I2 **Kong Christian IX Land** *reg.* Greenland
127 I2 **Kong Frederik VI Kyst** *coastal area* Greenland
119 C3 **Kongolo** Dem. Rep. Congo
93 E4 **Kongsberg** Norway
93 F3 **Kongsvinger** Norway
77 D3 **Kongur Shan** *mt.* China
100 C2 **Königswinter** Ger.
103 D1 **Konin** Pol.
109 C2 **Konjic** Bos. & Herz.
122 A2 **Konkiep** *watercourse* Namibia
91 C1 **Konotop** Ukr.
102 B2 **Konstanz** Ger.
115 C3 **Kontagora** Nigeria
63 B2 **Kon Tum** Vietnam
63 B2 **Kon Tum, Cao Nguyên** *plat.* Vietnam
80 B2 **Konya** Turkey
100 C3 **Konz** Ger.
86 E3 **Konzhakovskiy Kamen', Gora** *mt.* Russia
134 C1 **Kooskia** U.S.A.
128 C3 **Kootenay Lake** Can.
122 B3 **Kootjieskolk** S. Africa
92 □B2 **Kópasker** Iceland
108 B1 **Koper** Slovenia
93 G4 **Kopparberg** Sweden
109 C1 **Koprivnica** Croatia
89 F3 **Korablino** Russia
73 C3 **Koraput** India
101 D2 **Korbach** Ger.
109 D2 **Korçë** Albania
109 C2 **Korčula** Croatia
109 C2 **Korčula** *i.* Croatia
70 C2 **Korea Bay** *g.* China/N. Korea
65 B2 **Korea, North** *country* Asia
65 B2 **Korea, South** *country* Asia
65 B3 **Korea Strait** Japan/S. Korea
91 D2 **Korenovsk** Russia
90 B1 **Korets'** Ukr.
111 C2 **Körfez** Turkey
114 B4 **Korhogo** Côte d'Ivoire
Korinthos Greece *see* **Corinth**
103 D2 **Kris-hegy** *h.* Hungary
109 D2 **Koritnik** *mt.* Albania/Kosovo
67 D3 **Kōriyama** Japan
80 B2 **Korkuteli** Turkey
68 B2 **Korla** China
103 D2 **Körmend** Hungary
114 B3 **Koro** Mali
131 D1 **Koroc** *r.* Can.
91 D1 **Korocha** Russia
119 D3 **Korogwe** Tanz.
59 C2 **Koror** Palau
90 B1 **Korosten'** Ukr.
90 B1 **Korostyshiv** Ukr.
115 D3 **Koro Toro** Chad
91 C2 **Korsun'-Shevchenkivs'kyy** Ukr.
103 E1 **Korsze** Pol.
100 A2 **Kortrijk** Belgium
83 L3 **Koryakskaya Sopka, Vulkan** *vol.* Russia
83 M2 **Koryakskoye Nagor'ye** *mts* Russia
86 D2 **Koryazhma** Russia
91 C1 **Koryukivka** Ukr.
111 C3 **Kos** Greece
111 C3 **Kos** *i.* Greece
65 B2 **Kosan** N. Korea
103 D1 **Kościan** Pol.
53 C3 **Kosciuszko, Mount** Austr.
68 B1 **Kosh-Agach** Russia
103 E2 **Košice** Slovakia
92 H2 **Koskullskulle** Sweden
65 B2 **Kosŏng** N. Korea
109 D2 **Kosovo** *country* Europe
Kosovska Mitrovica Kosovo *see* **Mitrovicë**
48 E2 **Kosrae** *atoll* Micronesia
114 B4 **Kossou, Lac de** *l.* Côte d'Ivoire
76 C1 **Kostanay** Kazakh.
110 B2 **Kostenets** Bulg.
123 C2 **Koster** S. Africa
117 B3 **Kosti** Sudan
86 C2 **Kostomuksha** Russia
90 B1 **Kostopil'** Ukr.
89 F2 **Kostroma** Russia
89 F2 **Kostroma** *r.* Russia
102 C1 **Kostrzyn nad Odrą** Pol.
103 D1 **Koszalin** Pol.
103 D2 **Kszeg** Hungary
74 B2 **Kota** India
60 B2 **Kotaagung** Indon.
61 C2 **Kotabaru** Indon.
61 C1 **Kota Belud** *Sabah* Malaysia
60 B1 **Kota Bharu** Malaysia
60 B2 **Kotabumi** Indon.
61 C1 **Kota Kinabalu** *Sabah* Malaysia
61 C1 **Kota Samarahan** *Sarawak* Malaysia
86 D3 **Kotel'nich** Russia
87 D4 **Kotel'nikovo** Russia
83 K1 **Kotel'nyy, Ostrov** *i.* Russia
101 E2 **Köthen (Anhalt)** Ger.
93 I3 **Kotka** Fin.
86 D2 **Kotlas** Russia
109 C2 **Kotor Varoš** Bos. & Herz.
87 D3 **Kotovo** Russia
91 E1 **Kotovsk** Russia
90 B2 **Kotovs'k** Ukr.
83 H2 **Kotuy** *r.* Russia
100 A2 **Koudekerke** Neth.
114 B3 **Koudougou** Burkina Faso
122 B3 **Kougaberge** *mts* S. Africa
118 B3 **Koulamoutou** Gabon
114 B3 **Koulikoro** Mali
114 A3 **Koundâra** Guinea
151 C1 **Kourou** Fr. Guiana
114 B3 **Kouroussa** Guinea
115 D3 **Kousséri** Cameroon
114 B3 **Koutiala** Mali
93 I3 **Kouvola** Fin.
92 J2 **Kovdor** Russia

90 A1 **Kovel'** Ukr.
89 F2 **Kovrov** Russia
54 B2 **Kowhitirangi** N.Z.
Koyamutthoor India *see* **Coimbatore**
111 C3 **Köyceğiz** Turkey
86 D2 **Koyda** Russia
126 A2 **Koyukuk** *r.* U.S.A.
111 B2 **Kozani** Greece
90 C1 **Kozelets'** Ukr.
89 E3 **Kozel'sk** Russia
73 B3 **Kozhikode** India
90 B2 **Kozyatyn** Ukr.
63 A3 **Krabi** Thai.
63 A2 **Kra Buri** Thai.
63 B2 **Krâchéh** Cambodia
93 E4 **Kragerø** Norway
100 B1 **Kraggenburg** Neth.
109 D2 **Kragujevac** Serbia
60 B2 **Krakatau** *i.* Indon.
103 D1 **Kraków** Pol.
91 D2 **Kramators'k** Ukr.
93 G3 **Kramfors** Sweden
111 B3 **Kranidi** Greece
86 E1 **Krasino** Russia
88 C2 **Krāslava** Latvia
101 F2 **Kraslice** Czech Rep.
89 D3 **Krasnapollye** Belarus
89 D3 **Krasnaya Gora** Russia
87 D3 **Krasnoarmeysk** Russia
91 D2 **Krasnoarmiys'k** Ukr.
86 D2 **Krasnoborsk** Russia
91 D2 **Krasnodar** Russia
91 D2 **Krasnodarskoye Vodokhranilishche** *resr* Russia
91 D2 **Krasnodon** Ukr.
88 C2 **Krasnogorodsk** Russia
91 D2 **Krasnohrad** Ukr.
91 C2 **Krasnohvardiys'ke** Ukr.
86 E3 **Krasnokamsk** Russia
89 D2 **Krasnomayskiy** Russia
91 C2 **Krasnoperekops'k** Ukr.
87 D3 **Krasnoslobodsk** Russia
86 E3 **Krasnoufimsk** Russia
83 H3 **Krasnoyarsk** Russia
89 F2 **Krasnoye-na-Volge** Russia
89 D3 **Krasnyy** Russia
89 E2 **Krasnyy Kholm** Russia
87 C4 **Krasnyy Luch** Ukr.
91 E2 **Krasnyy Sulin** Russia
90 B2 **Krasyliv** Ukr.
100 C2 **Krefeld** Ger.
91 C2 **Kremenchuk** Ukr.
91 C2 **Kremenchuts'ke Vodoskhovyshche** *resr* Ukr.
103 D2 **Křemešník** *h.* Czech Rep.
91 D2 **Kreminna** Ukr.
103 D2 **Krems an der Donau** Austria
89 D2 **Kresttsy** Russia
88 B2 **Kretinga** Lith.
100 C2 **Kreuzau** Ger.
100 C2 **Kreuztal** Ger.
118 A2 **Kribi** Cameroon
111 B3 **Krikellos** Greece
66 D1 **Kril'on, Mys** *c.* Russia
73 C3 **Krishna** *r.* India
73 C3 **Krishna, Mouths of the** India
75 C2 **Krishnanagar** India
93 E4 **Kristiansand** Norway
93 F4 **Kristianstad** Sweden
92 E3 **Kristiansund** Norway
93 F4 **Kristinehamn** Sweden
Kriti *i.* Greece *see* **Crete**
111 C3 **Kritiko Pelagos** *sea* Greece
Krivoy Rog Ukr. *see* **Kryvyy Rih**
109 C1 **Križevci** Croatia
108 B1 **Krk** *i.* Croatia
92 F3 **Krokom** Sweden
91 C1 **Krolevets'** Ukr.
101 E2 **Kronach** Ger.
63 B2 **Krŏng Kaôh Kŏng** Cambodia
127 I2 **Kronprins Frederik Bjerge** *nunataks* Greenland
123 C2 **Kroonstad** S. Africa
87 D4 **Kropotkin** Russia
103 E2 **Krosno** Pol.
103 D1 **Krotoszyn** Pol.
60 B2 **Krui** Indon.
109 C2 **Krujë** Albania
111 C2 **Krumovgrad** Bulg.
Krung Thep Thai. *see* **Bangkok**
88 C3 **Krupki** Belarus
109 D2 **Kruševac** Serbia
101 F2 **Krušné hory** *mts* Czech Rep.
128 A2 **Kruzof Island** U.S.A.
89 D3 **Krychaw** Belarus
91 D3 **Krymsk** Russia
91 C2 **Kryvyy Rih** Ukr.
114 B2 **Ksabi** Alg.
107 D2 **Ksar el Boukhari** Alg.
114 B1 **Ksar el Kebir** Morocco
89 E3 **Kshenskiy** Russia
78 B2 **Kū', Jabal al** *h.* Saudi Arabia
61 C1 **Kuala Belait** Brunei
60 B1 **Kuala Kerai** Malaysia
60 B1 **Kuala Lipis** Malaysia
60 B1 **Kuala Lumpur** Malaysia
61 C2 **Kualapembuang** Indon.
60 B1 **Kuala Terengganu** Malaysia
60 B2 **Kualatungal** Indon.
61 C1 **Kuamut** *Sabah* Malaysia
65 A1 **Kuandian** China
60 B1 **Kuantan** Malaysia
91 D2 **Kuban'** *r.* Russia
89 E2 **Kubenskoye, Ozero** *l.* Russia
110 C2 **Kubrat** Bulg.
61 C1 **Kubuang** Indon.
61 C1 **Kuching** *Sarawak* Malaysia
109 C2 **Kuçovë** Albania
61 C1 **Kudat** *Sabah* Malaysia
61 C2 **Kudus** Indon.
102 C2 **Kufstein** Austria
127 F2 **Kugaaruk** Can.
126 D2 **Kugluktuk** Can.
92 I3 **Kuhmo** Fin.
79 C2 **Kūhrān, Kūh-e** *mt.* Iran
Kuitin China *see* **Kuytun**
120 A2 **Kuito** Angola
92 I2 **Kuivaniemi** Fin.
65 B2 **Kujang** N. Korea
109 D2 **Kukës** Albania
111 C3 **Kula** Turkey
75 D2 **Kula Kangri** *mt.* Bhutan/China
76 B2 **Kulandy** Kazakh.
88 B2 **Kuldīga** Latvia
122 B1 **Kule** Botswana
101 E2 **Kulmbach** Ger.
77 C3 **Kŭlob** Tajik.
76 B2 **Kul'sary** Kazakh.
77 D1 **Kulunda** Russia
127 I2 **Kulusuk** Greenland
67 C3 **Kumagaya** Japan
67 B4 **Kumamoto** Japan
109 D2 **Kumanovo** Macedonia
114 B4 **Kumasi** Ghana
118 A2 **Kumba** Cameroon
78 B2 **Kumdah** Saudi Arabia
87 E3 **Kumertau** Russia
93 G4 **Kumla** Sweden
115 D3 **Kumo** Nigeria
62 A1 **Kumon Range** *mts* Myanmar
62 B2 **Kumphawapi** Thai.
Kumul China *see* **Hami**
66 D2 **Kunashir, Ostrov** *i.* Russia
120 A2 **Kunene** *r.* Angola/Namibia
77 D2 **Kungei Alatau** *mts* Kazakh./Kyrg.
93 F4 **Kungsbacka** Sweden
118 B2 **Kungu** Dem. Rep. Congo
86 E3 **Kungur** Russia
62 A1 **Kunhing** Myanmar
77 D3 **Kunlun Shan** *mts* China
62 B1 **Kunming** China
50 B1 **Kununurra** Austr.
92 I3 **Kuopio** Fin.
109 C1 **Kupa** *r.* Croatia/Slovenia
59 C3 **Kupang** Indon.
88 B2 **Kupiškis** Lith.
111 C2 **Küplü** Turkey
128 A2 **Kupreanof Island** U.S.A.
91 D2 **Kup"yans'k** Ukr.
77 E2 **Kuqa** China
67 B4 **Kurashiki** Japan
67 B3 **Kurayoshi** Japan
89 E3 **Kurchatov** Russia
81 C2 **Kurdistan** *reg.* Asia
67 B4 **Kure** Japan
88 B2 **Kuressaare** Estonia
86 F3 **Kurgan** Russia
93 H3 **Kurikka** Fin.
156 C3 **Kuril Trench** N. Pacific Ocean
89 E3 **Kurkino** Russia
117 B3 **Kurmuk** Sudan
73 B3 **Kurnool** India
53 D2 **Kurri Kurri** Austr.
89 E3 **Kursk** Russia
122 B2 **Kuruman** S. Africa
122 B2 **Kuruman** *watercourse* S. Africa
67 B4 **Kurume** Japan
83 I3 **Kurumkan** Russia
73 C4 **Kurunegala** Sri Lanka
111 C3 **Kuşadası** Turkey
111 C3 **Kuşadası, Gulf of** *b.* Turkey
111 C2 **Kuş Gölü** *l.* Turkey
91 D2 **Kushchevskaya** Russia
66 D2 **Kushiro** Japan
75 C2 **Kushtia** Bangl.
76 C1 **Kusmuryn** Kazakh.
66 D2 **Kussharo-ko** *l.* Japan
111 C3 **Kütahya** Turkey
81 C1 **Kutaisi** Georgia
109 C1 **Kutjevo** Croatia
103 D1 **Kutno** Pol.
118 B3 **Kutu** Dem. Rep. Congo
126 D2 **Kuujjua** *r.* Can.
131 D1 **Kuujjuaq** Can.
130 C1 **Kuujjuarapik** Can.
92 I2 **Kuusamo** Fin.
120 A2 **Kuvango** Angola
89 D2 **Kuvshinovo** Russia
78 B2 **Kuwait** *country* Asia
79 B2 **Kuwait** Kuwait
Kuybyshev Russia *see* **Samara**
91 D2 **Kuybysheve** Ukr.
87 D3 **Kuybyshevskoye Vodokhranilishche** *resr* Russia
77 E2 **Kuytun** China
111 C3 **Kuyucak** Turkey
87 D3 **Kuznetsk** Russia
90 B1 **Kuznetsovs'k** Ukr.
92 H1 **Kvalsund** Norway
123 D2 **KwaDukuza** S. Africa
123 D2 **KwaMashu** S. Africa
Kwangju S. Korea *see* **Gwangju**
65 B1 **Kwanmo-bong** *mt.* N. Korea
123 C3 **KwaNobuhle** S. Africa
122 B3 **KwaNonzame** S. Africa
123 C3 **Kwatinidubu** S. Africa
123 C2 **KwaZamokuhle** S. Africa
123 D2 **KwaZulu-Natal** *prov.* S. Africa
121 B2 **Kwekwe** Zimbabwe
118 B3 **Kwenge** *r.* Dem. Rep. Congo

103 D1 **Kwidzyn** Pol.
118 B3 **Kwilu** *r.* Angola/Dem. Rep. Congo
59 C3 **Kwoka** *mt.* Indon.
53 C3 **Kyabram** Austr.
62 A2 **Kyaikto** Myanmar
69 D1 **Kyakhta** Russia
52 A2 **Kyancutta** Austr.
62 A1 **Kyaukpadaung** Myanmar
62 A2 **Kyaukpyu** Myanmar
88 B3 **Kybartai** Lith.
62 A2 **Kyebogyi** Myanmar
62 A2 **Kyeintali** Myanmar
74 B1 **Kyelang** India
Kyiv Ukr. *see* **Kiev**
90 C1 **Kyivs'ke Vodoskhovyshche** *resr* Ukr.
Kyklades *is* Greece *see* **Cyclades**
129 D2 **Kyle** Can.
96 B2 **Kyle of Lochalsh** U.K.
100 C3 **Kyll** *r.* Ger.
111 B3 **Kyllini** *mt.* Greece
111 B3 **Kymi** Greece
52 B3 **Kyneton** Austr.
119 D2 **Kyoga, Lake** Uganda
53 D1 **Kyogle** Austr.
67 C4 **Kyōto** Japan
111 B3 **Kyparissia** Greece
111 B3 **Kyra Panagia** *i.* Greece
80 B2 **Kyrenia** Cyprus
77 D2 **Kyrgyzstan** *country* Asia
101 F1 **Kyritz** Ger.
92 H3 **Kyrönjoki** *r.* Fin.
86 E2 **Kyrta** Russia
86 D2 **Kyssa** Russia
111 B3 **Kythira** *i.* Greece
111 B3 **Kythnos** *i.* Greece
128 B2 **Kyuquot** Can.
67 B4 **Kyūshū** *i.* Japan
110 B2 **Kyustendil** Bulg.
92 H3 **Kyyjärvi** Fin.
68 C1 **Kyzyl** Russia
76 C2 **Kyzylkum Desert** Kazakh./Uzbek.
77 C2 **Kyzylorda** Kazakh.

L

145 C3 **La Angostura, Presa de** *resr* Mex.
117 C4 **Laascaanood** Somalia
150 B1 **La Asunción** Venez.
114 A2 **Laâyoune** Western Sahara
87 D4 **Laba** *r.* Russia
144 B2 **La Babia** Mex.
146 B3 **La Bahía, Islas de** *is* Hond.
152 B3 **La Banda** Arg.
104 B2 **La Baule-Escoublac** France
114 A3 **Labé** Guinea
128 A1 **Laberge, Lake** Can.
129 C2 **La Biche, Lac** *l.* Can.
87 D4 **Labinsk** Russia
64 B1 **Labo** Phil.
104 B3 **Labouheyre** France
131 D1 **Labrador** *reg.* Can.
131 D1 **Labrador City** Can.
158 C1 **Labrador Sea** Can./Greenland
150 B2 **Lábrea** Brazil
61 C1 **Labuan** Malaysia
60 B1 **Labuhanbilik** Indon.
59 C3 **Labuna** Indon.
63 A2 **Labutta** Myanmar
86 F2 **Labytnangi** Russia
109 C2 **Laç** Albania
105 C2 **La Capelle** France
Laccadive Islands India *see* **Lakshadweep**
129 E2 **Lac du Bonnet** Can.
146 B3 **La Ceiba** Hond.
53 B2 **Lachlan** *r.* Austr.
141 E1 **Lachute** Can.
105 D3 **La Ciotat** France
129 C2 **Lac La Biche** Can.
Lac la Martre Can. *see* **Whatî**
141 E1 **Lac-Mégantic** Can.
128 C2 **Lacombe** Can.
146 B4 **La Concepción** Panama
145 C3 **La Concordia** Mex.
108 A3 **Laconi** *Sardinia* Italy
141 E2 **Laconia** U.S.A.
128 C2 **La Crete** Can.
140 A2 **La Crosse** U.S.A.
144 B2 **La Cruz** Mex.
144 B2 **La Cuesta** Mex.
75 B1 **Ladakh Range** *mts* India/Pak.
122 B3 **Ladismith** S. Africa
79 D2 **Lādīz** Iran
86 C2 **Ladoga, Lake** Russia
Ladozhskoye Ozero *l.* Russia *see* **Ladoga, Lake**
128 B3 **Ladysmith** Can.
123 C2 **Ladysmith** S. Africa
59 D3 **Lae** P.N.G.
152 B3 **La Esmeralda** Bol.
93 F4 **Læsø** *i.* Denmark
143 C2 **La Fayette** U.S.A.
140 B2 **Lafayette** *IN* U.S.A.
142 B2 **Lafayette** *LA* U.S.A.
115 C4 **Lafia** Nigeria
104 B2 **La Flèche** France
143 D1 **La Follette** U.S.A.
131 C1 **Laforge** Can.
79 C2 **Lāft** Iran
108 A3 **La Galite** *i.* Tunisia
81 C1 **Lagan'** Russia
118 B2 **Lagdo, Lac de** *l.* Cameroon
152 C3 **Lages** Brazil
115 C1 **Laghouat** Alg.
155 D1 **Lagoa Santa** Brazil
114 A2 **La Gomera** *i.* Canary Islands
114 C4 **Lagos** Nigeria
106 B2 **Lagos** Port.
134 C1 **La Grande** U.S.A.
130 C1 **La Grande 3, Réservoir** *resr* Can.
131 C1 **La Grande 4, Réservoir** *resr* Can.
50 B1 **La Grange** Austr.
143 C2 **La Grange** U.S.A.
150 B1 **La Gran Sabana** *plat.* Venez.
152 D3 **Laguna** Brazil
144 A2 **Laguna, Picacho de la** *mt.* Mex.
150 A2 **Lagunas** Peru
La Habana Cuba *see* **Havana**
61 C1 **Lahad Datu** *Sabah* Malaysia
60 B2 **Lahat** Indon.
78 B3 **Laḥij** Yemen
81 C2 **Lāhījān** Iran
100 C2 **Lahnstein** Ger.
74 B1 **Lahore** Pak.
74 A2 **Lahri** Pak.
93 I3 **Lahti** Fin.
115 D4 **Laï** Chad
53 D1 **Laidley** Austr.
104 C2 **L'Aigle** France
111 B3 **Laimos, Akrotirio** *pt* Greece
122 B3 **Laingsburg** S. Africa
92 H2 **Lainioälven** *r.* Sweden
96 B1 **Lairg** U.K.
108 B1 **Laives** Italy
70 B2 **Laiwu** China
70 C2 **Laiyang** China
70 B2 **Laizhou** China
70 B2 **Laizhou Wan** *b.* China
50 C1 **Lajamanu** Austr.
144 B2 **La Junta** Mex.
136 C3 **La Junta** U.S.A.
121 C2 **Lake Cabora Bassa** *resr* Moz.
53 C2 **Lake Cargelligo** Austr.
53 D2 **Lake Cathie** Austr.
142 B2 **Lake Charles** U.S.A.
143 D2 **Lake City** *FL* U.S.A.
143 E2 **Lake City** *SC* U.S.A.
108 A1 **Lake Como** Italy
128 B3 **Lake Cowichan** Can.
108 B1 **Lake Garda** Italy
138 A2 **Lake Havasu City** U.S.A.
143 D3 **Lakeland** U.S.A.
128 C2 **Lake Louise** Can.
134 B1 **Lake Oswego** U.S.A.
54 A2 **Lake Paringa** N.Z.
142 B2 **Lake Providence** U.S.A.
54 B2 **Lake Pukaki** N.Z.
53 C3 **Lakes Entrance** Austr.
134 B2 **Lakeview** U.S.A.
136 B3 **Lakewood** *CO* U.S.A.
141 E2 **Lakewood** *NJ* U.S.A.
143 D3 **Lake Worth** U.S.A.
74 A2 **Lakhpat** India
74 B1 **Lakki Marwat** Pak.
111 B3 **Lakonikos Kolpos** *b.* Greece
92 H1 **Lakselv** Norway
73 B3 **Lakshadweep** India
107 C1 **L'Alcora** Spain
145 C3 **La Libertad** Guat.
106 B1 **Lalín** Spain
75 B2 **Lalitpur** India
129 D2 **La Loche** Can.
100 B2 **La Louvière** Belgium
108 A2 **La Maddalena** *Sardinia* Italy
61 C1 **Lamag** *Sabah* Malaysia
La Manche *str.* France/U.K. *see* **English Channel**
136 C3 **Lamar** U.S.A.
108 A3 **La Marmora, Punta** *mt.* *Sardinia* Italy
128 C1 **La Martre, Lac** *l.* Can.
118 B3 **Lambaréné** Gabon
122 A3 **Lambert's Bay** S. Africa
92 □A2 **Lambeyri** Iceland
106 B1 **Lamego** Port.
150 A3 **La Merced** Peru
79 C2 **Lāmerd** Iran
52 B3 **Lameroo** Austr.
139 C2 **Lamesa** U.S.A.
111 B3 **Lamia** Greece
137 E2 **Lamoni** U.S.A.
62 A2 **Lampang** Thai.
139 D2 **Lampasas** U.S.A.
145 B2 **Lampazos** Mex.
99 A2 **Lampeter** U.K.
62 A2 **Lamphun** Thai.
119 E3 **Lamu** Kenya
62 A2 **Lan, Loi** *mt.* Myanmar/Thai.
96 C3 **Lanark** U.K.
63 A2 **Lanbi Kyun** *i.* Myanmar
Lancang Jiang *r.* China *see* **Mekong**
98 B1 **Lancaster** U.K.
135 C4 **Lancaster** *CA* U.S.A.
140 C3 **Lancaster** *OH* U.S.A.
141 D2 **Lancaster** *PA* U.S.A.
143 D2 **Lancaster** *SC* U.S.A.
127 F2 **Lancaster Sound** *str.* Can.
Lanchow China *see* **Lanzhou**
102 C2 **Landeck** Austria
136 B2 **Lander** U.S.A.
99 A3 **Land's End** *pt* U.K.
102 C2 **Landshut** Ger.

93 F4 **Landskrona** Sweden
143 C2 **Lanett** U.S.A.
122 B2 **Langberg** *mts* S. Africa
137 D1 **Langdon** U.S.A.
93 F4 **Langeland** *i.* Denmark
101 D1 **Langen** Ger.
100 C1 **Langeoog** Ger.
100 C1 **Langeoog** *i.* Ger.
101 D2 **Langgöns** Ger.
92 ⃞A3 **Langjökull** Iceland
105 C3 **Langogne** France
104 B3 **Langon** France
105 D2 **Langres** France
60 A1 **Langsa** Indon.
62 B1 **Lang Sơn** Vietnam
101 D1 **Langwedel** Ger.
129 C2 **Lanigan** Can.
153 A4 **Lanín, Volcán** *vol.* Arg./Chile
81 C2 **Länkäran** Azer.
104 B2 **Lannion** France
140 C2 **Lansing** U.S.A.
71 B3 **Lanxi** China
117 B4 **Lanya** South Sudan
114 A2 **Lanzarote** *i.* Canary Islands
70 A2 **Lanzhou** China
64 B1 **Laoag City** Phil.
62 B1 **Lao Cai** Vietnam
70 B2 **Laohekou** China
68 C2 **Laojunmiao** China
65 B1 **Laoling** China
65 B1 **Lao Ling** *mts* China
68 C2 **Lao Mangnai** China
105 C2 **Laon** France
62 B2 **Laos** *country* Asia
65 B1 **Laotougou** China
154 C3 **Lapa** Brazil
114 A2 **La Palma** *i.* Canary Islands
146 C4 **La Palma** Panama
150 B1 **La Paragua** Venez.
152 B2 **La Paz** Bol.
144 A2 **La Paz** Mex.
150 B2 **La Pedrera** Col.
66 D1 **La Pérouse Strait** Japan/Russia
145 C2 **La Pesca** Mex.
144 B2 **La Piedad** Mex.
153 C4 **La Plata** Arg.
153 C4 **La Plata, Río de** *sea chan.* Arg./Uru.
106 B1 **La Pola** Spain
93 I3 **Lappeenranta** Fin.
92 H2 **Lappland** *reg.* Europe
111 C2 **Lâpseki** Turkey
83 J1 **Laptev Sea** Russia
Laptevykh, More *sea see* Laptev Sea
92 H3 **Lapua** Fin.
152 B3 **La Quiaca** Arg.
79 C2 **Lār** Iran
114 B1 **Larache** Morocco
136 B2 **Laramie** U.S.A.
136 B2 **Laramie Mountains** U.S.A.
154 B3 **Laranjeiras do Sul** Brazil
59 C3 **Larantuka** Indon.
59 C3 **Larat** *i.* Indon.
107 D2 **Larba** Alg.
106 C1 **Laredo** Spain
139 D3 **Laredo** U.S.A.
98 B3 **Largs** U.K.
152 B3 **La Rioja** Arg.
111 B3 **Larisa** Greece
74 A2 **Larkana** Pak.
80 B2 **Larnaca** Cyprus
97 D1 **Larne** U.K.
100 B2 **La Roche-en-Ardenne** Belgium
104 B2 **La Rochelle** France
104 B2 **La Roche-sur-Yon** France

107 C2 **La Roda** Spain
147 D3 **La Romana** Dom. Rep.
129 D2 **La Ronge** Can.
129 D2 **La Ronge, Lac** *l.* Can.
50 C1 **Larrimah** Austr.
55 P3 **Larsen Ice Shelf** Antarctica
93 F4 **Larvik** Norway
130 C2 **La Sarre** Can.
138 B2 **Las Cruces** U.S.A.
153 C4 **Las Flores** Arg.
153 B4 **Las Heras** Arg.
62 A1 **Lashio** Myanmar
74 A1 **Lashkar Gāh** Afgh.
109 C3 **La Sila** *reg.* Italy
152 B3 **Las Lomitas** Arg.
144 B2 **Las Nieves** Mex.
114 A2 **Las Palmas de Gran Canaria** Canary Islands
108 A2 **La Spezia** Italy
153 B5 **Las Plumas** Arg.
129 D2 **Last Mountain Lake** Can.
152 B3 **Las Tórtolas, Cerro** *mt.* Arg./Chile
118 B3 **Lastoursville** Gabon
109 C2 **Lastovo** *i.* Croatia
144 A2 **Las Tres Vírgenes, Volcán** *vol.* Mex.
146 C2 **Las Tunas** Cuba
144 B2 **Las Varas** *Chihuahua* Mex.
144 B2 **Las Varas** *Nayarit* Mex.
138 B1 **Las Vegas** *NM* U.S.A.
135 C3 **Las Vegas** *NV* U.S.A.
131 E1 **La Tabatière** Can.
80 B2 **Latakia** Syria
104 B3 **La Teste-de-Buch** France
108 B2 **Latina** Italy
147 D3 **La Tortuga, Isla** *i.* Venez.
64 B1 **La Trinidad** Phil.
89 E2 **Latskoye** Russia
131 C2 **La Tuque** Can.
88 B2 **Latvia** *country* Europe
102 C1 **Lauchhammer** Ger.
106 C1 **Laudio** Spain
101 E3 **Lauf an der Pegnitz** Ger.
102 C2 **Laufen** Switz.
51 D4 **Launceston** Austr.
99 A3 **Launceston** U.K.
62 A1 **Launggyaung** Myanmar
51 D1 **Laura** Austr.
142 C2 **Laurel** *MS* U.S.A.
134 E1 **Laurel** *MT* U.S.A.
109 C2 **Lauria** Italy
143 E2 **Laurinburg** U.S.A.
105 D2 **Lausanne** Switz.
61 C2 **Laut** *i.* Indon.
61 C2 **Laut Bali** *sea* Indon.
101 D2 **Lauterbach (Hessen)** Ger.
61 C2 **Laut Kecil, Kepulauan** *is* Indon.
100 C1 **Lauwersmeer** *l.* Neth.
104 B2 **Laval** France
107 C2 **La Vall d'Uixó** Spain
50 B2 **Laverton** Austr.
155 D2 **Lavras** Brazil
123 D2 **Lavumisa** Swaziland
61 C1 **Lawas** *Sarawak* Malaysia
62 A1 **Lawksawk** Myanmar
114 B3 **Lawra** Ghana
137 D3 **Lawrence** U.S.A.
142 C1 **Lawrenceburg** U.S.A.
139 D2 **Lawton** U.S.A.
78 A2 **Lawz, Jabal al** *mt.* Saudi Arabia
93 F4 **Laxå** Sweden
74 B1 **Layyah** Pak.
109 D2 **Lazarevac** Serbia
144 A1 **Lázaro Cárdenas** *Baja California* Mex.

144 B3 **Lázaro Cárdenas** *Michoacán* Mex.
88 B3 **Lazdijai** Lith.
136 C2 **Lead** U.S.A.
129 D2 **Leader** Can.
136 B3 **Leadville** U.S.A.
Leaf Bay Can. *see* Tasiujaq
129 D2 **Leaf Rapids** Can.
97 B2 **Leane, Lough** *l.* Ireland
80 B2 **Lebanon** *country* Asia
137 E3 **Leavenworth** U.S.A.
141 E2 **Lebanon** *MO* U.S.A.
141 E2 **Lebanon** *NH* U.S.A.
134 B2 **Lebanon** *OR* U.S.A.
141 D2 **Lebanon** *PA* U.S.A.
89 E3 **Lebedyan'** Russia
91 C1 **Lebedyn** Ukr.
104 C2 **Le Blanc** France
103 D1 **Lębork** Pol.
123 C1 **Lebowakgomo** S. Africa
106 B2 **Lebrija** Spain
153 A4 **Lebu** Chile
104 C3 **Le Bugue** France
109 C2 **Lecce** Italy
108 A1 **Lecco** Italy
102 C2 **Lech** *r.* Austria/Ger.
111 B3 **Lechaina** Greece
71 B3 **Lechang** China
102 B1 **Leck** Ger.
104 C3 **Lectoure** France
106 B1 **Ledesma** Spain
104 C2 **Le Dorat** France
128 C2 **Leduc** Can.
137 E1 **Leech Lake** U.S.A.
98 C2 **Leeds** U.K.
98 C2 **Leek** U.K.
100 C1 **Leer (Ostfriesland)** Ger.
143 D3 **Leesburg** U.S.A.
142 B2 **Leesville** U.S.A.
53 C2 **Leeton** Austr.
122 B3 **Leeu-Gamka** S. Africa
100 B1 **Leeuwarden** Neth.
50 A3 **Leeuwin, Cape** Austr.
147 D3 **Leeward Islands** Caribbean Sea
111 B3 **Lefkada** Greece
111 B3 **Lefkada** *i.* Greece
Lefkosia Cyprus *see* Nicosia
64 B1 **Legazpi** Phil.
108 B1 **Legnago** Italy
103 D1 **Legnica** Pol.
75 B1 **Leh** India
104 C2 **Le Havre** France
122 B1 **Lehututu** Botswana
103 D2 **Leibnitz** Austria
99 C2 **Leicester** U.K.
51 C1 **Leichhardt** *r.* Austr.
100 B1 **Leiden** Neth.
100 A2 **Leie** *r.* Belgium
52 A2 **Leigh Creek** Austr.
93 E3 **Leikanger** Norway
101 D1 **Leine** *r.* Ger.
97 C2 **Leinster** *reg.* Ireland
101 F2 **Leipzig** Ger.
92 F2 **Leiranger** Norway
106 B2 **Leiria** Port.
93 E4 **Leirvik** Norway
97 C2 **Leixlip** Ireland
71 B3 **Leiyang** China
71 B3 **Leizhou** China
71 A3 **Leizhou Bandao** *pen.* China
118 B3 **Lékana** Congo
100 B1 **Lelystad** Neth.
153 B6 **Le Maire, Estrecho de** *sea chan.* Arg.
Léman, Lac *l.* France/Switz. *see* Geneva, Lake
104 C2 **Le Mans** France

137 D2 **Le Mars** U.S.A.
154 C2 **Leme** Brazil
Lemesos Cyprus *see* **Limassol**
101 D1 **Lemförde** Ger.
127 G2 **Lemieux Islands** Can.
136 C1 **Lemmon** U.S.A.
135 C3 **Lemoore** U.S.A.
131 D1 **Le Moyne, Lac** *l.* Can.
62 A1 **Lemro** *r.* Myanmar
109 C2 **Le Murge** *hills* Italy
83 J2 **Lena** *r.* Russia
100 C1 **Lengerich** Ger.
71 B3 **Lengshuijiang** China
91 D2 **Lenine** Ukr.
Leningrad Russia *see* **St Petersburg**
91 D2 **Leningradskaya** Russia
77 D3 **Lenin Peak** Kyrg./Tajik.
Leninsk Kazakh. *see* **Baykonyr**
89 E3 **Leninskiy** Russia
100 A2 **Lens** Belgium
104 C1 **Lens** France
83 I2 **Lensk** Russia
103 D2 **Lenti** Hungary
109 C3 **Lentini** *Sicily* Italy
114 B3 **Léo** Burkina Faso
103 D2 **Leoben** Austria
99 B2 **Leominster** U.K.
144 B2 **León** Mex.
146 B3 **León** Nic.
106 B1 **León** Spain
122 A1 **Leonardville** Namibia
50 B2 **Leonora** Austr.
155 D2 **Leopoldina** Brazil
123 C1 **Lephalale** S. Africa
123 C1 **Lephepe** Botswana
123 C3 **Lephoi** S. Africa
71 B3 **Leping** China
105 C2 **Le Puy-en-Velay** France
150 A2 **Lérida** Col.
106 C1 **Lerma** Spain
111 C3 **Leros** *i.* Greece
130 C1 **Le Roy, Lac** *l.* Can.
93 F4 **Lerum** Sweden
96 □ **Lerwick** U.K.
111 C3 **Lesbos** *i.* Greece
147 C3 **Les Cayes** Haiti
69 C3 **Leshan** China
86 D2 **Leshukonskoye** Russia
109 D2 **Leskovac** Serbia
104 B2 **Lesneven** France
89 E2 **Lesnoye** Russia
83 H3 **Lesosibirsk** Russia
123 C2 **Lesotho** *country* Africa
66 B1 **Lesozavodsk** Russia
104 B2 **Les Sables-d'Olonne** France
147 D3 **Lesser Antilles** *is* Caribbean Sea
81 C1 **Lesser Caucasus** *mts* Asia
128 C2 **Lesser Slave Lake** Can.
58 B3 **Lesser Sunda Islands** *is* Indon.
105 C3 **Les Vans** France
Lesvos *i.* Greece *see* **Lesbos**
103 D1 **Leszno** Pol.
99 C3 **Letchworth Garden City** U.K.
128 C3 **Lethbridge** Can.
150 C1 **Lethem** Guyana
59 C3 **Leti, Kepulauan** *is* Indon.
150 B2 **Leticia** Col.
123 C1 **Letlhakeng** Botswana
104 C1 **Le Touquet-Paris-Plage** France
99 D3 **Le Tréport** France
63 A2 **Letsok-aw Kyun** *i.* Myanmar
123 C2 **Letsopa** S. Africa
97 C1 **Letterkenny** Ireland
105 C3 **Leucate, Étang de** *l.* France
60 A1 **Leuser, Gunung** *mt.* Indon.
100 B2 **Leuven** Belgium
92 F3 **Levanger** Norway
139 C2 **Levelland** U.S.A.
50 B1 **Lévêque, Cape** Austr.
100 C2 **Leverkusen** Ger.
103 D2 **Levice** Slovakia
54 C2 **Levin** N.Z.
131 C2 **Lévis** Can.
89 E3 **Lev Tolstoy** Russia
99 D3 **Lewes** U.K.
96 A1 **Lewis, Isle of** *i.* U.K.
140 C3 **Lewisburg** U.S.A.
134 D1 **Lewis Range** *mts* U.S.A.
134 C1 **Lewiston** *ID* U.S.A.
141 E2 **Lewiston** *ME* U.S.A.
134 E1 **Lewistown** U.S.A.
140 C3 **Lexington** *KY* U.S.A.
136 D2 **Lexington** *NE* U.S.A.
141 D3 **Lexington** *VA* U.S.A.
64 B1 **Leyte** *i.* Phil.
109 C2 **Lezhë** Albania
89 F2 **Lezhnevo** Russia
89 E3 **L'gov** Russia
68 C2 **Lharigarbo** China
75 D2 **Lhasa** China
75 C2 **Lhazê** China
60 A1 **Lhokseumawe** Indon.
111 B3 **Liakoura** *mt.* Greece
67 B3 **Liancourt Rocks** *i.* N. Pacific Ocean
71 B3 **Lianhua** China
71 B3 **Lianjiang** China
70 C1 **Lianshan** China
70 B2 **Lianyungang** China
71 B3 **Lianzhou** China
70 B2 **Liaocheng** China
70 C1 **Liaodong Bandao** *pen.* China
70 C1 **Liaodong Wan** *b.* China
65 A1 **Liao He** *r.* China
70 C1 **Liaoning** *prov.* China
65 A1 **Liaoyang** China
65 B1 **Liaoyuan** China
128 B1 **Liard** *r.* Can.
134 C1 **Libby** U.S.A.
118 B2 **Libenge** Dem. Rep. Congo
136 C3 **Liberal** U.S.A.
103 D1 **Liberec** Czech Rep.
114 B4 **Liberia** *country* Africa
146 B3 **Liberia** Costa Rica
150 B1 **Libertad** Venez.
100 B3 **Libin** Belgium
104 B3 **Libourne** France
118 A2 **Libreville** Gabon
115 D2 **Libya** *country* Africa
115 E2 **Libyan Desert** Egypt/Libya
116 A1 **Libyan Plateau** Egypt/Libya
108 B3 **Licata** *Sicily* Italy
Licheng China *see* **Lipu**
121 C2 **Lichinga** Moz.
101 E2 **Lichte** Ger.
123 C2 **Lichtenburg** S. Africa
101 E2 **Lichtenfels** Ger.
88 C3 **Lida** Belarus
93 F4 **Lidköping** Sweden
50 C2 **Liebig, Mount** Austr.
105 D2 **Liechtenstein** *country* Europe
100 B2 **Liège** Belgium
92 J3 **Lieksa** Fin.
119 C2 **Lienart** Dem. Rep. Congo
63 B2 **Liên Nghia** Vietnam
102 C2 **Lienz** Austria
88 B2 **Liepāja** Latvia
102 C2 **Liezen** Austria
97 C2 **Liffey** *r.* Ireland
97 C1 **Lifford** Ireland
53 C1 **Lightning Ridge** Austr.
121 C2 **Ligonha** *r.* Moz.
105 D3 **Ligurian Sea** France/Italy
119 C4 **Likasi** Dem. Rep. Congo
128 B2 **Likely** Can.
89 E2 **Likhoslavl'** Russia
61 B1 **Liku** Indon.
105 D3 **L'Île-Rousse** *Corsica* France
71 B3 **Liling** China
93 F4 **Lilla Edet** Sweden
100 B2 **Lille** Belgium
105 C1 **Lille** France
Lille Bælt *sea chan.* Denmark *see* **Little Belt**
93 F3 **Lillehammer** Norway
93 F4 **Lillestrøm** Norway
128 B2 **Lillooet** Can.
121 C2 **Lilongwe** Malawi
64 B2 **Liloy** Phil.
150 A3 **Lima** Peru
140 C2 **Lima** U.S.A.
80 B2 **Limassol** Cyprus
97 C1 **Limavady** U.K.
153 B4 **Limay** *r.* Arg.
101 F2 **Limbach-Oberfrohna** Ger.
88 B2 **Limbaži** Latvia
118 A2 **Limbe** Cameroon
100 D2 **Limburg an der Lahn** Ger.
122 B2 **Lime Acres** S. Africa
154 C2 **Limeira** Brazil
97 B2 **Limerick** Ireland
93 E4 **Limfjorden** *sea chan.* Denmark
111 C3 **Limnos** *i.* Greece
104 C2 **Limoges** France
136 C3 **Limon** U.S.A.
104 C3 **Limoux** France
123 C1 **Limpopo** *prov.* S. Africa
121 C3 **Limpopo** *r.* S. Africa/Zimbabwe
64 A1 **Linapacan** *i.* Phil.
153 A4 **Linares** Chile
145 C2 **Linares** Mex.
106 C2 **Linares** Spain
62 B1 **Lincang** China
Linchuan China *see* **Fuzhou**
98 C2 **Lincoln** U.K.
140 B2 **Lincoln** *IL* U.S.A.
141 F1 **Lincoln** *ME* U.S.A.
137 D2 **Lincoln** *NE* U.S.A.
151 C1 **Linden** Guyana
142 C1 **Linden** U.S.A.
119 C2 **Lindi** *r.* Dem. Rep. Congo
119 D3 **Lindi** Tanz.
Lindisfarne *i.* U.K. *see* **Holy Island**
80 A2 **Lindos** Greece
141 D2 **Lindsay** Can.
49 H2 **Line Islands** Kiribati
70 B2 **Linfen** China
64 B1 **Lingayen** Phil.
70 B2 **Lingbao** China
123 C3 **Lingelethu** S. Africa
123 C3 **Lingelihle** S. Africa
100 C1 **Lingen (Ems)** Ger.
60 B2 **Lingga, Kepulauan** *is* Indon.
71 B3 **Lingling** China
71 A3 **Lingshan** China
71 A4 **Lingshui** China
114 A3 **Linguère** Senegal
63 B2 **Linh, Ngok** *mt.* Vietnam
155 D1 **Linhares** Brazil
93 G4 **Linköping** Sweden
66 B1 **Linkou** China
70 B2 **Linqing** China
154 C2 **Lins** Brazil
136 C1 **Linton** U.S.A.
69 D2 **Linxi** China
69 C2 **Linxia** China
70 B2 **Linyi** *Shandong* China

70 B2 Linyi *Shandong* China
70 B2 Linying China
102 C2 Linz Austria
105 C3 Lion, Golfe du *g.* France
109 B3 Lipari Italy
108 B3 Lipari, Isole *is* Italy
89 E3 Lipetsk Russia
110 B1 Lipova Romania
101 D2 Lippstadt Ger.
71 B3 Lipu China
76 C1 Lisakovsk Kazakh.
118 C2 Lisala Dem. Rep. Congo
Lisboa Port. *see* Lisbon
106 B2 Lisbon Port.
97 C1 Lisburn U.K.
97 B2 Liscannor Bay Ireland
104 C2 Lisieux France
99 A3 Liskeard U.K.
89 E3 Liski Russia
53 D1 Lismore Austr.
97 C1 Lisnaskea U.K.
97 B2 Listowel Ireland
71 A3 Litang *Guangxi* China
68 C2 Litang *Sichuan* China
140 B3 Litchfield *IL* U.S.A.
137 E1 Litchfield *MN* U.S.A.
53 D2 Lithgow Austr.
111 B3 Lithino, Akrotirio *pt* Greece
88 B2 Lithuania *country* Europe
102 C1 Litoměřice Czech Rep.
146 C2 Little Abaco *i.* Bahamas
73 D3 Little Andaman *i.* India
93 E4 Little Belt *sea chan.* Denmark
137 E1 Little Falls U.S.A.
139 C2 Littlefield U.S.A.
99 C3 Littlehampton U.K.
122 A2 Little Karas Berg *plat.* Namibia
122 B3 Little Karoo *plat.* S. Africa
96 A2 Little Minch *sea chan.* U.K.
136 C1 Little Missouri *r.* U.S.A.
63 A3 Little Nicobar *i.* India
142 B2 Little Rock U.S.A.
141 E2 Littleton U.S.A.
70 B2 Liujiachang China
71 A3 Liupanshui China
71 A3 Liuzhou China
111 B3 Livadeia Greece
88 C2 Līvāni Latvia
50 B1 Liveringa Austr.
138 C2 Livermore, Mount U.S.A.
131 D2 Liverpool Can.
98 B2 Liverpool U.K.
127 F2 Liverpool, Cape Can.
53 C2 Liverpool Range *mts* Austr.
134 D1 Livingston *MT* U.S.A.
139 E2 Livingston *TX* U.S.A.
139 D2 Livingston, Lake U.S.A.
120 B2 Livingstone Zambia
109 C2 Livno Bos. & Herz.
89 E3 Livny Russia
140 C2 Livonia U.S.A.
108 B2 Livorno Italy
119 D3 Liwale Tanz.
70 B2 Liyang China
99 A4 Lizard Point U.K.
108 B1 Ljubljana Slovenia
93 G3 Ljungan *r.* Sweden
93 F4 Ljungby Sweden
93 G3 Ljusdal Sweden
93 G3 Ljusnan *r.* Sweden
99 B3 Llandeilo U.K.
99 B3 Llandovery U.K.
99 B2 Llandrindod Wells U.K.
98 B2 Llandudno U.K.
99 A3 Llanelli U.K.
98 A2 Llangefni U.K.
139 C2 Llano Estacado *plain* U.S.A.
150 B1 Llanos *plain* Col./Venez.
107 D1 Lleida Spain
99 A2 Lleyn Peninsula U.K.
107 C2 Llíria Spain
128 B2 Lloyd George, Mount Can.
129 D2 Lloyd Lake Can.
129 C2 Lloydminster Can.
152 B3 Llullaillaco, Volcán *vol.* Chile
123 C2 Lobatse Botswana
120 A2 Lobito Angola
101 F1 Loburg Ger.
96 B2 Lochaber *reg.* U.K.
104 C2 Loches France
96 B2 Lochgilphead U.K.
96 B1 Lochinver U.K.
96 A2 Lochmaddy U.K.
96 C2 Lochnagar *mt.* U.K.
52 A2 Lock Austr.
96 C3 Lockerbie U.K.
139 D3 Lockhart U.S.A.
141 D2 Lock Haven U.S.A.
141 D2 Lockport U.S.A.
63 B2 Lôc Ninh Vietnam
105 C3 Lodève France
86 C2 Lodeynoye Pole Russia
92 F2 Løding Norway
119 D2 Lodwar Kenya
103 D1 Łódź Pol.
62 B2 Loei Thai.
122 A3 Loeriesfontein S. Africa
92 F2 Lofoten *is* Norway
134 D2 Logan U.S.A.
126 B2 Logan, Mount Can.
140 B2 Logansport U.S.A.
108 B1 Logatec Slovenia
106 C1 Logroño Spain
101 D1 Löhne Ger.
101 D1 Lohne (Oldenburg) Ger.
62 A2 Loikaw Myanmar
104 B2 Loire *r.* France
150 A2 Loja Ecuador
106 C2 Loja Spain
92 I2 Lokan tekojärvi *resr* Fin.
74 B1 Lōkār Afgh.
100 B2 Lokeren Belgium
122 B1 Lokgwabe Botswana
119 D2 Lokichar Kenya
119 D2 Lokichokio Kenya
89 D2 Loknya Russia
115 C4 Lokoja Nigeria
89 D3 Lokot' Russia
88 C2 Loksa Estonia
127 G2 Loks Land *i.* Can.
119 D3 Loliondo Tanz.
93 F4 Lolland *i.* Denmark
122 B2 Lolwane S. Africa
110 B2 Lom Bulg.
93 E3 Lom Norway
119 C2 Lomami *r.* Dem. Rep. Congo
153 C4 Lomas de Zamora Arg.
61 C2 Lombok *i.* Indon.
61 C2 Lombok, Selat *sea chan.* Indon.
114 C4 Lomé Togo
118 C3 Lomela *r.* Dem. Rep. Congo
100 B2 Lommel Belgium
96 B2 Lomond, Loch *l.* U.K.
88 C2 Lomonosov Russia
135 B4 Lompoc U.S.A.
63 B2 Lom Sak Thai.
103 E1 Łomża Pol.
130 B2 London Can.
99 C3 London U.K.
140 C3 London U.S.A.
97 C1 Londonderry U.K.
50 B1 Londonderry, Cape Austr.
154 B2 Londrina Brazil
83 M2 Longa, Proliv *sea chan.* Russia
61 C1 Long Akah *Sarawak* Malaysia
143 E2 Long Bay U.S.A.
135 C4 Long Beach U.S.A.
97 C2 Longford Ireland
61 C2 Longiram Indon.
147 C2 Long Island Bahamas
130 C1 Long Island Can.
59 D3 Long Island P.N.G.
141 E2 Long Island U.S.A.
130 B2 Longlac Can.
130 B2 Long Lake Can.
136 B2 Longmont U.S.A.
70 A2 Longnan China
140 C2 Long Point Can.
71 B3 Longquan China
131 E2 Long Range Mountains Can.
51 D2 Longreach Austr.
99 D2 Long Stratton U.K.
98 B1 Longtown U.K.
105 D2 Longuyon France
139 E2 Longview *TX* U.S.A.
134 B1 Longview *WA* U.S.A.
70 A2 Longxi China
71 B3 Longxi Shan *mt.* China
63 B2 Long Xuyên Vietnam
71 B3 Longyan China
82 C1 Longyearbyen Svalbard
102 B2 Lons-le-Saunier France
143 E2 Lookout, Cape U.S.A.
97 B2 Loop Head Ireland
63 B2 Lop Buri Thai.
64 B1 Lopez Phil.
68 C2 Lop Nur *salt flat* China
118 B2 Lopori *r.* Dem. Rep. Congo
74 A2 Lora, Hāmūn-i- *dry lake* Afgh./Pak.
106 B2 Lora del Río Spain
140 C2 Lorain U.S.A.
74 A1 Loralai Pak.
107 C2 Lorca Spain
48 E5 Lord Howe Island Austr.
138 B2 Lordsburg U.S.A.
155 C2 Lorena Brazil
152 B2 Loreto Bol.
144 A2 Loreto Mex.
104 B2 Lorient France
96 B2 Lorn, Firth of *est.* U.K.
52 B3 Lorne Austr.
138 B1 Los Alamos U.S.A.
139 D3 Los Aldamas Mex.
153 A4 Los Ángeles Chile
135 C4 Los Angeles U.S.A.
135 B3 Los Banos U.S.A.
152 B3 Los Blancos Arg.
91 E1 Losevo Russia
108 B2 Lošinj *i.* Croatia
144 B2 Los Mochis Mex.
118 B2 Losombo Dem. Rep. Congo
147 D3 Los Roques, Islas *is* Venez.
96 C2 Lossiemouth U.K.
150 B1 Los Teques Venez.
152 A4 Los Vilos Chile
104 C3 Lot *r.* France
96 C1 Loth U.K.
119 D2 Lotikipi Plain Kenya/Sudan
118 C3 Loto Dem. Rep. Congo
89 E2 Lotoshino Russia
62 B1 Louangnamtha Laos
62 B2 Louangphabang Laos
118 B3 Loubomo Congo
104 B2 Loudéac France
71 B3 Loudi China
118 B3 Loudima Congo
114 A3 Louga Senegal
99 C2 Loughborough U.K.
97 B2 Loughrea Ireland
105 D2 Louhans France

97 B2 **Louisburgh** Ireland
142 B2 **Louisiana** *state* U.S.A.
140 B3 **Louisville** *KY* U.S.A.
142 C2 **Louisville** *MS* U.S.A.
86 C2 **Loukhi** Russia
130 C1 **Loups Marins, Lacs des** *lakes* Can.
104 B3 **Lourdes** France
151 C1 **Lourenço** Brazil
106 B1 **Lousã** Port.
53 C2 **Louth** Austr.
98 C2 **Louth** U.K.
Louvain Belgium *see* **Leuven**
89 D2 **Lovat'** *r.* Russia
110 B2 **Lovech** Bulg.
136 B2 **Loveland** U.S.A.
135 C2 **Lovelock** U.S.A.
139 C2 **Lovington** U.S.A.
119 C3 **Lowa** Dem. Rep. Congo
141 E2 **Lowell** U.S.A.
128 C3 **Lower Arrow Lake** Can.
54 B2 **Lower Hutt** N.Z.
97 C1 **Lower Lough Erne** *l.* U.K.
128 B2 **Lower Post** Can.
99 D2 **Lowestoft** U.K.
103 D1 **Łowicz** Pol.
141 D2 **Lowville** U.S.A.
52 B2 **Loxton** Austr.
Loyang China *see* **Luoyang**
48 F4 **Loyauté, Îles** *is* New Caledonia
89 D3 **Loyew** Belarus
92 F2 **Løypskardtinden** *mt.* Norway
109 C2 **Loznica** Serbia
91 D2 **Lozova** Ukr.
120 B2 **Luacano** Angola
70 B2 **Lu'an** China
120 A1 **Luanda** Angola
121 C2 **Luangwa** *r.* Zambia
121 B2 **Luanshya** Zambia
106 B1 **Luarca** Spain
120 B2 **Luau** Angola
103 E1 **Lubaczów** Pol.
120 A2 **Lubango** Angola
119 C3 **Lubao** Dem. Rep. Congo
103 E1 **Lubartów** Pol.
101 D1 **Lübbecke** Ger.
139 C2 **Lubbock** U.S.A.
101 E1 **Lübeck** Ger.
69 E2 **Lubei** China
87 E3 **Lubenka** Kazakh.
103 D1 **Lubin** Pol.
103 E1 **Lublin** Pol.
91 C1 **Lubny** Ukr.
61 C1 **Lubok Antu** *Sarawak* Malaysia
101 E1 **Lübow** Ger.
101 E1 **Lübtheen** Ger.
119 C3 **Lubudi** Dem. Rep. Congo
60 B2 **Lubuklinggau** Indon.
119 C4 **Lubumbashi** Dem. Rep. Congo
120 B2 **Lubungu** Zambia
119 C3 **Lubutu** Dem. Rep. Congo
120 A1 **Lucala** Angola
97 C2 **Lucan** Ireland
120 B1 **Lucapa** Angola
96 B3 **Luce Bay** U.K.
154 B2 **Lucélia** Brazil
64 B1 **Lucena** Phil.
106 C2 **Lucena** Spain
103 D2 **Lučenec** Slovakia
109 C2 **Lucera** Italy
105 D2 **Lucerne** Switz.
101 E1 **Lüchow (Wendland)** Ger.
120 A2 **Lucira** Angola
101 F1 **Luckenwalde** Ger.
122 B2 **Luckhoff** S. Africa
75 C2 **Lucknow** India
120 B2 **Lucusse** Angola
Lüda China *see* **Dalian**
100 C2 **Lüdenscheid** Ger.
101 E1 **Lüder** Ger.
120 A3 **Lüderitz** Namibia
74 B1 **Ludhiana** India
140 B2 **Ludington** U.S.A.
99 B2 **Ludlow** U.K.
135 C4 **Ludlow** U.S.A.
110 C2 **Ludogorie** *reg.* Bulg.
93 G3 **Ludvika** Sweden
102 B2 **Ludwigsburg** Ger.
101 F1 **Ludwigsfelde** Ger.
101 D3 **Ludwigshafen am Rhein** Ger.
101 E1 **Ludwigslust** Ger.
88 C2 **Ludza** Latvia
118 C3 **Luebo** Dem. Rep. Congo
120 A2 **Luena** Angola
70 A2 **Lüeyang** China
71 B3 **Lufeng** China
139 E2 **Lufkin** U.S.A.
88 C2 **Luga** Russia
88 C2 **Luga** *r.* Russia
105 D2 **Lugano** Switz.
121 C2 **Lugenda** *r.* Moz.
97 C2 **Lugnaquilla** *h.* Ireland
106 B1 **Lugo** Spain
110 B1 **Lugoj** Romania
91 D2 **Luhans'k** Ukr.
119 D3 **Luhombero** Tanz.
90 B1 **Luhyny** Ukr.
120 B2 **Luiana** Angola
118 C3 **Luilaka** *r.* Dem. Rep. Congo
105 D2 **Luino** Italy
92 I2 **Luiro** *r.* Fin.
118 C3 **Luiza** Dem. Rep. Congo
70 B2 **Lujiang** China
109 C2 **Lukavac** Bos. & Herz.
118 B3 **Lukenie** *r.* Dem. Rep. Congo
138 A2 **Lukeville** U.S.A.
89 E3 **Lukhovitsy** Russia
103 E1 **Łuków** Pol.
120 B2 **Lukulu** Zambia
92 H2 **Luleå** Sweden
92 H2 **Luleälven** *r.* Sweden
110 C2 **Lüleburgaz** Turkey
70 B2 **Lüliang Shan** *mts* China
61 C2 **Lumajang** Indon.
75 C1 **Lumajangdong Co** *salt l.* China
120 B2 **Lumbala Kaquengue** Angola
120 B2 **Lumbala N'guimbo** Angola
143 E2 **Lumberton** U.S.A.
61 C1 **Lumbis** Indon.
106 B1 **Lumbrales** Spain
63 B2 **Lumphăt** Cambodia
129 D2 **Lumsden** Can.
54 A3 **Lumsden** N.Z.
93 F4 **Lund** Sweden
121 C2 **Lundazi** Zambia
99 A3 **Lundy** *i.* U.K.
101 E1 **Lüneburg** Ger.
101 E1 **Lüneburger Heide** *reg.* Ger.
100 C2 **Lünen** Ger.
105 D2 **Lunéville** France
120 B2 **Lunga** *r.* Zambia
114 A4 **Lungi** Sierra Leone
62 A1 **Lunglei** India
120 B2 **Lungwebungu** *r.* Zambia
74 B2 **Luni** *r.* India
88 C3 **Luninyets** Belarus
114 A4 **Lunsar** Sierra Leone
77 E2 **Luntai** China
71 A3 **Luodian** China
71 B3 **Luoding** China
70 B2 **Luohe** China
70 B2 **Luoyang** China
121 B2 **Lupane** Zimbabwe
110 B1 **Lupeni** Romania
121 C2 **Lupilichi** Moz.
101 F2 **Luppa** Ger.
121 D2 **Lúrio** Moz.
121 D2 **Lurio** *r.* Moz.
121 B2 **Lusaka** Zambia
118 C3 **Lusambo** Dem. Rep. Congo
109 C2 **Lushnjë** Albania
136 C2 **Lusk** U.S.A.
76 B3 **Lüt, Kavīr-e** *des.* Iran
99 C3 **Luton** U.K.
61 C1 **Lutong** *Sarawak* Malaysia
129 C1 **Łutselk'e** Can.
90 B1 **Luts'k** Ukr.
122 B2 **Lutzputs** S. Africa
122 A3 **Lutzville** S. Africa
117 C4 **Luuq** Somalia
137 D2 **Luverne** U.S.A.
119 C3 **Luvua** *r.* Dem. Rep. Congo
123 D1 **Luvuvhu** *r.* S. Africa
119 D2 **Luwero** Uganda
59 C3 **Luwuk** Indon.
100 C3 **Luxembourg** *country* Europe
100 C3 **Luxembourg** Lux.
105 D2 **Luxeuil-les-Bains** France
123 C3 **Luxolweni** S. Africa
116 B2 **Luxor** Egypt
100 B2 **Luyksgestel** Neth.
86 D2 **Luza** Russia
Luzern Switz. *see* **Lucerne**
71 A3 **Luzhou** China
154 C1 **Luziânia** Brazil
151 D2 **Luzilândia** Brazil
64 B1 **Luzon** *i.* Phil.
71 C3 **Luzon Strait** Phil./Taiwan
90 A2 **L'viv** Ukr.
L'vov Ukr. *see* **L'viv**
88 C3 **Lyakhavichy** Belarus
92 G3 **Lycksele** Sweden
88 C3 **Lyel'chytsy** Belarus
88 C3 **Lyepyel'** Belarus
99 B3 **Lyme Bay** U.K.
141 D3 **Lynchburg** U.S.A.
129 D2 **Lynn Lake** Can.
129 D1 **Lynx Lake** Can.
105 C2 **Lyon** France
89 D2 **Lyozna** Belarus
86 E3 **Lys'va** Russia
91 D2 **Lysychans'k** Ukr.
98 B2 **Lytham St Anne's** U.K.
88 C3 **Lyuban'** Belarus
89 E2 **Lyubertsy** Russia
90 B1 **Lyubeshiv** Ukr.
89 F2 **Lyubim** Russia
91 D2 **Lyubotyn** Ukr.
89 D2 **Lyubytino** Russia
89 D3 **Lyudinovo** Russia

M

80 B2 **Ma'ān** Jordan
88 C2 **Maardu** Estonia
100 B2 **Maas** *r.* Neth.
100 B2 **Maaseik** Belgium
64 B1 **Maasin** Phil.
100 B2 **Maastricht** Neth.
121 C3 **Mabalane** Moz.
150 C1 **Mabaruma** Guyana
121 C3 **Mabote** Moz.
122 B2 **Mabule** Botswana
122 B1 **Mabutsane** Botswana
155 D2 **Macaé** Brazil
121 C2 **Macaloge** Moz.
126 E2 **MacAlpine Lake** Can.
71 B3 **Macao** *aut. reg.* China
151 C1 **Macapá** Brazil

150 A2 Macará Ecuador
155 D1 Macarani Brazil
123 D1 Macarretane Moz.
151 E2 Macas Ecuador
98 B2 Macclesfield U.K.
81 B2 Macdonald, Lake imp. l. Austr.
50 C2 Macdonnell Ranges mts Austr.
130 A1 MacDowell Lake Can.
106 B1 Macedo de Cavaleiros Port.
52 B3 Macedon mt. Austr.
109 D2 Macedonia country Europe
151 E2 Maceió Brazil
108 B2 Macerata Italy
52 A2 Macfarlane, Lake imp. l. Austr.
97 B3 Macgillycuddy's Reeks mts Ireland
74 A2 Mach Pak.
155 C2 Machado Brazil
121 C3 Machaila Moz.
119 D3 Machakos Kenya
150 A2 Machala Ecuador
68 C2 Machali China
121 C3 Machanga Moz.
70 B2 Macheng China
141 F2 Machias U.S.A.
150 A1 Machiques Venez.
150 A3 Machu Picchu tourist site Peru
123 D2 Macia Moz.
110 C1 Măcin Romania
114 B3 Macina Mali
53 D1 Macintyre r. Austr.
51 D2 Mackay Austr.
50 B2 Mackay, Lake imp. l. Austr.
129 C1 MacKay Lake Can.
128 B2 Mackenzie Can.
128 A1 Mackenzie r. Can.
126 B2 Mackenzie Bay Can.
126 D1 Mackenzie King Island Can.
128 A1 Mackenzie Mountains Can.
129 D2 Macklin Can.
53 D3 Macksville Austr.
53 D1 Maclean Austr.
50 A2 MacLeod, Lake dry lake Austr.
140 A2 Macomb U.S.A.
108 A2 Macomer Sardinia Italy
105 C2 Mâcon France
143 D2 Macon GA U.S.A.
137 E3 Macon MO U.S.A.
53 C2 Macquarie r. Austr.
48 E6 Macquarie Island S. Pacific Ocean
53 C2 Macquarie Marshes Austr.
97 B3 Macroom Ireland
41 A2 Macumba watercourse Austr.
145 C3 Macuspana Mex.
144 B2 Macuzari, Presa resr Mex.
123 D2 Madadeni S. Africa
121 □D3 Madagascar country Africa
115 D2 Madama Niger
111 B2 Madan Bulg.
59 D3 Madang P.N.G.
150 C2 Madeira r. Brazil
114 A1 Madeira terr. N. Atlantic Ocean
131 D2 Madeleine, Îles de la is Can.
144 B2 Madera Mex.
135 B3 Madera U.S.A.
118 B3 Madingou Congo
140 B3 Madison IN U.S.A.
137 D2 Madison SD U.S.A.
140 B2 Madison WI U.S.A.
140 C3 Madison WV U.S.A.
134 D1 Madison r. U.S.A.
138 B3 Madisonville U.S.A.
61 C2 Madiun Indon.
119 D2 Mado Gashi Kenya

88 C2 Madona Latvia
78 A2 Madrakah Saudi Arabia
Madras India see Chennai
134 B2 Madras U.S.A.
145 C2 Madre, Laguna lag. Mex.
145 B3 Madre del Sur, Sierra mts Mex.
144 B2 Madre Occidental, Sierra mts Mex.
145 B2 Madre Oriental, Sierra mts Mex.
106 C1 Madrid Spain
106 C2 Madridejos Spain
61 C2 Madura i. Indon.
61 C2 Madura, Selat sea chan. Indon.
73 B4 Madurai India
67 C3 Maebashi Japan
62 A2 Mae Hong Son Thai.
62 A1 Mae Sai Thai.
62 A2 Mae Sariang Thai.
62 A2 Mae Suai Thai.
123 C2 Mafeteng Lesotho
119 D3 Mafia Island Tanz.
119 D3 Mafinga Tanz.
154 C3 Mafra Brazil
83 L3 Magadan Russia
147 C4 Magangué Col.
144 A1 Magdalena Mex.
138 B2 Magdalena r. Mex.
144 A2 Magdalena, Bahía b. Mex.
101 E1 Magdeburg Ger.
153 A6 Magellan, Strait of Chile
97 C1 Magherafelt U.K.
87 E3 Magnitogorsk Russia
142 B2 Magnolia U.S.A.
131 D1 Magpie, Lac l. Can.
114 A3 Magta' Lahjar Maur.
151 D2 Maguarinho, Cabo c. Brazil
123 D2 Magude Moz.
62 A1 Magway Myanmar
Magwe Myanmar see Magway
81 C2 Mahābād Iran
74 B2 Mahajan India
121 □D2 Mahajanga Madag.
61 C2 Mahakam r. Indon.
123 C1 Mahalapye Botswana
121 □D2 Mahalevona Madag.
75 C2 Mahanadi r. India
121 □D2 Mahanoro Madag.
63 B2 Maha Sarakham Thai.
79 C2 Mahavavy r. Madag.
78 B2 Mahd adh Dhahab Saudi Arabia
150 C1 Mahdia Guyana
113 K7 Mahé i. Seychelles
74 B2 Mahesana India
74 B2 Mahi r. India
54 C1 Mahia Peninsula N.Z.
123 C2 Mahikeng S. Africa
89 D3 Mahilyow Belarus
74 B2 Mahuva India
110 C2 Mahya Dağı mt. Turkey
74 A1 Maidan Shahr Afgh.
99 D3 Maidstone Can.
115 D3 Maiduguri Nigeria
75 C2 Mailani India
74 B1 Maimanah Afgh.
101 D2 Main r. Ger.
118 B3 Mai-Ndombe, Lac l. Dem. Rep. Congo
101 E3 Main-Donau-Kanal canal Ger.
141 F1 Maine state U.S.A.
62 A1 Maingkwan Myanmar
96 C1 Mainland i. Scotland U.K.
96 □ Mainland i. Scotland U.K.

121 □D2 Maintirano Madag.
101 D2 Mainz Ger.
150 B1 Maiquetía Venez.
53 D2 Maitland N.S.W. Austr.
52 A2 Maitland S.A. Austr.
146 B3 Maíz, Islas del is Nic.
67 C3 Maizuru Japan
61 C2 Majene Indon.
106 D2 Majorca i. Spain
48 F2 Majuro atoll Marshall Is
123 C2 Majwemasweu S. Africa
118 B3 Makabana Congo
58 B3 Makale Indon.
77 E2 Makanshy Kazakh.
109 C2 Makarska Croatia
58 B3 Makassar Indon.
61 C2 Makassar, Selat str. Indon.
Makassar Strait Indon. see Makassar, Selat
76 B2 Makat Kazakh.
123 D2 Makatini Flats lowland S. Africa
114 A4 Makeni Sierra Leone
120 B3 Makgadikgadi depr. Botswana
87 D4 Makhachkala Russia
123 C1 Makhado S. Africa
76 B2 Makhambet Kazakh.
119 D3 Makindu Kenya
77 D1 Makinsk Kazakh.
91 D2 Makiyivka Ukr.
Makkah Saudi Arabia see Mecca
131 E1 Makkovik Can.
103 E2 Makó Hungary
118 B2 Makokou Gabon
119 D3 Makongolosi Tanz.
120 B3 Makopong Botswana
79 D2 Makran reg. Iran/Pak.
74 A2 Makran Coast Range mts Pak.
89 E2 Maksatikha Russia
81 C2 Mākū Iran
62 A1 Makum India
67 B4 Makurazaki Japan
115 C4 Makurdi Nigeria
92 G2 Malá Sweden
146 B4 Mala, Punta pt Panama
118 A2 Malabo Equat. Guinea
60 A1 Malacca, Strait of Indon./ Malaysia
134 D2 Malad City U.S.A.
88 C3 Maladzyechna Belarus
106 C2 Málaga Spain
97 B1 Málainn Mhóir Ireland
48 E3 Malaita i. Solomon Is
117 B4 Malakal South Sudan
48 F4 Malakula i. Vanuatu
61 C2 Malang Indon.
120 A1 Malanje Angola
93 G4 Mälaren l. Sweden
153 B4 Malargüe Arg.
80 B2 Malatya Turkey
121 C2 Malawi country Africa
Malawi, Lake Africa see Nyasa, Lake
89 D2 Malaya Vishera Russia
64 B2 Malaybalay Phil.
81 C2 Malāyer Iran
60 B1 Malaysia country Asia
81 C2 Malazgirt Turkey
103 D1 Malbork Pol.
101 F1 Malchin Ger.
100 A2 Maldegem Belgium
49 H3 Malden Island Kiribati
56 G6 Maldives country Indian Ocean
150 C4 Maldonado Uru.
56 G6 Male Maldives
111 B3 Maleas, Akrotirio pt Greece

103 D2 **Malé Karpaty** *hills* Slovakia
134 C2 **Malheur Lake** U.S.A.
114 B3 **Mali** *country* Africa
114 A3 **Mali** Guinea
58 C3 **Malili** Indon.
119 E3 **Malindi** Kenya
97 C1 **Malin Head** Ireland
111 C2 **Malkara** Turkey
88 C3 **Mal'kavichy** Belarus
110 C2 **Malko Tarnovo** Bulg.
53 C3 **Mallacoota** Austr.
53 C3 **Mallacoota Inlet** *b.* Austr.
96 B2 **Mallaig** U.K.
129 E1 **Mallery Lake** Can.
Mallorca *i.* Spain *see* **Majorca**
97 B2 **Mallow** Ireland
92 H2 **Malmberget** Sweden
100 C2 **Malmedy** Belgium
122 A3 **Malmesbury** S. Africa
93 F4 **Malmö** Sweden
62 B1 **Malong** China
118 C4 **Malonga** Dem. Rep. Congo
93 E3 **Måløy** Norway
89 E2 **Maloyaroslavets** Russia
89 E2 **Maloye Borisovo** Russia
85 H5 **Malta** *country* Europe
88 C2 **Malta** Latvia
134 E1 **Malta** U.S.A.
122 A1 **Maltahöhe** Namibia
98 C1 **Malton** U.K.
Maluku *is* Indon. *see* **Moluccas**
59 C3 **Maluku, Laut** *sea* Indon.
93 F3 **Malung** Sweden
123 C2 **Maluti Mountains** Lesotho
73 B3 **Malvan** India
142 B2 **Malvern** U.S.A.
90 B1 **Malyn** Ukr.
83 L2 **Malyy Anyuy** *r.* Russia
83 K2 **Malyy Lyakhovskiy, Ostrov** *i.* Russia
123 C2 **Mamafubedu** S. Africa
119 C2 **Mambasa** Dem. Rep. Congo
118 B2 **Mambéré** *r.* C.A.R.
123 C2 **Mamelodi** S. Africa
150 B3 **Mamoré** *r.* Bol./Brazil
114 A3 **Mamou** Guinea
61 C2 **Mamuju** Indon.
114 B4 **Man** Côte d'Ivoire
98 A1 **Man, Isle of** *i.* Irish Sea
150 B2 **Manacapuru** Brazil
107 D2 **Manacor** Spain
59 C2 **Manado** Indon.
146 B3 **Managua** Nic.
121 □D3 **Manakara** Madag.
78 B3 **Manākhah** Yemen
79 C2 **Manama** Bahrain
59 D3 **Manam Island** P.N.G.
121 □D3 **Mananara** *r.* Madag.
121 □D2 **Mananara Avaratra** Madag.
121 □D3 **Mananjary** Madag.
114 A3 **Manantali, Lac de** *l.* Mali
77 E2 **Manas Hu** *l.* China
59 C3 **Manatuto** East Timor
62 A2 **Man-aung Kyun** *i.* Myanmar
150 B2 **Manaus** Brazil
80 B2 **Manavgat** Turkey
98 B2 **Manchester** U.K.
141 E2 **Manchester** U.S.A.
121 □D3 **Mandabe** Madag.
93 E4 **Mandal** Norway
59 D3 **Mandala, Puncak** *mt.* Indon.
62 A1 **Mandalay** Myanmar
69 D1 **Mandalgovĭ** Mongolia
136 C1 **Mandan** U.S.A.
118 B1 **Mandara Mountains** Cameroon/Nigeria
108 A3 **Mandas** *Sardinia* Italy
100 C2 **Manderscheid** Ger.
74 B1 **Mandi** India
114 B3 **Mandiana** Guinea
75 C2 **Mandla** India
121 □D2 **Mandritsara** Madag.
74 B2 **Mandsaur** India
50 A3 **Mandurah** Austr.
73 B3 **Mandya** India
108 B1 **Manerbio** Italy
90 B1 **Manevychi** Ukr.
109 C2 **Manfredonia** Italy
114 B3 **Manga** Burkina Faso
118 B3 **Mangai** Dem. Rep. Congo
54 C1 **Mangakino** N.Z.
110 C2 **Mangalia** Romania
Mangalore India *see* **Mangaluru**
73 B3 **Mangaluru** India
123 C2 **Mangaung** S. Africa
61 B2 **Manggar** Indon.
76 B2 **Mangistau** Kazakh.
121 C2 **Mangochi** Malawi
59 C3 **Mangole** *i.* Indon.
154 B3 **Mangueirinha** Brazil
69 E1 **Mangui** China
137 D3 **Manhattan** U.S.A.
121 C3 **Manhica** Moz.
155 D2 **Manhuaçu** Brazil
121 □D2 **Mania** *r.* Madag.
108 B1 **Maniago** Italy
150 B2 **Manicoré** Brazil
131 D2 **Manicouagan** *r.* Can.
131 D1 **Manicouagan, Petit Lac** *l.* Can.
131 D1 **Manicouagan, Réservoir** *resr* Can.
79 B2 **Manīfah** Saudi Arabia
64 B1 **Manila** Phil.
53 D2 **Manilla** Austr.
111 C3 **Manisa** Turkey
140 B2 **Manistee** U.S.A.
129 E2 **Manitoba** *prov.* Can.
129 E2 **Manitoba, Lake** Can.
140 B1 **Manitou Islands** U.S.A.
130 B2 **Manitoulin Island** Can.
140 B2 **Manitowoc** U.S.A.
130 C2 **Maniwaki** Can.
150 A1 **Manizales** Col.
137 E2 **Mankato** U.S.A.
114 B4 **Mankono** Côte d'Ivoire
129 D3 **Mankota** Can.
73 C4 **Mankulam** Sri Lanka
74 B2 **Manmad** India
73 B4 **Mannar, Gulf of** India/Sri Lanka
101 D3 **Mannheim** Ger.
128 C2 **Manning** Can.
52 A2 **Mannum** Austr.
129 C2 **Mannville** Can.
59 C3 **Manokwari** Indon.
119 C3 **Manono** Dem. Rep. Congo
63 A2 **Manoron** Myanmar
105 D3 **Manosque** France
131 C1 **Manouane, Lac** *l.* Can.
107 D1 **Manresa** Spain
121 B2 **Mansa** Zambia
127 F2 **Mansel Island** Can.
92 I2 **Mansel'kya** *ridge* Fin./Russia
53 C3 **Mansfield** Austr.
98 C2 **Mansfield** U.K.
142 B2 **Mansfield** *LA* U.S.A.
140 C2 **Mansfield** *OH* U.S.A.
141 D2 **Mansfield** *PA* U.S.A.
150 A2 **Manta** Ecuador
143 E1 **Manteo** U.S.A.
104 C2 **Mantes-la-Jolie** France
155 C2 **Mantiqueira, Serra da** *mts* Brazil
Mantova Italy *see* **Mantua**
108 B1 **Mantua** Italy
151 C2 **Manuelzinho** Brazil
59 C3 **Manui** *i.* Indon.
54 B1 **Manukau** N.Z.
142 B2 **Many** U.S.A.
119 D3 **Manyoni** Tanz.
106 C2 **Manzanares** Spain
144 B3 **Manzanillo** Mex.
69 D1 **Manzhouli** China
123 D2 **Manzini** Swaziland
115 D3 **Mao** Chad
107 D2 **Maó** Spain
59 D3 **Maoke, Pegunungan** *mts* Indon.
123 C2 **Maokeng** S. Africa
65 A1 **Maokui Shan** *mt.* China
71 B3 **Maoming** China
121 C3 **Mapai** Moz.
75 C1 **Mapam Yumco** *l.* China
145 C3 **Mapastepec** Mex.
144 B2 **Mapimí** Mex.
144 B2 **Mapimí, Bolsón de** *des.* Mex.
121 C3 **Mapinhane** Moz.
129 D3 **Maple Creek** Can.
121 C3 **Maputo** Moz.
123 D2 **Maputo** *r.* Moz./S. Africa
120 A1 **Maquela do Zombo** Angola
153 B5 **Maquinchao** Arg.
137 E2 **Maquoketa** U.S.A.
150 B2 **Maraã** Brazil
151 D2 **Marabá** Brazil
151 C1 **Maracá, Ilha de** *i.* Brazil
150 A1 **Maracaibo** Venez.
150 A1 **Maracaibo, Lake** Venez.
152 C3 **Maracaju, Serra de** *hills* Brazil
150 B1 **Maracay** Venez.
115 D2 **Marādah** Libya
115 C3 **Maradi** Niger
81 C2 **Marāgheh** Iran
151 D2 **Marajó, Baía de** *est.* Brazil
151 C2 **Marajó, Ilha de** *i.* Brazil
79 C2 **Marākī** Iran
119 D2 **Maralal** Kenya
50 C3 **Maralinga** Austr.
81 C2 **Marand** Iran
150 A2 **Marañón** *r.* Peru
130 B2 **Marathon** Can.
143 D4 **Marathon** U.S.A.
106 C2 **Marbella** Spain
50 A2 **Marble Bar** Austr.
123 C1 **Marble Hall** S. Africa
101 D2 **Marburg** Ger.
123 D3 **Marburg** S. Africa
99 D2 **March** U.K.
100 B2 **Marche-en-Famenne** Belgium
106 B2 **Marchena** Spain
152 B4 **Mar Chiquita, Laguna** *l.* Arg.
141 E2 **Marcy, Mount** U.S.A.
74 B1 **Mardan** Pak.
153 C4 **Mar del Plata** Arg.
81 C2 **Mardin** Turkey
96 B2 **Maree, Loch** *l.* U.K.
108 B3 **Marettimo, Isola** *i. Sicily* Italy
89 D2 **Marevo** Russia
138 C2 **Marfa** U.S.A.
73 B3 **Margao** India
50 A3 **Margaret River** Austr.
147 D3 **Margarita, Isla de** *i.* Venez.
123 D3 **Margate** S. Africa
99 D3 **Margate** U.K.
119 C2 **Margherita Peak** Dem. Rep. Congo/Uganda
76 C3 **Mārgō, Dasht-e** *des.* Afgh.
91 C2 **Marhanets'** Ukr.
62 A1 **Mari** Myanmar
152 B3 **María Elena** Chile

156 C5 **Mariana Trench**
 N. Pacific Ocean
142 B2 **Marianna** *AR* U.S.A.
143 C1 **Marianna** *FL* U.S.A.
102 C2 **Mariánské Lázně** Czech Rep.
144 B2 **Marias, Islas** *is* Mex.
 78 B3 **Ma'rib** Yemen
109 C1 **Maribor** Slovenia
117 A4 **Maridi** *watercourse*
 South Sudan
 55 M2 **Marie Byrd Land** *reg.*
 Antarctica
147 D3 **Marie-Galante** *i.* Guadeloupe
 93 G3 **Mariehamn** Fin.
122 A1 **Mariental** Namibia
 93 F4 **Mariestad** Sweden
143 D2 **Marietta** *GA* U.S.A.
140 C3 **Marietta** *OH* U.S.A.
105 D3 **Marignane** France
 83 K3 **Marii, Mys** *pt* Russia
 88 B3 **Marijampol** Lith.
154 C2 **Marília** Brazil
106 B1 **Marín** Spain
109 C3 **Marina di Gioiosa Ionica** Italy
 88 C3 **Mar''ina Horka** Belarus
140 B1 **Marinette** U.S.A.
154 B2 **Maringá** Brazil
106 B2 **Marinha Grande** Port.
140 B2 **Marion** *IN* U.S.A.
140 C2 **Marion** *OH* U.S.A.
143 E2 **Marion** *SC* U.S.A.
140 C3 **Marion** *VA* U.S.A.
143 D2 **Marion, Lake** U.S.A.
 52 A3 **Marion Bay** Austr.
152 B3 **Mariscal José Félix
 Estigarribia** Para.
110 C2 **Maritsa** *r.* Bulg.
 91 D2 **Mariupol'** Ukr.
117 C4 **Marka** Somalia
123 C1 **Marken** S. Africa
100 B1 **Markermeer** *l.* Neth.
 83 I2 **Markha** *r.* Russia
 91 D2 **Markivka** Ukr.
142 B2 **Marksville** U.S.A.
101 D3 **Marktheidenfeld** Ger.
101 F2 **Marktredwitz** Ger.
100 C2 **Marl** Ger.
100 A3 **Marle** France
139 D2 **Marlin** U.S.A.
104 C3 **Marmande** France
111 C2 **Marmara, Sea of** *g.* Turkey
 Marmara Denizi *g.* Turkey *see*
 Marmara, Sea of
111 C3 **Marmaris** Turkey
104 C2 **Marne-la-Vallée** France
121 □D2 **Maroantsetra** Madag.
101 E2 **Maroldsweisach** Ger.
121 □D2 **Maromokotro** *mt.* Madag.
121 C2 **Marondera** Zimbabwe
151 C1 **Maroni** *r.* Fr. Guiana
118 B1 **Maroua** Cameroon
121 □D2 **Marovoay** Madag.
 49 I3 **Marquesas Islands** *is*
 Fr. Polynesia
140 B1 **Marquette** U.S.A.
117 A3 **Marra, Jebel** *mt.* Sudan
117 A3 **Marra, Jebel** *plat.* Sudan
123 D2 **Marracuene** Moz.
114 B1 **Marrakech** Morocco
 52 A1 **Marree** Austr.
121 C2 **Marromeu** Moz.
121 C2 **Marrupa** Moz.
116 B2 **Marsá al 'Alam** Egypt
115 D1 **Marsá al Burayqah** Libya
119 D2 **Marsabit** Kenya
108 B3 **Marsala** Sicily Italy
116 A1 **Marsá Maţrūḩ** Egypt
101 D2 **Marsberg** Ger.

108 B2 **Marsciano** Italy
 53 C2 **Marsden** Austr.
105 D3 **Marseille** France
137 D2 **Marshall** *MN* U.S.A.
137 E3 **Marshall** *MO* U.S.A.
139 E2 **Marshall** *TX* U.S.A.
 48 F2 **Marshall Islands** *country*
 N. Pacific Ocean
137 E2 **Marshalltown** U.S.A.
140 A2 **Marshfield** U.S.A.
143 E3 **Marsh Harbour** Bahamas
142 B3 **Marsh Island** U.S.A.
 88 A2 **Märsta** Sweden
 61 C2 **Martapura** *Kalimantan Selatan*
 Indon.
 60 B2 **Martapura** *Sumatera Selatan*
 Indon.
141 E2 **Martha's Vineyard** *i.* U.S.A.
105 D2 **Martigny** Switz.
103 D2 **Martin** Slovakia
136 C2 **Martin** U.S.A.
145 C3 **Martínez** Mex.
147 D3 **Martinique** *terr.* West Indies
141 D3 **Martinsburg** U.S.A.
140 D3 **Martinsville** U.S.A.
 76 B1 **Martok** Kazakh.
 54 C2 **Marton** N.Z.
107 D1 **Martorell** Spain
106 C2 **Martos** Spain
105 C3 **Marvejols** France
 76 C3 **Mary** Turkm.
 51 E2 **Maryborough** Austr.
122 B2 **Marydale** S. Africa
141 D3 **Maryland** *state* U.S.A.
137 D3 **Marysville** U.S.A.
137 E2 **Maryville** *MO* U.S.A.
143 D1 **Maryville** *TN* U.S.A.
119 D3 **Masai Steppe** *plain* Tanz.
119 D3 **Masaka** Uganda
 65 B2 **Masan** S. Korea
119 D4 **Masasi** Tanz.
 64 B1 **Masbate** Phil.
 64 B1 **Masbate** *i.* Phil.
123 C2 **Maseru** Lesotho
 76 B3 **Mashhad** Iran
123 D2 **Mashishing** S. Africa
 74 A2 **Mashkel, Hamun-i-** *salt flat*
 Pak.
123 C3 **Masibambane** S. Africa
 79 C3 **Masilah, Wādī al** *watercourse*
 Yemen
123 C2 **Masilo** S. Africa
119 D2 **Masindi** Uganda
 79 C2 **Maşīrah, Jazīrat** *i.* Oman
 79 C3 **Maşīrah, Khalīj** *b.* Oman
 81 C2 **Masjed Soleymān** Iran
 97 B2 **Mask, Lough** *l.* Ireland
121 □E2 **Masoala, Tanjona** *c.* Madag.
137 E2 **Mason City** U.S.A.
 Masqaţ Oman *see* **Muscat**
108 B2 **Massa** Italy
141 E2 **Massachusetts** *state* U.S.A.
141 E2 **Massachusetts Bay** U.S.A.
121 C3 **Massangena** Moz.
120 A1 **Massango** Angola
116 B3 **Massawa** Eritrea
141 E2 **Massena** U.S.A.
128 A2 **Masset** Can.
105 C2 **Massif Central** *mts* France
140 C2 **Massillon** U.S.A.
121 C3 **Massinga** Moz.
123 D1 **Massingir** Moz.
 78 A2 **Mastābah** Saudi Arabia
 54 C2 **Masterton** N.Z.
 74 A2 **Mastung** Pak.
 78 A2 **Mastūrah** Saudi Arabia
 88 C3 **Masty** Belarus
 67 B4 **Masuda** Japan

 Masuku Gabon *see* **Franceville**
121 C3 **Masvingo** Zimbabwe
 69 D1 **Matad** Mongolia
118 B3 **Matadi** Dem. Rep. Congo
146 B3 **Matagalpa** Nic.
130 C2 **Matagami** Can.
130 C2 **Matagami, Lac** *l.* Can.
139 D3 **Matagorda Island** U.S.A.
120 A2 **Matala** Angola
114 A3 **Matam** Senegal
144 B2 **Matamoros** *Coahuila* Mex.
145 C2 **Matamoros** *Tamaulipas* Mex.
119 D3 **Matandu** *r.* Tanz.
131 D2 **Matane** Can.
146 B2 **Matanzas** Cuba
 73 C4 **Matara** Sri Lanka
 61 C2 **Mataram** Indon.
 50 C1 **Mataranka** Austr.
107 D1 **Mataró** Spain
123 C3 **Matatiele** S. Africa
 54 A3 **Mataura** N.Z.
 49 G3 **Matā'utu** Wallis and Futuna Is
 54 C1 **Matawai** N.Z.
152 B2 **Mategua** Bol.
145 B2 **Matehuala** Mex.
109 C2 **Matera** Italy
139 D3 **Mathis** U.S.A.
 75 B2 **Mathura** India
 64 B2 **Mati** Phil.
 98 C2 **Matlock** U.K.
123 D2 **Matola** Moz.
 Matou China *see* **Pingguo**
 67 D3 **Matsue** Japan
 66 D2 **Matsumae** Japan
 67 C4 **Matsusaka** Japan
 67 B4 **Matsuyama** Japan
130 B1 **Mattagami** *r.* Can.
105 D2 **Matterhorn** *mt.* Italy/Switz.
134 C2 **Matterhorn** *mt.* U.S.A.
140 B3 **Mattoon** U.S.A.
150 B1 **Maturín** Venez.
123 C2 **Matwabeng** S. Africa
100 A2 **Maubeuge** France
104 C3 **Maubourguet** France
124 E5 **Maui** *i.* U.S.A.
140 C2 **Maumee** *r.* U.S.A.
120 B2 **Maun** Botswana
 62 A1 **Maungdaw** Myanmar
 50 C2 **Maurice, Lake** *imp. l.* Austr.
114 A3 **Mauritania** *country* Africa
113 K9 **Mauritius** *country*
 Indian Ocean
 78 B2 **Māwān, Khashm** *mt.*
 Saudi Arabia
118 B3 **Mawanga** Dem. Rep. Congo
 71 B3 **Mawei** China
 62 A1 **Mawkmai** Myanmar
 62 A1 **Mawlaik** Myanmar
 Mawlamyine Myanmar *see*
 Moulmein
 78 B2 **Mawqaq** Saudi Arabia
 78 B3 **Mawza'** Yemen
108 A3 **Maxia, Punta** *mt.* Sardinia
 Italy
 83 J2 **Maya** *r.* Russia
147 C2 **Mayaguana** *i.* Bahamas
 96 B3 **Maybole** U.K.
104 B2 **Mayenne** France
104 B2 **Mayenne** *r.* France
128 C2 **Mayerthorpe** Can.
140 B3 **Mayfield** U.S.A.
 87 D4 **Maykop** Russia
126 B2 **Mayo** Can.
118 B3 **Mayoko** Congo
121 D2 **Mayotte** *terr.* Africa
 83 J3 **Mayskiy** Russia
140 C3 **Maysville** U.S.A.
118 B3 **Mayumba** Gabon

Mayville

137 D1 Mayville U.S.A.
151 C2 Mazagão Brazil
104 C3 Mazamet France
77 D3 Mazar China
108 B3 Mazara del Vallo *Sicily* Italy
77 C3 Mazār-e Sharīf Afgh.
144 A2 Mazatán Mex.
146 A3 Mazatenango Guat.
144 B2 Mazatlán Mex.
88 B2 Mažeikiai Lith.
88 B2 Mazirbe Latvia
71 C3 Mazu Dao *i.* Taiwan
121 B3 Mazunga Zimbabwe
88 C3 Mazyr Belarus
123 D2 Mbabane Swaziland
118 B2 Mbaïki C.A.R.
121 C1 Mbala Zambia
119 D2 Mbale Uganda
118 B2 Mbalmayo Cameroon
118 B3 Mbandaka Dem. Rep. Congo
118 A2 Mbanga Cameroon
120 A1 M'banza Congo Angola
119 D3 Mbeya Tanz.
119 D4 Mbinga Tanz.
123 D2 Mbombela S. Africa
118 B2 Mbomo Congo
118 B2 Mbouda Cameroon
114 A3 Mbour Senegal
118 C3 Mbout Maur.
118 C3 Mbuji-Mayi Dem. Rep. Congo
119 D3 Mbuyuni Tanz.
139 D2 McAlester U.S.A.
139 D3 McAllen U.S.A.
128 B2 McBride Can.
134 C2 McCall U.S.A.
126 E2 McClintock Channel Can.
126 D2 McClure Strait Can.
142 B2 McComb U.S.A.
136 C2 McConaughy, Lake U.S.A.
136 C2 McCook U.S.A.
134 C2 McDermitt U.S.A.
134 D1 McDonald Peak U.S.A.
134 D1 McGuire, Mount U.S.A.
        McKinley, Mount *mt* U.S.A.
        see Denali
128 C2 McLennan Can.
128 B2 McLeod Lake Can.
134 B1 McMinnville *OR* U.S.A.
142 C1 McMinnville *TN* U.S.A.
137 D3 McPherson U.S.A.
123 C3 Mdantsane S. Africa
135 D3 Mead, Lake *resr* U.S.A.
129 D2 Meadow Lake Can.
140 C2 Meadville U.S.A.
66 D2 Meaken-dake *vol.* Japan
106 B1 Mealhada Port.
131 E1 Mealy Mountains Can.
128 C2 Meander River Can.
78 A2 Mecca Saudi Arabia
100 B2 Mechelen Belgium
100 B2 Mechelen Neth.
100 C2 Mechernich Ger.
100 C2 Meckenheim Ger.
106 B1 Meda Port.
60 A1 Medan Indon.
153 B5 Medanosa, Punta *pt* Arg.
73 C4 Medawachchiya Sri Lanka
107 D2 Médéa Alg.
150 A1 Medellín Col.
115 D1 Medenine Tunisia
134 B2 Medford U.S.A.
110 C1 Medgidia Romania
110 B1 Mediaş Romania
136 B2 Medicine Bow Mountains U.S.A.
136 B2 Medicine Bow Peak U.S.A.
129 C2 Medicine Hat Can.
137 D3 Medicine Lodge U.S.A.

155 D1 Medina Brazil
78 A2 Medina Saudi Arabia
106 C1 Medinaceli Spain
106 C1 Medina del Campo Spain
106 B1 Medina de Rioseco Spain
84 G5 Mediterranean Sea
129 C2 Medley Can.
87 E3 Mednogorsk Russia
83 L2 Medvezh'i, Ostrova *is* Russia
86 C2 Medvezh'yegorsk Russia
136 B2 Meekatharra Austr.
136 B2 Meeker U.S.A.
75 B2 Meerut India
100 A2 Meetkerke Belgium
111 B3 Megalopoli Greece
75 C2 Meghasani *mt.* India
80 A2 Megisti *i.* Greece
92 I1 Mehamn Norway
50 A2 Meharry, Mount Austr.
79 C2 Mehrān *watercourse* Iran
76 C3 Mehrestān Iran
74 B1 Mehtar Läm Afgh.
154 C1 Meia Ponte *r.* Brazil
118 B2 Meiganga Cameroon
65 B1 Meihekou China
        Meijiang China *see* Ningdu
62 A1 Meiktila Myanmar
101 E2 Meiningen Ger.
102 C1 Meißen Ger.
71 B3 Meizhou China
152 B3 Mejicana *mt.* Arg.
152 A3 Mejillones Chile
117 B3 Mek'elë Eth.
114 C2 Mekerrhane, Sebkha *salt pan* Alg.
114 B1 Meknès Morocco
63 B2 Mekong *r.* Asia
63 B3 Mekong, Mouths of the Vietnam
60 B1 Melaka Malaysia
53 B3 Melbourne Austr.
143 D3 Melbourne U.S.A.
108 A2 Mele, Capo *c* Italy
131 C1 Mélèzes, Rivière aux *r.* Can.
115 D3 Melfi Chad
109 C2 Melfi Italy
129 D2 Melfort Can.
92 F3 Melhus Norway
106 B1 Melide Spain
114 B1 Melilla N. Africa
91 D2 Melitopol' Ukr.
101 D1 Melle Ger.
93 F4 Mellerud Sweden
101 E2 Mellrichstadt Ger.
100 D1 Mellum *i.* Ger.
152 C4 Melo Uru.
115 C1 Melrhir, Chott *salt l.* Alg.
99 C2 Melton Mowbray U.K.
104 C2 Melun France
129 D2 Melville Can.
51 D1 Melville, Cape Austr.
131 E1 Melville, Lake Can.
50 C1 Melville Island Austr.
126 D1 Melville Island Can.
127 F2 Melville Peninsula Can.
102 C2 Memmingen Ger.
61 B1 Mempawah Indon.
80 B3 Memphis *tourist site* Egypt
142 B1 Memphis *TN* U.S.A.
139 C2 Memphis *TX* U.S.A.
91 C1 Mena Ukr.
142 B2 Mena U.S.A.
114 C3 Ménaka Mali
        Mènam Khong *r.* Laos/Thai. *see* Mekong
105 C3 Mende France
116 B3 Mendefera Eritrea
145 C2 Méndez Mex.

119 D2 Mendī Eth.
59 D3 Mendi P.N.G.
99 B3 Mendip Hills U.K.
153 B4 Mendoza Arg.
111 C3 Menemen Turkey
60 B2 Menggala Indon.
62 B1 Mengzi China
131 D1 Menihek Can.
52 B2 Menindee Austr.
52 B2 Menindee Lake Austr.
52 A3 Meningie Austr.
104 C2 Mennecy France
140 B1 Menominee U.S.A.
120 A2 Menongue Angola
        Menorca *i.* Spain *see* Minorca
60 A2 Mentawai, Kepulauan *is* Indon.
60 B2 Mentok Indon.
50 B2 Menzies Austr.
100 C1 Meppel Neth.
100 C1 Meppen Ger.
123 D1 Mepuze Moz.
123 C2 Mqheleng S. Africa
108 B1 Merano Italy
59 D3 Merauke Indon.
52 B2 Merbein Austr.
135 B3 Merced U.S.A.
152 C3 Mercedes Arg.
127 G2 Mercy, Cape Can.
139 C1 Meredith, Lake U.S.A.
91 D2 Merefa Ukr.
116 A3 Merga Oasis Sudan
63 A2 Mergui Archipelago *is* Myanmar
110 C2 Meriç *r.* Greece/Turkey
145 D2 Mérida Mex.
106 B2 Mérida Spain
150 A1 Mérida Venez.
142 C2 Meridian U.S.A.
53 C3 Merimbula Austr.
116 B3 Merowe Sudan
50 A3 Merredin Austr.
96 B3 Merrick *h.* U.K.
140 B1 Merrill U.S.A.
140 B2 Merrillville U.S.A.
128 B2 Merritt Can.
53 C2 Merrygoen Austr.
116 C3 Mersa Fatma Eritrea
100 C3 Mersch Lux.
101 E2 Merseburg Ger.
98 B2 Mersey *r.* U.K.
80 B2 Mersin Turkey
60 B1 Mersing Malaysia
99 D3 Mers-les-Bains France
74 B2 Merta India
99 B3 Merthyr Tydfil U.K.
106 B2 Mértola Port.
76 B2 Mertvyy Kultuk, Sor *dry lake* Kazakh.
119 D3 Meru *vol.* Tanz.
100 C3 Merzig Ger.
138 A2 Mesa U.S.A.
109 C2 Mesagne Italy
101 D2 Meschede Ger.
89 E3 Meshchovsk Russia
91 E2 Meshkovskaya Russia
111 B2 Mesimeri Greece
111 B3 Mesolongi Greece
121 D2 Messalo *r.* Moz.
109 C3 Messina Sicily Italy
109 C3 Messina, Strait of Italy
111 B3 Messiniakos Kolpos *g.* Greece
110 B2 Mesta *r.* Bulg.
150 B1 Meta *r.* Col./Venez.
127 G2 Meta Incognita Peninsula Can.
152 B3 Metán Arg.

111 B3 Methoni Greece
109 C2 Metković Croatia
60 B2 Metro Indon.
117 B4 Metu Eth.
105 D2 Metz France
86 C3 Meuse r. Belgium/France
139 D2 Mexia U.S.A.
144 A1 Mexicali Mex.
144 B2 Mexico country
Central America
137 E3 Mexico U.S.A.
125 I5 Mexico, Gulf of Mex./U.S.A.
145 C3 Mexico City Mex.
101 F1 Meyenburg Ger.
86 D2 Mezen' Russia
86 D2 Mezen' r. Russia
86 E1 Mezhdusharskiy, Ostrov i.
Russia
103 E2 Meztúr Hungary
144 B2 Mezquitic Mex.
88 C2 Mežvidi Latvia
121 C2 Mfuwe Zambia
123 D2 Mhlume Swaziland
74 B2 Mhow India
145 C3 Miahuatlán Mex.
106 B2 Miajadas Spain
143 D3 Miami FL U.S.A.
139 E1 Miami OK U.S.A.
143 D3 Miami Beach U.S.A.
81 C2 Miandoab Iran
121 ☐D2 Miandrivazo Madag.
81 C2 Mianeh Iran
74 B1 Mianwali Pak.
70 A2 Mianyang China
121 ☐D2 Miarinarivo Madag.
87 P2 Miass Russia
128 C2 Mica Creek Can.
103 E2 Michalovce Slovakia
140 B1 Michigan state U.S.A.
140 B2 Michigan, Lake U.S.A.
140 B2 Michigan City U.S.A.
130 B2 Michipicoten Island Can.
130 B2 Michipicoten River Can.
89 F3 Michurinsk Russia
48 D2 Micronesia, Federated States
of country N. Pacific Ocean
100 A2 Middelburg Neth.
123 C3 Middelburg E. Cape S. Africa
123 C2 Middelburg Mpumalanga
S. Africa
100 B2 Middelharnis Neth.
134 B2 Middle Alkali Lake U.S.A.
73 D3 Middle Andaman i. India
136 D2 Middle Loup r. U.S.A.
140 C3 Middlesboro U.S.A.
98 C1 Middlesbrough U.K.
141 E2 Middletown NY U.S.A.
140 C3 Middletown OH U.S.A.
78 B3 Midi Yemen
130 C2 Midland Can.
140 C2 Midland MI U.S.A.
139 C2 Midland TX U.S.A.
97 B3 Midleton Ireland
94 B1 Miðvágur Faroe Is.
109 D2 Midzhur mt. Bulgaria/Serbia
103 E1 Mielec Pol.
110 C1 Miercurea-Ciuc Romania
106 B1 Mieres del Camín Spain
101 E1 Mieste Ger.
145 C3 Miguel Alemán, Presa resr
Mex.
144 B2 Miguel Auza Mex.
144 B2 Miguel Hidalgo, Presa resr
Mex.
63 A2 Migyaunglaung Myanmar
89 E3 Mikhaylov Russia
Mikhaylovgrad Bulg. see
Montana

66 B2 Mikhaylovka Russia
77 D1 Mikhaylovskoye Russia
93 I3 Mikkeli Fin.
86 E2 Mikun' Russia
67 C3 Mikuni-sanmyaku mts Japan
108 A1 Milan Italy
121 C2 Milange Moz.
Milano Italy see Milan
111 C3 Milas Turkey
137 D1 Milbank U.S.A.
99 D2 Mildenhall U.K.
52 B2 Mildura Austr.
62 B1 Mile China
136 B1 Miles City U.S.A.
141 D3 Milford DE U.S.A.
135 D3 Milford UT U.S.A.
99 A3 Milford Haven U.K.
54 A2 Milford Sound N.Z.
107 D2 Miliana Alg.
116 B3 Milk, Wadi el watercourse
Sudan
83 L3 Mil'kovo Russia
129 C3 Milk River Can.
105 C3 Millau France
143 D2 Milledgeville U.S.A.
137 E1 Mille Lacs lakes U.S.A.
130 A2 Mille Lacs, Lac des l. Can.
137 D2 Miller U.S.A.
91 E2 Millerovo Russia
52 A2 Millers Creek Austr.
52 B3 Millicent Austr.
141 F1 Millinocket U.S.A.
53 D1 Millmerran Austr.
98 B1 Millom U.K.
128 C1 Mills Lake Can.
111 B3 Milos i. Greece
89 E3 Miloslavskoye Russia
91 E2 Milove Ukr.
52 B1 Milparinka Austr.
54 A3 Milton N.Z.
99 C2 Milton Keynes U.K.
140 B2 Milwaukee U.S.A.
104 B3 Mimizan France
118 B3 Mimongo Gabon
79 C2 Minab Iran
58 C2 Minahasa, Semenanjung pen.
Indon.
79 C2 Mina' Jabal 'Ali U.A.E.
60 B1 Minas Indon.
153 C4 Minas Uru.
155 D1 Minas Novas Brazil
145 C3 Minatitlán Mex.
62 A1 Minbu Myanmar
64 B2 Mindanao i. Phil.
101 D1 Minden Ger.
142 B2 Minden LA U.S.A.
137 D2 Minden NE U.S.A.
64 B1 Mindoro i. Phil.
64 A1 Mindoro Strait Phil.
118 B3 Mindouli Congo
99 B3 Minehead U.K.
154 B1 Mineiros Brazil
139 D2 Mineral Wells U.S.A.
77 E3 Minfeng China
119 C4 Minga Dem. Rep. Congo
81 C1 Mingäçevir Azer.
131 D1 Mingan Can.
52 B2 Mingary Austr.
70 B2 Mingguang China
62 A1 Mingin Myanmar
107 C2 Minglanilla Spain
119 D4 Mingoyo Tanz.
69 E1 Mingshui China
71 B3 Mingxi China
73 B4 Minicoy atoll India
50 A2 Minilya Austr.
131 D1 Minipi Lake Can.
130 A1 Miniss Lake Can.

115 C4 Minna Nigeria
137 E2 Minneapolis U.S.A.
129 E2 Minnedosa Can.
137 E2 Minnesota r. U.S.A.
137 E1 Minnesota state U.S.A.
106 B1 Miño r. Port./Spain
107 D1 Minorca i. Spain
136 C1 Minot U.S.A.
88 C3 Minsk Belarus
103 E1 Mińsk Mazowiecki Pol.
131 D2 Minto Can.
130 C1 Minto, Lac l. Can.
70 A2 Minxian China
155 C3 Mirabela Brazil
155 D1 Miralta Brazil
131 D2 Miramichi Can.
111 C3 Mirampellou, Kolpos b.
Greece
152 C3 Miranda Brazil
152 C2 Miranda r. Brazil
106 C1 Miranda de Ebro Spain
106 B1 Mirandela Port.
154 B2 Mirandópolis Brazil
79 C3 Mirbāṭ Oman
61 C1 Miri Sarawak Malaysia
153 C4 Mirim, Lagoa l. Brazil/Uru.
79 D2 Mirjāveh Iran
101 F1 Mirnyy Russia
74 A2 Mirpur Khas Pak.
111 B3 Mirtoö Pelagos sea Greece
65 B2 Miryang S. Korea
75 C2 Mirzapur India
66 B1 Mishan China
146 B3 Miskitos, Cayos is Nic.
103 E2 Miskolc Hungary
59 C3 Misoöl i. Indon.
115 D1 Miṣrātah Libya
130 B1 Missinaibi r. Can.
130 B2 Missinaibi Lake Can.
128 B3 Mission Can.
130 B1 Missisa Lake Can.
142 C2 Mississippi r. U.S.A.
142 C2 Mississippi state U.S.A.
142 C3 Mississippi Delta U.S.A.
134 D1 Missoula U.S.A.
137 E3 Missouri r. U.S.A.
137 E3 Missouri state U.S.A.
131 C2 Mistassibi r. Can.
130 C1 Mistassini, Lac l. Can.
131 D1 Mistastin Lake Can.
103 D2 Mistelbach Austria
131 D1 Mistinibi, Lac l. Can.
130 C1 Mistissini Can.
51 D2 Mitchell Austr.
51 D1 Mitchell r. Austr.
137 D2 Mitchell U.S.A.
97 B2 Mitchelstown Ireland
74 A2 Mithi Pak.
67 D3 Mito Japan
119 D3 Mitole Tanz.
109 D2 Mitrovicë Kosovo
53 D2 Mittagong Austr.
101 E2 Mittelhausen Ger.
101 D1 Mittellandkanal canal Ger.
101 F3 Mitterteich Ger.
150 A1 Mitú Col.
119 C4 Mitumba, Chaîne des mts
Dem. Rep. Congo
119 C3 Mitumba, Monts mts
Dem. Rep. Congo
118 B2 Mitzic Gabon
78 B2 Miyah, Wādī al watercourse
Saudi Arabia
67 C4 Miyake-jima i. Japan
66 D3 Miyako Japan
67 B4 Miyakonojō Japan
76 B2 Miyaly Kazakh.

Miyang China *see* **Mile**
67 B4 **Miyazaki** Japan
115 D1 **Mizdah** Libya
97 B3 **Mizen Head** Ireland
90 A2 **Mizhhirr"ya** Ukr.
93 G4 **Mjölby** Sweden
93 F3 **Mjøsa** *l.* Norway
119 D3 **Mkomazi** Tanz.
103 C1 **Mladá Boleslav** Czech Rep.
109 D2 **Mladenovac** Serbia
103 E1 **Mława** Pol.
123 C3 **Mlungisi** S. Africa
90 B1 **Mlyniv** Ukr.
123 C2 **Mmabatho** S. Africa
123 C2 **Mmathethe** Botswana
135 E3 **Moab** U.S.A.
123 D2 **Moamba** Moz.
119 C3 **Moba** Dem. Rep. Congo
118 C2 **Mobayi-Mbongo** Dem. Rep. Congo
137 E3 **Moberly** U.S.A.
142 C2 **Mobile** U.S.A.
142 C2 **Mobile Bay** U.S.A.
136 C1 **Mobridge** U.S.A.
121 D2 **Moçambique** Moz.
62 B1 **Môc Châu** Vietnam
78 B3 **Mocha** Yemen
123 C1 **Mochudi** Botswana
121 D2 **Mocimboa da Praia** Moz.
150 A1 **Mocoa** Col.
154 C2 **Mococa** Brazil
144 B2 **Mocorito** Mex.
144 B1 **Moctezuma** *Chihuahua* Mex.
145 B2 **Moctezuma** *San Luis Potosí* Mex.
144 B2 **Moctezuma** *Sonora* Mex.
121 C2 **Mocuba** Moz.
105 D2 **Modane** France
122 B2 **Modder** *r.* S. Africa
108 B2 **Modena** Italy
135 B3 **Modesto** U.S.A.
123 C1 **Modimolle** S. Africa
123 D1 **Modjadjiskloof** S. Africa
53 C3 **Moe** Austr.
100 C2 **Moers** Ger.
96 C3 **Moffat** U.K.
117 C4 **Mogadishu** Somalia
123 C1 **Mogalakwena** *r.* S. Africa
62 A1 **Mogaung** Myanmar
155 C2 **Mogi das Cruzes** Brazil
Mogilev Belarus *see* **Mahilyow**
154 C2 **Mogi Mirim** Brazil
83 I3 **Mogocha** Russia
62 A1 **Mogok** Myanmar
103 D2 **Mohács** Hungary
123 C3 **Mohale's Hoek** Lesotho
74 B1 **Mohali** India
79 C2 **Moḩammadābād** Iran
107 D2 **Mohammadia** Alg.
141 E2 **Mohawk** *r.* U.S.A.
119 D3 **Mohoro** Tanz.
90 B2 **Mohyliv-Podil's'kyy** Ukr.
110 C1 **Moinești** Romania
92 F2 **Mo i Rana** Norway
104 C3 **Moissac** France
135 C3 **Mojave** U.S.A.
135 C3 **Mojave Desert** U.S.A.
62 B1 **Mojiang** China
154 C2 **Moji-Guaçu** *r.* Brazil
54 B1 **Mokau** N.Z.
123 C2 **Mokhotlong** Lesotho
123 C1 **Mokopane** S. Africa
65 B3 **Mokpo** S. Korea
145 C2 **Molango** Mex.
Moldavia *country* Europe *see* **Moldova**
92 E3 **Molde** Norway
90 B2 **Moldova** *country* Europe
110 B1 **Moldoveanu, Vârful** *mt.* Romania
90 B2 **Moldovei Centrale, Podișul** *plat.* Moldova
123 C1 **Molepolole** Botswana
88 C2 **Moltai** Lith.
109 C2 **Molfetta** Italy
107 C1 **Molina de Aragón** Spain
150 A3 **Mollendo** Peru
53 C2 **Molong** Austr.
122 B2 **Molopo** *watercourse* Botswana/S. Africa
118 B2 **Moloundou** Cameroon
59 C3 **Moluccas** *is* Indon.
Molucca Sea Indon. *see* **Maluku, Laut**
52 B2 **Momba** Austr.
119 D3 **Mombasa** Kenya
154 B1 **Mombuca, Serra da** *hills* Brazil
93 F4 **Møn** *i.* Denmark
105 D3 **Monaco** *country* Europe
96 B2 **Monadhliath Mountains** U.K.
97 C1 **Monaghan** Ireland
89 D3 **Monastyrshchina** Russia
90 B2 **Monastyryshche** Ukr.
66 D2 **Monbetsu** Japan
108 A1 **Moncalieri** Italy
107 C1 **Moncayo** *mt.* Spain
86 C2 **Monchegorsk** Russia
100 C2 **Mönchengladbach** Ger.
144 B2 **Monclova** Mex.
131 D2 **Moncton** Can.
106 B1 **Mondego** *r.* Port.
108 A2 **Mondovì** Italy
111 B3 **Monemvasia** Greece
66 D1 **Moneron, Ostrov** *i.* Russia
137 E3 **Monett** U.S.A.
108 B1 **Monfalcone** Italy
106 B1 **Monforte de Lemos** Spain
62 B1 **Mông Cai** Vietnam
62 B1 **Mong Lin** Myanmar
68 C1 **Mongolia** *country* Asia
62 A1 **Mong Pawk** Myanmar
62 A1 **Mong Ping** Myanmar
120 B2 **Mongu** Zambia
135 C3 **Monitor Range** *mts* U.S.A.
114 C4 **Mono** *r.* Benin/Togo
135 C3 **Mono Lake** U.S.A.
109 C2 **Monopoli** Italy
107 C1 **Monreal del Campo** Spain
142 B2 **Monroe** *LA* U.S.A.
140 B2 **Monroe** *WI* U.S.A.
142 C2 **Monroeville** U.S.A.
114 A4 **Monrovia** Liberia
100 A2 **Mons** Belgium
122 B3 **Montagu** S. Africa
109 C3 **Montalto** *mt.* Italy
110 B2 **Montana** Bulg.
134 E1 **Montana** *state* U.S.A.
104 C2 **Montargis** France
104 C3 **Montauban** France
141 E2 **Montauk Point** U.S.A.
123 C2 **Mont-aux-Sources** *mt.* Lesotho
105 C2 **Montbard** France
105 C2 **Montbrison** France
100 B3 **Montcornet** France
104 B3 **Mont-de-Marsan** France
104 C2 **Montdidier** France
151 C2 **Monte Alegre** Brazil
105 D3 **Monte-Carlo** Monaco
152 C4 **Monte Caseros** Arg.
146 C3 **Montego Bay** Jamaica
105 C3 **Montélimar** France
109 C2 **Montella** Italy
145 C2 **Montemorelos** Mex.
104 B2 **Montendre** France
109 C2 **Montenegro** *country* Europe
121 C2 **Montepuez** Moz.
108 B2 **Montepulciano** Italy
135 B3 **Monterey** U.S.A.
135 B3 **Monterey Bay** U.S.A.
150 A1 **Montería** Col.
152 B2 **Montero** Bol.
145 B2 **Monterrey** Mex.
109 C2 **Montesano sulla Marcellana** Italy
109 C2 **Monte Sant'Angelo** Italy
151 E3 **Monte Santo** Brazil
108 A2 **Monte Santu, Capo di** *c.* *Sardinia* Italy
155 D1 **Montes Claros** Brazil
153 C4 **Montevideo** Uru.
137 D2 **Montevideo** U.S.A.
136 B3 **Monte Vista** U.S.A.
142 C2 **Montgomery** U.S.A.
105 D2 **Monthey** Switz.
142 B2 **Monticello** *AR* U.S.A.
135 E3 **Monticello** *UT* U.S.A.
104 C2 **Montignac** France
105 D2 **Montigny-le-Roi** France
106 C2 **Montilla** Spain
131 D2 **Mont-Joli** Can.
130 C2 **Mont-Laurier** Can.
104 C2 **Montluçon** France
131 C2 **Montmagny** Can.
104 C2 **Montmorillon** France
51 E2 **Monto** Austr.
134 D2 **Montpelier** *ID* U.S.A.
141 E2 **Montpelier** *VT* U.S.A.
105 C3 **Montpellier** France
130 C2 **Montréal** Can.
129 D2 **Montreal Lake** Can.
129 D2 **Montreal Lake** Can.
99 D3 **Montreuil** France
105 D2 **Montreux** Switz.
96 C2 **Montrose** U.K.
136 B3 **Montrose** U.S.A.
147 D3 **Montserrat** *terr.* West Indies
62 A1 **Monywa** Myanmar
108 A1 **Monza** Italy
107 D1 **Monzón** Spain
123 C1 **Mookane** Botswana
123 C1 **Mookgophong** S. Africa
53 D1 **Moonie** Austr.
53 C1 **Moonie** *r.* Austr.
52 A2 **Moonta** Austr.
50 A2 **Moore, Lake** *imp. l.* Austr.
137 D1 **Moorhead** U.S.A.
53 C3 **Mooroopna** Austr.
122 A3 **Moorreesburg** S. Africa
130 B1 **Moose** *r.* Can.
130 B1 **Moose Factory** Can.
141 F1 **Moosehead Lake** U.S.A.
129 D2 **Moose Jaw** Can.
137 E1 **Moose Lake** U.S.A.
129 D2 **Moosomin** Can.
130 B1 **Moosonee** Can.
52 B2 **Mootwingee** Austr.
123 C1 **Mopane** S. Africa
114 B3 **Mopti** Mali
150 A3 **Moquegua** Peru
93 F3 **Mora** Sweden
137 E1 **Mora** U.S.A.
75 B2 **Moradabad** India
121 □D2 **Moramanga** Madag.
103 D2 **Morava** *r.* Europe
96 B2 **Moray Firth** *b.* U.K.
100 C3 **Morbach** Ger.
74 B2 **Morbi** India
104 B3 **Morcenx** France
69 E1 **Mordaga** China
129 E3 **Morden** Can.
91 E1 **Mordovo** Russia

98 B1 **Morecambe** U.K.
98 B1 **Morecambe Bay** U.K.
53 C1 **Moree** Austr.
59 D3 **Morehead** P.N.G.
140 C3 **Morehead** U.S.A.
143 E2 **Morehead City** U.S.A.
145 B3 **Morelia** Mex.
107 C1 **Morella** Spain
106 B2 **Morena, Sierra** *mts* Spain
110 C2 **Moreni** Romania
128 A2 **Moresby, Mount** Can.
142 B3 **Morgan City** U.S.A.
143 D1 **Morganton** U.S.A.
140 D3 **Morgantown** U.S.A.
105 D2 **Morges** Switz.
77 C3 **Morghāb, Daryā-ye** *r.* Afgh.
66 D2 **Mori** Japan
128 B2 **Morice Lake** Can.
66 D3 **Morioka** Japan
53 D2 **Morisset** Austr.
104 B2 **Morlaix** France
51 C1 **Mornington Island** Austr.
59 D3 **Morobe** P.N.G.
114 B1 **Morocco** *country* Africa
119 D3 **Morogoro** Tanz.
64 B2 **Moro Gulf** Phil.
122 B2 **Morokweng** S. Africa
121 □D3 **Morombe** Madag.
68 C1 **Mörön** Mongolia
121 □D3 **Morondava** Madag.
121 D2 **Moroni** Comoros
59 C2 **Morotai** *i.* Indon.
119 D2 **Moroto** Uganda
98 C1 **Morpeth** U.K.
86 F2 **Morrasale** Russia
154 C1 **Morrinhos** Brazil
129 E3 **Morris** Can.
137 D1 **Morris** U.S.A.
143 D1 **Morristown** U.S.A.
87 D3 **Morshansk** Russia
154 B1 **Mortes, Rio das** *r.* Brazil
52 B3 **Mortlake** Austr.
53 D3 **Moruya** Austr.
96 B2 **Morvern** *reg.* U.K.
53 C3 **Morwell** Austr.
102 B2 **Mosbach** Ger.
89 E2 **Moscow** Russia
134 C1 **Moscow** U.S.A.
100 C2 **Mosel** *r.* Ger.
105 D2 **Moselle** *r.* France
134 C1 **Moses Lake** U.S.A.
92 □A3 **Mosfellsbær** Iceland
54 B3 **Mosgiel** N.Z.
89 D2 **Moshenskoye** Russia
119 D3 **Moshi** Tanz.
92 F2 **Mosjøen** Norway
Moskva Russia *see* **Moscow**
103 D2 **Mosonmagyaróvár** Hungary
146 B3 **Mosquitos, Costa de** *coastal area* Nic.
146 B4 **Mosquitos, Golfo de los** *b.* Panama
93 F4 **Moss** Norway
122 B3 **Mossel Bay** S. Africa
122 B3 **Mossel Bay** S. Africa
118 B3 **Mossendjo** Congo
52 B2 **Mossgiel** Austr.
51 D1 **Mossman** Austr.
151 E2 **Mossoró** Brazil
53 D2 **Moss Vale** Austr.
102 C1 **Most** Czech Rep.
114 C1 **Mostaganem** Alg.
109 C2 **Mostar** Bos. & Herz.
152 C4 **Mostardas** Brazil
81 C2 **Mosul** Iraq
93 G4 **Motala** Sweden
96 C3 **Motherwell** U.K.
107 C2 **Motilla del Palancar** Spain
122 B1 **Motokwe** Botswana
106 C2 **Motril** Spain
110 B2 **Motru** Romania
63 A2 **Mottama, Gulf of** Myanmar
145 D2 **Motul** Mex.
111 C3 **Moudros** Greece
118 B3 **Mouila** Gabon
52 B3 **Moulamein** Austr.
105 C2 **Moulins** France
63 A2 **Moulmein** Myanmar
143 D2 **Moultrie** U.S.A.
143 E2 **Moultrie, Lake** U.S.A.
140 B3 **Mound City** U.S.A.
115 D4 **Moundou** Chad
137 E3 **Mountain Grove** U.S.A.
142 B1 **Mountain Home** *AR* U.S.A.
134 C2 **Mountain Home** *ID* U.S.A.
143 D1 **Mount Airy** U.S.A.
52 A3 **Mount Barker** Austr.
53 C3 **Mount Beauty** Austr.
121 C2 **Mount Darwin** Zimbabwe
141 F2 **Mount Desert Island** U.S.A.
123 C3 **Mount Fletcher** S. Africa
123 C3 **Mount Frere** S. Africa
52 B3 **Mount Gambier** Austr.
59 D3 **Mount Hagen** P.N.G.
53 C2 **Mount Hope** Austr.
51 C2 **Mount Isa** Austr.
50 A2 **Mount Magnet** Austr.
52 B2 **Mount Manara** Austr.
54 C1 **Mount Maunganui** N.Z.
111 B2 **Mount Olympus** Greece
137 E2 **Mount Pleasant** *IA* U.S.A.
140 C2 **Mount Pleasant** *MI* U.S.A.
139 E2 **Mount Pleasant** *TX* U.S.A.
99 A3 **Mount's Bay** U.K.
134 B2 **Mount Shasta** U.S.A.
140 B3 **Mount Vernon** *IL* U.S.A.
140 C2 **Mount Vernon** *OH* U.S.A.
134 B1 **Mount Vernon** *WA* U.S.A.
51 D2 **Moura** Austr.
115 E3 **Mourdi, Dépression du** *depr.* Chad
97 C1 **Mourne Mountains** *hills* U.K.
100 A2 **Mouscron** Belgium
115 D3 **Moussoro** Chad
58 C2 **Moutong** Indon.
115 C2 **Mouydir, Monts du** *plat.* Alg.
100 B3 **Mouzon** France
97 B1 **Moy** *r.* Ireland
117 B4 **Moyale** Eth.
123 C3 **Moyeni** Lesotho
76 B2 **Mo'ynoq** Uzbek.
77 D2 **Moyynty** Kazakh.
121 C3 **Mozambique** *country* Africa
113 I9 **Mozambique Channel** Africa
89 E2 **Mozhaysk** Russia
119 D3 **Mpanda** Tanz.
121 C2 **Mpika** Zambia
121 C1 **Mporokoso** Zambia
123 C2 **Mpumalanga** *prov.* S. Africa
62 A1 **Mrauk-U** Myanmar
88 C2 **Mshinskaya** Russia
107 D2 **M'Sila** Alg.
89 D2 **Msta** *r.* Russia
89 D2 **Mstinskiy Most** Russia
89 D3 **Mstsislaw** Belarus
123 C3 **Mthatha** S. Africa
89 E3 **Mtsensk** Russia
119 E4 **Mtwara** Tanz.
118 B3 **Muanda** Dem. Rep. Congo
63 B2 **Muang Không** Laos
62 B1 **Muang Ngoy** Laos
62 B2 **Muang Pakbeng** Laos
62 B1 **Muang Sing** Laos
62 B2 **Muang Vangviang** Laos
60 B1 **Muar** Malaysia
60 B2 **Muarabungo** Indon.
60 B2 **Muaradua** Indon.
61 C2 **Muaralaung** Indon.
60 A2 **Muarasiberut** Indon.
60 B2 **Muaratembesi** Indon.
61 C2 **Muarateweh** Indon.
119 D2 **Mubende** Uganda
115 D3 **Mubi** Nigeria
120 B2 **Muconda** Angola
155 E1 **Mucuri** Brazil
155 E1 **Mucuri** *r.* Brazil
66 A2 **Mudanjiang** China
66 A1 **Mudan Jiang** *r.* China
111 C2 **Mudanya** Turkey
101 E1 **Müden (Örtze)** Ger.
53 C2 **Mudgee** Austr.
63 A2 **Mudon** Myanmar
80 B1 **Mudurnu** Turkey
121 C2 **Mueda** Moz.
121 B2 **Mufulira** Zambia
120 B2 **Mufumbwe** Zambia
111 C3 **Muğla** Turkey
116 B2 **Muhammad Qol** Sudan
101 F2 **Mühlberg/Elbe** Ger.
101 E2 **Mühlhausen/Thüringen** Ger.
121 C2 **Muite** Moz.
65 B2 **Muju** S. Korea
90 A2 **Mukacheve** Ukr.
61 C1 **Mukah** *Sarawak* Malaysia
79 B3 **Mukalla** Yemen
63 B2 **Mukdahan** Thai.
50 A3 **Mukinbudin** Austr.
60 B2 **Mukomuko** Indon.
121 C2 **Mulanje, Mount** Malawi
101 F2 **Mulde** *r.* Ger.
144 A2 **Mulegé** Mex.
139 C2 **Muleshoe** U.S.A.
106 C2 **Mulhacén** *mt.* Spain
100 C2 **Mülheim an der Ruhr** Ger.
105 D2 **Mulhouse** France
66 B2 **Muling** China
66 B1 **Muling He** *r.* China
96 B2 **Mull** *i.* U.K.
53 C2 **Mullaley** Austr.
136 C2 **Mullen** U.S.A.
61 C1 **Muller, Pegunungan** *mts* Indon.
50 A2 **Mullewa** Austr.
97 C2 **Mullingar** Ireland
96 B3 **Mull of Galloway** *c.* U.K.
96 B3 **Mull of Kintyre** *hd* U.K.
96 A3 **Mull of Oa** *hd* U.K.
120 B2 **Mulobezi** Zambia
74 B1 **Multan** Pak.
73 B3 **Mumbai** India
120 B2 **Mumbwa** Zambia
145 D2 **Muna** Mex.
101 E2 **Münchberg** Ger.
München Ger. *see* **Munich**
140 B2 **Muncie** U.S.A.
50 B3 **Mundrabilla** Austr.
119 C2 **Mungbere** Dem. Rep. Congo
75 C2 **Munger** India
52 A1 **Mungeranie** Austr.
53 C1 **Mungindi** Austr.
102 C2 **Munich** Ger.
155 D2 **Muniz Freire** Brazil
101 E1 **Munster** *Niedersachsen* Ger.
100 C2 **Münster** *Nordrhein-Westfalen* Ger.
97 B2 **Munster** *reg.* Ireland
100 C2 **Münsterland** *reg.* Ger.
62 B1 **Mường Nhe** Vietnam
92 H2 **Muonio** Fin.
92 H2 **Muonioälven** *r.* Fin./Sweden
Muqdisho Somalia *see* **Mogadishu**
103 D2 **Mur** *r.* Austria
119 C3 **Muramvya** Burundi

Murang'a

119 D3	Murang'a Kenya
81 B2	Murat r. Turkey
111 C2	Muratlı Turkey
50 A2	Murchison watercourse Austr.
107 C2	Murcia Spain
111 C2	Mürefte Turkey
110 B1	Mureşul r. Romania
104 C3	Muret France
142 C1	Murfreesboro U.S.A.
77 D3	Murghob Tajik.
155 D2	Muriaé Brazil
120 B1	Muriege Angola
101 F1	Müritz l. Ger.
86 C2	Murmansk Russia
87 D3	Murom Russia
66 D2	Muroran Japan
106 B1	Muros Spain
67 B4	Muroto Japan
67 B4	Muroto-zaki pt Japan
143 D1	Murphy U.S.A.
53 C1	Murra Murra Austr.
52 A3	Murray r. Austr.
128 B2	Murray r. Can.
140 B3	Murray U.S.A.
143 D2	Murray, Lake U.S.A.
52 A3	Murray Bridge Austr.
122 B3	Murraysburg S. Africa
52 B3	Murrayville Austr.
52 B2	Murrumbidgee r. Austr.
121 C2	Murrupula Moz.
53 D2	Murrurundi Austr.
109 C1	Murska Sobota Slovenia
54 C1	Murupara N.Z.
49 I4	Mururoa atoll Fr. Polynesia
	Murwara India see Katni
53 D1	Murwillumbah Austr.
115 D2	Murzūq Libya
115 D2	Murzuq, Idhān des. Libya
81 C2	Muş Turkey
110 B2	Musala mt. Bulg.
65 B1	Musan N. Korea
78 B3	Musaymir Yemen
79 C2	Muscat Oman
137 E2	Muscatine U.S.A.
50 C2	Musgrave Ranges mts Austr.
118 B3	Mushie Dem. Rep. Congo
60 B2	Musi r. Indon.
123 D1	Musina S. Africa
140 B2	Muskegon U.S.A.
139 D1	Muskogee U.S.A.
128 B2	Muskwa r. Can.
74 A1	Muslimbagh Pak.
78 A3	Musmar Sudan
119 D3	Musoma Tanz.
96 C3	Musselburgh U.K.
88 B2	Mustjala Estonia
53 D2	Muswellbrook Austr.
116 A2	Mūṭ Egypt
121 C2	Mutare Zimbabwe
66 D2	Mutsu Japan
121 C2	Mutuali Moz.
92 I2	Muurola Fin.
70 A2	Mu Us Shadi des. China
120 A1	Muxaluando Angola
86 C2	Muyezerskiy Russia
119 D3	Muyinga Burundi
74 B1	Muzaffargarh Pak.
75 C2	Muzaffarpur India
144 B2	Múzquiz Mex.
75 C1	Muz Shan mt. China
119 C3	Mwanza Dem. Rep. Congo
119 D3	Mwanza Tanz.
118 C3	Mweka Dem. Rep. Congo
121 B2	Mwenda Zambia
118 C3	Mwene-Ditu Dem. Rep. Congo
121 C3	Mwenezi Zimbabwe

119 C3	Mweru, Lake Dem. Rep. Congo/Zambia
118 C3	Mwimba Dem. Rep. Congo
120 B2	Mwinilunga Zambia
88 C3	Myadzyel Belarus
62 A2	Myanaung Myanmar
62 A1	Myanmar country Asia
63 A2	Myaungmya Myanmar
63 A2	Myeik Myanmar
	Myeik Kyunzu is Myanmar see Mergui Archipelago
62 A1	Myingyan Myanmar
62 A1	Myitkyina Myanmar
91 C2	Mykolayiv Ukr.
111 C3	Mykonos Greece
111 C3	Mykonos i. Greece
86 E2	Myla Russia
75 D2	Mymensingh Bangl.
67 C3	Myōkō Japan
65 B1	Myŏnggan N. Korea
88 C2	Myory Belarus
92 □B3	Mýrdalsjökull Iceland
90 C1	Myrhorod Ukr.
90 C2	Myronivka Ukr.
143 E2	Myrtle Beach U.S.A.
53 C3	Myrtleford Austr.
134 B2	Myrtle Point U.S.A.
89 E2	Myshkin Russia
103 C1	Myślibórz Pol.
	Mysore India see Mysuru
83 N2	Mys Shmidta Russia
73 B3	Mysuru India
63 B2	My Tho Vietnam
111 C3	Mytilini Greece
89 E3	Mytishchi Russia
123 C3	Mzamomhle S. Africa
121 C2	Mzimba Malawi
121 C2	Mzuzu Malawi

N

97 C2	Naas Ireland
122 A2	Nababeep S. Africa
87 E3	Naberezhnyye Chelny Russia
59 D3	Nabire Indon.
80 B2	Nāblus West Bank
121 D2	Nacala Moz.
63 A2	Nachuge India
139 E2	Nacogdoches U.S.A.
144 B1	Nacozari de García Mex.
74 B2	Nadiad India
90 A2	Nadvirna Ukr.
86 C2	Nadvoitsy Russia
86 G2	Nadym Russia
93 F4	Næstved Denmark
111 B3	Nafpaktos Greece
111 B3	Nafplio Greece
115 D1	Nafūsah, Jabal hills Libya
78 B2	Nafy Saudi Arabia
64 B1	Naga Phil.
130 B1	Nagagami r. Can.
67 C3	Nagano Japan
67 C3	Nagaoka Japan
75 D2	Nagaon India
74 B1	Nagar India
74 B2	Nagar Parkar Pak.
67 A4	Nagasaki Japan
67 B4	Nagato Japan
74 B2	Nagaur India
73 B4	Nagercoil India
74 A2	Nagha Kalat Pak.
75 C2	Nagina India
81 C1	Nagorno-Karabakh disp. terr. Azer.
67 C3	Nagoya Japan
75 B2	Nagpur India

68 C2	Nagqu China
103 D2	Nagyatád Hungary
103 D2	Nagykanizsa Hungary
128 B1	Nahanni Butte Can.
76 A3	Nahāvand Iran
101 E1	Nahrendorf Ger.
153 A5	Nahuel Huapí, Lago l. Arg.
131 D1	Nain Can.
81 D2	Nā'īn Iran
96 C2	Nairn U.K.
119 D3	Nairobi Kenya
119 D3	Naivasha Kenya
81 D2	Najafābād Iran
78 B2	Najd reg. Saudi Arabia
106 C1	Nájera Spain
65 C1	Najin N. Korea
78 B3	Najrān Saudi Arabia
	Nakambé r. Burkina Faso/Ghana see White Volta
67 C3	Nakatsugawa Japan
78 A3	Nakfa Eritrea
66 B2	Nakhodka Russia
63 B2	Nakhon Pathom Thai.
63 B2	Nakhon Ratchasima Thai.
63 B2	Nakhon Sawan Thai.
63 A3	Nakhon Si Thammarat Thai.
130 B1	Nakina Can.
121 C1	Nakonde Zambia
93 F4	Nakskov Denmark
119 D3	Nakuru Kenya
128 C2	Nakusp Can.
75 D2	Nalbari India
87 D4	Nal'chik Russia
115 D1	Nālūt Libya
123 C2	Namahadi S. Africa
77 D2	Namangan Uzbek.
122 A2	Namaqualand reg. S. Africa
51 E2	Nambour Austr.
53 D2	Nambucca Heads Austr.
75 D1	Nam Co salt l. China
62 B1	Nam Đinh Vietnam
120 A3	Namib Desert Namibia
120 A2	Namibe Angola
120 A3	Namibia country Africa
72 D2	Namjagbarwa Feng mt. China
59 C3	Namlea Indon.
53 C2	Namoi r. Austr.
134 C2	Nampa U.S.A.
114 B3	Nampala Mali
65 B2	Namp'o N. Korea
121 C2	Nampula Moz.
62 A1	Namrup India
62 A1	Namsang Myanmar
92 F3	Namsos Norway
62 A2	Nam Tok Thai.
83 J2	Namtsy Russia
62 A1	Namtu Myanmar
100 B2	Namur Belgium
120 B2	Namwala Zambia
65 B2	Namwon S. Korea
62 A1	Namya Ra Myanmar
62 B2	Nan Thai.
128 B3	Nanaimo Can.
71 B3	Nan'an China
122 A1	Nananib Plateau Namibia
67 C3	Nanao Japan
71 B3	Nanchang Jiangxi China
71 B3	Nanchang Jiangxi China
70 A2	Nanchong China
63 A3	Nancowry i. India
105 D2	Nancy France
75 C1	Nanda Devi mt. India
71 A3	Nandan China
73 B3	Nanded India
74 B2	Nandurbar India
73 B3	Nandyal India
71 B3	Nanfeng China

118 B2 **Nanga Eboko** Cameroon
61 C2 **Nangahpinoh** Indon.
74 B1 **Nanga Parbat** *mt.* Pak.
61 C2 **Nangatayap** Indon.
70 B2 **Nangong** China
119 D3 **Nangulangwa** Tanz.
70 C2 **Nanhui** China
70 B2 **Nanjing** China
Nanking China *see* **Nanjing**
120 A2 **Nankova** Angola
71 B3 **Nan Ling** *mts* China
71 A3 **Nanning** China
127 H2 **Nanortalik** Greenland
71 A3 **Nanpan Jiang** *r.* China
75 C2 **Nanpara** India
71 B3 **Nanping** China
Nansei-shotō *is* Japan *see* **Ryukyu Islands**
104 B2 **Nantes** France
70 C2 **Nantong** China
141 F2 **Nantucket Island** U.S.A.
155 D1 **Nanuque** Brazil
64 B2 **Nanusa, Kepulauan** *is* Indon.
71 B3 **Nanxiong** China
70 B2 **Nanyang** China
70 B2 **Nanzhang** China
107 D2 **Nao, Cabo de la** *c.* Spain
131 C1 **Naococane, Lac** *l.* Can.
135 B3 **Napa** U.S.A.
126 D2 **Napaktulik Lake** Can.
127 H2 **Napasoq** Greenland
54 C1 **Napier** N.Z.
108 B2 **Naples** Italy
143 D3 **Naples** U.S.A.
150 A2 **Napo** *r.* Ecuador/Peru
Napoli Italy *see* **Naples**
114 B3 **Nara** Mali
93 I4 **Narach** Belarus
52 B3 **Naracoorte** Austr.
145 C2 **Naranjos** Mex.
63 B3 **Narathiwat** Thai.
105 C3 **Narbonne** France
63 A2 **Narcondam Island** India
127 G1 **Nares Strait** Can./Greenland
122 A1 **Narib** Namibia
87 D4 **Narimanov** Russia
67 D3 **Narita** Japan
74 B2 **Narmada** *r.* India
74 B2 **Narnaul** India
108 B2 **Narni** Italy
90 B1 **Narodychi** Ukr.
89 E2 **Naro-Fominsk** Russia
53 D3 **Narooma** Austr.
88 C3 **Narowlya** Belarus
53 C2 **Narrabri** Austr.
53 C2 **Narrandera** Austr.
53 C2 **Narromine** Austr.
88 C2 **Narva** Estonia
88 C2 **Narva Bay** Estonia/Russia
92 G2 **Narvik** Norway
88 C2 **Narvskoye Vodokhranilishche** *resr* Estonia/Russia
86 E2 **Nar'yan-Mar** Russia
77 D2 **Naryn** Kyrg.
74 B2 **Nashik** India
141 E2 **Nashua** U.S.A.
142 C1 **Nashville** U.S.A.
49 I5 **Nasinu** Fiji
117 B4 **Nasir** South Sudan
128 B2 **Nass** *r.* Can.
146 C2 **Nassau** Bahamas
116 B2 **Nasser, Lake** *resr* Egypt
93 F4 **Nässjö** Sweden
130 C1 **Nastapoca** *r.* Can.
130 C1 **Nastapoka Islands** Can.
67 D3 **Nasushiobara** Japan
120 B3 **Nata** Botswana
151 E2 **Natal** Brazil
131 D1 **Natashquan** Can.
131 D1 **Natashquan** *r.* Can.
142 B2 **Natchez** U.S.A.
142 B2 **Natchitoches** U.S.A.
53 C3 **Nathalia** Austr.
107 D1 **Nati, Punta** *pt* Spain
114 C3 **Natitingou** Benin
151 D3 **Natividade** Brazil
67 D3 **Natori** Japan
131 D1 **Natuashish** Can.
61 B1 **Natuna, Kepulauan** *is* Indon.
61 B1 **Natuna Besar** *i.* Indon.
120 A3 **Nauchas** Namibia
101 F1 **Nauen** Ger.
88 B2 **Naujoji Akmen** Lith.
74 A2 **Naukot** Pak.
101 E2 **Naumburg (Saale)** Ger.
48 F3 **Nauru** *country* S. Pacific Ocean
145 C2 **Nautla** Mex.
88 C3 **Navahrudak** Belarus
106 B2 **Navalmoral de la Mata** Spain
106 B2 **Navalvillar de Pela** Spain
97 C2 **Navan** Ireland
88 C2 **Navapolatsk** Belarus
83 M2 **Navarin, Mys** *c.* Russia
153 B6 **Navarino, Isla** *i.* Chile
96 B1 **Naver** *r.* U.K.
73 B3 **Navi Mumbai** India
89 D3 **Navlya** Russia
110 C2 **Năvodari** Romania
77 C2 **Navoiy** Uzbek.
144 B2 **Navojoa** Mex.
144 B2 **Navolato** Mex.
74 A2 **Nawabshah** Pak.
62 A1 **Nawnghkio** Myanmar
62 A1 **Nawngleng** Myanmar
81 C2 **Naxçıvan** Azer.
111 C3 **Naxos** *i.* Greece
144 B2 **Nayar** Mex.
66 D2 **Nayoro** Japan
144 B2 **Nazas** Mex.
144 B2 **Nazas** *r.* Mex.
150 A3 **Nazca** Peru
80 B2 **Nazerat** Israel
111 C3 **Nazilli** Turkey
117 B4 **Nazrēt** Eth.
79 C2 **Nazwá** Oman
121 B1 **Nchelenge** Zambia
122 B1 **Ncojane** Botswana
120 A1 **N'dalatando** Angola
118 C2 **Ndélé** C.A.R.
118 B3 **Ndendé** Gabon
115 D3 **Ndjamena** Chad
121 B2 **Ndola** Zambia
97 C1 **Neagh, Lough** *l.* U.K.
50 C2 **Neale, Lake** *imp. l.* Austr.
111 B2 **Nea Roda** Greece
99 B3 **Neath** U.K.
53 C1 **Nebine Creek** *r.* Austr.
150 B1 **Neblina, Pico da** *mt.* Brazil
89 D2 **Nebolchi** Russia
136 C2 **Nebraska** *state* U.S.A.
137 D2 **Nebraska City** U.S.A.
108 B3 **Nebrodi, Monti** *mts Sicily* Italy
153 C4 **Necochea** Arg.
131 C1 **Nedlouc, Lac** *l.* Can.
135 D4 **Needles** U.S.A.
74 B2 **Neemuch** India
129 E2 **Neepawa** Can.
87 E3 **Neftekamsk** Russia
82 F2 **Nefteyugansk** Russia
120 A1 **Negage** Angola
117 B4 **Negēlē** Eth.
150 A2 **Negra, Punta** *pt* Peru
63 A2 **Negrais, Cape** Myanmar
153 B5 **Negro** *r.* Arg.
150 C2 **Negro** *r.* S. America
152 C4 **Negro** *r.* Uru.
106 B2 **Negro, Cabo** *c.* Morocco
64 B2 **Negros** *i.* Phil.
69 E1 **Nehe** China
70 A3 **Neijiang** China
129 D2 **Neilburg** Can.
150 A1 **Neiva** Col.
129 E2 **Nejanilini Lake** Can.
117 B4 **Nek'emtē** Eth.
89 F2 **Nekrasovskoye** Russia
89 D2 **Nelidovo** Russia
73 B3 **Nellore** India
128 C3 **Nelson** Can.
129 E2 **Nelson** *r.* Can.
54 B2 **Nelson** N.Z.
52 B3 **Nelson, Cape** Austr.
53 D2 **Nelson Bay** Austr.
129 E2 **Nelson House** Can.
134 E1 **Nelson Reservoir** U.S.A.
114 B3 **Néma** Maur.
88 B2 **Neman** Russia
104 C2 **Nemours** France
66 D2 **Nemuro** Japan
90 B2 **Nemyriv** Ukr.
97 B2 **Nenagh** Ireland
99 D2 **Nene** *r.* U.K.
69 E1 **Nenjiang** China
137 E3 **Neosho** U.S.A.
75 C2 **Nepal** *country* Asia
75 C2 **Nepalganj** Nepal
135 D3 **Nephi** U.S.A.
97 B1 **Nephin** *h.* Ireland
97 B1 **Nephin Beg Range** *hills* Ireland
131 D2 **Nepisiguit** *r.* Can.
119 C2 **Nepoko** *r.* Dem. Rep. Congo
104 C3 **Nérac** France
53 D1 **Nerang** Austr.
69 D1 **Nerchinsk** Russia
89 F2 **Nerekhta** Russia
109 C2 **Neretva** *r.* Bos. & Herz./Croatia
120 B2 **Neriquinha** Angola
88 B3 **Neris** *r.* Lith.
89 E2 **Nerl'** *r.* Russia
86 F2 **Nerokhi** Russia
154 C1 **Nerópolis** Brazil
83 J3 **Neryungri** Russia
92 □C2 **Neskaupstaður** Iceland
96 B2 **Ness, Loch** *l.* U.K.
136 D3 **Ness City** U.S.A.
111 B2 **Nestos** *r.* Greece
100 B1 **Netherlands** *country* Europe
127 G2 **Nettilling Lake** Can.
101 F1 **Neubrandenburg** Ger.
105 D2 **Neuchâtel** Switz.
100 C2 **Neuerburg** Ger.
100 B3 **Neufchâteau** Belgium
105 D2 **Neufchâteau** France
104 C2 **Neufchâtel-en-Bray** France
101 D2 **Neuhof** Ger.
102 B1 **Neumünster** Ger.
102 B2 **Neunkirchen** Ger.
153 B4 **Neuquén** Arg.
153 B4 **Neuquén** *r.* Arg.
101 F1 **Neuruppin** Ger.
100 C2 **Neuss** Ger.
101 D1 **Neustadt am Rübenberge** Ger.
101 E3 **Neustadt an der Aisch** Ger.
101 F1 **Neustrelitz** Ger.
100 C2 **Neuwied** Ger.
137 E3 **Nevada** U.S.A.
135 C3 **Nevada** *state* U.S.A.
106 C2 **Nevada, Sierra** *mts* Spain
135 B2 **Nevada, Sierra** *mts* U.S.A.
88 C2 **Nevel'** Russia
105 C2 **Nevers** France

53 C2 Nevertire Austr.
109 C2 Nevesinje Bos. & Herz.
87 C4 Nevinnomyssk Russia
128 B2 New Aiyansh Can.
140 B3 New Albany U.S.A.
151 C1 New Amsterdam Guyana
141 E2 Newark NJ U.S.A.
140 C2 Newark OH U.S.A.
98 C2 Newark-on-Trent U.K.
141 E2 New Bedford U.S.A.
143 E1 New Bern U.S.A.
143 D2 Newberry U.S.A.
139 E2 New Boston U.S.A.
139 D3 New Braunfels U.S.A.
97 C2 Newbridge Ireland
48 E3 New Britain i. P.N.G.
131 D2 New Brunswick prov. Can.
99 C3 Newbury U.K.
64 A1 New Busuanga Phil.
48 E4 New Caledonia terr. S. Pacific Ocean
53 D2 Newcastle Austr.
123 C2 Newcastle S. Africa
97 D1 Newcastle U.K.
140 C2 New Castle U.S.A.
136 C2 Newcastle U.S.A.
98 B2 Newcastle-under-Lyme U.K.
98 C1 Newcastle upon Tyne U.K.
97 B2 Newcastle West Ireland
74 B2 New Delhi India
128 C3 New Denver Can.
53 D2 New England Range mts Austr.
131 E2 Newfoundland i. Can.
131 E1 Newfoundland and Labrador prov. Can.
131 D2 New Glasgow Can.
59 D3 New Guinea i. Indon./P.N.G.
141 E2 New Hampshire state U.S.A.
141 E2 New Haven U.S.A.
128 B2 New Hazelton Can.
New Hebrides country S. Pacific Ocean see Vanuatu
142 B2 New Iberia U.S.A.
48 E3 New Ireland i. P.N.G.
141 E3 New Jersey state U.S.A.
130 C2 New Liskeard Can.
50 A2 Newman Austr.
138 B2 New Mexico state U.S.A.
142 B3 New Orleans U.S.A.
140 C2 New Philadelphia U.S.A.
54 B1 New Plymouth N.Z.
99 C3 Newport England U.K.
99 B3 Newport Wales U.K.
142 B1 Newport AR U.S.A.
134 B2 Newport OR U.S.A.
141 E2 Newport RI U.S.A.
141 E2 Newport VT U.S.A.
134 C1 Newport WA U.S.A.
141 D3 Newport News U.S.A.
143 E3 New Providence i. Bahamas
99 A3 Newquay U.K.
142 B2 New Roads U.S.A.
97 C2 New Ross Ireland
97 C1 Newry U.K.
83 K1 New Siberia Islands Russia
52 B2 New South Wales state Austr.
137 D3 Newton IA U.S.A.
137 D4 Newton KS U.S.A.
99 B3 Newton Abbot U.K.
96 B3 Newton Stewart U.K.
97 B2 Newtown Ireland
99 B2 Newtown U.K.
136 C1 New Town U.S.A.
97 D1 Newtownabbey U.K.
97 D1 Newtownards U.K.
96 C3 Newtown St Boswells U.K.
97 C1 Newtownstewart U.K.

137 E2 New Ulm U.S.A.
141 E2 New York U.S.A.
141 E2 New York state U.S.A.
54 B2 New Zealand country Oceania
79 C2 Neyriz Iran
76 B3 Neyshābūr Iran
145 C3 Nezahualcóyotl, Presa resr Mex.
61 B1 Ngabang Indon.
75 C2 Ngamring China
75 C1 Ngangla Ringco salt l. China
77 E3 Nganglong Kangri mt. China
75 C1 Nganglong Kangri mts China
75 C1 Ngangzê Co salt l. China
62 A2 Ngao Thai.
118 B2 Ngaoundéré Cameroon
54 C1 Ngaruawahia N.Z.
62 A2 Ngathainggyaung Myanmar
121 D2 Ngazidja i. Comoros
118 B3 Ngo Congo
115 C4 Ngol Bembo Nigeria
68 C2 Ngoring Hu l. China
115 D3 Ngourti Niger
115 D3 Nguigmi Niger
59 D2 Ngulu atoll Micronesia
115 D3 Nguru Nigeria
123 D2 Ngwelezana S. Africa
121 C2 Nhamalabu Moz.
63 B2 Nha Trang Vietnam
52 B3 Nhill Austr.
123 D2 Nhlangano Swaziland
51 C1 Nhulunbuy Austr.
141 D2 Niagara Falls U.S.A.
114 C3 Niamey Niger
119 C2 Niangara Dem. Rep. Congo
114 B3 Niangay, Lac l. Mali
60 A1 Nias i. Indon.
146 B3 Nicaragua country Central America
146 B3 Nicaragua, Lake Nic.
105 D3 Nice France
73 D4 Nicobar Islands India
80 B2 Nicosia Cyprus
146 B4 Nicoya, Golfo de b. Costa Rica
88 B2 Nida Lith.
103 E1 Nidzica Pol.
102 B1 Niebüll Ger.
101 D2 Niederaula Ger.
118 B2 Niefang Equat. Guinea
101 F1 Niemegk Ger.
101 D1 Nienburg (Weser) Ger.
100 B1 Nieuwe Niedorp Neth.
151 C1 Nieuw Nickerie Suriname
122 A3 Nieuwoudtville S. Africa
100 A2 Nieuwpoort Belgium
80 B2 Niğde Turkey
115 C3 Niger country Africa
115 C4 Niger r. Africa
115 C4 Niger, Mouths of the Nigeria
115 C3 Nigeria country Africa
130 B2 Nighthawk Lake Can.
111 B2 Nigrita Greece
67 C3 Niigata Japan
67 B4 Niihama Japan
67 C4 Nii-jima i. Japan
67 C3 Niitsu Japan
100 B2 Nijmegen Neth.
100 C1 Nijverdal Neth.
92 J2 Nikel' Russia
83 M3 Nikol'skoye Russia
91 C2 Nikopol' Ukr.
80 B1 Niksar Turkey
79 D2 Nīkshahr Iran
109 C2 Nikšić Montenegro
116 B1 Nile r. Africa
140 B2 Niles U.S.A.
74 A1 Nīlī Afgh.
105 C3 Nîmes France

53 C3 Nimmitabel Austr.
117 B4 Nimule Sudan
53 C1 Nindigully Austr.
73 B3 Nine Degree Channel India
53 C3 Ninety Mile Beach Austr.
54 B1 Ninety Mile Beach N.Z.
70 C3 Ningbo China
71 B3 Ningde China
71 B3 Ningdu China
70 B2 Ningguo China
71 C3 Ninghai China
Ningjiang China see Songyuan
68 C2 Ningjing Shan mts China
70 A2 Ningxia Huizu Zizhiqu aut. reg. China
70 B2 Ningyang China
62 B1 Ninh Binh Vietnam
63 B2 Ninh Hoa Vietnam
66 D2 Ninohe Japan
137 D2 Niobrara r. U.S.A.
114 B3 Niono Mali
114 B3 Nioro Mali
104 B2 Niort France
129 D2 Nipawin Can.
130 B2 Nipigon Can.
130 B2 Nipigon, Lake Can.
131 D1 Nipishish Lake Can.
130 C2 Nipissing, Lake Can.
135 C3 Nipton U.S.A.
151 D3 Niquelândia Brazil
73 B3 Nirmal India
109 D2 Niš Serbia
109 D2 Nišava r. Serbia
108 B3 Niscemi Sicily Italy
67 B4 Nishino-omote Japan
155 D2 Niterói Brazil
96 C3 Nith r. U.K.
103 D2 Nitra Slovakia
49 G4 Niue terr. S. Pacific Ocean
92 H3 Nivala Fin.
100 B2 Nivelles Belgium
73 B3 Nizamabad India
81 E1 Nizhnekamsk Russia
83 H3 Nizhneudinsk Russia
82 G2 Nizhnevartovsk Russia
89 F3 Nizhniy Kislyay Russia
87 D3 Nizhniy Lomov Russia
87 D3 Nizhniy Novgorod Russia
86 E2 Nizhniy Odes Russia
86 E3 Nizhniy Tagil Russia
83 G2 Nizhnyaya Tunguska r. Russia
91 C1 Nizhyn Ukr.
119 D3 Njinjo Tanz.
119 D3 Njombe Tanz.
121 D2 Nkhotakota Malawi
118 A2 Nkongsamba Cameroon
123 C3 Nkululeko S. Africa
123 C3 Nkwenkwezi S. Africa
67 B4 Nobeoka Japan
52 B1 Noccundra Austr.
144 A1 Nogales Mex.
138 A2 Nogales U.S.A.
104 C2 Nogent-le-Rotrou France
89 E2 Noginsk Russia
74 B2 Nohar India
100 C3 Nohfelden Ger.
104 B2 Noirmoutier, Île de i. France
104 B2 Noirmoutier-en-l'Île France
67 C4 Nojima-zaki c. Japan
74 B2 Nokha India
93 H3 Nokia Fin.
74 A2 Nok Kundi Pak.
118 B2 Nola C.A.R.
86 D3 Nolinsk Russia
123 C3 Nomonde S. Africa
123 D2 Nondweni S. Africa

62 B2 **Nong Khai** Thai.
52 A2 **Nonning** Austr.
144 B2 **Nonoava** Mex.
65 B2 **Nonsan** S. Korea
63 B2 **Nonthaburi** Thai.
122 B3 **Nonzwakazi** S. Africa
77 C3 **Norak** Tajik.
141 D1 **Noranda** Can.
82 C1 **Nordaustlandet** *i.* Svalbard
128 C2 **Nordegg** Can.
100 C1 **Norden** Ger.
83 H1 **Nordenshel'da, Arkhipelag** *is* Russia
100 C1 **Norderney** Ger.
100 C1 **Norderney** *i.* Ger.
101 E1 **Norderstedt** Ger.
93 E3 **Nordfjordeid** Norway
101 E2 **Nordhausen** Ger.
101 D1 **Nordholz** Ger.
100 C1 **Nordhorn** Ger.
Nordkapp *c.* Norway *see* **North Cape**
92 F3 **Nordli** Norway
102 C2 **Nördlingen** Ger.
92 G3 **Nordmaling** Sweden
94 B1 **Norðoyar** *is* Faroe Is
97 C2 **Nore** *r.* Ireland
137 D2 **Norfolk** *NE* U.S.A.
141 D3 **Norfolk** *VA* U.S.A.
48 F4 **Norfolk Island** *terr.* S. Pacific Ocean
93 E3 **Norheimsund** Norway
82 G2 **Noril'sk** Russia
75 C2 **Norkyung** China
139 D1 **Norman** U.S.A.
Normandes, Îles *is* English Chan. *see* **Channel Islands**
51 D1 **Normanton** Austr.
93 G4 **Norrköping** Sweden
93 G4 **Norrtälje** Sweden
50 B3 **Norseman** Austr.
92 G3 **Norsjö** Sweden
98 C1 **Northallerton** U.K.
50 A2 **Northampton** Austr.
99 C2 **Northampton** U.K.
73 D3 **North Andaman** *i.* India
129 D2 **North Battleford** Can.
130 C2 **North Bay** Can.
130 C1 **North Belcher Islands** Can.
96 C2 **North Berwick** U.K.
92 I1 **North Cape** Norway
54 B1 **North Cape** N.Z.
130 A1 **North Caribou Lake** Can.
143 E1 **North Carolina** *state* U.S.A.
130 B2 **North Channel** *lake channel* Can.
96 A3 **North Channel** U.K.
128 B3 **North Cowichan** Can.
136 C1 **North Dakota** *state* U.S.A.
99 C3 **North Downs** *hills* U.K.
143 E3 **Northeast Providence Channel** Bahamas
101 D2 **Northeim** Ger.
122 A2 **Northern Cape** *prov.* S. Africa
129 E2 **Northern Indian Lake** Can.
97 C1 **Northern Ireland** *prov.* U.K.
48 D1 **Northern Mariana Islands** *terr.* N. Pacific Ocean
50 C1 **Northern Territory** *admin. div.* Austr.
96 C2 **North Esk** *r.* U.K.
137 E2 **Northfield** U.S.A.
99 D3 **North Foreland** *c.* U.K.
54 B1 **North Island** N.Z.
129 E2 **North Knife Lake** Can.
65 B1 **North Korea** *country* Asia
62 A1 **North Lakhimpur** India
128 B1 **North Nahanni** *r.* Can.
136 C2 **North Platte** U.S.A.
136 C2 **North Platte** *r.* U.S.A.
96 C1 **North Ronaldsay** *i.* U.K.
94 D2 **North Sea** Europe
130 A1 **North Spirit Lake** Can.
53 D1 **North Stradbroke Island** Austr.
54 B1 **North Taranaki Bight** *b.* N.Z.
130 C1 **North Twin Island** Can.
98 B1 **North Tyne** *r.* U.K.
96 A2 **North Uist** *i.* U.K.
131 D2 **Northumberland Strait** Can.
122 C2 **North West** *prov.* S. Africa
50 A2 **North West Cape** Austr.
143 E3 **Northwest Providence Channel** Bahamas
131 E1 **North West River** Can.
128 B1 **Northwest Territories** *admin. div.* Can.
98 C1 **North York Moors** *moorland* U.K.
140 C3 **Norton** U.S.A.
121 C2 **Norton** Zimbabwe
140 C2 **Norwalk** U.S.A.
93 F3 **Norway** *country* Europe
129 E2 **Norway House** Can.
160 A3 **Norwegian Sea** N. Atlantic Ocean
99 D2 **Norwich** U.K.
141 E2 **Norwich** *CT* U.S.A.
141 D2 **Norwich** *NY* U.S.A.
66 D2 **Noshiro** Japan
91 C1 **Nosivka** Ukr.
122 B2 **Nosop** *watercourse* Africa
86 E2 **Nosovaya** Russia
79 C2 **Noşratābād** Iran
Nossob *watercourse* Africa *see* **Nosop**
103 D1 **Noteć** *r.* Pol.
93 E4 **Notodden** Norway
67 C3 **Noto-hantō** *pen.* Japan
131 D2 **Notre-Dame, Monts** *mts* Can.
131 E2 **Notre Dame Bay** Can.
130 C1 **Nottaway** *r.* Can.
99 C2 **Nottingham** U.K.
114 A2 **Nouâdhibou** Maur.
114 A3 **Nouakchott** Maur.
114 A3 **Nouâmghâr** Maur.
48 F4 **Nouméa** New Caledonia
114 B3 **Nouna** Burkina Faso
154 B2 **Nova Esperança** Brazil
155 D2 **Nova Friburgo** Brazil
109 C1 **Nova Gradiška** Croatia
154 C2 **Nova Granada** Brazil
155 D2 **Nova Iguaçu** Brazil
91 C2 **Nova Kakhovka** Ukr.
155 D1 **Nova Lima** Brazil
154 B2 **Nova Londrina** Brazil
91 C2 **Nova Odesa** Ukr.
131 D2 **Nova Scotia** *prov.* Can.
155 D1 **Nova Venécia** Brazil
83 K1 **Novaya Sibir', Ostrov** *i.* Russia
86 E1 **Novaya Zemlya** *is* Russia
103 D2 **Nové Zámky** Slovakia
91 C1 **Novhorod-Sivers'kyy** Ukr.
110 B2 **Novi Iskar** Bulg.
108 A2 **Novi Ligure** Italy
109 D2 **Novi Pazar** Serbia
109 C1 **Novi Sad** Serbia
87 D3 **Novoanninskiy** Russia
150 B2 **Novo Aripuanã** Brazil
91 D2 **Novoazovs'k** Ukr.
91 E2 **Novocherkassk** Russia
86 D2 **Novodvinsk** Russia
152 C3 **Novo Hamburgo** Brazil
154 C2 **Novo Horizonte** Brazil
90 B1 **Novohrad-Volyns'kyy** Ukr.
103 D2 **Novo mesto** Slovenia
91 D3 **Novomikhaylovskiy** Russia
89 E3 **Novomoskovsk** Russia
91 D2 **Novomoskovs'k** Ukr.
91 C2 **Novomyrhorod** Ukr.
91 C2 **Novooleksiyivka** Ukr.
150 B1 **Novo Paraíso** Brazil
91 D2 **Novopskov** Ukr.
91 D3 **Novorossiysk** Russia
88 C2 **Novorzhev** Russia
87 E3 **Novosergiyevka** Russia
91 D2 **Novoshakhtinsk** Russia
82 G3 **Novosibirsk** Russia
Novosibirskiye Ostrova *is* Russia *see* **New Siberia Islands**
89 E3 **Novosil'** Russia
89 D2 **Novosokol'niki** Russia
91 C2 **Novotroyits'ke** Ukr.
91 C2 **Novoukrayinka** Ukr.
90 A1 **Novovolyns'k** Ukr.
89 D3 **Novozybkov** Russia
103 D2 **Nový Jičín** Czech Rep.
86 E2 **Novyy Bor** Russia
91 D1 **Novyy Oskol** Russia
86 G2 **Novyy Port** Russia
82 G2 **Novyy Urengoy** Russia
69 E1 **Novyy Urgal** Russia
103 D1 **Nowogard** Pol.
53 D2 **Nowra** Austr.
81 D2 **Nowshahr** Iran
74 B1 **Nowshera** Pak.
103 E2 **Nowy Sącz** Pol.
103 E2 **Nowy Targ** Pol.
87 G2 **Noyabr'sk** Russia
105 C2 **Noyon** France
68 C2 **Noyon** Mongolia
121 C2 **Nsanje** Malawi
118 B3 **Ntandembele** Dem. Rep. Congo
111 B3 **Ntoro, Kavo** *pt* Greece
119 D3 **Ntungamo** Uganda
79 C2 **Nu'aym** *reg.* Oman
116 B2 **Nubian Desert** Sudan
129 E1 **Nueltin Lake** Can.
153 A5 **Nueva Lubecka** Arg.
145 B2 **Nueva Rosita** Mex.
144 B1 **Nuevo Casas Grandes** Mex.
144 B2 **Nuevo Ideal** Mex.
145 C2 **Nuevo Laredo** Mex.
117 C4 **Nugaal** *watercourse* Somalia
117 C4 **Nugaaleed, Dooxo** *val.* Somalia
105 C2 **Nuits-St-Georges** France
Nu Jiang *r.* China/Myanmar *see* **Salween**
49 G4 **Nuku'alofa** Tonga
49 I3 **Nuku Hiva** *i.* Fr. Polynesia
76 B2 **Nukus** Uzbek.
50 B2 **Nullagine** Austr.
50 B3 **Nullarbor Plain** Austr.
115 D4 **Numan** Nigeria
67 C3 **Numazu** Japan
93 E3 **Numedal** *val.* Norway
59 C3 **Numfoor** *i.* Indon.
53 C3 **Numurkah** Austr.
Nunap Isua *c.* Greenland *see* **Farewell, Cape**
127 G3 **Nunavik** *reg.* Can.
129 E1 **Nunavut** *admin. div.* Can.
99 C2 **Nuneaton** U.K.
106 B1 **Nuñomoral** Spain
108 A2 **Nuoro** *Sardinia* Italy
78 B2 **Nuqrah** Saudi Arabia
101 E3 **Nuremberg** Ger.
52 A2 **Nuriootpa** Austr.
92 I3 **Nurmes** Fin.
Nürnberg Ger. *see* **Nuremberg**

Nu Shan

62 A1 Nu Shan mts China
74 A2 Nushki Pak.
127 H2 Nuuk Greenland
127 H2 Nuussuaq Greenland
127 H2 Nuussuaq pen. Greenland
78 A2 Nuwaybi' al Muzayyinah Egypt
122 B3 Nuweveldberge mts S. Africa
86 F2 Nyagan' Russia
75 D1 Nyainqêntanglha Feng mt. China
75 D2 Nyainqêntanglha Shan mts China
117 A3 Nyala Sudan
86 D2 Nyandoma Russia
118 B3 Nyanga r. Gabon
121 C2 Nyanga Zimbabwe
Nyang'oma Kenya see Kogelo
121 C1 Nyasa, Lake Africa
93 F4 Nyborg Denmark
92 I1 Nyborg Norway
93 G4 Nybro Sweden
119 D3 Nyeri Kenya
68 C3 Nyingchi China
103 E2 Nyíregyháza Hungary
93 F4 Nykøbing Falster Denmark
93 G4 Nyköping Sweden
53 C2 Nymagee Austr.
93 G4 Nynäshamn Sweden
53 C2 Nyngan Austr.
88 B3 Nyoman r. Belarus/Lith.
105 D3 Nyons France
86 E2 Nyrob Russia
134 C2 Nyssa U.S.A.
119 C3 Nyunzu Dem. Rep. Congo
91 C2 Nyzhn'ohirs'kyy Ukr.
119 D3 Nzega Tanz.
114 B4 Nzérékoré Guinea
120 A1 N'zeto Angola

O

136 C2 Oahe, Lake U.S.A.
124 E5 O'ahu i. U.S.A.
52 B2 Oakbank Austr.
142 B2 Oakdale U.S.A.
53 C1 Oakey Austr.
134 B1 Oak Harbor U.S.A.
140 C3 Oak Hill U.S.A.
135 B3 Oakland U.S.A.
52 B2 Oakover r. Austr.
134 B2 Oakridge U.S.A.
143 D1 Oak Ridge U.S.A.
54 B3 Oamaru N.Z.
64 B1 Oas Phil.
145 C3 Oaxaca Mex.
86 F2 Ob' r. Russia
118 B2 Obala Cameroon
96 B2 Oban U.K.
106 B1 O Barco Spain
53 C2 Oberon Austr.
101 F3 Oberpfälzer Wald mts Ger.
101 F3 Oberviechtach Ger.
59 C3 Obi i. Indon.
151 C2 Óbidos Brazil
66 D2 Obihiro Japan
69 E1 Obluch'ye Russia
89 E2 Obninsk Russia
119 C2 Obo C.A.R.
117 C3 Obock Djibouti
118 B3 Obouya Congo
89 E3 Oboyan' Russia
144 B2 Obregón, Presa resr Mex.
109 D2 Obrenovac Serbia
87 E3 Obshchiy Syrt hills Kazakh./ Russia

86 G2 Obskaya Guba sea chan. Russia
114 B4 Obuasi Ghana
90 C1 Obukhiv Ukr.
86 D2 Ob"yachevo Russia
143 D3 Ocala U.S.A.
144 B2 Ocampo Mex.
106 C2 Ocaña Spain
150 A1 Occidental, Cordillera mts Col.
150 A3 Occidental, Cordillera mts Peru
141 D3 Ocean City U.S.A.
128 B2 Ocean Falls Can.
135 C4 Oceanside U.S.A.
91 C2 Ochakiv Ukr.
86 E3 Ocher Russia
101 E3 Ochsenfurt Ger.
143 D2 Oconee r. U.S.A.
145 C3 Ocosingo Mex.
58 C3 Ocussi enclave East Timor
116 B2 Oda, Jebel mt. Sudan
66 D2 Ōdate Japan
67 C3 Odawara Japan
93 E3 Odda Norway
106 B2 Odemira Port.
111 C3 Ödemiş Turkey
93 F4 Odense Denmark
101 D3 Odenwald reg. Ger.
102 C1 Oderbucht b. Ger.
Odesa Ukr. see Odessa
90 C2 Odessa Ukr.
139 C2 Odessa U.S.A.
114 B4 Odienné Côte d'Ivoire
103 D2 Odra r. Ger./Pol.
151 D2 Oeiras Brazil
100 D2 Oelde Ger.
136 C2 Oelrichs U.S.A.
101 F2 Oelsnitz/Vogtland Ger.
100 B1 Oenkerk Neth.
109 C2 Ofanto r. Italy
102 B2 Offenbach am Main Ger.
100 C2 Offenburg Ger.
117 C4 Ogaden reg. Eth.
66 C3 Oga-hantō pen. Japan
67 C3 Ōgaki Japan
136 C2 Ogallala U.S.A.
115 C4 Ogbomoso Nigeria
134 D2 Ogden U.S.A.
141 D2 Ogdensburg U.S.A.
126 B2 Ogilvie r. Can.
126 B2 Ogilvie Mountains Can.
143 D2 Oglethorpe, Mount U.S.A.
130 B1 Ogoki r. Can.
130 B1 Ogoki Reservoir Can.
88 B2 Ogre Latvia
109 C1 Ogulin Croatia
140 B3 Ohio r. U.S.A.
140 C2 Ohio state U.S.A.
101 E2 Ohrdruf Ger.
109 D2 Ohrid Macedonia
111 B2 Ohrid, Lake l. Albania/ Macedonia
151 C1 Oiapoque Brazil
141 D2 Oil City U.S.A.
100 A3 Oise r. France
67 B4 Ōita Japan
144 B2 Ojinaga Mex.
152 B3 Ojos del Salado, Nevado mt. Arg./Chile
89 F2 Oka r. Russia
120 A3 Okahandja Namibia
120 A3 Okakarara Namibia
128 C3 Okanagan Falls Can.
128 C3 Okanagan Lake Can.
134 C1 Okanogan U.S.A.
134 C1 Okanogan r. U.S.A.
74 B1 Okara Pak.

120 B2 Okavango r. Africa
120 B2 Okavango Delta swamp Botswana
67 C3 Okaya Japan
67 B4 Okayama Japan
67 C4 Okazaki Japan
143 D3 Okeechobee, Lake U.S.A.
143 D2 Okefenokee Swamp U.S.A.
99 A3 Okehampton U.K.
74 A2 Okha India
83 K3 Okha Russia
75 C2 Okhaldhunga Nepal
83 K3 Okhota r. Russia
83 K3 Okhotsk Russia
156 C2 Okhotsk, Sea of Japan/Russia
91 C1 Okhtyrka Ukr.
69 E3 Okinawa i. Japan
67 B3 Oki-shotō is Japan
139 D1 Oklahoma state U.S.A.
139 D1 Oklahoma City U.S.A.
139 D1 Okmulgee U.S.A.
78 A2 Oko, Wadi watercourse Sudan
118 B3 Okondja Gabon
128 C2 Okotoks Can.
89 D3 Okovskiy Les for. Russia
118 B3 Okoyo Congo
92 H1 Øksfjord Norway
62 A2 Oktwin Myanmar
86 D2 Oktyabr'skiy Arkhangel'skaya Oblast' Russia
83 L3 Oktyabr'skiy Kamchatskiy Kray Russia
87 E3 Oktyabr'skiy Respublika Bashkortostan Russia
86 F2 Oktyabr'skoye Russia
83 H1 Oktyabr'skoy Revolyutsii, Ostrov i. Russia
89 D2 Okulovka Russia
66 C2 Ōkushiri-tō i. Japan
93 G4 □A3 Ólafsvík Iceland
93 G4 Öland i. Sweden
52 B2 Olary Austr.
153 B4 Olavarría Arg.
103 D1 Oława Pol.
108 A2 Olbia Sardinia Italy
126 B2 Old Crow Can.
101 D1 Oldenburg Ger.
102 C1 Oldenburg in Holstein Ger.
100 C1 Oldenzaal Neth.
97 B3 Old Head of Kinsale Ireland
128 C2 Olds Can.
129 D2 Old Wives Lake Can.
141 D2 Olean U.S.A.
103 E1 Olecko Pol.
83 J2 Olekminsk Russia
91 C2 Oleksandriya Ukr.
86 C2 Olenegorsk Russia
83 I2 Olenek Russia
83 I2 Olenek r. Russia
89 D2 Olenino Russia
90 B1 Olevs'k Ukr.
106 B2 Olhão Port.
122 A2 Olifants watercourse Namibia
123 D1 Olifants S. Africa
123 D1 Olifants r. Northern S. Africa
123 A3 Olifants r. W. Cape S. Africa
122 B2 Olifantshoek S. Africa
154 C2 Olímpia Brazil
151 E2 Olinda Brazil
123 C1 Oliphants Drift Botswana
107 C2 Oliva Spain
155 D2 Oliveira Brazil
106 B2 Olivenza Spain
152 B3 Ollagüe Chile
150 A2 Olmos Peru
140 B3 Olney U.S.A.
103 D2 Olomouc Czech Rep.
64 B1 Olongapo Phil.

104 B3 **Oloron-Ste-Marie** France
107 D1 **Olot** Spain
69 D1 **Olovyannaya** Russia
83 L2 **Oloy** *r.* Russia
100 C2 **Olpe** Ger.
103 E1 **Olsztyn** Pol.
110 B2 **Olt** *r.* Romania
81 C1 **Oltu** Turkey
111 B3 **Olympia** *tourist site* Greece
134 B1 **Olympia** U.S.A.
134 B1 **Olympus, Mount** U.S.A.
83 M3 **Olyutorskiy, Mys** *c.* Russia
97 C1 **Omagh** U.K.
137 D2 **Omaha** U.S.A.
79 C2 **Oman** *country* Asia
79 C2 **Oman, Gulf of** Asia
120 A3 **Omaruru** Namibia
120 B2 **Omatako** *watercourse* Namibia
116 B3 **Omdurman** Sudan
53 C3 **Omeo** Austr.
145 C3 **Ometepec** Mex.
78 A3 **Om Hajër** Eritrea
128 B2 **Omineca Mountains** Can.
67 C3 **Ōmiya** Japan
100 C1 **Ommen** Neth.
83 L2 **Omolon** *r.* Russia
100 B3 **Omont** France
82 F3 **Omsk** Russia
83 L2 **Omsukchan** Russia
110 C1 **Omu, Vârful** *mt.* Romania
67 A4 **Ōmura** Japan
141 D3 **Onancock** U.S.A.
140 C1 **Onaping Lake** Can.
131 C2 **Onatchiway, Lac** *l.* Can.
120 A2 **Oncócua** Angola
122 B3 **Onderstedorings** S. Africa
120 A2 **Ondjiva** Angola
86 C2 **Onega** Russia
86 C2 **Onega** *r.* Russia
141 D2 **Oneida Lake** U.S.A.
137 D2 **O'Neill** U.S.A.
141 D2 **Oneonta** U.S.A.
110 C1 **Onești** Romania
Onezhskoye, Ozero *l.* Russia *see* **Onezhskoye Ozero**
86 C2 **Onezhskoye Ozero** *l.* Russia
122 B2 **Ongers** *watercourse* S. Africa
65 B2 **Ongjin** N. Korea
73 C3 **Ongole** India
121 D3 **Onilahy** *r.* Madag.
115 C4 **Onitsha** Nigeria
122 A2 **Onseepkans** S. Africa
50 A2 **Onslow** Austr.
143 E2 **Onslow Bay** U.S.A.
130 A1 **Ontario** *prov.* Can.
134 C2 **Ontario** U.S.A.
141 D2 **Ontario, Lake** Can./U.S.A.
51 C2 **Oodnadatta** Austr.
Oostende Belgium *see* **Ostend**
100 B2 **Oosterhout** Neth.
100 A2 **Oosterschelde** *est.* Neth.
100 B1 **Oost-Vlieland** Neth.
128 B2 **Ootsa Lake** Can.
128 B2 **Ootsa Lake** Can.
118 C3 **Opala** Dem. Rep. Congo
130 C1 **Opataca, Lac** *l.* Can.
103 D2 **Opava** Czech Rep.
143 C2 **Opelika** U.S.A.
142 B2 **Opelousas** U.S.A.
130 C1 **Opinaca, Réservoir** *resr* Can.
131 D1 **Opiscotéo, Lac** *l.* Can.
88 C2 **Opochka** Russia
144 A2 **Opodepe** Mex.
103 D1 **Opole** Pol.
106 B1 **Oporto** Port.
54 C1 **Opotiki** N.Z.
93 E3 **Oppdal** Norway
54 B1 **Opunake** N.Z.
120 A2 **Opuwo** Namibia
110 B1 **Oradea** Romania
Orahovac Kosovo *see* **Rahovec**
114 B1 **Oran** Alg.
152 B3 **Orán** Arg.
65 B1 **Ŏrang** N. Korea
53 C2 **Orange** Austr.
105 C3 **Orange** France
122 A2 **Orange** *r.* Namibia/S. Africa
139 E2 **Orange** U.S.A.
143 D2 **Orangeburg** U.S.A.
140 C2 **Orangeville** Can.
101 F1 **Oranienburg** Ger.
122 A2 **Oranjemund** Namibia
120 B3 **Orapa** Botswana
110 B1 **Orăștie** Romania
108 B2 **Orbetello** Italy
53 C3 **Orbost** Austr.
50 B1 **Ord, Mount** *h.* Austr.
106 B1 **Ordes** Spain
Ordos China *see* **Dongsheng**
80 B1 **Ordu** Turkey
Ordzhonikidze Russia *see* **Vladikavkaz**
91 C2 **Ordzhonikidze** Ukr.
93 G4 **Örebro** Sweden
134 B2 **Oregon** *state* U.S.A.
134 B1 **Oregon City** U.S.A.
87 C3 **Orekhovo-Zuyevo** Russia
89 E3 **Orel** Russia
83 K3 **Orel', Ozero** *l.* Russia
135 D2 **Orem** U.S.A.
111 C3 **Ören** Turkey
87 E3 **Orenburg** Russia
54 A3 **Orepuki** N.Z.
93 F4 **Öresund** *str.* Denmark/Sweden
99 D2 **Orford Ness** *hd* U.K.
111 C3 **Orhaneli** Turkey
111 C2 **Orhangazi** Turkey
83 I3 **Orhon Gol** *r.* Mongolia
152 B2 **Oriental, Cordillera** *mts* Bol.
150 A1 **Oriental, Cordillera** *mts* Col.
150 A3 **Oriental, Cordillera** *mts* Peru
107 C2 **Orihuela** Spain
91 D2 **Orikhiv** Ukr.
130 C2 **Orillia** Can.
150 B1 **Orinoco** *r.* Col./Venez.
150 B1 **Orinoco, Delta del** Venez.
93 H4 **Orissaare** Estonia
108 A3 **Oristano** *Sardinia* Italy
93 I3 **Orivesi** *l.* Fin.
151 C2 **Oriximiná** Brazil
145 C3 **Orizaba** Mex.
145 C3 **Orizaba, Pico de** *vol.* Mex.
92 E3 **Orkanger** Norway
93 F4 **Örkelljunga** Sweden
92 E3 **Orkla** *r.* Norway
96 C1 **Orkney Islands** U.K.
154 C2 **Orlândia** Brazil
143 D3 **Orlando** U.S.A.
104 C2 **Orléans** France
74 A2 **Ormara** Pak.
64 B1 **Ormoc** Phil.
98 B2 **Ormskirk** U.K.
92 G3 **Örnsköldsvik** Sweden
114 B3 **Orodara** Burkina Faso
134 C1 **Orofino** U.S.A.
Oroqen Zizhiqi China *see* **Alihe**
64 B2 **Oroquieta** Phil.
108 A2 **Orosei** *Sardinia* Italy
108 A2 **Orosei, Golfo di** *b. Sardinia* Italy
103 E2 **Orosháza** Hungary
135 B3 **Oroville** U.S.A.
52 A2 **Orroroo** Austr.
89 D3 **Orsha** Belarus
87 E3 **Orsk** Russia
93 E3 **Ørsta** Norway
106 B1 **Ortegal, Cabo** *c.* Spain
104 B3 **Orthez** France
106 B1 **Ortigueira** Spain
137 D1 **Ortonville** U.S.A.
83 J2 **Orulgan, Khrebet** *mts* Russia
Orūmīyeh, Daryācheh-ye *salt l.* Iran *see* **Urmia, Lake**
152 B2 **Oruro** Bol.
108 B2 **Orvieto** Italy
146 B4 **Osa, Península de** *pen.* Costa Rica
137 E3 **Osage** *r.* U.S.A.
67 C4 **Ōsaka** Japan
66 D3 **Ōsaki** Japan
110 B2 **Osam** *r.* Bulg.
101 E1 **Oschersleben (Bode)** Ger.
108 A2 **Oschiri** *Sardinia* Italy
89 E3 **Osetr** *r.* Russia
77 D2 **Osh** Kyrg.
120 A2 **Oshakati** Namibia
130 C2 **Oshawa** Can.
66 C2 **Ō-shima** *i.* Japan
67 C4 **Ō-shima** *i.* Japan
140 B2 **Oshkosh** U.S.A.
81 C2 **Oshnavīyeh** Iran
118 B3 **Oshwe** Dem. Rep. Congo
109 C1 **Osijek** Croatia
128 B2 **Osilinka** *r.* Can.
108 B2 **Osimo** Italy
123 D2 **oSizweni** S. Africa
137 E2 **Oskaloosa** U.S.A.
93 G4 **Oskarshamn** Sweden
89 E3 **Oskol** *r.* Russia
93 F4 **Oslo** Norway
93 F4 **Oslofjorden** *sea chan.* Norway
80 B1 **Osmancık** Turkey
111 C2 **Osmaneli** Turkey
80 B2 **Osmaniye** Turkey
88 C2 **Os'mino** Russia
100 D1 **Osnabrück** Ger.
115 C4 **Osogbo** Nigeria
153 A5 **Osorno** Chile
106 C1 **Osorno** Spain
128 C3 **Osoyoos** Can.
100 B2 **Oss** Neth.
51 D4 **Ossa, Mount** Austr.
83 L3 **Ossora** Russia
89 D2 **Ostashkov** Russia
101 D1 **Oste** *r.* Ger.
100 A2 **Ostend** Belgium
101 E1 **Osterburg (Altmark)** Ger.
93 F3 **Österdalälven** *r.* Sweden
101 D1 **Osterholz-Scharmbeck** Ger.
101 E2 **Osterode am Harz** Ger.
92 F3 **Östersund** Sweden
Ostfriesische Inseln *is* Ger. *see* **East Frisian Islands**
100 C1 **Ostfriesland** *reg.* Ger.
93 G3 **Östhammar** Sweden
103 D2 **Ostrava** Czech Rep.
103 D1 **Ostróda** Pol.
89 E3 **Ostrogozhsk** Russia
103 E1 **Ostrołęka** Pol.
101 F2 **Ostrov** Czech Rep.
88 C2 **Ostrov** Russia
103 E1 **Ostrowiec Świętokrzyski** Pol.
103 E1 **Ostrów Mazowiecka** Pol.
103 D1 **Ostrów Wielkopolski** Pol.
67 B4 **Ōsumi-kaikyō** *sea chan.* Japan
67 B4 **Ōsumi-shotō** *is* Japan
106 B2 **Osuna** Spain
141 D2 **Oswego** U.S.A.
99 B2 **Oswestry** U.K.

67 C3 **Ōta** Japan
54 B3 **Otago Peninsula** N.Z.
54 C2 **Otaki** N.Z.
66 D2 **Otaru** Japan
120 A2 **Otavi** Namibia
134 C1 **Othello** U.S.A.
120 A3 **Otjiwarongo** Namibia
117 B3 **Otoro, Jebel** *mt.* Sudan
93 E4 **Otra** *r.* Norway
109 C2 **Otranto, Strait of** Albania/Italy
67 C3 **Ōtsu** Japan
93 E3 **Otta** Norway
130 C2 **Ottawa** Can.
130 C2 **Ottawa** *r.* Can.
140 B2 **Ottawa** *IL* U.S.A.
137 D3 **Ottawa** *KS* U.S.A.
130 B1 **Otter Rapids** Can.
100 B2 **Ottignies** Belgium
137 E2 **Ottumwa** U.S.A.
150 A2 **Otuzco** Peru
52 B3 **Otway, Cape** Austr.
142 B2 **Ouachita** *r.* U.S.A.
142 B2 **Ouachita, Lake** U.S.A.
142 B2 **Ouachita Mountains** U.S.A.
118 C2 **Ouadda** C.A.R.
115 D3 **Ouaddaï** *reg.* Chad
114 B3 **Ouagadougou** Burkina Faso
114 B3 **Ouahigouya** Burkina Faso
114 B3 **Oualâta** Maur.
118 C2 **Ouanda Djallé** C.A.R.
114 B2 **Ouarâne** *reg.* Maur.
115 C1 **Ouargla** Alg.
114 B1 **Ouarzazate** Morocco
100 A2 **Oudenaarde** Belgium
122 B3 **Oudtshoorn** S. Africa
107 C2 **Oued Tlélat** Alg.
104 A2 **Ouessant, Île d'** *i.* France
118 B2 **Ouesso** Congo
114 B1 **Oujda** Morocco
107 D2 **Ouled Farès** Alg.
92 I2 **Oulu** Fin.
92 I3 **Oulujärvi** *l.* Fin.
108 A1 **Oulx** Italy
115 E3 **Oum-Chalouba** Chad
115 D3 **Oum-Hadjer** Chad
115 E3 **Ounianga Kébir** Chad
100 B2 **Oupeye** Belgium
106 B1 **Ourense** Spain
154 C2 **Ourinhos** Brazil
155 D2 **Ouro Preto** Brazil
100 B2 **Ourthe** *r.* Belgium
98 C2 **Ouse** *r.* U.K.
131 D2 **Outardes, Rivière aux** *r.* Can.
131 D1 **Outardes Quatre, Réservoir** *resr* Can.
96 A2 **Outer Hebrides** *is* U.K.
120 A3 **Outjo** Namibia
129 D2 **Outlook** Can.
92 I3 **Outokumpu** Fin.
52 B3 **Ouyen** Austr.
106 B1 **Ovar** Port.
92 H2 **Överkalix** Sweden
135 D3 **Overton** U.S.A.
92 H2 **Övertorneå** Sweden
106 B1 **Oviedo** Spain
93 E3 **Øvre Årdal** Norway
93 F3 **Øvre Rendal** Norway
90 B1 **Ovruch** Ukr.
118 B3 **Owando** Congo
67 C4 **Owase** Japan
137 E2 **Owatonna** U.S.A.
140 B3 **Owensboro** U.S.A.
135 C3 **Owens Lake** U.S.A.
130 B2 **Owen Sound** Can.
115 C4 **Owerri** Nigeria
140 C2 **Owosso** U.S.A.
134 C2 **Owyhee** U.S.A.
134 C2 **Owyhee** *r.* U.S.A.
54 B2 **Oxford** N.Z.
99 C3 **Oxford** U.K.
142 C2 **Oxford** U.S.A.
129 E2 **Oxford Lake** Can.
52 B2 **Oxley** Austr.
97 B1 **Ox Mountains** *hills* Ireland
135 C4 **Oxnard** U.S.A.
67 C3 **Oyama** Japan
118 B2 **Oyem** Gabon
129 C2 **Oyen** Can.
105 D2 **Oyonnax** France
64 B2 **Ozamis** Phil.
142 C2 **Ozark** U.S.A.
137 E3 **Ozark Plateau** U.S.A.
137 E3 **Ozarks, Lake of the** U.S.A.
83 L3 **Ozernovskiy** Russia
88 B3 **Ozersk** Russia
89 E3 **Ozery** Russia
87 D3 **Ozinki** Russia

P

127 H2 **Paamiut** Greenland
122 A3 **Paarl** S. Africa
103 D1 **Pabianice** Pol.
75 C2 **Pabna** Bangl.
74 A2 **Pab Range** *mts* Pak.
109 C3 **Pachino** *Sicily* Italy
145 C2 **Pachuca** Mex.
156 **Pacific Ocean**
103 D1 **Paczków** Pol.
60 B2 **Padang** Indon.
60 B1 **Padang Endau** Malaysia
60 B2 **Padangpanjang** Indon.
60 A1 **Padangsidimpuan** Indon.
101 D2 **Paderborn** Ger.
Padova Italy *see* **Padua**
139 D3 **Padre Island** U.S.A.
52 B3 **Padthaway** Austr.
108 B1 **Padua** Italy
140 B3 **Paducah** *KY* U.S.A.
139 C2 **Paducah** *TX* U.S.A.
65 B1 **Paegam** N. Korea
Paengnyŏng-do *i.* S. Korea *see* **Baengnyeong-do**
54 C1 **Paeroa** N.Z.
Pafos Cyprus *see* **Paphos**
109 C2 **Pag** Croatia
64 B2 **Pagadian** Phil.
60 B2 **Pagai Selatan** *i.* Indon.
60 B2 **Pagai Utara** *i.* Indon.
59 D1 **Pagan** *i.* N. Mariana Is
61 C2 **Pagatan** Indon.
138 A1 **Page** U.S.A.
88 B2 **Paggiai** Lith.
136 B3 **Pagosa Springs** U.S.A.
88 C2 **Paide** Estonia
93 I3 **Päijänne** *l.* Fin.
75 C2 **Paikü Co** *l.* China
138 A1 **Painted Desert** U.S.A.
96 B3 **Paisley** U.K.
92 H2 **Pajala** Sweden
150 B1 **Pakaraima Mountains** S. America
150 C1 **Pakaraima Mountains** S. America
74 A2 **Pakistan** *country* Asia
62 A1 **Pakokku** Myanmar
88 B2 **Pakruojis** Lith.
103 D2 **Paks** Hungary
130 A1 **Pakwash Lake** Can.
62 B2 **Pakxan** Laos
63 B2 **Pakxé** Laos
115 D4 **Pala** Chad
60 B2 **Palabuhanratu, Teluk** *b.* Indon.
111 C3 **Palaikastro** Greece
111 B3 **Palaiochora** Greece
122 B1 **Palamakoloi** Botswana
107 D1 **Palamós** Spain
83 L3 **Palana** Russia
64 B1 **Palanan** Phil.
61 C2 **Palangkaraya** Indon.
74 B2 **Palanpur** India
120 B3 **Palapye** Botswana
83 L2 **Palatka** Russia
143 D3 **Palatka** U.S.A.
59 C2 **Palau** *country* N. Pacific Ocean
63 A2 **Palaw** Myanmar
64 A2 **Palawan** *i.* Phil.
93 H4 **Paldiski** Estonia
60 B2 **Palembang** Indon.
106 C1 **Palencia** Spain
145 C3 **Palenque** Mex.
108 B3 **Palermo** *Sicily* Italy
139 D2 **Palestine** U.S.A.
62 A1 **Paletwa** Myanmar
74 B2 **Pali** India
48 E2 **Palikir** Micronesia
109 C2 **Palinuro, Capo** *c.* Italy
111 B3 **Paliouri, Akrotirio** *pt* Greece
100 B3 **Paliseul** Belgium
92 I3 **Paljakka** *h.* Fin.
88 C2 **Palkino** Russia
73 B4 **Palk Strait** India/Sri Lanka
54 C2 **Palliser, Cape** N.Z.
49 I3 **Palliser, Îles** *is* Fr. Polynesia
106 B2 **Palma del Río** Spain
107 D2 **Palma de Mallorca** Spain
154 B3 **Palmas** *Paraná* Brazil
151 D3 **Palmas** *Tocantins* Brazil
114 B4 **Palmas, Cape** Liberia
154 C3 **Palmeira** Brazil
151 D2 **Palmeirais** Brazil
55 P2 **Palmer Land** *reg.* Antarctica
54 C2 **Palmerston North** N.Z.
109 C3 **Palmi** Italy
145 C2 **Palmillas** Mex.
150 A1 **Palmira** Col.
135 C4 **Palm Springs** U.S.A.
49 H2 **Palmyra Atoll** N. Pacific Ocean
117 B3 **Paloich** South Sudan
145 C3 **Palomares** Mex.
107 C2 **Palos, Cabo de** *c.* Spain
92 I3 **Paltamo** Fin.
58 B3 **Palu** Indon.
83 M2 **Palyavaam** *r.* Russia
104 C3 **Pamiers** France
77 D3 **Pamir** *mts* Asia
143 E1 **Pamlico Sound** *sea chan.* U.S.A.
152 B2 **Pampa Grande** Bol.
153 B4 **Pampas** *reg.* Arg.
150 A1 **Pamplona** Col.
107 C1 **Pamplona** Spain
111 D2 **Pamukova** Turkey
60 B2 **Panaitan** *i.* Indon.
73 B3 **Panaji** India
146 B4 **Panama** *country* Central America
146 C4 **Panamá, Canal de** Panama
146 C4 **Panama, Gulf of** Panama
146 C4 **Panama City** Panama
142 C2 **Panama City** U.S.A.
135 C3 **Panamint Range** *mts* U.S.A.
61 B1 **Panarik** Indon.
64 B1 **Panay** *i.* Phil.
109 D2 **Pančevo** Serbia
64 B1 **Pandan** Phil.

75 C2 **Pandaria** India
73 B3 **Pandharpur** India
61 C2 **Panevėžys** Lith.
61 C2 **Pangkalanbuun** Indon.
60 A1 **Pangkalansusu** Indon.
60 B2 **Pangkalpinang** Indon.
127 G2 **Pangnirtung** Can.
86 G2 **Pangody** Russia
89 F3 **Panino** Russia
74 B2 **Panipat** India
74 A2 **Panjgur** Pak.
65 C1 **Pan Ling** *mts* China
75 C2 **Panna** India
50 A2 **Pannawonica** Austr.
54 B2 **Panorama** Brazil
65 B1 **Panshi** China
145 C2 **Pánuco** Mex.
62 B1 **Panzhihua** China
109 C3 **Paola** Italy
63 B2 **Paôy Pêt** Cambodia
103 D2 **Pápa** Hungary
54 B1 **Papakura** N.Z.
145 C2 **Papantla** Mex.
49 I4 **Papeete** Fr. Polynesia
100 C1 **Papenburg** Ger.
80 B2 **Paphos** Cyprus
59 D3 **Papua, Gulf of** P.N.G.
59 D3 **Papua New Guinea** *country*
       Oceania
50 A2 **Paraburdoo** Austr.
154 C1 **Paracatu** Brazil
155 C1 **Paracatu** *r.* Brazil
52 A2 **Parachilna** Austr.
109 D2 **Paraćin** Serbia
155 D1 **Pará de Minas** Brazil
135 B3 **Paradise** U.S.A.
142 B1 **Paragould** U.S.A.
151 C3 **Paraguai** *r.* Brazil
152 C3 **Paraguay** *r.* Arg./Para.
152 C3 **Paraguay** *country* S. America
155 D2 **Paraíba do Sul** *r.* Brazil
154 B1 **Paraíso** Brazil
145 C3 **Paraíso** Mex.
114 C4 **Parakou** Benin
151 C1 **Paramaribo** Suriname
83 L3 **Paramushir, Ostrov** *i.* Russia
152 B4 **Paraná** Arg.
154 A3 **Paraná** *r.* S. America
154 C3 **Paranaguá** Brazil
154 B1 **Paranaíba** Brazil
154 B2 **Paranaíba** *r.* Brazil
154 B2 **Paranapanema** *r.* Brazil
154 B2 **Paranapiacaba, Serra** *mts*
       Brazil
154 B2 **Paranavaí** Brazil
54 B2 **Paraparaumu** N.Z.
155 D2 **Paratimirim** Brazil
154 B1 **Paraúna** Brazil
105 C2 **Paray-le-Monial** France
73 B3 **Parbhani** India
101 E1 **Parchim** Ger.
155 E1 **Pardo** *r. Bahia* Brazil
154 B2 **Pardo** *r. Mato Grosso do Sul*
       Brazil
154 C2 **Pardo** *r. São Paulo* Brazil
103 D1 **Pardubice** Czech Rep.
150 B3 **Parecis, Serra dos** *hills* Brazil
130 C2 **Parent, Lac** *l.* Can.
58 B3 **Parepare** Indon.
92 D2 **Parfino** Russia
111 B3 **Parga** Greece
109 C3 **Parghelia** Italy
147 D3 **Paria, Gulf of** Trin. and Tob./
       Venez.
150 B1 **Parima, Serra** *mts* Brazil
151 C2 **Parintins** Brazil
104 C2 **Paris** France
142 C1 **Paris** *TN* U.S.A.

139 D2 **Paris** *TX* U.S.A.
93 H3 **Parkano** Fin.
138 A2 **Parker** U.S.A.
140 C3 **Parkersburg** U.S.A.
53 C2 **Parkes** Austr.
140 A1 **Park Falls** U.S.A.
137 D1 **Park Rapids** U.S.A.
108 B2 **Parma** Italy
151 E2 **Parnaíba** *r.* Brazil
151 D2 **Parnaíba** *r.* Brazil
54 B2 **Parnassus** N.Z.
111 B3 **Parnonas** *mts* Greece
88 C2 **Pärnu** Estonia
65 B2 **Paro-ho** *l.* S. Korea
52 B2 **Paroo** *watercourse* Austr.
       Paropamisus *mts* Afgh. *see*
       Safēd Köh, Silsilah-ye
111 C3 **Paros** *i.* Greece
144 B2 **Parras** Mex.
126 C2 **Parry, Cape** Can.
126 D1 **Parry Islands** Can.
130 C2 **Parry Sound** Can.
79 C2 **Pārsian** Iran
137 D3 **Parsons** U.S.A.
101 D2 **Partenstein** Ger.
104 B2 **Parthenay** France
97 B2 **Partry Mountains** *hills* Ireland
151 C2 **Paru** *r.* Brazil
135 C4 **Pasadena** U.S.A.
62 A2 **Pasawng** Myanmar
142 C2 **Pascagoula** U.S.A.
110 C1 **Pașcani** Romania
134 C1 **Pasco** U.S.A.
102 C1 **Pasewalk** Ger.
129 D2 **Pasfield Lake** Can.
64 B1 **Pasig** Phil.
60 B1 **Pasir Putih** Malaysia
74 A2 **Pasni** Pak.
153 A5 **Paso Río Mayo** Arg.
135 B3 **Paso Robles** U.S.A.
155 D2 **Passa Tempo** Brazil
102 C2 **Passau** Ger.
152 C3 **Passo Fundo** Brazil
155 C2 **Passos** Brazil
88 C3 **Pastavy** Belarus
150 A2 **Pastaza** *r.* Peru
150 A1 **Pasto** Col.
61 C2 **Pasuruan** Indon.
88 B2 **Pasvalys** Lith.
153 A6 **Patagonia** *reg.* Arg.
75 C2 **Patan** Nepal
54 B1 **Patea** N.Z.
141 E2 **Paterson** U.S.A.
       Pathein Myanmar *see* **Bassein**
136 B2 **Pathfinder Reservoir** U.S.A.
61 C2 **Pati** Indon.
62 A1 **Patkai Bum** *mts* India/
       Myanmar
111 C3 **Patmos** *i.* Greece
75 C2 **Patna** India
81 C2 **Patnos** Turkey
154 B3 **Pato Branco** Brazil
152 C4 **Patos, Lagoa dos** *l.* Brazil
155 C1 **Patos de Minas** Brazil
152 B4 **Patquía** Arg.
111 B3 **Patras** Greece
75 C2 **Patratu** India
154 C1 **Patrocínio** Brazil
63 B3 **Pattani** Thai.
63 B2 **Pattaya** Thai.
128 B2 **Pattullo, Mount** Can.
129 D2 **Patuanak** Can.
144 B3 **Pátzcuaro** Mex.
104 B3 **Pau** France
104 B2 **Pauillac** France
62 A1 **Pauk** Myanmar
151 D2 **Paulistana** Brazil
151 E2 **Paulo Afonso** Brazil

123 D2 **Paulpietersburg** S. Africa
139 D2 **Pauls Valley** U.S.A.
62 A2 **Paungde** Myanmar
155 D1 **Pavão** Brazil
108 A1 **Pavia** Italy
88 B2 **Pāvilosta** Latvia
110 C2 **Pavlikeni** Bulg.
77 D1 **Pavlodar** Kazakh.
91 C2 **Pavlohrad** Ukr.
91 E1 **Pavlovsk** Russia
91 E1 **Pavlovskaya** Russia
60 B2 **Payakumbuh** Indon.
134 C2 **Payette** U.S.A.
134 C2 **Payette** *r.* U.S.A.
86 F2 **Pay-Khoy, Khrebet** *hills* Russia
152 C4 **Paysandú** Uru.
81 C1 **Pazar** Turkey
110 B2 **Pazardzhik** Bulg.
111 C3 **Pazarköy** Turkey
108 B1 **Pazin** Croatia
63 A2 **Pe** Myanmar
128 C2 **Peace** *r.* Can.
128 C2 **Peace River** Can.
135 E3 **Peale, Mount** U.S.A.
142 C2 **Pearl** *r.* U.S.A.
139 D3 **Pearsall** U.S.A.
121 C2 **Pebane** Moz.
       Peč Kosovo *see* **Pejë**
155 D1 **Peçanha** Brazil
86 E2 **Pechora** Russia
86 E2 **Pechora** *r.* Russia
88 C2 **Pechory** Russia
139 C2 **Pecos** U.S.A.
139 C3 **Pecos** *r.* U.S.A.
103 D2 **Pécs** Hungary
155 D1 **Pedra Azul** Brazil
154 C2 **Pedregulho** Brazil
151 D2 **Pedreiras** Brazil
73 C4 **Pedro, Point** Sri Lanka
151 D2 **Pedro Afonso** Brazil
154 B1 **Pedro Gomes** Brazil
152 C3 **Pedro Juan Caballero** Para.
96 C3 **Peebles** U.K.
143 E2 **Pee Dee** *r.* U.S.A.
126 C2 **Peel** *r.* Can.
98 A1 **Peel** Isle of Man
128 C2 **Peerless Lake** Can.
54 B2 **Pegasus Bay** N.Z.
101 E3 **Pegnitz** Ger.
62 A2 **Pegu** Myanmar
62 A2 **Pegu Yoma** *mts* Myanmar
153 B4 **Pehuajó** Arg.
101 E1 **Peine** Ger.
88 C2 **Peipus, Lake** Estonia/Russia
154 B2 **Peixe** *r.* Brazil
109 D2 **Pejë** Kosovo
61 B2 **Pekalongan** Indon.
60 B1 **Pekan** Malaysia
60 B1 **Pekanbaru** Indon.
       Peking China *see* **Beijing**
130 B2 **Pelee Island** Can.
59 C3 **Peleng** *i.* Indon.
92 I2 **Pelkosenniemi** Fin.
122 A2 **Pella** S. Africa
59 D3 **Pelleluhu Islands** P.N.G.
92 H2 **Pello** Fin.
61 B2 **Pelly** *r.* Can.
128 A1 **Pelly Mountains** Can.
152 C4 **Pelotas** Brazil
152 C3 **Pelotas, Rio das** *r.* Brazil
141 F1 **Pemadumcook Lake** U.S.A.
61 B2 **Pemangkat** Indon.
60 A1 **Pematangsiantar** Indon.
121 D2 **Pemba** Moz.
120 B2 **Pemba** Zambia
119 D3 **Pemba Island** Tanz.
128 B2 **Pemberton** Can.
137 D1 **Pembina** *r.* Can./U.S.A.

Pembroke

130 C2 **Pembroke** Can.
99 A3 **Pembroke** U.K.
145 C2 **Peña Nevada, Cerro** mt. Mex.
154 B2 **Penápolis** Brazil
106 B1 **Peñaranda de Bracamonte** Spain
107 C1 **Peñarroya** mt. Spain
106 B2 **Peñarroya-Pueblonuevo** Spain
106 B1 **Peñas, Cabo de** c. Spain
153 A5 **Penas, Golfo de** g. Chile
134 C1 **Pendleton** U.S.A.
128 B2 **Pendleton Bay** Can.
134 C1 **Pend Oreille Lake** U.S.A.
74 B3 **Penganga** r. India
123 D1 **Penge** S. Africa
70 C2 **Penglai** China
71 A3 **Pengshui** China
106 B2 **Peniche** Port.
98 B1 **Penicuik** U.K.
108 B2 **Penne** Italy
98 B1 **Pennines** hills U.K.
141 D2 **Pennsylvania** state U.S.A.
127 G2 **Penny Icecap** Can.
141 F2 **Penobscot** r. U.S.A.
52 B3 **Penola** Austr.
50 C3 **Penong** Austr.
49 H3 **Penrhyn** atoll Cook Is
98 B1 **Penrith** U.K.
142 C2 **Pensacola** U.S.A.
55 Q1 **Pensacola Mountains** Antarctica
61 C1 **Pensiangan** Sabah Malaysia
128 C3 **Penticton** Can.
96 C1 **Pentland Firth** sea chan. U.K.
99 B2 **Penygadair** h. U.K.
87 D3 **Penza** Russia
99 A3 **Penzance** U.K.
140 B2 **Peoria** U.S.A.
107 C1 **Perales del Alfambra** Spain
51 E2 **Percy Isles** Austr.
86 F2 **Peregrebnoye** Russia
150 A1 **Pereira** Col.
154 B2 **Pereira Barreto** Brazil
90 A2 **Peremyshlyany** Ukr.
89 E2 **Pereslavl'-Zalesskiy** Russia
91 C1 **Pereyaslav-Khmel'nyts'kyy** Ukr.
153 B4 **Pergamino** Arg.
92 H3 **Perhonjoki** r. Fin.
131 C1 **Péribonka, Lac** l. Can.
152 B3 **Perico** Arg.
144 B2 **Pericos** Mex.
104 C2 **Périgueux** France
147 C4 **Perijá, Sierra de** mts Venez.
153 A5 **Perito Moreno** Arg.
101 E1 **Perleberg** Ger.
86 E3 **Perm'** Russia
52 A2 **Pernatty Lagoon** imp. l. Austr.
105 C2 **Péronne** France
145 C3 **Perote** Mex.
104 C3 **Perpignan** France
99 A3 **Perranporth** U.K.
143 D2 **Perry** FL U.S.A.
143 D2 **Perry** GA U.S.A.
137 E2 **Perry** IA U.S.A.
139 C1 **Perryton** U.S.A.
137 F3 **Perryville** U.S.A.
99 B2 **Pershore** U.K.
91 D2 **Pershotravens'k** Ukr.
  Persian Gulf Asia see **The Gulf**
50 A3 **Perth** Austr.
96 C2 **Perth** U.K.
105 D3 **Pertuis** France
108 A2 **Pertusato, Capo** c. Corsica France
150 A2 **Peru** country S. America
157 H4 **Peru-Chile Trench** S. Pacific Ocean

108 B2 **Perugia** Italy
154 C2 **Peruíbe** Brazil
100 A2 **Péruwelz** Belgium
90 C2 **Pervomays'k** Ukr.
91 C2 **Pervomays'ke** Ukr.
89 F1 **Pervomayskiy** Russia
91 D2 **Pervomays'kyy** Ukr.
108 B2 **Pesaro** Italy
108 B2 **Pescara** Italy
108 B2 **Pescara** r. Italy
74 B1 **Peshawar** Pak.
109 D2 **Peshkopi** Albania
109 C1 **Pesnica** Slovenia
89 E2 **Pestovo** Russia
144 B3 **Petatlán** Mex.
140 B2 **Petenwell Lake** U.S.A.
52 A2 **Peterborough** Austr.
130 C2 **Peterborough** Can.
99 C2 **Peterborough** U.K.
96 D2 **Peterhead** U.K.
50 B2 **Petermann Ranges** mts Austr.
129 D2 **Peter Pond Lake** Can.
128 A2 **Petersburg** AK U.S.A.
141 D3 **Petersburg** VA U.S.A.
101 D1 **Petershagen** Ger.
131 E1 **Petit Mécatina** r. Can.
145 D2 **Peto** Mex.
140 C1 **Petoskey** U.S.A.
80 B2 **Petra** tourist site Jordan
66 B2 **Petra Velikogo, Zaliv** b. Russia
111 B2 **Petrich** Bulg.
151 D2 **Petrolina** Brazil
83 L3 **Petropavlovsk-Kamchatskiy** Russia
77 C1 **Petropavlovsk** Kazakh.
110 B1 **Petroșani** Romania
89 F3 **Petrovskoye** Russia
86 C2 **Petrozavodsk** Russia
123 C2 **Petrusburg** S. Africa
123 C2 **Petrus Steyn** S. Africa
122 B3 **Petrusville** S. Africa
89 E2 **Petushki** Russia
60 A1 **Peureula** Indon.
83 M2 **Pevek** Russia
102 B2 **Pforzheim** Ger.
102 C2 **Pfunds** Austria
101 D3 **Pfungstadt** Ger.
123 C2 **Phahameng** S. Africa
123 D1 **Phalaborwa** S. Africa
74 B2 **Phalodi** India
63 B2 **Phang Hoei, San Khao** mts Thai.
63 A3 **Phangnga** Thai.
62 B1 **Phăng Xi Păng** mt. Vietnam
63 B2 **Phan Rang-Thap Cham** Vietnam
63 B2 **Phan Thiết** Vietnam
63 B3 **Phatthalung** Thai.
62 A2 **Phayao** Thai.
129 D2 **Phelps Lake** Can.
143 C2 **Phenix City** U.S.A.
63 A2 **Phet Buri** Thai.
63 B2 **Phichit** Thai.
141 D3 **Philadelphia** U.S.A.
136 C2 **Philip** U.S.A.
100 B2 **Philippeville** Belgium
100 A2 **Philippine** Neth.
64 B1 **Philippines** country Asia
64 B1 **Philippine Sea** N. Pacific Ocean
126 B2 **Philip Smith Mountains** U.S.A.
122 B3 **Philipstown** S. Africa
53 C3 **Phillip Island** Austr.
137 D3 **Phillipsburg** U.S.A.
123 C2 **Phiritona** S. Africa
63 B2 **Phitsanulok** Thai.
63 B2 **Phnom Penh** Cambodia

  Phnum Pénh Cambodia see **Phnom Penh**
138 A2 **Phoenix** U.S.A.
49 G3 **Phoenix Islands** Kiribati
63 B2 **Phon** Thai.
62 B1 **Phôngsali** Laos
62 B2 **Phônsavan** Laos
62 B2 **Phônsavan** mt. Laos
62 B2 **Phrae** Thai.
63 A3 **Phuket** Thai.
62 A2 **Phumiphon, Khuan** Thai.
123 C2 **Phuthaditjhaba** S. Africa
62 A2 **Phyu** Myanmar
108 A1 **Piacenza** Italy
110 C1 **Piatra Neamț** Romania
151 D2 **Piauí** r. Brazil
108 B1 **Piave** r. Italy
117 B4 **Pibor** r. South Sudan
117 B4 **Pibor Post** South Sudan
142 C2 **Picayune** U.S.A.
152 B3 **Pichanal** Arg.
144 A2 **Pichilingue** Mex.
98 C1 **Pickering** U.K.
130 A1 **Pickle Lake** Can.
151 D2 **Picos** Brazil
153 B5 **Pico Truncado** Arg.
130 B3 **Picton** Can.
150 B3 **Piedras, Río de las** r. Peru
145 C3 **Piedras Negras** Guat.
145 B2 **Piedras Negras** Mex.
93 I3 **Pieksämäki** Fin.
92 I3 **Pielinen** l. Fin.
136 C2 **Pierre** U.S.A.
105 C3 **Pierrelatte** France
123 D2 **Pietermaritzburg** S. Africa
110 B1 **Pietrosa** mt. Romania
128 C2 **Pigeon Lake** Can.
153 B4 **Pigüé** Arg.
92 I3 **Pihtipudas** Fin.
145 C3 **Pijijiapan** Mex.
136 C3 **Pikes Peak** U.S.A.
122 A3 **Piketberg** S. Africa
140 C3 **Pikeville** U.S.A.
103 D1 **Piła** Pol.
152 C3 **Pilar** Arg.
152 C3 **Pilar** Para.
50 A2 **Pilbara** reg. Austr.
53 C2 **Pilliga** Austr.
154 C1 **Pilões, Serra dos** mts Brazil
150 B3 **Pimenta Bueno** Brazil
153 C4 **Pinamar** Arg.
80 B2 **Pınarbaşı** Turkey
146 B2 **Pinar del Río** Cuba
103 E1 **Pińczów** Pol.
151 D2 **Pindaré** r. Brazil
  Pindos mts Greece see **Pindus Mountains**
111 B2 **Pindus Mountains** Greece
142 B2 **Pine Bluff** U.S.A.
50 C1 **Pine Creek** Austr.
136 B2 **Pinedale** U.S.A.
86 D2 **Pinega** Russia
129 D2 **Pinehouse Lake** Can.
111 B3 **Pineios** r. Greece
128 C1 **Pine Point (abandoned)** Can.
136 C2 **Pine Ridge** U.S.A.
123 D2 **Pinetown** S. Africa
70 B2 **Pingdingshan** China
71 A3 **Pingguo** China
71 B3 **Pingjiang** China
71 A3 **Pingliang** China
71 C3 **P'ingtung** Taiwan
71 A3 **Pingxiang** Guangxi China
71 B3 **Pingxiang** Jiangxi China
70 B2 **Pingyin** China
151 D2 **Pinheiro** Brazil
101 D1 **Pinneberg** Ger.
145 C3 **Pinotepa Nacional** Mex.

88 C3 Pinsk Belarus
135 D3 Pioche U.S.A.
119 C3 Piodi Dem. Rep. Congo
103 E1 Pionki Pol.
103 D1 Piotrków Trybunalski Pol.
137 D2 Pipestone U.S.A.
131 C2 Pipmuacan, Réservoir resr Can.
154 B2 Piquiri r. Brazil
154 C1 Piracanjuba Brazil
154 C2 Piracicaba Brazil
155 D1 Piracicaba r. Brazil
111 B3 Piraeus Greece
154 C2 Piraí do Sul Brazil
154 C2 Pirajuí Brazil
154 B1 Piranhas Brazil
151 E2 Piranhas r. Brazil
155 D1 Pirapora Brazil
154 C1 Pirassununga Brazil
154 C1 Pires do Rio Brazil
151 D2 Piripiri Brazil
59 C3 Piru Indon.
108 B2 Pisa Italy
152 A2 Pisagua Chile
150 A3 Pisco Peru
102 C2 Písek Czech Rep.
79 D2 Pīshīn Iran
145 D2 Pisté Mex.
109 C2 Pisticci Italy
108 B2 Pistoia Italy
106 C1 Pisuerga r. Spain
134 B2 Pit r. U.S.A.
151 E3 Pitanga Brazil
49 J4 Pitangui Brazil
92 H2 Pitcairn Island i. Pitcairn Is
92 H2 Piteå Sweden
92 H2 Piteälven r. Sweden
110 B2 Piteşti Romania
75 C2 Pithoragarh India
96 C2 Pitlochry U.K.
128 B2 Pitt Island Can.
137 E3 Pittsburg U.S.A.
141 D2 Pittsburgh U.S.A.
141 E2 Pittsfield U.S.A.
53 D1 Pittsworth Austr.
155 C2 Piumhi Brazil
150 A2 Piura Peru
90 C2 Pivdennyy Buh r. Ukr.
131 E2 Placentia Can.
135 B3 Placerville U.S.A.
146 C2 Placetas Cuba
139 C2 Plainview U.S.A.
154 C1 Planaltina Brazil
142 B2 Plaquemine U.S.A.
106 B1 Plasencia Spain
147 C4 Plato Col.
137 D2 Platte r. U.S.A.
141 E2 Plattsburgh U.S.A.
101 F1 Plau am See Ger.
101 F2 Plauen Ger.
101 F1 Plauer See l. Ger.
89 E3 Plavsk Russia
129 E2 Playgreen Lake Can.
63 B2 Plây Ku Vietnam
153 B4 Plaza Huincul Arg.
139 D3 Pleasanton U.S.A.
54 B2 Pleasant Point N.Z.
104 C2 Pleaux France
130 B1 Pledger Lake Can.
54 C1 Plenty, Bay of g. N.Z.
136 C1 Plentywood U.S.A.
128 B2 Plesetsk Russia
131 C1 Plétipi, Lac l. Can.
100 C2 Plettenberg Ger.
123 B3 Plettenberg Bay S. Africa
110 B2 Pleven Bulg.
109 C2 Pljevlja Montenegro
109 C2 Ploče Croatia

103 D1 Płock Pol.
109 C2 Pločno mt. Bos. & Herz.
104 B2 Ploemeur France
110 C2 Ploieşti Romania
89 F2 Ploskoye Russia
104 B2 Plouzané France
110 B2 Plovdiv Bulg.
88 B2 Plungė Lith.
88 C3 Plyeshchanitsy Belarus
99 A3 Plymouth U.K.
140 B2 Plymouth U.S.A.
147 D3 Plymouth (abandoned)
Montserrat
88 C2 Plyussa Russia
102 C2 Plzeň Czech Rep.
114 B3 Pô Burkina Faso
108 B1 Po r. Italy
77 E2 Pobeda Peak China/Kyrg.
142 B1 Pocahontas U.S.A.
134 D2 Pocatello U.S.A.
90 B1 Pochayiv Ukr.
89 D3 Pochep Russia
89 D3 Pochinok Russia
145 C3 Pochutla Mex.
141 D3 Pocomoke City U.S.A.
155 C2 Poços de Caldas Brazil
89 D2 Poddor'ye Russia
91 D1 Podgorenskiy Russia
109 C2 Podgorica Montenegro
82 G3 Podgornoye Russia
83 H2 Podkamennaya Tunguska r.
Russia
89 E2 Podol'sk Russia
109 D2 Podujevo Kosovo see
Podujevë
122 A2 Pofadder S. Africa
89 D3 Pogar Russia
109 D2 Pogradec Albania
65 B2 Pohang S. Korea
48 E2 Pohnpei atoll Micronesia
110 B2 Poiana Mare Romania
118 C3 Poie Dem. Rep. Congo
118 B3 Pointe-Noire Congo
126 D2 Point Lake Can.
140 C3 Point Pleasant U.S.A.
104 C2 Poitiers France
74 B2 Pokaran India
75 C2 Pokhara Nepal
83 J2 Pokrovsk Russia
91 D2 Pokrovskoye Russia
138 A1 Polacca U.S.A.
103 D1 Poland country Europe
88 C2 Polatsk Belarus
61 C2 Polewali Indon.
118 B2 Poli Cameroon
102 C1 Police Pol.
109 C2 Policoro Italy
105 D2 Poligny France
64 B1 Polillo Islands Phil.
90 B1 Polis'ke (abandoned) Ukr.
103 D1 Polkowice Pol.
109 C3 Pollino, Monte mt. Italy
91 D2 Polohy Ukr.
123 C1 Polokwane S. Africa
123 C1 Polokwane r. S. Africa
90 B1 Polonne Ukr.
134 D1 Polson U.S.A.
91 C2 Poltava Ukr.
66 B2 Poltavka Russia
91 D2 Poltavskaya Russia
88 C2 Põlva Estonia
111 B3 Polygyros Greece
106 B2 Pombal Port.
102 C1 Pomeranian Bay Ger./Pol.
108 B2 Pomezia Italy
92 I2 Pomokaira reg. Fin.
110 C2 Pomorie Bulg.

Pomorska, Zatoka b. Ger./Pol.
see Pomeranian Bay
155 D1 Pompéu Brazil
139 C1 Ponca City U.S.A.
147 D3 Ponce Puerto Rico
127 F2 Pond Inlet Can.
106 B1 Ponferrada Spain
117 A4 Pongo watercourse
South Sudan
123 D2 Pongola r. S. Africa
128 C2 Ponoka Can.
84 D5 Ponta Delgada
Arquipélago dos Açores
154 B3 Ponta Grossa Brazil
154 C1 Pontalina Brazil
105 D2 Pont-à-Mousson France
105 D2 Pontarlier France
102 B2 Pontcharra France
142 B2 Pontchartrain, Lake U.S.A.
106 B2 Ponte de Sor Port.
129 D3 Ponteix Can.
150 C3 Pontes e Lacerda Brazil
106 B1 Pontevedra Spain
140 B2 Pontiac IL U.S.A.
140 C2 Pontiac MI U.S.A.
61 B2 Pontianak Indon.
104 B2 Pontivy France
151 C1 Pontoetoe Suriname
129 E2 Ponton Can.
99 B3 Pontypool U.K.
108 B2 Ponziane, Isole is Italy
99 C3 Poole U.K.
Poona India see Pune
52 B2 Pooncarie Austr.
152 B2 Poopó, Lago de l. Bol.
150 A1 Popayán Col.
83 I2 Popigay r. Russia
52 B2 Popiltah Austr.
129 E2 Poplar r. Can.
137 E3 Poplar Bluff U.S.A.
118 B3 Popokabaka Dem. Rep. Congo
110 C2 Popovo Bulg.
103 E2 Poprad Slovakia
151 D3 Porangatu Brazil
74 A2 Porbandar India
126 B2 Porcupine r. Can./U.S.A.
108 B1 Poreč Croatia
54 B2 Porirua N.Z.
88 C2 Porkhov Russia
104 B2 Pornic France
83 K3 Poronaysk Russia
111 B3 Poros Greece
93 E4 Porsgrunn Norway
97 C1 Portadown U.K.
97 D1 Portaferry U.K.
140 B2 Portage U.S.A.
129 E3 Portage la Prairie Can.
128 B3 Port Alberni Can.
106 B2 Portalegre Port.
139 C2 Portales U.S.A.
128 A2 Port Alexander U.S.A.
128 B2 Port Alice Can.
134 B1 Port Angeles U.S.A.
51 D4 Port Arthur Austr.
139 E3 Port Arthur U.S.A.
96 A3 Port Askaig U.K.
52 A2 Port Augusta Austr.
147 C3 Port-au-Prince Haiti
131 E1 Port aux Choix Can.
73 D3 Port Blair India
52 B3 Port Campbell Austr.
54 B3 Port Chalmers N.Z.
143 D3 Port Charlotte U.S.A.
147 C3 Port-de-Paix Haiti
128 A2 Port Edward Can.
155 D1 Porteirinha Brazil
151 C2 Portel Brazil
130 B2 Port Elgin Can.

Port Elizabeth

123 C3	**Port Elizabeth** S. Africa	
96 A3	**Port Ellen** U.K.	
98 A1	**Port Erin** Isle of Man	
122 A3	**Porterville** S. Africa	
135 C3	**Porterville** U.S.A.	
52 B3	**Port Fairy** Austr.	
54 C1	**Port Fitzroy** N.Z.	
118 A3	**Port-Gentil** Gabon	
115 C4	**Port Harcourt** Nigeria	
128 B2	**Port Hardy** Can.	
	Port Harrison Can. *see*	
	Inukjuak	
131 D2	**Port Hawkesbury** Can.	
50 A2	**Port Hedland** Austr.	
99 A2	**Porthmadog** U.K.	
131 E1	**Port Hope Simpson** Can.	
140 C2	**Port Huron** U.S.A.	
106 B2	**Portimão** Port.	
53 C2	**Portland** N.S.W. Austr.	
52 B3	**Portland** Vic. Austr.	
141 E2	**Portland** ME U.S.A.	
134 B1	**Portland** OR U.S.A.	
128 A2	**Portland Canal** inlet Can.	
97 C2	**Portlaoise** Ireland	
139 D3	**Port Lavaca** U.S.A.	
52 A2	**Port Lincoln** Austr.	
114 A4	**Port Loko** Sierra Leone	
113 K9	**Port Louis** Mauritius	
53 D2	**Port Macquarie** Austr.	
128 B2	**Port McNeill** Can.	
131 D2	**Port-Menier** Can.	
59 D3	**Port Moresby** P.N.G.	
122 A2	**Port Nolloth** S. Africa	
	Port-Nouveau-Québec Can.	
	see Kangiqsualujjuaq	
	Porto Port. *see* Oporto	
150 B2	**Porto Acre** Brazil	
152 C4	**Porto Alegre** Brazil	
151 C3	**Porto Artur** Brazil	
151 C3	**Porto dos Gaúchos Óbidos**	
	Brazil	
150 C3	**Porto Esperidião** Brazil	
108 D2	**Portoferraio** Italy	
96 A1	**Port of Ness** U.K.	
151 D2	**Porto Franco** Brazil	
147 D3	**Port of Spain** Trin. and Tob.	
108 B1	**Portogruaro** Italy	
108 B2	**Portomaggiore** Italy	
154 B2	**Porto Mendes** Brazil	
152 C3	**Porto Murtinho** Brazil	
151 D3	**Porto Nacional** Brazil	
114 C4	**Porto-Novo** Benin	
154 B2	**Porto Primavera, Represa** resr	
	Brazil	
155 E1	**Porto Seguro** Brazil	
108 B2	**Porto Tolle** Italy	
108 A2	**Porto Torres** Sardinia Italy	
105 D3	**Porto-Vecchio** Corsica France	
150 B2	**Porto Velho** Brazil	
150 A2	**Portoviejo** Ecuador	
52 B3	**Port Phillip Bay** Austr.	
52 A2	**Port Pirie** Austr.	
96 A2	**Portree** U.K.	
128 B3	**Port Renfrew** Can.	
97 C1	**Portrush** U.K.	
116 B1	**Port Said** Egypt	
143 C3	**Port St Joe** U.S.A.	
123 C3	**Port St Johns** S. Africa	
123 D3	**Port Shepstone** S. Africa	
99 C3	**Portsmouth** U.K.	
141 E2	**Portsmouth** NH U.S.A.	
140 C3	**Portsmouth** OH U.S.A.	
141 D3	**Portsmouth** VA U.S.A.	
97 C1	**Portstewart** U.K.	
116 B3	**Port Sudan** Sudan	
142 C3	**Port Sulphur** U.S.A.	
99 B3	**Port Talbot** U.K.	
106 B2	**Portugal** country Europe	
97 B2	**Portumna** Ireland	
105 C3	**Port-Vendres** France	
48 F4	**Port Vila** Vanuatu	
93 I3	**Porvoo** Fin.	
152 C3	**Posadas** Arg.	
89 E2	**Poshekhon'ye** Russia	
92 I2	**Posio** Fin.	
58 C3	**Poso** Indon.	
151 D3	**Posse** Brazil	
101 E2	**Pößneck** Ger.	
139 C2	**Post** U.S.A.	
	Poste-de-la-Baleine Can. *see*	
	Kuujjuarapik	
122 B2	**Postmasburg** S. Africa	
109 C2	**Posušje** Bos. & Herz.	
139 E1	**Poteau** U.S.A.	
109 C2	**Potenza** Italy	
151 D2	**Poti** r. Brazil	
81 C1	**Poti** Georgia	
115 D3	**Potiskum** Nigeria	
141 D3	**Potomac, South Branch** r.	
	U.S.A.	
152 B2	**Potosí** Bol.	
64 B1	**Pototan** Phil.	
138 C3	**Potrero del Llano** Mex.	
101 F1	**Potsdam** Ger.	
141 E2	**Potsdam** U.S.A.	
141 D2	**Pottstown** U.S.A.	
141 D2	**Pottsville** U.S.A.	
131 E2	**Pouch Cove** Can.	
141 E2	**Poughkeepsie** U.S.A.	
98 B2	**Poulton-le-Fylde** U.K.	
155 C2	**Pouso Alegre** Brazil	
63 B2	**Poŭthĭsăt** Cambodia	
103 D2	**Považská Bystrica** Slovakia	
109 C2	**Povlen** mt. Serbia	
106 B1	**Póvoa de Varzim** Port.	
136 B2	**Powell** U.S.A.	
135 D3	**Powell, Lake** resr U.S.A.	
128 B3	**Powell River** Can.	
154 B1	**Poxoréo** Brazil	
71 B3	**Poyang** China	
71 B3	**Poyang Hu** l. China	
109 D2	**Požarevac** Serbia	
145 C2	**Poza Rica** Mex.	
109 C1	**Požega** Croatia	
109 D2	**Požega** Serbia	
79 D2	**Pozm Tīāb** Iran	
103 D1	**Poznań** Pol.	
106 C2	**Pozoblanco** Spain	
108 B2	**Pozzuoli** Italy	
60 B2	**Prabumulih** Indon.	
102 C2	**Prachatice** Czech Rep.	
63 A2	**Prachuap Khiri Khan** Thai.	
155 E1	**Prado** Brazil	
102 C1	**Prague** Czech Rep.	
	Praha Czech Rep. *see*	
	Prague	
112 C5	**Praia** Cape Verde	
139 C2	**Prairie Dog Town Fork** r.	
	U.S.A.	
140 A2	**Prairie du Chien** U.S.A.	
60 A1	**Prapat** Indon.	
154 C1	**Prata** Brazil	
105 E3	**Prato** Italy	
137 D3	**Pratt** U.S.A.	
61 C2	**Praya** Indon.	
63 B2	**Preăh Vihéar** Cambodia	
89 F2	**Prechistoye** Russia	
129 D2	**Preeceville** Can.	
88 C2	**Preiļi** Latvia	
53 C2	**Premer** Austr.	
105 C2	**Prémery** France	
101 F1	**Premnitz** Ger.	
102 C1	**Prenzlau** Ger.	
63 A2	**Preparis Island** Cocos Is	
63 A2	**Preparis North Channel**	
	Cocos Is	
63 A2	**Preparis South Channel**	
	Cocos Is	
103 D2	**Přerov** Czech Rep.	
138 A2	**Prescott** U.S.A.	
109 D2	**Preševo** Serbia	
152 B3	**Presidencia Roque Sáenz**	
	Peña Arg.	
151 D2	**Presidente Dutra** Brazil	
154 B2	**Presidente Epitácio** Brazil	
64 B2	**Presidente Manuel A Roxas**	
	Phil.	
154 B2	**Presidente Prudente** Brazil	
138 C3	**Presidio** U.S.A.	
103 E2	**Prešov** Slovakia	
141 F1	**Presque Isle** U.S.A.	
101 F2	**Pressel** Ger.	
98 B2	**Preston** U.K.	
134 D2	**Preston** U.S.A.	
96 B3	**Prestwick** U.K.	
155 C1	**Preto** r. Brazil	
123 C2	**Pretoria** S. Africa	
111 B3	**Preveza** Greece	
63 B2	**Prey Vêng** Cambodia	
109 C2	**Priboj** Serbia	
135 D3	**Price** U.S.A.	
88 B3	**Prienai** Lith.	
122 B2	**Prieska** S. Africa	
103 D2	**Prievidza** Slovakia	
109 C2	**Prijedor** Bos. & Herz.	
	Prikaspiyskaya Nizmennost'	
	lowland Kazakh./Russia *see*	
	Caspian Lowland	
109 D2	**Prilep** Macedonia	
91 D2	**Primorsko-Akhtarsk** Russia	
129 D2	**Primrose Lake** Can.	
129 D2	**Prince Albert** Can.	
122 B3	**Prince Albert** S. Africa	
126 D2	**Prince Albert Peninsula** Can.	
122 B3	**Prince Albert Road** S. Africa	
126 C2	**Prince Edward, Cape** Can.	
122 A3	**Prince Alfred Hamlet**	
	S. Africa	
127 F2	**Prince Charles Island** Can.	
55 E2	**Prince Charles Mountains**	
	Antarctica	
131 D2	**Prince Edward Island** prov.	
	Can.	
113 I11	**Prince Edward Islands**	
	Indian Ocean	
128 B2	**Prince George** Can.	
126 E2	**Prince of Wales Island** Can.	
128 A2	**Prince of Wales Island** U.S.A.	
126 D2	**Prince of Wales Strait** Can.	
126 D1	**Prince Patrick Island** Can.	
126 E2	**Prince Regent Inlet** sea chan.	
	Can.	
128 A2	**Prince Rupert** Can.	
51 D1	**Princess Charlotte Bay** Austr.	
128 B2	**Princess Royal Island** Can.	
128 B3	**Princeton** Can.	
134 B2	**Prineville** U.S.A.	
90 B1	**Pripet** r. Belarus/Ukr.	
90 A1	**Pripet Marshes** Belarus/Ukr.	
109 D2	**Prishtinë** Kosovo	
	Priština Kosovo *see* Prishtinë	
101 F1	**Pritzwalk** Ger.	
109 C2	**Privlaka** Croatia	
89 F2	**Privolzhsk** Russia	
109 D2	**Prizren** Kosovo	
151 C1	**Professor van Blommestein**	
	Meer resr Suriname	
145 D2	**Progreso** Mex.	
81 C1	**Prokhladnyy** Russia	
109 D2	**Prokuplje** Serbia	
87 D4	**Proletarskaya**	
	Vodokhranilishche l. Russia	
126 C3	**Prophet** r. Can.	
128 B2	**Prophet River** Can.	

51 D2 **Proserpine** Austr.
89 E3 **Protvino** Russia
110 C2 **Provadia** Bulg.
141 E2 **Providence** U.S.A.
146 B3 **Providencia, Isla de** *i.* Caribbean Sea
83 N2 **Provideniya** Russia
135 D2 **Provo** U.S.A.
129 C2 **Provost** Can.
154 B3 **Prudentópolis** Brazil
126 B2 **Prudhoe Bay** U.S.A.
100 C2 **Prüm** Ger.
105 D3 **Prunelli-di-Fiumorbo** *Corsica* France
103 E1 **Pruszków** Pol.
110 C1 **Prut** *r.* Europe
91 C1 **Pryluky** Ukr.
91 D2 **Prymors'k** Ukr.
139 D1 **Pryor** U.S.A.
Prypyats' *r.* Belarus *see* **Pripet**
103 E2 **Przemyśl** Pol.
111 C3 **Psara** *i.* Greece
81 C1 **Psebay** Russia
91 D3 **Pshekha** *r.* Russia
88 C2 **Pskov** Russia
88 C2 **Pskov, Lake** Estonia/Russia
111 B2 **Ptolemaïda** Greece
109 C1 **Ptuj** Slovenia
150 A2 **Pucallpa** Peru
71 B3 **Pucheng** China
103 D1 **Puck** Pol.
92 I2 **Pudasjärvi** Fin.
86 C2 **Pudozh** Russia
Puduchcheri India *see* **Puducherry**
73 B3 **Puducherry** India
145 C3 **Puebla** Mex.
136 C3 **Pueblo** U.S.A.
153 B4 **Puelén** Arg.
106 C2 **Puente Genil** Spain
153 A5 **Puerto Aisén** Chile
152 B2 **Puerto Alegre** Bol.
145 C3 **Puerto Ángel** Mex.
146 B4 **Puerto Armuelles** Panama
150 B1 **Puerto Ayacucho** Venez.
146 B3 **Puerto Cabezas** Nic.
150 B1 **Puerto Carreño** Col.
153 A5 **Puerto Cisnes** Chile
144 A2 **Puerto Cortés** Mex.
145 C3 **Puerto Escondido** Mex.
152 B2 **Puerto Frey** Bol.
150 B1 **Puerto Inírida** Col.
152 C2 **Puerto Isabel** Bol.
150 A2 **Puerto Leguizamo** Col.
144 A2 **Puerto Libertad** Mex.
146 B3 **Puerto Limón** Costa Rica
106 C2 **Puertollano** Spain
153 B5 **Puerto Madryn** Arg.
150 B3 **Puerto Maldonado** Peru
153 A5 **Puerto Montt** Chile
153 A6 **Puerto Natales** Chile
150 B1 **Puerto Nuevo** Col.
144 A1 **Puerto Peñasco** Mex.
152 C3 **Puerto Pinasco** Para.
147 C3 **Puerto Plata** Dom. Rep.
150 A2 **Puerto Portillo** Peru
64 A2 **Puerto Princesa** Phil.
147 D3 **Puerto Rico** *terr.* West Indies
158 B3 **Puerto Rico Trench** Caribbean Sea
146 A3 **Puerto San José** Guat.
153 B6 **Puerto Santa Cruz** Arg.
144 B2 **Puerto Vallarta** Mex.
87 D3 **Pugachev** Russia
74 B2 **Pugal** India
54 B2 **Pukaki, Lake** N.Z.
129 D2 **Pukatawagan** Can.
65 B1 **Pukchin** N. Korea
65 B1 **Pukch'ŏng** N. Korea
54 B1 **Pukekohe** N.Z.
65 B1 **Puksubaek-san** *mt.* N. Korea
108 B2 **Pula** Croatia
108 A3 **Pula** *Sardinia* Italy
152 B3 **Pulacayo** Bol.
77 C3 **Pul-e Khumrī** Afgh.
92 I3 **Pulkkila** Fin.
134 C1 **Pullman** U.S.A.
64 B1 **Pulog, Mount** Phil.
150 A2 **Puná, Isla** *i.* Ecuador
54 B2 **Punakaiki** N.Z.
123 D1 **Punda Maria** S. Africa
73 B3 **Pune** India
65 B1 **P'ungsan** N. Korea
121 C2 **Púnguè** *r.* Moz.
153 B4 **Punta Alta** Arg.
153 A6 **Punta Arenas** Chile
146 B3 **Puntarenas** Costa Rica
117 C4 **Puntland** *reg.* Somalia
150 A1 **Punto Fijo** Venez.
92 I3 **Puolanka** Fin.
82 G2 **Pur** *r.* Russia
75 C3 **Puri** India
100 B1 **Purmerend** Neth.
75 C2 **Purnia** India
75 C2 **Puruliya** India
150 B2 **Purus** *r.* Brazil/Peru
61 B2 **Purwakarta** Indon.
65 B1 **Puryŏng** N. Korea
Pusan S. Korea *see* **Busan**
88 C2 **Pushkinskiye Gory** Russia
88 C2 **Pustoshka** Russia
62 A1 **Putao** Myanmar
71 B3 **Putian** China
Puting China *see* **De'an**
61 C2 **Puting, Tanjung** *pt* Indon.
101 F1 **Putlitz** Ger.
58 A2 **Putrajaya** Malaysia
102 C1 **Puttgarden** Ger.
150 A2 **Putumayo** *r.* Col.
61 C1 **Putusibau** Indon.
91 C1 **Putyvl'** Ukr.
127 F2 **Puvirnituq** Can.
70 B2 **Puyang** China
104 C3 **Puylaurens** France
99 A2 **Pwllheli** U.K.
63 A2 **Pyapon** Myanmar
82 G2 **Pyasina** *r.* Russia
87 D4 **Pyatigorsk** Russia
91 C2 **P"yatykhatky** Ukr.
62 A2 **Pyè** Myanmar
88 C3 **Pyetrykaw** Belarus
93 H3 **Pyhäjärvi** *l.* Fin.
92 H3 **Pyhäjoki** *r.* Fin.
92 I3 **Pyhäsalmi** Fin.
62 A2 **Pyinmana** Myanmar
65 B2 **Pyŏksŏng** N. Korea
65 B2 **P'yŏnggang** N. Korea
65 B2 **P'yŏngsan** N. Korea
65 B2 **P'yŏngyang** N. Korea
135 C2 **Pyramid Lake** U.S.A.
80 B3 **Pyramids of Giza** *tourist site* Egypt
107 D1 **Pyrenees** *mts* Europe
111 B3 **Pyrgos** Greece
91 C1 **Pyryatyn** Ukr.
103 C1 **Pyrzyce** Pol.
88 C2 **Pytalovo** Russia
111 B3 **Pyxaria** *mt.* Greece

Q

127 G1 **Qaanaaq** Greenland
123 C3 **Qacha's Nek** Lesotho
68 C2 **Qaidam Pendi** *basin* China
74 A1 **Qalāt** Afgh.
78 B2 **Qal'at Bīshah** Saudi Arabia
129 E1 **Qamanirjuaq Lake** Can.
Qamanittuaq Can. *see* **Baker Lake**
79 C3 **Qamar, Ghubbat al** *b.* Yemen
78 B3 **Qam Hadīl** Saudi Arabia
77 C3 **Qarshi** Uzbek.
78 B2 **Qaryat al Ulyā** Saudi Arabia
127 H2 **Qasigiannguit** Greenland
79 D2 **Qaşr-e Qand** Iran
81 C2 **Qaşr-e Shīrīn** Iran
127 H2 **Qassimiut** Greenland
78 B3 **Qa'tabah** Yemen
79 C2 **Qatar** *country* Asia
116 A2 **Qattara Depression** Egypt
81 C1 **Qazax** Azer.
81 C2 **Qazvīn** Iran
127 H2 **Qeqertarsuaq** *i.* Greenland
127 H2 **Qeqertarsuatsiaat** Greenland
127 H2 **Qeqertarsuup Tunua** *b.* Greenland
79 C2 **Qeshm** Iran
70 A3 **Qianjiang** *Chongqing* China
70 B2 **Qianjiang** *Hubei* China
65 A1 **Qian Shan** *mts* China
70 C2 **Qidong** China
68 B2 **Qiemo** China
71 A3 **Qijiang** China
68 C2 **Qijiaojing** China
127 G2 **Qikiqtarjuaq** Can.
74 A2 **Qila Ladgasht** Pak.
68 C2 **Qilian Shan** *mts* China
127 I2 **Qillak** *i.* Greenland
70 B3 **Qimen** China
127 G1 **Qimusseriarsuaq** *b.* Greenland
116 B2 **Qinā** Egypt
70 C2 **Qingdao** China
68 C2 **Qinghai Hu** *salt l.* China
68 C2 **Qinghai Nanshan** *mts* China
70 A2 **Qingyang** China
71 B3 **Qingyuan** *Guangdong* China
65 A1 **Qingyuan** *Liaoning* China
Qingzang Gaoyuan *plat.* China *see* **Tibet, Plateau of**
70 B2 **Qingzhou** China
70 B2 **Qinhuangdao** China
70 A2 **Qin Ling** *mts* China
Qinting China *see* **Lianhua**
70 B2 **Qinyang** China
71 A3 **Qinzhou** China
71 B4 **Qionghai** China
68 C2 **Qionglai Shan** *mts* China
71 B4 **Qiongshan** China
69 E1 **Qiqihar** China
79 C2 **Qīr** Iran
66 B1 **Qitaihe** China
70 B2 **Qixian** China
Qogir Feng *mt.* China/Pak. *see* **K2**
81 D2 **Qom** Iran
Qomolangma Feng *mt.* China/Nepal *see* **Everest, Mount**
76 B2 **Qo'ng'irot** Uzbek.
Qoqek China *see* **Tacheng**
77 D2 **Qo'qon** Uzbek.
76 B2 **Qoraqalpog'iston** Uzbek.
100 C1 **Quakenbrück** Ger.
63 B2 **Quang Ngai** Vietnam
63 B2 **Quang Tri** Vietnam
71 B3 **Quanzhou** *Fujian* China
71 B3 **Quanzhou** *Guangxi* China
108 A3 **Quartu Sant'Elena** *Sardinia* Italy
138 A2 **Quartzsite** U.S.A.
81 C1 **Quba** Azer.
53 C3 **Queanbeyan** Austr.

Québec

131 C2	**Québec** Can.	
130 C1	**Québec** *prov.* Can.	
101 E2	**Quedlinburg** Ger.	
128 A2	**Queen Charlotte** Can.	
128 B2	**Queen Charlotte Sound** *sea chan.* Can.	
128 B2	**Queen Charlotte Strait** Can.	
126 D1	**Queen Elizabeth Islands** Can.	
55 A1	**Queen Elizabeth Land** *reg.* Antarctica	
126 E2	**Queen Maud Gulf** Can.	
55 B2	**Queen Maud Land** *reg.* Antarctica	
55 N1	**Queen Maud Mountains** Antarctica	
52 B1	**Queensland** *state* Austr.	
51 D4	**Queenstown** Austr.	
54 A3	**Queenstown** N.Z.	
123 C3	**Queenstown** S. Africa	
121 C2	**Quelimane** Moz.	
138 B2	**Quemado** U.S.A.	
154 B2	**Querência do Norte** Brazil	
145 B2	**Querétaro** Mex.	
101 E2	**Querfurt** Ger.	
128 B2	**Quesnel** Can.	
128 B2	**Quesnel Lake** Can.	
74 A1	**Quetta** Pak.	
64 A2	**Quezon** Phil.	
64 B1	**Quezon City** Phil.	
120 A2	**Quibala** Angola	
150 A1	**Quibdó** Col.	
104 B2	**Quiberon** France	
104 C3	**Quillan** France	
153 C4	**Quilmes** Arg.	
	Quilon India *see* **Kollam**	
51 D2	**Quilpie** Austr.	
153 A4	**Quilpué** Chile	
120 A1	**Quimbele** Angola	
152 B3	**Quimilí** Arg.	
104 B2	**Quimper** France	
104 B2	**Quimperlé** France	
137 E3	**Quincy** *IL* U.S.A.	
141 E2	**Quincy** *MA* U.S.A.	
107 C1	**Quinto** Spain	
121 D2	**Quionga** Moz.	
53 D2	**Quirindi** Austr.	
120 A2	**Quitapa** Angola	
150 A2	**Quito** Ecuador	
151 E2	**Quixadá** Brazil	
71 A3	**Qujing** China	
52 A2	**Quorn** Austr.	
79 C2	**Qurayat** Oman	
77 C3	**Qürghonteppa** Tajik.	
63 B2	**Quy Nhơn** Vietnam	
71 B3	**Quzhou** China	

R

103 D2	**Raab** *r.* Austria	
92 H3	**Raahe** Fin.	
100 C1	**Raalte** Neth.	
61 C1	**Raas** *i.* Indon.	
61 C2	**Raba** Indon.	
114 B1	**Rabat** Morocco	
48 E3	**Rabaul** P.N.G.	
78 A2	**Rābigh** Saudi Arabia	
131 E2	**Race, Cape** Can.	
63 B3	**Rach Gia** Vietnam	
140 B2	**Racine** U.S.A.	
78 B3	**Radā'** Yemen	
110 C1	**Rădăuţi** Romania	
140 B3	**Radcliff** U.S.A.	
74 B2	**Radhanpur** India	
130 C1	**Radisson** Can.	
103 E1	**Radom** Pol.	
103 D1	**Radomsko** Pol.	
90 B1	**Radomyshl'** Ukr.	
109 D2	**Radoviš** Macedonia	
88 B2	**Radviliškis** Lith.	
78 A2	**Radwá, Jabal** *mt.* Saudi Arabia	
90 B1	**Radyvyliv** Ukr.	
75 C2	**Rae Bareli** India	
100 C2	**Raeren** Belgium	
54 C1	**Raetihi** N.Z.	
152 B4	**Rafaela** Arg.	
118 C2	**Rafaï** C.A.R.	
78 B2	**Rafḩā'** Saudi Arabia	
79 C1	**Rafsanjān** Iran	
64 B2	**Ragang, Mount** *vol.* Phil.	
109 B3	**Ragusa** *Sicily* Italy	
59 C3	**Raha** Indon.	
88 D3	**Rahachow** Belarus	
74 B2	**Rahimyar Khan** Pak.	
109 D2	**Rahovec** Kosovo	
73 B3	**Raichur** India	
62 A1	**Raigarh** India	
128 C2	**Rainbow Lake** Can.	
134 B1	**Rainier, Mount** *vol.* U.S.A.	
130 A2	**Rainy Lake** Can./U.S.A.	
129 E3	**Rainy River** Can.	
75 C2	**Raipur** India	
93 H3	**Raisio** Fin.	
73 C3	**Rajahmundry** India	
61 C1	**Rajang** *r. Sarawak* Malaysia	
74 B2	**Rajanpur** Pak.	
73 B4	**Rajapalayam** India	
74 B2	**Rajasthan Canal** India	
74 B2	**Rajgarh** India	
74 B2	**Rajkot** India	
74 B2	**Rajpur** India	
75 C2	**Rajshahi** Bangl.	
54 B2	**Rakaia** *r.* N.Z.	
90 A2	**Rakhiv** Ukr.	
91 D1	**Rakitnoye** Russia	
88 C2	**Rakke** Estonia	
88 C2	**Rakvere** Estonia	
143 E1	**Raleigh** U.S.A.	
48 F2	**Ralik Chain** *is* Marshall Is	
117 B3	**Ramciel** S. Sudan	
74 B2	**Ramgarh** India	
81 C2	**Rāmhormoz** Iran	
	Ramlat Rabyānah *des.* Libya *see* **Rebiana Sand Sea**	
110 C1	**Râmnicu Sărat** Romania	
110 B1	**Râmnicu Vâlcea** Romania	
89 E3	**Ramon'** Russia	
123 C1	**Ramotswa** Botswana	
75 B2	**Rampur** India	
62 A2	**Ramree Island** Myanmar	
98 A1	**Ramsey** Isle of Man	
99 D3	**Ramsgate** U.K.	
75 C2	**Ranaghat** India	
61 C1	**Ranau** *Sabah* Malaysia	
153 A4	**Rancagua** Chile	
75 C2	**Ranchi** India	
93 F4	**Randers** Denmark	
54 B2	**Rangiora** N.Z.	
54 C1	**Rangitaiki** *r.* N.Z.	
62 A2	**Rangoon** Myanmar	
75 C2	**Rangpur** Bangl.	
129 E1	**Rankin Inlet** Can.	
53 C2	**Rankin's Springs** Austr.	
96 B2	**Rannoch Moor** *moorland* U.K.	
63 A3	**Ranong** Thai.	
61 C1	**Ransiki** Indon.	
61 C2	**Rantaupanjang** Indon.	
60 A1	**Rantauprapat** Indon.	
92 I2	**Ranua** Fin.	
78 B2	**Ranyah, Wādī** *watercourse* Saudi Arabia	
49 I4	**Rapa** *i.* Fr. Polynesia	
136 C2	**Rapid City** U.S.A.	
88 B2	**Rapla** Estonia	
74 A2	**Rapur** India	
49 H4	**Rarotonga** *i.* Cook Is	
153 B5	**Rasa, Punta** *pt* Arg.	
79 C2	**Ra's al Khaymah** U.A.E.	
117 B3	**Ras Dejen** *mt.* Eth.	
88 B2	**Raseiniai** Lith.	
81 C2	**Rasht** Iran	
74 A2	**Ras Koh** *mt.* Pak.	
88 C2	**Rasony** Belarus	
87 D3	**Rasskazovo** Russia	
79 C2	**Ras Tannūrah** Saudi Arabia	
101 D1	**Rastede** Ger.	
93 F3	**Rätan** Sweden	
74 B2	**Ratangarh** India	
63 A2	**Rat Buri** Thai.	
62 A1	**Rathedaung** Myanmar	
101 F1	**Rathenow** Ger.	
97 C1	**Rathlin Island** U.K.	
74 B2	**Ratlam** India	
73 B3	**Ratnagiri** India	
73 C4	**Ratnapura** Sri Lanka	
90 A1	**Ratne** Ukr.	
138 C1	**Raton** U.S.A.	
96 D2	**Rattray Head** U.K.	
101 E1	**Ratzeburg** Ger.	
92 □B2	**Raufarhöfn** Iceland	
54 C1	**Raukumara Range** *mts* N.Z.	
93 H3	**Rauma** Fin.	
61 C2	**Raung, Gunung** *vol.* Indon.	
75 C2	**Raurkela** India	
134 D1	**Ravalli** U.S.A.	
81 C2	**Ravānsar** Iran	
108 B2	**Ravenna** Italy	
102 B2	**Ravensburg** Ger.	
74 B1	**Ravi** *r.* Pak.	
74 B1	**Rawalpindi** Pak.	
103 D1	**Rawicz** Pol.	
50 B3	**Rawlinna** Austr.	
136 B2	**Rawlins** U.S.A.	
153 B5	**Rawson** Arg.	
73 C3	**Rayagada** India	
69 E1	**Raychikhinsk** Russia	
78 B3	**Raydah** Yemen	
87 E3	**Rayevskiy** Russia	
81 B1	**Raymond** U.S.A.	
53 D2	**Raymond Terrace** Austr.	
139 D3	**Raymondville** U.S.A.	
145 C2	**Rayón** Mex.	
63 B2	**Rayong** Thai.	
78 A2	**Rayyis** Saudi Arabia	
104 B2	**Raz, Pointe du** *pt* France	
81 C2	**Razāzah, Buḩayrat ar** *l.* Iraq	
110 C2	**Razgrad** Bulg.	
110 C2	**Razim, Lacul** *lag.* Romania	
110 B2	**Razlog** Bulg.	
104 B2	**Ré, Île de** *i.* France	
99 C3	**Reading** U.K.	
141 D2	**Reading** U.S.A.	
115 E2	**Rebiana Sand Sea** *des.* Libya	
66 D1	**Rebun-tō** *i.* Japan	
50 B3	**Recherche, Archipelago of the** *is* Austr.	
89 D3	**Rechytsa** Belarus	
151 E2	**Recife** Brazil	
123 C3	**Recife, Cape** S. Africa	
100 C2	**Recklinghausen** Ger.	
152 C3	**Reconquista** Arg.	
142 B2	**Red** *r.* U.S.A.	
131 E1	**Red Bay** Can.	
135 B2	**Red Bluff** U.S.A.	
98 C1	**Redcar** U.K.	
129 C2	**Redcliff** Can.	
52 B2	**Red Cliffs** Austr.	
128 C2	**Red Deer** Can.	
126 D3	**Red Deer** *r.* Can.	
129 D2	**Red Deer Lake** Can.	
134 B2	**Redding** U.S.A.	
99 C2	**Redditch** U.K.	

137	D2	Redfield U.S.A.
130	A1	Red Lake Can.
137	E1	Red Lakes U.S.A.
134	E1	Red Lodge U.S.A.
134	B2	Redmond U.S.A.
137	D2	Red Oak U.S.A.
106	B2	Redondo Port.
159	B2	Red Sea Africa/Asia
128	B1	Redstone r. Can.
100	B1	Reduzum Neth.
137	E2	Red Wing U.S.A.
137	D2	Redwood Falls U.S.A.
97	C2	Ree, Lough l. Ireland
134	B2	Reedsport U.S.A.
54	B2	Reefton N.Z.
102	C2	Regen Ger.
155	E1	Regência Brazil
102	C2	Regensburg Ger.
114	C2	Reggane Alg.
109	C3	Reggio di Calabria Italy
108	B2	Reggio nell'Emilia Italy
110	B1	Reghin Romania
129	D2	Regina Can.
122	A1	Rehoboth Namibia
101	F2	Reichenbach im Vogtland Ger.
143	E1	Reidsville U.S.A.
99	C3	Reigate U.K.
105	C2	Reims France
101	E1	Reinbek Ger.
129	D2	Reindeer r. Can.
129	E2	Reindeer Island Can.
129	D2	Reindeer Lake Can.
92	F2	Reine Norway
100	C3	Reinsfeld Ger.
123	C2	Reitz S. Africa
122	B2	Reivilo S. Africa
129	D1	Reliance Can.
107	D2	Relizane Alg.
79	C2	Remeshk Iran
105	D2	Remiremont France
100	C2	Remscheid Ger.
102	B1	Rendsburg Ger.
141	D1	Renfrew Can.
60	B2	Rengat Indon.
90	B2	Reni Ukr.
52	B2	Renmark Austr.
100	D2	Rennerod Ger.
104	B2	Rennes France
129	D1	Rennie Lake Can.
108	B2	Reno r. Italy
135	C3	Reno U.S.A.
70	A3	Renshou China
140	B2	Rensselaer U.S.A.
75	C2	Renukut India
54	B2	Renwick N.Z.
58	C3	Reo Indon.
136	D3	Republican r. U.S.A.
127	F2	Repulse Bay Can.
150	A2	Requena Peru
107	C2	Requena Spain
154	B2	Reserva Brazil
152	C3	Resistencia Arg.
110	B1	Reşiţa Romania
126	E2	Resolute Can.
127	G2	Resolution Island Can.
105	C2	Rethel France
111	B3	Rethymno Greece
113	K9	Réunion terr. Indian Ocean
107	D1	Reus Spain
102	B2	Reutlingen Ger.
128	C2	Revelstoke Can.
144	A3	Revillagigedo, Islas is Mex.
128	A2	Revillagigedo Island U.S.A.
75	C2	Rewa India
134	D2	Rexburg U.S.A.
92	□A3	Reykjanestá pt Iceland
92	□A3	Reykjavík Iceland
145	C2	Reynosa Mex.
88	C2	Rēzekne Latvia
		Rhein r. Ger. see Rhine
100	C1	Rheine Ger.
101	F1	Rheinsberg Ger.
		Rhin r. France see Rhine
100	C2	Rhine r. Europe
140	B1	Rhinelander U.S.A.
101	F1	Rhinluch marsh Ger.
101	F1	Rhinow Ger.
141	E2	Rhode Island state U.S.A.
111	C3	Rhodes Greece
111	C3	Rhodes i. Greece
110	B2	Rhodope Mountains Bulg./Greece
105	C3	Rhône r. France/Switz.
		Rhuthun U.K. see Ruthin
98	B2	Rhyl U.K.
154	C1	Rianápolis Brazil
60	B1	Riau, Kepulauan is Indon.
106	B1	Ribadeo Spain
106	B1	Ribadesella/Ribeseya Spain
154	B2	Ribas do Rio Pardo Brazil
121	C2	Ribáuè Moz.
98	B2	Ribble r. U.K.
154	C2	Ribeira r. Brazil
154	C2	Ribeirão Preto Brazil
104	C2	Ribérac France
152	B2	Riberalta Bol.
90	B2	Rîbniţa Moldova
102	C1	Ribnitz-Damgarten Ger.
140	A1	Rice Lake U.S.A.
123	D2	Richards Bay S. Africa
126	B2	Richardson Mountains Can.
135	D3	Richfield U.S.A.
134	C1	Richland U.S.A.
140	A2	Richland Center U.S.A.
53	D2	Richmond N.S.W. Austr.
51	D2	Richmond Qld Austr.
54	B2	Richmond N.Z.
122	B3	Richmond S. Africa
98	C1	Richmond U.K.
140	C3	Richmond IN U.S.A.
140	C3	Richmond KY U.S.A.
141	D3	Richmond VA U.S.A.
130	C2	Rideau Lakes Can.
135	C3	Ridgecrest U.S.A.
102	C1	Riesa Ger.
100	D1	Rieste Ger.
123	B2	Riet r. S. Africa
101	D2	Rietberg Ger.
108	B2	Rieti Italy
136	B3	Rifle U.S.A.
88	B2	Rīga Latvia
88	B2	Riga, Gulf of Estonia/Latvia
134	D2	Rigby U.S.A.
131	E1	Rigolet Can.
93	H3	Riihimäki Fin.
108	B1	Rijeka Croatia
134	C2	Riley U.S.A.
78	B2	Rimah, Wādī ar watercourse Saudi Arabia
103	E2	Rimavská Sobota Slovakia
129	C2	Rimbey Can.
108	B2	Rimini Italy
131	D2	Rimouski Can.
93	F3	Ringebu Norway
93	E4	Ringkøbing Denmark
92	G2	Ringvassøya i. Norway
59	C3	Rinteln Ger.
150	A2	Riobamba Ecuador
150	B3	Rio Branco Brazil
154	C3	Rio Branco do Sul Brazil
154	B2	Rio Brilhante Brazil
154	C2	Rio Claro Brazil
153	B4	Río Colorado Arg.
153	B4	Río Cuarto Arg.
155	D2	Rio de Janeiro Brazil
153	B6	Río Gallegos Arg.
153	B6	Río Grande Arg.
152	C4	Rio Grande Brazil
144	B2	Río Grande Mex.
139	D3	Rio Grande r. Mex./U.S.A.
139	D3	Rio Grande City U.S.A.
150	A1	Riohacha Col.
150	A2	Rioja Peru
145	D2	Río Lagartos Mex.
105	C2	Riom France
152	B2	Río Mulatos Bol.
154	C3	Rio Negro Brazil
155	D1	Rio Pardo de Minas Brazil
138	B1	Rio Rancho U.S.A.
150	A2	Rio Tigre Ecuador
154	B1	Rio Verde Brazil
145	C2	Río Verde Mex.
154	B1	Rio Verde de Mato Grosso Brazil
90	C1	Ripky Ukr.
98	C2	Ripley U.K.
107	D1	Ripoll Spain
98	C1	Ripon U.K.
66	D1	Rishiri-tō i. Japan
93	E4	Risør Norway
122	B2	Ritchie S. Africa
63	A2	Ritchie's Archipelago is India
134	C1	Ritzville U.S.A.
152	B3	Rivadavia Arg.
108	B1	Riva del Garda Italy
146	B3	Rivas Nic.
152	C4	Rivera Uru.
129	D2	Riverhurst Can.
52	B2	Riverina reg. Austr.
122	B3	Riversdale S. Africa
135	C4	Riverside U.S.A.
136	B2	Riverton U.S.A.
131	D2	Riverview Can.
104	C3	Rivesaltes France
131	D2	Rivière-du-Loup Can.
90	B1	Rivne Ukr.
54	B2	Riwaka N.Z.
78	B2	Riyadh Saudi Arabia
81	C1	Rize Turkey
70	B2	Rizhao China
105	C2	Roanne France
141	D3	Roanoke U.S.A.
143	E1	Roanoke r. U.S.A.
143	E1	Roanoke Rapids U.S.A.
52	A3	Robe Austr.
101	F1	Röbel/Müritz Ger.
130	C1	Robert-Bourassa, Réservoir resr Can.
92	H3	Robertsfors Sweden
122	A3	Robertson S. Africa
114	A4	Robertsport Liberia
131	C2	Roberval Can.
50	A2	Robinson Ranges hills Austr.
52	B2	Robinvale Austr.
129	C2	Roblin Can.
128	C2	Robson, Mount Can.
152	C4	Rocha Uru.
98	B2	Rochdale U.K.
154	B1	Rochedo Brazil
100	B2	Rochefort Belgium
104	B2	Rochefort France
137	E2	Rochester MN U.S.A.
141	E2	Rochester NH U.S.A.
141	D2	Rochester NY U.S.A.
140	B2	Rockford U.S.A.
51	E2	Rockhampton Austr.
143	D2	Rock Hill U.S.A.
50	A3	Rockingham Austr.
140	A2	Rock Island U.S.A.
136	B1	Rock Springs MT U.S.A.
139	C3	Rocksprings U.S.A.
136	B2	Rock Springs WY U.S.A.

136 C3 **Rocky Ford** U.S.A.
143 E1 **Rocky Mount** U.S.A.
128 C2 **Rocky Mountain House** Can.
124 G3 **Rocky Mountains** Can./U.S.A.
100 B3 **Rocroi** France
102 C1 **Rødbyhavn** Denmark
131 E1 **Roddickton** Can.
104 C3 **Rodez** France
89 F2 **Rodniki** Russia
Rodos Greece *see* Rhodes
Rodos *i.* Greece *see* Rhodes
50 A2 **Roebourne** Austr.
50 B1 **Roebuck Bay** Austr.
123 C1 **Roedtan** S. Africa
100 B2 **Roermond** Neth.
100 A2 **Roeselare** Belgium
127 F2 **Roes Welcome Sound** *sea chan.* Can.
142 B1 **Rogers** U.S.A.
122 B3 **Roggeveldberge** *esc.* S. Africa
92 G2 **Rognan** Norway
134 B2 **Rogue** *r.* U.S.A.
88 B2 **Roja** Latvia
60 B1 **Rokan** *r.* Indon.
88 C2 **Rokiškis** Lith.
90 B1 **Rokytne** Ukr.
154 B2 **Rolândia** Brazil
137 E3 **Rolla** U.S.A.
51 D2 **Roma** Austr.
Roma Lesotho
Roma Italy *see* Rome
123 C2 **Roma** U.S.A.
139 D3 **Roma** U.S.A.
143 E2 **Romain, Cape** U.S.A.
110 C1 **Roman** Romania
59 C3 **Romang, Pulau** *i.* Indon.
110 B1 **Romania** *country* Europe
91 C3 **Roman-Kosh** *mt.* Ukr.
69 D1 **Romanovka** Russia
105 D2 **Rombas** France
64 B1 **Romblon** Phil.
108 B2 **Rome** Italy
143 C2 **Rome** GA U.S.A.
141 D2 **Rome** NY U.S.A.
99 D3 **Romford** U.K.
105 C2 **Romilly-sur-Seine** France
91 C1 **Romny** Ukr.
104 C2 **Romorantin-Lanthenay** France
99 C3 **Romsey** U.K.
96 □ **Ronas Hill** U.K.
151 C3 **Roncador, Serra do** *hills* Brazil
106 B2 **Ronda** Spain
154 B2 **Rondon** Brazil
154 B1 **Rondonópolis** Brazil
74 B1 **Rondu** Pak.
71 A3 **Rong'an** China
71 A3 **Rongjiang** China
62 A1 **Rongklang Range** *mts* Myanmar
Rongmei China *see* Hefeng
93 F4 **Rønne** Denmark
55 P2 **Ronne Ice Shelf** Antarctica
101 D1 **Ronnenberg** Ger.
100 A2 **Ronse** Belgium
75 B2 **Roorkee** India
100 B2 **Roosendaal** Neth.
135 E2 **Roosevelt** U.S.A.
128 B2 **Roosevelt, Mount** Can.
55 K2 **Roosevelt Sub-glacial Island** Antarctica
104 B3 **Roquefort** France
150 B1 **Roraima, Mount** Guyana
93 F3 **Røros** Norway
153 B4 **Rosario** Arg.
144 A1 **Rosario** *Baja California* Mex.
144 B2 **Rosario** *Sinaloa* Mex.

144 B2 **Rosario** *Sonora* Mex.
151 C3 **Rosário Oeste** Brazil
144 A2 **Rosarito** Mex.
109 C3 **Rosarno** Italy
104 B2 **Roscoff** France
97 B2 **Roscommon** Ireland
97 C2 **Roscrea** Ireland
147 D3 **Roseau** Dominica
137 D1 **Roseau** U.S.A.
134 B2 **Roseburg** U.S.A.
139 D3 **Rosenberg** U.S.A.
101 D1 **Rosengarten** Ger.
102 C2 **Rosenheim** Ger.
129 D2 **Rosetown** Can.
122 A2 **Rosh Pinah** Namibia
110 C2 **Roșiori de Vede** Romania
93 F4 **Roskilde** Denmark
89 D3 **Roslavl'** Russia
109 C3 **Rossano** Italy
97 B1 **Rossan Point** Ireland
55 K1 **Ross Ice Shelf** Antarctica
131 D2 **Rossignol, Lake** Can.
128 C3 **Rossland** Can.
97 C2 **Rosslare** Ireland
114 A3 **Rosso** Maur.
105 D3 **Rosso, Capo** *c. Corsica* France
99 B3 **Ross-on-Wye** U.K.
91 D1 **Rossosh'** Russia
128 A1 **Ross River** Can.
55 K2 **Ross Sea** Antarctica
92 F2 **Ressvatnet** *l.* Norway
79 C2 **Rostāq** Iran
129 D2 **Rosthern** Can.
102 C1 **Rostock** Ger.
89 E2 **Rostov** Russia
91 D2 **Rostov-na-Donu** Russia
92 H2 **Rosvik** Sweden
138 C2 **Roswell** U.S.A.
59 D2 **Rota** *i.* N. Mariana Is
59 C3 **Rote** *i.* Indon.
101 D1 **Rotenburg (Wümme)** Ger.
102 C2 **Roth** Ger.
98 C1 **Rothbury** U.K.
98 C2 **Rotherham** U.K.
96 B3 **Rothesay** U.K.
53 C2 **Roto** Austr.
105 D3 **Rotondo, Monte** *mt. Corsica* France
54 C1 **Rotorua** N.Z.
54 C1 **Rotorua, Lake** N.Z.
101 E2 **Rottenbach** Ger.
102 C2 **Rottenmann** Austria
100 B2 **Rotterdam** Neth.
102 B2 **Rottweil** Ger.
49 F3 **Rotuma** *i.* Fiji
105 C1 **Roubaix** France
104 C2 **Rouen** France
Roulers Belgium *see* Roeselare
53 D2 **Round Mountain** Austr.
131 E2 **Round Pond** *l.* Can.
139 D2 **Round Rock** U.S.A.
134 E1 **Roundup** U.S.A.
96 C1 **Rousay** *i.* U.K.
130 C2 **Rouyn-Noranda** Can.
92 I2 **Rovaniemi** Fin.
91 D3 **Roven'ki** Russia
91 D2 **Roven'ky** Ukr.
108 B1 **Rovereto** Italy
63 B2 **Rôviĕng Tbong** Cambodia
108 B1 **Rovigo** Italy
108 B1 **Rovinj** Croatia
53 C1 **Rowena** Austr.
64 B1 **Roxas** *Capiz* Phil.
64 B1 **Roxas** *Oriental Mindoro* Phil.
64 A1 **Roxas** *Palawan* Phil.
52 A2 **Roxby Downs** Austr.
138 C1 **Roy** U.S.A.
140 B1 **Royale, Isle** *i.* U.S.A.

99 D3 **Royal Tunbridge Wells** U.K.
104 B2 **Royan** France
99 C2 **Royston** U.K.
90 C2 **Rozdil'na** Ukr.
91 C2 **Rozdol'ne** Ukr.
100 B3 **Rozoy-sur-Serre** France
87 D3 **Rtishchevo** Russia
54 C1 **Ruapehu, Mount** *vol.* N.Z.
54 A3 **Ruapuke Island** N.Z.
78 B3 **Rub' al Khālī** *des.* Saudi Arabia
91 D2 **Rubizhne** Ukr.
77 E1 **Rubtsovsk** Russia
135 C2 **Ruby Mountains** U.S.A.
66 C2 **Rudnaya Pristan'** Russia
89 D3 **Rudnya** Russia
76 C1 **Rudnyy** Kazakh.
82 E1 **Rudol'fa, Ostrov** *i.* Russia
101 E2 **Rudolstadt** Ger.
119 D3 **Rufiji** *r.* Tanz.
153 B4 **Rufino** Arg.
121 B2 **Rufunsa** Zambia
70 C2 **Rugao** China
99 C2 **Rugby** U.K.
136 C1 **Rugby** U.S.A.
102 C1 **Rügen** *i.* Ger.
101 E2 **Ruhla** Ger.
88 B2 **Ruhnu** *i.* Estonia
100 C2 **Ruhr** *r.* Ger.
71 C3 **Rui'an** China
138 B2 **Ruidoso** U.S.A.
144 B2 **Ruiz** Mex.
119 D3 **Rukwa, Lake** Tanz.
96 A2 **Rum** *i.* U.K.
109 C1 **Ruma** Serbia
78 B2 **Rumāh** Saudi Arabia
117 A4 **Rumbek** South Sudan
105 D2 **Rumilly** France
50 C1 **Rum Jungle (abandoned)** Austr.
54 B2 **Runanga** N.Z.
98 B2 **Runcorn** U.K.
120 A2 **Rundu** Namibia
68 B2 **Ruoqiang** China
130 C1 **Rupert** *r.* Can.
130 C1 **Rupert Bay** Can.
121 C2 **Rusape** Zimbabwe
110 C2 **Ruse** Bulg.
77 D3 **Rūshon** Tajik.
136 C2 **Rushville** U.S.A.
53 C3 **Rushworth** Austr.
129 D2 **Russell** Can.
54 B1 **Russell** N.Z.
142 C2 **Russellville** AL U.S.A.
142 B1 **Russellville** AR U.S.A.
140 B3 **Russellville** KY U.S.A.
101 D2 **Rüsselsheim** Ger.
82 F2 **Russia** *country* Asia/Europe
123 C2 **Rustenburg** S. Africa
142 B2 **Ruston** U.S.A.
98 B2 **Ruthin** U.K.
141 E2 **Rutland** U.S.A.
119 E4 **Ruvuma** *r.* Moz./Tanz.
79 C2 **Ruweis** U.A.E.
77 C1 **Ruzayevka** Kazakh.
87 D3 **Ruzayevka** Russia
119 C3 **Rwanda** *country* Africa
89 F3 **Ryazan'** Russia
89 F3 **Ryazhsk** Russia
86 C2 **Rybachiy, Poluostrov** *pen.* Russia
89 E2 **Rybinsk** Russia
89 E2 **Rybinskoye Vodokhranilishche** *resr* Russia
103 D1 **Rybnik** Pol.
89 E3 **Rybnoye** Russia
99 D3 **Rye** U.K.
89 D3 **Ryl'sk** Russia
67 C3 **Ryōtsu** Japan

69 E3 **Ryukyu Islands** Japan
103 E1 **Rzeszów** Pol.
89 D2 **Rzhev** Russia

S

79 C2 **Sa'ādatābād** Iran
101 E2 **Saale** *r.* Ger.
101 E2 **Saalfeld/Saale** Ger.
102 B2 **Saarbrücken** Ger.
88 B2 **Saaremaa** *i.* Estonia
92 I2 **Saarenkylä** Fin.
93 I3 **Saarijärvi** Fin.
102 B2 **Saarlouis** Ger.
80 B2 **Sab' Ābār** Syria
107 D1 **Sabadell** Spain
61 C1 **Sabah** *state* Malaysia
61 C2 **Sabalana** *i.* Indon.
155 D1 **Sabará** Brazil
108 B2 **Sabaudia** Italy
115 D2 **Sabhā** Libya
123 D2 **Sabie** *r.* Moz./S. Africa
145 B2 **Sabinas** Mex.
145 B2 **Sabinas Hidalgo** Mex.
131 D2 **Sable, Cape** Can.
143 D3 **Sable, Cape** U.S.A.
131 E2 **Sable Island** Can.
106 B1 **Sabugal** Port.
78 B3 **Şabyā** Saudi Arabia
76 B3 **Sabzevār** Iran
120 A2 **Sachanga** Angola
65 B3 **Sacheon** S. Korea
130 A1 **Sachigo Lake** Can.
126 C2 **Sachs Harbour** Can.
135 B3 **Sacramento** U.S.A.
138 B2 **Sacramento Mountains** U.S.A.
135 B2 **Sacramento Valley** U.S.A.
123 C3 **Sada** S. Africa
107 C1 **Sádaba** Spain
78 B3 **Şa'dah** Yemen
62 A1 **Sadiya** India
67 C3 **Sadoga-shima** *i.* Japan
107 D2 **Sa Dragonera** *i.* Spain
76 C3 **Safēd Kōh, Silsilah-ye** *mts* Afgh.
93 F4 **Säffle** Sweden
138 B2 **Safford** U.S.A.
99 D2 **Saffron Walden** U.K.
114 B1 **Safi** Morocco
86 D2 **Safonovo** *Arkhangel'skaya Oblast'* Russia
89 D2 **Safonovo** *Smolenskaya Oblast'* Russia
75 C2 **Saga** China
67 B4 **Saga** Japan
62 A1 **Sagaing** Myanmar
67 C3 **Sagamihara** Japan
75 B2 **Sagar** India
140 C2 **Saginaw** U.S.A.
140 C2 **Saginaw Bay** U.S.A.
106 B2 **Sagres** Port.
146 B2 **Sagua la Grande** Cuba
141 F1 **Saguenay** *r.* Can.
107 C2 **Sagunto** Spain
76 B2 **Sagyndyk, Mys** *pt* Kazakh.
106 B1 **Sahagún** Spain
114 C3 **Sahara** *des.* Africa
Saharan Atlas *mts* Alg. *see* **Atlas Saharien**
75 B2 **Saharanpur** India
75 C2 **Saharsa** India
114 B3 **Sahel** *reg.* Africa
144 B2 **Sahuayo** Mex.
78 B2 **Şāḩūq** *reg.* Saudi Arabia
Saïda Lebanon *see* **Sidon**
75 C2 **Saidpur** Bangl.
Saigon Vietnam *see* **Ho Chi Minh City**
62 A1 **Saiha** India
69 D2 **Saihan Tal** China
67 B4 **Saiki** Japan
93 I3 **Saimaa** *l.* Fin.
144 B2 **Sain Alto** Mex.
96 C3 **St Abb's Head** U.K.
99 C3 **St Albans** U.K.
99 B3 **St Aldhelm's Head** U.K.
96 C2 **St Andrews** U.K.
131 E1 **St Anthony** Can.
134 D2 **St Anthony** U.S.A.
52 B3 **St Arnaud** Austr.
131 E1 **St-Augustin** Can.
131 E1 **St Augustin** *r.* Can.
143 D3 **St Augustine** U.S.A.
99 A3 **St Austell** U.K.
104 C2 **St-Avertin** France
98 B1 **St Bees Head** U.K.
105 D3 **St-Bonnet-en-Champsaur** France
99 A3 **St Bride's Bay** U.K.
104 B2 **St-Brieuc** France
130 C2 **St Catharines** Can.
99 C3 **St Catherine's Point** U.K.
137 E3 **St Charles** U.S.A.
140 C2 **St Clair, Lake** Can./U.S.A.
105 D2 **St-Claude** France
137 E1 **St Cloud** U.S.A.
140 A1 **St Croix** *r.* U.S.A.
147 D3 **St Croix** *i.* Virgin Is (U.S.A.)
105 C2 **St-Dizier** France
131 D2 **Ste-Anne-des-Monts** Can.
105 D2 **St-Égrève** France
126 B2 **St Elias Mountains** Can.
131 D1 **Ste-Marguerite** *r.* Can.
129 E2 **Sainte Rose du Lac** Can.
104 B2 **Saintes** France
105 C2 **St-Étienne** France
108 A2 **St-Florent** *Corsica* France
105 C2 **St-Flour** France
136 C3 **St Francis** U.S.A.
104 C3 **St-Gaudens** France
53 C1 **St George** Austr.
135 D3 **St George** U.S.A.
143 D3 **St George Island** U.S.A.
131 C2 **St-Georges** Can.
147 D3 **St George's** Grenada
97 C3 **St George's Channel** Ireland/U.K.
105 D2 **St Gotthard Pass** Switz.
113 E8 **St Helena** *i.* S. Atlantic Ocean
113 E8 **St Helena, Ascension and Tristan da Cunha** *terr.* S. Atlantic Ocean
122 A3 **St Helena Bay** S. Africa
122 A3 **St Helena Bay** S. Africa
98 B2 **St Helens** U.K.
134 B1 **St Helens, Mount** *vol.* U.S.A.
95 C4 **St Helier** Channel Is
100 B2 **St-Hubert** Belgium
141 E1 **St-Hyacinthe** Can.
140 C1 **St Ignace** U.S.A.
130 B2 **St Ignace Island** Can.
99 A3 **St Ives** U.K.
128 A2 **St James, Cape** Can.
131 C2 **St-Jean, Lac** *l.* Can.
104 B2 **St-Jean-d'Angély** France
104 B2 **St-Jean-de-Monts** France
130 C2 **St-Jean-sur-Richelieu** Can.
141 E1 **St-Jérôme** Can.
134 C1 **St Joe** *r.* U.S.A.
131 D2 **Saint John** Can.
141 F1 **St John** *r.* U.S.A.
147 D3 **St John's** Antigua
131 E2 **St John's** Can.
138 B2 **St Johns** U.S.A.
141 E2 **St Johnsbury** U.S.A.
137 E3 **St Joseph** U.S.A.
130 A1 **St Joseph, Lake** Can.
130 B2 **St Joseph Island** Can.
104 C2 **St-Junien** France
94 B2 **St Kilda** *is* U.K.
147 D3 **St Kitts and Nevis** *country* West Indies
St-Laurent, Golfe du *g.* Can. *see* **St Lawrence, Gulf of**
151 C1 **St-Laurent-du-Maroni** Fr. Guiana
131 D2 **St Lawrence** *inlet* Can.
131 D2 **St Lawrence, Gulf of** Can.
83 N2 **St Lawrence Island** U.S.A.
104 B2 **St-Lô** France
114 A3 **St-Louis** Senegal
137 E3 **St Louis** U.S.A.
137 E1 **St Louis** *r.* U.S.A.
147 D3 **St Lucia** *country* West Indies
123 D2 **St Lucia Estuary** S. Africa
104 B2 **St-Malo** France
104 B2 **St-Malo, Golfe de** *g.* France
122 A3 **St Martin, Cape** S. Africa
141 D2 **St Marys** U.S.A.
130 C2 **St-Maurice** *r.* Can.
104 B2 **St-Nazaire** France
104 C1 **St-Omer** France
129 C2 **St Paul** Can.
137 E2 **St Paul** U.S.A.
137 E2 **St Peter** U.S.A.
95 C4 **St Peter Port** Channel Is
89 D2 **St Petersburg** Russia
143 D3 **St Petersburg** U.S.A.
131 E2 **St-Pierre** St Pierre and Miquelon
131 E2 **St Pierre and Miquelon** *terr.* N. America
104 B2 **St-Pierre-d'Oléron** France
105 C2 **St-Pourçain-sur-Sioule** France
131 D2 **St Quentin** Can.
105 C2 **St-Quentin** France
131 D2 **St-Siméon** Can.
129 E2 **St Theresa Point** Can.
130 B2 **St Thomas** Can.
105 D3 **St-Tropez** France
105 D3 **St-Tropez, Cap de** *c.* France
52 A3 **St Vincent, Gulf** Austr.
147 D3 **St Vincent and the Grenadines** *country* West Indies
100 C2 **St-Vith** Belgium
129 D2 **St Walburg** Can.
104 C2 **St-Yrieix-la-Perche** France
59 D1 **Saipan** *i.* N. Mariana Is
152 B2 **Sajama, Nevado** *mt.* Bol.
122 B2 **Sak** *watercourse* S. Africa
67 C4 **Sakai** Japan
67 B4 **Sakaide** Japan
78 B2 **Sakākah** Saudi Arabia
136 C1 **Sakakawea, Lake** U.S.A.
111 D2 **Sakarya** *r.* Turkey
66 C3 **Sakata** Japan
65 B1 **Sakchu** N. Korea
83 K3 **Sakhalin** *i.* Russia
123 C2 **Sakhile** S. Africa
81 C1 **Şäki** Azer.
88 B3 **Šakiai** Lith.
69 E3 **Sakishima-shotō** *is* Japan
62 B2 **Sakon Nakhon** Thai.
122 B3 **Sakrivier** S. Africa
67 D3 **Sakura** Japan
91 C2 **Saky** Ukr.
93 G4 **Sala** Sweden
130 C2 **Salaberry-de-Valleyfield** Can.

88 B2 **Salacgrīva** Latvia
109 C2 **Sala Consilina** Italy
135 C4 **Salada, Laguna** *salt l.* Mex.
152 B4 **Salado** *r.* Arg.
145 C2 **Salado** *r.* Mex.
114 B4 **Salaga** Ghana
122 B1 **Salajwe** Botswana
115 D3 **Salal** Chad
78 A2 **Salâla** Sudan
79 C3 **Şalālah** Oman
145 B2 **Salamanca** Mex.
106 B1 **Salamanca** Spain
106 B1 **Salas** Spain
63 B2 **Salavan** Laos
59 C3 **Salawati** *i.* Indon.
104 C2 **Salbris** France
88 C3 **Šalčininkai** Lith.
106 C1 **Saldaña** Spain
122 A3 **Saldanha** S. Africa
88 B2 **Saldus** Latvia
53 C3 **Sale** Austr.
86 F2 **Salekhard** Russia
73 B3 **Salem** India
137 E3 **Salem** *MO* U.S.A.
134 B2 **Salem** *OR* U.S.A.
96 B2 **Salen** U.K.
109 B2 **Salerno** Italy
98 B2 **Salford** U.K.
151 E2 **Salgado** *r.* Brazil
103 D2 **Salgótarján** Hungary
151 E2 **Salgueiro** Brazil
136 B3 **Salida** U.S.A.
111 C3 **Salihli** Turkey
88 C3 **Salihorsk** Belarus
121 C2 **Salima** Malawi
121 C2 **Salimo** Moz.
137 D3 **Salina** U.S.A.
108 B3 **Salina, Isola** *i.* Italy
145 C3 **Salina Cruz** Mex.
155 D1 **Salinas** Brazil
144 B2 **Salinas** Mex.
135 B3 **Salinas** U.S.A.
107 D2 **Salines, Cap de ses** *c.* Spain
151 D2 **Salinópolis** Brazil
99 C3 **Salisbury** U.K.
141 D3 **Salisbury** *MD* U.S.A.
143 D1 **Salisbury** *NC* U.S.A.
99 B3 **Salisbury Plain** U.K.
151 D2 **Salitre** *r.* Brazil
92 I2 **Salla** Fin.
127 F2 **Salluit** Can.
75 C2 **Sallyana** Nepal
81 C2 **Salmās** Iran
134 D1 **Salmon** U.S.A.
134 C1 **Salmon** *r.* U.S.A.
128 C2 **Salmon Arm** Can.
134 C2 **Salmon River Mountains** U.S.A.
100 C3 **Salmtal** Ger.
93 H3 **Salo** Fin.
87 D4 **Sal'sk** Russia
122 B3 **Salt** *watercourse* S. Africa
138 A2 **Salt** *r.* U.S.A.
152 B3 **Salta** Arg.
145 B2 **Saltillo** Mex.
134 D2 **Salt Lake City** U.S.A.
154 C2 **Salto** Brazil
152 C4 **Salto** Uru.
155 E1 **Salto da Divisa** Brazil
154 B2 **Salto del Guairá** Para.
135 C4 **Salton Sea** *salt l.* U.S.A.
143 D2 **Saluda** U.S.A.
108 A2 **Saluzzo** Italy
151 E3 **Salvador** Brazil
79 C2 **Salwah** Saudi Arabia
62 A1 **Salween** *r.* China/Myanmar
81 C2 **Salyan** Azer.
102 C2 **Salzburg** Austria
101 E1 **Salzgitter** Ger.
101 D2 **Salzkotten** Ger.
101 E1 **Salzwedel** Ger.
144 B1 **Samalayuca** Mex.
66 D2 **Samani** Japan
64 B1 **Samar** *i.* Phil.
87 E3 **Samara** Russia
61 C2 **Samarinda** Indon.
77 C3 **Samarqand** Uzbek.
81 C2 **Sāmarrā'** Iraq
81 C1 **Şamaxı** Azer.
119 C3 **Samba** Dem. Rep. Congo
61 C1 **Sambaliung** *mts* Indon.
75 C2 **Sambalpur** India
61 C2 **Sambar, Tanjung** *pt* Indon.
61 B1 **Sambas** Indon.
121 E2 **Sambava** Madag.
90 A2 **Sambir** Ukr.
153 C4 **Samborombón, Bahía** *b.* Arg.
65 B2 **Samcheok** S. Korea
81 C2 **Samdi Dag** *mt.* Turkey
119 D3 **Same** Tanz.
78 B2 **Samīrah** Saudi Arabia
65 B1 **Samjiyŏn** N. Korea
49 G3 **Samoa** *country* S. Pacific Ocean
109 C1 **Samobor** Croatia
111 C3 **Samos** *i.* Greece
111 C2 **Samothraki** Greece
111 C2 **Samothraki** *i.* Greece
61 C2 **Sampit** Indon.
119 C3 **Sampwe** Dem. Rep. Congo
63 B2 **Sâmraông** Cambodia
139 E2 **Sam Rayburn Reservoir** U.S.A.
80 B1 **Samsun** Turkey
81 C1 **Samt'redia** Georgia
63 B3 **Samui, Ko** *i.* Thai.
63 B2 **Samut Songkhram** Thai.
114 B3 **San** Mali
78 B3 **Şan'ā'** Yemen
118 A2 **Sanaga** *r.* Cameroon
81 C2 **Sanandaj** Iran
146 B3 **San Andrés, Isla de** *i.* Caribbean Sea
138 B2 **San Andres Mountains** U.S.A.
145 C3 **San Andrés Tuxtla** Mex.
139 C2 **San Angelo** U.S.A.
139 D3 **San Antonio** U.S.A.
135 C4 **San Antonio, Mount** U.S.A.
152 B3 **San Antonio de los Cobres** Arg.
153 B5 **San Antonio Oeste** Arg.
108 B2 **San Benedetto del Tronto** Italy
144 A3 **San Benedicto, Isla** *i.* Mex.
135 C4 **San Bernardino** U.S.A.
135 C4 **San Bernardino Mountains** U.S.A.
143 C3 **San Blas, Cape** U.S.A.
152 B2 **San Borja** Bol.
144 B2 **San Buenaventura** Mex.
64 B1 **San Carlos** Phil.
147 D4 **San Carlos** Venez.
153 A5 **San Carlos de Bariloche** Arg.
147 C4 **San Carlos del Zulia** Venez.
135 C4 **San Clemente Island** U.S.A.
104 C2 **Sancoins** France
150 A1 **San Cristóbal** Venez.
145 C3 **San Cristóbal de las Casas** Mex.
146 C2 **Sancti Spíritus** Cuba
61 C1 **Sandakan** *Sabah* Malaysia
93 E3 **Sandane** Norway
111 B2 **Sandanski** Bulg.
96 C1 **Sanday** *i.* U.K.
139 C2 **Sanderson** U.S.A.
150 B3 **Sandia** Peru
135 C4 **San Diego** U.S.A.
80 B2 **Sandıklı** Turkey
93 E4 **Sandnes** Norway
92 F2 **Sandnessjøen** Norway
118 C3 **Sandoa** Dem. Rep. Congo
103 E1 **Sandomierz** Pol.
89 E2 **Sandovo** Russia
94 B1 **Sandoy** *i.* Faroe Is
134 C1 **Sandpoint** U.S.A.
71 B3 **Sandu** China
94 B1 **Sandur** Faroe Is
140 C2 **Sandusky** U.S.A.
122 A3 **Sandveld** *mts* S. Africa
93 F4 **Sandvika** Norway
93 G3 **Sandviken** Sweden
131 E1 **Sandwich Bay** Can.
129 D2 **Sandy Bay** Can.
51 E2 **Sandy Cape** Austr.
130 A1 **Sandy Lake** Can.
130 A1 **Sandy Lake** Can.
144 A1 **San Felipe** *Baja California* Mex.
145 B2 **San Felipe** *Guanajuato* Mex.
150 B1 **San Felipe** Venez.
144 A2 **San Fernando** *Baja California* Mex.
145 C2 **San Fernando** *Tamaulipas* Mex.
64 B1 **San Fernando** *La Union* Phil.
64 B1 **San Fernando** *Pampanga* Phil.
106 B2 **San Fernando** Spain
147 D3 **San Fernando** Trin. and Tob.
150 B1 **San Fernando de Apure** Venez.
143 D3 **Sanford** *FL* U.S.A.
141 E2 **Sanford** *ME* U.S.A.
152 B4 **San Francisco** Arg.
135 B3 **San Francisco** U.S.A.
74 B3 **Sangamner** India
83 J2 **Sangar** Russia
108 A3 **San Gavino Monreale** *Sardinia* Italy
101 E2 **Sangerhausen** Ger.
61 C1 **Sanggau** Indon.
118 B3 **Sangha** *r.* Congo
109 C3 **San Giovanni in Fiore** Italy
64 B2 **Sangir** *i.* Indon.
59 C2 **Sangir, Kepulauan** *is* Indon.
65 B2 **Sangju** S. Korea
61 C1 **Sangkulirang** Indon.
73 B3 **Sangli** India
118 B2 **Sangmélima** Cameroon
121 C3 **Sango** Zimbabwe
136 B3 **Sangre de Cristo Range** *mts* U.S.A.
75 C2 **Sangsang** China
144 A2 **San Hipólito, Punta** *pt* Mex.
144 A2 **San Ignacio** Mex.
130 C1 **Sanikiluaq** Can.
71 A3 **Sanjiang** China
135 B3 **San Joaquin** *r.* U.S.A.
153 B5 **San Jorge, Golfo de** *g.* Arg.
146 B4 **San José** Costa Rica
64 B1 **San Jose** *Nueva Ecija* Phil.
64 B1 **San Jose** *Occidental Mindoro* Phil.
135 B3 **San Jose** U.S.A.
144 A2 **San José, Isla** *i.* Mex.
144 B2 **San José de Bavicora** Mex.
64 B1 **San Jose de Buenavista** Phil.
144 A2 **San José de Comondú** Mex.
144 B2 **San José del Cabo** Mex.
150 A1 **San José del Guaviare** Col.
152 B4 **San Juan** Arg.
146 B3 **San Juan** *r.* Costa Rica/Nic.
147 D3 **San Juan** Puerto Rico
135 D3 **San Juan** *r.* U.S.A.

Sarbāz

145 C3	San Juan Bautista Tuxtepec Mex.	
134 B1	San Juan Islands U.S.A.	
144 B2	San Juanito Mex.	
136 B3	San Juan Mountains U.S.A.	
153 B5	San Julián Arg.	
75 C2	Sankh r. India	
105 D2	Sankt Gallen Switz.	
105 D2	Sankt Moritz Switz.	
	Sankt-Peterburg Russia see St Petersburg	
102 C2	Sankt Veit an der Glan Austria	
100 C3	Sankt Wendel Ger.	
80 B2	Şanlıurfa Turkey	
138 B3	San Lorenzo Mex.	
106 B2	Sanlúcar de Barrameda Spain	
153 B4	San Luis Arg.	
145 B2	San Luis de la Paz Mex.	
138 A2	San Luisito Mex.	
135 B3	San Luis Obispo U.S.A.	
145 B2	San Luis Potosí Mex.	
144 A1	San Luis Río Colorado Mex.	
139 D3	San Marcos U.S.A.	
108 B2	San Marino country Europe	
108 B2	San Marino San Marino	
144 B2	San Martín de Bolaños Mex.	
153 A5	San Martín de los Andes Arg.	
153 B5	San Matías, Golfo g. Arg.	
70 B2	Sanmenxia China	
146 B3	San Miguel El Salvador	
152 B3	San Miguel de Tucumán Arg.	
145 C3	San Miguel Sola de Vega Mex.	
71 B3	Sanming China	
153 B4	San Nicolás de los Arroyos Arg.	
135 C4	San Nicolas Island U.S.A.	
123 C2	Sannieshof S. Africa	
103 E2	Sanok Pol.	
64 B1	San Pablo Phil.	
144 B2	San Pablo Balleza Mex.	
152 B3	San Pedro Arg.	
152 B2	San Pedro Bol.	
114 B4	San-Pédro Côte d'Ivoire	
144 A2	San Pedro Mex.	
138 A2	San Pedro watercourse U.S.A.	
106 B2	San Pedro, Sierra de mts Spain	
144 B2	San Pedro de las Colonias Mex.	
146 B3	San Pedro Sula Hond.	
108 A3	San Pietro, Isola di i. Sardinia Italy	
144 A1	San Quintín, Cabo c. Mex.	
153 B4	San Rafael Arg.	
108 A2	Sanremo Italy	
146 B3	San Salvador El Salvador	
152 B3	San Salvador de Jujuy Arg.	
107 C1	San Sebastián Spain	
107 C1	San Sebastián Spain	
109 C2	San Severo Italy	
109 C2	Sanski Most Bos. & Herz.	
152 B2	Santa Ana Bol.	
146 B3	Santa Ana El Salvador	
144 A1	Santa Ana Mex.	
135 C4	Santa Ana U.S.A.	
144 B2	Santa Bárbara Mex.	
135 C4	Santa Barbara U.S.A.	
154 B1	Santa Bárbara, Serra de hills Brazil	
152 B3	Santa Catalina Chile	
150 B2	Santa Clara Cuba	
146 C2	Santa Clara Cuba	
135 C4	Santa Clarita U.S.A.	
109 C3	Santa Croce, Capo c. Sicily Italy	
153 B6	Santa Cruz r. Arg.	
152 B2	Santa Cruz Bol.	
64 C1	Santa Cruz Phil.	
135 B3	Santa Cruz U.S.A.	
145 C3	Santa Cruz Barillas Guat.	
155 E1	Santa Cruz Cabrália Brazil	
107 C2	Santa Cruz de Moya Spain	
114 A2	Santa Cruz de Tenerife Canary Islands	
135 C4	Santa Cruz Island U.S.A.	
48 F3	Santa Cruz Islands Solomon Is	
152 B4	Santa Fe Arg.	
138 B1	Santa Fe U.S.A.	
154 B1	Santa Helena de Goiás Brazil	
153 B4	Santa Isabel Arg.	
154 B1	Santa Luisa, Serra de hills Brazil	
152 C3	Santa Maria Brazil	
144 B1	Santa María r. Mex.	
135 B4	Santa Maria U.S.A.	
123 D2	Santa Maria, Cabo de c. Moz.	
106 B2	Santa Maria, Cabo de c. Port.	
151 D2	Santa Maria das Barreiras Brazil	
109 C3	Santa Maria di Leuca, Capo c. Italy	
150 A1	Santa Marta Col.	
135 C4	Santa Monica U.S.A.	
151 C2	Santana Amapá Brazil	
151 D3	Santana Bahia Brazil	
106 C1	Santander Spain	
108 A3	Sant'Antioco Sardinia Italy	
108 A3	Sant'Antioco, Isola di i. Sardinia Italy	
107 D2	Sant Antoni de Portmany Spain	
151 C2	Santarém Brazil	
106 B2	Santarém Port.	
154 B1	Santa Rita do Araguaia Brazil	
153 B4	Santa Rosa Arg.	
152 C3	Santa Rosa Brazil	
135 B3	Santa Rosa CA U.S.A.	
138 C2	Santa Rosa NM U.S.A.	
146 B3	Santa Rosa de Copán Hond.	
135 B4	Santa Rosa Island U.S.A.	
144 A2	Santa Rosalía Mex.	
107 D2	Sant Francesc de Formentera Spain	
152 C3	Santiago Brazil	
153 A4	Santiago Chile	
147 C3	Santiago Dom. Rep.	
144 B2	Santiago Mex.	
146 B4	Santiago Panama	
64 B1	Santiago Phil.	
106 B1	Santiago de Compostela Spain	
144 B2	Santiago Ixcuintla Mex.	
144 B2	Santiago Papasquiaro Mex.	
107 D2	Sant Joan de Labritja Spain	
107 D1	Sant Jordi, Golf de g. Spain	
155 D2	Santo Amaro de Campos Brazil	
155 D2	Santo André Brazil	
152 C3	Santo Ângelo Brazil	
154 B2	Santo Antônio da Platina Brazil	
151 E3	Santo Antônio de Jesus Brazil	
150 B2	Santo Antônio do Içá Brazil	
155 C2	Santo Antônio do Monte Brazil	
147 D3	Santo Domingo Dom. Rep.	
138 B1	Santo Domingo Pueblo U.S.A.	
111 C3	Santorini i. Greece	
155 C2	Santos Brazil	
152 C3	Santo Tomé Arg.	
153 A5	San Valentín, Cerro mt. Chile	
146 B3	San Vicente El Salvador	
144 A1	San Vicente Mex.	
150 A3	San Vicente de Cañete Peru	
108 B2	San Vincenzo Italy	
108 B3	San Vito, Capo c. Sicily Italy	
71 A4	Sanya China	
155 C2	São Bernardo do Campo Brazil	
152 C3	São Borja Brazil	
154 C2	São Carlos Brazil	
151 C3	São Félix do Araguaia Brazil	
151 C2	São Félix do Xingu Brazil	
155 D2	São Fidélis Brazil	
155 D1	São Francisco Brazil	
151 E3	São Francisco r. Brazil	
154 C3	São Francisco, Ilha de i. Brazil	
152 C4	São Francisco do Sul Brazil	
152 C4	São Gabriel Brazil	
150 B2	São Gabriel da Cachoeira Brazil	
155 D2	São Gonçalo Brazil	
155 C1	São Gotardo Brazil	
155 D2	São João da Barra Brazil	
155 C2	São João da Boa Vista Brazil	
106 B1	São João da Madeira Port.	
155 D1	São João do Paraíso Brazil	
155 D2	São João Nepomuceno Brazil	
154 C2	São Joaquim da Barra Brazil	
154 C2	São José do Rio Preto Brazil	
154 C3	São José dos Campos Brazil	
154 C3	São José dos Pinhais Brazil	
152 C3	São Lourenço Brazil	
151 D2	São Luís Brazil	
154 B2	São Manuel Brazil	
154 C1	São Marcos r. Brazil	
151 D2	São Marcos, Baía de b. Brazil	
155 E1	São Mateus Brazil	
155 C2	São Paulo Brazil	
151 D2	São Raimundo Nonato Brazil	
155 C1	São Romão Brazil	
155 C2	São Sebastião, Ilha de i. Brazil	
154 C2	São Sebastião do Paraíso Brazil	
154 B1	São Simão Brazil	
154 B1	São Simão, Barragem de resr Brazil	
59 C2	Sao-Siu Indon.	
113 F6	São Tomé São Tomé and Príncipe	
155 D2	São Tomé, Cabo de c. Brazil	
113 F6	São Tomé and Príncipe country Africa	
155 C2	São Vicente Brazil	
106 B2	São Vicente, Cabo de c. Port.	
59 C3	Saparua Indon.	
89 F3	Sapozhok Russia	
66 D2	Sapporo Japan	
109 C2	Capri Italy	
81 C2	Saqqez Iran	
81 C2	Sarāb Iran	
63 B2	Sara Buri Thai.	
109 C2	Sarajevo Bos. & Herz.	
76 B1	Saraktash Russia	
141 E2	Saranac Lake U.S.A.	
109 D2	Sarandë Albania	
64 B2	Sarangani Islands Phil.	
87 D3	Saransk Russia	
87 E3	Sarapul Russia	
143 D3	Sarasota U.S.A.	
90 B2	Sarata Ukr.	
136 B2	Saratoga U.S.A.	
141 E2	Saratoga Springs U.S.A.	
61 C1	Saratok Sarawak Malaysia	
87 D3	Saratov Russia	
79 D2	Sarāvān Iran	
61 C1	Sarawak state Malaysia	
110 C2	Saray Turkey	
111 C3	Sarayköy Turkey	
79 D2	Sarbāz Iran	

235

74 B2 **Sardarshahr** India
Sardegna *i.* Italy *see* **Sardinia**
108 A2 **Sardinia** *i.* Italy
92 G2 **Sarektjåkkå** *mt.* Sweden
77 C3 **Sar-e Pul** Afgh.
158 B3 **Sargasso Sea** N. Atlantic Ocean
74 B1 **Sargodha** Pak.
115 D4 **Sarh** Chad
79 D2 **Sarhad** *reg.* Iran
81 D2 **Sārī** Iran
111 C3 **Sarıgöl** Turkey
81 C1 **Sarıkamış** Turkey
61 C1 **Sarikei** *Sarawak* Malaysia
51 D2 **Sarina** Austr.
65 B2 **Sariwŏn** N. Korea
111 C2 **Sarıyer** Turkey
78 B2 **Sark, Safrā' as** *esc.* Saudi Arabia
77 D2 **Sarkand** Kazakh.
111 C2 **Şarköy** Turkey
59 D3 **Sarmi** Indon.
140 C2 **Sarnia** Can.
90 B1 **Sarny** Ukr.
60 B2 **Sarolangun** Indon.
111 B3 **Saronikos Kolpos** *g.* Greece
111 C2 **Saros Körfezi** *b.* Turkey
87 D3 **Sarov** Russia
105 D2 **Sarrebourg** France
106 B1 **Sarria** Spain
107 C1 **Sarrión** Spain
105 D3 **Sartène** *Corsica* France
103 D2 **Sárvár** Hungary
77 D1 **Saryarka** *plain* Kazakh.
76 B2 **Sarykamyshskoye Ozero** *salt l.* Turkm./Uzbek.
77 D2 **Saryozek** Kazakh.
77 D2 **Saryshagan** Kazakh.
82 F3 **Sarysu** *watercourse* Kazakh.
77 D3 **Sary-Tash** Kyrg.
75 C2 **Sasaram** India
67 A4 **Sasebo** Japan
129 D2 **Saskatchewan** *prov.* Can.
129 D2 **Saskatchewan** *r.* Can.
129 D2 **Saskatoon** Can.
83 I2 **Saskylakh** Russia
123 C2 **Sasolburg** S. Africa
87 D3 **Sasovo** Russia
114 B4 **Sassandra** Côte d'Ivoire
108 A2 **Sassari** *Sardinia* Italy
102 C1 **Sassnitz** Ger.
114 A3 **Satadougou** Mali
123 D1 **Satara** S. Africa
75 C2 **Satna** India
74 B2 **Satpura Range** *mts* India
67 B4 **Satsuma-Sendai** Japan
63 B2 **Sattahip** Thai.
110 B1 **Satu Mare** Romania
63 B3 **Satun** Thai.
144 B2 **Saucillo** Mex.
93 E4 **Sauda** Norway
92 □B2 **Sauðárkrókur** Iceland
78 B2 **Saudi Arabia** *country* Asia
105 C3 **Saugues** France
105 C2 **Saulieu** France
130 B2 **Sault Sainte Marie** Can.
140 C1 **Sault Sainte Marie** U.S.A.
77 C1 **Saumalkol'** Kazakh.
59 C3 **Saumlakki** Indon.
104 B2 **Saumur** France
120 B1 **Saurimo** Angola
109 D2 **Sava** *r.* Europe
49 G3 **Savai'i** *i.* Samoa
91 E1 **Savala** *r.* Russia
143 D2 **Savannah** *GA* U.S.A.
142 C1 **Savannah** *TN* U.S.A.
143 D2 **Savannah** *r.* U.S.A.
63 B2 **Savannakhét** Laos
130 A1 **Savant Lake** Can.
111 C3 **Savaştepe** Turkey
89 F2 **Savino** Russia
86 D2 **Savinskiy** Russia
108 A2 **Savona** Italy
93 I3 **Savonlinna** Fin.
92 I2 **Savukoski** Fin.
Savu Sea Indon. *see* **Sawu, Laut**
74 B2 **Sawai Madhopur** India
62 A2 **Sawankhalok** Thai.
136 B3 **Sawatch Range** *mts* U.S.A.
53 D2 **Sawtell** Austr.
59 C3 **Sawu, Laut** *sea* Indon.
79 C3 **Sayḩūt** Yemen
69 D2 **Saynshand** Mongolia
141 D2 **Sayre** U.S.A.
144 B3 **Sayula** *Jalisco* Mex.
145 C3 **Sayula** *Veracruz* Mex.
128 B2 **Sayward** Can.
89 E2 **Sazonovo** Russia
114 B2 **Sbaa** Alg.
98 B1 **Scafell Pike** *h.* U.K.
109 C3 **Scalea** Italy
96 C1 **Scapa Flow** *inlet* U.K.
130 C2 **Scarborough** Can.
147 D3 **Scarborough** Trin. and Tob.
98 C1 **Scarborough** U.K.
64 A1 **Scarborough Reef** *sea feature* S. China Sea
96 A2 **Scarinish** U.K.
Scarpanto *i.* Greece *see* **Karpathos**
105 D2 **Schaffhausen** Switz.
100 B1 **Schagen** Neth.
102 C2 **Schärding** Austria
100 A2 **Scharendijke** Neth.
101 D1 **Scharhörn** *i.* Ger.
101 D1 **Scheeßel** Ger.
131 D1 **Schefferville** Can.
135 D3 **Schell Creek Range** *mts* U.S.A.
141 E2 **Schenectady** U.S.A.
101 E3 **Scheßlitz** Ger.
100 C1 **Schiermonnikoog** *i.* Neth.
108 B1 **Schio** Italy
101 F2 **Schkeuditz** Ger.
101 E1 **Schladen** Ger.
101 E2 **Schleiz** Ger.
102 B1 **Schleswig** Ger.
101 D2 **Schloß Holte-Stukenbrock** Ger.
101 D2 **Schlüchtern** Ger.
101 E3 **Schlüsselfeld** Ger.
101 D2 **Schmallenberg** Ger.
101 D1 **Schneverdingen** Ger.
101 E1 **Schönebeck (Elbe)** Ger.
101 E1 **Schöningen** Ger.
100 B2 **Schoonhoven** Neth.
59 D3 **Schouten Islands** P.N.G.
102 B2 **Schwäbische Alb** *mts* Ger.
102 C2 **Schwandorf** Ger.
61 C2 **Schwaner, Pegunungan** *mts* Indon.
101 E1 **Schwarzenbek** Ger.
101 F2 **Schwarzenberg/Erzgebirge** Ger.
122 A2 **Schwarzrand** *mts* Namibia
Schwarzwald *mts* Ger. *see* **Black Forest**
102 C2 **Schwaz** Austria
102 C1 **Schwedt/Oder** Ger.
101 E2 **Schweinfurt** Ger.
101 E1 **Schwerin** Ger.
101 E1 **Schweriner See** *l.* Ger.
105 D2 **Schwyz** Switz.
108 B3 **Sciacca** *Sicily* Italy
95 B4 **Scilly, Isles of** U.K.
140 C3 **Scioto** *r.* U.S.A.
136 B1 **Scobey** U.S.A.
53 D2 **Scone** Austr.
55 R3 **Scotia Ridge** S. Atlantic Ocean
158 C8 **Scotia Sea** S. Atlantic Ocean
96 C2 **Scotland** *admin. div.* U.K.
128 B2 **Scott, Cape** Can.
123 D3 **Scottburgh** S. Africa
136 C3 **Scott City** U.S.A.
136 C2 **Scottsbluff** U.S.A.
142 C2 **Scottsboro** U.S.A.
96 B1 **Scourie** U.K.
141 D2 **Scranton** U.S.A.
98 C2 **Scunthorpe** U.K.
105 E2 **Scuol** Switz.
129 E2 **Seal** *r.* Can.
122 B3 **Seal, Cape** S. Africa
52 B3 **Sea Lake** Austr.
139 D3 **Sealy** U.S.A.
142 B1 **Searcy** U.S.A.
98 B1 **Seascale** U.K.
134 B1 **Seattle** U.S.A.
141 E2 **Sebago Lake** U.S.A.
144 A2 **Sebastián Vizcaíno, Bahía** *b.* Mex.
110 B1 **Sebeş** Romania
60 B2 **Sebesi** *i.* Indon.
88 C2 **Sebezh** Russia
80 B1 **Şebinkarahisar** Turkey
143 D3 **Sebring** U.S.A.
128 B3 **Sechelt** Can.
150 A2 **Sechura** Peru
73 B3 **Secunderabad** India
137 E3 **Sedalia** U.S.A.
105 C2 **Sedan** France
54 B2 **Seddon** N.Z.
138 A2 **Sedona** U.S.A.
101 E2 **Seeburg** Ger.
101 E1 **Seehausen (Altmark)** Ger.
122 A2 **Seeheim** Namibia
104 C2 **Sées** France
101 E2 **Seesen** Ger.
101 E1 **Seevetal** Ger.
123 C1 **Sefare** Botswana
60 B1 **Segamat** Malaysia
86 C2 **Segezha** Russia
114 B3 **Ségou** Mali
106 C1 **Segovia** Spain
115 D2 **Séguédine** Niger
114 B4 **Séguéla** Côte d'Ivoire
139 D3 **Seguin** U.S.A.
107 C2 **Segura** *r.* Spain
106 C2 **Segura, Sierra de** *mts* Spain
120 B3 **Sehithwa** Botswana
93 H3 **Seinäjoki** Fin.
104 C2 **Seine** *r.* France
104 B2 **Seine, Baie de** *b.* France
103 E1 **Sejny** Pol.
60 B2 **Sekayu** Indon.
114 B4 **Sekondi** Ghana
59 C3 **Selaru** *i.* Indon.
61 C2 **Selatan, Tanjung** *pt* Indon.
126 A2 **Selawik** U.S.A.
58 C3 **Selayar, Pulau** *i.* Indon.
98 C2 **Selby** U.K.
120 B3 **Selebi-Phikwe** Botswana
105 D2 **Sélestat** France
92 □A3 **Selfoss** Iceland
114 A3 **Sélibabi** Maur.
138 A1 **Seligman** U.S.A.
116 A2 **Selîma Oasis** Sudan
111 C3 **Selimiye** Turkey
114 B3 **Sélingué, Lac de** *l.* Mali
89 D2 **Selizharovo** Russia
93 E4 **Seljord** Norway
129 E2 **Selkirk** Can.
96 C3 **Selkirk** U.K.
128 C2 **Selkirk Mountains** Can.

142 C2 **Selma** *AL* U.S.A.
135 C3 **Selma** *CA* U.S.A.
89 D3 **Sel'tso** Russia
150 A2 **Selvas** *reg.* Brazil
134 C1 **Selway** *r.* U.S.A.
129 D1 **Selwyn Lake** Can.
128 A1 **Selwyn Mountains** Can.
51 C2 **Selwyn Range** *hills* Austr.
60 B2 **Semangka, Teluk** *b.* Indon.
61 C2 **Semarang** Indon.
61 B1 **Sematan** *Sarawak* Malaysia
118 B2 **Sembé** Congo
81 C2 **Şemdinli** Turkey
91 C1 **Semenivka** Ukr.
86 D3 **Semenov** Russia
61 C2 **Semeru, Gunung** *vol.* Indon.
77 E1 **Semey** Kazakh.
89 E3 **Semiluki** Russia
136 B2 **Seminoe Reservoir** U.S.A.
139 C2 **Seminole** U.S.A.
143 D2 **Seminole, Lake** U.S.A.
61 C1 **Semitau** Indon.
81 D2 **Semnān** Iran
61 C1 **Semporna** *Sabah* Malaysia
105 C2 **Semur-en-Auxois** France
150 B2 **Sena Madureira** Brazil
120 B2 **Senanga** Zambia
67 D3 **Sendai** Japan
114 A3 **Senegal** *country* Africa
114 A3 **Sénégal** *r.* Maur./Senegal
102 C1 **Senftenberg** Ger.
119 D3 **Sengerema** Tanz.
151 D3 **Senhor do Bonfim** Brazil
108 B2 **Senigallia** Italy
109 B2 **Senj** Croatia
92 G2 **Senja** *i.* Norway
122 B2 **Senlac** S. Africa
104 C2 **Senlis** France
63 B2 **Sênmônoŭrôm** Cambodia
117 B3 **Sennar** Sudan
130 C2 **Senneterre** Can.
123 C3 **Senqu** *r.* Lesotho
105 C2 **Sens** France
109 D1 **Senta** Serbia
128 B2 **Sentinel Peak** Can.
123 C1 **Senwabarwana** S. Africa
65 B2 **Seocheon** S. Korea
65 B2 **Seongnam** S. Korea
75 B2 **Seoni** India
65 B2 **Seosan** S. Korea
65 B2 **Seoul** S. Korea
155 D2 **Sepetiba, Baía de** *b.* Brazil
59 D3 **Sepik** *r.* P.N.G.
61 C1 **Sepinang** Indon.
131 D1 **Sept-Îles** Can.
59 C3 **Seram** *i.* Indon.
59 C3 **Seram, Laut** *sea* Indon.
60 B2 **Serang** Indon.
109 D2 **Serbia** *country* Europe
76 B3 **Serdar** Turkm.
89 E3 **Serebryanyye Prudy** Russia
60 B1 **Seremban** Malaysia
119 D3 **Serengeti Plain** Tanz.
87 D3 **Sergach** Russia
89 E2 **Sergiyev Posad** Russia
74 A1 **Serhetabat** Turkm.
61 C1 **Seria** Brunei
61 C1 **Serian** *Sarawak* Malaysia
111 B3 **Serifos** *i.* Greece
80 B2 **Serik** Turkey
59 C3 **Sermata, Kepulauan** *is* Indon.
86 F3 **Serov** Russia
120 B3 **Serowe** Botswana
106 B2 **Serpa** Port.
89 E3 **Serpukhov** Russia
151 D3 **Serra da Mesa, Represa** *resr* Brazil
154 B1 **Serranópolis** Brazil
100 A3 **Serre** *r.* France
111 B2 **Serres** Greece
151 E3 **Serrinha** Brazil
155 D1 **Serro** Brazil
154 C2 **Sertãozinho** Brazil
61 C2 **Seruyan** *r.* Indon.
68 C2 **Sêrxü** China
120 A2 **Sesfontein** Namibia
108 B2 **Sessa Aurunca** Italy
108 A2 **Sestri Levante** Italy
105 C3 **Sète** France
155 D1 **Sete Lagoas** Brazil
92 G2 **Setermoen** Norway
93 E4 **Setesdal** *val.* Norway
115 C1 **Sétif** Alg.
67 B4 **Seto-naikai** *sea* Japan
114 B1 **Settat** Morocco
98 B1 **Settle** U.K.
106 B2 **Setúbal** Port.
106 B2 **Setúbal, Baía de** *b.* Port.
130 A1 **Seul, Lac** *l.* Can.
76 A2 **Sevan, Lake** Armenia
Sevana Lich *l.* Armenia *see* **Sevan, Lake**
91 C3 **Sevastopol'** Ukr.
105 C3 **Sévérac-le-Château** France
130 B1 **Severn** *r.* Can.
122 B2 **Severn** S. Africa
99 B3 **Severn** *r.* U.K.
86 D2 **Severnaya Dvina** *r.* Russia
83 H1 **Severnaya Zemlya** *is* Russia
86 D2 **Severnyy** *Nenetskiy Avtonomnyy Okrug* Russia
86 F2 **Severnyy** *Respublika Komi* Russia
82 E1 **Severnyy, Ostrov** *i.* Russia
86 C2 **Severodvinsk** Russia
86 C2 **Severomorsk** Russia
91 D3 **Severskaya** Russia
135 D3 **Sevier** *r.* U.S.A.
135 D3 **Sevier Lake** U.S.A.
Sevilla Spain *see* **Seville**
106 B2 **Seville** Spain
128 A2 **Sewell Inlet** Can.
128 C2 **Sexsmith** Can.
144 B2 **Sextín** *r.* Mex.
86 G1 **Seyakha** Russia
113 J7 **Seychelles** *country* Indian Ocean
92 □C2 **Seyðisfjörður** Iceland
91 C1 **Seym** *r.* Russia/Ukr.
83 L2 **Seymchan** Russia
53 C3 **Seymour** Austr.
140 B3 **Seymour** *IN* U.S.A.
139 D2 **Seymour** *TX* U.S.A.
105 C2 **Sézanne** France
110 C1 **Sfântu Gheorghe** Romania
115 D1 **Sfax** Tunisia
's-Gravenhage Neth. *see* **The Hague**
96 A2 **Sgurr Alasdair** *h.* U.K.
70 A2 **Shaanxi** *prov.* China
91 D2 **Shabel'skoye** Russia
77 D3 **Shache** China
55 R1 **Shackleton Range** *mts* Antarctica
99 B3 **Shaftesbury** U.K.
75 C2 **Shahdol** India
77 C3 **Shāh Fōlād** *mt.* Afgh.
75 B2 **Shahjahanpur** India
81 D2 **Shahr-e Kord** Iran
81 D2 **Shahreẓā** Iran
77 C3 **Shahrisabz** Uzbek.
81 D2 **Shāhrūd** Iran
89 E2 **Shakhovskaya** Russia
91 E2 **Shakhty** Russia
86 D3 **Shakhun'ya** Russia
66 D2 **Shakotan-misaki** *c.* Japan
76 B2 **Shalkar** Kazakh.
68 C2 **Shaluli Shan** *mts* China
129 E2 **Shamattawa** Can.
139 C1 **Shamrock** U.S.A.
70 B2 **Shancheng** China
68 C2 **Shandan** China
70 B2 **Shandong** *prov.* China
70 C2 **Shandong Bandao** *pen.* China
121 B2 **Shangani** *r.* Zimbabwe
70 C2 **Shanghai** China
70 C2 **Shanghai** *mun.* China
71 B3 **Shanghang** China
70 A2 **Shangluo** China
71 B3 **Shangrao** China
70 B2 **Shangshui** China
70 C2 **Shangyu** China
69 E1 **Shangzhi** China
97 B2 **Shannon** *r.* Ireland
97 B2 **Shannon, Mouth of the** Ireland
71 B3 **Shantou** China
70 B2 **Shanxi** *prov.* China
71 B3 **Shaoguan** China
71 B3 **Shaowu** China
70 C2 **Shaoxing** China
71 B3 **Shaoyang** China
116 C2 **Shaqrā'** Saudi Arabia
90 B2 **Sharhorod** Ukr.
79 C2 **Sharjah** U.A.E.
88 C2 **Sharkawshchyna** Belarus
50 A2 **Shark Bay** Austr.
78 A2 **Sharm ash Shaykh** Egypt
140 C2 **Sharon** U.S.A.
86 D3 **Shar'ya** Russia
121 B3 **Shashe** *r.* Botswana/Zimbabwe
117 B4 **Shashemenē** Eth.
134 B2 **Shasta, Mount** *vol.* U.S.A.
134 B2 **Shasta Lake** U.S.A.
156 D3 **Shatsky Rise** *sea feature* N. Pacific Ocean
89 E2 **Shatura** Russia
129 D3 **Shaunavon** Can.
140 B2 **Shawano** U.S.A.
131 C2 **Shawinigan** Can.
139 D1 **Shawnee** U.S.A.
50 B2 **Shay Gap (abandoned)** Austr.
89 E3 **Shchekino** Russia
89 E2 **Shchelkovo** Russia
89 E3 **Shchigry** Russia
91 C1 **Shchors** Ukr.
88 B3 **Shchuchyn** Belarus
91 D1 **Shebekino** Russia
117 C4 **Shebelē Wenz, Wabē** *r.* Eth./Somalia
140 B2 **Sheboygan** U.S.A.
91 D3 **Shebsh** *r.* Russia
97 C2 **Sheelin, Lough** *l.* Ireland
98 C2 **Sheffield** U.K.
89 E2 **Sheksna** Russia
89 E2 **Sheksninskoye Vodokhranilishche** *resr* Russia
83 M2 **Shelagskiy, Mys** *pt* Russia
131 D2 **Shelburne** Can.
134 D1 **Shelby** U.S.A.
140 B3 **Shelbyville** *IN* U.S.A.
142 C1 **Shelbyville** *TN* U.S.A.
83 L2 **Shelikhova, Zaliv** *g.* Russia
129 D2 **Shellbrook** Can.
134 B1 **Shelton** U.S.A.
137 D2 **Shenandoah** U.S.A.
141 D3 **Shenandoah** *r.* U.S.A.
141 D3 **Shenandoah Mountains** U.S.A.
118 A2 **Shendam** Nigeria
86 D2 **Shenkursk** Russia
65 A1 **Shenyang** China

71 B3 **Shenzhen** China
90 B1 **Shepetivka** Ukr.
53 C3 **Shepparton** Austr.
99 D3 **Sheppey, Isle of** *i.* U.K.
131 D2 **Sherbrooke** *N.S.* Can.
131 C2 **Sherbrooke** *Que.* Can.
116 B3 **Shereiq** Sudan
136 B2 **Sheridan** U.S.A.
139 D2 **Sherman** U.S.A.
100 B2 **'s-Hertogenbosch** Neth.
96 □ **Shetland Islands** U.K.
76 B2 **Shetpe** Kazakh.
Shevchenko Kazakh. *see* **Aktau**
137 D1 **Sheyenne** *r.* U.S.A.
79 B3 **Shibām** Yemen
66 D2 **Shibetsu** Japan
77 C3 **Shibirghān** Afgh.
71 B3 **Shicheng** China
96 B2 **Shiel, Loch** *l.* U.K.
77 E2 **Shihezi** China
Shijiao China *see* **Fogang**
70 B2 **Shijiazhuang** China
74 A2 **Shikarpur** Pak.
67 B4 **Shikoku** *i.* Japan
66 D2 **Shikotsu-ko** *l.* Japan
86 D2 **Shilega** Russia
75 C2 **Shiliguri** India
75 D2 **Shillong** India
89 F3 **Shilovo** Russia
117 C3 **Shimbiris** *mt.* Somalia
67 C3 **Shimizu** Japan
Shimoga India *see* **Shivamogga**
67 B4 **Shimonoseki** Japan
96 B1 **Shin, Loch** *l.* U.K.
67 C4 **Shingū** Japan
123 D1 **Shingwedzi** S. Africa
123 D1 **Shingwedzi** *r.* S. Africa
119 D3 **Shinyanga** Tanz.
67 C4 **Shiono-misaki** *c.* Japan
138 B1 **Shiprock** U.S.A.
71 A3 **Shiqian** China
70 A2 **Shiquan** China
Shiquanhe China *see* **Gar**
Shiquan He *r.* China/Pak. *see* **Indus**
67 C3 **Shirane-san** *mt.* Japan
81 D3 **Shīrāz** Iran
66 D2 **Shiretoko-misaki** *c.* Japan
66 D2 **Shiriya-zaki** *c.* Japan
74 B2 **Shiv** India
73 B3 **Shivamogga** India
69 D1 **Shiveegovĭ** Mongolia
75 B2 **Shivpuri** India
70 B2 **Shiyan** China
70 B2 **Shizhong** China
70 A2 **Shizuishan** China
67 C4 **Shizuoka** Japan
89 D3 **Shklow** Belarus
109 C2 **Shkodër** Albania
83 H1 **Shmidta, Ostrov** *i.* Russia
135 C3 **Shoshone** U.S.A.
135 C3 **Shoshone Mountains** U.S.A.
123 C1 **Shoshong** Botswana
91 C1 **Shostka** Ukr.
70 B2 **Shouxian** China
138 A2 **Show Low** U.S.A.
91 C2 **Shpola** Ukr.
142 B2 **Shreveport** U.S.A.
99 B2 **Shrewsbury** U.K.
62 A1 **Shuangjiang** China
87 E4 **Shubarkudyk** Kazakh.
116 B1 **Shubrā al Khaymah** Egypt
89 D2 **Shugozero** Russia
120 B2 **Shumba** Zimbabwe
110 C2 **Shumen** Bulg.
88 C2 **Shumilina** Belarus
89 D3 **Shumyachi** Russia
126 A2 **Shungnak** U.S.A.
78 B3 **Shuqrah** Yemen
89 F2 **Shushkodom** Russia
81 C2 **Shūshtar** Iran
128 C2 **Shuswap Lake** Can.
89 F2 **Shuya** Russia
89 F2 **Shuyskoye** Russia
62 A1 **Shwebo** Myanmar
62 A1 **Shwedwin** Myanmar
62 A2 **Shwegyin** Myanmar
77 D2 **Shyganak** Kazakh.
77 C2 **Shymkent** Kazakh.
91 C2 **Shyroke** Ukr.
59 C3 **Sia** Indon.
74 A2 **Siahan Range** *mts* Pak.
74 B1 **Sialkot** Pak.
64 B2 **Siargao** *i.* Phil.
88 B2 **Šiauliai** Lith.
109 C2 **Šibenik** Croatia
83 I2 **Siberia** *reg.* Russia
60 A2 **Siberut** *i.* Indon.
74 A2 **Sibi** Pak.
110 B1 **Sibiu** Romania
60 A1 **Sibolga** Indon.
61 C1 **Sibu** *Sarawak* Malaysia
118 B2 **Sibut** C.A.R.
64 B1 **Sibuyan** *i.* Phil.
64 B1 **Sibuyan Sea** Phil.
128 C2 **Sicamous** Can.
63 A3 **Sichon** Thai.
70 A2 **Sichuan** *prov.* China
70 A3 **Sichuan Pendi** *basin* China
105 D3 **Sicié, Cap** *c.* France
Sicilia *i.* Italy *see* **Sicily**
108 B3 **Sicilian Channel** Italy/Tunisia
108 B3 **Sicily** *i.* Italy
150 A3 **Sicuani** Peru
111 C3 **Sideros, Akrotirio** *pt* Greece
74 B2 **Sidhpur** India
107 D2 **Sidi Aïssa** Alg.
107 D2 **Sidi Ali** Alg.
114 B1 **Sidi Bel Abbès** Alg.
114 A2 **Sidi Ifni** Morocco
60 A1 **Sidikalang** Indon.
96 C2 **Sidlaw Hills** U.K.
99 B3 **Sidmouth** U.K.
134 B1 **Sidney** Can.
136 C1 **Sidney** *MT* U.S.A.
136 C2 **Sidney** *NE* U.S.A.
140 C2 **Sidney** *OH* U.S.A.
143 D2 **Sidney Lanier, Lake** U.S.A.
80 B2 **Sidon** Lebanon
154 B2 **Sidrolândia** Brazil
103 E1 **Siedlce** Pol.
100 C2 **Sieg** *r.* Ger.
100 D2 **Siegen** Ger.
63 B2 **Siĕm Réab** Cambodia
108 B2 **Siena** Italy
103 D1 **Sieradz** Pol.
153 B5 **Sierra Grande** Arg.
114 A4 **Sierra Leone** *country* Africa
144 B2 **Sierra Mojada** Mex.
138 A2 **Sierra Vista** U.S.A.
105 D2 **Sierre** Switz.
111 B3 **Sifnos** *i.* Greece
107 C2 **Sig** Alg.
127 H2 **Sigguup Nunaa** *pen.* Greenland
103 E2 **Sighetu Marmației** Romania
110 B1 **Sighișoara** Romania
60 A1 **Sigli** Indon.
92 □B2 **Siglufjörður** Iceland
102 B2 **Sigmaringen** Ger.
100 B3 **Signy-l'Abbaye** France
106 C1 **Sigüenza** Spain
114 B3 **Siguiri** Guinea
88 B2 **Sigulda** Latvia
63 B2 **Sihanoukville** Cambodia
92 I3 **Siilinjärvi** Fin.
81 C2 **Siirt** Turkey
60 B2 **Sijunjung** Indon.
74 B2 **Sikar** India
114 B3 **Sikasso** Mali
137 F3 **Sikeston** U.S.A.
66 B2 **Sikhote-Alin'** *mts* Russia
111 C3 **Sikinos** *i.* Greece
75 C2 **Sikkim** *state* India
144 B2 **Silao** Mex.
75 D2 **Silchar** India
77 D1 **Siletyteniz, Ozero** *salt l.* Kazakh.
75 C2 **Silgarhi** Nepal
80 B2 **Silifke** Turkey
75 C1 **Siling Co** *salt l.* China
110 C2 **Silistra** Bulg.
80 A1 **Silivri** Turkey
93 F3 **Siljan** *l.* Sweden
93 E4 **Silkeborg** Denmark
88 C2 **Sillamäe** Estonia
142 B1 **Siloam Springs** U.S.A.
123 D2 **Silobela** S. Africa
88 B2 **Šilut** Lith.
81 C2 **Silvan** Turkey
138 B2 **Silver City** U.S.A.
136 B3 **Silverton** U.S.A.
62 B1 **Simao** China
130 C2 **Simard, Lac** *l.* Can.
111 C3 **Simav** Turkey
111 C3 **Simav Dağları** *mts* Turkey
118 C2 **Simba** Dem. Rep. Congo
141 D2 **Simcoe, Lake** Can.
60 A1 **Simeulue** *i.* Indon.
91 C3 **Simferopol'** Ukr.
110 B1 **Şimleu Silvaniei** Romania
100 C3 **Simmern/Hunsrück** Ger.
129 D2 **Simonhouse** Can.
51 C2 **Simpson Desert** Austr.
93 F4 **Simrishamn** Sweden
60 A1 **Sinabang** Indon.
116 B2 **Sinai** *pen.* Egypt
71 A3 **Sinan** China
65 B2 **Sinanju** N. Korea
62 A1 **Sinbo** Myanmar
150 A1 **Sincelejo** Col.
111 C3 **Sındırgı** Turkey
86 E2 **Sindor** Russia
111 C2 **Sinekçi** Turkey
106 B2 **Sines** Port.
106 B2 **Sines, Cabo de** *c.* Port.
75 C2 **Singahi** India
60 B1 **Singapore** *country* Asia
61 C2 **Singaraja** Indon.
119 D3 **Singida** Tanz.
62 A1 **Singkaling Hkamti** Myanmar
61 B1 **Singkawang** Indon.
60 A1 **Singkil** Indon.
53 D2 **Singleton** Austr.
62 A1 **Singu** Myanmar
108 A2 **Siniscola** *Sardinia* Italy
109 C2 **Sinj** Croatia
116 B3 **Sinkat** Sudan
Sinkiang Uighur Autonomous Region *aut. reg.* China *see* **Xinjiang Uygur Zizhiqu**
80 B1 **Sinop** Turkey
65 B1 **Sinp'o** N. Korea
61 C1 **Sintang** Indon.
100 B2 **Sint Anthonis** Neth.
100 A2 **Sint-Laureins** Belgium
147 D3 **Sint Maarten** *i.* West Indies
147 D3 **Sint Maarten** *terr.* West Indies
100 B2 **Sint-Niklaas** Belgium
139 D3 **Sinton** U.S.A.
65 A1 **Sinŭiju** N. Korea
103 D2 **Siófok** Hungary

105 D2 **Sion** Switz.
137 D2 **Sioux Center** U.S.A.
137 D2 **Sioux City** U.S.A.
137 D2 **Sioux Falls** U.S.A.
130 A1 **Sioux Lookout** Can.
65 A1 **Siping** China
129 E2 **Sipiwesk Lake** Can.
60 A2 **Sipura** i. Indon.
93 E4 **Sira** r. Norway
 Siracusa Italy see **Syracuse**
51 C1 **Sir Edward Pellew Group** is Austr.
116 B1 **Sirhān, Wādī an** watercourse Saudi Arabia
79 C2 **Sirik** Iran
62 B2 **Siri Kit, Khuan** Thai.
128 B1 **Sir James MacBrien, Mount** Can.
79 C2 **Sīrjān** Iran
81 C2 **Şırnak** Turkey
74 B2 **Sirohi** India
74 B2 **Sirsa** India
115 D1 **Sirte** Libya
115 D1 **Sirte, Gulf of** Libya
88 B2 **Širvintos** Lith.
145 C2 **Sisal** Mex.
122 B2 **Sishen** S. Africa
81 C2 **Sisian** Armenia
129 D2 **Sisipuk Lake** Can.
63 B2 **Sisŏphŏn** Cambodia
105 D3 **Sisteron** France
75 C2 **Sitapur** India
123 D2 **Siteki** Swaziland
128 A2 **Sitka** U.S.A.
100 B2 **Sittard** Neth.
62 A2 **Sittaung** r. Myanmar
 Sittwe Myanmar see **Akyab**
61 C2 **Situbondo** Indon.
80 B2 **Sivas** Turkey
62 A1 **Sivasagar** India
111 C3 **Sivaslı** Turkey
80 B2 **Siverek** Turkey
80 B2 **Sivrihisar** Turkey
116 A2 **Siwah** Egypt
74 B1 **Siwalik Range** mts India/ Nepal
105 D3 **Six-Fours-les-Plages** France
70 B2 **Sixian** China
123 C2 **Siyabuswa** S. Africa
 Sjælland i. Denmark see **Zealand**
109 D2 **Sjenica** Serbia
92 G2 **Sjøvegan** Norway
91 C2 **Skadovs'k** Ukr.
93 F4 **Skagen** Denmark
93 E4 **Skagerrak** str. Denmark/ Norway
134 B1 **Skagit** r. U.S.A.
128 A2 **Skagway** U.S.A.
74 B1 **Skardu** Pak.
103 E1 **Skarżysko-Kamienna** Pol.
103 D2 **Skawina** Pol.
128 B2 **Skeena** r. Can.
128 B2 **Skeena Mountains** Can.
98 D2 **Skegness** U.K.
92 H3 **Skellefteå** Sweden
92 H3 **Skellefteälven** r. Sweden
97 C2 **Skerries** Ireland
111 B3 **Skiathos** i. Greece
97 B3 **Skibbereen** Ireland
92 □B2 **Skiðadalsjökull** glacier Iceland
98 B1 **Skiddaw** h. U.K.
93 E4 **Skien** Norway
103 E1 **Skierniewice** Pol.
115 C1 **Skikda** Alg.
52 B3 **Skipton** Austr.
98 B2 **Skipton** U.K.

93 E4 **Skive** Denmark
92 H1 **Skjervøy** Norway
111 B3 **Skopelos** i. Greece
89 E3 **Skopin** Russia
109 D2 **Skopje** Macedonia
93 F4 **Skövde** Sweden
141 F2 **Skowhegan** U.S.A.
88 B2 **Skrunda** Latvia
128 A1 **Skukum, Mount** Can.
123 D1 **Skukuza** S. Africa
88 B2 **Skuodas** Lith.
96 A2 **Skye** i. U.K.
111 B3 **Skyros** Greece
111 B3 **Skyros** i. Greece
93 F4 **Slagelse** Denmark
97 C2 **Slaney** r. Ireland
110 B2 **Slatina** Croatia
110 B2 **Slatina** Romania
129 C1 **Slave** r. Can.
114 C4 **Slave Coast** Africa
128 C2 **Slave Lake** Can.
82 G3 **Slavgorod** Russia
109 C1 **Slavonski Brod** Croatia
90 B1 **Slavuta** Ukr.
90 C1 **Slavutych** Ukr.
91 D2 **Slavyansk-na-Kubani** Russia
89 D3 **Slawharad** Belarus
103 D1 **Sławno** Pol.
97 A2 **Slea Head** Ireland
130 C1 **Sleeper Islands** Can.
97 D1 **Slieve Donard** h. U.K.
 Slieve Gamph hills Ireland see **Ox Mountains**
97 B1 **Sligo** Ireland
97 B1 **Sligo Bay** Ireland
93 G4 **Slite** Sweden
110 C2 **Sliven** Bulg.
110 C2 **Slobozia** Romania
128 C3 **Slocan** Can.
88 C3 **Slonim** Belarus
100 B1 **Sloten** Neth.
99 C3 **Slough** U.K.
103 D2 **Slovakia** country Europe
108 B1 **Slovenia** country Europe
91 D2 **Slov"yans'k** Ukr.
90 B1 **Sluch** r. Ukr.
103 D1 **Słupsk** Pol.
88 C3 **Slutsk** Belarus
97 A2 **Slyne Head** Ireland
131 D1 **Smallwood Reservoir** Can.
88 C3 **Smalyavichy** Belarus
88 C3 **Smarhon'** Belarus
129 D2 **Smeaton** Can.
109 D2 **Smederevo** Serbia
109 D2 **Smederevska Palanka** Serbia
91 C2 **Smila** Ukr.
88 C2 **Smiltene** Latvia
128 B2 **Smithers** Can.
143 E1 **Smithfield** U.S.A.
141 D3 **Smith Mountain Lake** U.S.A.
130 C2 **Smiths Falls** Can.
137 D3 **Smoky Hills** U.S.A.
92 E3 **Smøla** i. Norway
89 D3 **Smolensk** Russia
110 B2 **Smolyan** Bulg.
130 B2 **Smooth Rock Falls** Can.
 Smyrna Turkey see **İzmir**
92 □B3 **Snæfell** mt. Iceland
98 A1 **Snaefell** h. Isle of Man
132 B2 **Snake** r. U.S.A.
134 D2 **Snake River Plain** U.S.A.
100 B1 **Sneek** Neth.
97 B3 **Sneem** Ireland
122 B3 **Sneeuberge** mts S. Africa
108 B1 **Snežnik** mt. Slovenia
91 C2 **Snihurivka** Ukr.
93 E3 **Snøhetta** mt. Norway

129 D1 **Snowbird Lake** Can.
98 A2 **Snowdon** mt. U.K.
 Snowdrift Can. see **Łutselk'e**
129 C1 **Snowdrift** r. Can.
138 A2 **Snowflake** U.S.A.
129 D2 **Snow Lake** Can.
52 A2 **Snowtown** Austr.
53 C3 **Snowy** r. Austr.
53 C3 **Snowy Mountains** Austr.
139 C2 **Snyder** U.S.A.
121 □D2 **Soalala** Madag.
117 B4 **Sobat** r. South Sudan
89 F2 **Sobinka** Russia
151 D3 **Sobradinho, Barragem de** resr Brazil
151 D2 **Sobral** Brazil
87 C4 **Sochi** Russia
49 H4 **Society Islands** Fr. Polynesia
150 A1 **Socorro** Col.
138 B2 **Socorro** U.S.A.
144 A3 **Socorro, Isla** i. Mex.
56 F6 **Socotra** i. Yemen
63 B3 **Soc Trăng** Vietnam
106 C2 **Socuéllamos** Spain
92 I2 **Sodankylä** Fin.
134 D2 **Soda Springs** U.S.A.
93 G3 **Söderhamn** Sweden
93 G4 **Södertälje** Sweden
116 A3 **Sodiri** Sudan
117 B4 **Sodo** Eth.
93 G3 **Södra Kvarken** str. Fin./ Sweden
100 D2 **Soest** Ger.
110 B2 **Sofia** Bulg.
 Sofiya Bulg. see **Sofia**
68 C2 **Sog** China
93 E3 **Sognefjorden** inlet Norway
111 D2 **Söğüt** Turkey
100 B2 **Soignies** Belgium
105 C2 **Soissons** France
90 A1 **Sokal'** Ukr.
111 C3 **Söke** Turkey
81 C1 **Sokhumi** Georgia
114 C4 **Sokodé** Togo
89 F2 **Sokol** Russia
101 F2 **Sokolov** Czech Rep.
115 C3 **Sokoto** Nigeria
115 C3 **Sokoto** r. Nigeria
90 B2 **Sokyryany** Ukr.
73 B3 **Solapur** India
135 B3 **Soledad** U.S.A.
89 F2 **Soligalich** Russia
99 C2 **Solihull** U.K.
86 E3 **Solikamsk** Russia
87 E3 **Sol'-Iletsk** Russia
100 C2 **Solingen** Ger.
92 G3 **Sollefteå** Sweden
93 G4 **Sollentuna** Sweden
101 D2 **Solling** hills Ger.
89 E2 **Solnechnogorsk** Russia
60 B2 **Solok** Indon.
48 E3 **Solomon Islands** country S. Pacific Ocean
48 E3 **Solomon Sea** S. Pacific Ocean
105 D2 **Solothurn** Switz.
101 D1 **Soltau** Ger.
89 D2 **Sol'tsy** Russia
96 C3 **Solway Firth** est. U.K.
120 B2 **Solwezi** Zambia
111 C3 **Soma** Turkey
117 C4 **Somalia** country Africa
117 A4 **Somaliland** disp. terr. Somalia
120 B1 **Sombo** Angola
109 C1 **Sombor** Serbia
144 B2 **Sombrerete** Mex.
140 C3 **Somerset** U.S.A.
123 C3 **Somerset East** S. Africa

126 E2 **Somerset Island** Can.
122 A3 **Somerset West** S. Africa
101 E2 **Sömmerda** Ger.
75 C2 **Son** r. India
65 C1 **Sŏnbong** N. Korea
93 E4 **Sønderborg** Denmark
101 E2 **Sondershausen** Ger.
Søndre Strømfjord inlet
Greenland see **Kangerlussuaq**
62 B1 **Sông Đa, Hô** resr Vietnam
119 D4 **Songea** Tanz.
65 B1 **Sŏnggan** N. Korea
65 B1 **Songhua Hu** resr China
Sŏngjin N. Korea see
Kimch'aek
63 B3 **Songkhla** Thai.
65 B2 **Songnim** N. Korea
120 A1 **Songo** Angola
121 C2 **Songo** Moz.
69 E1 **Songyuan** China
Sonid Youqi China see
Saihan Tal
89 E2 **Sonkovo** Russia
62 B1 **Sơn La** Vietnam
74 A2 **Sonmiani** Pak.
101 E2 **Sonneberg** Ger.
138 A2 **Sonoita** Mex.
144 A2 **Sonora** r. Mex.
135 B3 **Sonora** CA U.S.A.
139 C2 **Sonora** TX U.S.A.
117 A4 **Sopo** watercourse
South Sudan
103 D2 **Sopron** Hungary
108 B2 **Sora** Italy
130 C2 **Sorel** Can.
51 D4 **Sorell** Austr.
106 C1 **Soria** Spain
90 B2 **Soroca** Moldova
154 C2 **Sorocaba** Brazil
87 E3 **Sorochinsk** Russia
59 D2 **Sorol** atoll Micronesia
59 C3 **Sorong** Indon.
119 D2 **Soroti** Uganda
92 H1 **Sørøya** i. Norway
92 G2 **Sorsele** Sweden
64 B2 **Sorsogon** Phil.
86 C2 **Sortavala** Russia
92 G2 **Sortland** Norway
123 C2 **Soshanguve** S. Africa
89 E3 **Sosna** r. Russia
153 B4 **Sosneado** mt. Arg.
86 E2 **Sosnogorsk** Russia
86 D2 **Sosnovka** Russia
88 C2 **Sosnovyy Bor** Russia
103 D1 **Sosnowiec** Pol.
91 D2 **Sosyka** r. Russia
145 C2 **Soto la Marina** Mex.
118 B2 **Souanké** Congo
104 C3 **Souillac** France
Sŏul S. Korea see **Seoul**
104 B2 **Soulac-sur-Mer** France
104 B3 **Soulom** France
Soûr Lebanon see **Tyre**
107 D2 **Sour el Ghozlane** Alg.
129 D3 **Souris** Man. Can.
131 D2 **Souris** P.E.I. Can.
129 E3 **Souris** r. Can.
151 E2 **Sousa** Brazil
115 D1 **Sousse** Tunisia
104 B3 **Soustons** France
122 B3 **South Africa** country Africa
99 C3 **Southampton** U.K.
127 F2 **Southampton Island** Can.
73 D3 **South Andaman** i. India
52 A1 **South Australia** state Austr.
130 B2 **South Baymouth** Can.
140 B2 **South Bend** U.S.A.
143 D2 **South Carolina** state U.S.A.
156 B4 **South China Sea**
N. Pacific Ocean
136 C2 **South Dakota** state U.S.A.
99 C3 **South Downs** hills U.K.
129 D2 **Southend** Can.
99 D3 **Southend-on-Sea** U.K.
54 B2 **Southern Alps** mts N.Z.
50 A3 **Southern Cross** Austr.
129 E2 **Southern Indian Lake** Can.
159 **Southern Ocean**
143 E1 **Southern Pines** U.S.A.
96 B3 **Southern Uplands** hills U.K.
149 F6 **South Georgia and the
South Sandwich Islands** terr.
S. Atlantic Ocean
96 A2 **South Harris** pen. U.K.
129 E1 **South Henik Lake** Can.
54 B2 **South Island** N.Z.
65 B2 **South Korea** country Asia
135 B3 **South Lake Tahoe** U.S.A.
55 Q4 **South Orkney Islands**
S. Atlantic Ocean
81 C1 **South Ossetia** disp. terr.
Georgia
136 C2 **South Platte** r. U.S.A.
98 B2 **Southport** U.K.
143 E2 **Southport** U.S.A.
96 C1 **South Ronaldsay** i. U.K.
123 D3 **South Sand Bluff** pt S. Africa
129 D2 **South Saskatchewan** r. Can.
55 I2 **South Seal** r. Can.
55 P3 **South Shetland Islands**
Antarctica
98 C1 **South Shields** U.K.
117 A4 **South Sudan** country Africa
54 B1 **South Taranaki Bight** b. N.Z.
130 C1 **South Twin Island** Can.
96 A2 **South Uist** i. U.K.
53 D2 **South West Rocks** Austr.
99 D2 **Southwold** U.K.
109 C3 **Soverato** Italy
88 B2 **Sovetsk** Russia
86 F2 **Sovetskiy** Russia
91 C2 **Sovyets'kyy** Ukr.
123 C2 **Soweto** S. Africa
66 D1 **Sōya-misaki** c. Japan
90 C1 **Sozh** r. Europe
110 C2 **Sozopol** Bulg.
106 C1 **Spain** country Europe
99 C2 **Spalding** U.K.
135 D2 **Spanish Fork** U.S.A.
97 B2 **Spanish Point** Ireland
108 B3 **Sparagio, Monte** mt. Sicily
Italy
135 C3 **Sparks** U.S.A.
140 A2 **Sparta** U.S.A.
143 D2 **Spartanburg** U.S.A.
111 B3 **Sparti** Greece
109 C3 **Spartivento, Capo** c. Italy
89 D3 **Spas-Demensk** Russia
89 F2 **Spas-Klepiki** Russia
66 B2 **Spassk-Dal'niy** Russia
89 F3 **Spassk-Ryazanskiy** Russia
111 B3 **Spatha, Akrotirio** pt Greece
136 C2 **Spearfish** U.S.A.
139 C1 **Spearman** U.S.A.
137 D2 **Spencer** U.S.A.
52 A2 **Spencer Gulf** est. Austr.
98 C1 **Spennymoor** U.K.
54 B2 **Spenser Mountains** N.Z.
101 D2 **Spessart** reg. Ger.
96 C2 **Spey** r. U.K.
102 B2 **Speyer** Ger.
100 C1 **Spiekeroog** i. Ger.
100 B2 **Spijkenisse** Neth.
128 C2 **Spirit River** Can.
103 E2 **Spišská Nová Ves** Slovakia
82 C1 **Spitsbergen** i. Svalbard
102 C2 **Spittal an der Drau** Austria
109 C2 **Split** Croatia
129 E2 **Split Lake** Can.
129 E2 **Split Lake** Can.
134 C1 **Spokane** U.S.A.
140 A1 **Spooner** U.S.A.
102 C1 **Spree** r. Ger.
122 A2 **Springbok** S. Africa
131 E2 **Springdale** Can.
142 B1 **Springdale** U.S.A.
101 D1 **Springe** Ger.
138 C1 **Springer** U.S.A.
138 B2 **Springerville** U.S.A.
136 C3 **Springfield** CO U.S.A.
140 B3 **Springfield** IL U.S.A.
141 E2 **Springfield** MA U.S.A.
137 E3 **Springfield** MO U.S.A.
140 C3 **Springfield** OH U.S.A.
134 B2 **Springfield** OR U.S.A.
123 C3 **Springfontein** S. Africa
131 D2 **Springhill** Can.
143 D3 **Spring Hill** U.S.A.
54 B2 **Springs Junction** N.Z.
98 D2 **Spurn Head** U.K.
128 B3 **Squamish** Can.
109 C3 **Squillace, Golfo di** g. Italy
Srbija country Europe see
Serbia
109 C2 **Srebrenica** Bos. & Herz.
110 C2 **Sredets** Bulg.
83 L3 **Sredinnyy Khrebet** mts Russia
83 L2 **Srednekolymsk** Russia
**Sredne-Russkaya
Vozvyshennost'** hills Russia see
Central Russian Upland
**Sredne-Sibirskoye
Ploskogor'ye** plat. Russia see
Central Siberian Plateau
69 D1 **Sretensk** Russia
61 C1 **Sri Aman** Sarawak Malaysia
73 B4 **Sri Jayewardenepura Kotte**
Sri Lanka
73 C3 **Srikakulam** India
73 C4 **Sri Lanka** country Asia
74 B1 **Srinagar** India
73 B3 **Srivardhan** India
101 D1 **Stade** Ger.
101 E1 **Stadensen** Ger.
100 C1 **Stadskanaal** Neth.
101 D2 **Stadtallendorf** Ger.
101 D1 **Stadthagen** Ger.
99 B2 **Stafford** U.K.
99 C3 **Staines-upon-Thames** U.K.
91 D2 **Stakhanov** Ukr.
Stalingrad Russia see
Volgograd
103 E1 **Stalowa Wola** Pol.
99 C2 **Stamford** U.K.
141 E2 **Stamford** CT U.S.A.
139 D2 **Stamford** TX U.S.A.
122 A1 **Stampriet** Namibia
92 F2 **Stamsund** Norway
123 C2 **Standerton** S. Africa
140 C2 **Standish** U.S.A.
153 C6 **Stanley** Falkland Is
136 C1 **Stanley** U.S.A.
83 I3 **Stanovoye Nagor'ye** mts
Russia
83 J3 **Stanovoy Khrebet** mts Russia
53 D1 **Stanthorpe** Austr.
103 E1 **Starachowice** Pol.
Stara Planina mts Bulgaria/
Serbia see **Balkan Mountains**
89 D2 **Staraya Russa** Russia
89 D2 **Staraya Toropa** Russia
110 C2 **Stara Zagora** Bulg.
103 D1 **Stargard Szczeciński** Pol.
142 C2 **Starkville** U.S.A.

91 D2 **Starobil's'k** Ukr.
89 D3 **Starodub** Russia
103 D1 **Starogard Gdański** Pol.
90 B2 **Starokostyantyniv** Ukr.
91 D2 **Starominskaya** Russia
91 D2 **Staroshcherbinovskaya** Russia
91 D2 **Starotitarovskaya** Russia
89 F3 **Staroyur'yevo** Russia
99 B3 **Start Point** U.K.
88 C3 **Staryya Darohi** Belarus
89 E3 **Staryy Oskol** Russia
101 E2 **Staßfurt** Ger.
141 D2 **State College** U.S.A.
143 D2 **Statesboro** U.S.A.
143 D1 **Statesville** U.S.A.
93 E4 **Stavanger** Norway
87 D4 **Stavropol'** Russia
87 D4 **Stavropol'skaya Vozvyshennost'** *hills* Russia
52 B3 **Stawell** Austr.
123 C2 **Steadville** S. Africa
136 B2 **Steamboat Springs** U.S.A.
101 E2 **Stedten** Ger.
128 C2 **Steen River** Can.
134 C2 **Steens Mountain** U.S.A.
100 C1 **Steenwijk** Neth.
126 D2 **Stefansson Island** Can.
101 E3 **Steigerwald** *mts* Ger.
129 E3 **Steinbach** Can.
100 C1 **Steinfurt** Ger.
120 A3 **Steinhausen** Namibia
92 F3 **Steinkjer** Norway
122 A2 **Steinkopf** S. Africa
122 B2 **Stella** S. Africa
105 D2 **Stenay** France
101 E1 **Stendal** Ger.
Stepanakert Azer. *see* **Xankändi**
131 E2 **Stephenville** Can.
139 D2 **Stephenville** U.S.A.
122 B3 **Sterling** S. Africa
136 C2 **Sterling** *CO* U.S.A.
140 B2 **Sterling** *IL* U.S.A.
87 E3 **Sterlitamak** Russia
101 E1 **Sternberg** Ger.
128 C2 **Stettler** Can.
140 C2 **Steubenville** U.S.A.
99 C3 **Stevenage** U.K.
129 E2 **Stevenson Lake** Can.
126 B2 **Stevens Village** U.S.A.
128 B2 **Stewart** Can.
126 B2 **Stewart** *r.* Can.
54 A3 **Stewart Island** N.Z.
127 F2 **Stewart Lake** Can.
102 C2 **Steyr** Austria
122 B3 **Steytlerville** S. Africa
128 A2 **Stikine** *r.* Can.
128 A2 **Stikine Plateau** Can.
122 B3 **Stilbaai** S. Africa
139 D1 **Stillwater** U.S.A.
109 D2 **Štip** Macedonia
96 C2 **Stirling** U.K.
92 F3 **Stjørdalshalsen** Norway
103 D2 **Stockerau** Austria
93 G4 **Stockholm** Sweden
98 B2 **Stockport** U.K.
135 B3 **Stockton** U.S.A.
98 C1 **Stockton-on-Tees** U.K.
63 B2 **Stœng Trêng** Cambodia
96 B1 **Stoer, Point of** U.K.
98 B2 **Stoke-on-Trent** U.K.
109 D2 **Stol** *mt.* Serbia
109 C2 **Stolac** Bos. & Herz.
100 C2 **Stolberg (Rheinland)** Ger.
88 C3 **Stolin** Belarus
101 F2 **Stollberg** Ger.
101 D1 **Stolzenau** Ger.
96 C2 **Stonehaven** U.K.
129 E2 **Stonewall** Can.
129 D2 **Stony Rapids** Can.
92 G2 **Storavan** *l.* Sweden
Store Bælt *sea chan.* Denmark *see* **Great Belt**
92 F3 **Støren** Norway
92 F2 **Storforshei** Norway
126 D2 **Storkerson Peninsula** Can.
137 D2 **Storm Lake** U.S.A.
93 E3 **Stornosa** *mt.* Norway
96 A1 **Stornoway** U.K.
86 E2 **Storozhevsk** Russia
90 B2 **Storozhynets'** Ukr.
92 F3 **Storsjön** *l.* Sweden
92 H2 **Storslett** Norway
92 G2 **Storuman** Sweden
99 C2 **Stour** *r. England* U.K.
99 C3 **Stour** *r. England* U.K.
130 A1 **Stout Lake** Can.
88 C3 **Stowbtsy** Belarus
97 C1 **Strabane** U.K.
102 C2 **Strakonice** Czech Rep.
102 C1 **Stralsund** Ger.
122 A3 **Strand** S. Africa
93 E3 **Stranda** Norway
97 D1 **Strangford Lough** *inlet* U.K.
96 B3 **Stranraer** U.K.
105 D2 **Strasbourg** France
140 C2 **Stratford** Can.
54 B1 **Stratford** N.Z.
139 C1 **Stratford** U.S.A.
99 C2 **Stratford-upon-Avon** U.K.
128 C2 **Strathmore** Can.
96 C2 **Strathspey** *val.* U.K.
102 C2 **Straubing** Ger.
51 C3 **Streaky Bay** Austr.
140 B2 **Streator** U.S.A.
110 B2 **Strehaia** Romania
153 B5 **Stroeder** Arg.
101 D1 **Ströhen** Ger.
109 C3 **Stromboli, Isola** *i.* Italy
96 C1 **Stromness** U.K.
92 G3 **Strömsund** Sweden
96 C1 **Stronsay** *i.* U.K.
53 D2 **Stroud** Austr.
99 B3 **Stroud** U.K.
100 C1 **Strücklingen (Saterland)** Ger.
109 D2 **Struga** Macedonia
88 C2 **Strugi-Krasnyye** Russia
122 B3 **Struis Bay** S. Africa
109 D2 **Strumica** Macedonia
122 B2 **Strydenburg** S. Africa
111 B2 **Strymonas** *r.* Greece
90 A2 **Stryy** Ukr.
128 B2 **Stuart Lake** Can.
130 A1 **Stull Lake** Can.
89 E3 **Stupino** Russia
140 B2 **Sturgeon Bay** U.S.A.
130 C2 **Sturgeon Falls** Can.
130 A2 **Sturgeon Lake** Can.
140 B2 **Sturgis** *MI* U.S.A.
136 C2 **Sturgis** *SD* U.S.A.
50 B1 **Sturt Creek** *watercourse* Austr.
52 B1 **Sturt Stony Desert** Austr.
123 C3 **Stutterheim** S. Africa
102 B2 **Stuttgart** Ger.
142 B2 **Stuttgart** U.S.A.
92 □A2 **Stykkishólmur** Iceland
90 B1 **Styr** *r.* Belarus/Ukr.
155 D1 **Suaçuí Grande** *r.* Brazil
116 B3 **Suakin** Sudan
78 A3 **Suara** Eritrea
109 C1 **Subotica** Serbia
110 C1 **Suceava** Romania
97 B2 **Suck** *r.* Ireland
152 B2 **Sucre** Bol.
154 B2 **Sucuriú** *r.* Brazil
89 E2 **Suda** Russia
91 C3 **Sudak** Ukr.
117 A3 **Sudan** *country* Africa
130 B2 **Sudbury** Can.
117 A4 **Sudd** *swamp* South Sudan
89 F2 **Sudislavl'** Russia
89 F2 **Sudogda** Russia
94 B1 **Suðuroy** *i.* Faroe Is
107 C2 **Sueca** Spain
116 B2 **Suez** Egypt
116 B2 **Suez, Gulf of** Egypt
80 B2 **Suez Canal** Egypt
141 D3 **Suffolk** U.S.A.
116 B2 **Sūhāj** Egypt
79 C2 **Şuḩār** Oman
69 D1 **Sühbaatar** Mongolia
101 E2 **Suhl** Ger.
109 C1 **Suhopolje** Croatia
70 B2 **Suide** China
66 B2 **Suifenhe** China
69 E1 **Suihua** China
70 A2 **Suining** China
70 B2 **Suiping** China
70 B2 **Suiyang** China
70 B2 **Suizhou** China
74 B2 **Sujangarh** India
74 B1 **Sujanpur** India
74 A2 **Sujawal** Pak.
60 B2 **Sukabumi** Indon.
61 B2 **Sukadana** Indon.
61 C2 **Sukaraja** Indon.
89 E3 **Sukhinichi** Russia
89 F2 **Sukhona** *r.* Russia
62 A2 **Sukhothai** Thai.
74 A2 **Sukkur** Pak.
89 E2 **Sukromny** Russia
59 C3 **Sula, Kepulauan** *is* Indon.
74 A1 **Sulaiman Range** *mts* Pak.
Sulawesi *i.* Indon. *see* **Celebes**
150 A2 **Sullana** Peru
137 E3 **Sullivan** U.S.A.
139 D2 **Sulphur Springs** U.S.A.
64 B2 **Sulu Archipelago** *is* Phil.
64 A2 **Sulu Sea** N. Pacific Ocean
101 E3 **Sulzbach-Rosenberg** Ger.
79 C2 **Sumāil** Oman
Sumatera *i.* Indon. *see* **Sumatra**
60 A1 **Sumatra** *i.* Indon.
58 C3 **Sumba** *i.* Indon.
61 C2 **Sumbawa** *i.* Indon.
61 C2 **Sumbawabesar** Indon.
119 D3 **Sumbawanga** Tanz.
120 A2 **Sumbe** Angola
96 □ **Sumburgh** U.K.
96 □ **Sumburgh Head** U.K.
61 C2 **Sumenep** Indon.
67 D4 **Sumisu-jima** *i.* Japan
131 D2 **Summerside** Can.
140 C3 **Summersville** U.S.A.
128 B2 **Summit Lake** Can.
103 D2 **Šumperk** Czech Rep.
81 C1 **Sumqayıt** Azer.
143 D2 **Sumter** U.S.A.
91 C1 **Sumy** Ukr.
75 D2 **Sunamganj** Bangl.
65 B2 **Sunan** N. Korea
79 C2 **Şunaynah** Oman
52 B3 **Sunbury** Austr.
141 D2 **Sunbury** U.S.A.
65 B3 **Suncheon** S. Korea
65 B2 **Sunch'ŏn** N. Korea
123 C2 **Sun City** S. Africa
60 B2 **Sunda, Selat** *str.* Indon.
136 C2 **Sundance** U.S.A.
75 C2 **Sundarbans** *coastal area* Bangl./India

98 C1 **Sunderland** U.K.
128 C2 **Sundre** Can.
93 G3 **Sundsvall** Sweden
123 D2 **Sundumbili** S. Africa
60 B2 **Sungailiat** Indon.
60 B2 **Sungaipenuh** Indon.
60 B1 **Sungai Petani** Malaysia
80 B1 **Sungurlu** Turkey
93 E3 **Sunndalsøra** Norway
134 C1 **Sunnyside** U.S.A.
135 B3 **Sunnyvale** U.S.A.
83 I2 **Suntar** Russia
74 A2 **Suntsar** Pak.
114 B4 **Sunyani** Ghana
82 D2 **Suoyarvi** Russia
138 A2 **Superior** *AZ* U.S.A.
137 D2 **Superior** *NE* U.S.A.
140 A1 **Superior** *WI* U.S.A.
140 B1 **Superior, Lake** Can./U.S.A.
89 D3 **Suponevo** Russia
81 C2 **Sūq ash Shuyūkh** Iraq
70 B2 **Suqian** China
78 A2 **Sūq Suwayq** Saudi Arabia
79 C2 **Şūr** Oman
74 A2 **Surab** Pak.
61 C2 **Surabaya** Indon.
61 C2 **Surakarta** Indon.
74 B2 **Surat** India
74 B2 **Suratgarh** India
63 A3 **Surat Thani** Thai.
89 D3 **Surazh** Russia
109 D2 **Surdulica** Serbia
74 B2 **Surendranagar** India
82 F2 **Surgut** Russia
64 B2 **Surigao** Phil.
63 B2 **Surin** Thai.
151 C1 **Suriname** *country* S. America
Surt Libya *see* **Sirte**
Surt, Khalīj *g.* Libya *see* **Sirte, Gulf of**
60 B2 **Surulangun** Indon.
89 F2 **Susanino** Russia
135 B2 **Susanville** U.S.A.
80 B1 **Suşehri** Turkey
131 D2 **Sussex** Can.
101 D1 **Süstedt** Ger.
100 C1 **Sustrum** Ger.
83 K2 **Susuman** Russia
111 C3 **Susurluk** Turkey
75 B1 **Sutak** India
122 B3 **Sutherland** S. Africa
99 C2 **Sutton Coldfield** U.K.
66 D2 **Suttsu** Japan
49 F4 **Suva** Fiji
89 E3 **Suvorov** Russia
103 E1 **Suwałki** Pol.
63 B2 **Suwannaphum** Thai.
143 D3 **Suwannee** *r.* U.S.A.
Suweis, Qanâ el *canal* Egypt *see* **Suez Canal**
65 B2 **Suwon** S. Korea
79 C2 **Sūzā** Iran
89 F2 **Suzdal'** Russia
70 B2 **Suzhou** *Anhui* China
70 C2 **Suzhou** *Jiangsu* China
67 C3 **Suzu** Japan
67 C3 **Suzu-misaki** *pt* Japan
82 B1 **Svalbard** *terr.* Arctic Ocean
91 D2 **Svatove** Ukr.
63 B2 **Svay Riĕng** Cambodia
93 F3 **Sveg** Sweden
88 C2 **Švenčionys** Lith.
93 F4 **Svendborg** Denmark
Sverdlovsk Russia *see* **Yekaterinburg**
109 D2 **Sveti Nikole** Macedonia
88 B3 **Svetlogorsk** Russia
88 B3 **Svetlyy** Russia
93 I3 **Svetogorsk** Russia
110 C2 **Svilengrad** Bulg.
110 B2 **Svinecea Mare, Vârful** *mt.* Romania
110 C2 **Svishtov** Bulg.
103 D2 **Svitavy** Czech Rep.
91 C2 **Svitlovods'k** Ukr.
69 E1 **Svobodnyy** Russia
92 F2 **Svolvær** Norway
88 C3 **Svyetlahorsk** Belarus
143 D2 **Swainsboro** U.S.A.
120 A3 **Swakopmund** Namibia
52 B3 **Swan Hill** Austr.
128 C2 **Swan Hills** Can.
129 D2 **Swan Lake** Can.
129 D2 **Swan River** Can.
53 D2 **Swansea** Austr.
99 B3 **Swansea** U.K.
123 C2 **Swartruggens** S. Africa
Swatow China *see* **Shantou**
123 D2 **Swaziland** *country* Africa
93 G3 **Sweden** *country* Europe
139 C2 **Sweetwater** U.S.A.
136 B2 **Sweetwater** *r.* U.S.A.
122 B3 **Swellendam** S. Africa
103 D1 **Świdnica** Pol.
103 D1 **Świdwin** Pol.
103 D1 **Świebodzin** Pol.
103 D1 **Świecie** Pol.
129 D2 **Swift Current** Can.
97 C1 **Swilly, Lough** *inlet* Ireland
99 C3 **Swindon** U.K.
102 C1 **Świnoujście** Pol.
105 D2 **Switzerland** *country* Europe
97 C2 **Swords** Ireland
88 C3 **Syanno** Belarus
89 D2 **Sychevka** Russia
53 D2 **Sydney** Austr.
131 D2 **Sydney** Can.
131 D2 **Sydney Mines** Can.
91 D2 **Syeverodonets'k** Ukr.
86 E2 **Syktyvkar** Russia
142 C2 **Sylacauga** U.S.A.
75 D2 **Sylhet** Bangl.
102 B1 **Sylt** *i.* Ger.
111 C3 **Symi** *i.* Greece
91 D2 **Synel'nykove** Ukr.
109 C3 **Syracuse** *Sicily* Italy
136 C3 **Syracuse** *KS* U.S.A.
141 D2 **Syracuse** *NY* U.S.A.
77 C2 **Syrdar'ya** *r.* Asia
80 B2 **Syria** *country* Asia
80 B2 **Syrian Desert** Asia
111 B3 **Syros** *i.* Greece
87 D3 **Syzran'** Russia
102 C1 **Szczecin** Pol.
103 D1 **Szczecinek** Pol.
103 E1 **Szczytno** Pol.
103 E2 **Szeged** Hungary
103 D2 **Székesfehérvár** Hungary
103 D2 **Szekszárd** Hungary
103 E2 **Szentes** Hungary
103 D2 **Szentgotthárd** Hungary
103 D2 **Szigetvár** Hungary
103 E2 **Szolnok** Hungary
103 D2 **Szombathely** Hungary

T

78 B2 **Tābah** Saudi Arabia
76 B3 **Ţabas** Iran
81 D3 **Tābask, Kūh-e** *mt.* Iran
150 B2 **Tabatinga** Brazil
114 B2 **Tabelbala** Alg.
129 C3 **Taber** Can.
102 C2 **Tábor** Czech Rep.
119 D3 **Tabora** Tanz.
114 B4 **Tabou** Côte d'Ivoire
81 C2 **Tabrīz** Iran
78 A2 **Tabūk** Saudi Arabia
77 E2 **Tacheng** China
102 C2 **Tachov** Czech Rep.
64 B1 **Tacloban** Phil.
150 A3 **Tacna** Peru
134 B1 **Tacoma** U.S.A.
152 C4 **Tacuarembó** Uru.
138 B3 **Tacupeto** Mex.
117 C3 **Tadjourah** Djibouti
80 B2 **Tadmur** Syria
129 E2 **Tadoule Lake** Can.
65 B2 **Taebaek** S. Korea
Taegu S. Korea *see* **Daegu**
Taejŏn S. Korea *see* **Daejeon**
107 C1 **Tafalla** Spain
152 B3 **Tafi Viejo** Arg.
79 D2 **Taftān, Kūh-e** *mt.* Iran
91 D2 **Taganrog** Russia
91 D2 **Taganrog, Gulf of** Russia/Ukr.
62 A1 **Tagaung** Myanmar
64 B1 **Tagaytay City** Phil.
64 B2 **Tagbilaran** Phil.
64 B1 **Tagudin** Phil.
64 B2 **Tagum** Phil.
106 B2 **Tagus** *r.* Port./Spain
60 B1 **Tahan, Gunung** *mt.* Malaysia
115 C2 **Tahat, Mont** *mt.* Alg.
69 E1 **Tahe** China
49 I4 **Tahiti** *i.* Fr. Polynesia
139 E1 **Tahlequah** U.S.A.
135 B3 **Tahoe, Lake** U.S.A.
135 B3 **Tahoe City** U.S.A.
126 D2 **Tahoe Lake** Can.
115 C3 **Tahoua** Niger
79 C2 **Tahrūd** Iran
128 B3 **Tahsis** Can.
70 B2 **Tai'an** China
71 C3 **Taibei** Taiwan
Taibus Qi China *see* **Baochang**
54 C1 **Taihape** N.Z.
70 C2 **Tai Hu** *l.* China
52 A3 **Tailem Bend** Austr.
71 C3 **Tainan** Taiwan
155 D1 **Taiobeiras** Brazil
60 B1 **Taiping** Malaysia
71 B3 **Taishan** China
153 A5 **Taitao, Península de** *pen.* Chile
71 C3 **T'aitung** Taiwan
92 I2 **Taivalkoski** Fin.
92 H2 **Taivaskero** *h.* Fin.
71 C3 **Taiwan** *country* Asia
71 B3 **Taiwan Strait** China/Taiwan
70 B2 **Taiyuan** China
71 C3 **Taizhong** Taiwan
70 B2 **Taizhou** *Jiangsu* China
71 C3 **Taizhou** *Zhejiang* China
78 B3 **Ta'izz** Yemen
77 D3 **Tajikistan** *country* Asia
75 B2 **Taj Mahal** *tourist site* India
Tajo *r.* Port. *see* **Tagus**
58 A1 **Tak** Thai.
54 B2 **Takaka** N.Z.
67 B4 **Takamatsu** Japan
67 C3 **Takaoka** Japan
54 B1 **Takapuna** N.Z.
67 C3 **Takasaki** Japan
122 B1 **Takatokwane** Botswana
67 C3 **Takayama** Japan
Takefu Japan *see* **Echizen**
60 A1 **Takengon** Indon.
63 B2 **Ta Khmau** Cambodia
66 D2 **Takikawa** Japan
128 B2 **Takla Lake** Can.

128 B2 **Takla Landing** Can.
77 E3 **Taklimakan Desert** China
Taklimakan Shamo *des.* China *see* **Taklimakan Desert**
128 A2 **Taku** *r.* Can./U.S.A.
63 A3 **Takua Pa** Thai.
115 C4 **Takum** Nigeria
88 C3 **Talachyn** Belarus
74 B1 **Talagang** Pak.
150 A2 **Talara** Peru
59 C2 **Talaud, Kepulauan** *is* Indon.
106 C2 **Talavera de la Reina** Spain
153 A4 **Talca** Chile
153 A4 **Talcahuano** Chile
89 E2 **Taldom** Russia
77 D2 **Taldykorgan** Kazakh.
59 C3 **Taliabu** *i.* Indon.
64 B1 **Talisay** Phil.
61 C2 **Taliwang** Indon.
81 C2 **Tall 'Afar** Iraq
143 D2 **Tallahassee** U.S.A.
88 B2 **Tallinn** Estonia
142 B2 **Tallulah** U.S.A.
104 B2 **Talmont-St-Hilaire** France
90 C2 **Tal'ne** Ukr.
117 B3 **Talodi** Sudan
91 E1 **Talovaya** Russia
126 E2 **Taloyoak** Can.
88 B2 **Talsi** Latvia
152 A3 **Taltal** Chile
129 C1 **Taltson** *r.* Can.
60 A1 **Talu** Indon.
53 C1 **Talwood** Austr.
114 B4 **Tamale** Ghana
115 C2 **Tamanrasset** Alg.
99 A3 **Tamar** *r.* U.K.
145 C2 **Tamazunchale** Mex.
114 A3 **Tambacounda** Senegal
61 B1 **Tambelan, Kepulauan** *is* Indon.
91 E1 **Tambov** Russia
145 C2 **Tamiahua, Laguna de** *lag.* Mex.
143 D3 **Tampa** U.S.A.
143 D3 **Tampa Bay** U.S.A.
93 H3 **Tampere** Fin.
145 C2 **Tampico** Mex.
69 D1 **Tamsagbulag** Mongolia
102 C2 **Tamsweg** Austria
53 D2 **Tamworth** Austr.
99 C2 **Tamworth** U.K.
119 E3 **Tana** *r.* Kenya
117 B3 **Tana, Lake** Eth.
67 C4 **Tanabe** Japan
92 I1 **Tana Bru** Norway
61 C2 **Tanahgrogot** Indon.
58 C3 **Tanahjampea** *i.* Indon.
50 C1 **Tanami Desert** Austr.
126 A2 **Tanana** U.S.A.
108 A1 **Tanaro** *r.* Italy
65 B1 **Tanch'ŏn** N. Korea
64 B2 **Tandag** Phil.
110 C2 **Ţăndărei** Romania
153 C4 **Tandil** Arg.
74 A2 **Tando Adam** Pak.
74 A2 **Tando Muhammad Khan** Pak.
114 B2 **Tanezrouft** *reg.* Alg./Mali
119 D3 **Tanga** Tanz.
119 C3 **Tanganyika, Lake** Africa
Tanger Morocco *see* **Tangier**
101 E1 **Tangermünde** Ger.
75 C1 **Tanggula Shan** *mts* China
114 B1 **Tangier** Morocco
75 C1 **Tangra Yumco** *salt l.* China
70 B2 **Tangshan** China
68 C2 **Taniantaweng Shan** *mts* China
59 C3 **Tanimbar, Kepulauan** *is* Indon.
64 B2 **Tanjay** Phil.
60 A1 **Tanjungbalai** Indon.
61 B2 **Tanjungpandan** Indon.
60 B1 **Tanjungpinang** Indon.
61 C1 **Tanjungredeb** Indon.
61 C1 **Tanjungselor** Indon.
74 B1 **Tank** Pak.
115 C3 **Tanout** Niger
75 C2 **Tansen** Nepal
116 B1 **Ţanţā** Egypt
119 D3 **Tanzania** *country* Africa
69 E1 **Taonan** China
138 B1 **Taos** U.S.A.
114 B2 **Taoudenni** Mali
88 C2 **Tapa** Estonia
145 C3 **Tapachula** Mex.
151 C2 **Tapajós** *r.* Brazil
60 A1 **Tapaktuan** Indon.
145 C3 **Tapanatepec** Mex.
150 B2 **Tapauá** Brazil
114 B4 **Tapeta** Liberia
141 D3 **Tappahannock** U.S.A.
74 B2 **Tapti** *r.* India
150 B2 **Tapurucuara** Brazil
154 A1 **Taquarí** *r.* Brazil
154 B1 **Taquari, Serra do** *hills* Brazil
154 C2 **Taquaritinga** Brazil
115 D4 **Taraba** *r.* Nigeria
Ţarābulus Libya *see* **Tripoli**
61 C1 **Tarakan** Indon.
88 A3 **Taran, Mys** *pt* Russia
54 B1 **Taranaki, Mount** *vol.* N.Z.
106 C1 **Tarancón** Spain
109 C2 **Taranto** Italy
109 C2 **Taranto, Golfo di** *g.* Italy
150 A2 **Tarapoto** Peru
91 E2 **Tarasovskiy** Russia
150 A2 **Tarauacá** Brazil
150 B2 **Tarauacá** *r.* Brazil
48 F2 **Tarawa** *atoll* Kiribati
77 D2 **Taraz** Kazakh.
107 C1 **Tarazona** Spain
77 E2 **Tarbagatay, Khrebet** *mts* Kazakh.
96 A2 **Tarbert** *Scotland* U.K.
96 B3 **Tarbert** *Scotland* U.K.
104 C3 **Tarbes** France
96 B2 **Tarbet** U.K.
51 C3 **Tarcoola** Austr.
53 D2 **Taree** Austr.
110 C2 **Târgovişte** Romania
110 B1 **Târgu Jiu** Romania
110 B1 **Târgu Mureş** Romania
110 C1 **Târgu Neamţ** Romania
79 C2 **Tarif** U.A.E.
152 B3 **Tarija** Bol.
79 B3 **Tarīm** Yemen
77 E3 **Tarim Basin** China
77 E2 **Tarim He** *r.* China
Tarim Pendi *basin* China *see* **Tarim Basin**
59 D3 **Taritatu** *r.* Indon.
82 G2 **Tarko-Sale** Russia
114 B4 **Tarkwa** Ghana
64 B1 **Tarlac** Phil.
68 C2 **Tarlag** China
92 G2 **Tärnaby** Sweden
77 C3 **Tarnak Rōd** *r.* Afgh.
110 B1 **Târnăveni** Romania
103 E1 **Tarnobrzeg** Pol.
103 E1 **Tarnów** Pol.
75 C1 **Taro Co** *salt l.* China
114 B1 **Taroudannt** Morocco
69 E1 **Tarqi** China
108 B2 **Tarquinia** Italy
107 D1 **Tarragona** Spain
107 D1 **Tàrrega** Spain
80 B2 **Tarsus** Turkey
152 B3 **Tartagal** Arg.
104 B3 **Tartas** France
88 C2 **Tartu** Estonia
80 B2 **Ţarţūs** Syria
155 D1 **Tarumirim** Brazil
89 E3 **Tarusa** Russia
108 B1 **Tarvisio** Italy
81 D3 **Tashk, Daryācheh-ye** *l.* Iran
Tashkent Uzbek. *see* **Toshkent**
127 I2 **Tasiilaq** Greenland
131 D1 **Tasiujaq** Can.
76 B1 **Taskala** Kazakh.
77 E2 **Taskesken** Kazakh.
54 B2 **Tasman Bay** N.Z.
51 D4 **Tasmania** *state* Austr.
54 B2 **Tasman Mountains** N.Z.
156 D8 **Tasman Sea** S. Pacific Ocean
103 D2 **Tatabánya** Hungary
90 B2 **Tatarbunary** Ukr.
83 K3 **Tatarskiy Proliv** *str.* Russia
67 C4 **Tateyama** Japan
128 C1 **Tathlina Lake** Can.
78 B3 **Tathlīth** Saudi Arabia
78 B2 **Tathlīth, Wādī** *watercourse* Saudi Arabia
53 C3 **Tathra** Austr.
62 A1 **Tatkon** Myanmar
128 B2 **Tatla Lake** Can.
103 D2 **Tatra Mountains** *mts* Pol./Slovakia
Tatry *mts* Pol./Slovakia *see* **Tatra Mountains**
154 C2 **Tatuí** Brazil
139 C2 **Tatum** U.S.A.
81 C2 **Tatvan** Turkey
151 D2 **Tauá** Brazil
155 C2 **Taubaté** Brazil
101 D3 **Tauberbischofsheim** Ger.
54 C1 **Taumarunui** N.Z.
62 A1 **Taunggyi** Myanmar
62 A2 **Taung-ngu** Myanmar
62 A2 **Taungup** Myanmar
99 B3 **Taunton** U.K.
100 C2 **Taunus** *hills* Ger.
54 C1 **Taupo** N.Z.
54 C1 **Taupo, Lake** N.Z.
88 B2 **Taurag** Lith.
54 C1 **Tauranga** N.Z.
80 B2 **Taurus Mountains** Turkey
111 C3 **Tavas** Turkey
86 F3 **Tavda** Russia
106 B2 **Tavira** Port.
99 A3 **Tavistock** U.K.
63 A2 **Tavoy** Myanmar
111 C3 **Tavşanlı** Turkey
99 A3 **Taw** *r.* U.K.
140 C2 **Tawas City** U.S.A.
61 C1 **Tawau** *Sabah* Malaysia
64 A2 **Tawi-Tawi** *i.* Phil.
145 C3 **Taxco** Mex.
76 B2 **Taxiatosh** Uzbek.
77 D3 **Taxkorgan** China
96 C2 **Tay** *r.* U.K.
96 C2 **Tay, Firth of** *est.* U.K.
96 B2 **Tay, Loch** *l.* U.K.
128 B2 **Taylor** Can.
139 D2 **Taylor** U.S.A.
140 B3 **Taylorville** U.S.A.
78 A2 **Taymā'** Saudi Arabia
83 H2 **Taymura** *r.* Russia
83 H2 **Taymyr, Ozero** *l.* Russia
Taymyr, Poluostrov *pen.* Russia *see* **Taymyr Peninsula**
83 G2 **Taymyr Peninsula** Russia
63 B2 **Tây Ninh** Vietnam
64 A1 **Taytay** Phil.

Taz

82 G2 **Taz** r. Russia
114 D1 **Taza** Morocco
129 D2 **Tazin Lake** Can.
86 G2 **Tazovskaya Guba** sea chan. Russia
81 C1 **Tbilisi** Georgia
91 E2 **Tbilisskaya** Russia
118 B3 **Tchibanga** Gabon
118 B2 **Tcholliré** Cameroon
103 D1 **Tczew** Pol.
144 B2 **Teacapán** Mex.
54 A3 **Te Anau** N.Z.
54 A3 **Te Anau, Lake** N.Z.
145 C3 **Teapa** Mex.
54 C1 **Te Awamutu** N.Z.
115 C1 **Tébessa** Alg.
60 B2 **Tebingtinggi** Sumatera Selatan Indon.
60 A1 **Tebingtinggi** Sumatera Utara Indon.
114 B4 **Techiman** Ghana
144 B3 **Tecomán** Mex.
144 B2 **Tecoripa** Mex.
145 B3 **Técpan** Mex.
144 B2 **Tecuala** Mex.
110 C1 **Tecuci** Romania
68 C1 **Teeli** Russia
98 C1 **Tees** r. U.K.
111 C3 **Tefenni** Turkey
61 B2 **Tegal** Indon.
146 B3 **Tegucigalpa** Hond.
115 C3 **Teguidda-n-Tessoumt** Niger
114 B4 **Téhini** Côte d'Ivoire
81 D2 **Tehrān** Iran
145 C3 **Tehuacán** Mex.
145 C3 **Tehuantepec, Gulf of** Mex.
145 C3 **Tehuantepec, Istmo de** isth. Mex.
99 A2 **Teifi** r. U.K.
Te Ika-a-Māui i. N.Z. see North Island
76 C3 **Tejen** Turkm.
76 C3 **Tejen** r. Turkm.
Tejo r. Spain see Tagus
145 B3 **Tejupilco** Mex.
54 B2 **Tekapo, Lake** N.Z.
145 D2 **Tekax** Mex.
116 B3 **Tekezē Wenz** r. Eritrea/Eth.
111 C2 **Tekirdağ** Turkey
54 C1 **Te Kuiti** N.Z.
75 C2 **Tel** r. India
81 C1 **Telavi** Georgia
80 B2 **Tel Aviv-Yafo** Israel
145 D2 **Telchac Puerto** Mex.
128 A2 **Telegraph Creek** Can.
154 B2 **Telêmaco Borba** Brazil
99 B2 **Telford** U.K.
60 B2 **Telo** Indon.
86 F2 **Telpoziz, Gora** mt. Russia
88 B2 **Telšiai** Lith.
61 B2 **Telukbatang** Indon.
60 A1 **Telukdalam** Indon.
60 B1 **Teluk Intan** Malaysia
130 C2 **Temagami Lake** Can.
61 C2 **Temanggung** Indon.
123 C2 **Temba** S. Africa
60 B2 **Tembilahan** Indon.
120 A1 **Tembo Aluma** Angola
99 B2 **Teme** r. U.K.
60 B1 **Temerluh** Malaysia
77 D1 **Temirtau** Kazakh.
53 C2 **Temora** Austr.
139 D2 **Temple** U.S.A.
97 C2 **Templemore** Ireland
145 C2 **Tempoal** Mex.
91 D2 **Temryuk** Russia
153 A4 **Temuco** Chile
54 B2 **Temuka** N.Z.

145 C2 **Tenabo** Mex.
73 C3 **Tenali** India
63 A2 **Tenasserim** Myanmar
99 A3 **Tenby** U.K.
117 C3 **Tendaho** Eth.
105 D3 **Tende** France
108 A2 **Tende, Col de** pass France/Italy
73 D4 **Ten Degree Channel** India
67 D3 **Tendō** Japan
114 B3 **Ténenkou** Mali
115 D3 **Ténéré, Erg du** des. Niger
115 D2 **Ténéré du Tafassâsset** des. Niger
114 A2 **Tenerife** i. Canary Islands
107 D2 **Ténès** Alg.
61 C2 **Tengah, Kepulauan** is Indon.
62 A1 **Tengchong** China
62 A1 **Tenggarong** Indon.
70 A2 **Tengger Shamo** des. China
71 B3 **Tengxian** China
119 C4 **Tenke** Dem. Rep. Congo
114 B3 **Tenkodogo** Burkina Faso
51 C1 **Tennant Creek** Austr.
142 C1 **Tennessee** r. U.S.A.
142 C1 **Tennessee** state U.S.A.
145 C3 **Tenosique** Mex.
53 D1 **Tenterfield** Austr.
154 D1 **Teodoro Sampaio** Brazil
155 D1 **Teófilo Otoni** Brazil
61 C2 **Teopisca** Mex.
61 C2 **Tepache** Mex.
54 B1 **Te Paki** N.Z.
144 B3 **Tepalcatepec** Mex.
144 B2 **Tepatitlán** Mex.
144 B2 **Tepehuanes** Mex.
109 D2 **Tepelenë** Albania
144 B2 **Tepic** Mex.
102 C1 **Teplice** Czech Rep.
89 E3 **Teploye** Russia
144 B2 **Tequila** Mex.
108 B2 **Teramo** Italy
89 E3 **Terbuny** Russia
90 B2 **Terebovlya** Ukr.
87 D4 **Terek** r. Russia
151 D2 **Teresina** Brazil
155 D2 **Teresópolis** Brazil
63 A3 **Teressa Island** India
80 B1 **Terme** Turkey
108 B3 **Termini Imerese** Sicily Italy
145 C3 **Términos, Laguna de** lag. Mex.
77 C3 **Termiz** Uzbek.
109 B2 **Térmoli** Italy
59 C2 **Ternate** Indon.
100 A2 **Terneuzen** Neth.
108 B2 **Terni** Italy
90 B2 **Ternopil'** Ukr.
128 B2 **Terrace** Can.
130 B2 **Terrace Bay** Can.
122 B2 **Terra Firma** S. Africa
140 B3 **Terre Haute** U.S.A.
131 E2 **Terrenceville** Can.
100 B1 **Terschelling** i. Neth.
108 A3 **Tertenia** Sardinia Italy
107 C1 **Teruel** Spain
92 H2 **Tervola** Fin.
109 C2 **Tešanj** Bos. & Herz.
116 B3 **Teseney** Eritrea
66 D2 **Teshio-gawa** r. Japan
128 A1 **Teslin** Can.
128 A1 **Teslin Lake** Can.
154 B1 **Tesouro** Brazil
115 C3 **Tessaoua** Niger
121 C2 **Tete** Moz.
90 C1 **Teteriv** r. Ukr.
101 F1 **Teterow** Ger.
90 B2 **Tetiyiv** Ukr.

114 B1 **Tétouan** Morocco
109 D2 **Tetovo** Macedonia
152 B3 **Teuco** r. Arg.
144 B2 **Teul de González Ortega** Mex.
101 D1 **Teutoburger Wald** hills Ger.
Tevere r. Italy see Tiber
54 A3 **Teviot** N.Z.
Te Waipounamu i. N.Z. see South Island
51 E2 **Tewantin** Austr.
54 C2 **Te Wharau** N.Z.
139 E2 **Texarkana** U.S.A.
53 D1 **Texas** Austr.
139 D2 **Texas** state U.S.A.
139 E3 **Texas City** U.S.A.
100 B1 **Texel** i. Neth.
139 D2 **Texoma, Lake** U.S.A.
123 C2 **Teyateyaneng** Lesotho
89 F2 **Teykovo** Russia
89 F2 **Teza** r. Russia
75 D2 **Tezpur** India
129 E1 **Tha-anne** r. Can.
123 C2 **Thabana-Ntlenyana** mt. Lesotho
123 C2 **Thaba Putsoa** mt. Lesotho
123 C1 **Thabazimbi** S. Africa
123 C2 **Thabong** S. Africa
63 A2 **Thagyettaw** Myanmar
62 B1 **Thai Binh** Vietnam
63 B2 **Thailand** country Asia
63 B2 **Thailand, Gulf of** Asia
62 B1 **Thai Nguyên** Vietnam
62 B2 **Thakhèk** Laos
63 A3 **Thalang** Thai.
74 B1 **Thal Desert** Pak.
101 E2 **Thale** Ger.
62 B2 **Tha Li** Thai.
123 C1 **Thamaga** Botswana
116 C3 **Thamar, Jabal** mt. Yemen
79 C3 **Thamarit** Oman
130 B2 **Thames** r. Can.
54 C1 **Thames** N.Z.
99 D3 **Thames** est. U.K.
99 D3 **Thames** r. U.K.
63 A2 **Thanbyuzayat** Myanmar
62 A2 **Thandwè** Myanmar
62 B2 **Thanh Hoa** Vietnam
73 B3 **Thanjavur** India
63 A2 **Thanlyin** Myanmar
74 A2 **Thano Bula Khan** Pak.
62 B1 **Than Uyên** Vietnam
74 A2 **Thar Desert** India/Pak.
52 B1 **Thargomindah** Austr.
81 C2 **Tharthār, Buḩayrat ath** l. Iraq
111 B2 **Thasos** i. Greece
62 B1 **Thât Khê** Vietnam
62 A2 **Thaton** Myanmar
74 A2 **Thatta** Pak.
62 A1 **Thaungdut** Myanmar
62 A2 **Thayawadi** Myanmar
62 A1 **Thayetmyo** Myanmar
62 A1 **Thazi** Myanmar
146 C2 **The Bahamas** country West Indies
98 B1 **The Cheviot** h. U.K.
134 B1 **The Dalles** U.S.A.
99 C2 **The Fens** reg. U.K.
114 A3 **The Gambia** country Africa
The Great Oasis Egypt see Khārijah, Wāḩāt al
79 C2 **The Gulf** Asia
100 B1 **The Hague** Neth.
129 E1 **Thelon** r. Can.
101 E2 **Themar** Ger.
96 A1 **The Minch** sea chan. U.K.
150 B2 **Theodore Roosevelt** r. Brazil
129 D2 **The Pas** Can.

111 B2 **Thermaïkos Kolpos** *g.* Greece
136 B2 **Thermopolis** U.S.A.
53 C3 **The Rock** Austr.
130 B2 **Thessalon** Can.
111 B2 **Thessaloniki** Greece
99 D2 **Thetford** U.K.
131 C2 **Thetford Mines** Can.
62 A1 **The Triangle** *mts* Myanmar
131 D1 **Thévenet, Lac** *l.* Can.
99 D2 **The Wash** *b.* U.K.
139 D2 **The Woodlands** U.S.A.
142 B3 **Thibodaux** U.S.A.
129 E2 **Thicket Portage** Can.
137 D1 **Thief River Falls** U.S.A.
105 C2 **Thiers** France
119 D3 **Thika** Kenya
73 B4 **Thiladhunmathi** Maldives
75 C2 **Thimphu** Bhutan
105 D2 **Thionville** France
Thira *i.* Greece *see* **Santorini**
98 C1 **Thirsk** U.K.
73 B4 **Thiruvananthapuram** India
93 E4 **Thisted** Denmark
129 E1 **Thlewiaza** *r.* Can.
62 A2 **Thoen** Thai.
123 D1 **Thohoyandou** S. Africa
101 E1 **Thomasburg** Ger.
97 C2 **Thomastown** Ireland
143 D2 **Thomasville** U.S.A.
100 C2 **Thommen** Belgium
129 E2 **Thompson** Can.
128 E3 **Thompson** *r.* U.S.A.
134 C1 **Thompson Falls** U.S.A.
128 B2 **Thompson Sound** Can.
Thoothukudi India *see* **Tuticorin**
96 C3 **Thornhill** U.K.
55 C2 **Thorshavnheiane** *reg.* Antarctica
104 B2 **Thouars** France
128 C2 **Three Hills** Can.
63 A2 **Three Pagodas Pass** Myanmar/Thai.
114 B4 **Three Points, Cape** Ghana
73 B3 **Thrissur** India
63 B2 **Thu Dâu Môt** Vietnam
100 B2 **Thuin** Belgium
127 G1 **Thule Air Base** Greenland
121 B3 **Thuli** Zimbabwe
130 B2 **Thunder Bay** Can.
63 A3 **Thung Song** Thai.
101 E2 **Thüringer Becken** *reg.* Ger.
101 E2 **Thüringer Wald** *mts* Ger.
97 C2 **Thurles** Ireland
96 C1 **Thurso** U.K.
96 C1 **Thurso** *r.* U.K.
151 D2 **Tianguá** Brazil
70 B2 **Tianjin** China
70 B2 **Tianjin** *mun.* China
71 A3 **Tianlin** China
70 B2 **Tianmen** China
70 A2 **Tianshui** China
154 B2 **Tibagi** *r.* Brazil
118 B2 **Tibati** Cameroon
108 B2 **Tiber** *r.* Italy
Tiberias, Lake Israel *see* **Galilee, Sea of**
115 D2 **Tibesti** *mts* Chad
Tibet *aut. reg.* China *see* **Xizang Zizhiqu**
68 B2 **Tibet, Plateau of** China
Tibet Autonomous Region *aut. reg.* China *see* **Xizang Zizhiqu**
115 D2 **Tībīstī, Sarīr** *des.* Libya
52 B1 **Tibooburra** Austr.
144 A2 **Tiburón, Isla** *i.* Mex.
114 B3 **Tîchît** Maur.
114 A2 **Tichla** Western Sahara
145 D2 **Ticul** Mex.
114 A3 **Tidjikja** Maur.
100 B2 **Tiel** Neth.
65 A1 **Tieling** China
100 A2 **Tielt** Belgium
100 B2 **Tienen** Belgium
68 B2 **Tien Shan** *mts* China/Kyrg.
Tientsin China *see* **Tianjin**
93 G3 **Tierp** Sweden
145 C3 **Tierra Blanca** Mex.
145 C3 **Tierra Colorada** Mex.
153 B6 **Tierra del Fuego, Isla Grande de** *i.* Arg./Chile
154 C2 **Tietê** Brazil
Tiflis Georgia *see* **Tbilisi**
143 D2 **Tifton** U.S.A.
Tighina Moldova *see* **Bender**
131 D2 **Tignish** Can.
150 A2 **Tigre** *r.* Ecuador/Peru
81 C2 **Tigris** *r.* Asia
145 C2 **Tihuatlán** Mex.
144 A1 **Tijuana** Mex.
91 E2 **Tikhoretsk** Russia
89 D2 **Tikhvin** Russia
89 D2 **Tikhvinskaya Gryada** *ridge* Russia
54 C1 **Tikokino** N.Z.
81 C2 **Tikrīt** Iraq
83 J2 **Tiksi** Russia
100 B2 **Tilburg** Neth.
152 B3 **Tilcara** Arg.
52 B1 **Tilcha (abandoned)** Austr.
114 C3 **Tillabéri** Niger
134 B1 **Tillamook** U.S.A.
63 A3 **Tillanchong Island** India
111 C3 **Tilos** *i.* Greece
52 B2 **Tilpa** Austr.
86 F2 **Til'tim** Russia
89 E3 **Tim** Russia
86 D2 **Timanskiy Kryazh** *ridge* Russia
54 B2 **Timaru** N.Z.
91 D2 **Timashevsk** Russia
114 B3 **Timbedgha** Maur.
50 C1 **Timber Creek** Austr.
114 B3 **Timbuktu** Mali
114 C2 **Timimoun** Alg.
111 B2 **Timiou Prodromou, Akrotirio** *pt* Greece
110 B1 **Timiş** *r.* Romania
110 B1 **Timişoara** Romania
130 B2 **Timmins** Can.
89 E2 **Timokhino** Russia
151 D2 **Timon** Brazil
59 C3 **Timor** *i.* East Timor/Indonesia
Timor-Leste *country* Asia *see* **East Timor**
58 C3 **Timor Sea** Austr./Indon.
93 G3 **Timrå** Sweden
114 B2 **Tindouf** Alg.
75 C2 **Tingri** China
93 F4 **Tingsryd** Sweden
59 D2 **Tinian** *i.* N. Mariana Is
152 B3 **Tinogasta** Arg.
111 C3 **Tinos** Greece
111 C3 **Tinos** *i.* Greece
115 C2 **Tinrhert, Hamada de** Alg.
62 A1 **Tinsukia** India
107 D2 **Tipasa** Alg.
97 B2 **Tipperary** Ireland
109 C2 **Tirana** Albania
Tiranë Albania *see* **Tirana**
108 B1 **Tirano** Italy
90 B2 **Tiraspol** Moldova
111 C3 **Tire** Turkey
96 A2 **Tiree** *i.* U.K.
74 B1 **Tirich Mir** *mt.* Pak.
73 B3 **Tiruchchirappalli** India
73 B4 **Tirunelveli** India
73 B3 **Tirupati** India
73 B3 **Tiruppattur** India
73 B3 **Tiruppur** India
109 D1 **Tisa** *r.* Serbia
129 D2 **Tisdale** Can.
107 D2 **Tissemsilt** Alg.
152 B2 **Titicaca, Lake** Bol./Peru
75 C2 **Titlagarh** India
110 C2 **Titu** Romania
143 D3 **Titusville** U.S.A.
99 B3 **Tiverton** U.K.
108 B2 **Tivoli** Italy
79 C2 **Ţīwī** Oman
145 D2 **Tizimín** Mex.
107 D2 **Tizi Ouzou** Alg.
114 B2 **Tiznit** Morocco
145 C3 **Tlacotalpán** Mex.
144 B2 **Tlahualilo** Mex.
145 C3 **Tlapa** Mex.
145 C3 **Tlaxcala** Mex.
145 C3 **Tlaxiaco** Mex.
114 B1 **Tlemcen** Alg.
123 C1 **Tlokweng** Botswana
128 B2 **Toad River** Can.
121 □D2 **Toamasina** Madag.
60 A1 **Toba, Danau** *l.* Indon.
74 A1 **Toba and Kakar Ranges** *mts* Pak.
147 D3 **Tobago** *i.* Trin. and Tob.
59 C2 **Tobelo** Indon.
130 B2 **Tobermory** Can.
96 A2 **Tobermory** U.K.
129 D2 **Tobin Lake** Can.
60 B2 **Toboali** Indon.
86 F3 **Tobol'sk** Russia
76 C1 **Tobyl** *r.* Kazakh./Russia
151 D2 **Tocantinópolis** Brazil
151 D2 **Tocantins** *r.* Brazil
143 D2 **Toccoa** U.S.A.
108 A1 **Toce** *r.* Italy
152 A3 **Tocopilla** Chile
53 C3 **Tocumwal** Austr.
144 A2 **Todos Santos** Mex.
128 B3 **Tofino** Can.
96 □ **Toft** U.K.
49 G4 **Tofua** *i.* Tonga
59 C3 **Togian, Kepulauan** *is* Indon.
114 C4 **Togo** *country* Africa
74 B2 **Tohana** India
126 B2 **Tok** U.S.A.
116 B3 **Tokar** Sudan
69 E3 **Tokara-rettō** *is* Japan
91 E1 **Tokarevka** Russia
49 G3 **Tokelau** *terr.* S. Pacific Ocean
91 D2 **Tokmak** Ukr.
77 D2 **Tokmok** Kyrg.
54 C1 **Tokoroa** N.Z.
68 B2 **Toksun** China
67 B4 **Tokushima** Japan
67 C3 **Tōkyō** Japan
121 □D3 **Tôlañaro** Madag.
154 B2 **Toledo** Brazil
106 C2 **Toledo** Spain
140 C2 **Toledo** U.S.A.
106 C2 **Toledo, Montes de** *mts* Spain
142 B2 **Toledo Bend Reservoir** U.S.A.
121 □D3 **Toliara** Madag.
58 C2 **Tolitoli** Indon.
108 B1 **Tolmezzo** Italy
104 B3 **Tolosa** Spain
145 C3 **Toluca** Mex.
87 D3 **Tol'yatti** Russia
140 A2 **Tomah** U.S.A.
66 D2 **Tomakomai** Japan
106 B2 **Tomar** Port.
103 E1 **Tomaszów Lubelski** Pol.
103 E1 **Tomaszów Mazowiecki** Pol.

Tomatlán

144	B3	Tomatlán Mex.
142	C2	Tombigbee r. U.S.A.
155	D2	Tombos Brazil
		Tombouctou Mali see Timbuktu
120	A2	Tombua Angola
123	C1	Tom Burke S. Africa
53	C2	Tomingley Austr.
58	C3	Tomini, Teluk g. Indon.
109	C2	Tomislavgrad Bos. & Herz.
50	A2	Tom Price Austr.
82	G3	Tomsk Russia
93	F4	Tomtabacken h. Sweden
145	C3	Tonalá Mex.
150	B2	Tonantins Brazil
59	C2	Tondano Indon.
49	G4	Tonga country S. Pacific Ocean
49	G4	Tongatapu Group is Tonga
71	B3	Tongcheng China
70	A2	Tongchuan China
71	A3	Tongdao China
100	B2	Tongeren Belgium
62	B1	Tonghai China
65	B1	Tonghua China
65	B2	Tongjosŏn-man b. N. Korea
62	B1	Tongking, Gulf of China/Vietnam
69	E2	Tongliao China
70	B2	Tongling China
52	B2	Tongo Austr.
71	A3	Tongren China
		Tongshan China see Xuzhou
		Tongtian He r. China see Yangtze
96	B1	Tongue U.K.
65	B3	Tongyeong S. Korea
69	E2	Tongyu China
65	A1	Tongyuanpu China
74	B2	Tonk India
63	B2	Tonle Sap l. Cambodia
135	C3	Tonopah U.S.A.
93	F4	Tønsberg Norway
135	D2	Tooele U.S.A.
52	B3	Tooleybuc Austr.
53	D1	Toowoomba Austr.
137	D3	Topeka U.S.A.
144	B2	Topia Mex.
144	B2	Topolobampo Mex.
86	C2	Topozero, Ozero l. Russia
134	B1	Toppenish U.S.A.
111	C3	Torbalı Turkey
76	B3	Torbat-e Ḥeydarīyeh Iran
76	C3	Torbat-e Jām Iran
106	C1	Tordesillas Spain
107	C1	Tordesilos Spain
107	D1	Torelló Spain
101	F2	Torgau Ger.
76	C2	Torgay Kazakh.
100	A2	Torhout Belgium
		Torino Italy see Turin
154	B1	Torixoréu Brazil
106	B1	Tormes r. Spain
92	H2	Torneälven r. Sweden
127	G3	Torngat Mountains Can.
92	H2	Tornio Fin.
106	B1	Toro Spain
130	C2	Toronto Can.
119	D2	Tororo Uganda
		Toros Dağları mts Turkey see Taurus Mountains
99	B3	Torquay U.K.
106	B2	Torrão Port.
106	B1	Torre mt. Port.
107	D1	Torreblanca Spain
106	C1	Torrecerredo mt. Spain
106	B1	Torre de Moncorvo Port.
106	C1	Torrelavega Spain
106	C2	Torremolinos Spain

52	A2	Torrens, Lake imp. l. Austr.
107	C2	Torrent Spain
144	B2	Torreón Mex.
106	B2	Torres Novas Port.
106	B2	Torres Vedras Port.
107	C2	Torrevieja Spain
96	B2	Torridon U.K.
106	C2	Torrijos Spain
141	E2	Torrington CT U.S.A.
136	C2	Torrington WY U.S.A.
107	D1	Torroella de Montgrí Spain
94	B1	Tórshavn Faroe Is
108	A3	Tortolì Sardinia Italy
107	D1	Tortosa Spain
103	D1	Toruń Pol.
97	B1	Tory Island Ireland
89	D2	Torzhok Russia
122	B2	Tosca S. Africa
108	B2	Toscano, Arcipelago is Italy
77	C2	Toshkent Uzbek.
89	D2	Tosno Russia
152	B3	Tostado Arg.
101	D1	Tostedt Ger.
80	B1	Tosya Turkey
86	D3	Tot'ma Russia
67	B3	Tottori Japan
114	B4	Touba Côte d'Ivoire
114	B1	Toubkal, Jebel mt. Morocco
114	B3	Tougan Burkina Faso
115	C1	Touggourt Alg.
105	D2	Toul France
105	D3	Toulon France
104	C3	Toulouse France
100	A2	Tournai Belgium
105	C2	Tournus France
151	E2	Touros Brazil
104	C2	Tours France
115	D2	Tousside, Pic mt. Chad
122	B3	Touwsrivier S. Africa
66	D2	Towada Japan
134	D1	Townsend U.S.A.
51	D1	Townsville Austr.
77	E2	Toxkan He r. China
66	D2	Tōya-ko l. Japan
67	C3	Toyama Japan
67	C3	Toyota Japan
115	C1	Tozeur Tunisia
81	C1	T'q'varcheli Georgia
		Trâblous Lebanon see Tripoli
80	B1	Trabzon Turkey
106	B2	Trafalgar, Cabo c. Spain
128	C3	Trail Can.
88	B3	Trakai Lith.
97	B2	Tralee Ireland
97	C2	Tramore Ireland
63	A3	Trang Thai.
59	D3	Trangan i. Indon.
55	I2	Transantarctic Mountains Antarctica
90	B2	Transnistria disp. terr. Moldova
110	B1	Transylvanian Alps mts Romania
108	B3	Trapani Sicily Italy
53	C3	Traralgon Austr.
63	B2	Trat Thai.
102	C2	Traunstein Ger.
140	B2	Traverse City U.S.A.
103	D2	Třebíč Czech Rep.
109	C2	Trebinje Bos. & Herz.
103	E2	Trebišov Slovakia
109	C1	Trebnje Slovenia
153	C4	Treinta y Tres Uru.
153	B5	Trelew Arg.
93	F4	Trelleborg Sweden
130	C2	Tremblant, Mont h. Can.
109	C2	Tremiti, Isole is Italy
134	D2	Tremonton U.S.A.

107	D1	Tremp Spain
103	D2	Trenčín Slovakia
153	B4	Trenque Lauquén Arg.
98	C2	Trent r. U.K.
108	B1	Trento Italy
141	D2	Trenton Can.
137	E2	Trenton MO U.S.A.
141	E2	Trenton NJ U.S.A.
131	E2	Trepassey Can.
153	B4	Tres Arroyos Arg.
155	C2	Três Corações Brazil
154	B1	Três Lagoas Brazil
153	A5	Tres Lagos Arg.
155	C1	Três Marias, Represa resr Brazil
155	C2	Três Pontas Brazil
153	B5	Tres Puntas, Cabo c. Arg.
155	D2	Três Rios Brazil
101	F1	Treuenbrietzen Ger.
108	A1	Treviglio Italy
108	B1	Treviso Italy
99	A3	Trevose Head U.K.
109	C3	Tricase Italy
53	C2	Trida Austr.
100	C3	Trier Ger.
108	B1	Trieste Italy
108	B1	Triglav mt. Slovenia
59	D3	Trikora, Puncak mt. Indon.
97	C2	Trim Ireland
73	C4	Trincomalee Sri Lanka
154	C1	Trindade Brazil
152	B2	Trinidad Bol.
147	D3	Trinidad i. Trin. and Tob.
136	C3	Trinidad U.S.A.
147	D3	Trinidad and Tobago country West Indies
131	E2	Trinity Bay Can.
111	B3	Tripoli Greece
80	B2	Tripoli Lebanon
115	D1	Tripoli Libya
113	D10	Tristan da Cunha i. S. Atlantic Ocean
		Trivandrum India see Thiruvananthapuram
108	B2	Trivento Italy
103	D2	Trnava Slovakia
109	C2	Trogir Croatia
109	C2	Troia Italy
100	C2	Troisdorf Ger.
131	C2	Trois-Rivières Can.
86	E2	Troitsko-Pechorsk Russia
151	C2	Trombetas r. Brazil
123	C3	Trompsburg S. Africa
92	G2	Tromsø Norway
92	F3	Trondheim Norway
128	C2	Trout Lake Can.
128	B1	Trout Lake N.W.T. Can.
130	A1	Trout Lake Ont. Can.
99	B3	Trowbridge U.K.
142	C2	Troy AL U.S.A.
141	E2	Troy NY U.S.A.
105	C2	Troyes France
109	D2	Trstenik Serbia
89	D3	Trubchevsk Russia
106	B1	Truchas Spain
79	C2	Trucial Coast U.A.E.
146	B3	Trujillo Hond.
150	A2	Trujillo Peru
106	B2	Trujillo Spain
147	C4	Trujillo Venez.
142	B1	Trumann U.S.A.
131	D2	Truro Can.
99	A3	Truro U.K.
138	B2	Truth or Consequences U.S.A.
103	D2	Trutnov Czech Rep.
93	F3	Trysil Norway
103	D1	Trzebiatów Pol.

68 B1 **Tsagaannuur** Mongolia
121 □D2 **Tsaratanana, Massif du** *mts* Madag.
110 C2 **Tsarevo** Bulg.
122 A2 **Tses** Namibia
122 B1 **Tsetseng** Botswana
68 C1 **Tsetserleg** *Arhangay* Mongolia
68 C1 **Tsetserleg** *Hövsgöl* Mongolia
122 B2 **Tshabong** Botswana
122 B1 **Tshane** Botswana
118 B3 **Tshela** Dem. Rep. Congo
118 C3 **Tshikapa** Dem. Rep. Congo
118 C3 **Tshikapa** *r.* Dem. Rep. Congo
123 D1 **Tshipise** S. Africa
118 C3 **Tshitanzu** Dem. Rep. Congo
118 C3 **Tshuapa** *r.* Dem. Rep. Congo
Tshwane S. Africa *see* **Pretoria**
87 D4 **Tsimlyanskoye Vodokhranilishche** *resr* Russia
Tsingtao China *see* **Qingdao**
Tsining China *see* **Ulan Qab**
121 □D2 **Tsiroanomandidy** Madag.
123 C3 **Tsomo** S. Africa
67 C4 **Tsu** Japan
67 D3 **Tsuchiura** Japan
66 D2 **Tsugarū-kaikyō** *str.* Japan
120 A2 **Tsumeb** Namibia
122 A1 **Tsumis Park** Namibia
120 B2 **Tsumkwe** Namibia
67 C3 **Tsuruga** Japan
66 C3 **Tsuruoka** Japan
67 A4 **Tsushima** *is* Japan
Tsushima-kaikyō *str.* Japan/S. Korea *see* **Korea Strait**
67 B3 **Tsuyama** Japan
123 C2 **Tswelelang** S. Africa
91 C2 **Tsyurupyns'k** Ukr.
Tthenaagoo Can. *see* **Nahanni Butte**
59 C3 **Tual** Indon.
97 B2 **Tuam** Ireland
91 D3 **Tuapse** Russia
54 A3 **Tuatapere** N.Z.
96 A1 **Tuath, Loch a'** *b.* U.K.
138 A1 **Tuba City** U.S.A.
61 C2 **Tuban** Indon.
152 D3 **Tubarão** Brazil
102 B2 **Tübingen** Ger.
115 E1 **Tubruq** Libya
49 H4 **Tubuai** Fr. Polynesia
49 I4 **Tubuai** *i.* Fr. Polynesia
144 A1 **Tubutama** Mex.
152 C2 **Tucavaca** Bol.
128 B1 **Tuchitua** Can.
138 A2 **Tucson** U.S.A.
139 C1 **Tucumcari** U.S.A.
150 B1 **Tucupita** Venez.
151 D2 **Tucuruí** Brazil
151 D2 **Tucuruí, Represa de** *resr* Brazil
107 C1 **Tudela** Spain
106 B1 **Tuela** *r.* Port.
62 A1 **Tuensang** India
64 B1 **Tuguegarao** Phil.
106 B1 **Tui** Spain
59 C3 **Tukangbesi, Kepulauan** *is* Indon.
126 C2 **Tuktoyaktuk** Can.
88 B2 **Tukums** Latvia
145 C2 **Tula** Mex.
89 E3 **Tula** Russia
145 C2 **Tulancingo** Mex.
135 C3 **Tulare** U.S.A.
138 B2 **Tularosa** U.S.A.
110 C1 **Tulcea** Romania
90 B2 **Tul'chyn** Ukr.
129 E1 **Tulemalu Lake** Can.
139 C2 **Tulia** U.S.A.
142 C1 **Tullahoma** U.S.A.
97 C2 **Tullamore** Ireland
104 C2 **Tulle** France
51 D1 **Tully** Austr.
139 D1 **Tulsa** U.S.A.
150 A1 **Tumaco** Col.
123 C2 **Tumahole** S. Africa
73 B3 **Tumakuru** India
93 G4 **Tumba** Sweden
118 B3 **Tumba, Lac** *l.* Dem. Rep. Congo
53 C3 **Tumbarumba** Austr.
150 A2 **Tumbes** Peru
128 B2 **Tumbler Ridge** Can.
52 A2 **Tumby Bay** Austr.
65 B1 **Tumen** China
150 B1 **Tumereng** Guyana
64 A2 **Tumindao** *i.* Phil.
Tumkur India *see* **Tumakuru**
74 A2 **Tump** Pak.
151 C1 **Tumucumaque, Serra** *hills* Brazil
53 C3 **Tumut** Austr.
80 B2 **Tunceli** Turkey
53 D2 **Tuncurry** Austr.
119 D4 **Tunduru** Tanz.
110 C2 **Tundzha** *r.* Bulg.
128 B1 **Tungsten (abandoned)** Can.
115 D1 **Tunis** Tunisia
115 C1 **Tunisia** *country* Africa
150 A1 **Tunja** Col.
92 F3 **Tunnsjøen** *l.* Norway
Tunxi China *see* **Huangshan**
154 B2 **Tupã** Brazil
154 C1 **Tupaciguara** Brazil
142 C2 **Tupelo** U.S.A.
152 B3 **Tupiza** Bol.
76 B2 **Tupkaragan, Mys** *pt* Kazakh.
83 H2 **Tura** Russia
86 F3 **Tura** *r.* Russia
78 B2 **Turabah** Saudi Arabia
83 J3 **Turana, Khrebet** *mts* Russia
54 C1 **Turangi** N.Z.
76 B2 **Turan Lowland** Asia
78 A1 **Ţurayf** Saudi Arabia
88 B2 **Turba** Estonia
74 A2 **Turbat** Pak.
150 A1 **Turbo** Col.
110 B1 **Turda** Romania
Turfan China *see* **Turpan**
111 C3 **Turgutlu** Turkey
80 B1 **Turhal** Turkey
107 C2 **Turia** *r.* Spain
108 A1 **Turin** Italy
86 F3 **Turinsk** Russia
90 A1 **Turiys'k** Ukr.
119 D2 **Turkana, Lake** *salt l.* Eth./Kenya
80 B2 **Turkey** *country* Asia/Europe
77 C2 **Turkistan** Kazakh.
76 C3 **Türkmenabat** Turkm.
76 B2 **Türkmenbaşy** Turkm.
76 B2 **Turkmenistan** *country* Asia
147 C2 **Turks and Caicos Islands** *terr.* West Indies
93 H3 **Turku** Fin.
135 B3 **Turlock** U.S.A.
54 C2 **Turnagain, Cape** N.Z.
100 B2 **Turnhout** Belgium
129 D2 **Turnor Lake** Can.
110 B2 **Turnu Măgurele** Romania
68 B2 **Turpan** China
77 D2 **Turugart Pass** China/Kyrg.
142 C2 **Tuscaloosa** U.S.A.
142 C2 **Tuskegee** U.S.A.
73 B4 **Tuticorin** India
120 B3 **Tutume** Botswana
49 F3 **Tuvalu** *country* S. Pacific Ocean
78 B2 **Tuwayq, Jabal** *hills* Saudi Arabia
78 B2 **Tuwayq, Jabal** *mts* Saudi Arabia
78 A2 **Tuwwal** Saudi Arabia
144 B2 **Tuxpan** *Nayarit* Mex.
145 C2 **Tuxpan** *Veracruz* Mex.
145 C3 **Tuxtla Gutiérrez** Mex.
62 B1 **Tuyên Quang** Vietnam
63 B2 **Tuy Hoa** Vietnam
80 B2 **Tuz, Lake** *salt l.* Turkey
Tuz Gölü *salt l.* Turkey *see* **Tuz, Lake**
81 C2 **Tuz Khurmātū** Iraq
109 C2 **Tuzla** Bos. & Herz.
91 E2 **Tuzlov** *r.* Russia
89 E2 **Tver'** Russia
98 B1 **Tweed** *r.* U.K.
122 A2 **Twee Rivier** Namibia
135 C4 **Twentynine Palms** U.S.A.
131 E2 **Twillingate** Can.
134 D2 **Twin Falls** U.S.A.
137 E1 **Two Harbors** U.S.A.
129 C2 **Two Hills** Can.
139 D2 **Tyler** U.S.A.
83 J3 **Tynda** Russia
93 F3 **Tynset** Norway
80 B2 **Tyre** Lebanon
111 B3 **Tyrnavos** Greece
52 B3 **Tyrrell, Lake** *dry lake* Austr.
108 B2 **Tyrrhenian Sea** France/Italy
87 E3 **Tyul'gan** Russia
86 F3 **Tyumen'** Russia
83 J2 **Tyung** *r.* Russia
99 A3 **Tywi** *r.* U.K.
123 D1 **Tzaneen** S. Africa

U

120 B2 **Uamanda** Angola
155 D2 **Ubá** Brazil
155 D1 **Ubaí** Brazil
151 E3 **Ubaitaba** Brazil
118 B3 **Ubangi** *r.* C.A.R./Dem. Rep. Congo
67 B4 **Ube** Japan
106 C2 **Úbeda** Spain
154 C1 **Uberaba** Brazil
154 C1 **Uberlândia** Brazil
106 B1 **Ubiña, Peña** *mt.* Spain
123 D2 **Ubombo** S. Africa
63 B2 **Ubon Ratchathani** Thai.
119 C3 **Ubundu** Dem. Rep. Congo
150 A2 **Ucayali** *r.* Peru
74 B2 **Uch** Pak.
66 D2 **Uchiura-wan** *b.* Japan
83 J3 **Uchur** *r.* Russia
128 B3 **Ucluelet** Can.
74 B2 **Udaipur** India
91 C1 **Uday** *r.* Ukr.
93 F4 **Uddevalla** Sweden
92 G2 **Uddjaure** *l.* Sweden
100 B2 **Uden** Neth.
74 B1 **Udhampur** India
108 B1 **Udine** Italy
89 E2 **Udomlya** Russia
62 B2 **Udon Thani** Thai.
73 B3 **Udupi** India
83 K3 **Udyl', Ozero** *l.* Russia
67 C3 **Ueda** Japan
58 C3 **Uekuli** Indon.
118 C2 **Uele** *r.* Dem. Rep. Congo
101 E1 **Uelzen** Ger.
119 C2 **Uere** *r.* Dem. Rep. Congo
87 E3 **Ufa** Russia
119 D3 **Ugalla** *r.* Tanz.

119 D2 **Uganda** *country* Africa
89 E2 **Uglich** Russia
89 D2 **Uglovka** Russia
89 D3 **Ugra** Russia
103 D2 **Uherské Hradiště** Czech Rep.
101 E2 **Uichteritz** Ger.
96 A2 **Uig** U.K.
120 A1 **Uíge** Angola
65 B2 **Uijeongbu** S. Korea
135 D2 **Uinta Mountains** U.S.A.
65 B2 **Uiseong** S. Korea
120 A3 **Uis Mine** Namibia
123 C3 **Uitenhage** S. Africa
100 C1 **Uithuizen** Neth.
74 B2 **Ujjain** India
89 F3 **Ukholovo** Russia
62 A1 **Ukhrul** India
86 E2 **Ukhta** Russia
135 B3 **Ukiah** U.S.A.
127 H2 **Ukkusissat** Greenland
88 B2 **Ukmerg** Lith.
90 C2 **Ukraine** *country* Europe
Ulaanbaatar Mongolia *see* **Ulan Bator**
68 C1 **Ulaangom** Mongolia
69 D1 **Ulan Bator** Mongolia
Ulanhad China *see* **Chifeng**
69 E1 **Ulanhot** China
87 D4 **Ulan-Khol** Russia
70 B1 **Ulan Qab** China
69 D1 **Ulan-Ude** Russia
75 D1 **Ulan Ul Hu** *l.* China
Uleåborg Fin. *see* **Oulu**
88 C2 **Ülenurme** Estonia
69 D1 **Uliastai** China
68 C1 **Uliastay** Mongolia
59 D2 **Ulithi** *atoll* Micronesia
65 B2 **Uljin** S. Korea
53 D3 **Ulladulla** Austr.
96 B2 **Ullapool** U.K.
65 C2 **Ulleung-do** *i.* S. Korea
98 B1 **Ullswater** *l.* U.K.
102 B2 **Ulm** Ger.
65 B2 **Ulsan** S. Korea
96 □ **Ulsta** U.K.
97 C1 **Ulster** *reg.* Ireland/U.K.
52 B3 **Ultima** Austr.
111 C3 **Ulubey** Turkey
111 C2 **Uludağ** *mt.* Turkey
126 D2 **Ulukhaktok** Can.
123 D2 **Ulundi** S. Africa
77 E2 **Ulungur Hu** *l.* China
50 C2 **Uluru** *h.* Austr.
98 B1 **Ulverston** U.K.
87 D3 **Ul'yanovsk** Russia
136 C3 **Ulysses** U.S.A.
90 C2 **Uman'** Ukr.
86 C2 **Umba** Russia
59 D3 **Umboi** *i.* P.N.G.
92 H3 **Umeå** Sweden
92 H3 **Umeälven** *r.* Sweden
127 I2 **Umiiviip Kangertiva** *inlet* Greenland
126 D2 **Umingmaktok** Can.
123 D2 **Umlazi** S. Africa
117 A3 **Umm Keddada** Sudan
78 A2 **Umm Lajj** Saudi Arabia
117 B3 **Umm Ruwaba** Sudan
115 E1 **Umm Sa'ad** Libya
134 B2 **Umpqua** *r.* U.S.A.
120 A2 **Umpulo** Angola
154 B2 **Umuarama** Brazil
109 C1 **Una** *r.* Bos. & Herz./Croatia
155 E1 **Una** Brazil
154 C1 **Unaí** Brazil
78 B2 **'Unayzah** Saudi Arabia
136 C1 **Underwood** U.S.A.
89 D3 **Unecha** Russia
53 C2 **Ungarie** Austr.
52 A2 **Ungarra** Austr.
127 G2 **Ungava, Péninsule d'** *pen.* Can.
127 G3 **Ungava Bay** Can.
90 B2 **Ungheni** Moldova
Unguja *i.* Tanz. *see* **Zanzibar Island**
154 B3 **União da Vitória** Brazil
150 B2 **Unini** *r.* Brazil
142 C1 **Union City** U.S.A.
122 B3 **Uniondale** S. Africa
141 D3 **Uniontown** U.S.A.
79 C2 **United Arab Emirates** *country* Asia
95 C3 **United Kingdom** *country* Europe
132 D3 **United States of America** *country* N. America
129 D2 **Unity** Can.
96 □ **Unst** *i.* U.K.
101 E2 **Unstrut** *r.* Ger.
89 E3 **Upa** *r.* Russia
119 C3 **Upemba, Lac** *l.* Dem. Rep. Congo
122 B2 **Upington** S. Africa
134 B2 **Upper Alkali Lake** U.S.A.
128 C2 **Upper Arrow Lake** Can.
134 B2 **Upper Klamath Lake** U.S.A.
128 B1 **Upper Liard** Can.
97 C1 **Upper Lough Erne** *l.* U.K.
93 G4 **Uppsala** Sweden
78 B2 **'Uqlat aş Şuqūr** Saudi Arabia
Urad Qianqi China *see* **Xishanzui**
76 B2 **Ural** *r.* Kazakh./Russia
53 D2 **Uralla** Austr.
87 E3 **Ural Mountains** Russia
76 B1 **Ural'sk** Kazakh.
Ural'skiy Khrebet *mts* Russia *see* **Ural Mountains**
119 D3 **Urambo** Tanz.
53 C3 **Urana** Austr.
129 D2 **Uranium City** Can.
86 F2 **Uray** Russia
98 C1 **Ure** *r.* U.K.
86 D3 **Uren'** Russia
144 A2 **Ures** Mex.
76 C2 **Urganch** Uzbek.
100 B1 **Urk** Neth.
111 C3 **Urla** Turkey
81 C2 **Urmia, Lake** *salt l.* Iran
Uroševac Kosovo *see* **Ferizaj**
144 B2 **Uruáchic** Mex.
151 D3 **Uruaçu** Brazil
144 B3 **Uruapan** Mex.
150 A3 **Urubamba** *r.* Peru
151 C2 **Urucará** Brazil
151 D2 **Uruçuí** Brazil
151 C2 **Urucurituba** Brazil
152 C3 **Uruguaiana** Brazil
153 C4 **Uruguay** *country* S. America
Urumchi China *see* **Ürümqi**
68 B2 **Ürümqi** China
53 D2 **Urunga** Austr.
110 C2 **Urziceni** Romania
67 B4 **Usa** Japan
82 E2 **Usa** *r.* Russia
111 C3 **Uşak** Turkey
82 G1 **Ushakova, Ostrov** *i.* Russia
77 E2 **Usharal** Kazakh.
77 D2 **Ushtobe** Kazakh.
153 B6 **Ushuaia** Arg.
86 E2 **Usinsk** Russia
88 C3 **Uskhodni** Belarus
89 E3 **Usman'** Russia
86 D2 **Usogorsk** Russia
104 C2 **Ussel** France
66 B2 **Ussuriysk** Russia
108 B3 **Ustica, Isola di** *i. Sicily* Italy
83 H3 **Ust'-Ilimsk** Russia
86 E2 **Ust'-Ilych** Russia
103 D1 **Ustka** Pol.
83 L3 **Ust'-Kamchatsk** Russia
77 E2 **Ust'-Kamenogorsk** Kazakh.
86 F2 **Ust'-Kara** Russia
86 E2 **Ust'-Kulom** Russia
83 I3 **Ust'-Kut** Russia
91 D2 **Ust'-Labinsk** Russia
88 C2 **Ust'-Luga** Russia
86 E2 **Ust'-Nem** Russia
83 K2 **Ust'-Nera** Russia
83 K2 **Ust'-Omchug** Russia
83 H3 **Ust'-Ordynskiy** Russia
86 E2 **Ust'-Tsil'ma** Russia
86 D2 **Ust'-Ura** Russia
76 B2 **Ustyurt Plateau** Kazakh./Uzbek.
89 E2 **Ustyuzhna** Russia
89 D2 **Usvyaty** Russia
135 D3 **Utah** *state* U.S.A.
135 D2 **Utah Lake** U.S.A.
93 I4 **Utena** Lith.
123 D2 **uThukela** *r.* S. Africa
141 D2 **Utica** U.S.A.
107 C2 **Utiel** Spain
128 C2 **Utikuma Lake** Can.
100 B1 **Utrecht** Neth.
106 B2 **Utrera** Spain
92 I2 **Utsjoki** Fin.
67 C3 **Utsunomiya** Japan
87 D4 **Utta** Russia
62 B2 **Uttaradit** Thai.
127 H2 **Uummannaq Fjord** *inlet* Greenland
93 H3 **Uusikaupunki** Fin.
139 D3 **Uvalde** U.S.A.
119 D3 **Uvinza** Tanz.
68 C1 **Uvs Nuur** *salt l.* Mongolia
67 B4 **Uwajima** Japan
78 A2 **'Uwayriḍ, Ḥarrat al** *lava field* Saudi Arabia
116 A2 **Uweinat, Jebel** *mt.* Sudan
83 H3 **Uyar** Russia
115 C4 **Uyo** Nigeria
152 B3 **Uyuni, Salar de** *salt flat* Bol.
76 C2 **Uzbekistan** *country* Asia
104 C2 **Uzerche** France
105 C3 **Uzès** France
90 C1 **Uzh** *r.* Ukr.
90 A2 **Uzhhorod** Ukr.
109 C2 **Užice** Serbia
89 E3 **Uzlovaya** Russia
111 C3 **Üzümlü** Turkey
111 C2 **Uzunköprü** Turkey

V

123 B2 **Vaal** *r.* S. Africa
123 C2 **Vaal Dam** S. Africa
123 C1 **Vaalwater** S. Africa
92 H3 **Vaasa** Fin.
103 D2 **Vác** Hungary
152 C3 **Vacaria** Brazil
154 B2 **Vacaria, Serra** *hills* Brazil
135 B3 **Vacaville** U.S.A.
74 B2 **Vadodara** India
92 I1 **Vadsø** Norway
105 D2 **Vaduz** Liechtenstein
94 B1 **Vágar** *i.* Faroe Is
94 B1 **Vágur** Faroe Is
103 D2 **Váh** *r.* Slovakia
49 F3 **Vaiaku** Tuvalu
88 B2 **Vaida** Estonia

136 B3 Vail U.S.A.
79 C2 Vakīlābād Iran
108 B1 Valdagno Italy
89 C2 Valday Russia
89 D2 Valdayskaya Vozvyshennost' hills Russia
106 D2 Valdecañas, Embalse de resr Spain
93 G4 Valdemarsvik Sweden
106 C2 Valdepeñas Spain
153 B5 Valdés, Península pen. Arg.
153 A4 Valdivia Chile
130 C2 Val-d'Or Can.
143 D2 Valdosta U.S.A.
128 C2 Valemount Can.
105 C3 Valence France
107 C2 Valencia Spain
150 B1 Valencia Venez.
107 C2 Valencia, Golfo de g. Spain
100 A2 Valenciennes France
136 C2 Valentine U.S.A.
64 B1 Valenzuela Phil.
150 A1 Valera Venez.
109 C2 Valjevo Serbia
88 C2 Valka Latvia
93 H3 Valkeakoski Fin.
100 B2 Valkenswaard Neth.
91 D2 Valky Ukr.
55 D1 Valkyrie Dome Antarctica
145 D2 Valladolid Mex.
106 C1 Valladolid Spain
93 E4 Valle Norway
145 C2 Vallecillos Mex.
150 B1 Valle de la Pascua Venez.
144 B1 Valledupar Col.
145 C2 Valle Hermoso Mex.
135 B3 Vallejo U.S.A.
152 A3 Vallenar Chile
85 H5 Valletta Malta
137 D1 Valley City U.S.A.
134 B2 Valley Falls U.S.A.
128 C2 Valleyview Can.
107 C2 Valls Spain
129 D3 Val Marie Can.
88 C2 Valmiera Latvia
88 C3 Valozhyn Belarus
153 A4 Valparaíso Brazil
152 A4 Valparaíso Chile
105 C3 Vals, Tanjung c. Indon.
59 D3 Vals, Tanjung c. Indon.
74 B2 Valsad India
122 B2 Valspan S. Africa
91 D1 Valuyki Russia
106 B2 Valverde del Camino Spain
81 C2 Van Turkey
81 C2 Van, Lake salt l. Turkey
141 F1 Van Buren U.S.A.
128 B3 Vancouver Can.
134 B1 Vancouver U.S.A.
128 B3 Vancouver Island Can.
140 B3 Vandalia U.S.A.
123 C2 Vanderbijlpark S. Africa
128 B2 Vanderhoof Can.
88 C2 Vändra Estonia
93 F4 Vänern l. Sweden
93 F4 Vänersborg Sweden
121 □D3 Vangaindrano Madag.
Van Gölü salt l. Turkey see Van, Lake
138 C2 Van Horn U.S.A.
59 D3 Vanimo P.N.G.
83 K3 Vanino Russia
104 B2 Vannes France
Van Rees, Pegunungan mts Indon.
122 A3 Vanrhynsdorp S. Africa
93 H3 Vantaa Fin.
49 F4 Vanua Levu i. Fiji

48 E3 Vanuatu country S. Pacific Ocean
140 C2 Van Wert U.S.A.
122 B3 Van Wyksvlei S. Africa
122 B2 Van Zylsrus S. Africa
75 C2 Varanasi India
92 I1 Varangerfjorden sea chan. Norway
92 I1 Varangerhalvøya pen. Norway
109 C1 Varaždin Croatia
93 F4 Varberg Sweden
109 D2 Vardar r. Macedonia
93 E4 Varde Denmark
92 J1 Vardø Norway
100 D1 Varel Ger.
88 B3 Varna Lith.
108 A1 Varese Italy
155 C2 Varginha Brazil
93 I3 Varkaus Fin.
110 C2 Varna Bulg.
93 F4 Värnamo Sweden
155 D1 Várzea da Palma Brazil
86 C2 Varzino Russia
Vasa Fin. see Vaasa
88 C2 Vasknarva Estonia
110 C1 Vaslui Romania
93 G4 Västerås Sweden
93 G3 Västerdalälven r. Sweden
88 A2 Västerhaninge Sweden
93 G4 Västervik Sweden
108 B2 Vasto Italy
90 C1 Vasyl'kiv Ukr.
93 C2 Vatan France
108 B2 Vatican City Europe
92 □B3 Vatnajökull Iceland
110 C1 Vatra Dornei Romania
93 F4 Vättern l. Sweden
138 B2 Vaughn U.S.A.
105 C3 Vauvert France
49 G4 Vava'u Group is Tonga
88 B3 Vawkavysk Belarus
93 F4 Växjö Sweden
86 E1 Vaygach, Ostrov i. Russia
101 D1 Vechta Ger.
110 C2 Vedea r. Romania
100 C1 Veendam Neth.
100 B1 Veenendaal Neth.
129 C2 Vegreville Can.
106 B2 Vejer de la Frontera Spain
93 E4 Vejle Denmark
109 D2 Velbüzhdki Prokhod pass Bulg./Macedonia
100 B2 Veldhoven Neth.
109 B2 Velebit mts Croatia
100 C2 Velen Ger.
109 C1 Velenje Slovenia
109 D2 Veles Macedonia
106 C2 Vélez-Málaga Spain
155 D1 Velhas r. Brazil
109 D2 Velika Plana Serbia
88 C2 Velikaya r. Russia
89 D2 Velikiye Luki Russia
89 D2 Velikiy Novgorod Russia
86 D2 Velikiy Ustyug Russia
110 C2 Veliko Tarnovo Bulg.
109 B2 Veli Lošinj Croatia
89 D2 Velizh Russia
86 D2 Vel'sk Russia
101 F1 Velten Ger.
91 D1 Velykyy Burluk Ukr.
108 B2 Venafro Italy
104 C2 Vendôme France
89 E3 Venev Russia
Venezia Italy see Venice
150 B1 Venezuela country S. America
150 A1 Venezuela, Golfo de g. Venez.
108 B1 Venice Italy
143 D3 Venice U.S.A.

108 B1 Venice, Gulf of Europe
100 C2 Venlo Neth.
100 B2 Venray Neth.
88 B2 Venta r. Latvia/Lith.
88 B2 Venta Lith.
123 C3 Venterstad S. Africa
99 C3 Ventnor U.K.
88 B2 Ventspils Latvia
135 C4 Ventura U.S.A.
139 C3 Venustiano Carranza, Presa resr Mex.
107 C2 Vera Spain
145 C3 Veracruz Mex.
74 B2 Veraval India
108 A1 Verbania Italy
108 A1 Vercelli Italy
105 D3 Vercors reg. France
92 F3 Verdalsøra Norway
154 B1 Verde r. Goiás Brazil
154 B2 Verde r. Mato Grosso do Sul Brazil
144 B2 Verde r. Mex.
138 A2 Verde r. U.S.A.
155 D1 Verde Grande r. Brazil
101 D1 Verden (Aller) Ger.
154 B1 Verdinho, Serra de mts Brazil
108 A2 Verdon r. France
105 D2 Verdun France
123 C2 Vereeniging S. Africa
106 B1 Verín Spain
91 D3 Verkhnebakanskiy Russia
92 J2 Verkhnetulomskiy Russia
91 E1 Verkhniy Mamon Russia
89 E3 Verkhov'ye Russia
90 A2 Verkhovyna Ukr.
83 J2 Verkhoyanskiy Khrebet mts Russia
129 C2 Vermilion Can.
137 D2 Vermillion U.S.A.
130 A2 Vermillion Bay Can.
141 E2 Vermont state U.S.A.
135 E2 Vernal U.S.A.
128 C2 Vernon Can.
139 D2 Vernon U.S.A.
143 D3 Vero Beach U.S.A.
111 B2 Veroia Greece
108 B1 Verona Italy
104 C2 Versailles France
104 B2 Vertou France
123 C2 Verulam S. Africa
100 B2 Verviers Belgium
105 C2 Vervins France
105 D3 Vescovato Corsica France
87 E3 Veselaya, Gora mt. Russia
91 C2 Vesele Ukr.
105 D2 Vesoul France
92 F2 Vesterålen is Norway
94 B1 Vestfjorden sea chan. Norway
94 B1 Vestmanna Faroe Is
93 E3 Vestnes Norway
108 B2 Vesuvius vol. Italy
89 E2 Ves'yegonsk Russia
93 G4 Vetlanda Sweden
86 D3 Vetluga Russia
100 A2 Veurne Belgium
105 D2 Vevey Switz.
91 D1 Veydelevka Russia
80 B1 Vezirköprü Turkey
151 D2 Viana Brazil
106 B1 Viana do Castelo Port.
62 B1 Viangchan Laos see Vientiane
111 C3 Viangphoukha Laos
154 C1 Viannos Greece
154 C1 Vianópolis Brazil
108 B2 Viareggio Italy
93 E4 Viborg Denmark
109 C3 Vibo Valentia Italy
107 C1 Vic Spain

144 A1 **Vicente Guerrero** Mex.
108 B1 **Vicenza** Italy
105 C2 **Vichy** France
142 B2 **Vicksburg** U.S.A.
155 D2 **Viçosa** Brazil
52 A3 **Victor Harbor** Austr.
50 C1 **Victoria** *r.* Austr.
52 B3 **Victoria** *state* Austr.
128 B3 **Victoria** Can.
153 A4 **Victoria** Chile
113 K7 **Victoria** Seychelles
139 D3 **Victoria** U.S.A.
119 D3 **Victoria, Lake** Africa
52 B2 **Victoria, Lake** Austr.
62 A1 **Victoria, Mount** Myanmar
59 D3 **Victoria, Mount** P.N.G.
120 B2 **Victoria Falls** Zambia/Zimbabwe
126 D2 **Victoria Island** Can.
50 C1 **Victoria River Downs** Austr.
122 B3 **Victoria West** S. Africa
135 C4 **Victorville** U.S.A.
110 C2 **Videle** Romania
92 □A2 **Víðidalsá** Iceland
153 B5 **Viedma** Arg.
153 A5 **Viedma, Lago** *l.* Arg.
100 B2 **Vielsalm** Belgium
101 E2 **Vienenburg** Ger.
103 D2 **Vienna** Austria
105 C2 **Vienne** France
104 C2 **Vienne** *r.* France
62 B2 **Vientiane** Laos
100 C2 **Viersen** Ger.
104 C2 **Vierzon** France
144 B2 **Viesca** Mex.
109 C2 **Vieste** Italy
62 B2 **Vietnam** *country* Asia
62 B1 **Viêt Tri** Vietnam
64 B1 **Vigan** Phil.
108 A1 **Vigevano** Italy
106 B1 **Vigo** Spain
73 C3 **Vijayawada** India
92 □B3 **Vík** Iceland
129 C2 **Viking** Can.
150 C3 **Vila Bela da Santíssima Trindade** Brazil
106 B2 **Vila Franca de Xira** Port.
106 B1 **Vilagarcía de Arousa** Spain
106 B1 **Vilalba** Spain
106 B1 **Vila Nova de Gaia** Port.
107 D1 **Vilanova i la Geltrú** Spain
106 B1 **Vila Real** Port.
106 B1 **Vilar Formoso** Port.
155 D2 **Vila Velha** Brazil
150 A3 **Vilcabamba, Cordillera** *mts* Peru
92 G3 **Vilhelmina** Sweden
150 B3 **Vilhena** Brazil
88 C2 **Viljandi** Estonia
88 B3 **Vilkaviškis** Lith.
83 H1 **Vil'kitskogo, Proliv** *str.* Russia
144 B1 **Villa Ahumada** Mex.
106 B1 **Villablino** Spain
102 C2 **Villach** Austria
144 B2 **Villa de Cos** Mex.
152 B4 **Villa Dolores** Arg.
145 C3 **Villa Flores** Mex.
145 C2 **Villagrán** Mex.
145 C3 **Villahermosa** Mex.
144 A2 **Villa Insurgentes** Mex.
152 B4 **Villa María** Arg.
152 B3 **Villa Montes** Bol.
144 B2 **Villanueva** Mex.
106 B2 **Villanueva de la Serena** Spain
106 C2 **Villanueva de los Infantes** Spain
152 C3 **Villa Ocampo** Arg.
108 A3 **Villaputzu** *Sardinia* Italy
152 C3 **Villarrica** Para.
106 C2 **Villarrobledo** Spain
152 B3 **Villa Unión** Arg.
144 B2 **Villa Unión** *Durango* Mex.
144 B2 **Villa Unión** *Sinaloa* Mex.
150 A1 **Villavicencio** Col.
152 B3 **Villazon** Bol.
107 C2 **Villena** Spain
104 C3 **Villeneuve-sur-Lot** France
142 B2 **Ville Platte** U.S.A.
105 C2 **Villeurbanne** France
102 B2 **Villingen** Ger.
88 C3 **Vilnius** Lith.
91 C2 **Vil'nohirs'k** Ukr.
91 D2 **Vil'nyans'k** Ukr.
100 B2 **Vilvoorde** Belgium
88 C3 **Vilyeyka** Belarus
83 J2 **Vilyuy** *r.* Russia
93 G4 **Vimmerby** Sweden
153 A4 **Viña del Mar** Chile
107 D1 **Vinaròs** Spain
140 B3 **Vincennes** U.S.A.
55 G3 **Vincennes Bay** Antarctica
141 D3 **Vineland** U.S.A.
62 B2 **Vinh** Vietnam
63 B2 **Vinh Long** Vietnam
139 D1 **Vinita** U.S.A.
90 B2 **Vinnytsya** Ukr.
55 O2 **Vinson, Mount** *mt.* Antarctica
93 E3 **Vinstra** Norway
108 B1 **Vipiteno** Italy
64 B1 **Virac** Phil.
129 D3 **Virden** Can.
104 B2 **Vire** France
120 A2 **Virei** Angola
155 D1 **Virgem da Lapa** Brazil
138 A1 **Virgin** *r.* U.S.A.
123 C2 **Virginia** S. Africa
137 E1 **Virginia** U.S.A.
141 D3 **Virginia** *state* U.S.A.
141 D3 **Virginia Beach** U.S.A.
135 C3 **Virginia City** U.S.A.
147 D3 **Virgin Islands (U.K.)** *terr.* West Indies
147 D3 **Virgin Islands (U.S.A.)** *terr.* West Indies
63 B2 **Virôchey** Cambodia
109 C1 **Virovitica** Croatia
100 B3 **Virton** Belgium
88 B2 **Virtsu** Estonia
109 C2 **Vis** *i.* Croatia
88 C2 **Visaginas** Lith.
135 C3 **Visalia** U.S.A.
74 B2 **Visavadar** India
64 B1 **Visayan Sea** Phil.
93 G4 **Visby** Sweden
126 D2 **Viscount Melville Sound** *sea chan.* Can.
151 D2 **Viseu** Brazil
106 B1 **Viseu** Port.
73 C3 **Vishakhapatnam** India
88 C2 **Viški** Latvia
109 C2 **Visoko** Bos. & Herz.
103 D1 **Vistula** *r.* Pol.
108 B2 **Viterbo** Italy
49 F4 **Viti Levu** *i.* Fiji
83 I3 **Vitim** *r.* Russia
155 D2 **Vitória** Brazil
151 D3 **Vitória da Conquista** Brazil
106 C1 **Vitoria-Gasteiz** Spain
104 B2 **Vitré** France
105 C2 **Vitry-le-François** France
89 D2 **Vitsyebsk** Belarus
105 D2 **Vittel** France
108 B3 **Vittoria** *Sicily* Italy
108 B1 **Vittorio Veneto** Italy
106 B1 **Viveiro** Spain
144 A2 **Vizcaíno, Sierra** *mts* Mex.
110 C2 **Vize** Turkey
73 C3 **Vizianagaram** India
100 B2 **Vlaardingen** Neth.
87 D4 **Vladikavkaz** Russia
89 F2 **Vladimir** Russia
66 B2 **Vladivostok** Russia
109 D2 **Vlasotince** Serbia
100 B1 **Vlieland** *i.* Neth.
100 A2 **Vlissingen** Neth.
109 C2 **Vlorë** Albania
102 C2 **Vöcklabruck** Austria
101 D2 **Vogelsberg** *hills* Ger.
119 D3 **Voi** Kenya
105 D2 **Voiron** France
131 D1 **Voisey's Bay** Can.
109 C1 **Vojvodina** *prov.* Serbia
92 J3 **Voknavolok** Russia
Volcano Bay Japan *see* **Uchiura-wan**
89 E2 **Volga** Russia
89 F2 **Volga** *r.* Russia
87 D4 **Volgodonsk** Russia
87 D4 **Volgograd** Russia
89 D2 **Volkhov** Russia
89 D1 **Volkhov** *r.* Russia
101 E2 **Volkstedt** Ger.
91 D2 **Volnovakha** Ukr.
90 B2 **Volochys'k** Ukr.
91 D2 **Volodars'ke** Ukr.
90 B1 **Volodars'k-Volyns'kyy** Ukr.
90 B1 **Volodymyrets'** Ukr.
90 A1 **Volodymyr-Volyns'kyy** Ukr.
89 E2 **Vologda** Russia
89 E2 **Volokolamsk** Russia
91 D1 **Volokonovka** Russia
111 B3 **Volos** Greece
88 C2 **Volosovo** Russia
89 D2 **Volot** Russia
89 E3 **Volovo** Russia
87 D3 **Vol'sk** Russia
114 C4 **Volta, Lake** *resr* Ghana
155 D2 **Volta Redonda** Brazil
87 D4 **Volzhskiy** Russia
92 □C2 **Vopnafjörður** Iceland
88 C3 **Voranava** Belarus
86 F2 **Vorkuta** Russia
88 B2 **Vormsi** *i.* Estonia
89 E3 **Voronezh** Russia
89 E3 **Voronezh** *r.* Russia
91 E1 **Vorontsovka** Russia
91 C2 **Vorskla** *r.* Russia
88 C2 **Võrtsjärv** *l.* Estonia
88 C2 **Võru** Estonia
122 B3 **Vosburg** S. Africa
105 D2 **Vosges** *mts* France
89 E2 **Voskresensk** Russia
93 E3 **Voss** Norway
83 H3 **Vostochnyy Sayan** *mts* Russia
86 E3 **Votkinsk** Russia
154 C2 **Votuporanga** Brazil
100 B3 **Vouziers** France
92 J2 **Voynitsa** Russia
91 C2 **Voznesens'k** Ukr.
93 E4 **Vrådal** Norway
66 B2 **Vrangel'** Russia
Vrangelya, Ostrov *i.* Russia *see* **Wrangel Island**
109 D2 **Vranje** Serbia
110 C2 **Vratnik** *pass* Bulg.
110 B2 **Vratsa** Bulg.
109 C1 **Vrbas** *r.* Bos. & Herz.
109 C1 **Vrbas** Serbia
122 A3 **Vredenburg** S. Africa
122 A3 **Vredendal** S. Africa
100 B3 **Vresse-sur-Semois** Belgium
109 D1 **Vršac** Serbia
122 B2 **Vryburg** S. Africa
123 D2 **Vryheid** S. Africa

89 D1	Vsevolozhsk Russia	
	Vučitrn Kosovo see Vushtrri	
109 C1	Vukovar Croatia	
86 E2	Vuktyl Russia	
123 C2	Vukuzakhe S. Africa	
109 B3	Vulcano, Isola i. Italy	
63 B2	Vung Tau Vietnam	
109 D2	Vushtrri Kosovo	
74 B2	Vyara India	
	Vyatka Russia see Kirov	
89 D2	Vyaz'ma Russia	
93 I3	Vyborg Russia	
88 C2	Vyerkhnyadzvinsk Belarus	
87 D3	Vyksa Russia	
90 B2	Vylkove Ukr.	
90 A2	Vynohradiv Ukr.	
89 D2	Vypolzovo Russia	
89 D2	Vyritsa Russia	
91 D2	Vyselki Russia	
90 C1	Vyshhorod Ukr.	
89 D2	Vyshniy-Volochek Russia	
103 D2	Vyškov Czech Rep.	
86 C2	Vytegra Russia	

W

114 B3	Wa Ghana	
100 B2	Waal r. Neth.	
100 B2	Waalwijk Neth.	
128 C2	Wabasca r. Can.	
128 C2	Wabasca-Desmarais Can.	
140 B3	Wabash r. U.S.A.	
129 E2	Wabowden Can.	
143 D3	Waccasassa Bay U.S.A.	
101 D2	Wächtersbach Ger.	
139 D2	Waco U.S.A.	
115 D2	Waddan Libya	
	Waddeneilanden is Neth. see	
	West Frisian Islands	
100 B1	Waddenzee sea chan. Neth.	
128 B2	Waddington, Mount Can.	
100 B1	Waddinxveen Neth.	
129 D2	Wadena Can.	
137 D1	Wadena U.S.A.	
74 A2	Wadh Pak.	
116 B2	Wadi Halfa Sudan	
116 B3	Wad Madani Sudan	
70 C2	Wafangdian China	
100 B2	Wageningen Neth.	
127 F2	Wager Bay Can.	
53 C3	Wagga Wagga Austr.	
137 D2	Wahoo U.S.A.	
137 D1	Wahpeton U.S.A.	
54 B2	Waiau r. N.Z.	
59 C3	Waigeo i. Indon.	
58 B3	Waikabubak Indon.	
52 A2	Waikerie Austr.	
54 B2	Waimate N.Z.	
75 B3	Wainganga r. India	
58 C3	Waingapu Indon.	
129 C2	Wainwright Can.	
54 B2	Waiouru N.Z.	
54 C1	Waipara N.Z.	
54 C1	Waipawa N.Z.	
54 B2	Wairau r. N.Z.	
54 C1	Wairoa N.Z.	
54 B2	Waitaki r. N.Z.	
54 B1	Waitara N.Z.	
54 B1	Waiuku N.Z.	
119 E2	Wajir Kenya	
67 C3	Wakasa-wan b. Japan	
54 A3	Wakatipu, Lake N.Z.	
129 D2	Wakaw Can.	
67 C4	Wakayama Japan	
136 D3	WaKeeney U.S.A.	
54 B2	Wakefield N.Z.	

98 C2	Wakefield U.K.	
48 F1	Wake Island N. Pacific Ocean	
66 D1	Wakkanai Japan	
123 D2	Wakkerstroom S. Africa	
103 D1	Wałbrzych Pol.	
53 D2	Walcha Austr.	
100 C1	Walchum Ger.	
103 D1	Wałcz Pol.	
99 B2	Wales admin. div. U.K.	
53 C2	Walgett Austr.	
119 C3	Walikale Dem. Rep. Congo	
135 C3	Walker Lake U.S.A.	
52 A2	Wallaroo Austr.	
98 B2	Wallasey U.K.	
134 C1	Walla Walla U.S.A.	
101 D3	Walldürn Ger.	
53 C2	Wallendbeen Austr.	
49 G3	Wallis and Futuna Islands	
	terr. S. Pacific Ocean	
96 □	Walls U.K.	
98 B1	Walney, Isle of i. U.K.	
99 C2	Walsall U.K.	
136 C3	Walsenburg U.S.A.	
101 D1	Walsrode Ger.	
143 D2	Walterboro U.S.A.	
120 A3	Walvis Bay Namibia	
119 C2	Wamba Dem. Rep. Congo	
52 B1	Wanaaring Austr.	
54 A2	Wanaka N.Z.	
54 A2	Wanaka, Lake N.Z.	
130 B3	Wanapitei Lake Can.	
66 B1	Wanda Shan mts China	
62 A1	Wanding China	
54 C1	Wanganui N.Z.	
53 C3	Wangaratta Austr.	
65 B1	Wangqing China	
62 A1	Wan Hsa-la Myanmar	
71 B4	Wanning China	
100 B2	Wanroij Neth.	
99 C3	Wantage U.K.	
70 A2	Wanyuan China	
70 A2	Wanzhou China	
73 B3	Warangal India	
101 D2	Warburg Ger.	
50 B2	Warburton Austr.	
52 A1	Warburton watercourse Austr.	
75 B2	Wardha India	
96 C1	Ward Hill U.K.	
128 B2	Ware Can.	
101 F1	Waren (Müritz) Ger.	
100 C2	Warendorf Ger.	
53 D1	Warialda Austr.	
122 A2	Warmbad Namibia	
135 C3	Warm Springs U.S.A.	
134 C2	Warner Lakes U.S.A.	
143 D2	Warner Robins U.S.A.	
152 B2	Warnes Bol.	
52 B3	Warracknabeal Austr.	
53 C2	Warrego r. Austr.	
53 C2	Warren Austr.	
142 B2	Warren AR U.S.A.	
140 C2	Warren OH U.S.A.	
141 D2	Warren PA U.S.A.	
97 C1	Warrenpoint U.K.	
137 E3	Warrensburg U.S.A.	
122 B2	Warrenton S. Africa	
115 C4	Warri Nigeria	
98 B2	Warrington U.K.	
52 B3	Warrnambool Austr.	
103 E1	Warsaw Pol.	
	Warszawa Pol. see Warsaw	
103 C1	Warta r. Pol.	
53 D1	Warwick Austr.	
99 C2	Warwick U.K.	
135 C3	Wasco U.S.A.	
136 C1	Washburn U.S.A.	
141 D3	Washington DC U.S.A.	

137 E2	Washington IA U.S.A.	
140 B3	Washington IN U.S.A.	
137 E3	Washington MO U.S.A.	
143 E1	Washington NC U.S.A.	
140 C2	Washington PA U.S.A.	
134 B1	Washington state U.S.A.	
141 E2	Washington, Mount U.S.A.	
140 C3	Washington Court House	
	U.S.A.	
74 A2	Washuk Pak.	
130 C1	Waskaganish Can.	
129 E2	Waskaiowaka Lake Can.	
122 A2	Wasser Namibia	
130 C2	Waswanipi, Lac l. Can.	
58 C3	Watampone Indon.	
141 E2	Waterbury U.S.A.	
129 D2	Waterbury Lake Can.	
97 C2	Waterford Ireland	
97 C2	Waterford Harbour Ireland	
137 E2	Waterloo U.S.A.	
123 C1	Waterpoort S. Africa	
141 D2	Watertown NY U.S.A.	
137 D2	Watertown SD U.S.A.	
140 B2	Watertown WI U.S.A.	
141 F2	Waterville U.S.A.	
99 C3	Watford U.K.	
136 C1	Watford City U.S.A.	
129 D2	Wathaman r. Can.	
139 D1	Watonga U.S.A.	
129 D2	Watrous Can.	
119 C2	Watsa Dem. Rep. Congo	
140 B2	Watseka U.S.A.	
118 C3	Watsi Kengo	
	Dem. Rep. Congo	
128 B1	Watson Lake Can.	
135 B3	Watsonville U.S.A.	
59 C3	Watubela, Kepulauan is	
	Indon.	
59 D3	Wau P.N.G.	
117 A4	Wau South Sudan	
53 D2	Wauchope Austr.	
140 B2	Waukegan U.S.A.	
139 D2	Waurika U.S.A.	
140 B2	Wausau U.S.A.	
99 D2	Waveney r. U.K.	
137 E2	Waverly U.S.A.	
143 D2	Waycross U.S.A.	
137 D2	Wayne U.S.A.	
143 D2	Waynesboro GA U.S.A.	
141 D3	Waynesboro VA U.S.A.	
143 D1	Waynesville U.S.A.	
74 B1	Wazirabad Pak.	
98 C1	Wear r. U.K.	
139 D2	Weatherford U.S.A.	
134 B2	Weaverville U.S.A.	
130 B1	Webequie Can.	
117 C4	Webi Shabeelle r. Somalia	
137 D1	Webster U.S.A.	
137 E2	Webster City U.S.A.	
55 Q2	Weddell Sea Antarctica	
100 B2	Weert Neth.	
53 C2	Wee Waa Austr.	
100 C2	Wegberg Ger.	
103 E1	Węgorzewo Pol.	
101 F3	Weiden in der Oberpfalz Ger.	
70 B2	Weifang China	
70 C2	Weihai China	
53 C1	Weilmoringle Austr.	
101 E2	Weimar Ger.	
70 A2	Weinan China	
51 D1	Weipa Austr.	
53 C2	Weir r. Austr.	
140 C2	Weirton U.S.A.	
62 B1	Weishan China	
101 E2	Weißenfels Ger.	
102 C2	Weißkugel mt. Austria/Italy	
103 D1	Wejherowo Pol.	
128 C1	Wekweètì Can.	

140 C3 **Welch** U.S.A.
117 B3 **Weldiya** Eth.
123 C2 **Welkom** S. Africa
99 C2 **Welland** *r.* U.K.
51 C1 **Wellesley Islands** Austr.
53 C2 **Wellington** Austr.
54 B2 **Wellington** N.Z.
122 A3 **Wellington** S. Africa
137 D3 **Wellington** U.S.A.
153 A5 **Wellington, Isla** *i.* Chile
53 C3 **Wellington, Lake** Austr.
128 B2 **Wells** Can.
99 B3 **Wells** U.K.
134 D2 **Wells** U.S.A.
50 B2 **Wells, Lake** *imp. l.* Austr.
54 B1 **Wellsford** N.Z.
98 D2 **Wells-next-the-Sea** U.K.
102 C2 **Wels** Austria
99 B2 **Welshpool** U.K.
123 C2 **Wembesi** S. Africa
130 C1 **Wemindji** Can.
134 B1 **Wenatchee** U.S.A.
154 C2 **Wenceslau Braz** Brazil
71 B4 **Wencheng** China
114 B4 **Wenchi** Ghana
70 C2 **Wendeng** China
101 E1 **Wendisch Evern** Ger.
117 B4 **Wendo** Eth.
134 D2 **Wendover** U.S.A.
71 B3 **Wengyuan** China
71 C3 **Wenling** China
71 A3 **Wenshan** China
52 B2 **Wentworth** Austr.
71 C3 **Wenzhou** China
123 C2 **Wepener** S. Africa
122 B2 **Werda** Botswana
101 F2 **Werdau** Ger.
101 F1 **Werder (Havel)** Ger.
101 F3 **Wernberg-Köblitz** Ger.
101 E2 **Wernigerode** Ger.
101 D2 **Werra** *r.* Ger.
53 D2 **Werris Creek** Austr.
101 D3 **Wertheim** Ger.
100 C2 **Wesel** Ger.
101 E1 **Wesendorf** Ger.
101 D1 **Weser** *r.* Ger.
101 D1 **Weser** *sea chan.* Ger.
51 C1 **Wessel, Cape** Austr.
51 C1 **Wessel Islands** Austr.
123 C2 **Wesselton** S. Africa
80 B2 **West Bank** *disp. terr.* Asia
140 B2 **West Bend** U.S.A.
99 C2 **West Bromwich** U.K.
100 C2 **Westerburg** Ger.
100 C1 **Westerholt** Ger.
50 B2 **Western Australia** *state* Austr.
122 B3 **Western Cape** *prov.* S. Africa
116 A2 **Western Desert** Egypt
73 B3 **Western Ghats** *mts* India
114 A2 **Western Sahara** *disp. terr.* Africa
100 A2 **Westerschelde** *est.* Neth.
100 C1 **Westerstede** Ger.
100 C2 **Westerwald** *hills* Ger.
153 B6 **West Falkland** *i.* Falkland Is
140 B3 **West Frankfort** U.S.A.
100 B1 **West Frisian Islands** *is* Neth.
147 D2 **West Indies** *is* Caribbean Sea
96 A1 **West Loch Roag** *b.* U.K.
128 C2 **Westlock** Can.
100 B2 **Westmalle** Belgium
142 B1 **West Memphis** U.S.A.
140 C3 **Weston** U.S.A.
99 B3 **Weston-super-Mare** U.K.
143 D3 **West Palm Beach** U.S.A.
137 E3 **West Plains** U.S.A.
137 D2 **West Point** U.S.A.
97 B2 **Westport** Ireland
54 B2 **Westport** N.Z.
129 D2 **Westray** Can.
96 C1 **Westray** *i.* U.K.
100 B1 **West-Terschelling** Neth.
140 C3 **West Virginia** *state* U.S.A.
53 C2 **West Wyalong** Austr.
134 D2 **West Yellowstone** U.S.A.
59 C3 **Wetar** *i.* Indon.
128 C2 **Wetaskiwin** Can.
101 D2 **Wetzlar** Ger.
59 D3 **Wewak** P.N.G.
97 C2 **Wexford** Ireland
129 D2 **Weyakwin** Can.
129 D3 **Weyburn** Can.
101 D1 **Weyhe** Ger.
99 B3 **Weymouth** U.K.
54 C1 **Whakatane** N.Z.
129 E1 **Whale Cove** Can.
96 □ **Whalsay** *i.* U.K.
54 B1 **Whangarei** N.Z.
98 C2 **Wharfe** *r.* U.K.
139 D3 **Wharton** U.S.A.
128 C1 **Whatî** Can.
136 B2 **Wheatland** U.S.A.
138 B1 **Wheeler Peak** *NM* U.S.A.
135 D3 **Wheeler Peak** *NV* U.S.A.
140 C2 **Wheeling** U.S.A.
98 B1 **Whernside** *h.* U.K.
128 B2 **Whistler** Can.
98 C1 **Whitby** U.K.
142 B2 **White** *r.* U.S.A.
50 B2 **White, Lake** *imp. l.* Austr.
131 E2 **White Bay** Can.
136 C1 **White Butte** *mt.* U.S.A.
52 B2 **White Cliffs** Austr.
128 C2 **Whitecourt** Can.
134 D1 **Whitefish** U.S.A.
98 B1 **Whitehaven** U.K.
97 D1 **Whitehead** U.K.
128 A1 **Whitehorse** Can.
142 B3 **White Lake** U.S.A.
135 C3 **White Mountain Peak** U.S.A.
116 B3 **White Nile** *r.* South Sudan/Uganda
86 C2 **White Sea** Russia
134 D1 **White Sulphur Springs** U.S.A.
143 E2 **Whiteville** U.S.A.
114 B3 **White Volta** *r.* Burkina Faso/Ghana
138 B2 **Whitewater Baldy** *mt.* U.S.A.
130 B1 **Whitewater Lake** Can.
129 D2 **Whitewood** Can.
96 B3 **Whithorn** U.K.
54 C1 **Whitianga** N.Z.
135 C3 **Whitney, Mount** U.S.A.
51 D2 **Whitsunday Island** Austr.
52 A2 **Whyalla** Austr.
100 A2 **Wichelen** Belgium
137 D3 **Wichita** U.S.A.
139 D2 **Wichita Falls** U.S.A.
96 C1 **Wick** U.K.
138 A2 **Wickenburg** U.S.A.
97 C2 **Wicklow** Ireland
97 D2 **Wicklow Head** Ireland
97 C2 **Wicklow Mountains** Ireland
98 B2 **Widnes** U.K.
101 D1 **Wiehengebirge** *hills* Ger.
100 C2 **Wiehl** Ger.
103 D1 **Wieluń** Pol.
Wien Austria *see* **Vienna**
103 D2 **Wiener Neustadt** Austria
100 B1 **Wieringerwerf** Neth.
100 D2 **Wiesbaden** Ger.
100 C1 **Wiesmoor** Ger.
103 D1 **Wieżyca** *h.* Pol.
99 C3 **Wight, Isle of** *i.* U.K.
96 B3 **Wigtown** U.K.
100 B2 **Wijchen** Neth.
52 B2 **Wilcannia** Austr.
123 C3 **Wild Coast** S. Africa
123 C2 **Wilge** *r.* S. Africa
100 D1 **Wilhelmshaven** Ger.
141 D2 **Wilkes-Barre** U.S.A.
55 H3 **Wilkes Land** *reg.* Antarctica
129 D2 **Wilkie** Can.
138 B2 **Willcox** U.S.A.
100 B2 **Willebroek** Belgium
147 D3 **Willemstad** Curaçao
52 B3 **William, Mount** Austr.
52 A1 **William Creek** Austr.
138 A1 **Williams** U.S.A.
141 D3 **Williamsburg** U.S.A.
128 B2 **Williams Lake** Can.
140 C3 **Williamson** U.S.A.
141 D2 **Williamsport** U.S.A.
143 E1 **Williamston** U.S.A.
122 B3 **Williston** S. Africa
136 C1 **Williston** U.S.A.
128 B2 **Williston Lake** Can.
135 B3 **Willits** U.S.A.
137 D1 **Willmar** U.S.A.
122 B3 **Willowmore** S. Africa
123 C3 **Willowvale** S. Africa
50 B2 **Wills, Lake** *imp. l.* Austr.
52 A3 **Willunga** Austr.
52 A2 **Wilmington** Austr.
141 D3 **Wilmington** *DE* U.S.A.
143 E2 **Wilmington** *NC* U.S.A.
100 D2 **Wilnsdorf** Ger.
143 E1 **Wilson** U.S.A.
53 C3 **Wilson's Promontory** *pen.* Austr.
100 B3 **Wiltz** Lux.
50 B2 **Wiluna** Austr.
99 C3 **Winchester** U.K.
140 C3 **Winchester** *KY* U.S.A.
141 D3 **Winchester** *VA* U.S.A.
98 B1 **Windermere** *l.* U.K.
120 A3 **Windhoek** Namibia
137 D2 **Windom** U.S.A.
51 D2 **Windorah** Austr.
136 B2 **Wind River Range** *mts* U.S.A.
53 D2 **Windsor** Austr.
130 B2 **Windsor** Can.
147 D3 **Windward Islands** Caribbean Sea
147 C3 **Windward Passage** Cuba/Haiti
137 D3 **Winfield** U.S.A.
100 A2 **Wingene** Belgium
53 D2 **Wingham** Austr.
130 B1 **Winisk** *r.* Can.
130 B1 **Winisk (abandoned)** Can.
130 B1 **Winisk Lake** Can.
63 A2 **Winkana** Myanmar
129 E3 **Winkler** Can.
114 B4 **Winneba** Ghana
140 B2 **Winnebago, Lake** U.S.A.
134 C2 **Winnemucca** U.S.A.
136 C2 **Winner** U.S.A.
142 B2 **Winnfield** U.S.A.
137 E1 **Winnibigoshish, Lake** U.S.A.
129 E3 **Winnipeg** Can.
129 E2 **Winnipeg** *r.* Can.
129 E2 **Winnipeg, Lake** Can.
129 D2 **Winnipegosis, Lake** Can.
141 E2 **Winnipesaukee, Lake** U.S.A.
142 B2 **Winnsboro** U.S.A.
137 E2 **Winona** *MN* U.S.A.
142 C2 **Winona** *MS* U.S.A.
100 C1 **Winschoten** Neth.
101 D1 **Winsen (Aller)** Ger.
101 E1 **Winsen (Luhe)** Ger.
138 A1 **Winslow** U.S.A.
143 D1 **Winston-Salem** U.S.A.
101 D2 **Winterberg** Ger.
143 D3 **Winter Haven** U.S.A.

100 C2 **Winterswijk** Neth.
105 D2 **Winterthur** Switz.
51 D2 **Winton** Austr.
54 A3 **Winton** N.Z.
52 A2 **Wirrabara** Austr.
99 D2 **Wisbech** U.K.
140 A2 **Wisconsin** *r.* U.S.A.
140 B2 **Wisconsin** *state* U.S.A.
140 B2 **Wisconsin Rapids** U.S.A.
Wisła *r.* Pol. *see* **Vistula**
101 E1 **Wismar** Ger.
98 D2 **Withernsea** U.K.
100 B1 **Witmarsum** Neth.
99 C3 **Witney** U.K.
123 D2 **Witrivier** S. Africa
101 F2 **Wittenberg, Lutherstadt** Ger.
101 E1 **Wittenberge** Ger.
101 E1 **Wittenburg** Ger.
101 E1 **Wittingen** Ger.
100 C3 **Wittlich** Ger.
100 C1 **Wittmund** Ger.
101 F1 **Wittstock/Dosse** Ger.
120 A3 **Witvlei** Namibia
101 D2 **Witzenhausen** Ger.
103 D1 **Władysławowo** Pol.
103 D1 **Włocławek** Pol.
53 C3 **Wodonga** Austr.
59 C3 **Wokam** *i.* Indon.
99 C3 **Woking** U.K.
101 F2 **Wolfen** Ger.
101 E1 **Wolfenbüttel** Ger.
101 D2 **Wolfhagen** Ger.
136 B1 **Wolf Point** U.S.A.
101 E1 **Wolfsburg** Ger.
100 C3 **Wolfstein** Ger.
131 D2 **Wolfville** Can.
102 C1 **Wolgast** Ger.
102 C1 **Wolin** Pol.
129 D2 **Wollaston Lake** Can.
129 D2 **Wollaston Lake** Can.
126 D2 **Wollaston Peninsula** Can.
53 D2 **Wollongong** Austr.
101 E2 **Wolmirsleben** Ger.
101 E1 **Wolmirstedt** Ger.
100 C1 **Wolvega** Neth.
99 B2 **Wolverhampton** U.K.
65 B2 **Wonju** S. Korea
128 B2 **Wonowon** Can.
65 B2 **Wŏnsan** N. Korea
53 C3 **Wonthaggi** Austr.
52 A2 **Woocalla** Austr.
51 C1 **Woodah, Isle** *i.* Austr.
99 D2 **Woodbridge** U.K.
136 B3 **Woodland Park** U.S.A.
50 C2 **Woodroffe, Mount** Austr.
51 C1 **Woods, Lake** *imp. l.* Austr.
129 E3 **Woods, Lake of the** Can./U.S.A.
53 C3 **Woods Point** Austr.
131 D2 **Woodstock** *N.B.* Can.
140 C2 **Woodstock** *Ont.* Can.
54 C2 **Woodville** N.Z.
139 D1 **Woodward** U.S.A.
53 D2 **Woolgoolga** Austr.
52 A2 **Woomera** Austr.
140 C2 **Wooster** U.S.A.
122 A3 **Worcester** S. Africa
99 B2 **Worcester** U.K.
141 E2 **Worcester** U.S.A.
102 C2 **Wörgl** Austria
98 B1 **Workington** U.K.
98 C2 **Worksop** U.K.
136 B2 **Worland** U.S.A.
101 D3 **Worms** Ger.
99 C3 **Worthing** U.K.
137 D2 **Worthington** U.S.A.
58 C3 **Wotu** Indon.
59 C3 **Wowoni** *i.* Indon.
83 N2 **Wrangel Island** Russia
128 A2 **Wrangell** U.S.A.
96 B1 **Wrath, Cape** U.K.
136 C2 **Wray** U.S.A.
122 A2 **Wreck Point** S. Africa
98 B2 **Wrexham** U.K.
136 B2 **Wright** U.S.A.
63 A2 **Wrightmyo** India
128 B1 **Wrigley** Can.
103 D1 **Wrocław** Pol.
103 D1 **Września** Pol.
70 B2 **Wu'an** China
70 A2 **Wuhai** China
70 B2 **Wuhan** China
70 B2 **Wuhu** China
Wujin China *see* **Changzhou**
115 C4 **Wukari** Nigeria
62 B1 **Wuliang Shan** *mts* China
59 C3 **Wuliaru** *i.* Indon.
71 A3 **Wumeng Shan** *mts* China
130 B1 **Wunnummin Lake** Can.
101 F2 **Wunsiedel** Ger.
101 D1 **Wunstorf** Ger.
62 A1 **Wuntho** Myanmar
100 C2 **Wuppertal** Ger.
122 A3 **Wuppertal** S. Africa
101 E2 **Wurzbach** Ger.
101 D3 **Würzburg** Ger.
101 F2 **Wurzen** Ger.
68 C2 **Wuwei** China
70 A2 **Wuxi** *Chongqing* China
70 C2 **Wuxi** *Jiangsu* China
Wuxing China *see* **Huzhou**
71 A3 **Wuxuan** China
Wuyang China *see* **Zhenyuan**
69 E1 **Wuyiling** China
71 B3 **Wuyishan** China
71 B3 **Wuyi Shan** *mts* China
70 A1 **Wuyuan** China
71 A4 **Wuzhishan** China
70 A2 **Wuzhong** China
71 B3 **Wuzhou** China
53 C2 **Wyangala Reservoir** Austr.
52 B3 **Wycheproof** Austr.
99 B3 **Wye** *r.* U.K.
50 B1 **Wyndham** Austr.
142 B1 **Wynne** U.S.A.
129 D2 **Wynyard** Can.
136 B2 **Wyoming** *state* U.S.A.
103 E1 **Wyszków** Pol.
140 C3 **Wytheville** U.S.A.

X

117 D3 **Xaafuun** Somalia
62 B2 **Xaignabouli** Laos
121 C3 **Xai-Xai** Moz.
145 C3 **Xalapa** Mex.
70 A1 **Xamba** China
62 A1 **Xamgyi'nyilha** China
62 B1 **Xam Nua** Laos
120 A2 **Xangongo** Angola
81 C2 **Xankändi** Azer.
111 B2 **Xanthi** Greece
150 B3 **Xapuri** Brazil
107 C2 **Xàtiva** Spain
Xiaguan China *see* **Dali**
71 B3 **Xiamen** China
70 A2 **Xi'an** China
70 A3 **Xianfeng** China
Xiangfan China *see* **Xiangyang**
Xianggang *aut. reg.* China *see* **Hong Kong**
Xianggang China *see* **Hong Kong**
Xiangjiang China *see* **Huichang**
71 B3 **Xiangtan** China
70 B2 **Xiangyang** China
70 B2 **Xiantao** China
70 A2 **Xianyang** China
70 B2 **Xiaogan** China
69 E1 **Xiao Hinggan Ling** *mts* China
70 C2 **Xiaoshan** China
62 B1 **Xichang** China
145 C2 **Xicohténcatl** Mex.
71 A3 **Xifeng** China
75 C2 **Xigazê** China
83 I4 **Xilinhot** China
70 B2 **Xincai** China
68 C2 **Xinghai** China
70 B2 **Xinghua** China
71 B3 **Xingning** China
70 A2 **Xingping** China
70 B2 **Xingtai** China
151 C2 **Xingu** *r.* Brazil
71 A3 **Xingyi** China
71 B3 **Xinhua** China
68 C2 **Xining** China
Xinjiang Uygur Autonomous Region *aut. reg.* China *see* **Xinjiang Uygur Zizhiqu**
75 C1 **Xinjiang Uygur Zizhiqu** *aut. reg.* China
Xinjing China *see* **Jingxi**
69 D2 **Xinkou** China
65 A1 **Xinmin** China
71 B3 **Xinning** China
70 B2 **Xintai** China
70 B2 **Xinxiang** China
70 B2 **Xinyang** China
70 B2 **Xinyi** China
71 C3 **Xinying** Taiwan
71 B3 **Xinyu** China
70 B2 **Xinzhou** China
71 C3 **Xinzhu** Taiwan
106 B1 **Xinzo de Limia** Spain
Xiongshan China *see* **Zhenghe**
68 C2 **Xiqing Shan** *mts* China
151 D3 **Xique-Xique** Brazil
70 A1 **Xishanzui** China
71 A3 **Xiushan** China
71 B3 **Xiuying** China
70 B2 **Xixia** China
Xixón Spain *see* **Gijón/Xixón**
68 B2 **Xizang Zizhiqu** *aut. reg.* China
76 B2 **Xo'jayli** Uzbek.
70 B2 **Xuancheng** China
71 A3 **Xuanwei** China
70 B2 **Xuchang** China
Xucheng China *see* **Xuwen**
117 C4 **Xuddur** Somalia
Xujiang China *see* **Guangchang**
71 B3 **Xun Jiang** *r.* China
71 B3 **Xunwu** China
107 C2 **Xúquer, Riu** *r.* Spain
71 B3 **Xuwen** China
71 A3 **Xuyong** China
70 B2 **Xuzhou** China

Y

117 B4 **Yabēlo** Eth.
69 D1 **Yablonovyy Khrebet** *mts* Russia
143 D1 **Yadkin** *r.* U.S.A.
75 C2 **Yadong** China

89 E2 **Yagnitsa** Russia
118 B1 **Yagoua** Cameroon
128 C3 **Yahk** Can.
144 B2 **Yahualica** Mex.
80 B2 **Yahyalı** Turkey
67 C4 **Yaizu** Japan
134 B1 **Yakima** U.S.A.
114 B3 **Yako** Burkina Faso
66 D2 **Yakumo** Japan
126 B3 **Yakutat** U.S.A.
83 J2 **Yakutsk** Russia
91 D2 **Yakymivka** Ukr.
63 B3 **Yala** Thai.
53 C3 **Yallourn** Austr.
111 C2 **Yalova** Turkey
91 C3 **Yalta** Ukr.
65 A1 **Yalu Jiang** *r.* China/N. Korea
67 D3 **Yamagata** Japan
67 B4 **Yamaguchi** Japan
Yamal, Poluostrov *pen.* Russia *see* **Yamal Peninsula**
86 F1 **Yamal Peninsula** Russia
53 D1 **Yamba** Austr.
117 A4 **Yambio** South Sudan
110 C2 **Yambol** Bulg.
86 G2 **Yamburg** Russia
62 A1 **Yamethin** Myanmar
114 B4 **Yamoussoukro** Côte d'Ivoire
90 B2 **Yampil'** Ukr.
75 C2 **Yamuna** *r.* India
75 D2 **Yamzho Yumco** *l.* China
83 K2 **Yana** *r.* Russia
70 A2 **Yan'an** China
150 A3 **Yanaoca** Peru
78 A2 **Yanbu' al Baḥr** Saudi Arabia
70 C2 **Yancheng** China
50 A3 **Yanchep** Austr.
70 B2 **Yangcheng** China
71 B3 **Yangchun** China
65 B2 **Yangdok** N. Korea
71 B3 **Yangjiang** China
Yangôn Myanmar *see* **Rangoon**
70 B2 **Yangquan** China
71 B3 **Yangshuo** China
70 C3 **Yangtze** *r.* China
69 E2 **Yangtze, Mouth of the** China
70 B2 **Yangzhou** China
65 B1 **Yanji** China
137 D2 **Yankton** U.S.A.
83 K2 **Yano-Indigirskaya Nizmennost'** *lowland* Russia
83 K2 **Yanskiy Zaliv** *g.* Russia
53 C1 **Yantabulla** Austr.
70 C2 **Yantai** China
118 B2 **Yaoundé** Cameroon
59 D2 **Yap** *i.* Micronesia
59 D3 **Yapen** *i.* Indon.
59 D3 **Yapen, Selat** *sea chan.* Indon.
144 A2 **Yaqui** *r.* Mex.
51 D2 **Yaraka** Austr.
86 D3 **Yaransk** Russia
48 F2 **Yaren** Nauru
78 B3 **Yarīm** Yemen
77 D3 **Yarkant He** *r.* China
75 D2 **Yarlung Zangbo** *r.* China
131 D2 **Yarmouth** Can.
86 F2 **Yarono** Russia
89 E2 **Yaroslavl'** Russia
66 B2 **Yaroslavskiy** Russia
53 C3 **Yarram** Austr.
89 D2 **Yartsevo** Russia
89 E3 **Yasnogorsk** Russia
63 B2 **Yasothon** Thai.
53 C2 **Yass** Austr.
111 C3 **Yatağan** Turkey
129 E1 **Yathkyed Lake** Can.
67 B4 **Yatsushiro** Japan
150 B2 **Yavarí** *r.* Brazil/Peru
75 B2 **Yavatmal** India
90 A2 **Yavoriv** Ukr.
67 B4 **Yawatahama** Japan
81 D2 **Yazd** Iran
142 B2 **Yazoo City** U.S.A.
111 B3 **Ydra** *i.* Greece
63 A2 **Ye** Myanmar
77 D3 **Yecheng** China
144 B2 **Yécora** Mex.
89 E3 **Yefremov** Russia
89 E2 **Yegor'yevsk** Russia
117 B4 **Yei** South Sudan
86 F3 **Yekaterinburg** Russia
77 D1 **Yekibastuz** Kazakh.
89 E3 **Yelets** Russia
114 A3 **Yélimané** Mali
96 □ **Yell** *i.* U.K.
128 C1 **Yellowknife** Can.
70 B2 **Yellow River** *r.* China
69 E2 **Yellow Sea** N. Pacific Ocean
136 C1 **Yellowstone** *r.* U.S.A.
136 A2 **Yellowstone Lake** U.S.A.
88 C3 **Yel'sk** Belarus
78 B3 **Yemen** *country* Asia
86 E2 **Yemva** Russia
91 D2 **Yenakiyeve** Ukr.
62 A1 **Yenangyaung** Myanmar
62 B1 **Yên Bai** Vietnam
114 B4 **Yendi** Ghana
111 C3 **Yenice** Turkey
111 C3 **Yenifoça** Turkey
68 C1 **Yenisey** *r.* Russia
65 B2 **Yeongdeok** S. Korea
53 C2 **Yeoval** Austr.
99 B3 **Yeovil** U.K.
51 E2 **Yeppoon** Austr.
83 I2 **Yerbogachen** Russia
81 C1 **Yerevan** Armenia
77 D1 **Yereymentau** Kazakh.
87 D3 **Yershov** Russia
Yertis *r.* Kazakh./Russia *see* **Irtysh**
65 B2 **Yesan** S. Korea
77 C1 **Yesil'** Kazakh.
77 D1 **Yesil'** *r.* Kazakh./Russia
111 C3 **Yeşilova** Turkey
99 A3 **Yes Tor** *h.* U.K.
53 D1 **Yetman** Austr.
62 A1 **Ye-U** Myanmar
104 B2 **Yeu, Île d'** *i.* France
91 C2 **Yevpatoriya** Ukr.
91 D2 **Yeya** *r.* Russia
91 D2 **Yeysk** Russia
88 C2 **Yezyaryshcha** Belarus
71 A3 **Yibin** China
70 B2 **Yichang** China
69 E1 **Yichun** *Heilong.* China
71 B3 **Yichun** *Jiangxi* China
110 C2 **Yıldız Dağları** *mts* Turkey
80 B2 **Yıldızeli** Turkey
70 A2 **Yinchuan** China
65 B1 **Yingchengzi** China
71 B3 **Yingde** China
70 C1 **Yingkou** China
70 B2 **Yingshan** *Hubei* China
70 A2 **Yingshan** *Sichuan* China
71 B3 **Yingtan** China
77 E2 **Yining** China
117 B4 **Yirga Alem** Eth.
70 B2 **Yishui** China
68 C2 **Yiwu** China
71 B3 **Yiyang** China
71 A3 **Yizhou** China
92 I2 **Yli-Kitka** *l.* Fin.
92 H2 **Ylitornio** Fin.
92 H3 **Ylivieska** Fin.
61 C2 **Yogyakarta** Indon.
118 B2 **Yoko** Cameroon
67 C3 **Yokohama** Japan
115 D4 **Yola** Nigeria
67 D3 **Yonezawa** Japan
71 B3 **Yong'an** China
71 B3 **Yongchun** China
70 A2 **Yongdeng** China
71 C3 **Yongkang** China
62 B1 **Yongsheng** China
71 B3 **Yongzhou** China
150 A1 **Yopal** Col.
50 A3 **York** Austr.
98 C2 **York** U.K.
137 D2 **York** *NE* U.S.A.
141 D3 **York** *PA* U.S.A.
51 D1 **York, Cape** Austr.
52 A3 **Yorke Peninsula** Austr.
52 A3 **Yorketown** Austr.
98 C2 **Yorkshire Wolds** *hills* U.K.
129 D2 **Yorkton** Can.
87 D3 **Yoshkar-Ola** Russia
97 C3 **Youghal** Ireland
53 C2 **Young** Austr.
52 A3 **Younghusband Peninsula** Austr.
140 C2 **Youngstown** U.S.A.
114 B3 **Youvarou** Mali
77 E2 **Youyi Feng** *mt.* China/Russia
80 B2 **Yozgat** Turkey
134 B2 **Yreka** U.S.A.
76 C2 **Yrgyz** Kazakh.
Yr Wyddfa *mt.* U.K. *see* **Snowdon**
105 C2 **Yssingeaux** France
93 F4 **Ystad** Sweden
Ysyk-Köl Kyrg. *see* **Balykchy**
77 D2 **Ysyk-Köl** *salt l.* Kyrg.
92 □A3 **Ytri-Rangá** *r.* Iceland
62 B1 **Yuanjiang** China
62 B1 **Yuan Jiang** *r.* China
62 B1 **Yuanmou** China
135 B3 **Yuba City** U.S.A.
66 D2 **Yūbari** Japan
145 C3 **Yucatán** *pen.* Mex.
146 B2 **Yucatan Channel** Cuba/Mex.
50 C2 **Yuendumu** Austr.
71 B3 **Yueyang** China
86 F2 **Yugorsk** Russia
83 L2 **Yukagirskoye Ploskogor'ye** *plat.* Russia
128 A1 **Yukon** *admin. div.* Can.
126 A2 **Yukon** *r.* Can./U.S.A.
71 B3 **Yulin** *Guangxi* China
70 A2 **Yulin** *Shaanxi* China
62 B1 **Yulong Xueshan** *mt.* China
138 A2 **Yuma** *AZ* U.S.A.
136 C2 **Yuma** *CO* U.S.A.
Yumen China *see* **Laojunmiao**
80 B2 **Yunak** Turkey
70 B2 **Yuncheng** China
71 B3 **Yunfu** China
62 B1 **Yunnan** *prov.* China
52 A2 **Yunta** Austr.
70 B2 **Yunyang** China
66 D3 **Yurihonjō** Japan
150 A2 **Yurimaguas** Peru
77 E3 **Yurungkax He** *r.* China
71 C3 **Yu Shan** *mt.* Taiwan
68 C2 **Yushu** China
Yushuwan China *see* **Huaihua**
81 C1 **Yusufeli** Turkey
77 E3 **Yutian** China
62 B1 **Yuxi** China
66 D2 **Yuzhno-Kuril'sk** Russia
83 K3 **Yuzhno-Sakhalinsk** Russia
91 C2 **Yuzhnoukrayins'k** Ukr.

82 E2 Yuzhnyy, Ostrov i. Russia
69 D2 Yuzhou China
104 C2 Yvetot France

Z

100 B1 Zaandam Neth.
69 D1 Zabaykal'sk Russia
78 B3 Zabid Yemen
Zābol Iran see Mehrestān
79 D2 Zābol Iran
144 B3 Zacapu Mex.
144 B2 Zacatecas Mex.
145 C3 Zacatepec Mex.
145 C3 Zacatlán Mex.
111 B3 Zacharo Greece
144 B2 Zacoalco Mex.
145 C2 Zacualtipán Mex.
109 C2 Zadar Croatia
63 A3 Zadetkyi Kyun i. Myanmar
89 E3 Zadonsk Russia
106 B2 Zafra Spain
109 C1 Zagreb Croatia
Zagros, Kūhhā-ye mts Iran see
Zagros Mountains
81 C2 Zagros Mountains Iran
79 D2 Zāhedān Iran
80 B2 Zahlé Lebanon
78 B3 Zahrān Saudi Arabia
Zaire country Africa see
Congo, Democratic
Republic of the
109 D2 Zaječar Serbia
89 E3 Zakharovo Russia
81 C2 Zakhū/Zaxo Iraq
111 B3 Zakynthos Greece
111 B3 Zakynthos i. Greece
103 D2 Zalaegerszeg Hungary
110 B1 Zalău Romania
78 B2 Zalim Saudi Arabia
117 A3 Zalingei Sudan
78 A2 Zalmā, Jabal az mt.
Saudi Arabia
128 C2 Zama City Can.
120 C2 Zambeze r. Moz.
120 C2 Zambezi r. Africa
Zambezi r. Moz. see Zambeze
120 B2 Zambezi Zambia
120 B2 Zambia country Africa
64 B2 Zamboanga Phil.
64 B2 Zamboanga Peninsula Phil.
106 B1 Zamora Spain
144 B3 Zamora de Hidalgo Mex.
103 E1 Zamość Pol.
75 B1 Zanda China
100 B2 Zandvliet Belgium
140 C3 Zanesville U.S.A.
81 C2 Zanjān Iran
75 B1 Zanskar Mountains India
Zante i. Greece see Zakynthos
119 D3 Zanzibar Tanz.
119 D3 Zanzibar Island Tanz.
89 D3 Zaokskiy Russia
115 C2 Zaouatallaz Alg.
89 D2 Zapadnaya Dvina r. Europe
89 D2 Zapadnaya Dvina Russia
68 B1 Zapadnyy Sayan reg. Russia
139 D3 Zapata U.S.A.
92 J2 Zapolyarnyy Russia
91 D2 Zaporizhzhya Ukr.
101 E2 Zappendorf Ger.
80 B2 Zara Turkey
145 B2 Zaragoza Mex.
107 C1 Zaragoza Spain
74 A1 Zarah Sharan Afgh.
76 B3 Zarand Iran

76 C3 Zaranj Afgh.
88 C2 Zarasai Lith.
89 E3 Zaraysk Russia
150 B1 Zaraza Venez.
115 C3 Zaria Nigeria
90 B1 Zarichne Ukr.
81 D3 Zarqān Iran
66 B2 Zarubino Russia
103 D1 Żary Pol.
115 D1 Zarzis Tunisia
123 C3 Zastron S. Africa
121 C3 Zavala Moz.
69 E1 Zavitinsk Russia
103 D1 Zawiercie Pol.
77 E2 Zaysan, Lake Kazakh.
Zaysan, Ozero l. Kazakh. see
Zaysan, Lake
90 B1 Zdolbuniv Ukr.
93 F4 Zealand i. Denmark
100 A2 Zeebrugge Belgium
123 C2 Zeerust S. Africa
101 F2 Zeil, Mount Austr.
101 F2 Zeitz Ger.
88 B3 Zelenogradsk Russia
82 E1 Zemlya Aleksandry i.
Russia
82 F1 Zemlya Vil'cheka i. Russia
107 D2 Zemmora Alg.
145 C3 Zempoaltépetl, Nudo de mt.
Mex.
65 B1 Zengfeng Shan mt. China
105 D2 Zermatt Switz.
91 E2 Zernograd Russia
101 E2 Zeulenroda Ger.
101 D1 Zeven Ger.
100 C2 Zevenaar Neth.
83 J3 Zeya Russia
79 C2 Zeydābād Iran
83 J3 Zeyskoye Vodokhranilishche
resr Russia
103 D1 Zgierz Pol.
88 B3 Zhabinka Belarus
76 A2 Zhalpaktal Kazakh.
77 C1 Zhaltyr Kazakh.
76 B2 Zhanakala Kazakh.
76 B2 Zhanaozen Kazakh.
Zhangde China see Anyang
71 C3 Zhanghua Taiwan
71 B3 Zhangjiajie China
70 B1 Zhangjiakou China
71 B3 Zhangping China
71 B3 Zhangshu China
68 C2 Zhangye China
71 B3 Zhangzhou China
87 D4 Zhanibek Kazakh.
71 B3 Zhanjiang China
71 B3 Zhao'an China
71 B3 Zhaoqing China
71 A3 Zhaotong China
75 C1 Zhari Namco salt l. China
77 E2 Zharkent Kazakh.
89 D2 Zharkovskiy Russia
77 E2 Zharma Kazakh.
90 C2 Zhashkiv Ukr.
Zhayyk r. Kazakh./Russia see
Ural
71 B3 Zhejiang prov. China
82 F1 Zhelaniya, Mys c. Russia
89 E3 Zheleznogorsk Russia
76 B2 Zhem r. Kazakh.
70 A2 Zhenba China
71 A3 Zheng'an China
70 B2 Zhenghe China
70 B2 Zhengzhou China
70 B2 Zhenjiang China
71 A3 Zhenyuan China
91 E1 Zherdevka Russia
86 D2 Zheshart Russia

77 D2 Zhetysuskiy Alatau mts China/
Kazakh.
77 C2 Zhezkazgan Karagandinskaya
Oblast' Kazakh.
77 C2 Zhezkazgan Karagandinskaya
Oblast' Kazakh.
68 C3 Zhigang China
83 J2 Zhigansk Russia
Zhi Qu r. China see Yangtze
Zhishan China see Lingling
76 C1 Zhitikara Kazakh.
88 D3 Zhlobin Belarus
90 B2 Zhmerynka Ukr.
74 A1 Zhob Pak.
83 L1 Zhokhova, Ostrov i. Russia
75 C2 Zhongba China
Zhonghe China see Xiushan
70 A2 Zhongning China
71 B3 Zhongshan Guangdong China
Zhongshan China see
Liupanshui
70 A2 Zhongwei China
Zhongxin China see
Xamgyi'nyilha
76 C2 Zhosaly Kazakh.
70 B2 Zhoukou China
70 C2 Zhoushan China
91 C2 Zhovti Vody Ukr.
65 A2 Zhuanghe China
70 B2 Zhucheng China
89 D3 Zhukovka Russia
89 E2 Zhukovskiy Russia
70 B2 Zhumadian China
Zhuoyang China see Suiping
71 B3 Zhuzhou Hunan China
71 B3 Zhuzhou Hunan China
90 A2 Zhydachiv Ukr.
88 C3 Zhytkavichy Belarus
90 B1 Zhytomyr Ukr.
103 D2 Žiar nad Hronom Slovakia
70 B2 Zibo China
103 D1 Zielona Góra Pol.
62 A1 Zigaing Myanmar
71 A3 Zigong China
114 A3 Ziguinchor Senegal
144 B3 Zihuatanejo Mex.
103 D2 Žilina Slovakia
83 H3 Zima Russia
145 C2 Zimapán Mex.
121 B2 Zimbabwe country Africa
114 A4 Zimmi Sierra Leone
110 C2 Zimnicea Romania
115 C3 Zinder Niger
78 B3 Zinjibār Yemen
103 D2 Zirc Hungary
62 A1 Ziro India
79 C2 Zīr Rūd Iran
103 D2 Zistersdorf Austria
145 B3 Zitácuaro Mex.
103 C1 Zittau Ger.
110 B2 Zlatitsa Bulg.
87 E3 Zlatoust Russia
103 D2 Zlín Czech Rep.
89 D3 Zlynka Russia
89 E3 Zmiyevka Russia
91 D2 Zmiyiv Ukr.
89 E3 Znamenka Orlovskaya Oblast'
Russia
91 E1 Znamenka Tambovskaya
Oblast' Russia
91 C2 Znam"yanka Ukr.
103 D2 Znojmo Czech Rep.
91 D1 Zolochiv Kharkivs'ka Oblast'
Ukr.
90 A2 Zolochiv L'vivs'ka Oblast' Ukr.
91 C2 Zolotonosha Ukr.
89 E3 Zolotukhino Russia
121 C2 Zomba Malawi

Zonguldak

80	B1	**Zonguldak** Turkey
105	D3	**Zonza** *Corsica* France
114	B4	**Zorzor** Liberia
115	D2	**Zouar** Chad
114	A2	**Zouérat** Maur.
109	D1	**Zrenjanin** Serbia
89	D2	**Zubtsov** Russia
105	D2	**Zug** Switz.
81	C1	**Zugdidi** Georgia
106	B2	**Zújar** *r.* Spain

100	C2	**Zülpich** Ger.
121	C2	**Zumbo** Moz.
145	C3	**Zumpango** Mex.
138	B1	**Zuni Mountains** U.S.A.
71	A3	**Zunyi** China
109	C1	**Županja** Croatia
105	D2	**Zürich** Switz.
100	C1	**Zutphen** Neth.
115	D1	**Zuwārah** Libya
90	C2	**Zvenyhorodka** Ukr.

121	C3	**Zvishavane** Zimbabwe
103	D2	**Zvolen** Slovakia
109	C2	**Zvornik** Bos. & Herz.
114	B4	**Zwedru** Liberia
123	C3	**Zwelitsha** S. Africa
103	D2	**Zwettl** Austria
101	F2	**Zwickau** Ger.
100	C1	**Zwolle** Neth.
83	L2	**Zyryanka** Russia

Acknowledgements

pages 34-35
Climatic map data:
Kottek, M., Grieser, J., Beck, C., Rudolf, B., and Rubel, F., 2006: World Map
of the Köppen-Geiger climate classification updated.
Meteorol. Z., 15, 259–263.
http://koeppen-geiger.vu-wien.ac.at

pages 36-37
World land cover map data:
© ESA 2010 and UCLouvain
Arino, O., Ramos, J., Kalogirou, V., Defourny, P., Achard, F., 2010.
GlobCover 2009. ESA Living Planet Symposium 2010, 28th June - 2nd July, Bergen, Norway, SP-686, ESA,
www.esa.int/due/globcover
http://due.esrin.esa.int/prjs/Results/20110202183257.pdf

pages 38-39
Population map data:
Center for International Earth Science Information Network (CIESIN), Columbia University; and Centro Internacional de Agricultura
Tropical (CIAT). 2005. Gridded Population of the World Version 3 (GPWv3). Palisades, NY: Socioeconomic
Data and Applications Center (SEDAC), Columbia University.
Available at: http://sedac.ciesin.columbia.edu/gpw
http://www.ciesin.columbia.edu

Cover
Aerial view of the Pilbara Landscape, Australia: © Tobias Titz/Getty Images